forward, rato-

MCSE

SQL Server™ 2000 Database Design and Implementation

Exam: 70-229

Thomas Moore,
MCSE, MCSD, MCDBA, MCT, CTT

MCSE TRAINING GUIDE (70-229): DESIGNING AND IMPLEMENTING DATABASES WITH MICROSOFT® SQL SERVER™ 2000 ENTERPRISE EDITION

International Standard Book Number: 0-7357-1129-1

Library of Congress Catalog Card Number: 2001087310

05 04 03 02   7 6 5 4 3 2 1

Interpretation of the printing code: The rightmost double-digit number is the year of the book's printing; the rightmost single-digit number is the number of the book's printing. For example, the printing code 02-1 shows that the first printing of the book occurred in 2002.

Printed in the United States of America

Trademarks

Warning and Disclaimer

PUBLISHER
David Culverwell

DIRECTOR OF PRODUCT DEVELOPMENT
Chuck Stewart

SENIOR ACQUISITIONS EDITOR
Jeff Riley

PRODUCTION MANAGER
Gina Kanouse

MANAGING EDITOR
Kristy Knoop

DEVELOPMENT EDITOR
Frederick Speers

PRODUCT MARKETING MANAGER
Amy Neidlinger

PROJECT EDITOR
Lori Lyons

COPY EDITOR
Margo Catts

INDEXER
Lisa Stumpf

PROOFREADER
Sarah Cisco

MANUFACTURING COORDINATOR
Jim Conway

BOOK DESIGNER
Louisa Klucznik

COVER DESIGNER
Aren Howell

COMPOSITION
Scan Communications Group, Inc.

MEDIA DEVELOPER
Jay Payne

Contents At a Glance

TABLE OF CONTENTS

Part I: Exam Preparation

6 Programming SQL Server 2000   329

10 Boosting Performance with Indexes   557

Part II   Final Review

Part III   Appendixes

About the Author

Thomas Moore, MCSE, MCSD, MCDBA, MCT, CTT, has been in the computer industry for more than 20 years. Thomas has a wide variety of expertise in all hardware environments and with most Microsoft Server products. "My first and lasting love, besides my wife and family, however, is programming." Thomas is comfortable in any programming language environment, achieving his MCSD and MCDBA certifications from their inception. Over the past 12 years he has been working for a variety of Microsoft partners and currently is a Systems Analyst for TechServices Web Development Group in Fort Wayne, Indiana, where he has been for the past three years. Thomas enjoys staying up-to-date, although like most of us, he finds it a challenge to keep up with the pace of the industry. Thomas's most recent certification achievements include being one of the first Windows 2000 MCSEs in the world and achieving the same standard as a SQL Server 2000 MCDBA.

Contributing Authors

Chris Miller is a database administrator on the Internet Operations team at GeoAccess in Lenexa, Kansas. He maintains several high-performance SQL Server boxes, tunes queries, manages an OLAP-based data repository, and generally fixes broken things—which is the nature of the job of a system administrator. He's been doing this for three years now and is having a blast working with some really smart people who are doing amazing things. Previously he worked as a team leader at a major wireless telecommunications company, although he doesn't thrive in a large corporate environment and dislikes managing people. Before that, he was a consultant and trainer, specializing in SQL Server, Exchange, and Microsoft Mail. Chris and his wife Jennifer live in Kansas City with their two dogs, Dogbert and Peekaboo.

Edward Tetz graduated in 1990 from Saint Lawrence College in Cornwall, Ontario, with a diploma in Business Administration. He spent a short time in computer sales, which turned into a computer support position. He has spent most of his time since then performing system and LAN support for small and large organizations. In 1994, he added training to his repertoire. He currently holds the following certifications: MCT, MCSE, MCDBA, CTT, A+, and CIW CI. He has experience with Apple Macintosh, IBM OS/2, Linux, and all Microsoft operating systems. He is an information technology coordinator and an instructor for PBSC and delivers training on many Microsoft products. Ed has published several certification titles for New Riders and can be reached through ed_tetz@hotmail.com.

ABOUT THE TECHNICAL REVIEWERS

These reviewers contributed their considerable hands-on expertise to the entire development process for *MCSE Training Guide (70-229): SQL Server 2000 Database Design and Implementation*. As the book was being written, these dedicated professionals reviewed all the material for technical content, organization, and flow. Their feedback was critical to ensuring that *MCSE Training Guide (70-229): SQL Server 2000 Database Design and Implementation* fits our reader's need for the highest-quality technical information.

David Besch has been a database administrator for eight years and is currently with GeoAccess, Inc, a software provider for the managed healthcare industry, located in Lenexa, Kansas. He is the author of *SQL 7.0 Database Design*, and he has been technical editor for several SQL Server books. David lives in Olathe, Kansas, with his wife Cheryl; two sons, Perrin and Matrim; and his cat, Blaise. When his children are not occupying his time, his activities include weightlifting, video editing, and home maintenance.

Sheldon Barry (B.A, B.ED, CCNA, CCAI, MCSE, MCT) is a technology trainer, writer, and consultant in Newfoundland, Canada. He is currently employed as Coordinating Instructor at Memorial University of Newfoundland in the postgraduate Information Technology Program (`http://www.ce.mun.ca/ppd/it_diploma.html`). Some of his previous employment positions have included technical writing, educational content consulting, high school department head, and high school teacher. Sheldon completed a Bachelor of Arts from Memorial University of Newfoundland in 1994 and then went on to complete a Bachelor of Education from Memorial in 1995. Since then, Sheldon has been working on a Masters of Education (Information Technology) Degree and is expected to complete by Spring 2002. He currently enjoys life with his wife, Kelly, his two little girls, Sarah and Anna, and loves to play soccer and golf. Sheldon can be reached at `sheldonb@mun.ca`.

DEDICATION

Thomas Moore

To my two sons, both of whom have been very understanding while Dad has been writing this book. Daniel, age 10, who seems to be more and more like me everyday; and Maxwell, age 6, whose insight and maturity never cease to amaze me.

ACKNOWLEDGMENTS

It is impossible to complete a project like this without considerable help and involvement from a number of different people from all walks of life and backgrounds. This book is no exception, and though at times the experience was rather trying, it was also rewarding. At times the participants threw about a little humor to make it a much more enjoyable task.

My initial thanks must go to my family. My wife, Joy; sons, Danny and Max; mother, Barbara, and brother Brian; as well as other friends and family members who helped me a great deal in maintaining my sanity and taking on additional tasks to leave me alone to do my work.

Considerable thanks to Ed Tetz and Chris Miller, whose direct input to the book took a great deal of the workload off my shoulders and assisted in multitudes when it came down to crunch time. Yes, Chris, the TOC was a considerable challenge, and I do agree about the "Kludgy piece ..." Ed, you have a true knack for what Microsoft will look for on the exam. Both gentlemen deserve accolades beyond what I can put here in print.

The technical reviewers for this book are nothing short of awesome. They were thorough and honest, and at times aggravating—but that is what makes for a good reviewer. Wayne Snyder, you are a godsend; your determination to check every last detail and correct the oversights from the contributing authors helped guarantee the accuracy and thorough coverage of all exam topics. David Besch, your input as well was greatly appreciated and the care and concern shown from someone who has "been there before and brought back a t-shirt" helped me recognize the importance of each element in the book. You also helped reform me, and I have now been converted to an SQL-92 coder. Sheldon Barry, although you came into the project late, you added to the technical depth of the book and your timeliness and response was prized. At the times when my work was less than accurate, you guys really came through. A couple of rather humorous quotes: "the 900 buts (bytes)" and "SQL Server Installation Screen (OSQL)." I hope they amused you as much as they did me.

For Elise Walter, Jeff Riley (formerly with New Riders, now with Que Certification), Chris Zahn, Frederick Speers, and anyone else at New Riders that I have failed to mention. This project could have never come off without your expertise, patience, assistance, and professionalism. Thank you, Frederick, for your guidance, suggestions, and psychotherapy, without which I am sure I would be in the nut-house by now. As well as to you, Jeff—your meticulous attention to detail and follow-up made writing this book a true experience, most of which was quite enjoyable.

A final word of thanks to John and Becky Sanderson of TechServices, Fort Wayne, Indiana, and all the rest of the staff of TechServices. The time given to do this book and just the opportunity to know and work with you all made my life richer than money could ever define.

— Thomas Moore

I would like to thank Jeff Riley, who brought me into this project, after months of trying to find something for me to work on; Fred Speers, who tied everyone together on the project; and the technical editors, who spotted everything that we missed. Finally, I would also like to thank my wife, Sharon, and our daughters, Emily and Mackenzie. They have been loving and supportive as always, and I have missed many hours with them as I wrote on this book. Thank you all.

—Edward Tetz

TELL US WHAT YOU THINK

As the reader of this book, you are the most important critic and commentator. We value your opinion and want to know what we're doing right, what we could do better, what areas you'd like to see us publish in, and any other words of wisdom you're willing to pass our way.

As Director of Product Development for Que Cetification, I welcome your comments. You can fax, email, or write me directly to let me know what you did or didn't like about this book—as well as what we can do to make our books stronger.

Please note that I cannot help you with technical problems related to the topic of this book, and that due to the high volume of mail I receive, I might not be able to reply to every message.

When you write, please be sure to include this book's title and author as well as your name and phone or fax number. I will carefully review your comments and share them with the author and editors who worked on the book.

Fax: 317-581-4663

Email: chuck.stewart@quepublishing.com

Mail: Chuck Stewart
         Director of Product Development
         Que Certification
         201 West 103rd Street
         Indianapolis, IN 46290 USA

How to Use This Book

Que Certification has made an effort in its Training Guide series to make the information as accessible as possible for the purposes of learning the certification material. Here, you have an opportunity to view the many instructional features that have been incorporated into the books to achieve that goal.

CHAPTER OPENER

Each chapter begins with a set of features designed to allow you to maximize study time for that material.

List of Objectives: Each chapter begins with a list of the objectives as stated by Microsoft.

Objective Explanations: Immediately following each objective is an explanation of it, providing context that defines it more meaningfully in relation to the exam. Because Microsoft can sometimes be vague in its objectives list, the objective explanations are designed to clarify any vagueness by relying on the authors' test-taking experience.

OBJECTIVES

Create and alter databases. Considerations include file groups, file placement, growth strategy, and space requirements.

- **Specify space management parameters. Parameters include autoshrink, growth increment, initial size, and maxsize.**
- **Specify file group and file placement. Considerations include logical and physical file placement.**
- **Specify transaction log placement. Considerations include bulk load operations and performance.**

▶ The placement of the files related to a SQL Server 2000 database environment helps to ensure optimum performance while minimizing administration. Recoverability can also be improved in the event of data corruption or hardware failures if appropriate measures are taken. On the exam, you must be prepared to respond to these requirements and properly configure the interactions with the file system.

Create and alter database objects. Objects include constraints, indexes, stored procedures, tables, triggers, user-defined functions, and views.

- **Specify table characteristics. Characteristics include cascading actions, CHECK constraints, clustered, defaults, FILLFACTOR, foreign keys, nonclustered, primary key, and UNIQUE constraints.**
- **Specify schema binding and encryption for stored procedures, triggers, user-defined functions, and views.**
- **Specify recompile settings for stored procedures.**
- **Specify index characteristics. Characteristics include clustered, FILLFACTOR, nonclustered, and uniqueness.**

C H A P T E R 3

Physical Database Design and Implementation

► An absolute necessity of building databases that interact with SQL Server 2000 is using the appropriate database objects to obtain a usable database system while improving response times and maintaining data integrity. There are considerations and trade-offs for choosing one technique over the other. The selection of the most appropriate method to obtain the desired result requires that you know where each is best implemented. The exam will test on the appropriate application of each of these objects.

Alter database objects to support replication and partitioned views.

• **Support merge, snapshot, and transactional replication models.**

• **Design a partitioning strategy.**

• **Design and create constraints and views.**

• **Resolve replication conflicts.**

► A variety of technologies exist in handling multiple server environments, knowing what each technology offers—as well its restrictions—helps you adapt a database system applied across multiple machines. Considerations for controlling data alterations, having the data available when needed, and responding to queries in a timely manner will be the aim of questions within this area of the exam.

Troubleshoot failed object creation.

► Troubleshooting is certainly a broad topic. In this chapter, the focus for troubleshooting is on the interactions with objects and the server as well as application settings that are required for an object to be created and used. On the exam, troubleshooting will be approached from a wide variety of angles. In the "real world," it is good practice to always view a procedure from a problem-solving perspective. Always be ready to ask yourself, "What could go wrong?" and "What can be done to resolve the problem?"

Chapter Outline: Learning always gets a boost when you can see both the forest and the trees. To give you a visual image of how the topics in a chapter fit together, you will find a chapter outline at the beginning of each chapter. You will also be able to use this for easy reference when looking for a particular topic.

► Disk configurations are a part of both the planning and the configuration of NT Server computers. To study for Planning Objective 1, you will need to look at both the following section and the material in Chapter 2, "Installation Part 1." As with many concepts, you should have a good handle on the terminology and know the best applications for different disk configurations. For the objectives of the NT Server exam, you will need to know only general disk configuration concepts—at a high level, not the nitty gritty. Make sure you memorize the concepts relating to partitioning and know the difference between the system and the boot partitions in an NT system (and the fact that the definitions of these are counter-intuitive). You should know that NT supports both FAT and NTFS partitions, as well as some of the advantages and disadvantages of each. You will also need to know about the fault-tolerance methods available in NT—stripe sets with parity and disk mirroring—including their definitions, hardware requirements, and advantages and disadvantages.

Of course, nothing substitutes for working with the concepts explained in this objective. If possible, get an NT system with some free disk space and play around with the Disk Administrator just to see how partitions are created and what they look like.

You might also want to look at some of the supplementary readings and scan TechNet for white papers on disk configuration.

► The best way to study for Planning Objective 2 is to read, memorize, and understand the use of each protocol. You should know what the protocols are, what they are used for, and what systems they are compatible with.

As with disk configuration, installing protocols on your NT Server is something that you plan for, not something you do just because it feels good to you at the time. Although it is much easier to add or remove a protocol than it is to reconfigure your hard drives, choosing a protocol is still an essential part of the planning process because specific protocols, like spoken languages, are designed to be used in certain circumstances. There is no point in learning to speak Mandarin Chinese if you are never around anyone who can understand you. Similarly, the NWLink protocol is used to interact with NetWare systems; therefore, if you do not have Novell servers on your network, you might want to rethink your plan to install it on your servers. We will discuss the uses of the major protocols in Chapter 7, "Connectivity." However, it is important that you have a good understanding of their uses here in the planning stage.

Study Strategies: Each topic presents its own learning challenge. To support you through this, Que has included strategies for how to best approach studying in order to retain the material in the chapter, particularly as it is addressed on the exam.

INSTRUCTIONAL FEATURES WITHIN THE CHAPTER

These books include a large amount and different kinds of information. The many different elements are designed to help you identify information by its purpose and importance to the exam and also to provide you with varied ways to learn the material. You will be able to determine how much attention to devote to certain elements, depending on what your goals are. By becoming familiar with the different presentations of information, you will know what information will be important to you as a test-taker and which information will be important to you as a practitioner.

EXAM TIP

Go with the Documentation If you run into this on the exam, the correct answer is likely to be one chosen based on the documentation and not on actual functionality. The capability to set a relationship to any unique column is not noted in documentation. The correct technique to use when answering an exam question would be one that involves a Foreign Key set to a Primary Key or Unique constraint.

Exam Tip: Exam Tips appear in the margins to provide specific exam-related advice. Such tips may address what material is covered (or not covered) on the exam, how it is covered, mnemonic devices, or particular quirks of that exam.

Note: Notes appear in the margins and contain various kinds of useful information, such as tips on the technology or administrative practices, historical background on terms and technologies, or side commentary on industry issues.

---

8 | Chapter 1   PLANNING

INTRODUCTION

Microsoft grew up around the personal computer industry and established itself as the preeminent maker of software products for personal computers. Microsoft has a vast portfolio of software products, but it is best known for its operating systems.

Microsoft's current operating system products, listed here, are undoubtedly well-known to anyone studying for the MCSE exams:

◆ Windows 95

◆ Windows NT Workstation

◆ Windows NT Server

NOTE

Master of the Server The Master database is crucial to the operations of SQL Server and should be considered as important as the most mission-critical database stored on the server. If it becomes damaged, the server ceases to function.

Some older operating system products—namely MS-DOS, Windows 3.1, and Windows for Workgroups—are still important to the operability of Windows NT Server, so don't be surprised if you hear them mentioned from time to time in this book.

Windows NT is the most powerful, the most secure, and perhaps the most elegant operating system Microsoft has yet produced. It languished for a while after it first appeared (in part because no one was sure why they needed it or what to do with it), but Microsoft has persisted with improving interoperability and performance. With the release of Windows NT 4 which offers a new Windows 95-like user interface, Windows NT has assumed a prominent place in today's world of network-based computing.

WINDOWS NT SERVER AMONG MICROSOFT OPERATING SYSTEMS

▶ As we already mentioned, Microsoft has three operating system products now competing in the marketplace: Windows 95, Windows NT Workstation, and Windows NT Server. Each of these operating systems has its advantages and disadvantages.

WARNING

Sharing Machines You seldom want SQL Server to share a machine with other applications, and certainly a SQL Server should never share a machine with a security server such as a Windows 2000 or Windows NT Domain controller.

Looking at the presentation of the desktop, the three look very much alike—so much so that you might have to click the Start button and read the banner on the left side of the menu to determine which operating system you are looking at. Each offers the familiar Windows 95 user interface featuring the Start button, the Recycling

Objective Coverage Text: In the text before an exam objective is specifically addressed, you will notice the objective is listed to help call your attention to that particular material.

Warning: In using sophisticated information technology, there is always potential for mistakes or even catastrophes that can occur through improper application of the technology. Warnings appear in the margins to alert you to such potential problems.

STEP BY STEP

5.2 Importing Data with the Import and Export Application

1. Start the Import and Export application by going to Start, clicking on Microsoft SQL Server, and then clicking on Import and Export Data. The DTS Import/Export Wizard opening screen appears as shown in Figure 5.4. Click the Next button.

2. Next up is the Choose a Data Source window, shown in Figure 5.5. This is where you get to choose where the data will be coming from for your copies. Click the drop-down box labeled Data Source and choose a data source type. For this example, choose Microsoft OLE DB Provider for SQL Server, but notice you can choose a lot of different data sources.

3. After you choose the data source, you need to pick a server. In the example shown in Figure 5.5, the local server is shown, with Windows Authentication. Change the database to Pubs and click the Next button.

FIGURE 5.5
The window where you can choose from which data source to read data.

Step by Step: Step by Steps are hands-on tutorial instructions that walk you through a particular task or function relevant to the exam objectives.

Figure: To improve readability, the figures have been placed in the margins wherever possible so they do not interrupt the main flow of text.

Using the Model Database

When you create a database for the first time, that database initially takes most of its attributes from the Model database. The Model database is a system database that SQL Server uses as a kind of template for database creations. It is a good and common practice to set the properties and contents of the Model database based on the majority of new databases that are to be created.

IN THE FIELD

OBJECT AND CODE REUSE

In practice, many objects are stored in the Model database to minimize the need to re-create these objects every time a database is created. Common elements placed in the Model often include specialized user-defined functions and data types that are present and frequently used by the development staff in their coding. In theory, objects are created for use in a single database, but all developers realize that object and code reuse is an important facet of easing the development process.

In the Field Sidebar: These more extensive discussions cover material that perhaps is not as directly relevant to the exam, but which is useful as reference material or in everyday practice. In the Field may also provide useful background or contextual information necessary for understanding the larger topic under consideration.

REVIEW BREAK

Physical Storage

Creating and altering databases involves selecting the physical volume type for each database file, setting the appropriate file properties, placing the objects into the files/filegroups, and ensuring appropriate adjustments are made as the database matures. The type of business needs that the database is being designed to meet helps to indicate the measures needed to ensure adequate performance.

Try to place onto separate volumes any files that might tend to compete with each other for read cycles during a single operation. Place log files away from the data to ensure adequate recovery and make sure that database properties have been set in such a way as to ensure that maintenance tasks can be performed.

Review Break: Crucial information is summarized at various points in the book in lists or tables. At the end of a particularly long section, you might come across a Review Break that is there just to wrap up one long objective and reinforce the key points before you shift your focus to the next section.

CASE STUDIES

Case Studies are presented throughout the book to provide you with another, more conceptual opportunity to apply the knowledge you are developing. They also reflect the "real-world" experiences of the authors in ways that prepare you not only for the exam but for actual network administration as well. In each Case Study, you will find similar elements: a description of a Scenario, the Essence of the Case, and an extended Analysis section.

CASE STUDY: EMERALD SHARP

ESSENCE OF THE CASE

▶ All new data that is entered in the main tables should automatically update pricing information in the foreign tables.

▶ Foreign pricing should be 10% less than domestic pricing.

▶ Like all organizations, they would like to have the prices synchronized with a minimum cost, effort, and time.

SCENARIO

Emerald Sharp is a large manufacturer of high-quality cut-glassware products. It enjoys a national reputation for its products, but until now has not exported any goods. Emerald Sharp manufactures cut-glassware products in both mass production and careful customized production, for those willing to pay additional fees. Now Emerald Sharp is running at a profit with its 300 highly skilled employees. The company has 30 factories located around the nation, all in remote areas. Emerald Sharp has out-competed all its rivals who manufacture similar products, which are in great demand because of their quality. Emerald Sharp wants to reach out to the world with its quality products by dedicating ten more factories as export manufacturers to locations around the world. The company therefore needs to somewhat alter its existing data model to accommodate the needs of the factories abroad. After altering the data model, its employees will start to enter the new data into the database. Emerald Sharp has set the international price for its products as 10% less than their domestic price on all models created after May 15th, 2001. Emerald Sharp sells identical products both domestically and internationally, and creates almost 25 new models of glassware each month.

You work as a contractor and are hired to construct and implement this scenario Emerald Sharp is in.

Essence of the Case: A bulleted list of the key problems or issues that need to be addressed in the Scenario.

Scenario: A few paragraphs describing a situation that professional practitioners in the field might face. A Scenario will deal with an issue relating to the objectives covered in the chapter, and it includes the kinds of details that make a difference.

Analysis: This is a lengthy description of the best way to handle the problems listed in the Essence of the Case. In this section, you might find a table summarizing the solutions, a worded example, or both.

CASE STUDY: EMERALD SHARP

ANALYSIS

You investigate the current scenario at Emerald Sharp and notice that Emerald Sharp sells to foreign countries at a discounted price of 10% less than the domestic price of goods on all models created after May 15, 2001. You have thought of a way to automate the process, so that Emerald Sharp will not have to manually create and populate a new table named ForeignPrice. You can create a trigger on the Product table and then write code to insert values into a new column or table named ForeignPrice. You decide to create

an INSERT trigger on the Products table. The INSERT trigger fires when products are added into the table. The trigger verifies that the Manufacture Date column of the record added is greater than May 15th, 2001. If it passes, it is entered into the table with an entry in the ForeignPrice column of 10% less than the domestic price. If the manufactured date of the product is not greater than May 15th, 2001, it is still entered into the table and has an entry in the ForeignPrice column that is equal to the domestic price.

CHAPTER SUMMARY

This chapter has considered a number of different subjects, all pertaining to the physical aspects of a database system. Although the exam concentrates on the new features in SQL Server 2000, you will find that almost all topics are addressed in some manner. In a real-world scenario, you will find that the best solution often involves a compromise, rather than the ideal. Many considerations, such as budget, time constraints, user knowledge, and technology bias might hamper your ability to achieve an optimum environment.

When in doubt, select the options that provide for the best performance in the system. Next to performance, a provision to minimize administrative effort would probably come in a close second. Performance is gained through the use of the optimum levels of hardware, especially options pertaining to the disk, controller, and volume configuration. Performance is gained in interactions between the database and file system, so appropriate placement of files, filegroups, and database objects becomes very important. Within the databases, selection of appropriate indexing, constraints, triggers, and other related processing all help as well.

To achieve minimal levels of administration, look to set up and utilize existing features that SQL Server can perform automatically. Be careful: Using too many of the features that are automated might detract from the system performance.

KEY TERMS

- constraint
- collation Sequence
- identity
- indexes
- stored procedures
- triggers
- user-defined functions (UDFs)
- views
- cascading actions
- CHECK constraints
- clustered index
- defaults
- FILLFACTOR
- Foreign Keys
- non-clustered index

Chapter Summary: Before the Apply Your Knowledge section, you will find a chapter summary that wraps up the chapter and reviews what you should have learned.

Key Terms: A list of key terms appears at the end of each chapter. These are terms that you should be sure you know and are comfortable defining and understanding when you go in to take the exam.

EXTENSIVE REVIEW AND SELF-TEST OPTIONS

At the end of each chapter, along with some summary elements, you will find a section called "Apply Your Knowledge" that gives you several different methods with which to test your understanding of the material and review what you have learned.

APPLY YOUR KNOWLEDGE

Exercises

2.1 Creating a One-to-Many Relationship

The purpose of this exercise is to show you how to create a basic one-to-many relationship between the Employee entity and the Course entity. Employees teach courses at Lloyd's Hospital. A single employee or teacher may teach many courses, such as blood composition and blood circulation, therefore creating a one-to-many relationship.

Estimated Time: 5 minutes.

1. Draw out the two entities, Employee and Course, as boxes, including the attributes defined in each as rows inside the box. Define a Primary Key element for each entity.

2. Creating a Foreign Key is required on the child table (Course) so that it can be related to the parent table (Employee). Create a Foreign Key named EmployeeID on the Course table that references the EmployeeID Primary Key in the Employee table.

3. Draw a line from the Employee entity to the Course entity, making a large dot at the end of the line pointing to Course. This indicates a one-to-many relationship, as shown in Figure 2.13.

2.2 Creating a Many-to-Many Relationship

This exercise demonstrates how to create a many-to-many relationship between the Trainee entity and the Course entity. Trainees enroll in courses taught at Lloyd's. A single trainee can enroll in many courses, and at the same time many trainees can enroll to a single course, thus developing a many-to-many relationship.

Estimated Time: 5 minutes.

1. Draw out the entities participating in this exercise; that is, the Trainee and Course entity. Include in each entity the attributes defined as rows inside the box.

2. Recall that a many-to-many relationship can only be implemented with the help of an associative entity as an intermediate. Create a new entity between Trainee and Course and name it TraineeCourse.

3. The new associative entity needs to link both the Course and Trainee entities. To do this, the associative entity must contain two Foreign Keys: TraineeID and CourseID.

4. After you have placed these two attributes onto the associative entity, draw two lines from the associative entity to both other entities, placing a

Exercises: These activities provide an opportunity for you to master specific hands-on tasks. Our goal is to increase your proficiency with the product or technology. You must be able to conduct these tasks in order to pass the exam.

Review Questions: These open-ended, short-answer questions allow you to quickly assess your comprehension of what you just read in the chapter. Instead of asking you to choose from a list of options, these questions require you to state the correct answers in your own words. Although you will not experience these kinds of questions on the exam, these questions will indeed test your level of comprehension of key concepts.

Review Questions

1. How does a DISTINCT query provide for useful reporting to the user?

2. What advantages can the use of a WHERE clause provide over the basic use of a SELECT or DELETE operation?

3. How would data in the form of dates be compared against data stored as characters?

4. What types of functions would be considered if the most important application issue centered around the use of network bandwidth?

5. When do data deletions and modifications affect data stored in other tables?

Answers to Review Questions

1. Configuring a Cascading Delete Action causes the deletion of a record to propagate deletions throughout the underlying related table. This option should be configured with caution, because the deletion of underlying data might not be desired. You need to set two tables up in a parent-child relationship, using appropriate Primary and Foreign Keys. Cascading Update Action performs a similar operation when key values are changed, propagating the new values to underlying child tables.

2. First, put the log files onto a volume other than where the data is stored to ensure optimum recoverability. If possible, use a mirror on the OS volume to minimize downtime in a system failure. If the data volume becomes corrupt, a restore can be performed to get that data back. Having the log on a separate volume means that you can recover additional data because the log volume should be unaffected by the damage to the data.

Exam Questions: These questions reflect the kinds of multiple-choice questions that appear on the Microsoft exams. Use them to become familiar with the exam question formats and to help you determine what you know and what you need to review or study more.

Exam Questions

1. In preparation for a major system upgrade, a large set of data changes are going to be made on a system. You would like to implement a number of changes without affecting any of the existing data. Which of the following operations do not affect any existing data values? Select all that apply:

   A. INSERT

   B. UPDATE

   C. Change column name

   D. Increase column length

   E. Decrease column length

2. You are creating a one-time report to supply the office staff with a revenue breakdown. The data source for the report contains cryptic column headings that cover several different categories.

Answers and Explanations: For each of the Review and Exam questions, you will find thorough explanations located at the end of the section.

Suggested Readings and Resources: The very last element in every chapter is a list of additional resources you can use if you want to go above and beyond certification-level material or if you need to spend more time on a particular subject that you are having trouble understanding.

Suggested Readings and Resources

1. Inside SQL Server 2000 – Kalen Delaney (www.insidesqlserver.com)

   Not a beginner book, but it fills in many of the gaps left out of the SQL Server Books Online documentation. Explains fully how SQL Server stores and processes data internally.

2. SQL Server 2000 Books Online

   • Creating and Maintaining Databases (Look particularly at the sections on indexes, views, and triggers.)

   • Transact-SQL Reference (Use this as a resource for the specific syntax requirements of each statement, as well as some code examples.)

   • Optimizing Database Performance (Focus on Database and Application Design.)

   • Troubleshooting Server and Database Troubleshooting

3. MSDN Online Internet Reference (http://msdn.microsoft.com)

   • Transact SQL Overview (/library/psdk/sql/ts_tsqlcon_61-k.htm)

   • Transact SQL Syntax Conventions (/library/psdk/sql/ts_syntaxc_9k-n.htm)

   • Transact SQL Tips (/library/psdk/sql/ac_8_qd_14_2k-3.htm)

Introduction

MCSE Training Guide (70-229): SQL Sever 2000 Database Design and Implementation is designed for advanced users, technicians, or system administrators with the goal of certification as a Microsoft Certified Systems Engineer (MCSE). It covers Exam 70-229, Designing and Implementing Databases with Microsoft SQL Server 2000 Enterprise Edition. This exam measures your ability to design and implement database solutions by using Microsoft SQL Server 2000 Enterprise Edition. In addition, the test measures the skills required to develop a logical data model, implement the physical database, retrieve and modify data, program business logic, tune and optimize data access, and design a database security plan.

This book is your one-stop shop. Everything you need to know to pass the exam is in here, and Microsoft has approved it as study material. You do not have to take a class in addition to buying this book to pass the exam. However, depending on your personal study habits or learning style, you may benefit from buying this book *and* taking a class.

Microsoft assumes that the typical candidate for this exam will have a minimum of one year experience implementing relational databases in a medium to very large network environment.

How This Book Helps You

This book takes you on a self-guided tour of all the areas covered by the Designing and Implementing Databases with Microsoft SQL Server 2000 Enterprise Edition exam and teaches you the specific skills you'll

need to achieve your MCSE certification. You'll also find helpful hints, tips, real-world examples, and exercises, as well as references to additional study materials. Specifically, this book is set up to help you in the following ways:

◆ **Organization.** The book is organized by individual exam objectives. Every objective you need to know for the Designing and Implementing Databases with Microsoft SQL Server 2000 Enterprise Edition exam is covered in this book. We have attempted to present the objectives in an order that is as close as possible to that listed by Microsoft. However, we have not hesitated to reorganize them where needed to make the material as easy as possible for you to learn. We have also attempted to make the information accessible in the following ways:

  • The full list of exam topics and objectives is included in this introduction.

  • Each chapter begins with a list of the objectives to be covered.

  • Each chapter also begins with an outline that provides you with an overview of the material and the page numbers where particular topics can be found.

  • The objectives are repeated where the material most directly relevant to it is covered (unless the whole chapter addresses a single objective).

  • Information on where the objectives are covered is also conveniently condensed on the CD that accompanies this book.

◆ **Instructional Features.** This book has been designed to provide you with multiple ways to learn and reinforce the exam material. The following are some of the helpful methods:

- *Case Studies.* Given the case study basis of the exam, we designed this *Training Guide* around them. Case studies appear in each chapter and also serve as the basis for exam questions.

- *Objective Explanations.* As mentioned previously, each chapter begins with a list of the objectives covered in the chapter. In addition, immediately following each objective is an explanation in a context that defines it more meaningfully.

- *Study Strategies.* The beginning of the chapter also includes strategies for approaching the studying and retaining of the material in the chapter, particularly as it is addressed on the exam.

- *Exam Tips.* Exam tips appear in the margin to provide specific exam-related advice. Such tips may address what material is covered (or not covered) on the exam, how it is covered, mnemonic devices, or particular quirks of that exam.

- *Review Breaks and Summaries.* Crucial information is summarized at various points in the book in lists or tables. Each chapter ends with a summary as well.

- *Key Terms.* A list of key terms appears at the end of each chapter.

- *Notes.* These appear in the margin and contain various kinds of useful information, such as tips on technology or administrative practices, historical background on terms and technologies, or side commentary on industry issues.

- *Warnings.* When using sophisticated information technology, there is always the potential for mistakes or even catastrophes that occur because of improper application of the technology. Warnings appear in the margin to alert you to such potential problems.

- *In the Field.* These more extensive discussions cover material that may not be directly relevant to the exam, but which is useful as reference material or in everyday practice. In the Field may also provide useful background or contextual information necessary for understanding the larger topic under consideration.

- *Exercises.* Found at the end of each chapter in the "Apply Your Knowledge" section, exercises are performance-based opportunities for you to learn and assess your knowledge.

◆ **Extensive Practice Test Options.** The book provides numerous opportunities for you to assess your knowledge and practice for the exam. The practice options include the following:

- *Review Questions.* These open-ended questions appear in the "Apply Your Knowledge" section at the end of each chapter. They allow you to quickly assess your comprehension of what you just read in the chapter. Answers to the questions are provided later in a separate section entitled "Answers to Review Questions."

- *Exam Questions.* These questions also appear in the "Apply Your Knowledge" section. Use them to help you determine what you know and what you need to review or study further. Answers and explanations for them are provided in a separate section entitled "Answers to Exam Questions."

- *Practice Exam*. A Practice Exam is included in the "Final Review" section. The Final Review section and the Practice Exam are discussed later in this section.

- *ExamGear*. The special Training Guide version of the *ExamGear* software included on the CD-ROM provides further opportunities for you to assess how well you understood the material in this book.

> **NOTE** For a description of the Que *ExamGear, Training Guide* software, please see Appendix D, "*Using the ExamGear, Training Guide Edition Software*."

◆ **Final Review.** This part of the book provides you with three valuable tools for preparing for the exam.

- *Fast Facts*. This condensed version of the information contained in the book will prove extremely useful for last-minute review.

- *Study and Exam Preparation Tips*. Read this section early on to help you develop study strategies. It also provides you with valuable exam-day tips and information on exam/question formats, such as adaptive tests and case study-based questions.

- *Practice*. A practice exam is included. Questions are written in styles similar to those used on the actual exam. Use it to assess your understanding of the material in the book.

The book includes several other features, such as a section titled "Suggested Readings and Resources " at the end of each chapter that directs you toward further information that could aid you in your exam preparation or your actual work. There are valuable appendixes

as well, including a glossary (Appendix A), an overview of the Microsoft certification program (Appendix B), and a description of what is on the CD-ROM (Appendix C).

These, and all the other book features mentioned previously, will supply you with thorough exam preparation.

For more information about the exam or the certification process, contact Microsoft:

Microsoft Education: 800-636-7544

Internet: `ftp://ftp.microsoft.com/ Services/MSEdCert`

World Wide Web: `http://www.microsoft.com/train_cert`

CompuServe Forum: GO MSEDCERT

WHAT EXAM 70-229: DESIGNING AND IMPLEMENTING DATABASES WITH MICROSOFT SQL SERVER 2000 ENTERPRISE EDITION COVERS

The Designing and Implementing Databases with Microsoft SQL Server 2000 Enterprise Edition exam (70-229) covers job skills in the following areas:

◆ Developing a Logical Data Model

◆ Implementing the Physical Database

◆ Retrieving and Modifying Data

◆ Programming Business Logic

◆ Tuning and Optimizing Data Access

◆ Designing a Database Security Plan

Before taking the exam, you should be proficient in the job skills represented by the following units, objectives, and subobjectives.

Developing a Logical Data Model

Define entities. Considerations include entity composition and normalization.

◆ Specify entity attributes.

◆ Specify degree or normalization.

Design entity keys. Considerations include Foreign Key constraints, Primary Key constraints, and UNIQUE constraints.

◆ Specify attributes that uniquely identify records.

◆ Specify attributes that reference other entities.

Design attribute domain integrity. Considerations include CHECK constraints, data types, and nullability.

◆ Specify scale and precision of allowable values for each attribute.

◆ Allow or prohibit NULL for each attribute.

◆ Specify allowable values for each attribute.

Implementing the Physical Database

Create and alter databases. Considerations include file groups, file placement, growth strategy, and space requirements.

◆ Specify space management parameters. Parameters include autoshrink, growth increment, initial size, and maxsize.

◆ Specify file group and file placement. Considerations include logical and physical file placement.

◆ Specify transaction log placement. Considerations include bulk-load operations and performance.

Create and alter database objects. Objects include constraints, indexes, stored procedures, tables, triggers, user-defined functions, and views.

◆ Specify table characteristics. Characteristics include cascading actions, CHECK constraints, clustered, defaults, FILLFACTOR, Foreign Keys, nonclustered, Primary Keys, and UNIQUE constraints.

◆ Specify schema binding and encryption for stored procedures, triggers, user-defined functions, and views.

◆ Specify recompile settings for stored procedures.

◆ Specify index characteristics. Characteristics include clustered, FILLFACTOR, nonclustered, and uniqueness.

Alter database objects to support replication and partitioned views.

◆ Support merge, snapshot, and transactional replication models.

◆ Design a partitioning strategy.

◆ Design and create constraints and views.

◆ Resolve replication conflicts.

Troubleshoot failed object creation.

Retrieving and Modifying Data

Import and export data. Methods include the bulk copy program, the Bulk Insert task, and Data Transformation Services (DTS).

Manipulate heterogeneous data. Methods include linked servers, OPENQUERY, OPENROWSET, and OPENXML.

Retrieve, filter, group, summarize, and modify data by using Transact-SQL.

Manage resultsets by using cursors and Transact-SQL. Considerations include locking models and appropriate usage.

Extract data in XML format. Considerations include output format and XML schema structure.

Programming Business Logic

Manage data manipulation by using stored procedures, transactions, triggers, user-defined functions, and views.

◆ Implement error handling in stored procedures, transactions, triggers, and user-defined functions.

◆ Pass and return parameters to and from stored procedures and user-defined functions.

◆ Validate data.

Enforce procedural business logic by using stored procedures, transactions, triggers, user-defined functions, and views.

◆ Specify trigger actions.

◆ Design and manage transactions

◆ Manage control of flow.

◆ Filter data by using stored procedures, triggers, user-defined functions, and views.

Troubleshoot and optimize programming objects. Objects include stored procedures, transactions, triggers, user-defined functions, and views.

Tuning and Optimizing Data Access

Analyze the query execution plan. Considerations include query processor operations and steps.

Capture, analyze, and replay SQL Profiler traces. Considerations include lock detection, performance tuning, and trace flags.

Create and implement indexing strategies. Considerations include clustered index, covering index, indexed views, nonclustered index, placement, and statistics.

Improve index use by using the Index Tuning wizard.

Monitor and troubleshoot database activity by using SQL Profiler.

Designing a Database Security Plan

Control data access by using stored procedures, triggers, user-defined functions, and views.

◆ Apply ownership chains.

◆ Use programming logic and objects. Considerations include implementing row-level security and restricting direct access to tables.

Define object-level security including column-level permissions by using GRANT, REVOKE, and DENY.

Create and manage application roles.

HARDWARE AND SOFTWARE YOU'LL NEED

As a self-paced study guide, *MCSE Training Guide (70-229): SQL Server 2000 Database Design and Implementation* is meant to help you understand concepts that must be refined through hands-on experience. To make the most of your studying, you need to have as much background on and experience with Microsoft SQL Server 2000 Enterprise Edition as possible. The best way to do this is to combine studying with work on Microsoft SQL Server 2000 Enterprise Edition. This section gives you a description of the minimum computer requirements you need to enjoy a solid practice environment.

◆ Windows 2000 Server, Advanced Server or DataCenter Server, or NT 4.0 SP5 or better. **Note:** Non-enterprise editions of SQL Server run on Windows 2000 Professional and Windows 98. These will satisfy *most* of the requirements for the book, with the exception of indexed views and distributed partitioned views.

◆ A server and a workstation computer on the Microsoft Hardware Compatibility List.

◆ Pentium 166MHZ (or better) processor.

◆ Hard disk space: SQL Server database components (95-270MB, 250MB typical); Analysis Services (50MB minimum, 130MB typical); English Query (80MB); Desktop Engine only (44MB); Books Online (15MB).

◆ VGA (or Super VGA) video adapter and monitor; 800×600 or higher resolution required for the SQL Server graphical tools.

◆ Mouse or equivalent pointing device (not required, but useful).

◆ CD-ROM drive.

◆ Network Interface Card (NIC) or modem connection to Internet.

◆ Internet access with Internet Explorer 5.0 or later.

◆ 64MB of RAM minimum, 128MB or more recommended.

You can obtain 120-day evaluation versions of the product as a download from Microsoft's product download page http://www.microsoft.com/sql/evaluation/ trial/2000.

It is easier to obtain access to the necessary computer hardware and software in a corporate business environment. It can be difficult, however, to allocate enough time within the busy workday to complete a self-study program. Most of your study time will occur after normal working hours, away from the everyday interruptions and pressures of your regular job.

ADVICE ON TAKING THE EXAM

More extensive tips are found in the Final Review section titled "Study and Exam Prep Tips," but keep this advice in mind as you study:

◆ **Read all the material.** Microsoft has been known to include material not expressly specified in the objectives. This book has included additional information not reflected in the objectives in an effort to give you the best possible preparation for the examination—and for the real-world experiences to come.

◆ **Do the Step by Steps and complete the Exercises in each chapter.** They will help you gain experience using the specified methodology or approach. All Microsoft exams are task- and experienced-based and require you to have experience actually performing the tasks upon which you will be tested.

◆ **Use the questions to assess your knowledge.** Don't just read the chapter content; use the questions to find out what you know and what you don't. You also need the experience of analyzing case studies. If you are struggling at all, study some more, review, and then assess your knowledge again.

◆ **Review the exam objectives.** Develop your own questions and examples for each topic listed. If you can develop and answer several questions for each topic, you should not find it difficult to pass the exam.

N O T E

Exam-Taking Advice   Although this book is designed to prepare you to take and pass the Designing and Implementing Databases with Microsoft SQL Server 2000 Enterprise Edition exam, there are no guarantees. Read this book, work through the questions and exercises, and when you feel confident, take the Assessment Exam and additional exams using the exam test software on the CD. This should tell you whether you are ready for the real thing.

When taking the actual certification exam, make sure you answer all the questions before your time limit expires. Do not spend too much time on any one question. If you are unsure, answer it as best as you can; then mark it for review when you have finished the rest of the questions. However, this advice will not apply if you are taking an adaptive exam. In that case, take your time on each question. There is no opportunity to go back to a question.

Remember, the primary object is not to pass the exam—it is to understand the material. After you understand the material, passing the exam should be simple. Knowledge is a pyramid; to build upward, you need a solid foundation. This book and the Microsoft Certified Professional programs are designed to ensure that you have that solid foundation.

Good luck!

QUE CERTIFICATION

The staff of Que Certification is committed to bringing you the very best in computer reference material. Each Que Certification book is the result of months of work by authors and staff who research and refine the information contained within its covers.

As part of this commitment to you, the reader, Que invites your input. Please let us know if you enjoy this book, if you have trouble with the information or examples presented, or if you have a suggestion for the next edition.

Please note, however, that Que staff cannot serve as a technical resource during your preparation for the Microsoft certification exams or for questions about software- or hardware-related problems. Please refer instead to the documentation that accompanies the Microsoft products or to the applications' Help systems.

If you have a question or comment about any Que book, there are several ways to contact Que Publishing. We will respond to as many readers as we can. Your name, address, or phone number will never become part of a mailing list or be used for any purpose other than to help us continue to bring you the best books possible. You can write to us at the following address:

Que Certification
Attn: Chuck Stewart
201 W. 103rd Street
Indianapolis, IN 46290

If you prefer, you can fax Que Certification at 317-581-4666.

You also can send email to Que at the following Internet address:

`feedback@quepublishing.com`

Que is an imprint of Pearson Education. To purchase a Que book, call 800-428-5331.

Thank you for selecting *MCSE Training Guide (70-229): SQL Server 2000 Database Design and Implementation.*

EXAM PREPARATION

1   Introduction to SQL Server 2000

2   Data Modeling

3   Physical Database Design

4   Querying and Modifying Data

5   Advanced Data Retrieval and Modification

6   Programming SQL Server 2000

7   Working with Views

8   Triggers

9   Stored Procedures and User-Defined Functions

10   Boosting Performance with Indexes

11   Implementing and Understanding Replication Methodologies

12   Monitoring SQL Server 2000

This first chapter gives you a birds-eye view of Microsoft SQL Server 2000, the various programs installed with the product, and the basic concepts you should know before continuing in the book. You will be interested to see what is actually included in the product and the facilities that are available.

Use this chapter to begin your preparation for passing the 70-229 exam; right from the start you will be gaining valuable exam tips. Each chapter begins by introducing the exam objectives and then follows by fleshing out the details. The following represents the specific Microsoft exam objectives that are covered in this chapter:

Knowledge of Microsoft SQL Server 2000 features and characteristics.

- **Standard features**

- **Features new to SQL Server 2000**

▶ As with all certification exams, you really have to spend time with the product. Often a good starting point to learning any technology is to simply know what it is and what it does. This objective provides a springboard to many topics covered in detail later in the book.

Be familiar with the programming environment and industry-standard coding language.

- **Transact SQL**

- **Command Language**

- **Methods of Execution**

- **The Query Analyzer**

▶ There should be no secret that this is a programming exam that will test your ability to provide working code. This objective will give you a starting point in understanding how to use the SQL coding language and SQL Server's coding environment.

CHAPTER 1

Introducing
SQL Server 2000

OBJECTIVES

Identify and manage environment restrictions.

- **SQL Server Limitations**
- **SQL Server as a Shared Resource**
- **Back Office Integration**
- **Important Numerical Restrictions**

▶ Knowledge of SQL Server limitations and installation requirements is a necessity for anyone attempting a SQL Server deployment, administration of a SQL Server, or implementing a database design for an existing server.

Familiarity with SQL Server tools, utilities, interface, and procedures.

▶ There are a lot of nooks and crannies in SQL Server and this version is no different then those of the past. With this objective you familiarize yourself with all the components of the software. SQL Server is much more than just a place to put databases, and knowledge of its intricacies will be an important part of attaining any certification goal.

Design for a medium to enterprise computing environment that uses SQL Server 2000 Enterprise Edition.

▶ Candidates for this exam work in a medium to enterprise computing environment that uses SQL Server 2000 Enterprise Edition. Therefore, you must know what separates the Enterprise Edition from the other editions.

OUTLINE

STUDY STRATEGIES

▶ Go to the SQL Server web site
`http://www.microsoft.com/sql` and read up on white papers, case studies, and the product information available.

▶ Frequently consult SQL Server Books Online. This is an immense resource included with the product. Everything you need to find out about SQL Server and the related technologies are in this resource.

▶ Practice, practice, practice. Learn by doing. There is no better learning tool than the time spent in front of the software itself. Use the exercises in this book and create additional ones of your own. Never be afraid to experiment and explore (though not every activity is recommended on a production machine).

INTRODUCTION

Welcome to the world of database development using SQL Server. If you are just starting out with the product, then this book will try to bring you along and quickly get you up to speed. If you are already familiar with this tremendous software, then you should look into what is new and fascinating with this 2000 release. This book covers a lot of new functionality.

This book explores all the attributes of SQL Server; it looks into the strengths of the product and points out some pitfalls and snags, as well. To really excel in database implementation and do well on the exam, you should use this book as a complete reference guide. Use the book also as a practical means of gaining experience as you complete a variety of exercises at the end of each chapter. These exercises are designed to simulate a production environment.

GETTING TO KNOW SQL SERVER 2000

Microsoft's database server is back and upgraded! It is creating huge amounts of excitement and interest throughout the database market. Before SQL Server had been in conjunction with Sybase, it was very unpopular and other database servers ruled the market. Now, with much development, SQL Server is one of the most powerful and robust servers available.

Features of SQL Server

▶ **Knowledge of Microsoft SQL Server 2000 features and characteristics**

These are just some of the many reasons why SQL Server has earned respect:

◆ Internet integration

◆ Scalability and availability

◆ Enterprise-level database features

◆ Ease of installation, deployment, and use

◆ Data warehousing

The SQL Server 2000 database engine includes integrated XML support. It also has features it needs to operate as the data storage component of the largest web sites. The SQL Server 2000 programming model is integrated with the Windows architecture for web application development, and SQL Server 2000 supports English Query and the Microsoft Search Service to allow for user-friendly queries and powerful search capabilities in web applications.

The same database engine can be used across platforms ranging from laptop computers running Microsoft Windows 98 through multiprocessor servers running Microsoft Windows 2000 Data Center. SQL Server 2000 Enterprise Edition supports features such as federated servers, indexed views, and large memory support that enable it to scale to the performance levels required by the largest web sites.

The SQL Server 2000 database engine supports features required by demanding environments. The database engine protects integrity while minimizing overhead. The engine is capable of managing thousands of users concurrently modifying the database. SQL Server 2000 distributed queries enable you to reference data from multiple sources as if it were a part of a single SQL Server 2000 database. Distributed transaction support protects the integrity of any updates of the data dispersed on multiple sources. Replication enables you to maintain multiple copies of data, while also ensuring synchronization.

SQL Server 2000 includes a complete set of administrative and development tools. SQL Server 2000 also supports a standards-based programming model, making the use of SQL Server databases and data warehouses a seamless part of building powerful systems. These features enable you to rapidly deliver SQL Server applications that can be implemented with a minimum of installation and administrative overhead.

SQL Server 2000 includes tools for extracting and analyzing summary data for online analytical processing. SQL Server also includes tools for visually designing databases and analyzing data using English-based questions.

Exam Questions about the New Features   You can expect to have one or more exam questions for each feature in the list of New Features. We have broken down the complete list of new features in SQL Server 2000 and have focused in on those you can expect on the exam. Those new features not likely to be seen on the exam have been omitted from this list.

New Features in SQL Server 2000

A great deal more functionality has been added to SQL Server in this 2000 release. Many of the features are extremely useful in the stages of design and implementation of databases. The features listed and described in this section represent the highlights of the new features most commonly of interest to developers and a necessity in exam preparation.

- ◆ XML support
- ◆ Federated database servers
- ◆ User-defined functions
- ◆ Indexed views
- ◆ New data types
- ◆ INSTEAD OF and AFTER triggers
- ◆ Cascading referential integrity constraints
- ◆ Collation enhancements
- ◆ Multiple instances of SQL Server
- ◆ Updateable distributed partitioned views

The relational database engine can return data as Extensible Markup Language (XML) documents. Additionally, XML can also be used to insert, update, and delete values in the database. XML is covered fully in Chapter 5, "Advanced Data Retrieval and Modification."

SQL Server 2000 supports distributed partitioned views that enable you to divide tables horizontally and place the data on multiple servers. A group of federated database servers can support the data storage requirements of the largest web sites and enterprise systems. Partitioned views are covered fully in Chapter 7, "Working with Views."

You can extend the programmability of SQL Server by creating your own Transact-SQL (T-SQL) functions. T-SQL is an extension of the language defined by SQL standards and the basis for programming in SQL Server. A user-defined function can return either a scalar value or a table. User-Defined Functions (UDFs) are covered fully in Chapter 9, "Stored Procedures and User-Defined Functions."

Indexed views can significantly improve the performance of an application where queries frequently perform certain joins or aggregations. An indexed view provides for a technique where fast access to data is enabled (indexing), associated with data display definitions (views), and where the result set of the view is materialized and stored and indexed in the database. Indexed views are covered fully in Chapter 7.

SQL Server 2000 introduces three new data types—bigint, sql_variant, and table—that are supported for variables and are the return types for user-defined functions. Data Types are covered in full in Chapter 2, "Data Modeling."

INSTEAD OF triggers are executed rather than the triggering action (for example, INSERT, UPDATE, DELETE). They can also be defined on views, in which case they greatly extend the types of updates a view can support. AFTER triggers fire after the triggering action. SQL Server 2000 introduces the capability to specify which AFTER triggers fire first and last. Triggers are covered fully in Chapter 8, "Constraints, Defaults, and Triggers."

Cascading actions enable you to control the actions SQL Server 2000 takes when deleting or changing data. If you attempt to update or delete a key to which existing foreign keys point, cascading actions will dictate the effects on the associated records. This is controlled by the new ON DELETE and ON UPDATE clauses in the REFERENCES clause of the CREATE TABLE and ALTER TABLE statements. Cascading Referential Integrity is covered fully in Chapter 3, "Physical Database Design."

SQL Server 2000 includes support for most collations supported in earlier versions of SQL Server, and introduces a new set of collations based on Windows collations. You can now specify collations at the database level or at the column level. Collations are covered fully in Chapter 3, "Physical Database Design."

SQL Server 2000 supports running multiple instances of the relational database engine on the same computer. Each computer can run one instance of the relational database engine from SQL Server version 6.5 or 7.0, along with one or more instances of the database engine from SQL Server 2000. Connecting to Multiple Instances of SQL Server is covered fully in Chapter 2, "Data Modeling."

SQL Server 2000 can partition tables horizontally across several servers, and define a distributed partitioned view on each member server so that it appears as if a full copy of the original table is stored on each server. Groups of servers running SQL Server that cooperate in this type of partitioning are called *federations* of servers. Partitioned views are covered fully in Chapter 7.

With all this fantastic new functionality, SQL Server 2000 has reached a level where it provides truly superior software value and performance.

SQL Server Implementation Requirements

The exam is geared for the Enterprise Version of Microsoft SQL Server 2000 edition, which is used as a production database server. It supports all features available in SQL Server 2000 and scales to the performance levels required to support the largest web sites and enterprise online transaction processing (OLTP) and data warehousing systems.

Requirements

A couple of things are required before you can set up your SQL Server. Internet Explorer 4.01 is needed solely for the Microsoft Management Console (MMC) and to view Help topics in Books Online. Certain hardware requirements must be met before SQL Server can be installed, some of which are listed in the next section. After making sure all the prerequisites are taken care of, you can then start the Setup Wizard by inserting the CD and clicking on Install SQL Server Components.

The following hardware is needed to install the Enterprise version of SQL Server 2000.

Minimum Hardware Requirements

◆ Computer:

Intel or compatible

Pentium 166MHz or higher

◆ Memory:

64MB minimum, 128MB or more recommended

◆ Hard disk space:

SQL Server database components: 95-270MB, 250MB typical

Analysis Services: 50MB minimum, 130MB typical

English Query: 80MB

Desktop Engine only: 44MB

Books Online: 15MB

◆ Monitor:

VGA or higher resolution

800 × 600 or higher resolution required for the SQL Server graphical tools

◆ Other Peripherals:

CD-ROM drive

You can obtain 120-day evaluation versions of the product as a download from Microsoft's product download page, `http://www.microsoft.com/sql/evaluation/trial/2000`.

STRUCTURED QUERY LANGUAGE (SQL)

▶ **Be familiar with the programming environment and industry-standard coding language.**

SQL is an industry-standard programming language used to insert, retrieve, modify, and delete data in a relational database. SQL also contains statements for defining and administering the objects in a database. SQL is the language supported by almost all database systems, and is the subject of published industry standards. SQL Server 2000 uses a version of the SQL language called Transact-SQL, or T-SQL.

Transact-SQL Language Elements

Transact-SQL is the language containing the commands used to administer SQL Server, to create and manage all objects in SQL Server, and to insert, retrieve, modify, and delete all data in tables.

T-SQL is an extension of the language defined in the SQL standards published by the International Standards Organization (ISO) and the American National Standards Institute (ANSI).

The basic elements of T-SQL are those used to view and edit the data in underlying tables and views. The basis for any database system is the handling of ACD operations which will use these T-SQL operations. ACD is an acronym used in data management for add, change, and delete. These four primary functions for Add (Insert), Change (Alter, Update), Delete, and T-SQL's capability to read and view data (known as "Querying" the data), are the basis for most SQL Server database activity.

In T-SQL you read data with a SELECT statement, add data with an INSERT operation, remove data with DELETE, and change data with UPDATE. T-SQL is presented throughout this book; for a detailed look into the structure and use of the language go to Chapter 6, "Programming SQL Server 2000."

Executing a Program

Executing T-SQL statements and other commands against a database can be achieved using a variety of techniques. You can develop front-end applications with Visual Basic, Visual C, Access, the Internet, or in combination with other data and programming interfaces. Commands can be executed through ODBC or OLE-DB standard libraries connecting to the server from virtually any computer. Statements can be executed directly on the server using the Query Analyzer or OSQL.

Query Analyzer

Figure 1.1. shows the Query Analyzer, which is your primary tool for executing Transact-SQL code, known as queries. This utility is discussed at great depth throughout the book. Most of the queries you execute are INSERT queries that add data, DELETE queries that remove data, SELECT queries that retrieve data, and UPDATE queries that change existing data. You can also create database objects such as views and indexes.

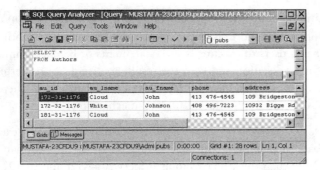

FIGURE 1.1
The Query Analyzer—your primary querying tool.

SQL Query Analyzer is an interactive, graphical tool that enables a database administrator or developer to write queries, execute multiple queries simultaneously, view results, analyze the query plan, and receive assistance to improve the query performance. The Execution Plan options graphically display the data retrieval methods chosen by the query optimizer.

Some queries, however, are not used to change data, but they will modify database and table design. These types of queries are called *data definition statements* and are used for tasks such as creating tables, indexes, views, and so on.

Not only can Query Analyzer execute any T-SQL statements, but it can also analyze them. Query Analyzer can report things such as how much time the queries took to run, how much time it took to read data from the hard disk, and so on.

If you think a particular query is inefficient, you can use tools built into the analyzer to diagnose the query to redesign the query in a way to achieve better performance. If you look at Figure 1.1, you can see a screen display of the Query Analyzer requesting all the data from the Authors table in the Pubs database. The bottom half is known as the Results Pane and contains the output of your query, which is known as a resultset.

ODBC Structured Query Language (OSQL)

OSQL is an interactive command prompt utility provided with SQL Server that replaces the ISQL utility used with SQL Server 6.5 and earlier versions. ISQL is still being supported for backward compatibility, but future versions of SQL Server will not support its use. Both ISQL and OSQL provide similar functionality. Both utilities enable users to execute T-SQL statements or batches from a server or workstation and view the results returned. ISQL performs this activity using the near obsolete DB-Library protocol, whereas OSQL uses industry-standard ODBC mechanisms.

The OSQL utility is similar to the Query Analyzer in that it executes batches of T-SQL code. The utility is run on the command line. Other than this, the two tools (Query Analyzer and OSQL) perform more or less the same function.

The question arises, "Then why use the OSQL utility?" The answer: One reason is scheduling.

It is possible to custom-schedule the OSQL utility. Say that you need to access sales figures on a daily basis. You could extract data manually every morning using the Query Analyzer, but this way would be too time consuming and ineffective. Or you could set up a job to automate the process. But the best and most efficient way would be to query with OSQL and save the results into a text file. You could then use scheduling to make that process automatic. The following represents the options for the OSQL utility:

```
OSQL[-?] ¦ [-L] ¦
    [
    {{-U login_id [-P password]} ¦ -E}
    [-S server_name[\instance_name]][-H wksta_name]
    [-d db_name][-l time_out][-t time_out][-h headers]
    [-s col_separator][-w column_width][-a packet_size]
    [-e][-I][-D data_source_name][-c cmd_end][-q "query"]
    [-Q "query"][-n][-m error_level][-r{0¦1}]
    [-i input_file][-o output_file][-p][-b][-u][-R][-O]
    ]
```

The -L parameter lists the locally configured servers and the names of the servers broadcasting on the network. Use -U to supply a login; if -U is omitted, the Windows login is passed in from environment variables, or alternatively, the operating system. If you omit the -P password option, you are prompted to provide your password. If neither the -U or the -P options are used, SQL Server 2000 attempts to connect using Windows Authentication mode. For more information on the other switches and particular examples, consult SQL Server Books Online.

Figure 1.2 illustrates the OSQL command prompt being used to execute a query that has been stored as a SQL script.

N O T E

OSQL Uses   OSQL can be used interactively to execute one or more T-SQL statements, display results in a text window, or save results to a text file. Its primary purpose, however, is to allow the scheduling of operations via the operating system scheduler, SQL Server scheduler, or any other schedule application provided by a third party.

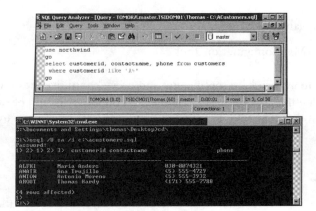

FIGURE 1.2
The OSQL Command Interface.

THE COMPLETE SQL SERVER 2000 SOFTWARE

▶ **Familiarity with SQL Server tools, utilities, interface, and procedures.**

Many tools and utilities are available for the SQL Server developer. After SQL Server is installed, you should know how to use these useful utilities to get the most out of SQL Server. After reading the following section, you should have a fair picture of what portion of the product performs the tasks that you want to do. For example, if you need to modify or insert data, you should know that the Query Analyzer and the Enterprise Manager are among your choices.

So far, this chapter has taken a quick look at the SQL Server Query Analyzer and OSQL, but many more useful programs and utilities are provided with the product that should be of great interest to you:

- ◆ Books Online
- ◆ Client Network utility
- ◆ Server Network utility
- ◆ Service Manager
- ◆ Enterprise Manager
- ◆ Profiler
- ◆ BCP
- ◆ English Query

◆ Analysis Services

◆ XML Configuration Tool

These tools each have specific uses and provide intuitive means of accessing the SQL Server environment. A brief explanation of each tool provides you with at least a point of initial discovery into its use.

SQL Server Databases

So, what exactly is a database? A database is similar to a work file folder, which contains information pertaining to related topics. In the same way, a *database* is a group of files used to store data pertaining to a single business process. Databases are organized in all database servers with components called fields, records, and tables.

A *field* is a single characteristic, attribute, or property that provides information about an object; for instance, salary or age provides information about an employee. A *record* is a complete set of all the fields/attributes combined together for a particular object. A record might include the salary, age, phone number, address, and name for a particular employee. A *table* is a group of all the records. A table might be set up for the employees holding hundreds of records, one record for each employee. A *database* is a group of all the tables. To continue with this example, a database might be set up for all the tables in the company, including employees, products, customers, and so on.

SQL Server is a relational database management system. A *relational database* contained within SQL Server is a collection of objects where data and other information are stored in multiple tables. The numerous tables are related in some way, either directly or indirectly via other tables. A relational database contains all database objects, structures, and the raw data pertaining to that database.

Default Databases

Some databases are created automatically when you install SQL Server. The default system databases should not be deleted because they may cause failure to your instance of SQL Server. The two sample databases are the Pubs and Northwind databases and may be removed, because they are there only to show you how a finished database functions.

Master

The Master database is provided to keep your instance of SQL Server functioning. This database records all the system information for the SQL Server instance. The Master database contains all information that is global to the server, including logins, error messages, system configuration, and the list of other databases that exist on the server. The Master database helps in tracking the location of primary files in order to view other user databases.

> **NOTE**
>
> **Master of the Server**   The Master database is crucial to the operations of SQL Server and should be considered as important as the most mission-critical database stored on the server. If it becomes damaged, the server ceases to function.

Msdb

The SQL Server Agent uses the Msdb database to store information about the scheduling of alerts, the definition of jobs, and the recording of the server operators to be contacted when a particular event occurs on the server.

Tempdb

The Tempdb contains all temporarily created stored procedures and tables and is generally used as a work area by SQL Server. Tempdb is where tasks that require memory are performed, such as join and sort operations. The temporary tables and objects created in a SQL Server session are dropped after SQL Server is shut down. Tempdb never saves information permanently. By default, the size of the Tempdb database automatically increases when needed and is restored to its default size (2.5MB) each time SQL Server is started.

Model

The Model database stores a complete template for creating new databases. When you create a new database, SQL Server copies the whole contents of the Model database into the new database you create.

Pubs

The Pubs database is a real-world example of a database serving as a learning tool. The Pubs database is a fictitious publisher's database containing publisher-specific tables and information such as authors and titles. The Pubs database may be dropped, because doing so does not affect the SQL Server environment whatsoever.

WARNING

> **Northwind Configuration**   The `Northwind` database is a poor example of the options to use in a live database. Don't use it as a measure for the options you need for your own database. Before selecting any option, know the impact of the option on the database and client connections as well as any applications-required settings.

Northwind

The `Northwind` database is the second example database. It is preferred by many Microsoft Access users who are new to SQL Server because it is the same sample database that was provided for Microsoft Access.

Contents of a Database

There are certain objects that are present within a database after it has been created. Many database objects are necessary for a database to function. For example, a table object is the basic object needed to store data; without a table, your database wouldn't get very far. An outline of the different database objects that you can use follows:

◆ **Table**. A table is the first thing you create in the database so that data may be stored. Tables may have many fields and records. A table is a data structure that may contain information of interest to users, table creator, or company. Tables, like spreadsheets, are made up of rows and columns.

◆ **View**. A view is an object used in displaying a subset of data from a table in different formats. This can be used to ensure security or reduce data redundancy. A view is a stored SQL query. You can assign permissions to a view to enable an administrator to forgo more granular permission assignments at the column level of a table.

◆ **User-Defined Function**. A user-defined function is a group of T-SQL statements that may be reused. It is similar to predefined functions, such as `ABS()`, which returns the absolute value of a number specified. User-defined functions can be created by a database developer and stored as database objects. Functions are subroutines used to encapsulate frequently performed logic. Any code that must perform the logic incorporated in a function can call the function rather than having to repeat all the function logic.

◆ **Stored Procedure**. Stored procedures are collections of T-SQL statements that execute as a single unit. Stored procedures are stored on the server and can execute faster than queries at the client, without any extra overhead.

◆ **Triggers**. A trigger is a stored procedure that automatically executes at the invocation of an `INSERT`, `DELETE`, or `UPDATE`.

Triggers can be used to validate the data being entered and to enforce data integrity.

◆ **Database roles**. Users can be assigned to various database roles that determine what access they have to which database objects. A role is a collection of users and permissions. Members of a role inherit the permissions associated with the role. A user may be a member of many roles, and the permissions are cumulative.

◆ **Database diagrams**. Database diagrams are graphically created outlines of how your database is structured. Database diagrams show how tables, and the fields that compose the table, are related.

◆ **Constraints**. A constraint is an attribute a column or table can take to restrict what users enter into your database. For example, you may want only unique values to be entered into a certain column. To do this, use a UNIQUE constraint.

◆ **Indexes**. An index is a database object that provides fast access to data in the rows of a table, based on key values. Indexes can also enforce uniqueness on the rows in a table. SQL Server supports clustered and nonclustered indexes. The Primary Key constraint of a table is automatically indexed.

Each database object has its own properties that make it an important piece of the entire picture. This book looks deep into the SQL Server object structure and looks independently at each part of SQL Server from multiple perspectives.

Client Network Utility

The Client Network utility is used to manage the client net-libraries and define server alias names. It can also be used to set the default options used by DB-Library applications. This tool is not very difficult to use. It can impact the connectivity of client computers accessing SQL Server. For the client and server to run on the same computer, they must be running the same network library. The Client Network utility is used to configure and even possibly change the network library in use on the client.

In some cases, an instance of SQL Server may be configured to listen on alternate network addresses. If this is done, client applications

> **NOTE**
>
> **The Client Network Utility** This utility is installed in SQL Server by default. It can be installed on other computers if you execute a Network Libraries Only installation, which is done by selecting Connectivity from the Installation Type selection screen.

connecting to that instance must explicitly specify the alternate address. Although applications could specify the alternate addresses on each connection request, it is easier to use the Client Network utility to set up an alias specifying the alternate addresses. Applications can then specify the alias name in place of the server network name in their connection requests. The starting screen of the Client Network utility looks like Figure 1.3.

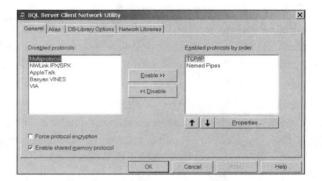

When you first run the Client Network utility by going to the Start menu and selecting Programs and Microsoft SQL Server, you will see four tabs: General, Alias, DB-Library, and Network Libraries. Each one is discussed in the following sections.

The General Tab

The General tab includes two boxes labeled Enabled Protocols and Disabled Protocols. The Client may communicate with SQL Server databases over any of the Network Libraries switched on in the Enabled box. If you select a library that is not supported by the server, the `Specified SQL Server Not Found` error will be reported.

The network libraries or net-libraries all have different properties that can be changed so that the client can communicate effectively.

You also have two arrows below the Enabled box. These boxes set the precedence of the network library. SQL Server tries to talk over the first mentioned net-library and works itself down to the bottom. For instance, if you want to make SQL Server communicate over the Named Pipes library, then you select it and press the Up arrow.

Alias Tab

In many organizations, several SQL Servers run simultaneously and each server is configured with different settings. For instance, one server may be running by having the TCP/IP net-library listen to port 1433. Another may be configured to listen to port 37337. Other servers have different settings for their client connections. In this case, you need to set server aliases. With an alias you have a method of assigning server-specific library configurations. The most common use of a server alias is to specify a particular network library to use to communicate with a specific server. In addition, an alias may be used to communicate with a SQL server that listens on a part other than the default.

The DB-Library Tab

SQL Server can be set up so that data can be retrieved using different tools. You can write T-SQL code by using the OSQL utility or the Query Analyzer, or you can also execute your custom-made programs. DB-Library is an interface dll to SQL Server. You can define applications using VB or C++ to call and use the functions inside the dll. The dll is an API that front-end programmers can access. The DB-Library API has not been enhanced beyond the level of SQL Server version 6.5. All DB-Library applications can work with SQL Server 2000, but only as 6.5-level clients. Features introduced in SQL Server 2000 and SQL Server version 7.0 are not supported for DB-Library applications.

As SQL Server changes, the DB-Library will also be changed, and therefore you will need to upgrade your DB-Library at times. To upgrade, you need to know information regarding the current DB-Library (version, size, date), which can be viewed from the DB-Library tab.

Network Libraries Tab

This tab displays the date and version number of all the network library files installed on your local system. Whenever files are outdated, you can upgrade then by installing the most recent service pack. You can check the readme file Microsoft provides with the service pack and compare it with the version numbers on this tab.

> **WARNING**
>
> **Front End Development** SQL Server 2000 does not include a programming environment for DB-Library for Microsoft Visual Basic. The existing DB-Library for Visual Basic applications can run against SQL Server 2000, but must be maintained using the software development tools from SQL Server version 6.5. All development of new Visual Basic applications that access SQL Server should use the Visual Basic data APIs such as ActiveX Data Objects (ADOs) and Remote Data Objects (RDOs).

> **NOTE**
>
> **Future Implementation** DB-Library is going to be de-implemented. OLE-DB and ODBC, in that order, are the preferred interfaces.

Server Network Utility

The Server Network utility works in a way similar to the Client Network utility because it is also used to configure net-libraries on which the server listens. Unlike the Client Network utility, which controls how applications connect to SQL Server, the Server Network utility tells on which network libraries SQL Server is listening.

This utility also contains Winsock Proxy information listed on the bottom of the general tab. By changing these proxy settings, SQL Server can listen for client calls through Microsoft Proxy Server. To do this, you need to check the Enable Winsock proxy check box and then supply the name of the proxy server as well as the port on which to listen.

Service Manager

This tool, shown in Figure 1.4, is quite simple in contrast to the others. The Service Manager is there only to stop, pause, start, and monitor SQL Server services. The easiest way to run the Service Manager is to double-click on its icon in the system tray.

FIGURE 1.4

The Service Manager, which is used to stop, start, and pause SQL Server services.

The Services drop-down list displays the services that can be controlled. These services include the MSSQLServer service, the Microsoft Search service, the MSDTC service, and the SQL Server Agent service.

You can find some "hidden" functionality in the Service Manager. Click the icon on the top left corner of the form and notice a selection named Options and Connect.

The Verify Service Control Action check box is checked by default. This controls whether an "Are You Sure?" dialog box appears when you stop a service.

The poll interval determines how frequently Service Manager looks for the status of the services that are monitored. The default interval is 5 seconds.

Profiler

After designing and deploying your databases, and giving access to users to modify data, you need to monitor how your server is functioning and make sure it's working the way it's supposed to work.

You can set up traces that monitor anything that happens to the server. These include knowing whether a login failed or succeeded, whether a query was executed, and other such events. Traces can be customized to monitor different angles of SQL Server at different times. The Profiler is shown in Figure 1.5.

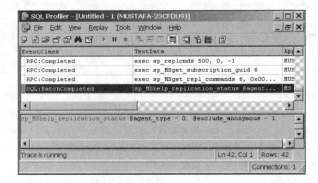

FIGURE 1.5
The SQL Server Profiler, used to monitor the SQL Server environment

Enterprise Manager

The Enterprise Manager is the primary graphical tool that performs many of the administrative tasks needed in SQL Server. With this tool, databases can be created as well as objects contained in them, such as views, tables, and so on. The Enterprise Manager is shown in Figure 1.6.

You use the Enterprise Manager to perform regular backups and restorations of databases. Server and database management and security can be maintained from here. Figure 1.6 shows the first screen of the Enterprise Manager. The Enterprise Manager is really a snap-in to the Microsoft Management Console (MMC). The MMC is a utility that Microsoft uses as an administrative interface for their associated products.

FIGURE 1.6
The easy-to-use SQL Server Enterprise
Manager.

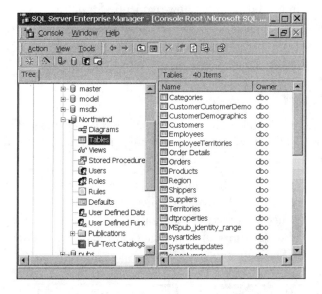

You can see two panes in the Enterprise Manager. The tree pane on the left is where the types of objects are displayed, and the contents pane is where the respective objects of the type selected are displayed.

The Enterprise Manager enables you to perform many of the tasks that require the use of T-SQL code at the click of a button. The Enterprise Manager enables you to easily manage and create databases, tables, indexes, and all other SQL Server objects. The Enterprise Manager enables you to delete and insert records. Using the SQL Server Enterprise Manager is one of the fastest and easiest ways to maintain and create databases and database objects. It is the primary tool used by SQL Server database administrators.

Registering Servers

The Enterprise Manager is an MMC snap-in that enables you to administer multiple SQL Servers from a single interface. Computers running SQL Server can be registered using the NetBIOS computer name, DNS Internet Host Name, or by TCP/IP address. Step by Step 1.1 walks you through the process of registering a server. Registering a server in the Enterprise Manager gives you access to the particular server and all the capabilities that were given to the login ID that was used in the registration process. This enables you to remotely monitor and manage multiple machines throughout the environment.

STEP BY STEP

1.1 Registering a Server Using the Enterprise Manager

1. Open the Enterprise Manager and click on a group. (Right-click if you want to create a new group.)

2. Right-click and choose New SQL Server Registration from the drop-down menu.

3. At the introductory screen, select Next to begin the registration process.

4. Select from the available list of servers. (You may also type in an IP address or other recognizable name not displayed.)

5. Select the type of security account you would like to use for this registration. The security account is used to determine the privileges of the administrating user.

6. Select or create a group to organize the interface and then click Next. The grouping has little practical purpose other than to place the servers to make them easier to manage.

7. Select Finish to complete the process and register the server.

After you have registered, you can change registration properties through the Enterprise Management Console (EMC).

Components of EMC

The Enterprise Management Console (EMC) is a full server and database management snap-in for the MMC. MMC is a common console framework for server and network management applications known as snap-ins. Snap-ins enable administrators to more effectively manage network resources. With several snap-ins placed into a single console it is possible to administer many applications from a single interface.

The EMC provides for administration over the SQL Server security environment, server and database configuration, statistical analysis and management, and provides a complete set of administrative tools. Essentially it is the only tool needed for day-to-day operations of a SQL Server environment.

Console Settings

As you work more with the Enterprise Manager and MMC in general, you will want to customize your administrative toolset and create your own consoles. In the Tools Menu of the console, Options will enable you to configure EMC and maintain your own personal settings. This is quite handy if multiple administrators share the same computer. Use Step by Step 1.2 to explore those options

STEP BY STEP

1.2 Customizing the Enterprise Management Console

1. From the Tools menu in the EMC, select Options. (If you want, you can set service-by-service polling intervals and configure console security.)

2. To configure user-by-user consoles, you must select the default Read/Store User Independent check box. This enables each administrator to have different console settings.

3. Select OK to close the window.

As you can see on the interface, it is also possible to set up a central server to store all registration information.

Bulk Copy Program

When databases are created in SQL Server, they need to be populated with data. You can certainly populate a database by using the Enterprise Manager or Query Analyzer, but why not use the Bulk Copy program? The main feature of the Bulk Copy program is to import or export data from text files to or from tables into other tables. As the name suggests, the "bulk" copy program is primarily used to shift large amounts of data from one place to another, and so it is used only in this case. The rate at which the bulk copy program transfers data from one place to another is about 2000 rows per second. The BCP.exe is stored in the C:\Program Files\Microsoft SQL Server\MSSQL\Binn folder and is run through the command prompt.

BOOKS ONLINE

With all programs comes documentation; SQL Server's documentation, and indeed Books Online, is a very helpful tool containing answers to many of the problems you run into in SQL Server. It is automatically installed when you successfully install SQL Server and is shown in Figure 1.7. This immense resource is discussed in greater detail near the end of this chapter.

Using Books Online

Books Online is an amazing resource that can answer literally any question about any topic related to SQL Server. From the opening screen, you can click any topic listed in the Contents pane. The first time you enter Books Online, you should peruse the Table of Contents to become familiar with its organization and to begin to feel comfortable with the depth of topic coverage.

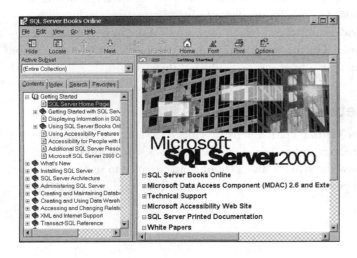

FIGURE 1.7
SQL Server Books Online preview.

Use the index pane to look up topics by key term or definition. The index is an alphabetical, cross-referenced alphabetic listing of all SQL Server and related terminology. It is easy to use and links you to the most probable locations to get assistance. If you know an exact word or statement in SQL Server, you can look it up. The Index tab mainly serves as a reference used to find coding statements used in T-SQL, but doesn't necessarily need to be used for this purpose. Code assistance can usually be found through context-sensitive searches that you can perform if you press the F1 key while you are coding.

If you still don't find what you're looking for, then you can click on the Search tab. This is useful when the exact terminology is not known. You can also use the tab to drill down deeper into a topic and attain more specific results. You can type in any keyword in the Search text box and expect to get information from every aspect on the topic. For example, if you type **enhancing performance**, and then press List Topics, you get over 50 topics.

If you find a topic that you think is interesting and well worth reading, you might want to keep it for later use and read it more thoroughly when you manage to get time. To do this, click on the Favorites tab and then click Add. This creates a shortcut to the page you were previously on.

General Contents

The Contents tab gives you an overview of what's contained in Books Online. It's divided into broad categories; each category divides into several others and each of those into smaller subcategories. The following sections list some of the categories or "books" and offer a brief summary of what they contain.

Getting Started

The Getting Started book provides overviews with links and the references to topics in the rest of the books, conventions (so you can know the syntax), and a list of contacts you can use for technical support. It also gives information on backward compatibility.

What's New?

This section, or book, contains a summarized overview of SQL Server features that are new—that is, for people who have already used the previous versions of SQL Server.

Installing SQL Server

The Installing SQL server book gives in-depth help on how to start, set up, and install a new instance of SQL Server 2000.

SQL Server Architecture

This book explains why and how everything works in SQL Server 2000.

Administering SQL Server

This book deals with how to administer SQL Server 2000 by looking at security, adding permissions, and so on.

Creating and Maintaining Databases

This book documents how to create and take care of databases and all tables, views, and objects presented in databases.

Creating and Using Data Warehouses

This book provides information on a more complex topic called data warehousing. It documents tools for data warehousing, creating data warehouses, and also understanding just what data warehouses are.

Accessing and Changing Relational Data

This book talks about different ways to access and manipulate data. It provides information on both advanced and basic techniques. It also gives information on locking, cursors, and the full-text searches.

XML and Internet Support

This chapter introduces the new feature of XML support in SQL Server. It gives most of the basics of retrieving XML data. However, you should know XML to an extent to understand this book.

Transact-SQL Reference

This is a reference to the whole Transact-SQL. It covers the complete syntax for each and every statement. This is a very useful tool for the SQL programmer.

Optimizing Database Performance

This book teaches you how to optimize SQL Server in the most efficient ways. If you use smart strategies in your database design, you can easily boost performance.

Replication

Replication is explained in this chapter, as well as replication tools, replication programming, and other information. Replication is a solution in which you can modify, copy, and distribute data across an enterprise.

Data Transformation Services

This book explains what DTS is and how to manage DTS. DTS is a graphical tool that enables you to consolidate and transform data from different sources into one or many destinations.

Analysis Services

This book explains Microsoft SQL Server 2000 Analysis Services, which are used for online analytical processing (OLAP) and also used for data mining. This points out the features of Analysis Services including architecture, administering, and troubleshooting.

English Query

This book explains what Microsoft English Query is and how you can create English Query applications from your databases. English Query enables end-users to pose questions in English rather than as a SQL query.

Meta Data Services

This book presents the basic of Meta Data Services, a set of services that enables you to manage meta data. Using Microsoft Meta Data Services requires that you understand meta data characteristics. Meta data describes the structure and meaning of data, as well as the structure and meaning of applications and processes. It is important to remember that meta data is abstract, has a context, and can be used for multiple purposes in a development environment.

Building SQL Server Applications

This is a huge book. It contains the whole T-SQL reference, as well as a programming reference for various client/server technologies. If you are writing programs that use ODBC, OLE DB, or ADO, then this is a good book for you.

Using SQL Server Tools

This book documents almost every utility that ships with SQL Server 2000, including utilities for administration and configuration, importation and transformation, and utilities that do everything SQL developers and administrators need to do.

Troubleshooting

The Troubleshooting section helps you resolve some of the common problems associated with the use of SQL Server. For additional resources in troubleshooting more involved problems, you can refer to the Microsoft technical online reference found at www.microsoft.com/technet. For SQL Server, the specific section is www.microsoft.com/technet/prodtechnol/sql/defaultasp.

Glossary

The Glossary is a dictionary of common terminology found throughout SQL Server 2000.

How-To

The How-To book is a how-to reference for specific procedures, such as installing, creating, or administering databases.

SQL SERVER 2000 LIMITATIONS

▶ **Identify and manage environment restrictions.**

You need to consider a few more things before you install SQL Server 2000 on any given computer. In most multi-SQL Server operations, the machine needs to participate in network security. An applications server such as SQL Server usually requires a large amount of resources exclusively available for its use. Also, appropriate permission sets need to be configured to ensure that sensitive data is not available where it shouldn't be.

SQL Server 2000 as a Resource

Participating as a network user, with access to resources through a login ID, is an important aspect of SQL Server. The service accounts that make up the database and agent engines are assigned a domain user account that will have administrative rights over the machine where it is installed.

> **WARNING**
>
> **Sharing Machines** You seldom want SQL Server to share a machine with other applications, and certainly a SQL Server should *never* share a machine with a security server such as a Windows 2000 or Windows NT Domain controller.

SQL Server 2000 Back Office Integration

SQL Server's capability to store data and handle scheduled procedures makes it an important portion of the Microsoft Server family. SQL Server can be used as the data support and back end of web sites running on IIS. SQL Server stores the data gathered by SMS in an enterprise infrastructure analysis. SQL Server can even supply information to the email system through Exchange.

SQL Server by the Numbers

A number of sources have provided impressive measurements of the capabilities of SQL Server 2000. Here are some of the impressive numbers:

◆ SQL Server allows maximized database capacity—approximately 1,000,000 terabytes. With this, you could store the name and address information for the entire population of the planet in a single database!

◆ Up to 16 simultaneous instances of SQL Server can be running.

◆ SQL Server supports up to 64 gigabytes of physical RAM.

Other statistics available that compare SQL Server to other products will change on a regular basis. Suffice it to say that Microsoft SQL Server is equal if not superior to other database engines in its class.

The following list provides some of the more important figures to keep in mind as you prepare any implementation:

◆ Databases per instance of SQL Server: 32,767

◆ Procedure nesting Levels: 32

◆ Columns per table: 1,024

◆ Columns per index or key: 16 with total byte size under 900 bytes

As you can see from the list of limitations, SQL Server can be used as the data storage software for virtually any size data structure.

SQL SERVER 2000 VERSIONS

▶ **Design for a medium to enterprise computing environment that uses SQL Server 2000 Enterprise Edition.**

SQL Server has different editions, and each has its own traits. Microsoft SQL Server 2000 is available in six editions, as described in the following sections.

SQL Server 2000 Enterprise Edition

Enterprise Edition is used as a production database server. This edition has all the features that are accessible in SQL Server 2000, and maintains performance and storage levels necessary to support the biggest web sites and enterprise online transaction processing (OLTP) and data warehousing systems. It is required for the use of Indexed views.

This edition is comprehensive: it includes the complete set of SQL Server database and analysis features and is uniquely characterized by several features that make it the most scalable and available edition of SQL Server 2000. It scales to the performance levels required to support large web sites, OLTP, and data warehousing. Its support for failover clustering also makes it ideal for any mission-critical line-of-business application. Additionally, this edition includes several advanced analysis features that are not included in SQL Server 2000 Standard Edition.

SQL Server 2000 Standard Edition

Standard Edition is used as a database server for a small organization or department-sized implementation. It does not include support for clustering, indexed views, distributed partitioned views, or log shipping. This is a more affordable option for small-sized and medium-sized organizations that do not require the advanced scalability, availability, performance, or analysis features of SQL Server 2000 Enterprise Edition. Standard Edition can be used on symmetric multiprocessing systems with up to 4 CPUs and 2GB of RAM.

Standard Edition includes the core functionality needed for non-mission-critical e-commerce, data warehousing, and line-of-business solutions. For instance, all the XML features present in Enterprise Edition are also included in Standard Edition. And although a handful of advanced OLAP features are reserved for Enterprise Edition, all data mining features and the core OLAP functionality are included in SQL Server 2000 Analysis Services in Standard Edition.

SQL Server 2000 Personal Edition

Mobile consumers who spend most of their time cut off from the network but execute programs that need SQL Server data storage space use Personal Edition. It is also used for standalone programs that require local SQL Server data storage on a client computer. It cannot act as a transactional replication publisher (subscriber only).

SQL Server 2000 Developer Edition

Developer Edition is used by programmers who design applications that use SQL Server 2000 as their data storage. Although the Developer Edition maintains all the features of the Enterprise Edition that enable developers to write and test applications, the Developer Edition is licensed for use only as a development and test system, not as a production server. It can be used to create and test indexed views.

SQL Server 2000 Developer Edition is the only edition of SQL Server 2000 that gives the licensee the right to download and install SQL Server 2000 Windows CE Edition (SQL Server CE) from `http://www.microsoft.com/sql`. The Developer Edition licensee also has the right to redistribute SQL Server CE-based applications to an unlimited number of devices at no additional cost beyond the purchase price of SQL Server 2000 Developer Edition.

SQL Server 2000 Windows CE Edition

Microsoft SQL Server 2000 Windows CE Edition (SQL Server CE) is for use as the data store on Windows CE devices. It is capable of replicating data with any edition of SQL Server 2000 so that you can keep Windows CE data synchronized with the primary database.

The SQL Server CE engine provides an essential set of relational database features—including an optimizing query processor and support for transactions and assorted data types—while it maintains a compact footprint that preserves system resources. Remote data access and merge replication, which work over Hypertext Transfer Protocol (HTTP) and support encryption, ensure that data from enterprise SQL Server databases is reliably delivered and that this data can be manipulated offline and synchronized later to the server. This makes SQL Server CE ideal for mobile and wireless scenarios.

SQL Server 2000 Enterprise Evaluation Edition

The Enterprise Evaluation Edition is a full-featured version available by a free download from the web. It is intended only for use in evaluating the features of SQL Server and stops running 120 days after it is initialized.

CASE STUDY: ACME GENERATORS

ESSENCE OF THE CASE

Here are the essential points in this case:

▶ Distributed environment

▶ Heterogeneous data sources

▶ Ability to integrate with IIS

▶ Data replication

SCENARIO

ACME Generators manufactures small electronic motors for use in a variety of mechanical devices. It is a medium-sized company of 150 employees with a manufacturing plant in Idaho and sales offices in Michigan, California, and Brazil. They require a database server to store all company data, provide access to data in sources across multiple platforms, and provide for front-end applications that will later be developed in Visual Basic and web applications developed for use on an IIS Server.

The software chosen must be able to handle data replication to and from the sales offices while maintaining ongoing updates from a fully automated manufacturing floor. Procedures will be updated to include information coming in from monitoring equipment that reports at various points during the manufacturing process.

The company executives have been looking into Microsoft SQL Server 2000 and would like to get information on how suitable it would be for the

CASE STUDY: ACME GENERATORS

continued

tasks. What are some of the features available in SQL Server that are suited to this deployment?

ANALYSIS

Microsoft SQL Server 2000 would be an excellent software choice in this situation. It handles well in a distributed environment so that all offices can gain access to the data they need.

SQL Server has many tools for interoperating in a heterogeneous environment that has multiple vendors and database products. SQL Server

uses ODBC and OLE-DB functionality to gain access to virtually any data stored anywhere.

SQL Server makes an excellent back-end database server for an Internet or intranet site. SQL Server and IIS integrate well to make data accessible over the Internet in a number of formats, including XML, HTML, and ADO.

With SQL Server replication, data can be transferred quickly and flexibly from one server to another. Options are available to maintain updateable copies at all locations if desired.

CHAPTER SUMMARY

This chapter was aimed at giving you an introduction to SQL Server. The tools and programs talked about in this chapter span the rest of this book and are examined at much greater depth. Use this chapter as a springboard to all the topics that you need to understand to be properly prepared for the 70-229 exam. This chapter has only outlined the basics of what is a large and diverse area of expertise.

KEY TERMS

- ADO
- Analysis Server
- BCP
- Books Online
- Cascading Referential Integrity
- Client Network utility
- collation
- constraints
- Data warehouse
- DELETE
- English Query
- Federated Database Server

CHAPTER SUMMARY

- HTML
- IIS
- index
- INSERT
- Internet host name
- OSQL
- Master database
- Microsoft Management Console (MMC)
- Model database
- MSDB database
- NetBIOS computer name
- ODBC
- OLE-DB
- online analytical processing (OLAP)
- online transaction processing (OLTP)
- partitioned views
- Profiler
- Query Analyzer

- relational database
- replication
- roles
- SELECT
- server network
- utility
- Service Manager
- stored procedures
- Structured Query Language (SQL)
- table
- TCP/IP
- tempdb
- Transact-SQL
- trigger
- UPDATE
- user-defined functions
- view
- XML

APPLY YOUR KNOWLEDGE

Exercises

1.1   Using the Enterprise Manager

In Exercise 1.1, you explore the Enterprise Manager interface to become comfortable with its layout.

Estimated Time: 5 minutes.

1. Open the Enterprise Manager and view the structure of the interface by choosing Start, Programs, Microsoft SQL Server.

2. Expand the SQL Server Group and Computer name by depressing the plus sign to the left of the name.

3. Expand databases and you should see the listing of system databases: Master, Model, Msdb, Tempdb, and the sample databases Northwind and Pubs.

   You may also see other user databases that have been previously created and the system's Distribution database if replication has been enabled.

4. Expand the Northwind database and view the variety of database object storage containers.

5. Click on tables to show the user and system tables in the right view pane.

6. Click on the Type column to sort the tables according to type. (You may have to click twice so that the user tables are all located at the top of the list).

Notice how easy it is to adjust the objects and place them into a desired sequence by name, owner, type, or creation date.

1.2   Using the Query Analyzer

In Exercise 1.2 you will run a couple of basic queries from the Query Analyzer and explore its interface.

Estimated Time: 5 minutes.

1. Open the Query Analyzer by choosing Start, Programs, Microsoft SQL Server.

2. Select OK to connect to the local server and supply login credentials if necessary.

3. On the left side of the screen is the object browser that enables the user to quickly look up names and syntax while creating and editing scripts.

4. Select the Northwind database from the Database drop-down list box in the toolbar.

5. Enter the following T-SQL query: **SELECT * FROM Customers**.

6. Run the query by pressing F5. (Alternatively, you can also select the Execute Query button from the toolbar.)

You can save the query if you want. It is also possible to save the query results or run the results straight to an output file, which you can do by selecting Results to File—in the Execute Mode drop-down list box on the toolbar, prior to running the query.

1.3   Creating a Database Diagram

In Exercise 1.3, you will draw a database diagram from the sample database, Northwind.

Estimated Time: 5 minutes.

1. Open the Enterprise Manager and view the structure of the interface by choosing Start, Programs, Microsoft SQL Server.

APPLY YOUR KNOWLEDGE

2. Expand the SQL Server Group, Server, Databases, and Northwind database and select the Diagrams container.

3. Right-click and select New Database Diagram. Select Next to bypass the introductory screen.

4. Select the Add Related Tables Automatically check box and leave the number of levels at the default of 1.

5. Select the Customers table and select Add. Select Next and Finish to draw the diagram.

Database diagrams are useful when you want to provide documentation about a database system. The diagrams show relationships and have a number of other useful features you can use to augment a diagram.

1.4   Using Books Online

In Exercise 1.4, you can explore Books Online and get used to using it as a learning tool.

Estimated Time: 5 minutes.

1. Open Books Online by choosing Start, Programs, Microsoft SQL Server.

2. Select the Contents tab and expand the Getting Started book.

3. Select the Getting Started book and read through the table to review the hyperlinks available.

4. Select the Index tab and enter the word **SELECT**.

5. Double-click Examples from the list of subheadings.

6. Select the Favorites tab and click Add to place SELECT Examples into the listing of Favorites.

You are sure to add and remove topics from your Favorites list on a regular basis as you study the product.

Review Questions

1. How is data queried from SQL Server?

2. Which versions of SQL Server have operating system requirements? What are these requirements?

3. What percentage of answers to potential exam questions can be obtained from within Books Online?

4. How is the Master database used?

5. What is the purpose of the Model database?

Exam Questions

1. You are the chief database administrator for a large manufacturing company. You need to install Microsoft SQL Server Enterprise for test purposes and have moderate storage capabilities. Which of the following systems suit your needs without requiring you to perform any alterations?

   A. Pentium 133, 256MB RAM, IE 5

   B. Pentium 200, 64MB RAM, IE 4

   C. Pentium 400, 128MB RAM, IE 3

   D. Pentium 400, 32MB RAM, IE 5

2. You are the database administrator for a small private educational institution. You would like to use SQL Server as a gateway to a variety of data sources that have been used for a number of different applications. As a primary goal you would like to get a copy of all data stored on the SQL Server. What technologies could be used to solve this problem? Select all that apply.

   A. OLE-DB

   B. ANSI

C. ISO

D. ODBC

E. Analysis Services

F. SQL Profiler

3. You are preparing a computer that is going to serve as a Windows 2000 domain controller. You would also like to install SQL Server for a database that will be used in your office. What is the preferred installation to use for these operations?

   A. Use one machine as a domain controller and a second as the database server.

   B. Install SQL Server first and then promote the machine to a domain controller.

   C. Promote the Windows 2000 machine to be a domain controller and then install SQL Server.

   D. A Windows 2000 domain controller cannot have SQL Server installed.

4. You are implementing a database for a chain of variety stores that share a central warehouse. Each of the stores tracks sales information and places orders from the central warehouse once a week. The server will use replication, indexed views, and analysis services for a variety of procedures. What version of SQL Server should be installed?

   A. SQL Server 2000 CE

   B. SQL Server 2000 Standard

   C. SQL Server 2000 Personal

   D. SQL Server 2000 Developer

   E. SQL Server 2000 Enterprise

5. You are a SQL Server database administrator preparing to install a series of laptops that will be used by your company's traveling sales force. The laptops are already loaded with Windows 98 and need to have SQL Server installed so that the salespeople can record orders through a custom Visual Basic application. When the salespeople return to the office, they execute another process to upload the information to a primary production server. What version of SQL Server do the laptops require?

   A. SQL Server 2000 CE

   B. SQL Server 2000 Standard

   C. SQL Server 2000 Personal

   D. SQL Server 2000 Developer

   E. SQL Server 2000 Enterprise

6. A large shipping company uses a dual processor SQL Server to track load information for a fleet of transport vehicles that handle shipments throughout North America. The data being collected is shared with other vendors. This company requires a technology that will provide a data structure and formatting rules, and that will be easily transferable between applications. Which technology is best suited for this structure?

   A. HTML

   B. IIS

   C. XML

   D. Replication

   E. Triggers

APPLY YOUR KNOWLEDGE

7. You are working on a database implementation in a production environment. You would like to perform analysis on the server hosting the database. You need to get detailed information on the types of queries being performed and the locking effects of all operations. Which tool should you use?

   A. Query Analyzer

   B. SQL Profiler

   C. Books Online

   D. Analysis Manager

   E. Enterprise Manager

Answers to Review Questions

1. Data can be read from a SQL Server database using a variety of techniques. The most common would be a front-end application designed with a Windows or Internet interface. Visual Basic, FrontPage, or Visual Interdev could be used to design such a front-end application. You can also query data using the OSQL command-line tool or use the Query Analyzer.

2. It probably goes without saying that each version has a specific focus. The CE version, of course, is for use on handheld computers that use Windows CE version 2.11 or later. The Developer Edition installs on Windows 2000 Professional and Windows NT Workstation 4.0, as well as on Microsoft Windows NT 4.0 servers and Windows 2000 servers. Personal Edition runs on non-server operating systems including Windows 2000 Professional, Windows NT Workstation 4.0, Windows Millennium Edition, and Windows 98, as well as servers.

3. The answer here is likely to be very close to 100%. SQL Server Books Online is an immense and complete SQL Server resource. Just about any question you have or database technology you would like to use or learn can be found within the application.

4. The Master database represents a given SQL Server installation. The Master database should be considered as important or more important than the most mission-critical database on the server. The Master database contains information for all databases and other objects stored on the server.

5. The Model database acts as a template for each newly created database. Every time you create a database, a copy of the objects and settings stored in the Model is used as a basis for the newly created database.

Answers to Exam Questions

1. **B.** To install SQL Server you need a minimum of a Pentium 166, 64MB of RAM (though more is recommended) and Internet Explorer 4 or above. See the section "Installation Requirements" for more information.

2. **A, D.** OLE-DB and ODBC are industry-standard technologies. They supply the standards for drivers that are supplied to allow data to be read from an underlying data source. ODBC (open database connectivity) is a mature interface supported by almost all database engines. OLE-DB is a set of driver APIs that has growing usage and allows for access to data in a generic form, as well. See the section "Executing a Program" for more information.

APPLY YOUR KNOWLEDGE

3. **A.** You should always avoid installing SQL Server on a domain controller. Although the configuration is possible, there are serious security implications in having an application server on the same machine as a network's security context. For more information, see "SQL Server 2000 as a Resource."

4. **E.** To use indexed views you must have either the Developer or Enterprise Editions. Because this server is for a production environment, not a test setup, the only choice is the Enterprise Edition. For more information see the section "SQL Server Versions."

5. **C.** The Personal Edition is probably most appropriate for this type of application because it is suited to mobile users that require SQL Server for data storage. However, if the application is using replication as a means of moving data from the laptops to the servers, it should be noted that the Personal Edition allows only for the subscriber options to be set. It cannot act as a publisher. For more information see "SQL Server Versions."

6. **C.** XML, now supported through a number of new features, provides a mechanism where the data can be transmitted from one application to the other while maintaining the data structure and other formatting provided by XML schemas and style sheets. For more information, refer to "Features of SQL Server 2000."

7. **B.** To perform analysis of this type, you would use the Profiler to gather detailed server-wide information. The Query Analyzer is more appropriate to analyze and improve upon the performance of singular queries and the Analysis Manager is used to configure data warehousing. For more information see the section "Features of SQL Server 2000."

Suggested Readings and Resources

- ◆ Holzner, Steven. *Inside XML*. New Riders Publishing, 2001.
- ◆ SQL Server 2000 Books Online
  - Getting Started with SQL Server Books Online
  - What's New in Microsoft SQL Server 2000
  - SQL Server Architecture Overview
  - XML and Internet Support Overview
- ◆ MSDN Online Internet Reference: (http://msdn.microsoft.com)
  - XML Online Developer Center: (/xml/default.asp)
  - Developer Resources for SQL Server: (/sqlserver)
- ◆ Technet Online Internet Reference: IT Resources for SQL Server (http://www.microsoft.com/technet/sql/default.asp)
- ◆ MS Press Online Internet Reference: Learning and Training Resources for IT Professionals / SQL Server 2000 (http://mspress.microsoft.com/it/feature/100500.htm)

The software to be used is not necessarily relevant to the database design, but because the software, SQL Server 2000 Enterprise Edition, is predetermined in this case, the features and limitations of the product as they relate to the database structure have been brought into this chapter. A complete breakdown of all SQL Server data types is covered here as a lead-in to Chapter 3, which covers SQL Server specifics in much more detail.

Define entities. Considerations include entity composition.

- **Specify entity, attributes, and relationships in a logical model.**

▶ This objective deals with creating and identifying entities and attributes in a data model. The coverage of this objective teaches you how an entity behaves during the three prominent phases of database normalization.

Define entities. Considering normalization and denormalization.

- **Specify degree of normalization.**

▶ For this objective, you will have to fully normalize a database structure and then decide whether denormalization of a database is appropriate in a given situation.

Design entity keys. Considerations include FOREIGN KEY constraints, PRIMARY KEY constraints, and UNIQUE constraints.

- **Specify attributes that uniquely identify records.**

- **Specify attributes that reference other entities.**

▶ Here you will learn how to undergo the process of creating FOREIGN KEY and PRIMARY KEY constraints and deciding on ways to uniquely identify records. You have to decide on which attribute or attributes will be required to uniquely identify records. This objective requires you to know how

CHAPTER 2

Database Design for SQL Server 2000

to create relationships by choosing FOREIGN KEY and PRIMARY KEY candidates.

Design attribute domain integrity. Considerations include CHECK constraints, data types, and nullability.

- **Specify scale and precision of allowable values for each attribute.**

- **Allow or prohibit NULL for each attribute.**

- **Specify allowable values for each attribute.**

▶ Domain integrity involves restricting the data entered to a domain or range of values. Using a variety of different data types, permitting different formats and allowing different ranges of values can define these domains. For this objective, you need to decide on whether NULLs are allowed and the values that are allowed on attributes.

Handle client/server configurations of 50 to 5,000 or more users.

- **One, two, and n tier operations.**

- **Internet applications. Web configurations that use Internet Information Server (IIS) or COM+.**

- **Heterogeneous databases using other non-SQL Server data sources.**

- **Very large database support.**

▶ Many types of environments exist. In some environments a database server is used on its own. In others the database server operates as only a small portion of the system with assistance from other machines and applications. The separations of this processing creates a tier effect. This chapter explores the roles of the software at various tiers and observes how the database servers function in each model.

STUDY STRATEGIES

▶ Database design is a large topic and can span many texts. I advise you to look at different articles and books with the many resources listed in the "Suggested Readings" section. Doing so is not required, but it ensures you a more thorough understanding of database design.

▶ Database design can sometimes get nerve-racking and so requires a lot of patience. Go through each step of the process in a slow and methodical manner. Don't be too rushed to put things into SQL Server until the design is ready.

INTRODUCTION

A strong database design is one of the primary factors in establishing a database that will provide good performance while minimizing the use of resources. One of the first steps after gathering information about a particular scenario is to begin the preparations of a database design by first determining its logical design. A logical design involves mapping out a database through the analysis of *entities, relationships,* and *attributes.* This is known as *Entity Relationship modeling,* which will be the first focus of this chapter.

Designing a good database does not require the knowledge of how databases are specifically implemented in SQL Server. In fact, often the logical design is prepared before any determination of the actual software to be used for the data storage. In cases where the software is predetermined, this should be taken into consideration during the logical design. Any particular limitations and features of the specific product would be handled as needed.

Preparing an appropriate database design often depends on how well you can comprehend a given scenario. Techniques are laid out through this chapter to help you comprehend and get information from a sample scenario. However, knowing the physical tasks for implementation of databases is necessary only when you want to apply and create the database in SQL Server. This chapter discusses the basic elements of a logical database structure. It also looks ahead to where and how the logical model evolves into the physical database itself.

Determining the database model, or ER-model on how tables relate to each other is known as putting together the logical database design, because you are just brainstorming how a database will be designed. When implementing the database itself onto SQL Server, you are applying the logical design to implement the physical database, which is the focus of the next chapter. In looking at the logical implementation, you must have a thorough understanding of relational databases themselves. The details of the physical SQL Server objects are in the next chapter, and the implementation of much of the physical side to databases is covered throughout this entire book.

This chapter also looks at some of the basics of application architectures. A variety of models for how a database is used and how SQL Server fits into a multiple data source environment are overviewed. Last, this chapter looks into some of the variety of environments that SQL Server fits into, covering database systems that can manage an extremely large quantity of data, users, and a variety of applications.

A Case Scenario Approach

This chapter covers the most important steps in designing a database. Detailed explanations are given that talk about database design concepts in depth. When designing a database model in the real world, you will also be given a particular scenario. The scenario often will take the form of sample documents and interview notes.

This chapter uses a case scenario to describe the current situation, problems, and changes a fictitious firm is undergoing. All chapters in this book contain a case study at the end to help drive home the ideas behind the chapter. This entire chapter, however, is based on a case scenario to help illustrate the process of database design point by point. It guides you through the process of deducing all entities (tables), attributes (columns), and relationships from a hospital scenario. The material is presented in this manner to better illustrate the process of and steps undergone in data modeling.

Case Scenario: Lloyd's Hospital

Lloyd's Hospital is one of the major hospitals in the city of Etmodsirch. It has as many as 1000 new patients each month and approximately 300 employees, including more than 160 doctors, surgeons, professors, and nurses. Lloyd's Hospital currently has at least 2000 beds and maintains highly sophisticated utilities, machinery, and robotics.

Lloyd's Hospital's business goals are in providing the highest quality care to individuals and the community, advancing in care through excellence in medical research, and educating future academic and practice leaders of the health care professions. Lloyd's Hospital is among the prominent hospitals in the city of Etmodsirch.

Lloyd's Hospital also provides diverse training opportunities for nurses and allied health care professionals. Lloyd's Hospital aims to serve the community as a public health advocate and provide support and services that respond to the area's health care needs through health education, health promotion, and access to care.

Because of numerous complaints on the extreme inefficiency of the current complex database, CEO John Patterson has made the decision to acquire a completely different database design. His requirement is to have a new database designed from scratch that will make the different processes that take place in Lloyd's more efficient. He gives you a brief overview of the current situation at Lloyd's:

"Our current patient registry exceeds 200,000 entries, and each entry contains detailed information about our patients. When patients come here for the first time, they are required to register into our catalog, filling in information such as their names and contact addresses. Approximately a thousand new patients register with us in a single month. We need a new registering design that will not only improve information access but will also decrease the time needed to enter the information.

We have 300 employees, most of whom work with a permanent contract, but some work on an hour-to-hour basis. Doctors specialize in different divisions, such as psychology and dermatology. Employees who are new adapt to the environment fairly quickly with the help of senior doctors. Each employee is placed into a single division, such as cardiology or dermatology. An ID card is granted to each employee, showing the division he belongs to. After employees hold a valid staff ID card, they are granted permission into the computer security organizational unit for the division.

The security host for the hospital is a set of organizational units (OU) within a Windows 2000 domain. There is a separate OU for each division of the hospital.

We also have a large selection of medicine available at our internal pharmacy, ranging from high blood pressure tablets to medicine for the common cold. The pharmacy is available to all our doctors, and medicine can be bought by any of our registered patients with an appropriate prescription or through a prescription from another facility or physician. Over-the-counter medications can be purchased by the general public, as well. Some of the medications are government-controlled substances that need to be monitored more closely. All our medicine is kept organized so that it may be found easily when needed. One particular problem exists in that our medicine stock is renewed every two days, making it difficult to maintain this level of organization.

We have a sophisticated array of machinery such as kidney and x-ray machines. These machines are kept in various labs, such as x-ray and blood labs, and can be accessed only by specialized doctors within these labs.

And with the introduction of our new academic facility, we offer different training opportunities for those interested. These training courses cover everything from surgery to medicine. Our educational facility is located within our campus beside the hospital proper and can accommodate numerous trainees."

With this information, you can begin designing a new data model in accordance with the current situation at Lloyd's Hospital. Realizing that this information is somewhat incomplete, you will have to make a few assumptions along the way. But first, you need a little background on relational databases and the modeling of such data. In an ideal situation, sample documents and full descriptions of all procedures that interact with the data would also be used as an aid to the development of the data model.

ENTITY RELATIONSHIP MODELING

▶ **Define entities. Considerations include entity composition.**

   • **Specify entity, attributes, and relationships in a logical model.**

Relational databases are databases in which data is organized into related objects rather than tied to a file. Each of the objects contained in a database is related to the others in some way. You'll often see the acronym RDBMS as an alternative to Relational Database Management System. Data RDBMS, such as SQL Server, also store other tidbits such as database security, database structure, and all other objects—including triggers, views, and stored procedures—pertaining to that database.

Based on the paper written by E.F. Codd in 1970, "A Relational Model of Data for Large Shared Data Banks," relational databases store sets of data in relations (often called tables). The tables are often related to one another, but this is not required.

The relational database design, also known as the Entity-Relationship model, was first developed by the database engineer Charles Bachman in 1960 and then later called the Entity-Relational model (ER model) in 1976 by Peter Chen. The Entity Relational model allows a database to be set up in a fairly simple and organized manner. The simplicity of a data model gives it the advantage of flexibility; this benefit enables you to easily create and enhance databases based on business requirements on the fly. Many other model formats are also commonly used, each having similar characteristics for diagramming a potential database structure. See Figure 2.1 for a sample ER model designed using Visio and a portion of the Northwind sample database.

Modeling data into entities is simple and any number of data modeling tools are available to assist in this design. Microsoft has the Visio product, which is an excellent design tool for a variety of purposes including databases, programming, flowcharting, network design, and more. Many third-party products are also available at little or no cost. However, the most commonly used tools—ERWIN and Embarcadero's products—are fairly expensive. Any of these tools will give you the desired functionality to document a logical design. A summary of some of the many products available and some related information is presented in Table 2.1. This chapter uses the Lloyd's Hospital case study as the medium to build a practical and efficient data model.

ERWIN

One of the most popular tools for ER model design used in a lot of business environments is ERWIN, now owned by Computer Associates.

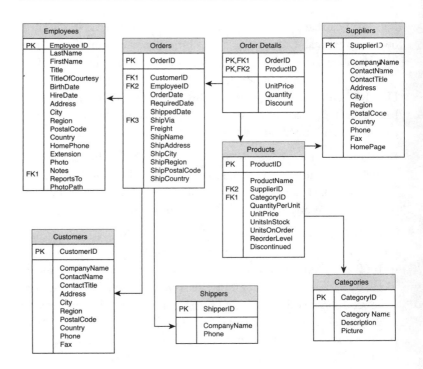

FIGURE 2.1
ER Source for Northwind.

TABLE 2.1		
DATABASE DESIGN SOFTWARE		
Product	*Source*	*License*
SmartDraw	www.smartdraw.com	Free 30-day full version
RFFlow	www.rff.com	Feature limited free trial
CaseStudio	www.casestudio.com	Feature limited free trial
DeZign	www.datanamic.com	Feature limited free trial
PDQ Lite	www.patton-patton.com	Free 15-day full version
Visio	www.microsoft.com	$7.50 30-day full version CD

An ER data model consists of three main components that are present in any model format:

◆ **Entities**. In data modeling, entities can be closely compared to the physical element of a table in SQL Server. An entity is a collection of related data elements such as customers or products.

◆ **Attributes**. Attributes are the characteristics given to an entity such as Salary and FirstName. Attributes of an entity represent a set of properties of a data element within an entity. They will become the columns or fields in the physical database.

◆ **Relationships**. Relationships show a logical link between two or more entities. A customer entity may be related to orders; a product entity may be related to sales.

The following three steps are involved in creating a basic data model:

1. Identify and create entities.

2. Create entity properties (attributes).

3. Identify relationships (one-to-many, one-to-one, many-to-many).

Entities

Entities are the main objects in an ER model because they contain all attributes and participate in relationships. Entities represent the things, places, people, and concepts involved in a real-world situation.

An easy way to identify candidates for entities is to keep a lookout for the nouns present in a case scenario. This method is not surprising because nouns resemble all the things an entity can represent. For example, look at this excerpt from the case study: "The pharmacy is available to all our doctors and medicine can be bought by any of our registered patients."

From the excerpt above, you can apparently determine entity candidates by looking at the nouns: Medicine, Patient, and Doctor.

Four steps need to be undertaken when determining entities for an ER diagram. The following four steps should be carefully observed because they are related to the first part of the Microsoft exam objective mentioned at the beginning of this chapter—defining entities.

1. Write down key nouns from the case study.

2. Identify which nouns are really needed as entities.

3. Draw the entities.

4. Write a brief description of each entity.

Now you can attempt to complete the first two steps of the data modeling process using the chapter case scenario.

STEP BY STEP

2.1 ER Modeling

Try out the following steps yourself, and then compare your results to the results listed following this Step by Step.

1. Write down the key nouns from the case scenario on a scrap piece of paper.

2. Identify which nouns are really going to be needed as entities.

Answer to Step by Step 2.1: The following are key nouns found in the case scenario representing a solution to Step by Step 2.1:

Patients	Doctors
Surgeons	Nurses
Training	Employees
Medicine	Labs
Machinery	Academic Faculty
Courses	Trainees

A standard documentation technique is to draw entities as rectangular boxes with enough space to hold many attributes. At this point, taking things one step at a time, you aren't quite ready to complete the attributes and relationships for your model. After you have identified the major nouns, you are ready to begin a diagram or sketch for the design. Rough paper or any of the previously mentioned software packages can be used for the design. These diagrams make up what is known as a *data model diagram*, better known as an *entity-relationship diagram.*(ERD)

STEP BY STEP

2.2 ER Modeling

To complete the entity portion of an ER model, you need to begin documenting the model. Try out these next two steps now to begin putting the picture together.

1. Draw the entities on paper and then, if desired, transfer them to computer.

2. Write a brief description of each entity.

Answer to Step by Step 2.2: The following are the nouns that would most logically be made into entities. These nouns should have enough significance to be used; the other nouns possibly would be contained within some of these entities.

Patient	Machinery
Employee	Course
Medicine	Trainee

Designing a good database at this stage still does not require you to acquire the knowledge of how databases are implemented in SQL Server; rather it depends on how well you can comprehend a given scenario and its elements. The next section takes a look at entity composition and the defining of attributes.

Defining Attributes

Identifying attributes is the next step in ensuring a successful data modeling process, and moreover is a part of the Microsoft exam objectives for this chapter, defining entity composition, and the sub-objective, specify entity attributes.

Attributes are characteristics or properties defined within a single entity, and they correspond to real-world properties of a place, thing, or concept. An attribute candidate is usually found by examining sentences in the case study that are in close proximity to its residing entity. For instance, take a look at this excerpt from the Lloyd's Hospital case study: "We have 300 employees, most of whom work with a permanent contract, but some work on an hour-to-hour basis." Think of attributes as properties of entities. Therefore, from the excerpt above, you probably should have guessed Contract as being a good candidate. because it is a property of an employee.

Some common issues in database design are:

◆ Should this be an entity or an attribute?

◆ Should this be an entity or a relationship?

One might model the Contract as an entity, and later make the relationship Employees work under a Contract. This is not the model used in this chapter, but it is worth mentioning that there are many different ways to model the same information. Each variation of a model may work and be correct. This is part of what makes data modeling a painstaking process that requires patience. Whatever model is chosen, try not to jump ahead to the next stage of modeling until you have considered some alternatives.

Try to find out the attributes that fit each of the Patient, Employee, Medicine, Machinery, Course, and Trainee entities. Test your results with the results provided in Figure 2.2. If you missed an attribute or added an extra attribute that isn't found below, don't feel that it is wrong. Attribute decision is a hard choice and is varied from person to person, depending on your perspective on the scenario. Also

EXAM TIP

Attributes on the Exam   On the exam you will not have to dream up your own attributes, but you may have to select from a list of potential attributes and place them into the correct entity.

remember that this simulation is missing a lot of information, so there are likely to be many more attributes than those listed.

Naming Attributes

For the case study of Lloyd's Hospital, attributes are defined as shown in Figure 2.2.

To create and identify attributes is a developed skill; there is no set method for doing so—you just need to practice. However, there are some good guidelines available that will help you in creating and choosing the best attributes for your data model. The first is how you name your entities. A good name makes an attribute look professional and helps in its readability. Here are some good guidelines that help in naming entities. Remember to always follow these to keep your design consistent.

◆ An entity or an attribute should be named in its singular form, thereby implying that it is only a single instance. An instance is a single occurrence of an entity.

◆ The use of underscores (_) in naming attributes is not a good habit because special characters have particular meanings in some software packages, and the mixture of text and other characters is difficult to type. Try to distinguish a word from another by using mixed case, as in DeliveryService rather than Delivery_Service.

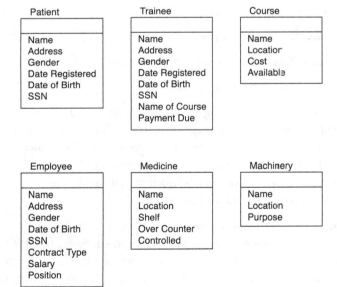

FIGURE 2.2

Attributes implementation in an Entity-Relationship diagram (ER diagram).

◆ Entity and attribute names should not exceed 128 characters because a table in SQL Server is restricted to that. In fact, names should be kept as small as possible while still providing a meaningful object title. Remember, entities will become tables in SQL Server.

◆ Entity names should be unique.

◆ Attributes within the same entity should not be the same as any other object name; any naming in SQL Server should be kept unique. Chapter 3 goes into more detail on this point.

Appropriate naming conventions are often developed as a corporate or development standard within an organization. Often mechanisms for shortening names or using common prefixing or suffixing may all be part of a programming team's standard.

Attribute Makeup

Now that you understand how to properly name attributes, it's time to look at how to break attributes down, a process more commonly known as *decomposing attributes*. Decomposing an attribute takes an attribute from its original form and divides it into its components. A good example of this is the breaking down of the Address attribute. An Address attribute may easily be broken down into attributes that store data as follows:

◆ **Street.** Stores the street address of the user.

◆ **City.** Stores where the user lives.

◆ **State.** Stores which state the user lives in.

◆ **Zip.** Stores the user's zip code.

This process of decomposing an attribute helps you develop a normalized database structure as defined later in this chapter during the discussion of the physical design. Decomposing is also a function of usage as well. If, for example, a person's name is only needed in its full form, then a decision may be made to not break it up into the separate attributes of first and last name.

Decomposing an attribute provides many benefits in contrast to general, built attributes that are not decomposed. First off, *data integrity* is improved. Data integrity is a measurement of how well data is kept consistent and flawless throughout the whole ER model.

When attributes are decomposed, different methods of ensuring data integrity can be applied to the broken-down segments rather than the attribute as a whole. For example, a Zip attribute can be checked as an integer and City as a string. Secondly, decomposing aids in sorting and improving data retrieval performance.

A generic attribute Address contains the street, city, state, and zip. To just get the state of a customer in Washington, you have to select the whole Address attribute and parse it to find Washington, thereby degrading performance because of the redundant data retrieved. If you just have four separate attributes, you can select the State column and get your results more quickly. This same rule applies to updating data. It's easier to update a single part of Address rather than parsing and then updating the whole Address attribute.

In most cases, an attribute is identified for each entity that will act as a key. This attribute could be a customer number, product number, or simply an attribute to serve no other purpose but to act as a key identifier. When an attribute is added solely for the sake of being an identifier, it is known as a *surrogate key*. Whether you use a natural or surrogate key, that key will represent an important part in establishing relationships. The term *Primary Key* is assigned to this attribute. Even though SQL Server does not mandate the use of a Primary Key, one should be defined simply as a matter of good practice.

R E V I E W   B R E A K

General Recap on Data Modeling

When designing a data model, you do not need to know how databases are actually implemented in SQL Server. In fact, the primary goal at this stage is picking the facts out of a given problem definition. A case scenario in whatever form it takes will describe the current situation, problems, and changes a firm is currently undergoing. You need to deduce all tables, columns, and relationships from this preparation.

Entities become the tables when a logical design is transferred to a physical database model. Each entity is made up of a number of properties or attributes that will later become the column definitions of the table. A relationship between entities creates a logical link between the entities and in the physical design will represent the Primary Key and Foreign Key relationship of a constraint.

DESIGNING ENTITY KEYS

▶ **Design entity keys. Considerations include FOREIGN KEY constraints, PRIMARY KEY constraints, and UNIQUE constraints.**

• **Specify attributes that uniquely identify records.**

• **Specify attributes that reference other entities.**

Entity key definition is an important part of designing the structure of an ER model. Two types of keys exist: Primary and Foreign. These keys are used in establishing relationships and also provide an easier and more efficient way to retrieve data in the physical implementation.

Primary Keys

Primary Keys consist of sets of attributes whose values uniquely identify the rows in an entity. Primary Keys give an ID to a row. They make the row unique throughout the entity. This means that rows can easily located by this identifier.

Primary Keys can only be used for columns or attributes that don't allow null values. Allowing null values would mean that a row would not be uniquely identified. Also, the attribute chosen to hold a Primary Key must have values unique throughout the entity.

Choosing a Primary Key for a column is relatively simple in contrast to choosing entities and attributes. Identifying Primary Keys is also part of the Microsoft exam objective, so it's advisable that you have a good grasp of designing entity keys. A Primary Key should be a numeric value if possible, but this is not a hard and fast rule.

To identify a Primary Key, a single investigation has to be taken: whether the column holds true when you ask whether this attribute can carry completely unique, known values throughout the entity.

If the answer is a solid yes, no more investigation is needed; the column is worthy of being named a Primary Key column. However, if you notice that none of the attributes in the entity can uniquely identify themselves, it's possible to add an additional surrogate attribute. In many cases surrogate keys are actually a preferred mechanism because the values never need to change. Some designers dislike its use because it adds a column to the data structure that has no particular correlation to the data.

> **NOTE**
>
> **Defining Primary Keys**   Primary Keys can be implemented on columns in SQL Server 2000 in three ways. The first is to use the stored procedure sp_primarykey. The second way is to create a primary key constraint on the column. Finally, you can create a unique index on a Primary Key candidate.

Primary Keys and Foreign Keys are an important aspect of setting up relationships. Whereas a Primary Key defines a unique value for a row in the entity, a Foreign Key is used as a mechanism for one entity's records to be related to another entity.

Foreign Keys

Foreign Keys help in the relational process between two entities. When a Primary Key is created on a parent entity, it is connected to another entity by linking to the other entity's Foreign Key. For example, in an invoice situation, there are usually two entities: one for invoice general information and the other for invoice details. The invoice details would contain a hook onto the invoice general entity through the use of a Foreign Key—potentially the invoice number or a surrogate key.

Foreign Keys help in the relational process. They define a parent/child relationship between records in an entity. For instance, we have a title entity and a publisher entity. Titles are published by publishers, and we want to identify which titles are published by which publisher. Rows in the titles entity are related to rows in the publisher entity. One way we can document this relationship is, when creating a new title row, we store the `publisherid` value with the title. The `publisherid` column in the title entity will contain values only from the `publisherid` column in the publisher entity (this column is the Primary Key of publisher). When we take values from the Primary Key of the publisher entity (or any entity) and store those values in rows of a child entity (like title), the `child` column is a Foreign Key.

Understanding Entity Relationships

Relationships are the final component in an ER model, allowing for a logical linkage between one entity and another. A relationship in an ER model connects the data elements of two entities that contain information about the same real-world element. The primary entity in a relationship provides some of the data, and other entities provide further related data. A relationship definition states how two entities are connected. This connection when the physical structure is developed will become Foreign Key connections to Primary Keys or other unique data elements.

Data Modeling and MS Exams
If you ever intend to sit the 70-100 exam, "Analyzing Requirements and Defining Solution Architectures," data modeling plays an important role in the exam, and surrogate keys are recommended for all structures. This exam is the core exam for the MCSD certification.

Relationships define a real-world connection or link between one entity and another. In the modeling process, you attempt to discover how things and which things are related to one another. Within the business problem you are modeling, each object requires full definition, including how it is related to other objects.

These relationships are usually defined as a numeric link connecting the entities together based on the number of data elements in one entity that are related to one or more full elements in another entity. It can be described as how many of one thing can relate to how many of something else. This property of a relationship is known as the *cardinality* of a relationship. In the Lloyd's Hospital example, patients buy or take drugs, so a Patient entity would probably be related to a Medicine entity.

Relationships can be made from one entity to another in essentially three different ways. These different relations are one-to-one, one-to-many, and many-to-many. The relationships between two entities is often called a *binary* relationship. The following sections describe how to identify, apply, and choose the correct relationships between the different entities in your model.

Although a binary relationship between two entities is common, there may be relationships between three entities (ternary), and more. Of course, an entity might be related to itself (unary or a self-referencing entity).

One-To-One

This type of relationship occurs when one row or data element of an entity is associated with only one row or element in the second entity. It is not surprising that one-to-one relationships are uncommon in the real world. They are used mostly when an entity has an extraordinarily large number of attributes, so the entity is split in two to make it more easy to manage, and applications perform better.

An extra entity might be desired during the development of the physical storage locations of the data. By separating off seldom-used data from more frequently used information, faster data retrieval and updates can be accommodated. For example, employees may have pictures but the pictures are not often retrieved by a front-end application and are therefore separated away in a separate entity. A one-to-one relationship is usually drawn on an ER diagram as a line with both ends having dots.

One-to-Many

One-to-many relationships exist when a single instance of an entity (the parent entity) relates to many instances of another entity (the child entity). One-to-many relationships are the most common relationships in the real world. For example, a customer may have many orders, and a manufactured product may have many components. A one-to-many relationship is usually drawn on an ER diagram as a line with the child end having a dot. The child end is a crow's foot in Chen and IE data models.

Many-to-Many

This type of relationship occurs when many rows or data elements in an entity are associated with many rows or data elements in another entity. For example, a many-to-many relationship occurs between the Trainee and Course entities. Many Trainees can enroll in a single course, and one trainee can be enrolled in numerous courses. This type of relationship is not uncommon in the real world. However, SQL Server doesn't actually directly implement many-to-many relationships. A many-to-many relationship is implemented using three entities. The two main entities are connected together using a third entity. The third entity contains keys and interrelationship information. Each entity is connected to the new entity as a one-to-many relationship. To discover the cardinality of a relationship, you look at the correlation between the entities. For example, a Trainee may take many Courses, and a Course may have many Trainees. The problem isn't SQL Server not implementing many-to-many relationships, but that relational databases in general cannot directly support this kind of relationship. Therefore, it is a combination of two, one-to-many ties.

Identifying Relationships

Remember, entities are the nouns in the model; akin to this, relationships are the verbs. This verb/noun concept is a key factor in determining entities and relationships and I advise beginners to use this. I once came across a saying, "One trick to discovering relationships between entities is to look closely at the entity definitions." I've particularly found that many beginners and even professionals use this method and find it extremely effective. Look back at the definitions you wrote for each entity in Step by Step 2.2:

◆ **Patient**. Stores information about the individual patients registered in Lloyd's Hospital to get treatment provided from doctors (EMPLOYEES).

◆ **Employee**. Tracks information, such as salary and contract, about the doctors and workers employed at Lloyd's Hospital who teach COURSES and treat PATIENTS.

◆ **Medicine**. Keeps a statistical list of the medicine available, which EMPLOYEES are allowed to prescribe for their ailing PATIENTS.

◆ **Machinery**. Holds miscellaneous details of the sophisticated machinery and utilities available at Lloyd's, only used by specialized EMPLOYEES.

◆ **Course**. Keeps information concerning the courses available at Lloyd's Hospital, taught to TRAINEES by EMPLOYEES.

◆ **Trainee**: Keeps track of the students learning the different COURSES available from Lloyd's EMPLOYEES.

From the preceding descriptions, you can construct a blueprint of an ER diagram after you summarize the information.

◆ A PATIENT is one who needs treatment from a doctor (EMPLOYEE).

◆ An EMPLOYEE helps a PATIENT with his/her expertise and can prescribe MEDICINE if needed.

◆ MEDICINE is used to aid PATIENTS and is prescribed by EMPLOYEES.

◆ MACHINERY helps EMPLOYEES in treating their PATIENTS.

◆ EMPLOYEES teach COURSES to TRAINEES.

◆ TRAINEES are those participating in the COURSES provided by Lloyd's Hospital.

Now you can construct a general overview of what your model is going to look like. This is shown in Figure 2.3.

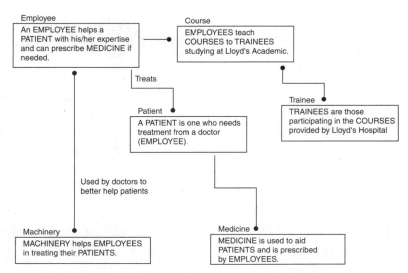

FIGURE 2.3
ER model overview.

So how are relationships actually implemented? They are implemented as parent and child entities. In all cases in the ER model, a key attribute from a child parent entity is attached to a related key value in a parent. All cardinality of relationships are implemented in this way. This means that whether you have a one-to-one, one-to-many, or many-to-many relationship, you always have the key of the child related to a parent.

As noted previously in the chapter, many-to-many relationships exist when many instances of one entity are related to many instances of another entity. The reason why many-to-many relationships are implemented a bit differently is that the ER relational model does not support many-to-many relationships. Nonetheless, establish many-to-many relationships by creating two one-to-many relationships and connecting them to a new entity.

This new entity is known as an *associate entity* or *join entity*. Resolving many-to-many relationships involves creating two one-to-many relationships from each of the original entities onto the associative entity. Take the many-to-many relationship between the Course entity and Trainee entity, for example. A many-to-many relationship needs to be resolved by creating an associative entity, TraineeCourse, and then linking a one-to-many relationship from the Course and Trainee entities to TraineeCourse. This process of resolving many-to-many relationships is shown in Figure 2.4.

FIGURE 2.4

A many-to-many relationship.

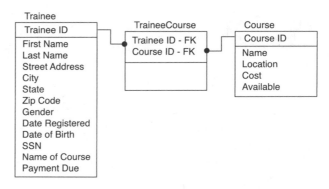

To help you better understand many-to-many relationships, the Course, Trainee, and Description entities along with sample data are shown in Figure 2.5.

One other many-to-many relationship also exists in the scenario. There is likely to be a many-to-many relationship between Employee and Machine, which is explored in the next section.

Setting up the relationships finalizes a draft of the ER model. This draft will undergo modifications as the database approaches a physical design. The next topic to discuss is potential alteration to the design that will improve efficiency of the data store.

FIGURE 2.5

Sample data after a many-to-many resolution.

Trainees	TraineeID	FirstName	LastName	ZipCode	City	State	Address	DuePayment
1	101	John	Jones	74832	Burford	CA	278 Mill Street	200.0000
2	207	Sue	Smith	73638	Delhi	CA	837 Phelan Street	300.0000
3	473	Bill	Brown	73833	Embro	CA	62 Dundas Street	400.0000
4	673	Joe	Samson	73345	Durham	CA	9304 Ferdale Avenue	200.0000
5	983	Sally	Hillery	78390	Wilson	CA	9 Center Drive	100.0000

Courses	CourseID	Number	Name	Cost	Available
1	1A	2378	Bed Baths	100	1
2	1B	6392	Sterilization	100	1
3	1C	7296	Introductory Meds	100	1
4	1D	1739	Advanced Meds	100	1
5	2A	1736	Cardio Therapy	100	1
6	2B	8363	ICU Care	100	1
7	2C	8923	Emergency Care	100	1
8	2D	7436	Post Operative Care	100	1
9	3A	7322	Post Natal	100	1
10	3B	4280	Doctor Assisting	100	1
11	3C	8370	Dietary Care	150	0
12	3D	1298	Medical Training	150	0
13	4A	7922	IV Therapy I	200	0
14	4B	2492	IV Therapy II	200	0
15	4C	0982	IV Therapy III	250	0
16	4D	3487	IV Therapy IV	250	0

	TraineeID	CourseID
1	101	3A
2	101	3B
3	207	2D
4	207	3A
5	207	3B
6	473	2A
7	473	2B
8	473	2C
9	473	2D
10	673	2C
11	673	2D
12	983	1A

Data Modeling Overview

We have completed our look at the basic elements of data modeling using the Entity Relationship approach. A general listing of attributes for each entity and the relationships between these entities is an important springboard for progressing through the database design to the eventual completed system.

Entities can correspond with each other in several different manners. If you look at a typical sales problem, it is easy to see some of these relationships. A salesman will have many customers, a customer will have many invoices, and an invoice will have many purchased products. The most common relationship is one-to-many, but the entire database system is sure to reveal a few many-to-many relationships as well. In the sales case, for example, many salesmen sell many products.

Although you now have a general listing of entities, relationships, and attributes, the logical design is not yet complete. Next you need to fine-tune the model with a process called *normalization*.

UNDERSTANDING DATABASE NORMALIZATION

▶ **Define entities. Considering normalization and denormalization.**

• **Specify degree of normalization.**

Normalization in general refers to how you implement and store data. (Normalization is a design process intended to eliminate duplicate data, it is not how you implement.) In a normalized entity, the redundant data is removed and the entity is simplified to its most basic form. This usually leads to a more involved entity structure with more entities. In the same way, database normalization and planned denormalization is the process of simplifying data and data design to achieve maximum performance and simplicity. This denormalization process involves the planned addition of redundant data.

Although both normalization and denormalization are valid, necessary processes, the two achieve opposite goals. They don't by themselves achieve maximum performance and simplicity, though they do strive for a perfect balance between performance (denormalization) and simplicity (normalization). Normalization means no duplicate data.

In 1970, Dr. E. F. Codd designed three regulations a relational database adheres to, known as *normal forms,* and today known as the first, second, and third normal forms. (Normal forms do exceed three, but the first three are the only ones widely used.) The goal of the initial database design is to simplify the database into the third normal form.

Before starting to normalize a database, look at the following guidelines:

◆ All columns should be decomposed (broken down to their most basic form).

◆ Many-to-many relationships should be converted to pairs of one-to-many relationships. This is not part of normalization, but part of the physical implementation.

◆ Primary and Foreign Keys should be created and identified.

Normalizing a database is seemingly good, but can hamper performance. In many cases a designer has to consider denormalizing a database, which is discussed a little later. The following sections discuss the three normal forms of a database and how to implement them.

First Normal Form

The first normal form, or 1NF, defines the foundation for the relational database system. Attributes should be atomic, which means that they cannot (or should not) be further broken down, based on the business needs for the use of the attribute. The first normal form defines that all attributes be atomic, which is to say they cannot be decomposed and must be non-repeating. In relational database terms, 1NF states that all attributes must be defined in their singular-most form; which means that attributes must be decomposed and not further divisible.

An attribute, which is not repeating, is known as an *atomic value,* which is a value that is represented only one time. You learned about the decomposition of attributes in the earlier discussion about having Street, City, State, and Zip fields rather than a general Address field. This is precisely what the 1NF does.

Successfully passing the 1NF eventually increases data access and performance. If there is ever a violation of the first normal form, it can easily be resolved. To know whether your database has violated the restrictions of 1NF, look at the attributes in an entity and then see whether the attribute repeats or is akin to any of the other attributes. If so, then you know that you are violating the first normal form.

To resolve this type of situation, find all the attributes that seem to be repeating. For example, take a look at a variation of the Employee entity where a repeated array of values holds information for an employee's multiple machine capabilities, as seen in Figure 2.6.

To resolve this type of situation, find all the attributes that seem to be repeating. Create a new entity with a name similar to the repeating attribute and place all repeatedly occurring attributes into it. For this example, if a machine entity didn't already exist it would be created. After creating a new entity and shifting repeated attributes into it, you have to create a key (a key that uniquely identifies each row in the new entity) and a related key in the Employee entity. In the example it is better treated as a many-to-many relationship. Many employees can run a machine and an employee can run many machines. This relationship would look similar to the illustration in Figure 2.7.

After eliminating duplicates and adding additional entities, you can then proceed with the second normal form and ensure that attributes are assigned to the most appropriate entity.

```
        Employee
 ┌──────────────────┐
 │ Employee ID      │
 ├──────────────────┤
 │ Name             │
 │ Address          │
 │ Gender           │
 │ Date of Birth    │
 │ SSN              │
 │ Contract Type    │
 │ Salary           │
 │ Position         │
 │ MachineName1     │
 │ MachineName2     │
 │ MachineName3     │
 └──────────────────┘
```

FIGURE 2.6
The Employee entity violating a restriction of 1NF.

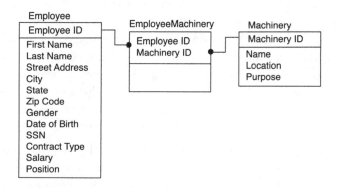

FIGURE 2.7
Employee/machinery relationship.

Second Normal Form

The first requirement of the second normal form is that it meets the requirements of the first normal form. The second requirement is that all non-key attributes are dependant on the entity key. To pass 2NF, every attribute in an entity must depend on the whole key, not just a part of it. A violation in 2NF occurs when these requirements are not met.

To know whether an entity is violating the restrictions of 2NF, see whether the attribute is dependant on only part of the Primary Key. 2NF applies in only those entities that have a compound Primary Key and a data element is dependent on only a portion of that key. In the example case there is no violation of 2NF, so Figure 2.8 uses a separate simple example to illustrate this point. In Figure 2.8, the partial dependence is true for the Square Footage attribute in that it is dependant on only the Warehouse ID and not the Region ID.

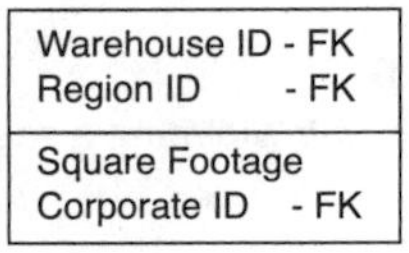

To resolve a 2NF violation, create a new entity for the partially-dependant attributes and then place these attributes inside it. Then create a key to make a relationship to the original entity. The 2NF ensures model flexibility and tries to ensure the prohibition of redundant data.

Meeting the second normal form brings the design closer to an efficient model. A final set of adjustments to consider is the third normal form.

| Warehouse ID - FK |
Region ID   - FK
Square Footage
Corporate ID   - FK

FIGURE 2.8
The RegionWarehouse entity violating a restriction of 2NF.

Third Normal Form

Third normal form shares a common objective like the other normal forms, in that its goal is to eliminate redundant data. However, it is more similar to the second normal form because it accomplishes this by cutting down interdependencies on non-key attributes. The third normal form ensures that you get the most consistency with the entity layout after you normalize the database. 3NF states that all non-Primary Key attributes must depend on the key. You cannot have any indirect or transitive dependencies, as described in the following paragraphs.

As stated previously, a database design's initial goal is to achieve the value and correctness of the third normal form to remove all data redundancy. The third normal form ensures elimination of data redundancy by eliminating interdependencies between non-key attributes.

Identifying a 3NF violation involves looking at an attribute and then asking whether this attribute depends on the availability of any other non-key attribute.

For example, examine the entity in Figure 2.9.

The `Trainee` entity is violating one of the restrictions of 3NF because it has three interdependent non-key attributes, which are `EnrolledCourseID`, `EnrolledCourse`, and `DateEnrolled`. These are referred to as *interdependent attributes* because they depend on the attribute `EnrolledCourseID`. To implement and resolve this 3NF violation, add the enrollment date to the `Course` table and eliminate the extra unnecessary columns. This eliminates the redundant data in an entity (see Figure 2.10).

FIGURE 2.9
The Trainee entity violating a restriction of 3NF.

Normalizing a design provides for efficient use of storage, but in many situations will affect performance. Planned redundancy or denormalization are often brought into the design to provide for better performance or to clarify data.

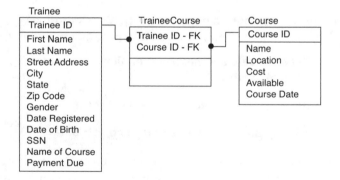

FIGURE 2.10
The Trainee entity is no longer violating 3NF.

When to Denormalize

Denormalization is the planned placement of redundant data to minimize table joins, reduce network traffic, eliminate repeated calculations, and provide for application-specific procedures. A database that is used primarily for decision support (as opposed to update-intensive transaction processing) may not have redundant updates and may be more understandable and efficient for queries if the design is not fully normalized. In data warehousing the results of calculations are often stored with the data, so that type of processing does not have to occur when the data is read. Many reporting systems also denormalize data to produce results specific to the application.

Normalization on the Exam   The exam will require that you know what to denormalize, as stated in the Microsoft exam sub-objective: "Specify degree of normalization." Normalization is not always the best design for a given database. Normalization creates numerous, small, interrelated tables. Processing the data in these tables can incur a great deal of extra work and other overhead to combine the related data. The extra processing reduces the performance of the database. In these situations, denormalizing the database slightly to simplify complex processes can improve performance.

Sometimes you'll encounter situations where a fully normalized data model just won't perform in the situation you place it in. In situations like this, you have to denormalize your database. A normalized database needs more join queries to gather information from multiple entities (because entities are divided into smaller entities when undergoing the process of normalization). Therefore, CPU usage might overwhelmingly increase, and cause an application to slow or freeze. In situations like this, denormalization is appropriate.

Normalization and denormalization processes begin to put a high-performance database system together in a logical fashion. Any seasoned database person knows, however, that performance isn't the only concern. It is necessary in any database system to minimize the administrative management needed to keep a database functional and accurate. The aim here is integrity.

Maintaining Data Integrity

▶ **Design attribute domain integrity. Considerations include CHECK constraints, data types, and nullability.**

   • **Specify scale and precision of allowable values for each attribute.**

   • **Allow or prohibit NULL for each attribute.**

   • **Specify allowable values for each attribute.**

Whether you have implemented or are in the process of implementing a data model, you will need to keep data integrity in mind as a key factor in verifying the correctness and uniqueness of data. Data integrity itself means preserving the correctness and verifying the consistency of data. When incorrect or inconsistent values and records are preserved in a database, it is said to have lost data integrity. For instance, a product in a Products table may have a Product_ID of 67. It would be up to the database designer to ensure that the same value is not inserted again. Or if a product ID is to have only numbers in it, it is the responsibility of the integrity regulations to prevent the entering of characters.

IN THE FIELD

GIGO

There is an old saying in the data processing environment that presents the end results of any operation as being determined by the data entering the operation: Garbage In gives Garbage Out, or GIGO. The process of maintaining integrity is an attempt to eliminate errors entering the system. No matter how good the design, maintaining data integrity determines how productive or usable a system is.

Many SQL Server techniques can be used to ensure data integrity is not lost. Before you can examine some of the techniques for the physical implementation, you need to break down the large topic of data integrity into some smaller, more manageable subtopics. Three types of data integrity can be enforced in your database: entity integrity, domain integrity, and referential integrity. All are discussed in detail in the sections that follow.

Entity Integrity

Applying entity integrity defines a unique row attribute as an identifier for individual entities. Generally, the regulations of this type of data integrity are easy to follow. Simple ways of enforcing this type of integrity are using Primary Keys, UNIQUE constraints, and unique indexes when the entity design moves into the physical stage of design. Entity integrity specifies that Primary Keys on every instance of an entity must be kept, must be unique, and have values other than null content.

Although SQL Server does not explicitly dictate that a table needs to have a Primary Key, it is a good practice to design a Primary Key for each table into the model. Many procedures in SQL Server require a unique identification for each row in an entity, which is no longer a concern if you establish a Primary Key. SQL Server creates a UNIQUE INDEX constraint to enforce a Primary Key's uniqueness. It also mandates no null content, so that every row in a table must have a value that denotes the row as a unique element of the entity.

Although indexing is discussed in Chapters 3 and 10, it is worth noting at this time that by default the Primary Key represents a clustered index. If left this way, the Primary Key places the data into sequence based on the key values.

Unique indexing, unique constraints, Primary Keys, and, in some cases, stored procedures can all be used to help you maintain entity integrity. There is also a mechanism for assigning a Primary Key or other attribute a sequential value. This sequential value is often referred to as an *auto-numbering attribute*. In SQL Server the appropriate term is an *Identity column*.

Using the IDENTITY property enforces uniqueness throughout attributes, which is one of the benefits of using a Primary Key. In SQL Server, the IDENTITY property creates a sequenced number each time a new row is created. This type of key on a column is often used as a surrogate Primary Key. Surrogate keys can be easily created to enforce uniqueness.

The IDENTITY property creates a column that contains sequenced numbers to distinguish one record from another, and thus behaves like a surrogate key. A good example of a column marked using the IDENTITY property is an ID column, such as CustomerID. If a column or attribute is marked with the IDENTITY property, SQL Server is obliged to maintain uniqueness throughout the column values. Remember, an IDENTITY property should be placed only when there is not a particular Primary Key candidate in mind. For example, consider the Course entity in the Lloyd's Hospital data model.

No attribute stays unique throughout the entity. Therefore, it would be proper to create your own candidate in this example: the CourseID attribute. This attribute has no meaning except that it enables you to uniquely identify a particular course. Primary Keys for the model are identified as shown in Figure 2.11.

Domain Integrity

Domain integrity involves restricting the data entered to a domain or range of values, thus preventing incorrect data from entering the system. You may, for example, not want to allow values greater than 2,500 from being entered into the database or prevent the entry of non-numeric data. There are many other types of domain integrity,

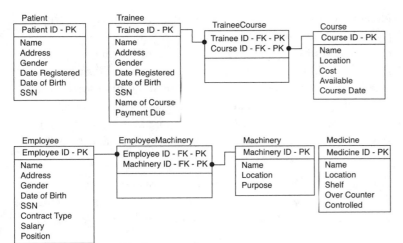

FIGURE 2.11

Primary keys identified for the Lloyd's Hospital data model.

as well as a large number of SQL Server technologies that can help you maintain this integrity.

We have already defined and showed the implementation of Foreign Keys. Foreign Keys help maintain domain integrity by ensuring that all rows of data in a child entity have a matching row of data in the parent entity. When a Foreign Key constraint is defined, it is not possible to add a new row in a child table that does not have an appropriate and related parent.

Many column properties help you maintain domain integrity. The data type chosen for a column enforces integrity by permitting only appropriate data in the column. Precision, the number of digits in a number, and scale, the number of digits to the right of the decimal place, can be used in conjunction with numeric data types to maintain accurate data. A complete listing of data types, their descriptions, and uses is given later in this chapter. Other column properties that assist in domain integrity are nullability, which determines whether an attribute is optional or mandatory, and default value, which can supply appropriate default input.

A *default* provides a predefined value placed when a value isn't specified on a column during data entry. Defaults can be used in conjunction with NULL where no data is entered to prevent errors or to just make it easier for someone to enter data. Default values can be attached to a column with the help of the DEFAULT column constraint. If most customers in the case study come from within the same region, a default value could be used and overridden by data entry when necessary.

Nullability is an aspect of database design that enforces integrity by placing a constraint that determines whether null values are allowed on a column or not. A null value is not a zero-length string ("") but it is referred to when absolutely no data is present. This is useful when a user must enter data for a column and cannot leave it blank. The null option can be set at the time of table creation using the NULL and NOT NULL options. If data is required for an attribute, it should have the NOT NULL property assigned to it, and NULL if the attribute value is optional.

Other aspects of SQL Server that enforce domain integrity require a little more work on the part of the designer, but can be implemented using a number of other mechanisms discussed in the next section.

Domain integrity can also involve the checking of data entered to ensure that it is valid based on business rules or other conditions of an application. A *business rule* is a logical rule that is used to run a business. Business rules can be enforced by a database system through the use of rules, stored procedures, triggers, and constraints. Each of these objects interacts in a different manner to prevent invalid data from entering the system.

A *rule* is a database object not connected directly to a column or table. It is bound to columns or user-defined data types to specify which data values are acceptable in a column. CHECK constraints can provide the same functionality with less overhead and are preferred because they are in the SQL-92 standard and are connected directly to a column or table.

Use of stored procedures allows actions to be performed in a controlled manner. They are precompiled collections of T-SQL statements stored under a name and processed as a single unit. Stored procedures can perform modifications in a predictable manner and maintain integrity through the logic developed by the designer.

A trigger provides a high degree of functionality but at a cost. A *trigger* is a stored procedure that executes when data in a specified table is modified. The data modification occurs and the trigger must react to the change. This means that a great deal more overhead is associated with a trigger, and it is therefore used only when other techniques lack the capability. Triggers are often created to enforce integrity or consistency among logically related data in different tables. Triggers are a complex mechanism and are covered in detail in Chapter 8, "Triggers."

Many types of constraints exist in SQL Server. A *constraint* is a property assigned to a table or column that prevents invalid data values from being entered. A UNIQUE or PRIMARY KEY constraint prevents you from inserting a duplicate value; a CHECK constraint prevents you from inserting a value that does not match a specified condition; and NOT NULL mandates a data value must be provided for the column. A constraint is processed on the server and catches an error before the data gets into the system. This is an important facet of handling data integrity because it is important to catch errors at the earliest moment to minimize the use of resources and processing overhead. Further expansion on this topic is found in Chapter 3, "Physical Database Design."

Referential Integrity

Referential integrity specifies that every Foreign Key value map to a Primary Key or other unique value in related tables. Referential integrity guarantees the smooth navigation in moving from entity to entity, so it is extremely important to ensure proper referential integrity definition. Referential integrity ensures that no orphaned records exist. Orphaned data is a term used when data in a child entity exists that points to a non-existent parent.

Setting up a Foreign Key constraint enforces referential integrity, and stored procedures and triggers can also be used to maintain the integrity. Past versions of SQL Server relied on triggers much more heavily than in SQL Server 2000, in which you find several new advanced features to maintain referential integrity. These new features of the physical implementation are discussed at length in Chapter 3.

Using Advanced Referential Integrity Options

Two new options exist for defining relationships to be used in a SQL Server database system. These options allow more control over the actions that can affect key values. Cascade Update Related Fields and Cascade Delete Related Records enable updates or deletions of key values to cascade through the tables defined to have Foreign Key relationships that can be traced back to the table on which the modification is made.

A cascading deletion occurs when you delete a row with a key referenced by Foreign Keys in existing rows in other tables. In that case, all rows containing those Foreign Keys are also deleted.

A cascading update occurs when you update a key value in a row, where the key value is referenced by Foreign Keys in existing rows in other tables. All the Foreign Key values are also updated to the new value specified for the key.

If cascading referential actions have also been defined on the target tables, the specified cascading actions are also taken for the rows in those tables.

Applications Maintaining Integrity

In many environments, it is possible to catch data integrity violations without using resources on the database server. Particularly in Internet applications, developers try to minimize the return trips needed to obtain accurate data entry. If errors can be caught at the user interface and corrected before the data is submitted to the database, then a more efficient system will result.

Some simple checks that can be performed include basic error checks to ensure that required fields do contain data and that the numerical and date entries are in valid ranges. You'll learn more about some of this functionality later in the chapter as it describes the different application architectures.

Using Appropriate Data Types

Traditionally, data is divided into three basic categories: numeric, alphanumeric, or character and binary. Other data types exist, however, and several require special handling in applications and design considerations.

Assigning a data type to an object defines four attributes of the object:

◆ The kind of data contained by the object

◆ The length of the data stored

◆ The precision of numeric data types

◆ The scale of numeric data types

Selecting an appropriate data type is an important decision that must take into account the application, usage of the data, and future trends. Particularly with numeric data you must be careful to select a type that is large enough to store the data. In character data types you want to be careful to not waste storage unnecessarily by configuring the size of the data to be larger than necessary.

Numeric Data Types

Numeric data can be defined as integer data, in a variety of sizes for whole numbers or one of several different types that accommodate decimal point storage for real numbers.

The bigint data type is an 8-byte integer type that is new to SQL Server 2000 and allows for the storage of very large integer numbers. A bigint supports values in the range from –9,223,372,036,854,775,808 through +9,223,372,036,854,775,807.

Other integer data types support a variety of smaller integers. The int data type, using 4 bytes of storage, supports values in the range from –2,147,483,648 through +2,147,483,647. The smallint data type uses 2 bytes and supports from –32,768 through +32,767, and the smallest integer data type tinyint, at only a single byte, supports values from 0 through 255.

Decimal and Numeric are functionally the same data type, and allow for the storage of a Fixed precision and scale numeric data from $-10^{38} + 1$ through $10^{38} - 1$. Depending on the precision chosen, this data type uses from 5 to 17 bytes for the storage of values as summarized in Table 2.2.

NOTE

Support for bigint A lot of the functions, statements, and system stored procedures that accepted int expressions for their parameters in the previous SQL Server versions have not been changed to support conversion of bigint expressions to those parameters. Thus, SQL Server converts bigint to int only when the bigint value is within the range supported by the int data type. A conversion error occurs at run time if the bigint expression contains a value outside the range supported by the int data type.

TABLE 2.2

DECIMAL AND NUMERIC STORAGE SIZES

Precision	Bytes
1–9	5
10–19	9
20–28	13
29–38	17

Two data types are used for storage of monetary values: smallmoney and money. These values are stored with a scale of four decimal places. The smallmoney data type consumes 4 bytes and allows for the storage of monetary values from –214,748.3648 through +214,748.3647, and the money data type, at 8 bytes, stores values from –922,337,203,685,477.5808 through +922,337,203,685,477.5807.

Character Data Types

Character data types are subdivided into two categories depending on the byte size of the characters being stored. Traditionally, character data consumed one byte per character, allowing for 255 different characters. This standard was found to be inflexible, so the Unicode standard was developed, in which each character uses two bytes of storage. This standard allows for approximately 64,000 different characters.

Each of these two data types have three variations for the storage of data: fixed-length, variable-length, and large character data. Non-Unicode data uses the char, varchar, and text data types, whereas Unicode data is stored in the nchar, nvarchar, and ntext types.

The char data type allows for the storage of fixed-length non-Unicode character data with lengths from 1 through 8,000. The varchar data type allows for the same sizes of data. The primary difference between the two is that the varchar uses storage space more efficiently and uses only the space necessary to store the data value, regardless of the maximum size a variable has been configured to store. The nchar and nvarchar are essentially the Unicode implementation of char and varchar, and allow for storage of up to 4,000 characters.

The text and ntext data types are used to store large variable-length character data. The text data type can store up to 2,147,483,647 characters, whereas ntext can store 1,073,741,823.

Binary Data Types

A number of data types are used to store binary data. The smallest is the bit data type, which supports Boolean operations and stores values of 0 or 1 in a single storage bit. Other binary data types are used to store binary strings and are stored as hexadecimal values.

Binary data is stored using the binary, varbinary, and image data types. A column assigned the binary data type must have the same fixed length of up to 8KB. In a column assigned the varbinary data type, entries can vary in size. Columns of image data can be used to store variable-length binary data exceeding 8KB, such as Microsoft Word documents, Microsoft Excel spreadsheets, and images that include bitmaps and other graphic files.

Specialty Data Types

Many data types are used in special circumstances to store data that does not directly qualify as numeric, character, or binary. Data types are available to store time and date information, globally unique identifiers (GUID), cursors, and tables.

Three data types support the storage of time and date information: datetime, smalldatetime, and timestamp. All three store dates and times, although the timestamp data type stores automatically generated binary values using 8 bytes of storage and is not used to store data.

Values with the datetime data type are stored as two 4-byte integers. The first 4 bytes store the number of days before or after the *base date*, which is January 1, 1900. The base date is the system reference date. Values for datetime earlier than January 1, 1753, are not permitted. The other 4 bytes store the time of day, represented as the number of milliseconds after midnight.

The smalldatetime data type stores dates and times of day with less precision than datetime. It stores them as two 2-byte integers. The first 2 bytes store the number of days after January 1, 1900. The other 2 bytes store the number of minutes since midnight. Dates range from January 1, 1900, through June 6, 2079.

The uniquidentifier data type stores a 16-byte data value known as a *globally unique identifier* or GUID. The GUID takes on the string format xxxxxxxx-xxxx-xxxx-xxxx-xxxxxxxxxxxx, in which each x is a hexadecimal digit. A GUID is long and obscure, but has the advantage of being guaranteed to be unique throughout the world.

The sql_variant is a generic data type that stores values of various SQL Server-supported data types, except text, ntext, image, timestamp, and sql_variant. It may be used in column definitions as well as in parameters, variables, and return values of user-defined functions. A sql_variant can have a maximum length of 8,016 bytes.

> **NOTE**
>
> **SQL-92 Standard Timestamp**   The T-SQL timestamp data type is not the same as the timestamp data type defined in the SQL-92 standard. The SQL-92 timestamp data type is equivalent to the T-SQL datetime data type.

The `table` data type is new to SQL Server in the 2000 release. It can be used to temporarily store a resultset for later use. The `table` data type is not used for defining column types within a structure; rather it is used in functions, stored procedures, and batches.

The `cursor` data type is another data type that is used only in functions, stored procedures, and batches. Its primary purpose is to allow the storage of a pointer to a resultset. Attributes of a T-SQL server cursor, such as its scrolling behavior and the query used to build the resultset on which the cursor operates, are set up using a `DECLARE CURSOR` operation within the procedure.

User-Defined Data Types

User-defined data types are stored as database objects and are based on any of the system data types. User-defined data types can be used when several tables must store the same type of data in a column and you must ensure that these columns have exactly the same data type, length, and nullability.

Using these data types can help you create tables more quickly and can also help you control the data in a predictable manner. Often a user-defined data type is created in the model database; it will then exist in all new user-defined databases created.

Data Types in a Logical Model

Data definition is a step that follows the ER modeling as the database system nears the stage where it can be designed for the actual physical implementation. If present at all, the data definition in the logical model is more a general characterization of the data as opposed to the specifics needed for the implementation. At this stage it is more important to simply categorize the data.

Between the logical modeling and the physical implementation, the actual software is chosen (though in the example case it was really predetermined). If developing a system from scratch where no software exists, the business needs are laid out, the logical model represented, and the system architecture is designed before any decisions are made about the physical design, software, and hardware. If certain software is already being used in a given business, then some of the logical design stages may be adjusted toward specific products. The next section looks at the architecture of different types of database systems from the smallest desktop environments to the large-scale Internet application becoming prevalent in today's IT environment.

Models and Uses

Now you have a model, and even have some ideas of how to control the model to maintain accuracy and prevent system breakdown due to loss of integrity. Many tools are available to prevent the bad data from getting in that could produce incorrect results. Imagine the result if a government agency bases its decisions that will affect an entire country on data that is inaccurate or misrepresented. (Governments have enough trouble making decisions with accurate data.)

So now you have a high-performance model that has been made as efficient possible through normalization principles. You may have even applied some planned redundancy (denormalization) in an effort to improve the performance and make the data more meaningful. But what about the storage? Now that you have attributes of all shapes and sizes, you need something to put them in. It is now time to look into the data itself.

THE CLIENT/SERVER MODEL

▶ **Handle client/server configurations of 50 to 5,000 or more users.**

- **One, two, and n tier operations**

- **Internet applications. Web configurations that use Internet Information Server (IIS) or COM+.**

- **Heterogeneous databases using other non-SQL Server data sources.**

- **Very large database support.**

There are essentially two different models in which database systems can be described: a client/server model and a desktop database system. SQL Server can be used in both instances to store data and allow for application interaction.

A client/server system divides the elements of a database system into two (or more) separate components, usually executing on two or more computers. The client component is responsible for the user interface and presents the data to the user in an attractive layout. This interface can be a Windows traditional form design or an HTML-based Internet design. The server is responsible for the data storage and actual manipulations of the data. This approach divides the processing and workload between the client, the server, and in some cases other machines as well.

The client/server model can be thought of as a number of workstation computers accessing a central database from a server computer. In a concise sentence, the client/server model expresses a connection between a client program running on a workstation computer requesting a service and/or data from the server. When the client application needs certain data, it fetches that data from the server. The server application in turn runs a search against the server database to find the desired records. After the records are found, the server sends them back to the client application.

In this way only data that is needed is sent back to the client, and thereby multiuser access is provided, in contrast to non-client/server desktop database systems that prefer singular access and have difficulty handling multiuser functionality. This process is shown in Figure 2.12.

In a non-client/server desktop architecture, the whole database resides on the client's machine; the client then processes the query locally on the database and finds records as required. This process results in wasted disk space and is difficult to set up in a multiple-user environment.

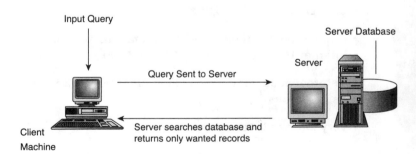

FIGURE 2.12
A basic overview of how Client/Server processes information.

The server is concerned with uses such as concurrency, security, and backing up data. The client-side application is implemented with a nice user interface and might contain queries and forms. The roles of each computer are not, however, carved in stone, and depending on the interactions required in any given system, many machines may take part. The process of dividing up processing across many machines creates a multi-layered environment. Each layer in the environment is referred to as a *tier* and each tier has a specific role to play in the overall system.

Application development and choice of model is a crossover stage between the logical development and the physical database structure. At times the choice of the number of tiers is accomplished before the physical database implementation. Others choose to prepare the database first. Neither is absolutely correct, but it is a good idea to have some idea of the model before determining the final physical data structure.

One- and Two-Tier Systems

A one-tier system in a PC environment dates back 25 or more years to an environment where the only way to share data was to use the "sneaker net" approach. In other words, copies of the data were made and distributed manually. This approach was adequate at best and caused many headaches for anyone trying to implement a multiple-user environment. Particularly difficult was the merging of updates from multiple copies of the data.

With a single-tier approach, one computer performs all the processing required to view, update, and store the data. Many products use this technique for small, single-user database systems, but this technique becomes overwhelming when the data is needed by multiple users sharing the same data. In this case, a two-tier with a central data store on a proper server is a better approach.

A two-tier architecture places the user interface and data on separate machines. The client application sends queries across the network to be resolved by the data engine running on the server. The server resolves the query and sends the necessary data back across the network for the client application to display. There are two different implementations of a two-tier system: "thin client" and "thick client," which is also known as "fat client."

In a thin approach the client application does little or no processing. A thin client just presents the data to the user and, when needed, communicates with the database engine on the server to work with the data. The thin client approach is best where the number of concurrent users accessing the data can be kept to a minimum. Because the server must perform the processing to validate the data as well as all other data manipulations, there is a lot of server overhead related to this approach. A thin client is a good approach for maintainability. If you need to upgrade software, for example, you do not have to do so on 1000 clients. It also works well for Internet applications.

The thick client approach offloads some of the work needed to validate and process the data from the server machine to the client machine. In this approach the client may make some of the determinations as to whether data should be sent to the server based on validity checks coded in the client application. This approach enables many more users to access the same database concurrently. On the down side, though, application maintenance is more demanding and higher performance is required from the client.

Although two-tier architectures allow for more flexibility and a larger number of users, it is still quite a limited architecture that can serve only small environments. When a larger number of concurrent user accesses is needed, a better choice of architecture is a multiple "n-tier" architecture or possibly an Internet architecture.

Three- or More Tier Systems

In a three-tier system, the client system presents the interface and interacts with the user. The database server manipulates the data, but there also exists a middle tier to control some of the operations. The middle tier can be represented by one or more machines that offload some processing from the database server, which allows for a very large number of users. There is usually no differentiation between three or more tiers and instead they are all categorized as n-tier systems.

In an n-tier system, processing is divided into three categories. Each category represents one of the three main tiers in the three-tier system, which is also carried forward in an n-tier system regardless of the number of layers of processing.

The presentation or client tier contains the components of the system that interact directly with the user. The sole purpose of this tier is to focus on the end user and present data in an attractive, organized, and meaningful fashion.

The middle tier, or business tier, is responsible for communicating with the database server and also sets up the rules by which communication will be established. The idea behind the business tier is to provide mechanisms to implement the business rules that need to be applied to validate data and also perform intermediate processing that may be needed to prepare the data for presentation to the user. For this reason the business tier is often separated into two divisions: interactions with the user and interactions with the database server. With this approach business rules can be separated from data access processes.

The final tier is the data tier, which is responsible for the execution of the data engine to perform all manipulations of the data. Access to the data tier is made through the middle tier. The data tier doesn't directly interact with the presentation layer.

Internet Applications

Internet applications can be said to fall under a two- or three-tier model, depending on the complexity and physical design. In an Internet application, the web server prepares the presentation elements to be displayed on the user's browser. If a middle tier server exists, then the web server is configured to interact with that server. If no middle tier server exists, then the web server interacts directly with the database server.

Depending on the implementation, the client's browser may also be considered a tier. If a set of records is sent to the browser by the web server to allow editing on the browser, then the client is considered a tier. In this case, a disconnected recordset or XML data is used for the client's data manipulation. If a round trip to the web server must take place to submit changes and interact with the data, then the client is not considered a tier—it is more just a mechanism to display the HTML that is sent by the web server. In this case the user tier is the Internet server that acts as the user and prepares the HTML for display.

Internet applications have the best scalability of all application architecture types, meaning that they can support the largest number of concurrent users. The drawback to using an Internet architecture is that it requires a greater number of development skills, and update conflict issues are inherent to the technology.

Although an Internet application is usually implemented so that the database can be accessed from anywhere in the world, it can also be used for internal purposes through a configured intranet. Under this principle, users can access the database from a corporate HTML or XML site.

Very Large Database Applications

SQL Server 2000 has high-speed optimizations that support very large database environments. Although previous versions lacked the capability to support larger systems, SQL Server 2000 and SQL Server 7.0 can effectively support terabyte-sized databases.

With the implementation of partitioned views in Enterprise Edition, servers can be scaled to meet the requirements of large Web sites and enterprise environments. Federated server implementations enable a large number of servers to assist in maintaining a complex large system.

Elements of the replication system can also help distribute data among a number of machines while providing mutual updatability and maintaining centralized control over the entire system.

Third-Party Database Interactions

SQL Server 2000 supports heterogeneous connectivity to any data source through the use of OLE-DB and ODBC drivers, which are available for most common databases. SQL Server can move data to and from these sources using Data Transformation Services (DTS), replication, and linked server operations. SQL Server can act as a gateway to any number of data sources and either handle a copy of the data itself or pass the processing to the third-party source.

The capability of SQL Server to act with almost any third-party source means that existing applications can continue to function in the environment undisturbed while SQL Server applications can also make use of the same data.

CASE STUDY: JONES & SONS

ESSENCE OF THE CASE:

▶ Current data design is devoid of fast access.

▶ Jones & Sons handles more clients each day and the processing is getting difficult.

▶ They need a re-creation of the data model.

SCENARIO

Starting as a small local bead trading company, Jones & Sons now exports and imports beads nationwide with headquarters in Detroit. Jones knew that the company would expand sometime in the distant future and so didn't worry too much about the inventory storage design he would use. His slothfulness backfired on him. There are many client interactions each day, and the current system, a poor inventory storage design created at an extremely low cost by one of the junior developers in town, just can't handle the volume. Jones and his staff have decided to implement a new design based on the original groundwork already existing. They hire you to implement a new database design that will expedite access and reduce data redundancy.

ANALYSIS

You request a copy of the original database design to see the flaws placed in it by the previous developer. You spot numerous defects affecting the design, some of which defy the foundations of database normalization, dependencies, and redundancy. After a moment of thought, you assume that the design did not even go through the process of database normalization, for if it did, all the deficiency and lack of flexibility would have been eliminated.

You decide to normalize the database until you find its best fit: the third normal form (3NF). You resolve all dependencies and interdependencies and eliminate attribute redundancy. Not only do Jones and his users see a great improvement in the overall data retrieval and modification, but they also notice an immense improvement in the hard disk space the database consumes, which is due to the effectiveness of the removal of repeated data.

CHAPTER SUMMARY

KEY TERMS

- client/server
- Relational Database Management System (RDBMS)
- entities
- attributes
- relationships
- entity decomposition
- Primary Key
- one-to-one relationship
- one-to-many relationship
- many-to-many relationship
- Foreign Key
- normalization
- denormalization

This chapter covered a lot on data modeling and database design concepts. You should have a firm grasp that the hub of data modeling circles is attributes and relationships. Nonetheless, other concepts were also covered.

Entities become tables in the physical design. Attributes become the columns of the tables. Relationships are used in the same manner in the physical database as they are in the logical model.

Normalizing the ER model helps remove redundant data. This normalization, however, can cause many small entities that need complex operations to print reports. Normalization can also be a detriment to server performance. In these instances, planned denormalization can provide for easier application development and better performance.

To complete the logical modeling, you define the data integrity rules. As you move toward the finalization of the logical model and into the physical design, you need to make other decisions based on data types and application development.

The process is never really finalized. As the database goes through its life cycle, changes will be needed to improve performance and/or meet the changing needs of the business. The next chapter elaborates on the integrity and design specifics for SQL Server. The physical implementation of the database will be a major exam focus.

Exercises

2.1 Creating a One-to-Many Relationship

The purpose of this exercise is to show you how to create a basic one-to-many relationship between the Employee entity and the Course entity. Employees teach courses at Lloyd's Hospital. A single employee or teacher may teach many courses, such as blood composition and blood circulation, therefore creating a one-to-many relationship.

Estimated Time: 5 minutes.

1. Draw out the two entities, Employee and Course, as boxes, including the attributes defined in each as rows inside the box. Define a Primary Key element for each entity.

2. Creating a Foreign Key is required on the child table (Course) so that it can be related to the parent table (Employee). Create a Foreign Key named EmployeeID on the Course table that references the EmployeeID Primary Key in the Employee table.

3. Draw a line from the Employee entity to the Course entity, making a large dot at the end of the line pointing to Course. This indicates a one-to-many relationship, as shown in Figure 2.13.

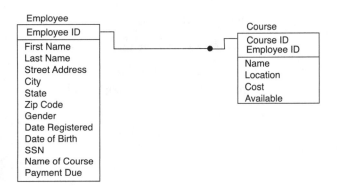

FIGURE 2.13

An example of a one-to-many relationship.

2.2 Creating a Many-to-Many Relationship

This exercise demonstrates how to create a many-to-many relationship between the Trainee entity and the Course entity. Trainees enroll in courses taught at Lloyd's. A single trainee can enroll in many courses, and at the same time many trainees can enroll to a single course, thus developing a many-to-many relationship.

Estimated Time: 5 minutes.

1. Draw out the entities participating in this exercise; that is, the Trainee and Course entity. Include in each entity the attributes defined as rows inside the box.

2. Recall that a many-to-many relationship can only be implemented with the help of an associative entity as an intermediate. Create a new entity between Trainee and Course and name it TraineeCourse.

3. The new associative entity needs to link both the Course and Trainee entities. To do this, the associative entity must contain two Foreign Keys: TraineeID and CourseID.

4. After you have placed these two attributes onto the associative entity, draw two lines from the associative entity to both other entities, placing a large dot at the ends of the lines pointing to the associative entity. The final model should look similar to the one in Figure 2.14.

2.3 Deciding on Primary Keys and Attribute Characteristics

This exercise demonstrates the use of characteristics and Primary Keys, as well how to identify them.

Estimated Time: 15 minutes

APPLY YOUR KNOWLEDGE

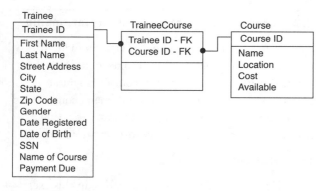

FIGURE 2.14
An example of a many-to-many relationship.

1. The entity to which you will be adding column constraints is the Employee entity. If you have not already copied out the Employee entity, do so now.

2. Now you will need to decide upon a Primary Key for this entity. You could use the employee's first name as a Primary Key, but doing so allows for duplicate values. Creating a Primary Key with the IDENTITY property enforces uniqueness on any attribute. Create a new attribute named EmployeeID that will be used as the Primary Key and mark it as IDENTITY.

3. You can decide which values are required and which values do not need to be entered; use NULL and NOT NULL to do this. Place NOT NULL for the FirstName, LastName, Hire_Date, SSN, Division, and Salary attributes. Place NULL beside the ContractType, Address, and Phone attributes.

4. To disallow changes on an attribute, use the NO CHANGES property. Because changes are not going to be made on the date an employee was hired, place this value beside the Hire_Date attribute.

5. The UNIQUE characteristic specifies that duplicate values not be permitted on any given column. In the Employee entity, the Phone, SSN, and Address attributes cannot have duplicate values; that is, no employee can have the same phone number as any other employee.

6. The final entity should look similar to the one in Figure 2.15. If you have not already copied out the entity, then copy it out.

	Employee	
	Employee ID	-IDENTITY
	First Name	-NOT NULL
	Last Name	-NOT NULL
	ContractType	-NULL
	Salary	-NOT NULL
	Division	-NOT NULL
UNIQUE	SSN	-NOT NULL
NO CHANGES	Hire_Date	-NOT NULL
UNIQUE	Phone	-NULL
UNIQUE	Address	-NULL

FIGURE 2.15
An example of choosing attribute characteristics.

Review Questions

1. How does data processing occur in the client/server model?

2. What are entities, attributes, and relationships?

3. Why would you want to decompose an attribute?

4. How are Foreign Keys related to Primary Keys?

5. Name four constraints that can be placed on columns. Why would you want to place constraints?

6. When would you consider denormalizing a database?

Exam Questions

1. You have prepared the logical design for a very large database system that will act as the back end for an Internet application, as well as being accessed from the corporate WAN. You need to support a large number of concurrent users who will be accessing the database at various bandwidth speeds. Which SQL Server technologies could assist in allowing the users access while providing good performance? Choose all that apply.

   A. Analysis services

   B. Replication

   C. Partitioned views

   D. English query

   E. Meta data services

2. You are designing a database that will be used for a small office. The client machines have minimal hard drive space and very little RAM. Other than the database server, there are no server-grade machines available. You have chosen a SQL Server in a client/server architecture as the best implementation for this system. Which application architecture is best suited for this system?

   A. Single-tier

   B. Two-tier thin client

   C. Two-tier thick client

   D. N-tier

   E. Internet

3. In a large office with hundreds of users, you have several servers that are centrally located in a secured room that only IT staff can access. One server is used as a security server and also acts as a DHCP server. A second dual processor server is running SQL Server and another machine runs an e-mail system with IIS operational. The office does not permit any other user access to the Internet nor does it expose any information to the Internet through a web site. You must select an application architecture suitable to this configuration. No other software is available on the servers. What application architecture would be best suited?

   A. Single-tier

   B. Two-tier thin client

   C. Two-tier thick client

   D. N-tier

   E. Internet

4. You are creating a database for a large government office. The Primary Key has already been established but you need to supply another column that has to have different values for each record. What data types could you use without creating additional constraints? Choose all that apply.

   A. `timestamp`

   B. `bigint`

   C. `uniqueidentifier`

   D. `nvarchar`

   E. `sql_variant`

APPLY YOUR KNOWLEDGE

5. You are creating a database for a large government office. The Primary Key has already been established, but you need to supply another column that has to have different values for each record. What implementation techniques are available other than data type selection? Choose all that apply.

   A. Identity

   B. Foreign Key

   C. Unique index

   D. Unique constraint

   E. Rule

6. You are putting together the logical design for a database. Tables to be included in the database are `Employees`, `Customers`, `Supplies`, `Products`, and `Sales`. The table used to store customer data has the following attributes: `CustomerID` (Primary Key), `CustomerName`, `StreetAddress`, `City`, `State`, `ZipCode`, `BalanceOwing`, `SalesmanID`, `SalesmanName`. Which of the following rules of normalization are not being maintained? Select all that apply.

   A. First normal form

   B. Second normal form

   C. Third normal form

   D. Decomposable normal form

   E. Boyce-Codd normal form

7. You are working for an automobile dealership that tracks inventory in a SQL Server database. The database contains information on the autos in stock. A partial listing of attributes is as follows: `VehicleIDNo(20 char)`, `InvoiceNo (bigint)`, `Make(20 char)`, `Model(15 char)`, `Year(smalldatetime)`, `Colorcode(int)`, `PurchasePrice(smallmoney)`, `StickerPrices (smallmoney)`. Which of the columns would you choose as a Primary Key?

   A. Use a compound key with `Make`, `Model`, and `Year`.

   B. Create a surrogate identity key.

   C. Use the `VehicleIDNo` as the key.

   D. Use the `InvoiceNo` as the key.

   E. Use a compound key with `InvoiceNo` and `VehicleIDNo`.

8. You are working in a database that has a `nchar(5)` attribute used to store solely numeric data. You want to minimize the amount of disk space used for storage and need to select an alternative data type. Which of the following data types would you select?

   A. `char(5)`

   B. `real`

   C. `smallint`

   D. `int`

   E. `bigint`

APPLY YOUR KNOWLEDGE

9. You are creating a historical database that stores information about important dates in history. You need to be able to store dates from the beginning of the 14th century. You want to minimize the storage space used by the data. Which data type would you use?

   A. `datetime`

   B. `smalldatetime`

   C. `bigint`

   D. `int`

   E. `char(8)`

10. You are preparing a database structure for a large construction company. At any one time the company is working on five or more job sites, and each site has between 25 and 200 homes. In charge of each site is a site supervisor who organizes the subcontractors at each phase of the building process (landscaping, framing, drywalling, electrical, plumbing, and so on). Any subcontractor who is planning on working on a given site must be found in a database of approved vendors. The company would like a structure that would allow for storage of the subcontractors' personal information and information about each site that includes the subcontractors assigned to the site. How would you set up this structure?

    A. A `Site` entity and a `Contractor` entity

    B. A `Site` entity, a `Contractor` entity, and a `Site/Contractor` entity

    C. A `Site` entity, a `Process` entity, and a `Contractor` entity

    D. A `Site` entity, a `Contractor` entity, and a `Site/Process` entity

11. A small manufacturing company has a considerable number of data sources because no standardization has occurred across any platform. One of the database servers has SQL Server installed; the others come from a variety of vendors. For a project you are working on, you need to gather data from the SQL Server and merge it together with data from two other sources. You then need to bring the data into Excel to do some charting. How would you accomplish this?

    A. Export the data from the other sources into a comma-delimited file for import to SQL Server. Then export from SQL Server the data that is to be imported into Excel.

    B. Export the data from all three sources so that it can be imported into Excel.

    C. Use SQL Server to transfer all the data from all sources directly into Excel.

    D. Use Excel to transfer data from all three sources into a spreadsheet.

12. A small scientific laboratory needs a powerful database server to perform analysis of complex measures performed on scientists' regular experiments. The lab requires exact accuracy with all calculations because the results determine the fracture points of various metals. Which data type offers the most accurate results?

    A. `smallmoney`

    B. `money`

    C. `float`

    D. `real`

    E. `decimal`

APPLY YOUR KNOWLEDGE

13. In a large department store, an inventory database is maintained for all products sold. Data is updated frequently by multiple computer terminals. Forty computer terminals throughout the offices and store can access the database simultaneously to perform updates. You want to minimize conflict situations and reduce the load on the server as much as possible. The client systems have very little processing power of their own. What architecture would you select for this system?

    A. Single-tier

    B. Two-tier thin client

    C. Two-tier thick client

    D. N-tier

    E. Internet

14. You are implementing a database for a military warehouse that needs to track the components that make up their equipment. Each piece of equipment has more than a hundred parts, each of which is made up of many smaller components. Any given aircraft has thousands of components from wheel assemblies to jet engines. A wheel assembly is made up of approximately 50 other components, each of which may come from a different supplier. Many of the separate parts are used in other components. What set of entities would be used in this structure?

    A. Suppliers, Equipment, Components, Parts

    B. Suppliers, Equipment, Components, Parts, Supplier/Parts

    C. Suppliers, Equipment, Components, Parts, Equipment/Parts

    D. Suppliers, Equipment, Components, Parts, Component/Parts

    E. Suppliers, Equipment, Components, Parts, Component/Equipment

Answers to Review Questions

1. The client/server model can be thought of as a connection between a client program or computer requesting a service or data from the server. When the client application needs certain data, it makes a call to the server. The server searches for only the specific data sought by the client and then fulfills the client's request by sending the requested data back to the client application.

2. An entity can be thought of as a table. Entities are usually represented as boxes. Attributes are the characteristics of the table.

    Attributes are usually represented as rows inside an entity. They can be thought of as the columns of a table.

    The Primary and Foreign Keys on those tables make up the relationships. They show the relationship of one table to another in a real-world situation.

3. Decomposing an attribute provides many benefits in contrast to using general-built attributes. Decomposing an attribute is done when data integrity is a key factor and also when data query performance needs to be improved. See "Optimizing Attributes."

4. A Foreign Key is a column or multiple columns whose values match the Primary Key of another table. Foreign Keys help in the relational process between two entities by connecting to a Primary Key. When a Primary Key is created on a parent

table, it is connected to another table by hooking onto the other table's Foreign Key. See the section "Foreign Keys."

5. The four constraints that can be placed on columns are `Default`, `Null`, `Duplicate`, and `Changes`. When the data model approaches perfection, certain measures must be taken to provide the most for your needs and to keep data integrity at its peak. These restrictions or constraints maintain the correctness of the data being entered.

6. Denormalization is undertaken when the database lacks performance. A database that has been normalized requires more join queries to gather information from multiple tables. Therefore, CPU usage might overwhelmingly increase and cause applications to freeze. In situations like this, denormalization is appropriate.

Answers To Exam Questions

1. **B, C.** Replication and partitioned views enable you to spread the load of a very large database system across several machines. The benefit of additional processing power and getting the data closer to the user could be recognized by both features, assuming they were properly partitioned and configured. For more information, see the section titled "The Client/Server Model."

2. **B.** With few resources on the clients, you have to make the clients as small as possible. N-tier or Internet could be potential solutions, but with the lack of sufficient processing power in the form of a server-grade machine, these would not suit this scenario. For more details, see the section "The Client/Server Model."

3. **E.** This is a good candidate for an Internet solution because you already have an IIS server available. Whether you have Internet access or not is irrelevant because everything can be performed in-house using an HTML or XML solution across the network. For more information, see the "Internet Applications" section.

4. **A, C.** By definition `timestamp` and `unique identifier` data types are guaranteed to be globally unique. The `timestamp` is an automatically entered value. The `uniqueidentifier` is usually entered using a `NEWID()` function to generate the `uniqueidentifier`. For more details, see the "Using Appropriate Data Types" section.

5. **A, C, D.** An Identity provides for uniqueness by incrementing a value continually, and therefore it is a standard choice for a column that requires a unique value. Unique indexes and unique constraints enforce the uniqueness of entered values and do not let any entry come into the system that already exists. For more information, see the section titled "Entity Integrity."

6. **A, C.** `Fullname` can be broken down into `firstname` and `lastname` and is therefore not in its most decomposed form. This breaks the first normal form rule of normalization. The salesman name should not be stored in this entity because it depends on the `salesmanID` and not the `customerID`. This breaks the third normal form rule of normalization. For more information, see "Understanding Database Normalization."

7. **B.** An automobile's VIN number, though unique, is character data and is much too large to use as a Primary Key. This is a perfect situation for an automatically incremented numeric surrogate key that will take up a lot less storage space. For more information, consult the section on "Primary Keys."

APPLY YOUR KNOWLEDGE

8. **D.** According to byte sizes, `int` would take a quarter of the space of the current `nchar(5)` setting. `Smallint` would even be better, but has an upper limit of 32,767. `Char(5)` would cut the space used in half but is not as good as using actual numeric storage. Whenever a variable is going to contain only numbers, numeric storage is always more efficient. For more details, see the "Using Appropriate Data Types" section.

9. **D.** This is a tricky question to resolve, and if it were not for the space restriction there would be a temptation to use characters for the storage. At 8 bytes a piece (double that of `int`) the easier technique would be to track days from the beginning of recorded time in an integer. (2001–1300)×365 1/4 requires 6 digits, and therefore `int` is the closest to the size required. `Datetime` allows dates in only the 1700s and `smalldatetime` in the 1900s. For more information, see the "Using Appropriate Data Types" section.

10. **B.** The many-to-many relationship in this scenario occurs because many contractors can work on a single site, and a single contractor can work at many sites. The connection needs to involve both sites and contractors for an appropriate relationship to be drawn. For further information, refer to the "Understanding Entity Relationships" section.

11. **C.** SQL Server is ideal for this situation. Depending on the actual details of the process, this can be performed directly using replication or data transformation services (DTS). Given the complexity of the scenario, it is likelier that DTS would be used because of its limitless flexibility. For more information, consult SQL Server Books OnLine.

12. **C.** `Float` gives accuracy up to 308 decimal places, which is almost ten times better than can be achieved with any of the other types. `Real` and `decimal` data types provide only 38 decimal places of accuracy at most, whereas `money` and `smallmoney` have accuracy to only the ten-thousandths. For more details, see the "Using Appropriate Data Types" section.

13. **D.** To minimize the amount of processing performed on a server, you would need to offload the processing onto the client by way of the two-tier thick client approach, or use a middle tier component such as an n-tier model. Because the client machines don't have much processing capability, the only remaining choice is to use the n-tier approach. For more information, see the "One- and Two-Tier Systems" section.

14. **D.** The many-to-many relationship in this process occurs because each part can be used in a number of different components. You can say that each component has many parts and each part can belong to a number of different components. For more details, see the section "Understanding Entity Relationships."

Suggested Readings and Resources

1. SQL Server Books Online

   - Relational Database Components

   - Relational Database Engine Architecture

   - Database Design Considerations

2. Graeme Simsion, *Data Modeling Essentials* (Van Nostrand Reinhold, 1994).

Create and alter databases. Considerations include file groups, file placement, growth strategy, and space requirements.

- **Specify space management parameters. Parameters include autoshrink, growth increment, initial size, and maxsize.**

- **Specify file group and file placement. Considerations include logical and physical file placement.**

- **Specify transaction log placement. Considerations include bulk load operations and performance.**

▶ The placement of the files related to a SQL Server 2000 database environment helps to ensure optimum performance while minimizing administration. Recoverability can also be improved in the event of data corruption or hardware failures if appropriate measures are taken. On the exam, you must be prepared to respond to these requirements and properly configure the interactions with the file system.

Create and alter database objects. Objects include constraints, indexes, stored procedures, tables, triggers, user-defined functions, and views.

- **Specify table characteristics. Characteristics include cascading actions, CHECK constraints, clustered, defaults, FILLFACTOR, foreign keys, nonclustered, primary key, and UNIQUE constraints.**

- **Specify schema binding and encryption for stored procedures, triggers, user-defined functions, and views.**

- **Specify recompile settings for stored procedures.**

- **Specify index characteristics. Characteristics include clustered, FILLFACTOR, nonclustered, and uniqueness.**

CHAPTER 3

Physical Database Design and Implementation

▶ An absolute necessity of building databases that interact with SQL Server 2000 is using the appropriate database objects to obtain a usable database system while improving response times and maintaining data integrity. There are considerations and trade-offs for choosing one technique over the other. The selection of the most appropriate method to obtain the desired result requires that you know where each is best implemented. The exam will test on the appropriate application of each of these objects.

Alter database objects to support replication and partitioned views.

• **Support merge, snapshot, and transactional replication models.**

• **Design a partitioning strategy.**

• **Design and create constraints and views.**

• **Resolve replication conflicts.**

▶ A variety of technologies exist in handling multiple server environments, knowing what each technology offers—as well its restrictions—helps you adapt a database system applied across multiple machines. Considerations for controlling data alterations, having the data available when needed, and responding to queries in a timely manner will be the aim of questions within this area of the exam.

Troubleshoot failed object creation.

▶ Troubleshooting is certainly a broad topic. In this chapter, the focus for troubleshooting is on the interactions with objects and the server as well as application settings that are required for an object to be created and used. On the exam, troubleshooting will be approached from a wide variety of angles. In the "real world," it is good practice to always view a procedure from a problem-solving perspective. Always be ready to ask yourself, "What could go wrong?" and "What can be done to resolve the problem?"

▶ Ensure that you have a thorough understanding of the variety of objects and technologies available within the realm of physical design. Know what each technique accomplishes (advantages) and also watch out for associated pitfalls (disadvantages).

▶ Understand the basics of the file system and its use by SQL Server. Know when to split off a portion of the database structure and storage to a separate physical disk drive.

▶ Know the interaction between SQL Server and the OS (operating system). Some of the physical design concepts that are discussed point out the role that the OS performs and the reason for its participation.

▶ Recognize the changes to the actual data structure and other areas of the database definition that might occur. Some technologies impact the database schema by applying their own objects.

▶ Watch out for "What's new in SQL Server 2000." Typically the exam tests on new features within the software, and this exam is certainly no different. The discussion of physical design topics reviews many important design and exam criteria, many of which are new features.

INTRODUCTION

Chapter 1, "Introduction to SQL Server 2000," looked at the modeling considerations and the logical structure of a database design. In moving from an idea to a logical structure to the actual physical elements, you must remember to consider elements that contribute to performance, reliability, and data integrity. Having a model of the system is one thing, but it must be able to meet the demands of an environment where inevitably the system must meet the intended goals of the company and add to the bottom line.

This chapter explores the aspects of the physical database design. It compares and contrasts the physical design and logical data modeling of Chapter 1 and then proceeds towards the implementation of a database system. Included are discussions of the file system, data structure, index structure, SQL Server objects, hardware, and finally, troubleshooting of the database design. Of particular interest to anyone preparing for the exam will be the discussion of schema binding and data partitioning. Because these two topics represent functionality that has been provided over and above the previous version, you can certainly expect questions on these areas when you take the exam.

In any physical design, the goal is to provide an efficient and responsive database system that also lends itself to appropriate maintenance tasks without becoming a database administrator's burden. At this stage of a database implementation, care is taken to provide a system structure that is usable, provides for optimum user response time, can be readily maintained, and above all meets the needs of the business for which it was designed.

As each of the physical design topics are discussed, pay close attention to the options that are available. Many different database technologies can be applied. Selecting the most appropriate technique to apply, based on what the problem warrants, is a very imperfect science. To become proficient in all these technologies, a developer must have a diverse background covering many data solutions. It would be beneficial, therefore, to try to experiment with as many different types of applications as possible. You will find that a manufacturing solution is considerably different from an online sales-oriented solution, which differs as well from a scientific application's solution, and so on.

The exam covers physical elements in numerous areas. The material contained in this chapter hits many of the exam topics. This chapter covers the exam objectives for the physical database design section of the Database Development SQL Server 2000 exam, including the hardware, the operating system, SQL Server, the database, all database objects, and the application. Many of these features are overviewed in this chapter but are further defined in other chapters throughout the book.

CREATING AND ALTERING DATABASES

▶ **Create and alter databases. Considerations include file groups, file placement, growth strategy, and space requirements.**

The file format in SQL Server 2000 has not significantly changed from the previous version (SQL Server 7). SQL Server uses a set of files to store the data, indexes, and log information for a database. A primary file also has some header information in it, providing SQL Server with necessary information about a database. Each database has a minimum of two files associated with it, one for the data and a second for the log. It is also possible to create multiple files for each of these purposes as described in the following paragraphs. File placement, and object placement within these files, plays an important role in the responsiveness of SQL Server. A database consists of two or more files with each file used for only a single database. A single file cannot be shared by multiple databases.

Each database has one or more files used to store indexes and data. The first file created for this purpose is referred to as the *primary* file. The primary file contains the information needed to start up a database and is also used to store some or all of the data. If desired, secondary files might be created to hold some of the data and other objects. Some databases might be large enough or complex enough in their design to have multiple secondary files used for storage.

Normally the *log* is maintained in a single file. The log file is used to store changes to the database before these changes are recorded in the data files themselves. The storage of information into log files in this manner enables SQL Server to use these files as an important part of its recovery process. Every time the SQL Server is started, it uses the log files for each of the databases to determine what units of work were still being handled at the time the server was stopped.

The file names given to all data and log files can be any desired name, although it is recommended that you select a name that gives some indication as to the content of the file. The file extensions for the primary data file, secondary data file(s), and log files can also be any chosen set of characters. It is recommended for consistency and standardization that the extensions be .mdf, .ndf, and .ldf for the primary, secondary, and log files, respectively.

Creating Database Files and Filegroups

All files needed for a database can be created through a single activity using SQL Server's Enterprise Manager, or with a single CREATE DATABASE Transact SQL statement. Either of these methods can be used to initialize all files and create the database and logs in a single step. The number of files you create and the placement of the files are addressed a little later in this chapter. (See the sections, "Using Filegroups" and "File Placement.")

The default names for the primary database and transaction log files are created using the database name you specified as the prefix—for example, *NewDatabase_Data*.mdf and *NewDatabase_Log*.ldf. These names and locations can be changed if desired from the default values provided for the new database file. The Transact SQL (T-SQL) syntax for creating a database is as follows:

```
CREATE DATABASE databasename
  [ON[<filespec>[,...n]]][,<filegroup>[,...n ]]][LOG
➥ON{<filespec>[,...n ]}]
[COLLATE collationname][FOR LOAD|FOR ATTACH]
 <filespec>::=
 [PRIMARY]
 ([NAME=logicalfilename,][FILENAME='physicalfilename']
 ➥[,SIZE=size][,MAXSIZE={size|UNLIMITED}]
  [,FILEGROWTH=growthincrement])
 [,...n]<filegroup>::=FILEGROUP filegroupname
 ➥<filespec>[,...n ]]
```

In the procedures that follow, you have the opportunity to create a database one step at a time. There are two techniques that can be used for these procedures. The first option uses the Create Database Wizard tool and Enterprise Manager in Step by Steps 3.1 and 3.2. The second option available provides for the syntax for the creation of a database using T-SQL code.

STEP BY STEP

3.1 Creating a Database Using the Create Database Wizard

1. Expand a server group, and then select the server in which to create a database.

2. On the Tools menu, click Wizards.

3. Expand Database.

4. Double-click Create Database Wizard.

5. Complete the steps in the wizard.

Or, if you prefer to use the Enterprise Manager:

STEP BY STEP

3.2 Creating a Database Using the Enterprise Manager

1. Expand a server group and then the server where the database is to be placed.

2. Right-click Databases, and then click New Database.

3. Enter a name for the database.

4. To specify how any specific file should grow, switch to the Data Files or Transaction Log tabs, highlight the file, select Automatically Grow File, then choose In Megabytes or By Percent and specify a value. To specify the file size limit, select Unrestricted Filegrowth or Restrict Filegrowth (MB) and specify a value.

To use T-SQL to create a database, use this code:

```
CREATE DATABASE MyDatabase
ON
(NAME = 'DataStore',
  FILENAME = 'd:\data directory\DataStore_MyDatabase.mdf',
  SIZE = 1MB, MAXSIZE = 5MB, FILEGROWTH = 1MB)
LOG ON
```

continues

continued

```
(NAME ='LogStore',
    FILENAME = 'e:\log directory\LogStore_MyDatabase.ldf ,
    SIZE = 1MB, MAXSIZE = 5MB, FILEGROWTH = 1MB)
```

You can use the CREATE DATABASE statement to create a database from script. Saving the script enables you to re-create a similar database on another server in the future. Any SQL Server object can have its creation script saved. The advantages of saving these scripts are discussed later in this chapter. Using the CREATE DATABASE statement to create a database using multiple files and log files would look similar to this:

```
CREATE DATABASE Example
ON
PRIMARY ( NAME = ExampleData,
FILENAME = 'c:\mssql\data\sampdat.mdf',
         SIZE = 10MB,
         MAXSIZE = 20MB,
         FILEGROWTH = 2MB),
       ( NAME = ExampleIndexes,
FILENAME = 'c:\mssql\data\sampind2.ndf',
SIZE = 10MB,
         MAXSIZE = 20MB,
         FILEGROWTH = 2MB),
       ( NAME = ExampleArchive,
FILENAME = 'c:\mssql\data\samparch.ndf',
SIZE = 10MB,
         MAXSIZE = 20MB,
         FILEGROWTH = 2MB)
LOG ON  ( NAME = ExampleLog1,
FILENAME = 'd:\mssql\log\samplog1.ldf',
SIZE = 10MB,
         MAXSIZE = 20MB,
         FILEGROWTH = 2MB),
       ( NAME = ExampleLog2,
FILENAME = 'd:\mssql\log\samplog2.ldf',
SIZE = 10MB,
         MAXSIZE = 20MB,
         FILEGROWTH = 2MB)
```

Important issues with regard to appropriate use of the CREATE DATABASE statement are as follows:

◆ The default growth increment measure is MB, but can also be specified with a KB or a % suffix. When % is specified, the growth increment size is the specified percentage of the size of the file at the time the increment occurs.

◆ A maximum of 32,767 databases can be defined on a server.

◆ The minimum size for a log file is 512K.

◆ Each database has an owner. The owner is the user who creates the database. The database owner can be changed through `sp_changedbowner`.

◆ The `Master` database should be backed up after a user database is created.

◆ The default unit of measure for the size and maxsize settings is MB if you supply a number, but no measure is provided. If no options are supplied, maxsize defaults to unlimited and the filegrowth is 10%.

At the time that you create the database and its associated files, you provide values to determine the initial file sizes, whether and how the files will grow, as well as some other basic database and file properties. The initial settings are used as a basis for future file system activities. If at a later date the initial settings are in need of alteration, you can perform this activity through the Enterprise Manager or by using the ALTER DATABASE T-SQL statement.

Using the Model Database

When you create a database for the first time, that database initially takes most of its attributes from the `Model` database. The `Model` database is a system database that SQL Server uses as a kind of template for database creations. It is a good and common practice to set the properties and contents of the `Model` database based on the majority of new databases that are to be created.

> **NOTE**
>
> **Selecting a Secure Partition** When interacting with a Windows 2000 or Windows NT Server operating system, ensure that all data is stored on an NTFS partition with appropriate security measures. NTFS provides for a flexible file system while maintaining a complete permission set for files and folders stored on disk. Using NTFS partitions helps prevent file tampering and allows for more flexible disk administration.

IN THE FIELD

OBJECT AND CODE REUSE

In practice, many objects are stored in the `Model` database to minimize the need to re-create these objects every time a database is created. Common elements placed in the `Model` often include specialized user-defined functions and data types that are present and frequently used by the development staff in their coding. In theory, objects are created for use in a single database, but all developers realize that object and code reuse is an important facet of easing the development process.

Often an object, such as a user-defined function, standard security role, or corporate information table, can be found in most if not all databases within a company. A property value, such as recovery level, might also have a standard implementation across all servers in the enterprise. If an object or property value is going to be present in most of the user databases, placing the object into the Model database or setting a property accordingly can save you the work of performing the activity as a post-creation task.

Using a Collation Sequence

A *collation sequence* is a set of rules governing over the characters that are used within a database and the means by which characters are sorted and compared. In SQL Server 2000 this sequence can be set on a database-by-database basis. In previous versions of SQL Server, the collation sequence was a server-wide setting. You therefore had to either perform a whole series of rebuilding actions to create a database that did not use the server collation, or install the database on a separate server altogether.

In SQL 2000 you can specify a non-default collation for any database on the server. This means that one database does not have to have the same characters or sorting rules as the rest of the databases on the server. If all but one or two of your databases have the same set of characters, then a single server can now implement the functionality that would have previously taken two separate machines.

To create a database with a non-default collating sequence, provide the COLLATE clause on the CREATE DATABASE command. You might also select the collation name from the drop-down box in the Enterprise Manager when you create the database from the GUI.

Be careful in the use of multiple collating sequences because it makes the transfer and entry of data more complex. It might also limit the application development environment and techniques normally used for data entry and editing.

Altering Database Properties

A number of the database properties affect the way in which some SQL Server commands operate. You can use the Enterprise Manager to make appropriate adjustments to some of the database properties. Alternatively you can use the ALTER DATABASE T-SQL statement to script these changes.

In altering a database, you can add or remove files and filegroups and/or modify attributes of the files and filegroups. ALTER DATABASE also enables you to set database properties, whereas in previous versions these properties could only be changed using the sp_dboption stored procedure.

Using Filegroups

In a lot of database scenarios, you will not implement more than one data file and one log file. In a number of instances, however, you might want to implement a *filegroup*. Filegroups enable a group of files to be handled as a single unit, and thus make implementations that require multiple files easier to accommodate. With filegroups, SQL Server provides an administrative mechanism of grouping files within a database. You might want to implement filegroups to spread data across more than one logical disk partition or physical disk drive. In some cases, this provides for increased performance as long as the hardware is sufficient to optimize reading and writing to multiple drives concurrently (see the section on "File Placement"). You might also have a performance gain through the appropriate placement of objects within these groups.

You can create a filegroup when a database is created, or you might add them in later when more files are needed or desired. After a filegroup has been assigned to a database, you cannot move its files to a different filegroup. Therefore, a file cannot be a member of more than one filegroup. SQL Server provides for a lot of flexibility in the implementation of filegroups. Tables, indexes, text, ntext, and image data can be associated with a specific filegroup, allocating all pages to one specific group. Filegroups can contain only data files; log files cannot be part of a filegroup.

Objects can easily be moved from one filegroup to another. Using the appropriate property page, you just select the new filegroup into which you wish to move the object.

Placement of Objects Within Filegroups

Placement of individual objects can aid in organizing data and at the same time provide for improved performance and recoverability. Many different objects can be assigned to separate files or filegroups.

WARNING

Be Sure of Your Collation Sequence After the collation sequence is set, it can be changed only through rebuilding of the database. If possible, collation decisions should be made during the logical design of the system so that you don't have to rebuild. Although collations can be different, if you want to change the sequence post creation, you will have to rebuild the database.

NOTE

Setting Options Using T-SQL The system-stored procedure sp_dboption can still be used to set database options, but Microsoft has stated that in future versions of SQL Server this functionality might not be supported.

For reasons given in the next few paragraphs, you might want to place the following objects into separate filegroups:

- ◆ Indexes
- ◆ A single table
- ◆ Text, ntext, or image columns

If you place indexes into their own filegroup, the index and data pages can be handled as separate physical read elements. If the associated filegroups are placed onto separate physical devices, then each can be read without interfering with the reading of the other. This is to say that while reading through an index in a sequential manner, the data can be accessed randomly without the need for manipulating the physical arm of a hard drive back and forth from the index and the data. This can improve performance and at the same time save on hardware wear and tear.

Placing an entire table onto its own filegroup offers many benefits. If you do so, you can back up a table without having to perform a much larger backup operation. Archived or seldom-used data can be separated from the data that is more readily needed. Of course the reverse is true: A table that needs to be more readily available within a database can be placed into its own filegroup to enable quicker access. In many instances, planned denormalization (the purposeful creation of redundant data) can be combined with this feature to obtain the best response.

Placing text, ntext, and image data in their own filegroup can improve application performance. Consider an application design that allows the data for these column types to be fetched only upon user request. Frequently, it is not necessary for a user to view pictures and extensive notes within a standard query. Not only does this accommodate better-performing hardware, but it can also provide faster query responses and less bandwidth saturation, because data that is not required is not sent across the network.

Considerations for Backup and Restore

Filegroups can provide for a more effective backup strategy for larger database environments. If a large database is placed across multiple filegroups, then the database can be backed up in smaller pieces.

This is an important aspect if the time to perform a full backup of the entire database is too lengthy.

To perform a backup in this manner, you would create a schedule to back up the individual filegroups (after an initial full database backup). In between each of the filegroup backups you then schedule log backups. Using this strategy enables you to break up an exceedingly large and long backup into more manageable increments.

After a determination has been made to use a filegroup strategy for storing data, always ensure that when a backup is performed against a filegroup that the indexes are also backed up at the same time. This is easily accomplished if the data and indexes are stored in the same filegroup. If they are located on separate filegroups, ensure that both the data and index filegroups are included in a single backup operation.

File Placement

After the decision has been made to go with filegroups, then comes the next major decision in the physical design: where to put the filegroups. Also, although logs are not stored into filegroups, they are stored in files and the placement of these files is very important.

Considerations in the placement within the file system depend on a number of variables. The first consideration is sequential versus random access. When a file is being read sequentially, the moving parts of the physical data device do less work (assuming no fragmentation). A large read/write process can use multiple physical devices at one time if they are placed on appropriate RAID hardware. Of course, there is also a software implementation of RAID that might not outperform the hardware one but is still beneficial.

Another consideration for file placement is system recoverability. When files are spread amongst multiple physical volumes, a fuller and faster recovery becomes possible in the event of hardware failure. Also, many other operations can benefit from appropriate file placement. The next four topics look at these considerations and discuss some of the instances where they each might be implemented.

> **WARNING**
>
> **SQL Server Does Not Enforce Backup**   Be aware that SQL Server does not enforce backup of data and index filegroups in a single operation. You must ensure that the files associated with the indexes tied to a particular data set are backed up with the data during a filegroup backup.

NOTE

> **Log Files**   Logs are not stored in filegroups. You can, however, use multiple log files and place them in different locations to obtain better and more varied maintenance and allow more storage space for log content.

Sequential/Random Access Considerations

Many processes performed within SQL Server can be classified as sequential or random. In a sequential process, the data or file can be read in a forward progression without having to locate the next data to be read. In a random process, the data is typically more spread out, and getting at the actual physical data requires multiple accesses.

Where possible, it is desirable to keep sequential processes running without physical interruption caused by other processes contending for the device. Using file placement strategies to keep random processes separate from sequential ones enables the configuration to minimize the competition over the placement of the read/write heads.

In an ideal configuration (somewhat tongue in cheek), you might want to separate the operating system from its page file. You would then place the log onto its one drive, separate from the data, with the data configured over a RAID volume as described in the following section. Take the seldom-used data (column or table data) and separate it from data that will be accessed more frequently. Place the indexes off on their own volume as well, and for about $150.00–$200,000.00, you have the optimum performance in a database server. In fact, while you're at it, why not throw in a couple of extra network cards and a few processors?

Obviously, in most production environments the database team must balance an ideal configuration with the company bottom line. For many of these volume placements, a definitive cost must be budgeted.

As a minimum requirement for almost any implementation, you should separate the normal sequential processing of the log files from the random processing of the data. You also improve recoverability by separating the data from the log and placing them on separate physical volumes. If the volume where the data is stored is damaged and must be restored from backup, you will still have access to the last log entries. The final log can be backed up and restored against the database, which gives something very close to 100% recoverability right to the point of failure.

An interesting and flexible strategy is to provide a separate drive solely for the log. This single volume does not have to participate in RAID architecture, but RAID might be desired for full recoverability. If you give the log the space of an entire volume, you give the log more room to grow and accumulate more of the log over time without the need for periodic emptying. Less frequent log backups are needed and the best possible log performance is achieved.

RAID Considerations

RAID (Redundant Array of Independent/Inexpensive Disks) is a technology where two or more disk drives can be configured in such a manner as to provide

◆ Larger volumes, because space on multiple disks is combined to form a single volume.

◆ Improved performance, by interacting with more than one physical disk at a time (disk striping).

◆ Safeguarding data, by providing mechanisms (mirror or parity) for redundant data storage.

RAID is classified under many categories, each category assigned as a number. For more information about RAID hardware or other interesting information, visit the web site of the RAID advisory board: http://www.raid-advisory.com/CIC.html. This book is concerned with only three RAID levels, 0 (zero), 1, and 5, although there are many different other qualifications for RAID.

RAID 0 (stripe set) provides for multiple simultaneous read/write access across two or more disks. There is no data redundancy and thus no fault tolerance. A striped implementation is valid when strong backups exist and recovery time is not relevant. It might also be considered if the data is considered somewhat trivial and loss of data is unimportant. Parity sets provide optimum performance with no waste space allocated to data redundancy. Microsoft recommends a 64K stripe size, which should be considered if you are using RAID 0.

RAID 1 (mirror) provides the exact duplication of one volume onto another. This solution offers quick recoverability but has a performance cost. Everything written to one volume is then written a second time to the alternate volume. A mirror implementation is valid for operating system drives or any other system where speed is not as important as recovery time in the event of a failure. In most implementations, if the first drive fails, the system has little or no downtime because it can operate fully on the mirror drive. Mirrors are a more costly form of fault tolerance than parity sets, losing a full 50% of available space to data redundancy.

An alternative form of mirroring, duplexing, involves not only the duplication of hard drives but also redundant drive controllers. In using duplexing, you achieve fault tolerance over the loss of the controller as well as hard drive failure. To achieve up-to-the minute recovery in any failure, you might want to place your log files on a mirror or duplexed volume.

RAID 5 (parity set) provides the best read performance while still giving the recoverability through data redundancy. In a parity set, the data is written across all the available drives in segments referred to as *stripes*. In each stripe, all but one drive will contain data, with the remaining drive containing the parity check information. Each time data is written, a checksum is calculated and written to the parity segment. If a failure causes the loss of a disk drive, the parity segment can be used to enable the stripe set to be regenerated. RAID 5 is usually referred to as a poor man's mirror because the more drives that are included in the set, the more cost-effective this solution. For example, if three drives are used, a third of the available space is lost to redundancy. If ten drives are used there is only a 10% loss of usable space.

IN THE FIELD

RAID: SOFTWARE VERSUS HARDWARE

Even though software implementations of RAID must be known to pass certification exams and will be found in production systems, they are not nearly regarded as reliable as hardware RAID. For any high-volume, mission-critical application, it is therefore preferred to set up data redundancy mechanisms at the hardware level.

Recoverability in the Event of Failure

Two primary concerns in most data environments are data recoverability in the event of the inevitable failures and considerations for minimal downtime. In the industry, one of the optimum ratings to strive for is the elusive "five nines" (99.999). This rating means that over any given period of time (generally accepted standard of 365 days minimum), the server remained online and servicing the end user 99.999 percent of the time. In other words, the total downtime for an entire year is a little over 5 minutes.

In an attempt to achieve as little downtime as possible, it is essential to consider a strategy that involves multiple servers and redundant other hardware, as well as other issues on each machine. Data redundancy, adequate backups, and some form of disaster recovery plan must all be a part of a complete solution. Most of the topics surrounding server clustering fall out of the scope of this book, although the partitioned views will be discussed at length within the section "Multiple Server Implementations," later in this chapter. Other multi-server functionality, such as data replication, is addressed in Chapter 11, "Implementing and Understanding Replication Methodologies."

Though most of the topics related to recoverability fall into the realm of administration, you need to give some consideration to these processes when you put together a physical design. The following three sections explain these considerations as they pertain to database design.

System and Data Recovery

Recovering from outages and minimizing data loss in the event of hardware failures involves prior planning, adequate backups, and the setting of appropriate database and server options. On the server, the recovery interval and service startup options can be adjusted to lessen the time it takes for a SQL Server to be online and operational after a power failure or other serious service interruption. In each database, the recovery model can be set to determine the log usage and amount of lost data activity upon failure. Backups are one of the most important aspects of recovery. Backups must be maintained in a diligent and thorough manner. Finally, a plan of action that is regularly practiced must be part of a workable solution.

Operating System Service Properties

In SQL Server 2000, two aspects of the server allow for a successful server database restart in the event of failure. The operating system's services can be configured to automatically start upon computer startup and can also be set up to respond to service interruptions. To set service properties, you must locate the MSSQLSERVER service. This service can be found in your administrative tools, Services for Windows 2000, or Control Panel Services for NT. For the configuration options as displayed using the Windows 2000 services properties, see Figures 3.1 and 3.2. The database recovery interval can be set for the number of minutes each database takes to start up after an outage or controlled server startup. You can find the Recovery

Interval option in the Enterprise Manager by right-clicking the server, selecting Properties from the pop-up menu, and navigating to the Database Settings tab.

FIGURE 3.1

General properties for operating system services.

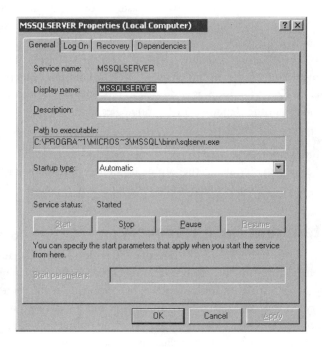

FIGURE 3.2

Recovery properties for operating system services.

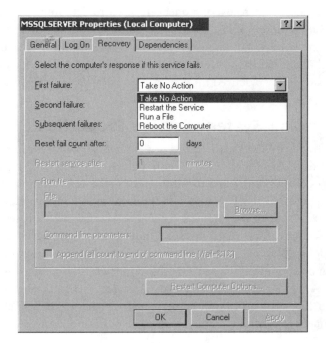

Use of Recovery Models

Some of the database properties that were available in previous releases of SQL Server have been combined to form what is referred to in SQL Server 2000 as *recovery models*. Setting the appropriate model can enable most if not all data activity to be recovered in the event of system failures. Three models are supported: Simple, Bulk-Logged, and Full.

The Simple recovery model ensures higher performance during bulk copy operations and maintains a smaller database log. However, the model does not support transaction log backups and, therefore, there will be data loss in the event of a failure because the database can be restored only to the point of the last full or differential database backup.

Bulk-Logged recovery also allows for high-performance bulk procedures that use minimal log space. Some data might be lost, but because you can perform log backups, usually the only loss will be bulk operations since the last backup.

If recoverability to a specific point in time with as little data loss as possible is the goal, then the Full recovery model should be set. The Full recovery model makes the heaviest use of the database logs.

Backup and Disaster Recovery

Usually backup and disaster recovery falls into the realm of the database and network administrators. In a total systems design strategy, a complete plan of recovery activity that includes a variety of scheduled backups and other tasks is documented and tested. This disaster recovery plan will be updated as needed, because test recovery and practicing the plan is sure to point out anything that might be otherwise missed. Though not a specific detail of implementation, the topic of recoverability would not be complete without at least the mention of a system-wide plan. Consider a regular exercise of simulating failures to test the plan.

Standby Servers and Log Shipping

A warm backup server or standby server is a lower-cost implementation that is often selected as an alternative to replication or clustering. The premise is to back up the production server on a regular basis, restoring it to a second machine that can be put into production in the event of failure in the first computer. A standby server can also assist in taking some of the workload from the production machine if it is used as a read-only query server.

In SQL Server 2000 you can use the Maintenance Plan Wizard to implement a standby server configuration. The wizard prompts you through the configuration of backups and regularly scheduled log shipments to the standby machine.

Space Requirements

Over time, the size of the database will need to be adjusted to accommodate new data or data removal. The configuration of the ideal server in any given situation will vary greatly. The applications that a server is intended to handle usually point toward the size of machine needed and its associated peripherals.

For a general guideline or minimum starting point, consider the following:

◆ **Multiple processors**. Preferred in most database environments (keep in mind that licensing models change).

◆ **RAM**. Can you ever have enough RAM? Start out with 1GB and don't be afraid to work your way up.

◆ **OS drive mirror**. Two physical disks set up in a physical or software mirror. In some cases, the use of two physical controllers provides for complete disk duplexing.

◆ **Data parity array**. A number of separate physical drives. A number of 4 to 6 usually provides an adequate size volume, but this might vary in larger systems.

◆ **Log volume**. One disk used for log storage. In some cases, this volume also stores data files for implementations that include archived data storage. You might also want to mirror this volume to ensure up-to-the-minute data recovery.

File Growth Strategies

SQL Server 2000 enables you to set database files so that they expand and shrink automatically as needed, eliminating the need for additional administration. By default, SQL Server enables data files to increase in size as needed for data storage. Therefore, a file can

NOTE

Licensing Models   With the release of SQL Server 2000, the licensing models available included Per Seat or Per Processor. The Per Server model has been discontinued.

grow to the point where all disk space is exhausted. You can specify that a file is not to grow beyond its creation size or implement a maximum size for file growth. Ensure that disk space is not exhausted by using the MAXSIZE option of the CREATE DATABASE or ALTER DATABASE statements to indicate the largest size to which a file can grow.

In a volatile environment, the database and its related files might frequently increase and decrease in size and this activity might be the desired operation of the server. In most instances, an implementation providing for more stability in the file system is the desired end result. A determination has to be made as to whether the database stays at about the same size or grows or shrinks over time. In most scenarios, a database grows over time and needs to be reduced only when data is archived.

When creating the files, you should set the SIZE, MAXSIZE, and FILEGROWTH parameters so that the database can increase in volume over time. The FILEGROWTH configuration should be implemented in larger increments so that growth within the file system isn't occupying too much of the server's resources. Growth of files occurs in the background and can be minimized by using a larger growth increment. Always provide a MAXSIZE entry even if the entry itself is close to the capacity of the volume.

Shrinking Files

File "shrinking" might be required as an application ages. In most operations, the older the data is, the less valuable its presence is among the mainstream data. As data ages, it is less likely to be queried and thus is passed over by most reads. It might become "wasted space" in the database and unnecessarily consume system resources. A system design usually includes means by which data is aged out into archive tables. After the archival process has completed, there might be a high percentage of empty space in the data files.

You can shrink each file within a database to remove unused pages. This applies to both data and log files. It is possible to shrink a database file manually or as a group. You use the DBCC statement with the SHRINKDATABASE or SHRINKFILE parameters (DBCC parameters are shown in the Fast Facts section in Part II "Final Review"). Use DBCC SHRINKDATABASE to shrink the size of the data files in the specified database, or you can selectively choose a specific file and shrink its size using DBCC SHRINKFILE.

You can set the database to automatically shrink at periodic intervals by right-clicking the database and selecting the database Properties page from within the Enterprise Manager.

Ongoing System Maintenance

After a database and associated files have been created and the implementation is complete, it's necessary to maintain the system using the periodic application of several commands. It might be necessary to adjust the database and file properties as the database system matures. In addition, DBCC (Database Consistency Checker) has a number of parameters to assist in regular maintenance activities.

As a starting point, use the SQL Server Maintenance Wizard to perform the necessary maintenance tasks. Adjust the scheduling of these tasks as needed to maintain a healthy server. Watch and adjust indexing and data structures because over time they will become fragmented. Indexing and data structures as well as other database objects are discussed more fully after the Review Break.

REVIEW BREAK

Physical Storage

Creating and altering databases involves selecting the physical volume type for each database file, setting the appropriate file properties, placing the objects into the files/filegroups, and ensuring appropriate adjustments are made as the database matures. The type of business needs that the database is being designed to meet helps to indicate the measures needed to ensure adequate performance.

Try to place onto separate volumes any files that might tend to compete with each other for read cycles during a single operation. Place log files away from the data to ensure adequate recovery and make sure that database properties have been set in such a way as to ensure that maintenance tasks can be performed.

CREATING AND ALTERING DATABASE OBJECTS

▶ **Create and alter database objects. Objects include constraints, indexes, stored procedures, tables, triggers, user-defined functions, and views.**

The next thing to consider is the creation of objects within the database. Database objects include constraints, indexes, stored procedures, tables, triggers, user-defined functions, views, and more. Each object is discussed in detail, paying particular attention to the impact on the system as a whole. In many implementations, there are several different approaches to meeting a particular need. Selecting the appropriate technique for a task requires trade-offs between functionality, performance, and resource utilization.

Each database contains a number of tables other than those used to store data. These tables store information that enables SQL Server to keep track of objects and procedures within the database. The sysobjects and syscomments system tables maintain entries containing the object definitions and other tracking information for each object. A number of other tables also exist to maintain information about specific objects. For more information regarding system tables, refer to SQL Server Books Online. These tables are used whenever SQL Server needs object information. You should never alter system tables directly but instead allow SQL Server to manipulate the entries as needed.

To help you secure the server, you might choose not to display system objects to the user from the Enterprise Manager interface. Also, hiding these objects from the user presents a cleaner interface to objects with which the user normally interacts. Step by Step 3.3 describes how to hide system objects:

STEP BY STEP

3.3 Setting Registration Options

1. Select the server from the Enterprise Manager interface.

2. Right-click to access the server menu.

3. Select the option to Edit SQL Server Registration Properties.

4. Clear the Show System Databases and System Objects check box.

Table Characteristics

The makeup of a table in SQL Server is more than just simply data definition. A complete table definition includes column descriptions, storage location, constraints, relationships with other tables, indexes, and keys, as well as table-level permissions and text indexing columns.

When defining tables, it is a good idea to have some form of data dictionary prepared to help you make appropriate choices for individual properties. A data dictionary defines data usage and is an extension of the logical data modeling discussed in Chapter 1. In SQL Server, the term "database diagram" is usually used rather than "dictionary," although a database diagram is not a complete data dictionary in the sense of documentation.

A *data dictionary* is a form of documentation generally considered a complete reference for the data it describes. The dictionary is usually a lot more than just a collection of data element definitions. A complete dictionary should include schema with reference keys and an entity-relationship model of the data elements or objects. A pseudo data dictionary can be represented using the database diagram tool provided with SQL Server. A partial dictionary for the Northwind database is illustrated in Figure 3.3.

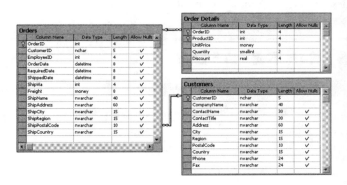

FIGURE 3.3

Database diagram showing column properties and table relationships.

Column Definition

After the file structure and content of each file has been determined, the tables themselves can be created and assigned to the files. If the purpose of the table is to hold data that is frequently accessed, then the file placement of the table should take that into consideration. Tables that hold archive data and other less frequently accessed data require less maintenance and don't have to be as responsive to user queries.

The initial definition of each column within a table consists of a name for the column, the type and length of data for the column, and an indicator as to whether the column must have data or allow NULL content. A number of additional column descriptors can be included to define characteristics of how the column obtains its value and how the column is treated within the table. A complete list of potential column descriptors is as follows:

◆ **Column Name.** Should be meaningful so as to describe the column content.

◆ **Data Type.** Any one of 25 possible definitions provides the basis for the data a column will contain. Choices include several possibilities for each data type. (Data types are discussed more fully later in this book.)

◆ **Length.** For many of the data types, the length is predetermined. You must, however, specify a length for character, Unicode (nCHAR), and binary data. A length must also be specified for variable-length data columns. If a char or nCHAR data type is only a single character, then no length has to be defined.

◆ **Allow Nulls.** You can provide an indicator for allowing NULL content for any variable except those assigned as primary keys.

◆ **Primary Key.** Enforces unique content for a column and can be used to relate other tables. Must contain a unique non-NULL value.

◆ **Description.** Provides an explanation of the column for documentation purposes. (This is an extended table property.)

◆ **Default Value.** Provides a value for a column when one is not explicitly given during data entry. A default object must be created and then bound to a column, but the preferred technique is to provide the default definition, directly attached to the column in the CREATE/ALTER table definition. It is defined at the database level and can be utilized by any number of columns in a database.

NOTE

Object Placement   Keep in mind when assigning objects to files that some objects can be placed away from the mainstream data through the use of filegroups. You can select the object placement from Table Design Properties in the Enterprise Manager or through the use of an ON clause in a CREATE/ALTER statement. SQL Server enables you to place the following table objects:

· Tables

· Indexes

· Text, nText, or Image data

◆ **Precision.** The number of digits in a numeric column.

◆ **Scale.** The number of digits to the right of a decimal point in a numeric column.

◆ **Identity.** Inserts a value automatically into a column, based on seed and increment definitions.

◆ **Identity Seed.** Provides the starting value for an Identity column.

◆ **Identity Increment.** Defines how an Identity will increase or decrease with each new row added to a table.

◆ **Is RowGuid.** Identifies a column that has been defined with the Unique Identifier data type as being the column to be used in conjunction with the ROWGUIDCOL function in a SELECT list.

◆ **Formula.** Provides a means of obtaining the column content through the use of a function or calculation.

◆ **Collation.** Can provide for a different character set or sort order than other data. (Use with extreme caution if at all because it impairs front-end development, capability and hampers data input and alteration processes.)

Many characteristics of column definitions affect other columns, tables, and databases. For a more complete definition of any of these properties, consult SQL Server Books Online.

Using *CHECK* Constraints

A CHECK constraint is one of several mechanisms that can be used to prevent incorrect data from entering the system. Restrictions on data entry can be applied at the table or column level through the use of a CHECK constraint. You might also apply more than a single check to any one column, in which case, the checks are evaluated in the order in which they were created.

A CHECK constraint represents any Boolean expression that is applied to the data to determine whether the data meets the criteria of the check. The advantage of using a check is that it is applied to the data before it enters the system. However, CHECK constraints do have less functionality than mechanisms, such as stored procedures or triggers. You can find a comparison of features for a number of these mechanisms with provisions for where each one is applied at the close of this section, just before the "Review Break."

One use for a CHECK constraint is to ensure that a value entered meets given criteria based on another value entered. A table-level CHECK constraint is defined at the bottom of the ALTER/CREATE TABLE statement, unlike a COLUMN CHECK constraint, which is defined as part of the column definition. For example, when a due date entered must be at least 30 days beyond an invoice date, a table-level constraint would be defined as:

```
(DueDate - InvoiceDate) >= 30
```

A column-level check might be used to ensure that data is within acceptable ranges, such as in the following:

```
InvoiceAmount >= 1 AND InvoiceAmount <= 25000
```

A check can also define the pattern or format in which data values are entered. You might, for example, want an invoice number to have an alphabetic character in the first position, followed by five numeric values, in which case, the check might look similar to the following:

```
InvoiceNumber LIKE '[A-Z][0-9][0-9][0-9][0-9][0-9]'
```

Finally, you might want to apply a check where an entry must be from a range of number choices within a list. An inventory item that must be one of a series of category choices might look similar to this:

```
ProductCategory IN ('HARDWARE', 'SOFTWARE', 'SERVICE')
```

A COLUMN CHECK (or other constraint) is stated as a portion of the column definition itself and applies only to the column where it is defined. A TABLE CHECK (or other constraint), on the other hand, is defined independently of any column, can be applied to more than one column, and must be used if more than one column is included in the constraint.

A table definition that is to define restrictions to a single column (minimum quantity ordered is 50), as well as a table constraint (date on which part is required must be later than when ordered), would be as follows:

```
CREATE TABLE ProductOrderLine
     (ProductLineKey  BigInt,
      OrderMatchKey   BigInt,
```

continues

continued

```
        ProductOrdered   Char(6),
        QtyOrdered       BigInt
          CONSTRAINT Over50 CHECK (QtyOrdered > 50),
        OrderDate        DateTime,
        RequiredDate     DateTime,
          CONSTRAINT CK_Date CHECK (RequiredDate >
          ➥OrderDate))
```

Usually a single table definition would provide clauses for key definition, indexing, and other elements that have been left out of the previous definition to focus in more closely on the use of CHECK constraints.

Index Organization

Putting the data into sequence to accommodate quick retrieval, and at the same time provide meaningful and usable output to an application, usually requires that a variety of indexes be defined. A *clustered index* provides the physical order of the data storage, whereas a *nonclustered index* provides an ordered list with pointers to the physical location of the data.

Indexing is most easily defined and understood if you compare the data and index storage of a database to that of a book. In a book, the data itself is placed onto the pages in a sequence that is meaningful if you read the book sequentially from cover to cover. An index at the back of the book enables you to read the data randomly. You can locate a topic by looking through a list of topics that is accompanied by a physical page reference to the place where the topic can be found. To read a single topic you need not skim through the entire book.

In a similar manner, data in a database can be handled randomly or in sequence. The location of a single record can be found in the database by looking it up in the index, rather than reading through all the rest of the data. Conversely, if a report is to be generated from all the data in a database, the data itself can be read sequentially in its entirety.

Index storage in SQL Server has a B-tree structured storage. The indexes are maintained in 8KB pages qualified as *root, intermediate,* and *leaf-level* pages. In a clustered index, the leaf level is the data itself, and all other levels represent index pages. In a nonclustered index, all pages contain indexes (see Figure 3.4).

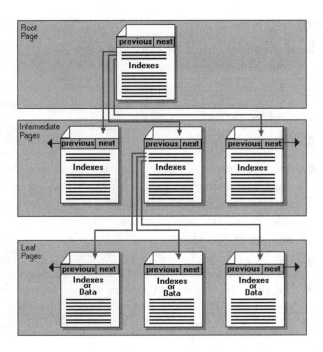

FIGURE 3.4
Illustration of the B-tree structure used for index storage.

If a clustered index has not been defined for a given table, then the data is stored in a "heap." A data heap does not maintain data in any particular order; it simply stores the data in the order in which it is entered. In some applications, where data is never retrieved in any particular order on a regular basis, this might actually be advantageous.

Indexes can be created using the T-SQL CREATE INDEX command. When you use the Enterprise Manager to create an index, you must access the table design and then reveal the table properties.

Step by Step 3.4 shows you how to use the Enterprise Manager to create an index.

STEP BY STEP

3.4 Selection of Index Creation from the Enterprise Manager

1. From the Enterprise Manager, select the table with which the index will be associated.

continues

continued

2. Right-click on the table name and select "Design Table" from the pop-up menu.

3. Select Table and Index Properties.

4. Click on the Indexes/Keys tab.

5. Click on the New button.

6. From the drop-down list boxes, select the column on which to base the index and whether the index is to be ascending or descending. If you are creating a compound index based on a number of columns, then add additional columns as needed.

7. Select a filegroup for the storage of the index.

8. If desired, you can make the index unique, supply fill factor and pad index values, make the index clustered (default is nonclustered), and choose to not recalculate statistics for the index.

9. Close the dialog box to save the index and exit table design properties and select OK to save the changes.

Create an index using the T-SQL CREATE INDEX. The following example creates a compound, nonclustered index that is 75% full:

```
CREATE INDEX IXProductItem
ON ProductOrderLine (OrderMateKey, ProductLineKey)
WITH FILLFACTOR = 75
```

Clustered Indexing

The selection of the appropriate column(s) on which to base a clustered index is important for a number of reasons. As previously mentioned, a clustered index represents the order in which the data is physically stored on the disk. For this reason, you can define only a single clustered index for any table. If you choose not to use a clustered index in a table, the data on disk will be stored in a heap. A clustered index, if present, has clustering keys that are used by all nonclustered indexes to determine the physical location of the data.

The basis for the index usually is determined by the order in which the majority of applications and queries want their output. The clustered index values are also present in other indexes and the size of the defined index should be kept as small as possible. When you select a clustering key, try to utilize a numeric data type because character types cause index storage to occupy much more space.

Always define a clustered index first before you define any of the nonclustered indexes. If you do these tasks in reverse order, then all nonclustered indexes rebuild themselves upon creation of the clustered index.

Nonclustered Indexing

Nonclustered indexes provide a means of retrieving the data from the database in an order other than that in which the data is physically stored. The only alternative to the use of these indexes would be provisions for a sort operation that would place undue overhead on the client system and might not produce the desired response times. A data sort implementation is usually performed only for one-time operations or for applications that will have very limited usage.

Although the creation of indexes saves time and resources in a lot of cases, avoid the creation of indexes that will rarely be utilized. Each time a record is added to a table, all indexes in the table must be updated, and this might also cause undue system overhead. For that reason, careful planning of index usage is necessary.

Unique Indexing

At times when indexes are created, it is important to guarantee that each value is distinctive. This is particularly important for a primary key. SQL Server automatically applies a unique index to a primary key to ensure that each key value uniquely defines a row in the table. You might want to create additional unique indexes for columns that are not going to be defined as the primary key.

Leaving Space for Inserts

Fill factor is the percent at which SQL Server fills leaf-level pages upon creation of indexes. Provision for empty pages enables the server to insert additional rows without performing a page-split operation. A page split occurs when a new row is inserted into a table that has no empty space for its placement. As the storage pages fill, page splits occur, which can hamper performance and increase fragmentation.

IN THE FIELD

MORE ON THE FILL FACTOR

You will normally find that queries (the reading of existing data) out-weigh data updates by a substantial margin. Providing the extra room slows down the query process. Therefore, you might not want to adjust the fill factor value at all.

Equally, setting the fill factor too low hampers read performance because the server must negotiate a series of empty pages to actually fetch the desired data. It is beneficial to specify a fill factor when you create an index on a table that already has data and will have a high volume of inserts. If you do not specify this setting when creating an index, the server default fill factor setting is chosen. The fill factor for the server is a configuration option set through the Enterprise Manager or the `sp_configure` stored procedure.

The percentage value for the fill factor is not maintained over time; it applies only at the time of creation. Therefore, if inserts into a table occur frequently, it's important to take maintenance measures for rebuilding the indexes to ensure that the empty space is put back in place. A specific index can be rebuilt using the `CREATE INDEX` T-SQL command with the `DROP EXISTING` option. Indexes can also be de-fragmented using the `DBCC INDEXDEFRAG` command, which also reapplies the fill factor.

The Pad Index setting is closely related to the setting for fill factor to allow space to be left in non-leaf levels. Pad Index cannot be specified by itself and can be used only if you supply a fill factor. You do not provide a value to this setting; it matches the setting given for the fill factor.

Maintaining Referential Integrity

When multiple tables maintained in a database are related to each other, some measures should be taken to ensure that the reliability of these relationships stays intact. To enforce referential integrity, you create a relationship between two tables. This can be done through the database diagram feature of the Enterprise Manager or through the CREATE and ALTER TABLE T-SQL statements. Normally, you relate the referencing or Foreign Key of one table to the Primary Key or other unique value of a second table.

Step by Step 3.5 shows you how to use a database diagram to define a relationship:

STEP BY STEP

3.5 Using the Wizard to Create a Relationship

1. From the Enterprise Manager, expand the tree view of the database you want to use and select Diagrams.

2. Right-click Diagrams and select New Database Diagram from the pop-up menu.

3. A wizard asks you for the tables to use in the diagram. Select the tables to be related and follow the wizard to completion.

4. Select the column to be related from the subsidiary table, and drag the column to the primary table.

5. Complete the desired options from the dialog, and press OK to establish the relationship (see Figure 3.5).

6. Exit the diagram, and select Yes to save the changes to the respective tables.

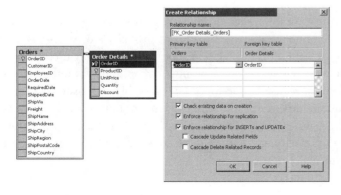

FIGURE 3.5
The Create Relationship dialog box as seen from the database diagram window.

Step by Step 3.6 shows you how to define a relationship from the Table Design Properties box:

STEP BY STEP

3.6 Using the Table Designer to Create a Relationship

1. From the Enterprise Manager, select the table that contains the Foreign Key element of the relationship.

2. Right-click on the table name that will represent the subsidiary table to be referenced, and select Design Table from the pop-up menu.

3. Select Table and Index Properties.

4. Click on the Relationships tab and click New.

5. Select the desired options from the dialog, and click Close to establish the relationship (see Figure 3.6).

6. Exit and save changes to the table.

You can define a relationship when creating or altering a table definition. The following example defines a relationship using T-SQL:

```
CREATE TABLE OrderDetails
    ( DetailsID          smallint,
      OrderID            smallint
        FOREIGN KEY (OrderID) REFERENCES Orders(OrderID),
      QtyOrdered bigint,
      WarehouseLocation  smallint
    )
```

The most common relationships are one-to-many, in which the unique value in one table has many subsidiary records in the second table. Another form of relationship, which is usually used to split a table with an extraordinary number of columns, is a one-to-one relationship. The use of one-to-one splits a table and associates a single unique value in one table with the same unique value in a second table. A many-to-many relationship can also be defined, but this form of referencing requires three tables and is really two separate one-to-many relationships.

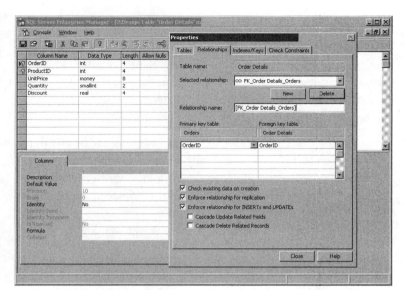

FIGURE 3.6
Create Relationship options dialog as seen from the table diagram window.

Utilizing referential integrity guidelines helps maintain the accuracy of data entered into the system. A database system uses referential integrity rules to prohibit subsidiary elements from being entered into the system unless a matching unique element is in the referenced table. The system also protects the data from changes and deletions, assuming that cascading actions (defined later in this chapter) have been carefully and properly implemented.

Primary and Foreign Keys

The definition of a Primary Key for each table, though not a requirement of the SQL Server database environment, is recommended. A Primary Key helps records maintain their identities as unique rows of a table and also provides a means of relating tables to other tables in the database to maintain normal forms. (For further information on normalization and normal forms, see Chapter 2, "Data Modeling.") A Foreign Key is defined in a subsidiary table as a pointer to the Primary Key or other unique value in the primary table.

Both Primary and Foreign Keys are defined in the form of a constraint. The pair of keys work together to accommodate table relationships. A Foreign Key refers back to the Primary Key in the parent table, forming a one-to-one or one-to-many relationship. (To see more about relationships, refer to Chapter 2.)

Primary Key Constraint

A Primary Key constraint enforces entity integrity in that it does not permit any two rows in a table to have the same key value. This enables each row to be uniquely defined in its own right. Although a Primary Key should be created when a table is initially created, it can be added or changed at any time after creation.

A Primary Key cannot have NULL content nor can there be any duplicate values. SQL Server automatically creates a unique index to enforce the exclusiveness of each value. If a Primary Key is referenced by a Foreign Key in another table, the Primary Key cannot be removed unless the Foreign Key relationship is removed first. A Primary Key is easily assigned in the table design window by either of the following actions:

◆ Right-click on the desired column name and select the Set Primary Key option. To select a compound key based on more than one column, hold down the Ctrl key while selecting multiple columns before right-clicking.

◆ Select the desired field and click the Set Primary Key button on the toolbar. To select a compound key based on more than one column, hold down the Ctrl key while selecting the appropriate columns.

Foreign Key Constraint

A Foreign Key constraint is defined so that a primary and subsidiary table can be linked together by a common value. A Foreign Key can be linked to any unique column in the main table; it does not necessarily have to be linked to the Primary Key. It can be linked to any column that is associated with a unique index.

With a Foreign Key defined, you cannot add a value to the Foreign Key column if a matching value is not present in the primary table. For instructions on setting a Foreign Key constraint, see the section on referential integrity, earlier in this chapter.

Note in the example shown in Figure 3.7 that there are matching Order IDs in the child Order Details table for only those Order IDs included in the parent Orders table. An Order ID must match from a child to a parent. If a child entry with an ID were not found in the parent table, then that is known as an *orphan child* and would be a breach of referential integrity rules.

WARNING

Documentation Discrepancy   The capability to set a relationship to any unique column is not noted in most SQL Server documentation. SQL Server Books Online reports that a Foreign Key must be set to a Primary Key or a UNIQUE constraint. In SQL Server, you can create a relationship against a Primary Key, unique index, or a UNIQUE constraint. You need not have a Primary Key or constraint. You can even set a unique index to ignore duplicates and the operation will still be permitted.

EXAM TIP

Go with the Documentation   If you run into this on the exam, the correct answer is likely to be one chosen based on the documentation and not on actual functionality. The capability to set a relationship to any unique column is not noted in documentation. The correct technique to use when answering an exam question would be one that involves a Foreign Key set to a Primary Key or Unique constraint.

Orders Table

Primary Key Order ID	Customer ID	Order Date
10249	TOMSP	5-Jul-1996
10250	HANAR	11-Nov-2000
10251	VICTE	8-Jul-1996
10252	SUPRD	9-Jul-1996
10253	HANAR	28-Nov-2000

Order Details Table

Foreign Key Order ID	Product ID	Unit Price	Quantity
10249	14	18.6	9
10249	51	42.4	40
10250	41	7.7	10
10250	51	42.4	35
10250	65	16.8	15
10251	22	16.8	6
10251	57	15.6	15
10251	65	16.8	20
10252	20	64.8	40
10252	33	2	25
10252	60	27.2	40
10253	31	10	20
10253	39	14.4	42
10253	49	18	40

FIGURE 3.7
Primary Key/Foreign Key referential integrity.

Using Cascade Action to Maintain Integrity

New to SQL Server with the 2000 release is a cascading action feature that many other database environments have been enjoying for quite some time. Cascading actions affect update and delete activity where an existing Foreign Key value is changed or removed. Cascade action is controlled through the CREATE and ALTER TABLE statements, with clauses for ON DELETE and ON UPDATE. You can also select these features using the Enterprise Manager.

In a cascading update, when you change the value of a key in a situation where a Foreign Key in another table references the key value, those changed values are reflected back to the other tables. A similar thing happens with a delete operation: if a record is deleted, then all subsidiary records in other tables are also deleted. For example, if an invoice record is deleted from an invoice table that has invoice details stored in another table and referenced by a Foreign Key, then the details would also be removed.

A series of cascading actions could easily result from the update or deletion of important keys. For example, the deletion of a customer could cause the deletion of all that customer's orders, which could cause the deletion of all its invoices, which in turn could cause the deletion of all the customer's invoice details. For this reason, careful system design is important and the potential archival of data through the use of triggers should be considered.

In the case of multiple cascading actions, all the triggers to be fired by the effects of the original deletion fire first. AFTER triggers then fire on the original table and then the AFTER triggers in the table chain subsequently fire.

> **EXAM TIP**
>
> **Cascading Actions Is a New Feature** You can expect that something about it will be asked on the exam. Also be prepared for the exam by knowing all the results and implications of cascading actions. For example, you might be asked what occurs when a record contained in the parent table is deleted, or has its key value changed.

Stored Procedures

A *stored procedure* is a set of T-SQL statements that can be saved as a database object for future and repeated executions. With stored procedures, you can enable a lot of the development and processing to be performed on the server, producing much more efficient and lightweight front-end applications. Any commands that can be entered via SQL Query tools can be included in a stored procedure.

Using stored procedures is a powerful and flexible technique for performing tasks within an application. A stored procedure, when it is first used, is compiled into an execution plan that remains in the procedure cache. This provides for some of the performance over ad-hoc operations. The performance improvements in SQL 7 and 2000 are not as drastic as in previous versions because changes in the way that other operations now execute provides them with some of the same benefits as stored procedures. A stored procedure can accept parameters, process operations against any number of databases, and return results to the calling process. Performance will be discussed in more detail in Chapter 12, "Monitoring SQL Server 2000."

The SQL Server 2000 implementation has many other capabilities that speed processing, secure data, reduce bandwidth usage, and enable advanced operations to be performed. Procedures that are repeatedly used will be held in memory in the SQL Server procedure cache for faster execution. A stored procedure, like other operations, can be encrypted to protect the details of the operation (the following section covers encryption). An application might need to send several operations across a network and respond conditionally to the results. This can be handled with a single call if the logic is contained in a single stored procedure. The use of local and global cursors can expose information to the application or other applications as needed, giving provisions for complex development processes with conversations between separate processes.

Temporary stored procedures used frequently in earlier versions are still supported by SQL Server, although improvements in other areas should eliminate or reduce the need for their use. The most significant improvement is the capability to compile and maintain most SQL operations in cache for prolonged periods.

Many system-stored procedures have already been created and are available upon installation of SQL Server. Extended stored procedures, which enable DLL files to be accessed from the operating system, are pre-established and present in the `Master` database.

The T-SQL `CREATE PROCEDURE` statement is used to create a stored procedure. This statement can be executed from the Query Analyzer or it is available through the Enterprise Manager by right-clicking on Stored Procedures under the database and choosing the New Stored Procedure option. The procedure is then saved within the current database as an object.

Encryption Can Secure Definitions

Data encryption is a mechanism that can be used to secure data, communications, procedures, and other sensitive information. When encryption techniques are applied, sensitive information is transformed into a non-readable form that must be decrypted to be viewed. Encryption slows performance, regardless of the method implemented, because extra processing cycles are required whenever encryption or decryption occurs. SQL Server can use data encryption at several levels:

◆ Login information

◆ Application role passwords

◆ Stored procedures

◆ Views

◆ User-defined functions

◆ Triggers

◆ Defaults

◆ Rules

◆ Data sent over the network

A variety of encryption procedures can be performed by a developer or administrator depending on what level of encryption is desired. SQL Server always encrypts login and role passwords within the system tables stored on the server. This automatic encryption of the login information stored on the server can be overridden using `sp_addlogin`, but this is not recommended. By default, however, application role passwords are not encrypted if they are provided across the network to invoke a role. The encryption of these passwords must be coded into the invoking application by utilizing the encryption capabilities of the `sp_setapprole` procedure as follows:

```
sp_setapprole 'SampleRole', (ENCRYPT N 'password'), 'odbc'
```

SQL Server can use SSL (Secure Sockets Layer) encryption across all network libraries, although multiprotocol encryption is still supported for backward compatibility reasons. A consideration in any SQL Server installation that uses multiple instances installed on the same server is that multiprotocol encryption is not supported by named instances of SQL Server.

Process definition encryption applied to stored procedures, defaults, rules, user-defined functions, triggers, and view definitions are all implemented in a similar fashion. The definition stored on the server is encrypted to prevent someone from viewing the details of the process. To encrypt these definitions, use the applicable CREATE statement, providing the WITH ENCRYPTION option as illustrated in the following VIEW definition:

```
CREATE VIEW SampleEncryptedView WITH ENCRYPTION AS
    SELECT FirstName, LastName, Wage FROM PayTable
```

Encryption can also serve the purpose of protecting the copyright that a developer might have over the processes created. In any case, before you encrypt a procedure, make sure you save a copy of the procedure to a file server or other backup mechanism, because future changes are difficult to implement if you do not have the original definition. To update any definition or remove encryption, simply supply the CREATE statement without the WITH ENCRYPTION option. This overwrites the encrypted process with a new version that is not encrypted.

Schema Binding

Schema binding involves attaching an underlying table definition to a view or user-defined function. Normally, if this process is not used, a function or view definition does not hold any data or other defining characteristics of a table. The definition is stored as a set of T-SQL statements and handled as a query or procedure. With binding, a view or function is connected to the underlying objects. Any attempt to change or remove the objects fails unless the binding has first been removed. Normally, you can create a view, but the underlying table might be changed so that the view no longer works. To prevent the underlying table from being changed, the view can be "schema-bound" to the table. Any table changes, which would break the view, are not allowed.

Indexed views require that a view be defined with the binding option and also that any user-defined functions referenced in the view must also be bound. In previous versions of SQL Server, it was not possible to define an index on a view. With the advent of binding, however, meaningful indexes can now be defined over a view that has been bound to the underlying objects. Other system options must be set to define an indexed view. These options are discussed later in the chapter in the "Indexed Views" section. More information on the use of all types of views can be found in Chapter 7, "Working With Views." The following example uses T-SQL of the creation of a schema-bound view:

```
CREATE VIEW SampleBoundView WITH SCHEMABINDING AS
        SELECT ProductID, Description, PurchPrice,
    PurchPrice * Markup AS SalesPrice
        FROM dbo.ProductTable
```

Recompilation of Procedures

Adding or altering indexes or changing a stored procedure causes SQL Server to automatically recompile the procedure. This optimization occurs the next time the stored procedure is run, but only after SQL Server is restarted. In instances where you want to force a recompilation, you can use the sp_recompile system-stored procedure. Alternatively, you can use the WITH RECOMPILE option when you create or execute a stored procedure. Stored procedures are dealt with in depth in Chapter 9, "Stored Procedures and User-Defined Functions."

Extended Stored Procedures

These procedures, like many of the system-stored procedures, are loaded automatically when you install SQL Server. Extended stored procedures access DLL files stored on the machine to enable the calling of the functions contained in the DLLs from within a SQL Server application. You might add to this set of procedures stored in the Master database using the sp_addextendedproc procedure as follows:

```
sp_addextendedproc 'MyFunction', 'MyFunctionSet.DLL'
```

The Many Meanings of "Schema"
The word *schema* has several different uses and definitions within SQL Server; the exam will leverage this and attempt to confuse the separate definitions. Make sure you are aware of how the term is used with relation to XML, Indexed Views, and maintaining metadata. For more information about these particulars, you can consult Chapter 5, "Advanced Data Retrieval and Modification," in the section on XML schema; Chapter 7, "Working With Views," in the section on indexed views; and Chapter 12, "Monitoring SQL Server 2000," in the section on metadata.

Trigger Utilization

Triggers are like stored procedures in that they contain a set of T-SQL statements saved for future execution. The big difference is that unlike stored procedures, triggers are executed automatically based on data activity in a table. A trigger may fire based on an UPDATE, INSERT, or DELETE operation.

In SQL Server 2000, triggers can be fired AFTER an operation completes (SQL Server default) or INSTEAD OF the triggering operation. An AFTER trigger can be used to archive data when it is deleted, send a notification that the new data has been added or changed, or to initiate any other process that you might want to automate based on data activity. An INSTEAD OF trigger can be used to perform more advanced activities (such as advanced data checking), to enable updates in a view to occur across multiple tables, and to perform many other functions that might be necessary in place of a triggering activity.

Many AFTER triggers can be specified for each INSERT, UPDATE, or DELETE action. If multiple triggers exist, you can specify the first and last trigger to fire. The others are fired in no particular order, and you cannot control that order. An AFTER trigger can be defined only on a table. Only one INSTEAD OF trigger can be defined for each of the triggering actions; however, an INSTEAD OF trigger can be defined on a view as well as a table.

In previous releases, you could use triggers to help enforce referential integrity constraints. This was difficult and required that you eliminate other elements, such as Foreign Key constraints. In SQL Server 2000, it is far more efficient to use cascading actions, discussed earlier in this chapter, for the purpose of cascading changes and deletions.

To define a trigger, you can select the Manage Triggers option from the Table Design window. You can also go to the table to which you want to attach a trigger, and you can find the option as an extension of the pop-up menu off the All Tasks option.

You can use the T-SQL CREATE TRIGGER statement to create triggers for all applicable operations. You can access this command from the Enterprise Manager by using the Managing Triggers option. Managing Triggers in the Enterprise Manager (and in other objects

as well) provides you with the shell of a CREATE statement even if you
are changing an existing trigger. The Enterprise Manager enables
you to change an existing trigger and the trigger will be first
dropped prior to re-creation. The ALTER TRIGGER statement is used
to change the definition of a trigger without dropping it first, and is
used only through T-SQL. An example of the creation of a trigger
using T-SQL is as follows:

```
CREATE TRIGGER UpdatedCustomer ON CustomerTable
FOR INSERT, UPDATE AS
        declare @phone nvarchar(20)
        declare @Contact nvarchar(100)
        select @phone = phoneno,
            @contact = contactname from inserted
        RAISERROR(50100, 1, 1, @Contact, @Phone)
```

This procedure is one of my favorite implementations for use in customer applications. In the case of customer information, an automated alert that sends an email message to the salesperson could be
defined around the error being raised. On an INSERT, a clerk or
salesperson may make an initial client contact call based on an email
that the alert may send. In the event of an UPDATE, the clerk could
call the client to ensure the new information is accurate. The benefit
is that the trigger automatically fires when new rows are added to
the table or changes are made to the customer information.

Consider some other possible implementations of triggers. A government database is present, which can be replicated into a local copy
of the database. Revenues are based on the capability to ferret out
new clients ahead of the competition. An INSERT trigger can fire an
email directly to the client with a promotional sales package
attached. The end result is that action occurs as quickly as possible,
which might provide an edge over the competition. For a more
complete guide to the use of triggers and other facets of this technology, see Chapter 8, "Triggers."

User-Defined Functions

In some applications, the functions available from the SQL Server
installation do not suit all needs. It is for these instances that user-
defined functions were intended. The functions can contain any
combination of T-SQL statements. These functions act similarly to
stored procedures with the exception that any errors occurring inside
the function cause the entire function to fail.

SQL Server supports three varieties of user-defined functions:

◆ Scalar functions

◆ Inline table-valued functions

◆ Multi-statement table-valued functions

The functions defined can accept parameters if needed and return either a scalar value or a table. A function cannot change any information outside the scope of the function and therefore maintains no information when processing has been completed. Other activities that are not permitted include returning information to the user and sending email. The CREATE FUNCTION statement is used to define a user-defined function similar to the following:

```
CREATE FUNCTION MyFunction (@Num1 smallint, @Num2 smallirt)
        RETURNS real AS
    BEGIN
    Declare @ReturnValue real
            If (@Num1 > @Num2)
             Set @ReturnValue = @Num1 * 2 + 30
            If (@Num1 = @Num2)
             Set @ReturnValue = @Num1 * 1.5 + 30
            If (@Num1 < @Num2)
             Set @ReturnValue = @Num1 * 1.25 + 30
            If (@Num1 < 0)
             Set @ReturnValue = @Num2 * 1.15 + 30
            Return(@ReturnValue)
            End
```

User-defined functions (UDFs) represent powerful functionality that has a wide variety of uses within the SQL Server environment. For more complete information on how to use UDFs see Chapter 9, "Stored Procedures and User-Defined Functions."

Focusing Interaction with Views

A view is a SELECT statement that is saved and given a name. In most respects, a view acts as a table. A VIEW name can be used in SELECT INSERT, UPDATE, and DELETE statements as if it were a table. No data is stored within views (except indexed views).

Often you would like to design an application that gives the user a list of specific columns out of a table but does not grant the user access to all data. A view can be used to limit what the user sees and the actions the user can perform over a portion of the data in a table.

An alternative to creating a view would be to handle column-level permissions over a table, which can be a true nightmare to administer. A new interface feature in SQL 2000 does enable you to use the GUI to set column-level permissions. However, this feature should be used as little as possible—if ever. (See Figures 3.8, 3.9, and 3.10 for column permission availability.) In previous releases, you could set column permissions, but only through the use of T-SQL commands. These illustrations shows that the GUI representations for column permissions are significantly different from standard permissions and thus stand out if they are set.

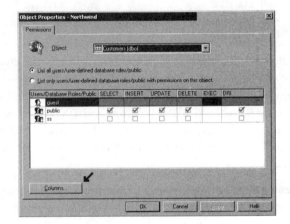

FIGURE 3.8
Command button now available on the interface to set column-level permissions.

FIGURE 3.9
Column Permissions dialog box, available from the GUI.

FIGURE 3.10
Permissions dialog box, showing that column permissions have been set.

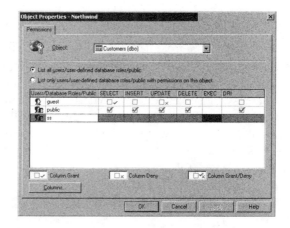

The problem with column-level permissions is the initial creation process of the permission is time-consuming, and the granularity of maintenance of the permissions requires extremely careful documentation. Imagine a table with 100 columns and 1000 or more users, groups, and roles. Trying to document and keep track of all the permissions set is an immense task that will overwhelm even the best administrator.

Use a view to simplify administration and provide a more meaningful perspective on the data for the user. The following example shows the creation of a view:

```
CREATE VIEW InStock AS
SELECT ProductID, Description, QTYOnHand FROM Products
WHERE QTYOnHand > 0
```

Indexed Views

If you want to use indexed views, a number of session-level options must be set On when you create the index. You need to set NUMERIC_ROUNDABORT Off. The options that need to be set On are as follows:

- ◆ ANSI_NULLS
- ◆ ANSI_PADDING
- ◆ ANSI_WARNINGS
- ◆ ARITHABORT
- ◆ CONCAT_NULL_YIELDS_NULL
- ◆ QUOTED_IDENTIFIERS

Other than setting the specific set of options, nothing more needs to be done for the optimizer to utilize an index with a query on a view. Essentially, the SQL SERVER Optimizer handles the view query in the same manner that it would a standard query against a table. The view cannot reference another view; only underlying tables are permitted and you must create the view with the SCEMABINDING option. Only the Enterprise and Developer editions support the creation of an indexed view.

There are limitations to the content of the SELECT statement for the view definition. They are as follows:

◆ No use of *.

◆ A column name used as a simple expression cannot be specified in more than one view column.

◆ No derived tables.

◆ Rowset functions are not permitted.

◆ UNION, Outer Joins, Subqueries, or Self-joins cannot be used only simple Joins.

◆ No TOP, ORDER BY, COMPUTE, or COMPUTE BY clause.

◆ DISTINCT is not permitted.

◆ COUNT(*) cannot be used, but COUNT_BIG(*) is allowed.

◆ Aggregate functions: AVG, MAX, MIN, STDEV, STDEVP, VAR, or VARP are not permitted.

◆ A SUM function cannot reference a nullable expression.

◆ No use of full-text predicates CONTAINS or FREETEXT.

> **EXAM TIP**
>
> **Know Your Options** A lot of specific options need to be in place to allow for Indexed Views. Make sure you are confident with the set of configuration features that are needed. Make sure that you read up on this topic as presented in Chapter 7, "Working with Views."

Partitioned Views

A partitioned view enables the creation of a view that spans a number of physical machines. These views can fall into one of two categories: local and distributed. A distinction is also made between views that are updateable and those that are read-only. The use of partitioned views can aid in the implementation of *federated database servers*, which are multiple machines set up to share the processing load. For more information on federated server implementations, see SQL Server Books Online, "Designing Federated Database Servers."

To use partitioned views, you horizontally split a single table into several smaller tables, each having the same column definitions. Set up the smaller tables to accept data in ranges and enforce the ranges using CHECK constraints. Then you can define the distributed view on each of the participating servers. Add linked server definitions on each of the member servers. An example of a distributed view definition is as follows:

```
CREATE VIEW AllProducts AS
        Select * FROM Server1.dbo.Products9999
UNION ALL
        Select * FROM Server2.dbo.Products19999
UNION ALL
        Select * FROM Server3.dbo.Products29999
```

Easing Data Entry with Defaults

A default is used to provide a value for a column so as to minimize data entry efforts or to provide an entry when the data is not known. A default provides a value for the column as a basis for initial input. Any data that is entered for the column overrides the default entry. You can apply a default definition to a column directly using the CREATE or ALTER TABLE statement or through the Design Table option from within the Enterprise Manager. You can also create a default as its own object and then bind it to one or more columns.

A default definition provided as part of a table definition is a standard and preferred method of implementing default entries. The advantages of this technique are that the default is dropped when the table is dropped and that the definition is stored within the table itself. A default object must be created and bound to the column in a two–step operation.

To create and bind a default object, use the following code:

```
CREATE DEFAULT StateDefault AS 'IN'
    sp_bindefault StateDefault, 'customers.state'
```

To create a default within a table definition, use the following:

```
CREATE TABLE SampleDefault
    ( SampleID           smallint NOT NULL
        CONSTRAINT UPKCL_SampleID PRIMARY KEY CLUSTERED,
      City               varchar(50)
        DEFAULT          ('Woodstock'),
      State              char(2)
        DEFAULT          ('NY')
    )
```

When an INSERT operation is performed on a table, you must supply values for all columns that do not have a default entry defined or that allow NULL content.

Application of Integrity Options

As discussed throughout this chapter, a number of techniques are available to maintain the integrity of the database. Each of these techniques will in part provide a usable, responsive system that prevents inappropriate data from getting into the system. Table 3.1 summarizes these techniques and provides some further detail as to what can be expected in their use.

TABLE 3.1

INTEGRITY MAINTENANCE OBJECTS

Technique	Integrity Achieved	Usage	Timing (Log)
Primary Key	Entity	Identify each row	Before
Foreign Key	Referential/Domain	Ensure no orphan child elements	Before
Unique Index	Entity	Ensure entries are exclusive	Before
Unique Constraint	Entity	No duplicate column values	Before
Identity	Entity	Auto-incremented values	Before
Check Constraint	Domain	Ensure correct column entry	Before
Not NULL	Domain	A value must be present	Before
Default	Domain	Provides initial value	Before
Rule	Domain	Ensure correct column entry	Before
Trigger	Referential/Domain	Respond to add, change, delete	After
Stored Procedures	Referential/Domain/Entity	Process-controlled operations	Before

Note from Table 3.1 that most integrity techniques are applied before the data is actually allowed into the system, and therefore operate faster with a much lower overhead. Triggers offer the most functionality, but at a cost: the data is allowed into the system and then reacted upon. If a trigger determines that data should not be permitted, it must be rolled back. Use triggers sparingly and only when the application requires the additional functionality.

When you define the table structure from the GUI, fill in the upper portion of the Design Table dialog box with column information by supplying the column name, selecting the appropriate data type from the drop-down list box, completing the Length field if the data type allows this to be adjusted, and setting whether the column is to allow NULL content. In the lower portion of the dialog box, you can optionally complete a description for the column, provide a default value, and, for numeric data types that allow for scale and precision, supply appropriate entries. If the column is to be an Identity column, select one of the integer data types, select Identity, and provide a starting value in the seed identification and an increment for the Identity. If the column is to be a row guid, select this option. If the column value is derived from a formula, specify the formula.

STEP BY STEP

3.7 Creating Tables, Indexes, and Constraints

1. Expand a server group, then the server, and then the database where the table is to be located.

2. Right-click Tables, and then select New Table.

3. Provide column definitions until all columns are defined.

4. Right-click on the column to be used as the Primary Key and select Set Primary Key.

5. In the top-left corner of the dialog box is a Table and Index Properties button that provides access to an area where you can provide further information to define the table.

6. Select the Relationships tab to define a Foreign Key.

7. Select the Indexes/Keys tab to define more indexing options.

8. Select the Check Constraints tab to define any constraint options for the table.

9. Close the Properties dialog box, and then save and exit to finish defining the table.

Using T-SQL code, you create the tables as follows:

```
CREATE TABLE projects
  ( project_id   smallint not Null
IDENTITY(1,1)
      PRIMARY KEY CLUSTERED,
    project_description        varchar(25)      NOT NULL
      DEFAULT '*Unknown*',
    start_date                 datetime         NOT NULL
      CHECK (start_date >= getdate()),
    completion_date            datetime         NOT NULL
      CHECK (completion_date >= getdate())
  )
```

Database Design, an Involved Process

Consider the functionality that is needed for any procedure that maintains the integrity of the data. In many cases, there are a number of choices that can be made between different techniques. The highest degree of functionality is achieved from stored procedures, followed closely by triggers. Also consider the basics of database design, regardless of application. Primary Keys, for example, serve a number of purposes and it is a good practice to implement them in almost any structure.

To achieve availability and performance, redundancy is the starting point. Data redundancy can be obtained at the table and database level through denormalization, and at the server level through the use of log shipping, replication, and/or partitioning. Each technique has a variety of requirements that must be closely adhered to.

There is no single, basic solution for any plan. Knowledge of the environment and how the data is going to be used will answer a number of the initial questions. There is no replacement for proper system development; you can't throw a technology at a problem and just hope it will go away. Research and plan the implementation and document each step of the way.

MULTIPLE SERVER IMPLEMENTATIONS

▶ **Alter database objects to support replication and partitioned views.**

Many high-demand implementations require the use of multiple servers to handle the workload. A variety of options exist for using SQL Server on multiple servers. Partitioning, log shipping, replication, federated servers, and clustering are all potential implementations for using multiple servers and obtaining load balancing.

Using log shipping is a way to have two separate servers that contain the same database split the query load away from the updating of data. The log information is periodically copied to a read-only, standby server that can then be used for query purposes, thereby offloading some of the work from the main production machine. For further information on log shipping implementations, see SQL Server Books Online, "Maintenance Planning Wizard." Microsoft failover clustering provides for availability by enabling a secondary server to take over activities if a primary server fails. For further information on failover clustering, see SQL Server Books Online, "Creating a Failover Cluster."

Partitioning and federated servers provide load balancing for a single application and work together to provide users with better response. This type of implementation is in place of a multiple server cluster where all machines load balance to share the workload. In a federation, each server is completely independent and it is the application and database design that implement the load balancing.

Replication places potentially updateable copies of the same data on multiple servers so that applications that allow for site independence can, at the same time, keep all copies of the data synchronized. Most models have a degree of latency or delay between the initial updates and the moment when all data is in agreement.

Use of Replication

Placing the same data on multiple servers, with each server closer to the user's location, can reduce the use of bandwidth and provide the user with faster update operations and retrieval of data. Replication is discussed in full in Chapter 11, "Implementing and Understanding Replication Methodologies," so this section focuses more or the specifics of designing a system to support the replication models.

These replication techniques can be applied to three replication models, as well as several different physical models. The physical aspects and models have no direct correlation. The replication model supplies the functionality, whereas the physical aspects lay out the placement and roles of individual servers.

Merge, snapshot, and transactional replication all involve essentially the same basic elements to begin with. However, each model has idiosyncrasies of its own that require some thought during the design of the implementation. For further information on replication, consult Chapter 11.

Partitioning to Achieve a Balance

Data partitioning as defined previously involves the horizontal division of a singular table into a number of smaller tables, each dealing with a range of data from the original and split off onto separate servers. Some configuration options can help gain performance when operating against partitions. Setting the Lazy Schema Validation option using sp_serveroption can optimize performance. Attempting to ensure that the correct query goes to the appropriate server also helps to improve performance while minimizing bandwidth use.

A partitioned view is considered to be updateable if a set of SELECT statements is combined into one resultset using UNION ALL operations, as was shown in the section "Partitioned Views." Indexes based on calculated columns are not permitted within any table definitions and all tables must have a Primary key and ANSI_PADDING set.

When you use a partitioned view to insert data, all columns must be included in the INSERT statement, even if the table definitions provide DEFAULTS or allow for NULL content. Also, IDENTITY columns cannot be referenced; therefore, no underlying tables can have IDENTITY columns nor are they permitted to have time-stamp columns.

Remote partitioned views require that you keep a few additional considerations in mind. A distributed transaction is automatically initiated to ensure that integrity is maintained throughout all operations, and the XACT_ABORT option must be set to ON Smallmoney and smalldatetime data types in the remote tables are mapped to money and datetime types locally.

Partition Creation Strategy

Partitions can be designed in a symmetric or asymmetric fashion, and although it is most useful to design symmetrically, the access requirements of a lot of systems necessitate an asymmetric design.

A symmetrical design is one in which all related data is placed on the same server so that most queries do not have to cross network boundaries to access the data. It is also easier to manage the data if the division of tables can be performed in such a manner that each server has the same amount of data.

In most real-world applications, data is accessed in a random fashion that can make the designer lean toward an asymmetric implementation. The design can be configured so that one server has a larger role and/or contains more data than the others. Performance can be improved if you weigh each server's use and make one server work harder on the partitioned applications because the other servers perform larger tasks that deal with other unrelated processes.

Designing for distributed partitioned views requires appropriate planning of front-end applications to ensure that, whenever possible, data queries are sent to the appropriate server. Middleware such as Microsoft Transaction Server or Application Server or other third-party equivalents, should attempt to match queries against data storage.

Constraint Considerations

Constraints need to be defined on each participating server so that only the data pertaining to the table(s) stored on that server is handled. Although CHECK constraints are not needed to return the correct results, they enable the query optimizer to more appropriately select the correct server to find the requested data.

EXAM TIP

Be Comfortable with Configuration
You are likely to find exam questions that will ask you to balance the work load and properly configure partitioned views. Ensure you are comfortable with the configuration required. To find out more information on these and other styles of views you can expect to see, refer to Chapter 7.

Spreading It Out

Multiple server operations balance the load so that updates are potentially separated from queries and query load can be spread across multiple machines.

Partitioned views drastically restrict the underlying table designs and require a number of options to be set when using indexes.

The application of the initial snapshot that begins the entire replication process can be compressed and/or saved to a CD so that some of the necessary communications can be offloaded. Doing so makes more efficient use of network bandwidth in slow-link or dial-up environments in particular.

TROUBLESHOOTING SQL SERVER OBJECTS

▶ **Troubleshoot failed object creation.**

Most problems associated with creating and/or accessing objects can be resolved through setting appropriate object access permissions. However, other elements that can hamper the creation or use of objects include (but are not limited to) the following:

◆ Backup and restore operations

◆ Other users' operations locking parts of the system

◆ Metadata corruption

◆ Hardware or resource problems

◆ Network connectivity

◆ Configuration settings

◆ Operating system

◆ Metadata corruption

A good starting point from which to resolve most problems is the wealth of feedback SQL Server gives in the form of OS Application

Event Log, SQL Server Logs, and the Current Activity Window, as well as the permission properties of the users, roles, and objects.

To create a database, you need to be a member of System Administrators or Database Creators server roles or have the Create Database permission. To create objects within a database, you must be a member of db_owner or db_ddladmin database roles or have the specific permission to create the object as given by statement-level permissions. Statement-level permissions can be found on the Permissions tab of the database Properties dialog box.

As databases and their objects are created, the system uses the default filegroup for the physical storage of the element. It is a good practice to create a storage group for user objects and make that the default filegroup. This way, as the user creates objects, those objects don't compete for storage with other data.

If a user lacks the permission to create or alter an object, an alternative is available that grants the user creation permission without giving the user too much control over the environment. An Application role that has permission to work with objects in this manner can be assigned to a stored procedure that creates the objects for the user. When the user executes the procedure, objects can be created or altered in a controlled manner.

Setting Server Configuration Options

Standard configuration settings are available through the Server Properties dialog box in the Enterprise Manager or can be accessed using the sp_configure stored procedure. Some of the more advanced options require that you enable Show Advanced Options.

```
sp_configure 'show advanced options', 1
reconfigure
```

Affinity Mask (Advanced)

Use this option in systems that have four or more processors. It increases performance when the system is under a heavy workload. You can specify which processors Microsoft SQL Server is to use. You can exclude SQL Server activity from processors that have been given specific workload assignments by the Windows NT 4.0 or Windows 2000 operating system.

Allow Updates

This option is used to allow the direct alteration of system tables. When Allow Updates is set to 1, any user with appropriate permissions can either update system tables directly with ad-hoc updates or create stored procedures that update system tables.

AWE Enabled (Advanced)

Address Windowing Extension (AWE) is an advanced option used to support up to a maximum of 64 gigabytes (GB) of physical memory.

C2 Audit Mode

Use C2 audit mode to review both successful and unsuccessful attempts to access statements and objects. Allowing for the documentation of system activity and observance of security policy violations, C2 auditing tracks C2 audit events and records them to a file in the \mssql\data directory or the \mssql$instancename\data directory for named instances of SQL Server. If the file reaches a size limit of 200 megabytes (MB), C2 auditing starts a new file.

Cost Threshold for Parallelism (Advanced)

Use this option to specify the threshold where SQL Server creates and executes parallel query plans. Parallel query plans are executed only when the estimated cost to execute a serial plan for the same query is higher than the value set. The cost refers to an estimated elapsed time in seconds that is required to execute a standard plan. Only set cost threshold for parallelism on symmetric multiprocessors.

Cursor Threshold (Advanced)

Use this option to indicate the number of rows in the cursor set at which cursor keysets are generated asynchronously. If you set Cursor Threshold to -1, all keysets are generated synchronously, which benefits small cursor sets. If you set Cursor Threshold to 0, all cursor keysets are generated asynchronously. With other values, the query optimizer compares the number of expected rows in the cursor set and builds the keyset asynchronously if it exceeds the number set in Cursor Threshold. Do not set Cursor Threshold too low because small result sets are better built synchronously.

Default Language

Use this option to specify the default language for all newly created logins.

Fill Factor (Advanced)

Use this option to specify how full the server should make each page when it creates a new index using existing data. The Fill Factor percentage affects performance because SQL Server must take time to split pages when they fill up. The default for Fill Factor of 0 (zero) does not mean that pages are 0% full. It is treated similarly to a fill factor value of 100 in that indexes are created with full data pages and nonclustered indexes with full leaf pages. The default setting is different from 100 in that SQL Server leaves some space within the upper level of the index tree.

Index Create Memory (Advanced)

Use this option to control the amount of memory used by index creation sorts. The Index Create Memory option is self-configuring and should operate without requiring adjustment. If difficulties are experienced creating indexes, consider increasing the value. Query sorts are controlled through the Min Memory Per Query option. The default value for this option is 0 (self-configuring).

Default Full-Text Language (Advanced)

Use the default full-text language option to specify a default language value for full-text indexed columns. The default value of this option is the language of the server.

Lightweight Pooling (Advanced)

This option provides a means of reducing the overhead associated with the excessive context switching sometimes seen in multiprocessor environments. When excessive context switching is present, lightweight pooling might provide better throughput.

Locks (Advanced)

The Locks option sets the maximum number of available locks, limiting the amount of memory the server uses. The default setting is 0, which enables SQL Server to allocate and deallocate locks dynamically based on changing system requirements.

Max Degree of Parallelism (Advanced)

This option limits the number of processors to use in parallel plan execution. The default value is 0 (actual number of CPUs) and the maximum is 32.

Max Server Memory/Min Server Memory

These two settings establish upper and lower limits to the amount of memory the database engine uses. The database engine starts with only the memory required to initialize. As the workload increases, it acquires additional memory. The database engine frees any of the acquired memory until it reaches the amount specified in Min Server Memory.

Max Text Repl Size

Specifies the maximum size (in bytes) of text and image data that can be added to a replicated column in a single INSERT, UPDATE, WRITETEXT, or UPDATETEXT statement.

Max Worker Threads (Advanced)

Configures the number of worker threads available to the server and its processes. SQL Server uses the threads so that one or more threads simultaneously support each network that SQL Server supports; another thread handles database checkpoints; and a pool of threads handles user connections.

Media Retention (Advanced)

Use the Media Retention option to provide a default for the length of time each backup should be retained. Overridden by the RETAIN-DAYS clause of the BACKUP statement, Media Retention helps protect backups from being overwritten until the specified number of days has elapsed.

Min Memory Per Query (Advanced)

Use this option to specify the minimum amount of memory that will be allocated for the execution of a query.

Nested Triggers

The Nested Triggers option enables actions that initiate another trigger to be performed. When the Nested Triggers option is set to 0, triggers cannot cascade. When the Nested Triggers option is set to the default setting of 1, triggers can cascade to as many as 32 levels.

Network Packet Size (Advanced)

Use this option to set the packet size used across the entire network. The default packet size is 4096 bytes. If an application does bulk copy operations, or sends or receives large amounts of text or image data, a packet size larger than the default can improve efficiency because it results in fewer network reads and writes. If an application sends and receives small amounts of information, you can set the packet size to 512 bytes, which is sufficient for most data transfers.

Open Objects (Advanced)

Use this option to set the maximum number of database objects that can be open at one time. Database objects are those objects defined in the sysobjects table: tables, views, rules, stored procedures, defaults, and triggers.

Priority Boost (Advanced)

This option specifies the processor scheduling priority. If you set this option to 1, SQL Server runs at a priority base of 13 in the Windows NT 4.0 or Windows 2000 Scheduler. The default is 0, which is a priority base of 7.

Query Governor Cost Limit (Advanced)

Specifies an upper limit for the time in which a query can run. Query cost refers to the estimated elapsed time, in seconds, required to execute a query.

Query Wait (Advanced)

Memory-intensive queries, such as those involving sorting and hashing, are queued when not enough memory is available to run the query. The query times out after a set amount of time that SQL Server calculates (25 times the estimated cost of the query) or the time amount specified by the non-negative value of the query wait.

Recovery Interval (Advanced)

Use this option to set the maximum number of minutes per database that the server needs to recover the database activity. The recovery process is initiated each time SQL Server starts or as the basis for completing a restore operation. The recovery process rolls back transactions that did not commit and rolls forward transactions that did commit. This configuration option sets an upper limit on the time it should take to recover each database. The default is 0, indicating automatic configuration by SQL Server. In practice, this means a recovery time of less than one minute and a checkpoint marker is placed into the transaction log approximately every one minute for active databases.

Remote Access

Use the Remote Access option to control logins from remote servers running SQL Server. Set Remote Access to 1 (default) to enable logins from remote servers. Set the option to 0 to secure a local server and prevent access from a remote server.

Remote Login Timeout

Use this option to specify the number of seconds to wait before returning from a failed remote login attempt.

Remote Proc Trans

This option protects the activities of a server-to-server process through the use of the Distributed Transaction Coordinator. Set Remote Proc Trans to 1 to provide an MS DTC-coordinated distributed transaction that protects the ACID properties of transactions. Sessions begun after setting this option to 1, inherit the configuration setting as their default.

Remote Query Timeout

This option is used to indicate the number of seconds that must elapse when processing a remote operation before the operation times out. The default of 600 sets a ten-minute wait.

Scan for Startup Process (Advanced)

Use this option to scan for automatic execution of stored procedures at startup time. If it is set to 1, SQL Server scans for and executes all automatically executed stored procedures defined on the server. The default value is 0 (do not scan).

Set Working Set Size (Advanced)

Reserves physical memory space for SQL Server that is equal to the server memory setting. SQL Server, based on workload and available resources, configures the server memory setting automatically. It varies dynamically between the Min Server Memory and Max Server Memory settings.

Two Digit Year Cutoff

Use the Two Digit Year Cutoff option to specify an integer from 1753 to 9999 that represents the last year for interpreting two-digit years as four-digit years.

User Connections (Advanced)

Use this option to specify the maximum number of simultaneous user connections. The actual number of user connections allowed also depends on the version of SQL Server you are using and the limits of your application(s) and hardware. SQL Server enables a maximum of 32,767 user connections.

User Options

The User Options option is used to specify global defaults for all users. A list of default query processing options is established for the duration of a user's work session. A user can override these defaults by using the SET statement. You can configure user options dynamically for new logins. After you change the setting of user options, new logins use the new setting; current logins are not affected.

Reconfigure

This option updates the server configuration. It is used after the application of sp_configure to change server settings and make the new settings take effect. Because some configuration options require that a server stop and restart before the currently running value can be updated, Reconfigure does not always update the currently running value. Use the With Override option of this command to force a value that might or might not meet ranges of allowed values or recommended settings.

Changing configuration options can easily be performed using T-SQL operations:

TSQL

USE master

```
EXEC sp_configure 'show advanced option', '1'

RECONFIGURE

GO

EXEC sp_configure 'recovery interval', '3'

RECONFIGURE WITH OVERRIDE
```

Step by Step 3.8 takes you through the setting of some common server options.

STEP BY STEP

3.8 Setting Server Configuration Options

1. Expand a server group, then right-click the server, and then select Properties.

2. Select the Database Settings tab.

3. Set the Recovery Interval to 3.

4. Select OK to save the setting.

Configuration Exam Considerations

The SQL Server configuration options are used to fine-tune the database environment. Many options provide a mechanism for an administrator or developer to obtain optimum performance and achieve a more secure and stable server. A total approach to an optimum environment also involves the proper use of database configuration options. Server property adjustments affect all the databases stored on the server where database configuration options are used to control a database and not affect other databases.

Setting Database Configuration Options

Standard database configuration settings are available through the Database Properties in the Enterprise Manager or can be accessed using the sp_dboption stored procedure. Some of the more advanced settings cannot be set singly; they must be set in combination with other settings.

There are five categories of database options:

◆ **Auto options**. AUTO_CLOSE, AUTO_CREATE_STATISTICS, AUTO_UPDATE_STATISTICS, and AUTO_SHRINK

◆ **Cursor options**. CURSOR_CLOSE_ON_COMMIT and CURSOR_DEFAULT LOCAL or GLOBAL

◆ **Recovery options**. RECOVERY FULL or BULK_LOGGED or SIMPLE and TORN_PAGE_DETECTION

◆ **SQL options**. ANSI_NULL_DEFAULT, ANSI_NULLS, ANSI_PADDING, ANSI_WARNINGS, ARITHABORT NUMERIC_ROUNDABORT, CONCAT_NULL_YIELDS_NULL, QUOTED_IDENTIFIER, and RECURSIVE_TRIGGERS

◆ **State options**. OFFLINE or ONLINE, READ_ONLY or READ_WRITE, SINGLE_USER or RESTRICTED_USER or MULTI_USER and WITH ROLLBACK AFTER or WITH ROLLBACK IMMEDIATE or NO_WAIT.

These options are described in the following sections, and are covered in alphabetical order.

ANSI_NULL_DEFAULT

This option enables the user to control the default nullability. When NULL or NOT NULL is not specified, a user-defined data type or a column definition uses the default setting for nullability. When this option is set to ON, all user-defined data types or columns that are not explicitly defined as NOT NULL during a CREATE TABLE or ALTER TABLE statement default to allowing null values. Columns that are defined with constraints follow constraint rules regardless of this setting.

ANSI_NULLS

When set to ON, all comparisons to a null value evaluate to NULL (unknown). When set to OFF, comparisons of non-Unicode values to a null value evaluate to TRUE if both values are NULL. By default, the ANSI_NULLS database option is OFF.

ANSI_PADDING

When set to ON, trailing blanks in character values inserted into varchar columns and trailing zeros in binary values inserted into varbinary columns are not trimmed. Values are not padded to the length of the column. When set to OFF, the trailing blanks and zeros are trimmed. This setting affects only the definition of new columns. It is recommended that ANSI_PADDING always be set to ON. SET ANSI_PADDING must be ON when creating or manipulating indexes on computed columns or indexed views.

ANSI_WARNINGS

When set to ON, errors or warnings are issued when conditions such as "divide by zero" occur or null values appear in aggregate functions. When set to OFF, no warnings are raised when null values appear in aggregate functions, and null values are returned when conditions such as "divide by zero" occur. By default, ANSI_WARNINGS is OFF.

ARITHABORT

When set to ON, an overflow or divide-by-zero error causes the query or batch to terminate. If the error occurs in a transaction, the transaction is rolled back. When set to OFF, a warning message is displayed if one of these errors occurs, but the query, batch, or transaction continues to process as if no error occurred.

AUTO_CLOSE

When set to ON, server resources are freed up as soon as the database is closed and shut down cleanly when the last user of the database exits. By default, this option is set to ON for all databases in the Desktop Engine, and OFF for all other editions. The database reopens automatically when a user tries to use the database again. When set to OFF, the database remains open even if no users are currently using it.

AUTO_CREATE_STATISTICS

When set to ON, statistics are automatically created on columns used in a predicate. Adding statistics improves query performance because the optimizer can better determine how to evaluate queries. If the statistics are not used, SQL Server automatically deletes them. When set to OFF, SQL Server does not automatically create statistics; instead, statistics can be manually created.

AUTO_SHRINK

When set to ON, the database files are set up for periodic shrinking. Any database-associated file, data, or log can be shrunk automatically. When set to OFF, the database files are not automatically shrunk during periodic checks for unused space. By default, this option is set to ON for all databases in SQL Server Desktop Edition, and OFF for all other editions, regardless of operating system.

AUTO_UPDATE_STATISTICS

When set to ON, existing statistics are automatically updated when the statistics become out-of-date because the data in the tables has changed. When set to OFF, existing statistics are not automatically updated; instead, statistics can be manually updated.

CONCAT_NULL_YIELDS_NULL

When set to ON, if one of the operands in a concatenation operation is NULL, the result of the operation is NULL. When set to OFF, concatenating a null value with a character string yields the character string as the result.

CURSOR_CLOSE_ON_COMMIT

When set to ON, any open cursors are closed automatically when a transaction using the cursor is committed. By default, this setting is OFF and cursors remain open across transaction boundaries, closing only when the connection is closed or when they are explicitly closed, which is usually when a procedure finishes.

CURSOR_DEFAULT LOCAL or GLOBAL

When CURSOR_DEFAULT LOCAL is set, and a cursor is not defined as GLOBAL when it is created, the scope of the cursor is local to the batch, stored procedure, or trigger. The cursor name is valid only within this scope. When CURSOR_DEFAULT GLOBAL is set, and a cursor is not defined as LOCAL when created, the scope of the cursor is global to the connection. The cursor name can be referenced in any stored procedure or batch the connection executes.

NUMERIC_ROUNDABORT

If set to ON, an error is generated when the loss of precision occurs in an expression. When set to OFF, losses of precision do not generate error messages and the result is rounded to the precision of the column or variable storing the result.

OFFLINE or ONLINE

When OFFLINE is specified, the database is closed and shut down cleanly and marked offline. The database cannot be modified while it is offline. When ONLINE is specified, the database is open and available for use.

QUOTED_IDENTIFIER

When set to ON, identifiers can be delimited by double quotation marks and literals must be delimited by single quotation marks. All strings delimited by double quotation marks are interpreted as object identifiers. Quoted identifiers do not have to follow the T-SQL rules for identifiers. They can be keywords and can include characters not generally allowed in T-SQL identifiers. When set to OFF (default), identifiers cannot be in quotation marks and must follow all T-SQL rules for identifiers. Literals can be delimited by either single or double quotation marks. Identifiers must be enclosed in square brackets ([ ]) if they contain spaces or other characters or key words.

READ_ONLY or READ_WRITE

When READ_ONLY is specified, users can retrieve data from the database but cannot modify the data. Automatic recovery is skipped at system startup and shrinking the database is not possible. No locking takes place in read-only databases, which can result in faster query performance. When READ_WRITE is specified, users can retrieve and modify data.

RECOVERY FULL or BULK_LOGGED or SIMPLE

When FULL is specified, database backups and transaction log backups are used to provide full recoverability from media failure. All operations, including bulk operations, such as SELECT INTO, CREATE INDEX, and bulk loading data, are fully logged. When BULK_LOGGED is specified, logging for all SELECT INTO, CREATE INDEX, and bulk loading data operations is minimal and therefore requires less log space. In exchange for better performance and less log space usage, the risk of exposure to loss is greater than with full recovery. When SIMPLE is specified, the database can be recovered only to the last full database backup or last differential backup.

RECURSIVE_TRIGGERS

When set to ON, triggers are enabled to fire recursively. When set to OFF (default), triggers cannot be fired recursively.

SINGLE_USER or RESTRICTED_USER or MULTI_USER

SINGLE_USER enables only one user at a time to connect to the database. All other user connections are broken. The timeframe for breaking the connection is controlled by the termination clause of the ALTER DATABASE statement. New connection attempts are refused. RESTRICTED_USER enables only members of the db_owner fixed database role and dbcreator and sysadmin fixed server roles to connect to the database, but it does not limit their number. MULTI_USER enables all users with the appropriate permissions to connect to the database.

TORN_PAGE_DETECTION

This recovery option enables SQL Server to detect incomplete I/O operations caused by power failures or other system outages. When set to ON, this option causes a bit to be reversed for each 512-byte sector in an 8-kilobyte (KB) database page as the page is written to disk. If a bit is in the wrong state when the page is later read by SQL Server, the page was written incorrectly; a torn page is therefore detected.

WITH <termination>

The termination clause of the ALTER DATABASE statement specifies how to terminate incomplete transactions. Breaking their connections to the database terminates transactions. If the termination clause is omitted, the ALTER DATABASE statement waits indefinitely, until the transactions commit or roll back on their own. ROLLBACK AFTER *'integer'* SECONDS waits for the specified number of seconds. ROLLBACK IMMEDIATE breaks unqualified connections immediately. NO_WAIT checks for connections before attempting to change the database state and causes the ALTER DATABASE statement to fail if certain connections exist. When the transition is to SINGLE_USER mode, the ALTER DATABASE statement fails if any other connections exist. When the transition is to RESTRICTED_USER mode, the ALTER DATABASE statement fails if any unqualified connections exist.

Similar to setting server configuration options, the process of setting database options is described in Step by Step 3.9.

STEP BY STEP

3.9 Setting Database Options

1. Expand a server group, and then expand the server where the database is to be placed.

---

2. Right-click Databases, and then click Properties.

---

3. Select the Options tab.

---

4. Change the appropriate desired settings and select OK to save.

T-SQL database options can be set programmatically, although this is not normally recommended. The following procedure illustrates how this can be done in those rare instances where it is desired:

TSQL

View settable database options:

```
Sp_dboption
```

View which options have been set on `Northwind` database:

```
Sp_dboption Northwind
```

Turn off an option:

```
Sp_dboption Northwind, 'autoclose', False
```

Turn on an option:

```
Sp_dboption Northwind, 'autoclose', True
```

Setting the Database Options

Database options are set to allow for application or procedural requirements and to provide for administrative configuration. You will interact with these settings to set up backups, allow for specific procedures, and provide appropriate access levels, depending on what is needed for a given process. Learn the settings that are required for each process and know the resulting effect on the system under different operating configurations.

CASE STUDY: ACME DISTRIBUTORS

ESSENCE OF THE CASE

Here are the essential points being addressed in this case:

- ▶ Budget is limited.

- ▶ High volume of updates.

- ▶ Downtime must be minimized.

- ▶ Data loss must be minimized if a failure occurs.

- ▶ Referential integrity must be configured for replication.

SCENARIO

ACME Distributors is a mail-order company with warehouse operations located in strategic locations throughout the United States. You are in charge of planning the physical server environment to be used in the implementation of a multi-server warehousing system. Each of the warehouses needs information on what the other warehouses have in stock and transactional replication has been chosen as the technique to deliver information among the warehouses.

Each warehouse is expected to handle about 1000 transactions of its own each day, as well as receive 9000 replicated transactions from other warehouses. You need to supply an environment that will function 24 hours a day, 7 days a week. You must pay particular attention to achieving an environment that has a minimum amount of downtime and data loss in the event of a failure.

With a limited budget, you have been asked to establish priorities within the system. A list should be prepared providing a range of choices from the minimum requirements to fulfill the needs of the system, and on the upper range, some alternatives that would still fall into a low-budget scenario.

ANALYSIS

This seems to be a far-too-typical situation, in which a company desires to have the optimum environment but is hesitant to invest the necessary funds to achieve the desired results.

To eliminate downtime, there are two separate possibilities. First, you can provide for failover clustering, which can incur a significant cost.

continues

CASE STUDY: ACME DISTRIBUTORS

continued

Second, you can include in the solution a mechanism where a middle-tier procedure can select the local server by default, but if the server is unavailable, the procedure can obtain the necessary information from one of the other warehouses. Although the later solution can appear less expensive at first, because hardware costs are lower, other factors, such as development, update ability, bandwidth, and licensing costs have to be considered.

Also worth considering is the use of a standby server or replication as a means of minimizing—though not eliminating—downtime. This would be a less expensive solution than failover clustering, but in the event of failure, you will have a small amount of downtime while adjusting the actual machine being used for production purposes. An additional advantage of this solution is the near elimination of data loss if a failure were to occur.

To minimize data loss in the event of failure, a number of options are available. On the less-expensive side, setting the database recovery mode to Full Recovery and adding a second disk volume can provide for the storage of the log files and allow for almost full data recovery. Other possibilities from less to more expensive would include RAID parity storage, RAID mirror storage, log shipping, replication, and failover clustering. As long as replication is already being planned for, this might be part of the desired solution.

To enable multiple warehouses to participate in replication and to share information, you must create a Primary Key constraint that combines both the location of the warehouse and the identifier for the data itself.

Here is the desired list:

- Minimum Requirements:

  Compound Primary Key

- Recommended Requirements:

  Second volume for transaction log and Full Recovery mode

  Frequent log backups and the development of a disaster recovery plan

  Data storage set up in RAID parity with OS mirrored

- Also Possible (Recommended Order):

  Replication to additional subscriber at each location

  Standby server with log shipping configured (achieves similar results as replication)

  Cost Restrictive

- Failover Clustering

CHAPTER SUMMARY

This chapter has considered a number of different subjects, all pertaining to the physical aspects of a database system. Although the exam concentrates on the new features in SQL Server 2000, you will find that almost all topics are addressed in some manner. In a real-world scenario, you will find that the best solution often involves a compromise, rather than the ideal. Many considerations, such as budget, time constraints, user knowledge, and technology bias might hamper your ability to achieve an optimum environment.

When in doubt, select the options that provide for the best performance in the system. Next to performance, a provision to minimize administrative effort would probably come in a close second. Performance is gained through the use of the optimum levels of hardware, especially options pertaining to the disk, controller, and volume configuration. Performance is gained in interactions between the database and file system, so appropriate placement of files, file-groups, and database objects becomes very important. Within the databases, selection of appropriate indexing, constraints, triggers, and other related processing all help as well.

To achieve minimal levels of administration, look to set up and utilize existing features that SQL Server can perform automatically. Be careful: Using too many of the features that are automated might detract from the system performance.

KEY TERMS

- constraint
- collation Sequence
- identity
- indexes
- stored procedures
- triggers
- user-defined functions (UDFs)
- views
- cascading actions
- CHECK constraints
- clustered index
- defaults
- FILLFACTOR
- Foreign Keys
- non-clustered index

CHAPTER SUMMARY

- Primary Key
- UNIQUE constraints
- UNIQUE index
- schema binding
- encryption
- recompile
- partitioned views
- merge replication

- RAID
- snapshot replication
- filegroups
- log
- rules
- roles
- UNIQUE constraint
- transactional replication

Exercises

The following set of exercises runs through the set of steps needed to create a basic physical environment. Each step requires that you have completed all subsequent steps and are thus better done in sequential order.

3.1 Creating a Database

In Exercise 3.1, you create a database with two data files and a single log file. The exercise makes the assumption that SQL Server 2000 has been installed into the default locations and uses this location for all files. You might want to alter the actual file locations.

Estimated Time: 5 minutes

1. If the SQL Query Analyzer is not already open, load it to enable you to create a database using T-SQL commands. Supply the logon connection information if requested.

2. Select the Master database from the database drop-down list box from the toolbar.

3. Type the following command to create the database and accompanying files:

```
CREATE DATABASE Sample ON
PRIMARY (NAME = 'SampleData', FILENAME =
'c:\Program Files\Microsoft SQL Server
➥\MSSQL\Data\SampData.mdf',
  SIZE = 10, MAXSIZE = 50, FILEGROWTH = 5),
FILEGROUP Archive (Name = 'ArchiveData',
➥FILENAME =
'c:\Program Files\Microsoft SQL Server
➥\MSSQL\Data\ArchData.ndf',
  SIZE = 10, MAXSIZE = 50, FILEGROWTH = 5)
LOG ON
  (NAME = 'LogStore', FILENAME =
'c:\Program Files\Microsoft SQL Server
➥\MSSQL\Data\SampLog.ldf',
    SIZE = 1MB, MAXSIZE = 5MB,
    ➥FILEGROWTH = 1MB)
Go
```

4. Execute the query. Check the Windows environment using the Explorer to ensure the files were actually created. You can check for the existence of the database and ensure the associated database properties were set up by running the sp_helpdb stored procedure.

Note that when the database is created that there are two resulting filegroups. The Primary filegroup is used for data storage and the Archive filegroup is used for the storage of noncurrent data.

3.2 Creating a Table

In Exercise 3.2, you create three tables within the database. One table contains contact information; the second is a table to list events in the upcoming year; the third table is for holding archive data for events that have already passed.

Estimated Time: 10 minutes

1. If the SQL Query Analyzer is not already open, load it to allow for the creation of the tables. Supply the logon connection information if requested.

2. Select the Sample database created in Exercise 3.1 from the database drop-down list box from the toolbar.

3. Type the following command to create the database and accompanying files:

```
CREATE TABLE Contacts
    ( ContactID     smallint   NOT
    ➥NULL
      CONSTRAINT  PKContact
      ➥PRIMARY KEY CLUSTERED,
    FirstName     varchar(25) NOT
    ➥NULL,
    LastName      varchar(25) NOT
    ➥NULL,
    PhoneNo       varchar(15) NULL,
    StreetAddress varchar(25) NULL,
    City          varchar(25) NULL,
    ZipCode       varchar(15) NULL )
```

continues

APPLY YOUR KNOWLEDGE

continued

```
CREATE TABLE Events
            ( EventID         smallint     NOT
              →NULL
                CONSTRAINT  PKEvent
                →PRIMARY KEY CLUSTERED,
              EventName       varchar(50) NOT
              →NULL,
              EventLocation varchar(50) NOT
              →NULL,
              ContactID       smallint     NOT
              →NULL,
              EventAddress   varchar(25) NULL,
              City            varchar(25) NULL,
              ZipCode         varchar(15) NULL )

CREATE TABLE EventArchive
            ( EventID         smallint     NOT
              →NULL
                CONSTRAINT  PKEventArch
                →PRIMARY KEY CLUSTERED,
              EventName       varchar(50) NOT
              →NULL,
              EventLocation varchar(50) NOT
              →NULL,
              ContactID       smallint     NOT
              →NULL,
              EventAddress   varchar(25) NULL,
              City            varchar(25) NULL,
              ZipCode         varchar(15) NULL )
              ON Archive
```

4. Execute the query. Check the Object Browser to ensure the files were actually created. Execute `sp_help` with the table name to ensure that each table was appropriately created as follows:

```
sp_help Contacts
Go
sp_help Events
Go
sp_help EventArchive
Go
```

Note that by supplying the `ON` clause for the `EventArchive` table that the table was placed onto a separate filegroup whereas the other tables were placed onto the `PRIMARY` file group. Also notice the existence of the Primary Key and an associated clustered index.

3.3   Setting Up Referential Integrity

In Exercise 3.3, you alter the tables so that the Contact IDs of the `Event` table become Foreign Keys pointing to the Contact ID in the `Contacts` table.

Estimated Time: 5 minutes

1. If the SQL Query Analyzer is not already open, load it to allow for the creation of the tables. Supply the logon connection information if requested.

2. Select the `Sample` database created in the previous exercise from the database drop-down list box from the toolbar.

3. Type the following command to create the database and accompanying files:

```
ALTER TABLE Events
        ADD CONSTRAINT  FKEventContactID
            FOREIGN KEY (ContactID)
            REFERENCES Contacts(ContactID)

ALTER TABLE EventArchive
        ADD CONSTRAINT  FKArchContactID
            FOREIGN KEY (ContactID)
            REFERENCES Contacts(ContactID)
```

4. Execute the query. Check the Object Browser to ensure the constraints were actually created. Execute `sp_help` with the table name to ensure each table was modified correctly:

```
sp_help Events
Go
sp_help EventArchive
Go
```

Note that new constraints were added that reference the appropriate column in the `Contacts` table.

APPLY YOUR KNOWLEDGE

Review Questions

1. How would you design a set of tables in a circumstance where the deletion of one record should cause the deletion of records in related tables?

2. What are the storage considerations in an extremely limited budget? What basic configuration requirements would be set up to ensure optimum data recoverability in the event of data corruption?

3. How do you use SQL Server 2000 technologies to maintain data integrity?

4. If data and indexes are stored in two different filegroups, what considerations are there for performing backups?

5. For what purposes does the term "schema" apply?

Exam Questions

1. You are working for a large international organization that supplies packaging materials for companies that require custom commercial designs. The number of products is becoming too large for the current computer system to handle and you need to provide a solution that will spread the load over the current server and a new machine coming into the system. Queries need to be performed over a wide variety of products and there is no predictable pattern to the queries. What is an appropriate technique to implement the changes?

   A. Configure replication using the new machine as a subscriber and the original machine as the publisher/distributor to balance the workload.

   B. Separate the table into two smaller tables and place one table on each server. Configure a partitioned view and appropriate constraints on each of the machines.

   C. Implement multi-server clustering so that each of the two servers can respond to data activities, thus achieving a balanced workload.

   D. Configure log shipping on both servers to have a copy of the data on each of the servers and propagate all changes to the alternate machine.

2. As a developer for a large healthcare provider, you are assigned the task of developing a process for updating a patient database. When a patient is transferred from one floor to another, an internal identifier, `CurrentRoomID`, which is used as the Primary Key, needs to be altered while the original key, `AdmittanceRoomID`, is still maintained. If a patient is moved more than once, only the original key and the current key need to be maintained. Several underlying tables have been configured for referential integrity against the patient table. These underlying tables must change in an appropriate manner to match with one or the other of the room keys in the patient table. These relationships will be altered based upon different situations in other tables. Figure 3.11 illustrates the `PatientTracker` table design exhibit. What method would you use to accommodate the update?

   A. Use the Cascade Update Related Fields option to have changes in the Primary Key automatically update the keys in all referenced tables.

   B. Use an indexed view to enable the user to make changes to multiple tables concurrently.

PatientTracker

Column Name	Condensed Type	Nullable	Data Type	Length
CurrentRoomID	char(3)	NOT NULL	char	3
AdmittanceRoomID	char(3)	NOT NULL	char	3
PatientID	int	NOT NULL	int	4
BedID	tinyint	NOT NULL	tinyint	1

FIGURE 3.11
`PatientTracker` table design exhibit.

APPLY YOUR KNOWLEDGE

C. Disable the Enforce Relationship for INSERTs and DELETEs option to enable an AFTER TRIGGER to handle the necessary changes.

D. Define an INSTEAD OF UPDATE TRIGGER to perform the necessary updates to all related tables.

3. A large organization needs to maintain IMAGE data on a database server. The data is scanned in from documents received from the federal government. Updates to the images are infrequent. When a change occurs, usually the old row of data is archived out of the system and the new document takes its place. Other column information that contains key identifiers about the nature of the document is frequently queried by an OLAP system. Statistical information on how the data was queried is also stored in additional columns. The actual document itself is rarely needed except in processes that print the image. Which of the following represents an appropriate storage configuration?

A. Place the IMAGE data into a filegroup of its own, but on the same volume as the remainder of the data. Place the log onto a volume of its own.

B. Place all the data onto one volume in a single file. Configure the volume as a RAID parity set and place the log into a volume of its own.

C. Place the IMAGE onto one volume in a file of its own and place the data and log files together on a second volume.

D. Place the IMAGE into a separate filegroup with the log on one volume and the remainder of the data on a second volume.

4. You are the administrator of a SQL Server 2000 computer. The server contains your company's Accounts database. Hundreds of users access the database each day. You have been experiencing power interruptions, and you want to protect the physical integrity of the Accounts database. You do not want to slow down server operations. What should you do?

A. Enable the torn page detection database option for each database.

B. Disable write caching on all disk controllers.

C. Create a database maintenance plan to check database integrity and make repairs each night.

D. Ensure that the write caching disk controllers have battery backups.

5. An Internet company sells outdoor hardware online to over 100,000 clients in various areas of the globe. Servicing the web site is a SQL Server whose performance is barely adequate to meet the needs of the site. You would like to apply a business rule to the existing system that will limit the outstanding balance of each customer. The outstanding balance is maintained as a denormalized column within the customer table. Orders are collected in a second table containing a trigger that updates the customer balance based on INSERT, UPDATE, and DELETE activity. Up to this point, care has been taken to remove any data from the table if the client balance is too high, so all data should meet the requirements of your new process. How would you apply the new data check?

A. Modify the existing trigger so that an order that allows the balance to exceed the limit is not permitted.

B. Create a check constraint with the No Check option enabled on the `customer` table, so that any inappropriate order is refused.

C. Create a rule that doesn't permit an order that exceeds the limit and bind the rule to the `Orders` table.

D. Create a new trigger on the `Orders` table that refuses an order that causes the balance to exceed the maximum. Apply the new trigger to only INSERT and UPDATE operations.

6. An existing sales catalog database structure exists on a system within your company. The company sells inventory from a single warehouse location that is across town from where the computer systems are located. The product table has been created with a non-clustered index based on the product ID, which is also the Primary Key. Non-clustered indexes exist on the product category column and also the storage location column. Most of the reporting done is ordered by product category. How would you change the existing index structure?

A. Change the definition of the Primary Key so that it is a clustered index.

B. Create a new clustered index based on the combination of storage location and product category.

C. Change the definition of the product category so that it is a clustered index.

D. Change the definition of the storage location so that it is a clustered index.

7. You are the sole IT person working in a small branch office for a non-profit organization that deals with natural resource conservation issues. A non-critical database is maintained on the data-base server. You have been given the task of configuring appropriate database properties that would allow for a minimum use of execution time and storage resources. Which of the following set of properties is most appropriate?

A. Full Recovery, Auto Shrink, Torn Page Detection

B. Bulk Recovery, Auto Shrink, Single User

C. Simple Recovery, Auto Close, Auto Shrink

D. Simple Recovery, Auto Shrink, Single User

E. Bulk Recovery, Auto Close, Auto Shrink

8. You are designing an application that will provide data entry clerks the capability of updating the data in several tables. You would like to ease entry and provide common input so the clerks need not enter data into all fields or enter redundant values. What types of technologies could you use to minimize the amount of input needed? Select all that apply.

A. Foreign Key

B. Cascading Update

C. Identity Column

D. Default

E. NULL

F. Primary Key

G. Unique Index

9. A database that you are working on is experiencing reduced performance. The database is used almost exclusively for reporting, with a large number of inserts occurring on a regular basis. Data is cycled out of the system four times a year as part of quarter-ending procedures. It is always impor-

APPLY YOUR KNOWLEDGE

tant to be able to attain a point-in-time restoration process. You would like to minimize the maintenance needed to accommodate increases and decreases in file storage space. Which option would assist the most in accomplishing the task?

A. SIMPLE RECOVERY

B. AUTOSHRINK

C. MAXSIZE

D. AUTOGROW

E. COLLATE

10. You are the administrator of a SQL Server 2000 computer. The server contains a database named Inventory. Users report that several storage locations in the UnitsStored field contain negative numbers. You examine the database's table structure. You correct all the negative numbers in the table. You must prevent the database from storing negative numbers. You also want to minimize use of server resources and physical I/O. Which statement should you execute?

A. ALTER TABLE dbo.StorageLocations ADD
   ➡CONSTRAINT
   CK_StorageLocations_UnitsStored
   CHECK (UnitsStored >= 0)

B. CREATE TRIGGER CK_UnitsStored On
   ➡StorageLocations
   FOR INSERT, UPDATE AS
   IF INSERTED.UnitsStored < 0 ROLLBACK TRAN

C. CREATE RULE CK_UnitsStored As @Units >= 0
   GO
   sp_bindrule 'CK_UnitsStored'
   'StorageLocations.UnitsStored'
       GO

D. CREATE PROC UpdateUnitsStored
   (@StorageLocationID int, @UnitsStored
   ➡bigint) AS
   IF @UnitsStored < 0
   RAISERROR (50099, 17)

```
ELSE
UPDATE StorageLocations
SET UnitsStored = @UnitsStored
WHERE StorageLocationID =
➡@StorageLocationID
```

11. You are the administrator of a SQL Server 2000 computer. The server contains a database named Inventory. In this database, the Parts table has a Primary Key that is used to identify each part stored in the company's warehouse. Each part has a unique UPC code that your company's accounting department uses to identify it. You want to maintain the referential integrity between the Parts table and the OrderDetails table. You want to minimize the amount of physical I/O that is used within the database. Which two T-SQL statements should you execute? (Each correct answer represents part of the solution. Choose two.)

A. CREATE UNIQUE INDEX IX_UPC On Parts(UPC)

B. CREATE UNIQUE INDEX IX_UPC On
   ➡OrderDetails(UPC)

C. CREATE TRIGGER UPCRI On OrderDetails
   FOR INSERT, UPDATE As
   If Not Exists (Select UPC From Parts
   Where Parts.UPC = inserted.UPC) BEGIN
       ROLLBACK TRAN
   END

D. CREATE TRIGGER UPCRI On Parts
   FOR INSERT, UPDATE As
   If Not Exists (Select UPC From Parts
   Where OrderDetails.UPC = inserted.UPC)
   ➡BEGIN
       ROLLBACK TRAN
   END

E. ALTER TABLE dbo.OrderDetails ADD
   ➡CONSTRAINT
   FK_OrderDetails_Parts FOREIGN KEY(UPC)
   REFERENCES dbo.Parts(UPC)

F. ALTER TABLE dbo.Parts ADD CONSTRAINT
   FK_Parts_OrderDetails FOREIGN KEY (UPC)
   REFERENCES dbo.Parts(UPC)

APPLY YOUR KNOWLEDGE

12. You are the database developer for a leasing company. Your database includes a table that is defined as follows:

```
CREATE TABLE Lease
(Id Int IDENTITY NOT NULL
   CONSTRAINT pk_lesse_id PRIMARY KEY
➡NONCLUSTERED,
Lastname varchar(50) NOT NULL,
FirstName varchar(50) NOT NULL,
SSNo char(9) NOT NULL,
Rating char(10) NULL,
Limit money NULL)
```

Each SSNo must be unique. You want the data to be physically stored in SSNo sequence. Which constraint should you add to the SSNo column on the Lease table?

A. UNIQUE CLUSTERED constraint

B. UNIQUE UNCLUSTERED constraint

C. PRIMARY KEY CLUSTERED constraint

D. PRIMARY KEY UNCLUSTERED constraint

13. You are building a database and you want to eliminate duplicate entry and minimize data storage wherever possible. You want to track the following information for employees and managers: First name, middle name, last name, employee identification number, address, date of hire, department, salary, and name of manager. Which table design should you use?

A. Table1: EmpID, MgrID, Firstname, Middlename, Lastname, Address, Hiredate, Dept, Salary. Table2: MgrID, Firstname, Middlename, Lastname.

B. Table1: EmpID, Firstname, Middlename, Lastname, Address, Hiredate, Dept, Salary. Table2: MgrID, Firstname, Middlename, Lastname. Table3: EmpID, MgrID.

C. Table1: EmpID, MgrID, Firstname, Middlename, Lastname, Address, Hiredate, Dept, Salary.

D. Table1: EmpID, Firstname, Middlename, Lastname, Address, Hiredate, Dept, Salary. Table2: EmpID, MgrID Table3: MgrID.

14. You are developing an application and need to create an inventory table on each of the databases located in New York, Detroit, Paris, London, Los Angeles, and Hong Kong. To accommodate a distributed environment, you must ensure that each row entered into the inventory table is unique across all locations. How can you create the inventory table?

A. Supply Identity columns using a different sequential starting value for each location and use an increment of 6.

B. Use the identity function. At first location, use IDENTITY(1,1), at second location use IDENTITY(100000,1), and so on.

C. Use a Uniqueidentifier as the key at each location.

D. Use TIMESTAMP column as the key at each location.

15. You are building a new database for a company with ten departments. Each department contains multiple employees. In addition, each employee might work for several departments. How should you logically model the relationship between the department entity and the employee entity?

A. A mandatory one-to-many relationship between department and employee.

B. An optional one-to-many relationship between department and employee.

C. Create a new entry; create a one-to-many relationship from the employee to the new entry; and create a one-to-many relationship from the department entry to the new entry.

D. Create a new entry; create a one-to-many relationship from the new entry to the employee entry; then create a one-to-many relationship from the entry to the department entry.

Answers to Review Questions

1. Configuring a Cascading Delete Action causes the deletion of a record to propagate deletions throughout the underlying related table. This option should be configured with caution, because the deletion of underlying data might not be desired. You need to set two tables up in a parent-child relationship, using appropriate Primary and Foreign Keys. Cascading Update Action performs a similar operation when key values are changed, propagating the new values to underlying child tables.

2. First, put the log files onto a volume other than where the data is stored to ensure optimum recoverability. If possible, use a mirror on the OS volume to minimize downtime in a system failure. If the data volume becomes corrupt, a restore can be performed to get that data back. Having the log on a separate volume means that you can recover additional data because the log volume should be unaffected by the damage to the data.

3. Referential integrity is used to create a link between two related tables. A Foreign Key in one table references a Primary Key or unique index in the other table. Any entry to the table in which the Foreign Key resides must have a matching

record in the table containing the Primary Key. Rules, constraints, triggers, and defaults all participate in maintaining data integrity.

4. Both filegroups must be backed up within the same backup set whenever the indexes are separated from the data. Care must be taken so that the indexes always maintain pointers to the corresponding data.

5. In SQL Server, there are several uses of the term "schema." Information, Database, XML, and Warehouse all use schema to define the structure of elements, whether they be statistics, data dictionaries, data structures, or cube dimensions.

Answers to Exam Questions

1. **B.** This is a perfect example of where partitioning a table into two smaller objects enables you to use two machines to help reduce the load on the overall application. Remember that failover clustering is the only form of clustering supported by SQL and therefore does not actually reduce the load; it only assists in obtaining an around-the-clock operation. Log shipping assists in offloading query load, but does little to reduce update load because it leaves the second server in a read-only state. Merge replication may enable updates to span many servers, but the associated overhead and data latency makes it a less than desirable alternative. For more information, see "Partitioning to Achieve a Balance."

2. **D.** The INSTEAD OF trigger was designed specifically for this type of situation and also to handle complicated updates where columns are defined as Timestamp, Calculated, or Identity. Cascade operations are inappropriate because the updated key is not always stored. Indexed views by themselves do not allow for the type of alteration

APPLY YOUR KNOWLEDGE

desired and would have to be complemented with the actions of a trigger. Disabling referential integrity is a poor solution to any problem, especially considering the medical nature of this application and the possible ramifications. For more information, see "Trigger Utilization."

3. **D.** Because the IMAGE data will seldom be accessed, it makes sense to get the remainder of the data away from the images while moving the log away from the data. This will help to improve performance while providing optimum recoverability in the event of a failure. For more information, see "Using Filegroups."

4. **D.** Good controllers suitable for database use will have a battery backup. The battery should be regularly tested under controlled circumstances. Disabling caching if currently in place is likely to affect performance, as will enabling torn page detection. Torn page detection might help point out whether data is being corrupted because of failures. A maintenance plan is recommended, although it is not an entire solution in its own right.

5. **A.** Because a trigger is already in place, it can easily be altered to perform the additional data check. A rule cannot provide the required functionality because you cannot compare the data. The CHECK constraint may be a viable solution but you would have to alter the trigger to check for an error and provide for nested operations. The number of triggers firing should be kept to a minimum. To accommodate additional triggers, you would have to check the order in which they are being fired and again set properties of the server and database accordingly. For more information, see "Trigger Utilization."

6. **C.** Because the majority of the reporting is going to be performed using the storage location, it

would be the likely candidate. The clustered index represents the physical order of the data and would minimize sorting operations when deriving the output. For more information, see "Index Organization."

7. **C.** Simple Recovery uses the least amount of log space for recording changes to the database. Full recovery uses the most space because it fully logs any bulk operations. Bulk recovery represents a mid-point between the two. Auto Close frees up resources at the earliest possible point during process execution, and Auto Shrink minimizes the space used in the file system by periodically reducing the files when there is too much unused space. For more information, see "Use of Recovery Models."

8. **B, C, D, E.** All these options have activities that provide or alter data so that it does not have to be performed as an entry operation. In the case of NULL, data need not be provided, possibly because the column contains non-critical information. For more information, see "Table Characteristics."

9. **D.** Use AUTOGROW to set the system so that the files will grow as needed for the addition of new data. You may want to perform a planned shrinkage of the database as part of the quarter-ending process and save on overhead by leaving the AUTOSHRINK option turned off. For more information, see "Creating Database Files and Filegroups."

10. **A.** You need to add a constraint to prevent negative data entry. The best method of implementing this functionality is a constraint. A trigger has too much overhead and the RULE is not accurately implemented. A procedure could handle the process but is normally only used for processes requiring more complex logic. For more information, see "Table Characteristics."

APPLY YOUR KNOWLEDGE

11. **A, E.** The UNIQUE constraint on the Parts table UPC column is required first, so that the FOREIGN KEY constraint can be applied from the OrderDetails.UPC column referencing Parts.UPC. This achieves the referential integrity requirement. It also reduces I/O required during joins between Parts and OrderDetails, which make use of the FOREIGN KEY constraint defined. For more information, see "Maintaining Referential Integrity."

12. **A.** To obtain the physical storage sequence of the data, you must use a clustered constraint or index. Although a Primary Key would also provide for the level of uniqueness, it is not the desired key for this table. For more information, see "Unique Indexing" in Chapter 10.

13. **C.** A single table could provide all the necessary information with no redundancy. The table could

easily be represented using a self-join operation to provide the desired reporting. Join operations will be discussed in detail in the next chapter.

14. **A.** Using identities in this fashion enables records to be entered that have no overlap. One location would use entry values 1, 7, 13, 19; the next would have 2, 8, 14, 20; the third 3, 9, 15, 21, and so on. For more information, see "Application of Integrity Options."

15. **C.** This is a many-to-many relationship scenario, which in SQL Server is implemented using three tables. The center table, often referred to as the connecting or joining table, is on the many side of both of the relationships to the other base table. For more information, see "Maintaining Referential Integrity."

Suggested Readings and Resources

1. Inside SQL Server 2000 – Kalen Delaney (www.insidesqlserver.com)

Not a beginner book, but it fills in many of the gaps left out of the SQL Server Books Online documentation. Explains fully how SQL Server stores and processes data internally.

2. SQL Server 2000 Books Online

   • Creating and Maintaining Databases (Look particularly at the sections on indexes, views, and triggers.)

   • Transact-SQL Reference (Use this as a resource for the specific syntax requirements of each statement, as well as some code examples.)

   • Optimizing Database Performance (Focus on Database and Application Design.)

   • Troubleshooting: Server and Database Troubleshooting

3. MSDN Online Internet Reference (http://msdn.microsoft.com)

   • Transact SQL Overview (/library/psdk/sql/ts_tsqlcon_6lyk.htm)

   • Transact SQL Syntax Conventions (/library/psdk/sql/ts_syntaxc_9kvn.htm)

   • Transact SQL Tips (/library/psdk/sql/ac_8_qd_14_2kc3.htm)

Retrieve data by using Transact-SQL.

▶ This objective requires you to know how to access data in different ways, providing for different "looks" into the data with user-friendly views and other reporting methods from the data source.

Filter data by using Transact-SQL.

▶ You don't often want all the data from the tables. Usually queries want to limit the number of columns and rows displayed from the database. You need to limit and specifically apply conditions over the data that is transmitted to the user interface.

Summarize data by using Transact-SQL.

▶ A database system needs to generate other information beyond just the data. Arithmetic, statistical analysis, and other operations are needed in a full-service database implementation.

Modify data by using Transact-SQL.

▶ This objective requires you to also know how to modify existing data in a table using statements such as UPDATE.

CHAPTER 4

Querying and Modifying Data

STUDY STRATEGIES

► This chapter is one you need to fully understand. Try reading this chapter more than once if needed.

► Be sure to follow the Step by Steps because practical work in this chapter is exceptionally vital. After reading through this chapter, practice creating queries using all the functions and methods mentioned in this chapter.

INTRODUCTION

After data is in the database, it is inevitable that the data will need to be accessed, changed, and reported on. To perform these basic operations, you need to be able to apply the programming constructs of Structured Query Language (SQL)—specifically, Microsoft's implementation referred to as Transact-SQL (T-SQL).

Understanding how to access and modify data is vital for any developer, beginner, or expert. This chapter discusses the not-so-tough topics of querying and modifying data, and then proceeds to the more advanced topics of data retrieval and modification.

DATA RETRIEVAL

Two utilities are built into SQL Server to allow for the interactive use of T-SQL. SQL Query Analyzer and the OSQL utility support using T-SQL interactively to view, process, and modify data. A third utility, the BCP utility, could be used to import or export large amounts of data.

SQL Query Analyzer and OSQL are used to:

◆ Execute T-SQL statements.

◆ Save the resultsets in a file.

◆ Show the results of a query to the user.

With SQL Query Analyzer, you can connect concurrently to numerous instances of SQL Server. However, the OSQL and BCP utilities enable you to work with only one instance at a time.

Queries in SQL Server refer to a set of T-SQL statements that are issued to the database to retrieve data. The most common method of data retrieval is using the SELECT T-SQL statement. The SELECT statement is the basis for the majority of the activity performed in data retrieval. It is the first statement for a SQL developer to master, as its use is varied and can involve many options.

The SQL *SELECT* Statement

Using the T-SQL SELECT statement is the most common way of accessing data. The majority of all data retrieval statements begins with these four fundamental parts of a SELECT operation:

◆ SELECT. Specifies the columns from the tables that need to be retrieved.

◆ FROM. Specifies where the table(s) and the columns are located.

◆ WHERE. Specifies a condition in order to filter data down.

◆ ORDER BY. Specifies how you want to order the data after it's been retrieved.

The following code illustrates the use of the standard clauses within a SELECT query:

```
EXAMPLE: SELECT * FROM Northwind.dbo.CUSTOMERS
              ORDER BY CompanyName
              (* retrieves all columns)
```

SELECT statements can be made very complex with the use of options that can join many tables together and with functions that can calculate and summarize data at the same time. SELECT statements also can often be as simple as one line of code that retrieves the requested data. The complete SELECT syntax is very involved with many optional portions. The complete syntax reference can be found in SQL Server Books Online (BOL) under "SELECT, SELECT (described)." Many of the options are used only under special circumstances. Take the following one-line code, for instance. Notice the simplicity required to code it and also note that at least the first two sub-statements are specified.

```
SELECT * FROM Pubs.dbo.AUTHORS
```

This statement retrieves all columns and rows from the authors table in the Pubs database.

The SELECT statement's syntax is relatively simple as shown in the following:

```
Select [all|distinct] columnlist
From tablelist
Where condition(s)
OrderBy columnname type
```

The descriptions for the arguments are shown in Table 4.1

TABLE 4.1	

THE ARGUMENTS OF THE BASIC SELECT STATEMENT

Argument	Description
All	Optional. Returns all rows, whether unique or not. This is the default.
Distinct	Optional. Selects only unique rows.
Column list	Required. The name of the column(s) you want to retrieve from the tables or * for all columns.
Table list	Required. Specifies in which table(s) the columns are stored. In cases of joins, you may have more than one table specified.
Where condition	Optional. These are conditions that limit the number of rows returned
Order By	Optional. This is a statement that tells how the resultset will be shown. This can be ordered as either ascending (ASC) or descending (DESC).

The first portion of the SELECT statement identifies which columns are going to come from table list. When specifying column names, be sure to use a comma-delimited list and don't place a comma after the final column name. When specifying column names, you can use an asterisk (*), designating that all columns are to be returned from the specified table or tables.

For example, if you created a table named Product with three columns—Product_ID, Name, and Price—and selected all columns from this table using the asterisk symbol, your resultset would first display the Product_ID column, then the Name column, and finally the Price column. When the asterisk is not used, however, columns are automatically rearranged in the output based on how you arrange the columns in the column list.

Anytime you create a data retrieval query, you have to specify where the data is coming from immediately after you specify which columns you want to access. When specifying table names in the SELECT statement, you may include one or more to collect information from more than one table. For example, examine the following basic query:

```
SELECT au_id, au_fname FROM Pubs.dbo.Authors
```

NOTE

Starting to Code   Note the naming convention used to supply table names. Four part names, Server.Owner.Database.Object, are discussed in Chapter 3. If the database you are using is already set, then you need not supply the database name or owner name. Before you try any of these examples, make sure the database is Pubs. To do this, type **USE PUBS** before the first query or select the Pubs database from the drop-down list box at the top of the Query Analyzer.

EXAM TIP

Faster Data Access   If retrieving data seems to take forever, a good idea may be to implement an indexing strategy. Chapter 10 discusses indexes, including index implementation.

This query selects the au_id and au_fname columns from the Authors table residing in the Pubs database. Notice that the column names au_id and au_fname were delimited with a comma. The example was just a basic query, which could have been made much more complex. You may want to filter the data, perhaps to select all authors with first names having the letter P, or only those authors living in California. This example could have even been more basic if you used an asterisk in the column selection sub-statement, which would select all columns from the Authors table.

Also, notice that the columns in the resultset, in the lower pane of the analyzer, were organized in the way they were specified in the column select list; that is, au_id was first displayed and then au_fname.

Changing Column Headers

Part of delivering a sound application in a business environment is development that provides a user-friendly interface for accessing the database. By default, the column headers that are displayed in the resultset are the same as the columns specified in the column select list, such as au_id and au_fname. But why not change this column header to a more understandable title? You can alias a column header without problem and in doing so increase the readability of the data. You can change the name of a resultset column by specifying the keyword AS, this being the traditional SQL-92 ANSI standard. Changing the column name with an equals sign (=) or implied assignment is also an alternative syntax choice.

IN THE FIELD

SQL-92 SYNTAX

SQL-92 ANSI standard coding mechanism is the method of choice when you are presented with syntax alternatives. SQL-92 standards are universally accepted by most SQL data engines.

Column names should be changed in cases where they are not user friendly. A good example is au_id. You could change this into a more readable column such as Author's ID. Even though T-SQL is Microsoft's implementation of SQL and does allow for a variety of syntax choices, the method usually selected by experienced developers is ANSI SQL-92. The AS option is used more frequently because it fits the ANSI SQL standard. The way in which you change a column header to an alias is as follows:

```
SELECT Au_id AS 'Author ID' FROM Authors.
```

The original column name is Au_id and the alias assigned to the column is 'Author ID'. The alias certainly provides for a much more meaningful heading. This alias can also be used as a means of renaming a column under a view definition.

There actually is no difference in using the equals assignment except that this method was introduced in a more recent version of SQL. Use the equals assignment as follows:

```
SELECT 'Author ID'=Au_id, 'First Name'= Au_fname,
'Last Name'=Au_lname FROM Authors
```

String Concatenation

Sometimes you need to show two columns as one by combining two columns together. When you do this, you are using a method called *string concatenation.* Concatenation can be thought of as joining strings together just as you can combine words into phrases. When done in a more involved application, concatenation can provide the means for taking individual string elements and combining them together as T-SQL syntax.

The operator used to perform the concatenation is the plus (+) sign. One reason to concatenate two columns together might be, for example, when you want to have a column named Full Name, which is created by combining both the last name and first name values. The only way you could combine the two columns is to use concatenation. For additional readabilty, insert a comma as follows:

```
SELECT Au_lname + ', ' + Au_fname As 'Full Name'
FROM Authors
```

This query concatenates the au_lname and au_fname columns to produce a new Full Name column with the name in the format "Smith, John." If you've programmed in Visual Basic before, this operator is equivalent to the ampersand (&).

As you can see, more than two strings can be concatenated together. Another example of concatenation occurs when you want to create an address column that combines the zip, state, and street of a person. At other times concatenation is used to create a code, such as in a magazine subscription identifier.

NOTE

Specifying AS   It is not mandatory for you to explicitly specify AS. The same resultset could have been generated using an implied assignment without including AS, as follows:

```
Select Au_id 'Author ID',
➥Au_fname 'First Name',
➥Au_lname 'Last Name'
➥From Authors
```

NOTE

Quotation Mark Usage   As you probably have already noticed, most column aliases have been enclosed with single quotation marks. This enclosure needs to be made when the column alias includes spaces. The alias name needs to be enclosed with brackets when the alias is a reserved SQL Server keyword.

The *DISTINCT* Keyword

A time may come where you will need to view or not view distinct records. Use of DISTINCT eliminates duplicate rows of any resultset. A SELECT query may return records with equal values, but using DISTINCT eliminates duplicates and leaves only singular values in the resultset. You might use the DISTINCT keyword when you need to know only whether a value exists, rather than how many records of a value exist. See Figure 4.1 for a contrast between listing all data values and DISTINCT data values.

This DISTINCT option, when specified, selects only the values that are unique throughout a pertaining row. The following statement selects all authors' states that are unique throughout the Authors table in the Pubs database. The finished resultset provides a list of states represented by the authors. No state would be listed more than once.

```
SELECT DISTINCT State FROM Authors
```

The DISTINCT keyword is optional with SUM, AVG, and COUNT. When DISTINCT is used, duplicate values are eliminated before the sum, average, or count is calculated.

At some point you may want to use DISTINCT on just one column of a resultset. If you really think about it for a while, it's clear that this doesn't really make sense, at least not without using aggregate functions for the other columns. Remember—the use of the keyword DISTINCT applies to the entire row, not just some columns.

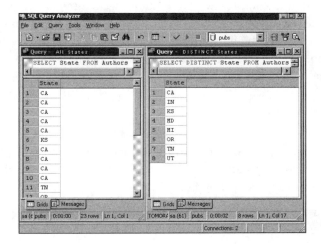

FIGURE 4.1
Limiting data to DISTINCT data values.

FROM Which Table?

When running any data retrieval query, it is compulsory to specify where the data is coming from. Specifying which tables are going to be accessed can be done with the FROM clause. FROM table lists do not necessarily have to be just standard tables. It is also valid to specify derived tables, joined tables, views, user-defined functions that return tables, and system functions that return tables.

A derived table is a subquery that retrieves rows from the database. A SELECT clause within a FROM clause of another SELECT, referred to by an alias, produces a derived table. The resulting rows take on a similar construct to that of a standard table.

Joined tables are used when you would like to combine records from multiple sources. Joining is a process whereby you can retrieve data from two or more tables based on logical relationships between the tables. Joining is discussed in detail later in Chapter 5.

The name of a view is often substituted for a table name. A view is stored as a query on the server and often provides necessary column restrictions and application considerations that makes it a beneficial data source. Views are discussed in detail in Chapter 7, "Working with Views."

User-defined functions can generate recordset output and in that form be used in place of a table name. A function can declare an internal table variable, insert rows into the variable, and then return the variable as its return value.

A class of user-defined functions known as in-line functions return the resultset of a SELECT statement as a variable of type table. User-defined functions are complex programming mechanisms that are covered in full in Chapter 9, "Stored Procedures and User-Defined Functions."

System functions often generate a set of records that can be envisioned as a table. These rowset functions return an object that can be used in place of a table reference in a T-SQL statement.

To increase the readability of queries, you can use table aliases similar to column aliases. Table aliases, however, are different. First, they are used to alias table names, and second, they don't make the user-interface more readable. Table aliases benefit the developer and save time as well as provide other coding benefits. Look at the following example:

```
Use Pubs
SELECT a.Au_id, a.Au_fname
FROM Authors AS a
```

It is also possible to have multiple table aliases assigned in the FROM statement. This is a very common practice to ease coding of columns from a variety of sources. It is also used in joining tables to provide more definition to the join operation. When using data from two or more tables, each table alias assignment is used in a prefix within the column list to ensure data pointers are defined to the correct table source:

```
SELECT a.Au_id, ta.Title_id FROM Authors AS a
INNER JOIN TitleAuthor AS ta
ON a.Au_id = ta.Au_id
```

This query selects Author ID from the Authors table and Title ID from the TitleAuthor table and groups them into one resultset. Joins are discussed in detail in Chapter 5. This is a powerful feature, especially when you need to create summary data. You can gather up the important information into a single resultset so that it can be coded more easily than it would be if you had to use the full table name as a prefix for every column name.

Data is displayed unconditionally for the columns selected, except in instances where data rows have been filtered by a HAVING or WHERE condition, or a JOIN operation that limits the rows.

The *WHERE* Clause

Now that you've seen the SELECT column list and FROM clause, it's time to move on to the additional optional specifications that enable you to further control what data is displayed. The WHERE clause is an optional specification that is used to limit the number of rows in the resultset based on defined restrictions. Restrictions are specified as conditional arguments, such as Salary>10000, LastName LIKE 'G%', or State = 'FL'. See "Filtering Data," later in this chapter.

Most SELECT statements are used to display several columns of data from a table, which requires that conditions be met pertinent to the application. The general SELECT, FROM, and WHERE format is illustrated in Step by Step 4.1:

STEP BY STEP

4.1 Displaying Data with the *SELECT* Statement

1. If it is not already open, load the SQL Query Analyzer. Supply the logon connection information if requested.

2. Across the top panel you will find a drop-down list box with which you can select the current database. From the drop-down menu select the `Northwind` database.

3. Enter the following query and Execute using F5 or the Execute key in the toolbar:

```
SELECT * FROM Customers
```

4. Use the following code to change the query so that the customer list is limited to only those customers whose names begin with *A*:

```
SELECT * FROM Customers WHERE CustomerID LIKE 'A%'
```

5. Execute the query and observe the results.

The WHERE clause is always executed first to discover which rows should be looked at before other operations needed by a given SELECT clause. This acts as a layer of filtration in a basic SELECT query. The WHERE clause is easy to use, yet is very powerful. There is considerable benefit in creating resultsets to be used in reports. Many operators can be used in conjunction with the WHERE clause to provide completely flexible filtration.

The WHERE and HAVING clauses in a SELECT statement control the rows from the source tables that are used to build the resultset. WHERE and HAVING are filters. They specify a series of search conditions, and only those rows that meet the terms of the search conditions are used to build the result set. HAVING is discussed later in Chapter 5, "Advanced Data Retrieval and Modification." To address it now would require that you first understand grouping of data, which falls out of the immediate scope of discussion.

After data selection has been determined, the actual data sent is ready for an ordering process if one has been defined. The ordering of data is optional and if it is not present in a request, the data is sent in an order determined at the data source.

ORDER Data

Putting data in order provides for a more meaningful display of data and enables the data to be presented in a manner that meets additional reporting requirements set by most front-end applications. The ORDER BY clause tells SQL to sort the data before returning it in a resultset. Step by Step 4.2 shows you how to place a list into alphabetical order.

STEP BY STEP

4.2 Ordering Data in a List

1. If not already open, load the SQL Query Analyzer. Supply the logon connection information if requested.

2. From the drop-down menu select the Northwind database.

3. Enter the following query and execute using F5 or the Execute key in the toolbar:

   SELECT * FROM Customers

4. Change the query so that the customer list is placed into alphabetical order by the Contact Name using the following code:

   SELECT * FROM Customers ORDER BY ContactName ASC

5. Execute the query and observe the results.

ORDER BY determines the sequence of data based on column(s) selected and sequencing requested: ascending (ASC) or descending (DESC). Descending orders rows from highest to lowest; ascending orders rows from lowest to highest.

The ORDER BY clause can include columns not mentioned in the SELECT list. There is no limit to the number of items in the ORDER BY clause; however, there is a limit of 8,060 bytes. The following is an example of its elementary use:

```
SELECT Au_fname
FROM Pubs.dbo.Authors
ORDER BY Au_id DESC
```

NOTE: **ASC/DESC** In the sample query the order is identified as ASC (Ascending). ASC is the default and can be optionally provided with the command. DESC must be provided if a descending sequence is desired.

NOTE: **Ordering NULL Values** When you are ordering rows that contain null values, the null-valued records are displayed first, provided that the default sort order is used (ASC).

Basic conditions and sequences used in the standard query can be greatly enhanced over what you have seen thus far. But you need this initial understanding of the rudiments of the language if you are going to use advanced features appropriately.

The Basic *SELECT* Statement

You have looked at the content of the basic element SELECT within the realm of T-SQL. Elements used in this command are useful in learning the concepts of the other commands and SQL elements. Many of the concepts of the SELECT statement can be applied in other statements.

The SELECT options must always be used in the correct sequence, which can be summarized by use of the anagram, S F W G H O C (Select From Where Group Having Order Compute). A mechanism I have used for years goes somewhat like this:

Some Funny Walrus Goes Hysterical Over CocaCola

Similar humorous statements have been constant reminders of correct syntax over the years. Nevertheless, the appropriate use of each of these options making up the seven letters in the acronym are crucial to the use of SQL Server.

You have learned about SELECT, FROM, WHERE, and ORDER in this section, and this chapter provides additional information on how to further use these options as you read ahead. GROUP BY, HAVING, and COMPUTE (BY) are discussed in detail in Chapter 5, "Advanced Data Retrieval and Modification."

FILTERING AND FORMATTING DATA

▶ **Filter data by using Transact-SQL.**

Formatting of data can be performed in T-SQL through a variety of statements, functions, and command options where the filtering of data is a much more basic concept. This unit is therefore separated into two basic divisions to cover what this objective entails. Formatting involves making the data look better and more meaningful to the end user. Filtering, on the other hand, is for determining the data to be selected based upon conditional requirements.

If you are going to understand this very broad objective, the first thing to do is to ask the most basic of questions: What is a comparison? A comparison involves taking two or more values, presenting them against each other and through a defined logical statement determining the winners and losers from the matchups. Essentially, the comparison comes down to a Boolean expression that has three possible outcomes. If two values are compared, the Boolean result is either positive, negative, or equal (greater than, less than, or equal to).

Filtering Data

Operators play an important part in determining the content of any conditional operations. An *operator* is a symbol specifying an action that is performed on one or more expressions. In SQL Server these operators are divided into a few elementary categories:

◆ Comparison operators

◆ Arithmetic operators

◆ Logical operators

◆ Assignment operators

◆ String concatenation operators

◆ Bitwise operators

◆ Unary operators

Each operator category represents a piece of functionality that provides many operators. In some instances there are several dozen operator choices.

Comparison Operators

Comparison operators can be used in conjunction with the WHERE and HAVING clauses to ensure filtration in a number of ways. Comparison operators can be used with character, numeric, or date data expressions. Table 4.2 lists all comparison operators that are valid in SQL Server.

TABLE 4.2

COMPARISON OPERATORS

Operator	Meaning
<	Less then
>	Greater than
=	Equal to
<=	Less than or equal to
>=	Greater than or equal to
!=	Not equal to
<>	Not equal to
!<	Not less than
!>	Not greater than

The following is an example of using comparison operators:

```
SELECT * FROM  Pubs.dbo.Publishers
WHERE Pub_id>9000
```

Step by Step 4.3 shows you how to use the comparison operators.

STEP BY STEP

4.3 Basic Comparisons

1. If it is not already open, load the SQL Query Analyzer. Supply the logon connection information if requested and select the Northwind database.

2. Enter a standard general query to test by entering and executing the following:

```
SELECT OrderID, CustomerID, OrderDate FROM Orders
```

3. Change and execute the query so that customers are shown for only OrderID greater than 11,000:

```
SELECT OrderID, CustomerID, OrderDate FROM Orders
 WHERE OrderID > 11000
```

4. Change and execute the query so that customers are shown for only `OrderID` less than 11,000:

```
SELECT OrderID, CustomerID, OrderDate FROM Orders
 WHERE OrderID < 11000
```

5. Change the query so that customers are shown for only `OrderID` greater than 11,000 yet less than 11,010:

```
SELECT OrderID, CustomerID, OrderDate FROM Orders
       WHERE OrderID > 11000 AND OrderID < 11010
```

You are not restricted to the use of only numeric data with comparison operators. You can also set up a comparison between character data and date data.

Examine the following query:

```
SELECT * from Authors
WHERE State='CA'
```

This returns all authors who live in the state of California.

Whereas comparison operators evaluate the differences between two or more values, arithmetic operators aid in processing mathematical functions against values.

Arithmetic Operators

Arithmetic operators perform mathematical operations on two expressions of any of the data types of the numeric data type category. For more information about data type categories, see Transact-SQL Syntax Conventions in SQL Server Books OnLine. A complete listing of the available arithmetic operators and their uses is shown in Table 4.3.

TABLE 4.3

ARITHMETIC OPERATORS

Operator	Meaning
+ (Add)	Addition
– (Subtract)	Subtraction
* (Multiply)	Multiplication
/ (Divide)	Division
% (Modulo)	Returns the integer remainder of a division

The plus (+) and minus (–) can also be used to perform arithmetic operations on date values.

Arithmetic operators help perform mathematical operations and have other similar uses in performing statistical operations. Logical operators act against values in a manner that provides for the implementation of multiple conditions.

Logical Operators

Logical operators, also known as Boolean operators, can also be used within the queries you execute. The three logical operators are AND, OR, and NOT. Their meanings are pretty straightforward: AND adds an additional filter condition to the one specified and returns TRUE only when both or all conditions specified are met. The OR logical operator adds another filter condition to the existing condition as well, but returns TRUE when either condition is met. NOT tells SQL to get everything in the query except for what it has specified. Here is an example of using AND, NOT, and OR:

```
SELECT title_id,type, advance
FROM titles
WHERE (type='business' or type= 'psychology')
AND NOT advance>5500
```

This query selects only records that are business-type or records that are psychology-type, both having an advance value not greater then 5500.

Note the parentheses around the type condition. They indicate that you want the AND NOT condition to apply to both types. If you wrote:

```
WHERE type = 'business' or type= 'psychology' AND NOT
➥advance>5500
```

You would get only psychology books where the advance is greater than 5,500. A contrasting use of the logical operators is shown in Figure 4.2.

Brackets can significantly alter the results of operations that use logical operators. Test all conditions and alter the precedence by using brackets. According to the order of operations, bracketed comparisons are performed first. The logical operators are evaluated in the order: ( ) first, then NOT, AND, and finally OR.

FIGURE 4.2

Comparison and contrast of logical operators.

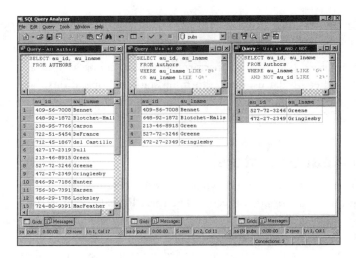

BETWEEN and *IN*

Ranges can also be specified when using the WHERE clause with the help of the BETWEEN keyword. Simply put, BETWEEN provides a range of values within which the data should lie; otherwise, the data does not meet the condition. BETWEEN is inclusive, meaning that the range includes the lower value specified and the upper value specified. The syntax in BETWEEN must be loval and hival, it does *not* work as expected if the hival is placed first in the expression.

Here is an example of how BETWEEN is used:

```
SELECT title_id, ytd_sales FROM titles
WHERE ytd_sales BETWEEN 1000 AND 11999
```

Remember, the values are inclusive.

You can also incorporate something known as a list when using the WHERE clause. Essentially, a list specifies the exact values a column may or may not take. If the record does not contain the value for the column specified in the IN list, it is not selected. IN determines whether a given value matches a set of values listed. For example:

```
SELECT state
FROM Authors
WHERE state IN ( 'TN', 'UT')
```

This example limits the values of state to only UT and TN. Authors that live in the states mentioned in the IN list will be the only ones listed. The next section talks about using the LIKE clause to perform wildcard searches, a further add-on to the WHERE clause. The use of IN is similar to that of EXISTS.

When a subquery is introduced with the keyword EXISTS, it functions as an existence test. The WHERE clause of the outer query tests for the existence of rows returned by the subquery. The subquery does not actually produce any data; it returns a value of TRUE or FALSE. The following is an example of the use of EXISTS to find only those publishers in the United States.

```
SELECT DISTINCT pub_name
FROM Pubs.dbo.Publishers
WHERE EXISTS
    (SELECT *
    FROM titles
    WHERE Pub_id = Publishers.Pub_id
    AND Country = 'USA')
```

IN THE FIELD

BETWEEN versus *IN*

If you had the choice of using either the BETWEEN or IN keyword, the BETWEEN keyword should usually be used. If the range includes lots of data with different values, BETWEEN is a lot more efficient.

Using the *LIKE* Clause

You can retrieve rows that are based on portions of character strings by using the LIKE predicate. The LIKE predicate determines whether a given character string matches a specified pattern. The types of data a LIKE statement can work with are char, varchar, nvarchar, nchar, datetime, smalldatetime, and text. A pattern specified in the LIKE predicate can include regular characters and wildcard characters. An example of the output generated using LIKE is given in Figure 4.3.

During pattern matching, regular characters must exactly match the characters specified in the column value. Wildcard characters can be matched with any character or set of characters according to the wildcard character used, as shown in Table 4.4.

The general syntax in which you submit a LIKE-style query is as follows:

```
Expression to be matched [NOT] LIKE pattern
```

Patterns to be matched are dependant on the wildcard operators that are used.

FIGURE 4.3
Using the LIKE predicate.

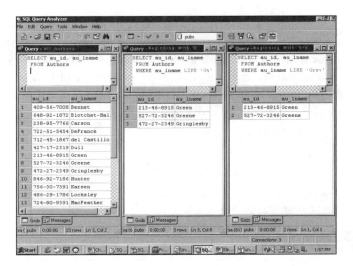

TABLE 4.4

THE WILDCARD CHARACTERS ALLOWED IN T-SQL

Character	Meaning
[ ]	Any one single character within the specified range ([f-j]) or set ([fghij])
_ (underscore)	Any one single character
%	Any number of zero or more characters
[^]	Any single character not in the specified range or set

The following example of how to use the LIKE clause uses the % wildcard to select all titles from the titles table where there is a character string match for 'computer'. (Full-text indexing could perform this search more efficiently if available; you should avoid LIKE searches that have a % wildcard at both the beginning and end.)

```
SELECT title
FROM titles
WHERE title LIKE '%computer%'
```

The following example uses the '[ ]' wildcard:

```
SELECT Au_id from Authors
WHERE Au_id LIKE '[0-2]%'
```

You can also use the NOT keyword with the LIKE predicate, which simply retrieves a query that does *not* contain records matching the specified elements in the LIKE clause. With character matching it is

---

WARNING

Full-Text Search   If your application repeatedly calls the LIKE predicate and performs numerous wildcard searches, you should consider using the MS Search Service if it is installed and in use on the server. Consider the value of the response time over the storage resources that the MS Search Service and full-text search capabilities require. MS Search Service is required to use full-text search. Full-text search allows you a variety of powerful wildcard searches. Full-text search is discussed later in Chapter 10.

sometimes more efficient to exclude characters with the use of NOT. It is common to use a negative test in particular when looking for values that represent true data, as in NOT NULL.

Selecting Rows Based on *NULL* Values

Before you can look at selecting and not selecting NULL values, you must understand what a NULL value is. A NULL value is a value given to a field that that has no value. Many people confuse NULL values with zero-length strings or the value zero, but such is not the case. NULL is just a fancy word for a value that is unknown.

In SQL Server, you can select the desired NULL values or reject them using IS NULL or IS NOT NULL. Don't enclose NULL in quotes because it is a keyword. Enclosing NULL in quotes would produce a character match for 'N', 'U', 'L', 'L', and not a NULL value. Look at the following example:

```
SELECT State FROM Pubs.dbo.Authors
WHERE State IS NOT NULL
```

As you have already noticed, this query selects all records where the State field is NOT NULL. NULL behaves in a different manner with regular comparison operators, (>, <, =, and so on). This behavior depends on the ANSI connection settings for the session.

When SET ANSI_NULLS is ON, a comparison in which one or more of the expressions is NULL returns UNKNOWN as the result of the comparison. A value that is not known cannot be compared against another value. Use the IS NULL or IS NOT NULL instead to test for NULL values. T-SQL does support an extension of the traditional behavior that allows for comparison operators to return TRUE or FALSE as a comparison result. If you set ANSI_NULLS OFF, comparisons to NULL return TRUE when the value being compared against is also a null. The comparison returns FALSE for any other value. Regardless of the ANSI_NULLS setting, NULL values are always considered equal for the purposes of the ORDER BY, GROUP BY, and DISTINCT keywords.

Returning *TOP* rows

Returning limited entries to only a few records is possible in T-SQL. You may, for instance, need to select the top three people in the school or maybe only return the top ten bestsellers; whatever the case may be, it can be accomplished. Use the following process shown in Step by Step 4.4 to return the highest and lowest values:

STEP BY STEP

4.4 Selecting TOP data

1. If it is not already open, load the SQL Query Analyzer. Supply the logon connection information if requested and select the Northwind database.

---

2. Enter a standard general query to test by entering and executing the following:

```
SELECT OrderID, CustomerID, OrderDate FROM Orders
 ORDER BY OrderDate ASC
```

---

3. Change and execute the query so that only the five earliest orders are shown:

```
SELECT TOP 5 OrderID, CustomerID, OrderDate FROM
➥Orders
 ORDER BY OrderDate ASC
```

---

4. Change and execute the query so that only the 5 most recent orders are displayed:

```
SELECT TOP 5 OrderID, CustomerID, OrderDate FROM
➥Orders
 ORDER BY OrderDate DESC
```

Limiting your selection to only a few records is made possible by the TOP clause. The TOP clause limits the number of rows returned in the resultset to a specified number or percentage.

TOP is generally simple and may be accomplished with the following syntax:

```
TOP n [percent]
```

In this syntax, *n* is a number that specifies how many rows are returned. If additionally [percent] is specified, *n* is the percent of rows that are to be returned in the resultset. Examine the following queries:

```
Select top 50 - returns the top 50 rows

Select top 50 percent - returns the top 50 percent of the
➥result-set rows

If a SELECT statement that includes TOP also has an ORDER
➥BY clause, the rows to be returned are selected from the
➥ordered result set. Look at the following example:SELECT
➥TOP 5 Au_fname
```

```
FROM Pubs.dbo.Authors
ORDER BY Au_fname
```

There is, however, an alternative to TOP. You can also limit the number of rows to return using SET ROWCOUNT N. The difference between these two is that the TOP keyword applies to the single SELECT statement in which it is specified. SET ROWCOUNT stays in effect until another SET ROWCOUNT statement is executed, such as SET ROWCOUNT 0 to turn the option off. The TOP *n* keyword is the preferred between the two and so should always be used when limited rows need to be returned.

You can optionally specify that the TOP keyword is to use the WITH TIES option, in which case any number of records can possibly be displayed. WITH TIES displays all records that are equivalent to the last matching element. If you are looking for the top 10 employees and there is a tie for tenth between two employees, 11 records would
be displayed. If the tie was for ninth or a higher position, only 10 records would be listed.

Bitwise and Unary Operators

Bitwise operators (see Table 4.5) are used on int, smallint, or tinyint data. The ~(Bitwise NOT) operator can also use bit data. All bitwise operators prform an operation on the one or more specified integer values as translated to binary expressions within T-SQL statements. For example, the ~(Bitwise NOT) operator changes binary 1s to 0s and 0s to 1s. To check bitwise operations, you can convert or calculate decimal values.

Bitwise operators perform bit manipulations between two expressions of any of the data types of the integer data type category.

TABLE 4.5

BITWISE OPERATORS

Operator	Meaning
&	Bitwise AND
|	Bitwise OR
^	Bitwise exclusive OR

The operands for bitwise operators can be any of the data types of the `integer` or `binary string` data type categories (except for the `image` data type), with the exception that both operands cannot be any of the data types of the `binary string` data type category.

Unary operators (see Table 4.6) perform an operation on only one expression of any of the data types of the `numeric` data type category.

The + (`Positive`) and - (`Negative`) operators can be used on any expression of any of the data types of the numeric data type category. The ~ (`Bitwise NOT`) operator can be used only on expressions of any of the data types of the `integer` data type category.

Learning to use the entire set of SQL Server operators will take a considerable amount of practice with a wide variety of applications. Obviously it is difficult, even in a book this size, to provide details and examples covering every one.

TABLE 4.6

UNARY OPERATORS

Operator	Meaning
+	Value is positive
-	Value is negative
~	Returns the ones complement of the number

Formatting the Data

Often data returned from the database is not presented in a manner that the end user can identify with and access in a reasonable manner. Many SQL Server functions allow for the alteration or more appropriate presentation to the user. If data is not in a type presentable to the user, then the CONVERT and CAST functions will be the first ones used.

Converting Data with *CONVERT* and *CAST* Functions

Data needs to be converted from one form to another when you are using diverse functions or data types that don't match up with the type needed by a particular function. Data can be converted from one data type to another with the CONVERT and CAST functions.

In converting data types, two things need to be supplied:

◆ The expression that needs to be converted

◆ The data type to convert the given expression to

Here are some notes that should be examined before converting:

◆ If you don't specify a length when converting, SQL Server automatically supplies a length of 30.

◆ CAST is based on the SQL-92 standard and is favored over CONVERT.

◆ SQL Server automatically converts certain data from one data type to another. For example, if a smallint is compared to an int, the smallint is automatically converted to int before the comparison proceeds. These are called *implicit transactions* because you don't have to use the CAST or CONVERT functions.

◆ When data is converted to a new data type and the data is too large for the new data type to handle, SQL Server displays an asterisk or identifies the problem with an error message, depending on the data types involved.

Both CONVERT and CAST have their particular strengths in handling individual types of data. The two functions are compared and contrasted in the next two sections.

The *CONVERT* Function

The CONVERT function transforms data from one data type to another. CONVERT is also used extensively with date operations to format a date. For use in date operations, see Books Online CAST and CONVERT.

The syntax is

```
CONVERT (data type [(length)], expression)
```

Where

◆ *Data type* is the data type you want to convert to

◆ *Expression* is the data being converted

The following example converts the `Price` column into a `CHAR` data type so that you can concatenate it with another string expression. Remember, concatenation can only be done using strings, so it must be converted:

```
SELECT 'The book costs ' + CONVERT(CHAR(5),price) AS 'Price
➥of book'
FROM titles
```

Using the *CAST* Function

The `CAST` function is similar to the `CONVERT` function in that it converts data. It is preferred over the `CONVERT` function because it's based on the SQL-92 standard. Of course, there is no harm in using either, but I personally use this more frequently. The syntax for `CAST` is:

```
CAST(expression AS data type)
```

Notice that the parameters are switched around in comparison to the `CONVERT` function.

`CAST` is usually preferred over `CONVERT` for operations with more advanced processing requirements.

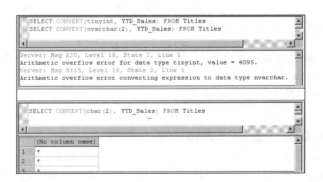

FIGURE 4.4
Data error clarification.

Data Filtering

Filtering of data is the selection of the required information, using supplied criteria, to create a resultset with only the requested data. Filtering minimizes the use of valuable bandwidth, provides for more efficient applications, and in general better suits the end user and business needs.

Formatting data is presenting the information so that more value is produced in the finished product. Formatting information can be as simple as placing output in the correct sequence; however, formatting can also mean the use of highly advanced procedures for the analysis and display of data.

DATA SUMMARY

▶ **Summarize data by using Transact-SQL.**

Summarizing information to provide results that collect data in a meaningful manner applies functions against the data that can perform calculations, make decisions, and provide answers by performing data analysis on behalf of the user.

All functions are either deterministic or nondeterministic. Whether a function is deterministic or nondeterministic is called the *determinism* of the function.

◆ Deterministic functions always return the same result any time they are called with a specific set of input values.

◆ Nondeterministic functions may return different results each time they are called with a specific set of input values.

For example, the DATEADD built-in function is deterministic because it always returns the same result for any given set of argument values for its three parameters. GETDATE is not deterministic because it is always invoked with the same argument, yet the value it returns changes each time it is executed.

Be careful with the use of appropriate functions because nondeterministic functions cannot be used in a lot of processes. An index cannot be created on a computed column if the expression references any nondeterministic functions, and a clustered index cannot be created on a view if the view references any nondeterministic functions.

Functions can be divided into categories that are each addressed separately over the remainder of this exam objective coverage.

Date Functions

In T-SQL, as with many other programming languages, date manipulation has been given special importance, by the many functions available. Dates are implemented as `datetime` and `smalldatetime` data types and need to be treated with special functions such as `DATEDIFF`. Dates cannot be added or subtracted using the regular operators. The date functions available in SQL Server enable you to change and manipulate dates easily; the dates must be in `datetime` or `smalldatetime` type. The next couple of sections cover the date functions found in SQL Server.

DATEADD

The `DATEADD` function adds a number to the part of the date you specify, such as month or day, and then returns the new `datetime` value. The syntax is

```
DATEADD (date_part, number, date)
```

Where:

◆ `Date_part` determines which unit of measure of time. A listing of the possible values accepted is shown in Table 4.7.

◆ `Number` determines the number by which you want to increase the `date_part`.

◆ `Date` is a `datetime` or `smalldatetime` value.

The `DATEADD` function adds an interval to a date you specify. For example, if the shipping dates of all invoices in the backorders table slip three days, you can get the new dates with this statement:

```
SELECT DATEADD(day, 3, shipdate)
FROM backorders
```

TABLE 4.7

POSSIBLE VALUES FOR DATE_PART

date_part *name*	*Abbreviations*
Year	yy, yyyy
Quarter	qq, q
Month	mm, m
Dayofyear	dy, y
Day	dd, d
Week	wk, ww
Hour	hh
Minute	mi, n
Second	ss, s
Millisecond	ms

The DATEDIFF function is used in a similar manner. This function, however, calculates the amount of time in dateparts between the second and first of two dates you specify.

DATEDIFF

Included in the various date manipulation functions is DATEDIFF. As the name suggests, DATEDIFF is a function that returns the difference between two date parts specified. The syntax for DATEDIFF is

```
DATEDIFF (date_part, start_date, end_date)
```

Where:

◆ date_part is the unit of time measure you want to find the difference between. The values this can take are shown earlier in Table 4.7.

◆ start_date is the beginning date for the calculation.

◆ end_date is the date being subtracted from start_date.

DATEDIFF subtracts the start date from the end date to produce the result. Look at the following example:

```
USE pubs
GO
SELECT pubdate, DATEDIFF(year, pubdate, getdate()) AS
➥'years difference'
FROM titles
```

The method of counting crossed boundaries such as minutes, seconds, and milliseconds makes the result given by DATEDIFF consistent across all data types. The result is a signed integer value equal to the number of date_part boundaries crossed between the first and second date. For example, the number of weeks between Monday, March 5, and Monday, March 12, is 1.

GETDATE

To get the current date, use the GETDATE function. This function can be useful when you are producing reports that need to be dated. The GETDATE function returns the current system date and can be used in a SELECT statement. The syntax for GETDATE is

```
GETDATE()
```

The following is an example of using GETDATE() to return the current date:

```
SELECT Getdate() as "today's date"
```

You can use GETDATE in designing a report to have the current date and time printed every time the report is produced. GETDATE is also useful for functions such as logging the time a transaction occurred on an account.

You can use GETDATE anywhere to return the current system date.

DATENAME

The DATENAME function can be used in determining the current date_part in the form of a string. You may, for instance, need to know specifically the day or month of a publication. The DATENAME function returns a character string representing the specified date part from the date. The syntax is

```
DATENAME (date_part, date)
```

Where:

◆ `date_part` determines which unit of time measure needs to be found. The values it can take were shown in Table 4.7.

◆ `date` is an expression denoting the date being used.

Here's an example of using `DATENAME` to find the name of the current month:

```
Select datename(mm,getdate()) as 'month'
```

The `DATEPART` and `DATENAME` functions produce the specified part of a `datetime` value (the year, quarter, day, hour, and so on) as either an integer or a string. Because `smalldatetime` is accurate only to the minute, when a `smalldatetime` value is used with either of these functions, the seconds and milliseconds returned are zero.

DATEPART

`DATEPART` is similar to `DATENAME` except that it returns an integer value indicating the date rather than a character string. The syntax for `DATEPART` is the same as for `DATENAME`.

The following is an example using `DATEPART` to find the current month and display it numerically:

```
SELECT datepart(mm,getdate()) AS 'month'
```

Many useful date functions give the developer flexibility in dealing with what is traditionally one of the more pesky data types: `Dates`. With history reflecting unfavorably on the storage of date information, it is important to consider this data type to be infinite in that dates need to remain unique as time progresses.

Numeric data types have always had useful functionality supplied with the programming environment in most languages. SQL Server is no exception with its adoption of a standard set of mathematical functions.

Using Mathematical Functions in T-SQL

A mathematical function performs a math operation on numeric expressions and returns the result of the operation. Math functions operate on any of the SQL Server numeric data types (`decimal`, `integer`, `float`, `real`, `money`, `smallmoney`, `smallint`, and tinyint). The precision of built-in operations on float data type data is six decimal places by default.

By default, a number passed to a mathematical function is interpreted as a decimal data type. The CAST or CONVERT functions can be used to change the data type to something else, such as a float. For example, the value returned by the FLOOR function has the data type of the input value. The input of this SELECT statement is a decimal, and FLOOR(123.34) returns 123, which is a decimal value.

You can use the diverse set of math functions provided by T-SQL to fulfill many database needs. SQL Server provided numerous mathematical functions so that you can perform the most complex calculations possible. These numerous functions are provided in most programming language environments. A compiled list of most of the important math functions is listed in Table 4.8.

TABLE 4.8

MATHEMATICAL FUNCTIONS IN T-SQL

Function	Parameters	Result
ABS	(Numeric expression)	Returns the absolute value of a number.
ACOS	(Float expression)	Angle (in radians) whose cosine is the specified float expression.
ASIN	(Float expression)	Angle (in radians) whose sine is the specified float expression.
ATAN	(Float expression)	Angle (in radians) whose tangent is the specified float expression.
ATN2	(Float expression1, float expression2)	Returns the angle in radians whose tangent is between the two given float expressions (also called arctangent).
CEILING	(Numeric expression)	Returns the smallest integer greater than or equal to the numeric expression.
COS	(Float expression)	The cosine of the specified expression.
COT	(Float expression)	Cotangent of the specified expression.
DEGREES	(Numeric expression)	Degrees converted from radians of the numeric expression.
EXP	(Float expression)	Exponential value of the specified expression.
FLOOR	(Numeric expression)	Largest integer less than or equal to the specified numeric expression.

continues

TABLE 4.8	*continued*

MATHEMATICAL FUNCTIONS IN T-SQL

Function	*Parameters*	*Result*
LOG	*(Float expression)*	Natural logarithm of the specified expression.
LOG10	*(Float expression)*	Base – 10 logarithm of the specified expression.
PI	( )	Returns 3.1415926535897931.
POWER	*(Numeric expression, y)*	Value of numeric expression to the power of y.
RADIANS	*(Numeric expression)*	Radians converted from degrees of the numeric expression.
RAND	(seed)	Random float value between zero and one.
ROUND	*(Numeric expression, length)*	Numeric expression rounded off to the precision (length) of a number.
SIGN	*(Numeric expression)*	Returns the positive, negative, or zero sign of a numeric expression.
SIN	*(Float expression)*	Trigonometric sine of the specified angle.
SQRT	*(Float expression)*	Square root of the specified expression.
TAN	*(Float expression)*	Tangent of the specified expression.
SQUARE	*(Float expression)*	Square of the specified expression.

The following example shows you a query that uses some of the many mathematical functions in SQL Server. Notice that when a query is non-data retrieval, as this one is, a FROM clause does not have to be specified.

```
SELECT pi() AS 'PI' , abs(-44) AS 'Absolute',
power(2,3) AS 'Power'
```

Discussion of mathematical functions would be an involved endeavor for this medium. This book does not set out to make mathematical geniuses out of every SQL developer. To become fully versed in all mathematical functions would require a significant education in the science of mathematics.

Character functions interact against alphanumeric data in a similar fashion as numeric data interacts with mathematical functions.

Character Functions

SQL Server also provides a full array of character (string) functions. Character functions enable you to easily manipulate attributes that are character-specific. Most of the functions provided in `table` are normally used and therefore you should regularly practice using them. For example, if you want to not include the blank spaces before a value or after a value, you could use the `LTRIM` and `RTRIM` functions. Table 4.9 is a compilation of the various character functions included in SQL Server's version of SQL.

TABLE 4.9

CHARACTER FUNCTIONS IN T-SQL

Function	Parameters	Result
+	*Expression1 + expression2*	Concatenates a string; brings two strings together.
ASCII	*String expression*	Gets the ASCII code value of the string.
CHAR	*Integer expression*	Changes the ASCII integer into a character.
LEN	*String expression*	Identifies the length of an expression in characters.
LOWER	*String expression*	Converts uppercase to lowercase.
LTRIM	*String expression*	Removes leading blanks.
PATINDEX	*Pattern, expression*	Returns the position of the beginning of the occurrence of the pattern. If the pattern is not found, it returns a zero.
REPLICATE	*String expression, integer expression*	Repeats a character expression the number of times specified.
REVERSE	*String expression*	Returns the reverse of a string expression.
RTRIM	*String expression*	Removes trailing blanks.
SPACE	*Integer expression*	Returns a string of repeated spaces.
STUFF	*String expression1, start, length, String expression2*	Deletes a specified length of characters and inserts another set of characters at a specified starting point.
SUBSTRING	*String expression, start, length*	Returns part of a string expression.
UPPER	*String expression*	Makes all lowercase letters uppercase.

Sometimes data is entered into a database with leading or trailing spaces. To retrieve data free of these spaces, use the trim functions: LTRIM and RTRIM.

```
SELECT RTRIM
(LTRIM(' this is an example          '))+'TESTER'
As 'example'
```

Concatenation processes are often performed to generate names from a fully normalized database, as shown in Figure 4.5.

You can change the direction of text or make an expression uppercase or lowercase by using these three functions: REVERSE, UPPER, and LOWER. Look at the following example:

```
SELECT UPPER('mustafa'),
LOWER('MUNAWAR'),
REVERSE('Mustafa')
```

Concatenation of a string value to a NULL string results in NULL. A check should be performed for string content in situations where concatenated information could be partially or completely NULL.

The *SUBSTRING* Function

It may be that you want to return a part of a string rather than the whole string. The SUBSTRING function, which returns a part of a character or binary string, can be used for this. The syntax for SUBSTRING is

```
SUBSTRING (expression, start, length)
```

FIGURE 4.5
Concatenation to formulate names from multiple columns.

Where:

◆ *Expression* is a character string, binary string, text, image, a column, or an expression that includes a column.

◆ *Start* is a number denoting the initial position of the sub-string.

◆ *Length* is a number denoting how long the sub-string is.

This example shows how SUBSTRING works:

```
SELECT Au_fname +' ' + au_lname AS 'full name',
    SUBSTRING (au_fname, 1,1) + SUBSTRING (au_lname, 1,1) AS
➥'initials'
    FROM authors
```

The next section looks at using DATALENGTH to count the number of bytes used to represent an expression.

DATALENGTH

You may need to know how many bytes long a string is. Of course, you could count the number of characters present in a string, but that would be a complete waste of time. You might also have problems differentiating standard one-byte strings and Unicode two-byte strings. For example, if you were creating an application with a first name column of a fixed length, you would need to observe previous tables with a first name column to get an estimate of the highest first name present to set the fixed length. An easy way to do this would be to use a function known as DATALENGTH in conjunction with MAX; in this way, you would certainly save time and get results. The DATALENGTH function returns the number of bytes used in an expression supplied. The syntax for DATALENGTH is

```
DATALENGTH (expression)
```

Where:

◆ *Expression* is the data you want to find the length of.

Filtering and formatting data can be carried further with elements of grouping and computing results. These features are defined further in Chapter 5, "Advanced Data Retrieval and Modification."

The final area of SQL Server functionality left to discuss is a series of functions that allow for a variety of system-level interactions.

System Functions

As you have seen in the previous two compilations, many functions are supplied to perform mathematical and character-manipulation operations. You can also use a third category of functions with the SELECT list known as system-specific functions. You can use system functions to retrieve special system or database information through T-SQL and the SELECT statement.

Table 4.10 shows a compilation of the numerous system functions available in T-SQL.

TABLE 4.10

DATABASE/SYSTEM FUNCTIONS
IN T-SQL

System Function	Parameters	Description
COL_LENGTH	(table name, column name)	The length of a column.
COL_NAME	(table_id, Column_id)	The name of a column.
DATALENGTH	(Expression)	The length of any expression in bytes.
DB_ID	(database_name)	The database's identification number.
DB_NAME	(database_ID)	The database's name.
GETANSINULL	(database_name)	Returns the default nullability for the database for this session.
HOST_ID	( )	The identification number for the workstation.
HOST_NAME	( )	The name of the workstation.
IDENT_INCR	(table or view)	Returns the increment value specified during the creation of an identity column in a table or view that has an identity column.
IDENT_SEED	(table or view)	The starting number for an identity column.
INDEX_COL	(table name, index_id,key_id)	The indexed column's name.
ISNULL	(expression, value)	Changes NULL values in the expression to a value specified.

continues

TABLE 4.10	*continued*

DATABASE/SYSTEM FUNCTIONS IN T-SQL

System Function	Parameters	Description
NULLIF	*(expression1, expression2)*	This gives a NULL value only if the two expressions are equivalent.
OBJECT_ID	*(object_name)*	The database object identification number.
OBJECT_NAME	*(Object_ID)*	The database object name.
STATS_DATE	*(Table_ID, Index_ID)*	The date that the statistics for a particular index were last updated.
SUSER_ID	*(login name)*	This is only used for backward compatibility. Use SUSER_SID instead.
SUSER_SID	*(login name)*	The user's login identification number.
SUSER_NAME	*(server_user_id)*	This is only used for backward compatibility. Use SUSER_SNAME instead.
SUSER_SNAME	*(server_user_id)*	The user's login identification name.
USER_ID	*(user_name)*	The user's database identification number.
USER_NAME	*(user_ID)*	The user's database username.

ISNULL can be useful when you want to convert all NULL values to a particular value. For example, look at the following query. This query converts all NULL values into zeros:

```
SELECT ISNULL (price, 0.0000), price
FROM titles
```

System functions, information schema views, or the system stored procedures can be used to gain access to system information without querying the system tables directly. System tables can change significantly between versions of SQL Server.

SQL Server provides system stored procedures or information schema views for obtaining information about the properties of data, such as the type of data in a column (numeric, text, and so on) or the length of a column. This type of information is called *meta data* and is maintained by SQL Server for all server and database objects. Meta data can be used to find out information about the structure of data, the contents of a server, or information that specifies the design of objects.

Although it is possible to obtain data through querying any of the system tables directly, the system tables may not provide the information required in the future. It is recommended that system stored procedures, system functions, and information schema views be used because the contents of the system tables may change in future releases.

Information Schema Views

Information schema views provide a method independent of the system tables to view meta data. These views enable applications to work properly even though significant changes may have been made to the system tables and more changes may be made in the future. An application that uses the views rather than a direct query against the system tables should function in the same manner in the future as it does in the current SQL Server release. The information schema views included in SQL Server conform to the SQL-92 Standard definition for the INFORMATION_SCHEMA.

Names used in the SQL-92 standard for these views are different from those used by SQL Server, though the names from SQL Server can equivalently be mapped to those of the standard. The following list shows the SQL-92 names and the SQL Server equivalents:

◆ A SQL-92 'Catalog' is a SQL Server 'Database'.

◆ 'Schema' in SQL-92 is an 'Owner' in SQL Server.

◆ 'Object' is the same in both SQL-92 and in SQL Server.

◆ A 'Domain' in SQL-92 is a user-defined data type in SQL Server.

When retrieving meta data from the information schema views, you must use a qualified name that includes the INFORMATION_SCHEMA in the position where you usually specify the user name. For example:

```
SELECT *
FROM Northwind.INFORMATION_SCHEMA.TABLES
```

For more information on the variety of meta data that can be obtained through the use of information schema views, use the Index tab of SQL Server Books Online. When you type **information schema**, the index shows links to all the appropriate views.

Many system stored procedures can also be used to find information about server and database objects. With many of the procedures, however, you can also perform actions against the server, whereas information schema views are used solely to obtain meta data.

System Stored Procedures

Many administrative and informational activities in SQL Server can be accomplished through the use of SQL Server's many system stored procedures. System stored procedures are available to perform a variety of activities from obtaining information about server settings and objects to managing processes on the server to performing maintenance activities and much more.

It is not possible to cover all the procedures in this book, and SQL Server Books Online has full definitions and examples for these procedures. At various points throughout the book, references will be made to those procedures you are likely to find on the exam and others that will serve useful purposes in the future.

REVIEW BREAK

> **EXAM TIP**
>
> **Exam Processes** Typical situations that are tested on the exam are:
>
> - Date conversion using appropriate date functions
>
> - String concatenation, including building and parsing functions
>
> - System application design, where system functions are used to programmatically control or manipulate the software functionality

Data Summary

Summarizing information requires that a variety of functions be applied against the data to produce useful information. Summarizing data will provide the end user with the best information source possible to meet the needs of a business.

To master the use of functions, you need to work with as many different situations as possible. Each individual problem requires the use of the set of functions necessary to accomplish the task. With such a diverse set of functions available, SQL Server can be used in a multitude of different situations. To recognize the diversity, you will need experience in an equal number of diverse situations.

MAKING DATA MODIFICATIONS

As time passes, new data will no doubt need to be inserted, redundant data will need to be deleted, and existing data will need to be updated. Data may be modified with a few simple lines of T-SQL. Data modification is always necessary when working with real-life situations. Think, for example, of an employee changing houses. His address would need to be modified, which could be done using the UPDATE statement.

Data modification is changing, deleting, or inserting data, and this section will teach you just that. Basically, there are three T-SQL statements that enable you to insert, delete, and update data; unsurprisingly, they are INSERT, DELETE, and UPDATE.

Inserting Data into Tables

Although there are many ways to insert data into an existing table, such as using the Enterprise Manager, this section deals with the primary coding method of using the INSERT statement.

The syntax of the INSERT INTO statement can be summarized as follows:

```
INSERT [INTO] table_or_view [(column_list)] VALUES
➥data_values
```

The statement causes the data values to be inserted as one or more rows into the named table. Column list is a comma-separated list of column names that can be used to indicate the columns for which data is supplied.

Remember, it's always a safe habit to practice modifying data on a test table. For these examples, use the table defined as follows:

```
CREATE TABLE TestTable
  ( age       int        NULL,
    month     varchar(8)  NULL,
    phone     varchar(15) NULL,
    gender    varchar(7)  NULL,
    haircolor varchar(14) NULL )
```

Now, to insert the data, enter the query as displayed in Figure 4.6.

FIGURE 4.6
Insert of data.

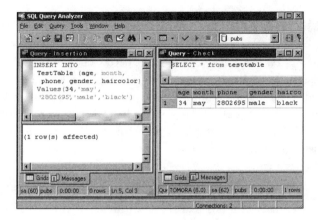

Alternatively, you can specify just the VALUES keyword, which is a more convenient method. Values is required unless you are doing INSERT, SELECT OR INSERT, or EXECUTE. The same results are produced with the following query:

```
INSERT INTO TestTable Values(34, 'may', '2802695', 'male',
➥'black')
```

Data inserted must meet the parameters defined by the table structure. This means that NOT NULL columns must have data provided either through input or through the use of column definitions that provide for their own values. A column can obtain its input value through a DEFAULT, IDENTITY, formula, or default object. Data must also meet all rules and constraints that have been defined in the table schema.

Data can be inserted into a table from the resultset of a SELECT query. When this is performed it enables a large amount of data to be extracted from a table or view and stored into another table.

INSERT INTO SELECT

A SELECT statement can be used within the INSERT statement to add values into a table from one or more other tables or views. Using a SELECT subquery is also a mechanism that enables more than one row to be inserted at one time. This type of INSERT statement is often used to insert data into a separate table from some other table or data source. In this manner the data can be copied or just separated off for handling of exceptions or specialty tasks. For example, imagine you would like to copy all your current employees into a customer table. This will enable your employees to make purchases and, of course, allow for an employee discount (not implemented in the Northwind example). The query to perform this operation might look similar to the following:

```
INSERT INTO Northwind.dbo.Customers
      SELECT EmployeeID, 'Northwind',
             FirstName + ' ' + LastName,
             'Employee', Address, City, Region,
             PostalCode, Country, HomePhone, NULL
         FROM Northwind.dbo.Employees
```

The SELECT list of the subquery must match the column list of the INSERT statement. If no column list is specified, the SELECT list must match the columns in the table or view being inserted into, as in the example. Note that NULL has been provided for a fax number at the end of the column list, because none is included in the employees table. The INSERT SELECT statement can be used to insert data from any viable source. This includes SQL Server tables, views, and sources outside SQL Server.

Values can be inserted from any number of sources using a variety of options available to an INSERT operation. As you will see next, this is a very flexible operation and virtually any data source can be used.

INSERT EXECUTE

An EXECUTE statement that returns data with SELECT or READTEXT statements can be used to return the insert values to an INSERT operation. Each resultset must be compatible with the columns in the table or in the column list being used by the INSERT. In this manner a stored procedure can be executed and the data returned as input to a table. If an operation returns data with the READTEXT statement, each individual READTEXT statement can return a maximum of 1MB. The execute operation can also be used with extended procedures (not available in previous versions of SQL Server).

Using an operation in this manner enables complex logic to be saved into a stored procedure, and the resulting output can be used for the insertion. For example, imagine you want to get a listing of top sales-people to establish year-end bonuses. You would like to place these records into a separate table. This operation would require four tables be queried on each of three servers and calculations be performed to determine each salesperson's ranking. If you create a procedure called pick_top_sales, the results of this procedure could be used to form the data for your table. The query would look similar to the following:

```
INSERT Top_Sales EXECUTE pick_top_sales
```

Using this facility, you can get virtually any data from anywhere and feed it to any destination.

SELECT INTO

The SELECT INTO statement can perform a data insertion and create the table for the data in a single operation. The new table is populated with the data provided by a FROM clause. A simple example of its use is as follows:

```
SELECT * INTO ObsoleteProducts
  FROM Products WHERE Discontinued = 1
```

In the example, the SELECT INTO creates a new table ObsoleteProducts with an identical structure as the products table. It then copies all data that meets the WHERE condition into this newly created table. It is possible to combine data from several tables or views into one table, and again a variety of sources can be used.

Deleting Data

Data that is not needed can be deleted using the DELETE statement. The DELETE statement removes one or more records from a table based on a condition in the WHERE clause. A simplified version of the DELETE statement is

```
DELETE table_ or_view FROM table_sources WHERE
➥search_condition
```

Table_or_view names a table or view from which the rows are to be deleted. All rows in table_or_view that meet the qualifications of the WHERE search condition are deleted. If a WHERE clause is not specified, all the rows in table_or_view are deleted.

If you would like to delete all rows, a fast, non-logged method is already supplied: TRUNCATE TABLE. It immediately frees all space used by indexes and data by that table, as opposed to DELETE, which should be used when partial data removal is desired.

Though both TRUNCATE TABLE and a DELETE statement with no WHERE clause remove all rows in a table, TRUNCATE TABLE is faster and uses fewer system and log resources. The DELETE statement removes rows one at a time, recording an entry in the transaction log for each row. TRUNCATE TABLE removes the data by de-allocating the data pages used to store the table's data, and only the page de-allocations are recorded in the log. TRUNCATE TABLE removes all rows from a table, but the table structure and its columns, constraints, and indexes remain intact. The counter used by any identity columns is reset to the seed value for the column. If you want to retain the identity counter, use DELETE instead. The following is an example of a DELETE statement:

```
DELETE from testTable
WHERE phone=2802695
```

Removal of data may impact other tables if cascading deletions has been specified for a relationship. This could mean the removal of other records based on a single DELETE operation. Also, a relationship definition may prevent the deletion of data and return an error condition to the operation.

Updating Data

Data that already exists may need to be modified with newer values as time passes; this type of data modification is known as *updating*. Data can be updated with the UPDATE statement, very much as it is deleted and inserted. An UPDATE execution is actually an INSERT and DELETE operation. The DELETE operation occurs when the old value is removed, and the INSERT occurs when the new value is added, thus creating an UPDATE effect. The basic syntax for the UPDATE statement is as follows:

```
UPDATE table_name

SET column_name = expression

WHERE condition
```

Where:

◆ table_name is the name of the table to be updated.

◆ column_name = expression is the new value assigned to a column.

◆ condition is a specified WHERE condition.

Take the query in Figure 4.7, for example, which updates the table created previously, TestTable.

Just as with the input of data, any alterations made to the data are subject to the rules and constraints as defined in the table schema. Any data modifications made that do not meet these defined standards result in errors being generated that the front-end application may have to trap and control.

FIGURE 4.7
UPDATE used against existing data.

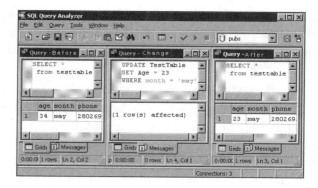

CASE STUDY: ADDRESS BOOK APPLICATION

ESSENCE OF THE CASE

▸ You created an address book application in Visual Basic.

▸ Beta testers commented that reporting of the results in the application was not properly performed.

▸ You implement a better and more organized way to display results.

SCENARIO

You have been working lately on an address book project in Visual Basic that uses SQL Server as the underlying database. You have created most of the program code and have already implemented the body of the project. So far, users can enter unlimited addresses and phone numbers through the easy-to-use graphical interface. After you have completed the project, you send it to a couple of beta testers to perfect the work. One strongly emphasized comment you receive is that the application lacks the proper reporting capabilities. The beta tester adds that retrieving a single address or phone number is a time-consuming process, because you have to scroll and manually find the address or phone number you want. He suggests that you program some sort of doodad into your application to allow easy address searching.

ANALYSIS

After reading the comment from one of the beta testers, you realize that reporting in your application is not functional. You decide to implement a

CASE STUDY: ADDRESS BOOK APPLICATION

search feature and an ordering feature, to make it easy to find a particular address or phone number. You look at the different data retrieval commands available in the T-SQL library and find the WHERE clause and LIKE predicate helpful. You alter your existing program to include this change by adding two components: first, searches that use the LIKE predicate, and second, the ordering of processed information. Now a user can, for example, order results by first name or last name and can perform partial word searches throughout the records. After altering the program code, you realize that the coding was not as difficult as you expected; however, this new change will save a great a great deal of time for the end user.

CHAPTER SUMMARY

This chapter has examined a lot of aspects of performing queries and modifying data. It started with tools to query data. These include the BCP and OSQL utilities and the SQL Query Analyzer. The BCP utility is used to insert large amounts of data into a table, whereas the OSQL utility and the Query Analyzer enable you to interactively modify and access data using T-SQL.

You also learned about the different parts of the "whole" SELECT statement. First is the SELECT *list* part, where you list the columns you want to access. Then the FROM clause determines from which table to access the data. After that is the WHERE clause, which can be used to limit or filter the data viewed. In this clause, you can connect various other functions to limit the data to your specifications. Some of these functions include LIKE, BETWEEN, IN, and IS NULL.

You also saw how to return the highest/lowest values using TOP n and ROWCOUNT. And you looked at the SUBSTRING function as well as various DATE, arithmetic, and system functions, which enable you to manipulate data and work with the database system.

The ORDER BY clause orders your data in either ascending or descending order.

You looked at the mathematical functions allowed in SQL. Some of these are ABS, which finds the absolute value, and ROUND, which rounds a number off to a given precision.

KEY TERMS

- SELECT statement
- column list
- FROM
- WHERE
- ORDER BY
- LIKE
- string concatenation
- CAST
- CONVERT
- TOP
- INSERT
- INSERT INTO
- DELETE

CHAPTER SUMMARY

Character functions can be used to manipulate the way strings look. LTRIM, for example, takes all leading blanks away. ASCII finds the ASCII code value for a string.

You looked at inserting and deleting data. Data can be inserted using the INSERT INTO statement. If you want to delete data, you can use the DELETE keyword. A faster non-logged method of deleting data all the rows in a table is to use the TRUNCATE TABLE statement.

APPLY YOUR KNOWLEDGE

Exercises

The following set of exercises takes you through the creation of a table structure, insertion of data, modification of existing data, and deletion of data.

4.1   Creation of Test Data

In Exercise 4.1 you initialize a table structure and insert some test data to be used by the remaining exercises in this chapter.

Estimated Time: 15 minutes.

1. If it is not already open, load the SQL Query Analyzer. Supply the logon connection information if requested.

2. Select the Master database from the database drop-down list box.

3. Enter the following query to initialize the database:

```
CREATE DATABASE TestData
ON
( NAME = TestData_data,
   FILENAME = 'c:\testdata.mdf',
   SIZE = 10,
   MAXSIZE = 50,
   FILEGROWTH = 5 )
LOG ON
( NAME = 'TestData_log',
   FILENAME = 'c:\testdata.ldf',
   SIZE = 5MB,
   MAXSIZE = 25MB,
   FILEGROWTH = 5MB )
GO
```

The database location could be altered if you wish. At the end of the chapter, you may want to go back and DROP the database, or leave it for future practice.

4. Enter the following query to initialize the two tables:

```
USE TestData
GO

CREATE TABLE publishers
( pub_id  char(4) NOT NULL CONSTRAINT
➥UPKCL_pubind PRIMARY KEY CLUSTERED,
   pub_name      varchar(40)      NULL,
   city          varchar(20)      NULL,
   state         char(2)          NULL,
   country       varchar(30)      NULL
 )
GO

CREATE TABLE employee
( emp_id  char(4) CONSTRAINT PK_emp_id
➥PRIMARY KEY NONCLUSTERED,
   firstname    varchar(20)      NOT NULL,
   lastname     varchar(30)      NOT NULL,
   salary       money            NOT NULL,
   datehired    datetime         NOT NULL,
   pub_id  char(4) NOT NULL
       CONSTRAINT myname FOREIGN KEY
       ➥REFERENCES publishers(pub_id)
 )
GO
```

Referential integrity has been set up on this definition. A later exercise illustrates the correct input procedure and then turns to the error conditions that may arise if data doesn't meet the requirements.

5. Enter the following query to enter some initial data.

```
INSERT Publishers VALUES (1, 'IM Publishing',
➥'Warsaw', 'PA', 'USA')
INSERT Publishers VALUES (2, 'UR Publishing',
➥'Harmony', 'TX', 'USA')
GO

INSERT Employee VALUES (1, 'John',
➥'Stevenson', 45000, '01/02/2001', 1)
INSERT Employee VALUES (2, 'Tim', 'Johns',
➥40000, '04/06/2000', 1)
INSERT Employee VALUES (3, 'Susan',
➥'Hilbury', 50000, '11/07/2000', 2)
INSERT Employee VALUES (4, 'Billy', 'Maxyor',
➥60000, '12/03/2000', 2)
GO
```

APPLY YOUR KNOWLEDGE

6. Ensure the data is correctly entered using a simple query:

```
SELECT * FROM Publishers
GO
SELECT * FROM Employee
GO
```

4.2   Database Interactions (ADD, CHANGE, DELETE)

In Exercise 4.2 you will use the data previously created to perform a variety of procedures and queries commonly issued against a database. Standard INSERT, UPDATE, and DELETE operations will be performed.

Estimated Time: 15 minutes.

1. You have already issued several INSERT statements in the previous exercise, so in this exercise you need add only a couple of additional rows. The exercise is performed from the Query Analyzer with the TestData database selected from the database drop-down list box.

2. Add an additional row to each of the tables by issuing the following queries:

```
INSERT Publishers VALUES (3, 'WR Publishing',
➡'Kingsville', 'CA', 'USA')
INSERT Employee VALUES (5, 'Kim', 'Jepsom',
➡30000, '03/05/2001', 3)
```

3. Change an existing record by issuing the following UPDATE operation:

```
UPDATE Employee
    SET firstname = 'William'
    WHERE firstname = 'Billy'
```

4. Remove an existing record using the following DELETE operation:

```
DELETE FROM Employee
    WHERE emp_id = 2
```

5. Check your results by querying the two tables:

```
SELECT * FROM Publishers
SELECT * FROM Employee
```

Try to determine what rules had to be followed to allow for input and removal of data. The next exercise illustrates conditions where errors might need to be trapped by a front-end application.

4.3   Error Conditions

Exercise 4.3 illustrates error conditions by attempting to add and remove data improperly against the referential integrity settings of the database.

Estimated Time: 15 minutes

1. The exercise is performed from the Query Analyzer with the TestData database selected from the database drop-down list box.

2. Attempt to remove an existing publisher that has Foreign Key records existing in another table:

```
DELETE FROM Publishers
    WHERE pub_id = 1
```

3. Attempt to insert a new employee record that has an invalid publisher identifier:

```
INSERT Employee VALUES
    (6, 'Joe', 'Smith', 20000, 06/04/2000, 9)
```

Note the type of errors that occur and the reasons for them. Error handling is covered fully in Chapter 9. If referential integrity is defined, then a primary entry must exist for every Foreign Key element. If a primary entry has such elements, it can't be removed. Of course, this activity could be affected by the cascading settings in the relationship. For more information on referential integrity and cascading operations, see Chapters 2 and 3.

APPLY YOUR KNOWLEDGE

Review Questions

1. How does a DISTINCT query provide for useful reporting to the user?

2. What advantages can the use of a WHERE clause provide over the basic use of a SELECT or DELETE operation?

3. How would data in the form of dates be compared against data stored as characters?

4. What types of functions would be considered if the most important application issue centered around the use of network bandwidth?

5. When do data deletions and modifications affect data stored in other tables?

Exam Questions

1. In preparation for a major system upgrade, a large set of data changes are going to be made on a system. You would like to implement a number of changes without affecting any of the existing data. Which of the following operations do not affect any existing data values? Select all that apply:

   A. INSERT

   B. UPDATE

   C. Change column name

   D. Increase column length

   E. Decrease column length

2. You are creating a one-time report to supply the office staff with a revenue breakdown. The data source for the report contains cryptic column headings that cover several different categories.

You must provide the report in a manner the users can easily understand. Which of the following would be the best solution? Select 2; each answer represents half of the correct solution.

   A. Provide friendly aliases for the table names.

   B. Provide friendly aliases for the column names.

   C. Create a VIEW with corresponding definition.

   D. Create a corresponding DEFAULT definition.

   E. Execute a corresponding query from the Analyzer.

   F. Create a front-end program to execute the required query.

3. You have implemented a database for an international research organization and are performing some test queries against the tables within the database. You would like to have a listing of the data from only the year 2000. Which of the following queries represents the best solution to the problem?

   A. SELECT * FROM Results
           WHERE ResultDate BETWEEN '01/01/2000'
       ➡AND '01/01/2001'

   B. SELECT * FROM Results
           WHERE ResultDate BETWEEN '12/31/1999'
       ➡AND '12/31/2000'

   C. SELECT * FROM Results
           WHERE ResultDate BETWEEN '12/31/1999'
       ➡AND '01/01/2001'

   D. SELECT * FROM Results
           WHERE ResultDate BETWEEN '01/01/2000'
       ➡AND '12/31/2000'

   E. SELECT * FROM Results
           WHERE ResultDate BETWEEN
       ➡'12/31/2000' AND '01/01/2000'

APPLY YOUR KNOWLEDGE

4. You have been given the assignment of preparing a set of user-friendly queries to produce a series of reports for a building construction supply company. You would like a query that places customers in order by country, region, and then city. Which of the following queries would solve the problem?

    A. SELECT * FROM Customers
           ORDER BY Country, State, City

    B. SELECT CustomerName, City, State, Country
           ORDER BY Country, State, City,
       CustomerName

    C. SELECT * FROM Customers
           ORDER BY City, State, Country

    D. SELECT CustomerName, City, State, Country
           ORDER BY City, State, Country,
       CustomerName

    E. SELECT CustomerName, City, State, Country
           ORDER BY CustomerName, City, State,
       Country

5. You are working on a database view that will be used by a group of salespeople to query a database for sales statistics. The report that you are debugging is printing duplicates for some states, and in some instances there are three or more duplicates. How would you try to resolve the problem?

    A. Correct the FROM clause

    B. Correct the WHERE clause

    C. Correct the TOP clause

    D. Correct the ORDER BY clause

    E. Correct the DISTINCT clause

6. You have entered a query using a TOP function to limit the number of records being viewed to five. When you see the results of the query, the dates

being viewed were not the first five in the data. What could be the source of the problem?

    A. The resultset has not been grouped.

    B. The data contains NULL values.

    C. There is an incorrect ORDER.

    D. Table aliases were used.

    E. Schema binding has been applied.

7. You work for a large manufacturing organization that maintains a large production database system on a single SQL Server 2000 machine. In attempting to enter a query to add a record to a table, you find that it is not possible. Which of the following is *not* a likely cause for the error?

    A. Data doesn't meet constraint.

    B. Referential integrity.

    C. Database is read-only.

    D. Permissions.

    E. Other applications are locking data.

    F. SQL Server Agent is not started.

8. A local branch of a large hotel chain maintains guest information on a single SQL Server 2000 computer. You are creating an application that will change the contents of a database programmatically through a Visual Basic interface on a local area network. Which technology would you utilize?

    A. ADO

    B. RDO

    C. DAO

    D. SQL DMO

    E. XML

APPLY YOUR KNOWLEDGE

9. You have been chosen by your development team to provide a set of queries that will print out a variety of reports from the Customer table. After opening the Query Analyzer, you discover that the test database and table you just created do not appear. Which of the following is likely to solve the problem?

   A. There was an error in the script you used to create the objects, and you need to correct the error and rerun the scripts.

   B. The Query Analyzer needs to be refreshed, thus giving it access to all objects in the system.

   C. You need to create the database and table from the Enterprise Manager to ensure that temporary objects are not used.

   D. You must restart the SQL Server service so that it has access to all newly created objects.

10. You are developing a query that will look for invalid entries in a table before implementing a new CHECK constraint. The constraint that you are implementing will enforce data entry into the gender column of the table. Which of the following queries will seek out records that have no value or are not male or female? (Select all that apply.)

    A.
    ```
    SELECT * FROM Employee
        WHERE Gndr = NULL or Gndr <> 'M' or
        ➥Gndr <> 'F'
        or Gndr <> 'm' or Gndr <> 'f'
    ```

    B.
    ```
    SELECT * FROM Employee
        WHERE Gndr = NULL and Gndr <> 'M'
        ➥and Gndr <> 'F'
        and Gndr <> 'm' and Gndr <> 'f'
    ```

    C.
    ```
    SELECT * FROM Employee
        WHERE Gndr IS NULL and Gndr <> 'M'
        ➥and Gndr <> 'F'
        and Gndr <> 'm' and Gndr <> 'f'
    ```

    D.
    ```
    SELECT * FROM Employee
        WHERE Gndr IS NULL or Gndr <> 'M'
        ➥or Gndr <> 'F'
        or Gndr <> 'm' or Gndr <> 'f'
    ```

    E.
    ```
    SELECT * FROM Employee
        WHERE Gndr IS NULL or (Gndr <> 'M'
        ➥and Gndr <> 'F'
        and Gndr <> 'm' and Gndr <> 'f')
    ```

    F.
    ```
    SELECT * FROM Employee
        WHERE Gndr IS NULL or Gndr NOT IN
        ➥('M', 'F', 'm', 'f')
    ```

11. A local manufacturing company uses a SQL Server to receive statistical information from various points on an assembly line. The information is gathered into a table called Production. Date information is maintained in a standard datetime column called Pdate. You would like to prepare a query that would list the production information from the preceding day. Which of the following queries solves the problem?

    A.
    ```
    SELECT * FROM Production
        WHERE Pdate = GetDate() - 1
    ```

    B.
    ```
    SELECT * FROM Production
        WHERE Pdate BETWEEN = GetDate()
        ➥- 2 AND GetDate()
    ```

    C.
    ```
    SELECT * FROM Production
        WHERE datediff(dd, PDate, getdate())
        ➥= 1
    ```

    D.
    ```
    SELECT * FROM Production
        WHERE datediff(dd, getdate(),
        ➥PDate) = 1
    ```

12. You are preparing to move a test database that you have been working on over the last several months over onto a production system. You are planning to go live with the new database sometime over the next few days. All the current data will be removed and replaced with production information when the system does go live. You

APPLY YOUR KNOWLEDGE

are performing some final tests when you notice that the column that is going to be used as the `ROWGUIDCOL` does not have any values. The ID is to be generated by the system and afterward used as a permanent value. How would you ensure that values are placed into this column as data is entered in the production system?

A. Correct the current data by providing the missing values and then add a constraint so that this doesn't happen again.

B. Correct the current data by providing the missing values and then add a `NEWID()` as a default for the column.

C. Correct the current data by providing the missing values and provide a formula to generate the value of the column.

D. Correct the current values by using an `UPDATE` operation and the `NEWID()` function and then add a `NEWID()` as a default for the column.

E. Empty the current table into a temporary table, add a default as `NEWID()`, and load the data back in using an `INSERT INTO` operation, omitting the ID column.

13. A local car dealership maintains a list of the current inventory on a single SQL Server. The machine also takes on a number of other networking roles for name resolution. Data is going to be moved off the existing machine in a move to create a dedicated database server. You would like to execute a query that copies all the data to a test database where the table already exists. Which of the following solves the problem?

```
A. INSERT INTO Test.dbo.Automobiles
        SELECT * FROM
        ➡Inventory.dbo.Automobiles
```

```
B. SELECT Test.dbo.Automobiles
        SELECT * FROM
        ➡Inventory.dbo.Automobiles
```

```
C. INSERT Test.dbo.Automobiles
        SELECT * FROM
        ➡Inventory.dbo.Automobiles
```

```
D. SELECT INTO Test.dbo.Automobiles
        SELECT * FROM
        ➡Inventory.dbo.Automobiles
```

```
E. INSERT INTO Inventory.dbo.Automobiles
        SELECT * FROM Test.dbo.Automobiles
```

14. An accounting system that has been recording company financial information for the past three years is being upgraded and having a number of additional columns added to the structure of several of the existing tables. You need to ensure that all existing data remains intact during these operations. Select two.

A. Set the database files to read-only.

B. Set the table properties to read-only.

C. Addition of columns shouldn't affect the database.

D. Set permissions on the database to prevent malicious updates.

E. Set column-level permissions to prevent updates to existing data.

15. You administer the database server for a large lumber and building materials supplier. You want to query the materials used by a single site. Which of the following queries would suit your needs?

```
A. SELECT Materials, Weight, Quantity
    FROM Inventory
            ORDER BY Site
```

```
B. SELECT Materials, Weight, Quantity
    FROM Inventory
            WHERE Site = 4
```

APPLY YOUR KNOWLEDGE

C. ```
SELECT Materials, Weight, Quantity
  FROM Inventory
        ORDER BY Quantity
```

D. ```
SELECT Materials, Weight, Quantity
  FROM Inventory
       ORDER BY Site, Quantity
```

E. ```
SELECT Materials, Weight, Quantity
  FROM Inventory
        where Materials = "Drywall"
```

# Answers To Review Questions

1. A DISTINCT query eliminates duplicate rows from a resultset, providing only a single copy of each row. This is usually most useful when you want to retrieve results on a small number of columns (one or two). With the use of DISTINCT you can list all the states where customers come from without duplicating any state, or you may want a listing of the topics of all employee experience without duplicating a topic. With this type of information you may be able to find gaps (no customers from a particular state or no employees with a desired talent) without needlessly searching through duplications of information.

2. A WHERE clause defined on a DELETE operation can prevent the accidental removal of every record in a table. Similarly, its use in a SELECT operation can allow for the listing of only desired data while filtering out data that does not meet the desired criteria.

3. There are many considerations for comparing date data with character data, including the actual format of the data storage, the native source and front-end application, as well as specifics of the required process. In general there are two approaches: to look at the comparison as a character comparison or a comparison between dates. Most applications will probably require date comparisons, and therefore a conversion of the character data into dates would be needed. Individual uses of a date and time that have been broken down into components is also common. If the application calls for other uses of the data in a character-related application, then turning the dates into characters may be performed. Some reporting applications have a requirement that all dates be received as character strings.

4. Functions that control data flow could include those that minimize the amount of data through the selection of columns and rows of data. Other functions control security and system interactions to permit the appropriate security and compression properties for all data being transmitted.

5. When table definitions include constraints and rules that can interact with foreign data, there is a possibility that those interactions can effect data in those sources. The most common forms of interaction involve the maintaining of referential integrity definitions. Optional Foreign Key constraints and cascading referential integrity can restrict, remove, or alter data in a foreign data source.

# Answers To Exam Questions

1. **A, C, D.** If you were to select UPDATE, the purpose of the command is exactly what you want to avoid. You should be able to increase the data storage size and alter a column name without affecting the internal data. However, decreasing the size for data storage results in data truncation or loss. INSERT used appropriately adds data but does not alter any existing values. For more information, see the section titled "Data Retrieval."
```

APPLY YOUR KNOWLEDGE

2. **B, E.** The key to this question is that this operation is going to be performed as a "one-time" thing, so the creation of data objects would likely be avoided and views would not be warranted. However, a script that performs the activity could easily be saved if needed in the future. Table aliases may help in your development, but in this scenario column aliases provide the end-user with the necessary data definition. For more information, see the section titled "Data Retrieval."

3. **D.** Dates are inclusive with the BETWEEN function. For further details on the use of the BETWEEN function, see the "BETWEEN and IN" section.

4. **A.** Assuming that all data from the table is needed, A is correct. It is not necessary to include all columns from a SELECT list when using ORDER. For appropriate use of ORDER BY, see the section "Ordering Data."

5. **E.** Appropriate use of the DISTINCT clause could eliminate the recurring data being noted. To diagnose this problem, the correct syntax must be implemented. The following code represents a plausible solution:

```
SELECT DISTINCT Country FROM Customers
    ORDER BY Country
```

For further details on the use of DISTINCT, see the section titled "The SQL SELECT Statement."

6. **C.** You are probably not ordering the data to achieve the desired results. Grouping of the resultset doesn't seem to be warranted because the question is asking for five rows. NULL values should not affect this query, though in some instances Null data can interfere with the results. See "Selecting Rows Based On NULL Values" for more information.

7. **F.** Each of the reasons excluding the agent are very possibly a cause of the symptoms being described. The SQL Server Agent handles non-data activity on the server related to Operators, Jobs, and Events configured on the system. If the Agent is not running only these particular processes are interrupted, not the entire database. For more information, refer to "SQL Server Agent" in SQL Server Books OnLine.

8. **A.** An XML implementation may be more suited to an active server page Internet application than a LAN application. RDO and DAO represent older technologies that aren't as efficient and versatile as ADO. SQL-DMO is for development of system applications that interact with SQL Server on a non-data level. For more details about any of the technologies, see SQL Server Books OnLine.

9. **B.** With all versions of SQL Server, the interface doesn't always show newly created objects. A periodic refresh in the Enterprise Manager and the object browser within the Query Analyzer is needed to assure accuracy of the display (see the note "Analyzer Connections").

10. **E, F.** Both E and F produce the desired results, though in this instance the IN may be easier to read and use and somewhat more efficient. The exam may ask you to choose the best of several working queries, in which case F would be the best answer. For more information on the use of IN see the section titled "BETWEEN and IN."

11. **C.** Date data types also include information for time, which causes many comparisons to not provide the desired results. Use the DATEDIFF function to prevent this problem. In this case the current date would be greater then the production date on

APPLY YOUR KNOWLEDGE

file, and therefore the first parameter must be PDate. For more information, see the "Date Functions" section of this chapter.

12. **E.** The most efficient and quickest way of performing this task would be to get the data out before you create the default. When the data is placed back without the ID, the default will generate the missing values. See DEFAULT use in Chapter 3.

13. **C.** The only query to use INSERT would work; INSERT INTO might have been appropriate if the table did not already exist. For more information, see the sections on "INSERT," "INSERT SELECT," and "INSERT INTO."

14. **C, D.** You don't want to set unnecessary read-only properties that wouldn't permit any alterations to the database or the records contained therein.

15. **B.** The query needed is a simple SELECT query with a WHERE condition for the site. For more information, see the section titled "The SQL SELECT statement".

Suggested Readings and Resources

1. SQL Server Books Online

   • Accessing and Changing Relational Data

2. Michael Reilly, Michelle Poolet, *SQL Server 2000 Design and TSQL Programming,* OSBORNE (December 2000).

3. Robin Dewson, *Beginning SQL Server Programming,* Wrox Press (June 2001).

In Chapter 4, we learned the basics of using the SELECT, INSERT, UPDATE, and DELETE statements. This chapter covers advanced techniques for writing queries to retrieve complex and summary data, along with how to import data into SQL Server from a variety of different systems and formats. Many complicated topics are covered in this chapter that are sure to provoke a couple of exam questions, especially the bits about GROUP BY and COMPUTE BY. Much of the query writing skills you learn in this chapter will also be really handy when you start looking at writing batches and scripts, which is covered in Chapter 6, "Programming SQL Server 2000."

Retrieve and filter data using Transact-SQL.

▶ You should know now to use the new and correct join syntax, derived tables, the IN operator, and the UNION operator.

Group Data using Transact-SQL.

▶ GROUP BY and HAVING, along with the COMPUTE and COMPUTE BY options of the SELECT statement, are integral parts of this objective, along with understanding the aggregate functions used to group data in SQL Server.

Summarize Data using Transact-SQL.

▶ You need to know how to use CUBE and ROLLUP, along with GROUP BY and aggregate functions, to summarize data.

Manipulate heterogeneous data. Methods include linked servers, OPENQUERY, and OPENROWSET.

▶ Sometimes the data you want to query isn't all on the same SQL Server, and sometimes it's not even stored in SQL Server at all. This objective says you should know about using SQL Server queries to retrieve data from other data sources.

CHAPTER 5

Advanced Data Retrieval and Modification

Extract data in XML format. Considerations include output format and XML schema structure.

▶ XML, the eXtensible Markup Language, has gained acceptance as a means to communicate data across platforms, especially over the Internet. This objective requires you to know how to retrieve data from SQL Server to exchange with other systems.

Import and manipulate data using OPENXML.

▶ This objective requires you to know how to read data in XML and manipulate it from SQL Server.

Import and export data. Methods include the bulk copy program, the Bulk Insert task, and Data Transformation Services.

▶ After you learn how to deal with importing and exporting data from XML, you need to learn how to import and export data from a variety of formats using the appropriate tools. The bulk copy program is used to move data to and from text files of various formats; BULK INSERT has the job of dealing with just data imports. Data Transformation Services provide a graphical interface for moving data between SQL Server and other formats.

STUDY STRATEGIES

▶ Practice, practice, practice. This chapter contains many examples on the various objectives covered; use these examples and play with the different types of syntax used. Type the examples into Query Analyzer and run them. Then see whether you can modify them to sort differently or group differently.

▶ There is more than one way to write nearly any query. Much of this chapter shows you different approaches to solving the same problem. The factor that establishes the SQL Server gurus from the SQL Server users is understanding the nuances between the methods, and not favoring one method over another, but using each appropriately.

▶ If you decide to play with some of your own data, understand that some of the queries covered here are very complex and take a while to run. If your queries are taking a distractingly long time to run, either skip ahead to the chapter on indexing, or find a way to work with a smaller test set.

RETRIEVE AND FILTER DATA USING TRANSACT-SQL

▶ **Retrieve and filter data using Transact-SQL.**

SQL Server is a relational database management system. This section focuses on the "Relational" part. It covers how tables relate to one another. In Chapter 2, you covered how Primary Keys and Foreign Keys are used in a database model, and how they impact storing data. This chapter shows you how to retrieve data from a relational database. This involves using the various join types: INNER, RIGHT, LEFT, and CROSS. You're also going to learn about using a technique called *derived tables* to simplify query writing.

A common data model is used throughout this chapter for the examples. This is to make life a bit easier for you. Here are the table layouts and some sample data:

```
CREATE TABLE Person (
        PersonID int IDENTITY(1,1) NOT NULL,
        FirstName varchar(50) NULL,
        LastName varchar(50) NOT NULL,
)
CREATE TABLE PersonAddress(
        PersonID int NOT NULL,
        AddressID int NOT NULL
)
CREATE TABLE Address (
        AddressID int IDENTITY(1,1) NOT NULL,
        StreetAddress varchar(250) NOT NULL,
        City varchar(50) NOT NULL,
        State varchar(50) NOT NULL,
        ZipCode char(5) NULL
)
CREATE TABLE Sales (
        PersonID int,
        ProductID int,
        QtyPurchased int,
        DatePurchased datetime
)
CREATE TABLE Product (
        ProductID int NOT NULL,
        ProductDescription varchar(15) NOT NULL
)
```

This model is for a many-to-many relationship between the Person table and the Address table. This means that one person can have several addresses, and several people can live at the same address. In addition, there is also a one-to-many relationship between Person and Sales, which means one person may have made several purchases, which are recorded in the Sales table. You may want to go ahead and build this structure in its own database on the server on which you're doing the examples.

Now insert some data into the sample schema and try it again. Some SELECT COUNT statements are at the bottom of the script to help you make sure you've got the correct number of rows in each table.

```
INSERT INTO Person VALUES ('Danny', 'Jones')
INSERT INTO Person VALUES ('Melissa', 'Jones')
INSERT INTO Person VALUES ('Scott', 'Smith')
INSERT INTO Person VALUES ('Alex', 'Riley')
INSERT INTO Person VALUES ('Chris', 'Avery')
INSERT INTO Person VALUES ('Jennifer', 'Avery')
INSERT INTO Person VALUES ('Bryan', 'Decker')
INSERT INTO Person VALUES ('Robin', 'Decker')
INSERT INTO Person VALUES ('Shelly', 'Alexander')

INSERT INTO Address VALUES ('1213 NW 97th Ct', 'SQL Town',
➥'MO', '64131')
INSERT INTO Address VALUES ('2721 SW 42nd Terr', 'Server
➥City', 'KS', '66212')
INSERT INTO Address VALUES ('1939 Overland St', 'Dell
➥Village', 'KS', '66213')
INSERT INTO Address VALUES ('9391 Nall Ave', 'Parrot
➥Township', 'MO', '64331')
INSERT INTO Address VALUES ('7737 Miner Dr', 'SQL Town',
➥'MO', '64132')
INSERT INTO Address VALUES ('5334 Shamrock Ln', 'Orange',
➥'KS', '66441')

INSERT INTO PersonAddress VALUES (1, 1)
INSERT INTO PersonAddress VALUES (2, 1)
INSERT INTO PersonAddress VALUES (3, 2)
INSERT INTO PersonAddress VALUES (4, 3)
INSERT INTO PersonAddress VALUES (5, 4)
INSERT INTO PersonAddress VALUES (6, 4)
INSERT INTO PersonAddress VALUES (7, 5)
INSERT INTO PersonAddress VALUES (8, 5)
INSERT INTO PersonAddress VALUES (9, 6)

INSERT INTO Sales VALUES (1, 37, 4, getdate())
INSERT INTO Sales VALUES (1, 38, 3, getdate())
INSERT INTO Sales VALUES (3, 39, 1, getdate())
INSERT INTO Sales VALUES (4, 51, 1, getdate())
INSERT INTO Sales VALUES (4, 47, 1, getdate())
INSERT INTO Sales VALUES (9, 37, 10, getdate())
INSERT INTO Sales VALUES (9, 38, 5, getdate())
INSERT INTO Sales VALUES (10, 41, 6, getdate())
INSERT INTO Product VALUES (37, 'Widget')
```

```
INSERT INTO Product VALUES (38, 'Grommet')
INSERT INTO Product VALUES (39, 'Spackle')
INSERT INTO Product VALUES (51, 'Sparkle Dust')
INSERT INTO Product VALUES (47, 'Shoe Polish')
INSERT INTO Product VALUES (38, 'Varnish')
INSERT INTO Product VALUES (41, 'Lava')
go

SELECT COUNT(*) FROM person --9 rows
SELECT COUNT(*) FROM address  --6 rows
SELECT COUNT(*) FROM PersonAddress --9 rows
SELECT COUNT(*) FROM Sales  --8 rows
SELECT COUNT(*) FROM Product  --7 rows
```

That's a lot of typing, but you'll end up using that data all the way through the chapter. Notice that several tables have data in them. You're probably wondering how to make them all work together. So now it's time to talk about join mechanics.

Join Mechanics

Whenever you query data from two tables, you need to find some way to relate the two tables together. If you need to select out the name and address of everyone in the example database, how would you go about doing it? You'd want to write a query that would relate the Person table to the Address table through the PersonAddress table.

Whenever you want to use a SQL statement to relate one table to another, it's called a *join*. In this case, you need two joins: one from the Person table to the PersonAddress table, and another one from the PersonAddress table to the Address table. Whenever you want to see a resultset that includes columns from several tables, you need to use a join.

There are three basic join types. An *inner join* shows results only where there are matches between the elements. In other words, if you query the database and want to see only the people who have addresses, you use an inner join. An inner join leaves out all the records that don't have a match.

An *outer join* can show all the records from one side of the relationship, records that match where they are available, and NULL values for records that do not have a match. An outer join between the Person and Sales tables can show you each person and the amount of purchases they've made, and show NULL values for people who haven't made purchases yet, but are in the Person table. An outer join shows all the same records as an inner join, plus all the records that don't match.

The final type of join is a *cross join*. A cross join returns all possible combinations of rows between the two sides of the join. The number of records in the resultset is equal to the number of records on one side of the join multiplied by the number of records on the other side of the join. No correlation is attempted between the two records; all the records from both sides are returned. Performing a cross join on two large tables is probably not a good idea. The number of rows in the return set, or in intermediate sets used by SQL Server, can get out of hand quickly, causing server-wide performance degradation.

IN THE FIELD

HOW MANY RECORDS?

If you have 100 records in the Person table, and 100 records in the Sales table, and then perform a cross join between the two tables, you'd end up with 10,000 records in your resultset (100×100 = 10,000).

Scale that up to a 50,000 record table and a 100 record table (5 million records) and you'll see some typical bad news that can result from a cross join. If you figure that each of those returned records contains about 300 bytes, you can end up with a resultset that weighs in at 1.5 gigabytes, which would probably overwhelm any client computer at which you aimed it.

NOTE

Order of Operations   Before some purist out there starts screaming and writing inflammatory post-publishing e-mails, a bit of clarification: Physically, SQL Server performs operations such as joining tables and filtering data in a WHERE clause in whatever order it decides is fastest. Logically, however, you can feel free to think of it doing things in join, then WHERE order. SQL Server doesn't re-order how it does things in such a way that will violate that rule.

In the grand scheme of SQL, joins are processed first. In other words, each join type description says, "will return all the records from one side...", which means the join returns all those records. What you put in the WHERE clause is applied after the joins are processed. So, bear in mind that when a join returns a specified set of records, the SQL statement may or may not return all those records, depending on what you've specified in the WHERE clause.

With all of that out of the way, let's look at each of the different join operators, starting with INNER JOIN.

Using *INNER JOIN*

The INNER JOIN statement is the easiest and most often used join statement. It's very simple; it relates one table to another table; and it returns a rowset where the two tables match up. For example:

```
SELECT *
FROM Person
          INNER JOIN Sales
                  on Person.PersonID = Sales.PersonID
```

What's that going to do? It returns all the rows where there is a person who has made a purchase. The columns returned are all the columns from both tables, with the columns from the Person table first.

The resultset is wider than you probably want:

PersonID	FirstName	LastName	PersonID	ProductID	QtyPurchased	DatePurchased
1	Danny	Jones	1	37	4	2001-07-22 16:50
1	Danny	Jones	1	38	3	2001-07-22 16:50
3	Scott	Smith	3	39	1	2001-07-22 16:50
4	Alex	Riley	4	51	1	2001-07-22 16:50
4	Alex	Riley	4	47	1	2001-07-22 16:50
9	Shelly	Alexander	9	37	10	2001-07-22 16:50
9	Shelly	Alexander	9	38	5	2001-07-22 16:50

That's probably not what you want in a resultset. You'll get a fairly useful resultset if you write the SELECT statement like this, specifying the column names, instead:

```
SELECT FirstName, LastName, ProductID, QtyPurchased
FROM Person
        INNER JOIN Sales
                ON Person.PersonID = Sales.PersonID
```

This query shows the people in the database to whom you have sold things. It doesn't show all the people in the database, because not everyone has bought something. It also shows some people more than once, because they bought several things.

Now look more closely at the statement after the keyword FROM. First, data is selected from the Person table, and followed by an INNER JOIN to the Sales table. The ON clause then tells SQL Server how the tables are related. That ON clause says to return rows where the PersonID column in the two tables is the same. Notice that the column name is specified as Person.PersonID. Both tables have a

PersonID column, so SQL Server gives you an error if you don't
specify which table the column comes from. SQL Server also gives
you an error if you write this:

```
SELECT PersonID, FirstName, LastName, ProductID,
➡QtyPurchased
FROM Person
        INNER JOIN Sales
                ON Person.PersonID = Sales.PersonID
```

This results in an error of Ambiguous column name 'PersonID'.
Once again, because the PersonID column appears more than once
in the set of joined tables, you need to specify which PersonID you
want, even though they are both going to have the same value after
the join.

The code sample is also representative of one way to indent and
style the SQL. It's valid to put the entire SQL statement on one line,
but it's also valid to wear dark socks with sandals, striped shorts, and
a plaid shirt. Use a consistent style when you are writing queries; it
makes them easier for you to read and for others to read.

That's all well and good, but how can you get a list of the addresses
for all the people to whom you've sold things? That goes something
like this:

```
SELECT Address.*
FROM Person
        INNER JOIN Sales
                ON Person.PersonID = Sales.PersonID
        INNER JOIN PersonAddress
                ON PersonAddress.PersonID = Person.PersonID
        INNER JOIN Address
                ON PersonAddress.AddressID = Address.AddressID
```

The Address.* in that statement specifies that you want to return all
the fields in the Address table, but you don't want the fields in the
rest of the tables. This is a convenient shortcut. Here's another neat
way to reduce typing:

```
SELECT A.*
FROM Person P
        INNER JOIN Sales S
                ON P.PersonID = S.PersonID
        INNER JOIN PersonAddress PA
                ON PA.PersonID = P.PersonID
        INNER JOIN Address A
                ON PA.AddressID = A.AddressID
```

This is an example of using table aliases. When you're doing complex joins, and you don't want to type the table name over and over again, you can alias the table to a different name. In this case, the Person table is aliased to P. After doing that, the only way you can access column names in the Person table is by using the P alias. You can't mix aliased and non-aliased names, so this does not work:

```
SELECT A.*
FROM Person P
        INNER JOIN Sales S
                ON P.PersonID = S.PersonID
        INNER JOIN PersonAddress PA
                ON PA.PersonID = P.PersonID
        INNER JOIN Address A
                ON PA.AddressID = A.AddressID
```

If you attempt to run that query, you get an error that says, the column prefix 'Person' does not match with a table name or alias name used in the query. That's because you aliased the table name to something else, so SQL Server can't use the real name for it anymore; it can use only the alias. Another form of table aliasing syntax is

```
SELECT A.*
FROM Person AS P
        INNER JOIN Sales AS S
                ON P.PersonID = S.PersonID
        INNER JOIN PersonAddress AS PA
                ON PA.PersonID = P.PersonID
        INNER JOIN Address AS A
                ON PA.AddressID = A.AddressID
```

The AS keyword is always optional, and if the point is to type less by using aliases, it should probably be left out.

On the topic of optional syntax, the keyword INNER is not required in the queries, either. If you want to write the query as follows, it works the same way:

```
SELECT A.*
FROM Person P
        JOIN Sales S
                ON P.PersonID = S.PersonID
        JOIN PersonAddress PA
                ON PA.PersonID = P.PersonID
        JOIN Address A
                ON PA.AddressID = A.AddressID
```

Arguably, this example requires less typing, but many people feel that the keyword INNER provides a little more insight into how the query works and is easier to read.

> **NOTE**
>
> **Using Aliases Effectively** You should use aliases that somehow abbreviate the table name in some consistent and standard way. For example, don't alias the first table as A, the second table as B, and so on, because you'll spend more time figuring out what the aliases mean than it would have taken to type in the full names in the first place. You should carefully measure tradeoffs between readability and brevity, and if you have to guess, lean toward readability.

One more variation on the theme of inner joins. Imagine that you need to join a table back onto itself. For example, you want to find all the people with the same last name in the Person table. You'd write a query like this one:

```
SELECT P1.FirstName, P2.FirstName, P1.LastName
FROM Person P1
      INNER JOIN Person P2
            ON P1.LastName = P2.LastName
            AND P1.FirstName < P2.FirstName
```

In this example, the same table is used twice, joined to itself. The example produces the following output:

```
FirstName FirstName LastName
Danny     Melissa   Jones
Chris     Jennifer  Avery
Bryan     Robin     Decker
```

The join also has an extra line in it. The P1.FirstName < P2.FirstName part prevents SQL Server from producing duplicate rows. Without that line in the JOIN clause, or at least in the WHERE clause, you'd have each couple showing up twice, once with each name first.

Now that you've seen how INNER JOIN works, it's time to move on to the outer joins.

Outer Joins

You can use an outer join when you want to return the entire list of rows from one side of the join, and the matching rows from the other side of the join. There are three types of outer joins: LEFT, RIGHT, and FULL. A RIGHT OUTER JOIN, often abbreviated RIGHT JOIN, returns all the rows belonging to the table on the right side of the join, and where there is a matching row on the table on the left side, it returns the matching data. Conversely, LEFT OUTER JOIN returns all the rows from the table on the left side, and where there is a matching row on the table on the right side, it returns the matching data. A FULL OUTER JOIN returns all the rows from both sides with correlations where they exist.

Most people read that for the first time and their eyes cross. Here are some examples to help you get back on track. Remember the query you saw earlier that returned all the records from Person with a matching record in Sales? This example returns all the records in Person, and matching records in Sales where they exist. First, using a LEFT JOIN:

```
SELECT FirstName, LastName, ProductID, QtyPurchased
FROM Person
        LEFT JOIN Sales
                ON Person.PersonID = Sales.PersonID
```

And then a RIGHT JOIN:

```
SELECT FirstName, LastName, ProductID, QtyPurchased
FROM Sales
        RIGHT JOIN Person
                ON Person.PersonID = Sales.PersonID
```

These two queries both return exactly the same resultset, because the order of the tables is different. The LEFT JOIN example does Person LEFT JOIN Sales and the RIGHT JOIN example does Sales RIGHT JOIN Person.

IN THE FIELD

RIGHT JOIN AND LEFT JOIN

As you've just read, LEFT JOIN and RIGHT JOIN both do the same thing. Why does Transact-SQL include both, and which should you use?

Typically, you should use LEFT JOIN whenever possible. There's no reason for this other than convention, and most Western languages read left to right, so people in Western cultures are more trained to think in that direction. So using LEFT JOIN will make your query easier for someone else to understand.

In other order-related issues, the order that the ON clause is in does not change how the clause works. For example, saying ON P.PersonID = S.PersonID is the same as S.PersonID = P.PersonID.

Now it's time to put together everything you've learned so far. You've got an INNER JOIN and an OUTER JOIN. You can use table aliases in an OUTER JOIN the same way as you do in an INNER JOIN, by the way. Table aliasing is a feature of the FROM clause, not the join type. Now here's a list of all the addresses in the database and what they bought, if they bought anything:

```
SELECT A.*, S.ProductID, S.QtyPurchased
FROM Person P
        LEFT JOIN Sales S
                ON P.PersonID = S.PersonID
        INNER JOIN PersonAddress PA
                ON PA.PersonID = P.PersonID
        INNER JOIN Address A
                on PA.AddressID = A.AddressID
```

Now, the FULL OUTER JOIN. Imagine that you want to query all the records from Person and Sales, and have the tables put together where possible, but you want all records shown from both tables, regardless of whether there was a correlation or not. Here's how you can do it:

```
SELECT FirstName, LastName, ProductID, QtyPurchased
FROM Person
        FULL JOIN Sales
                ON Person.PersonID = Sales.PersonID
```

That returns the following recordset:

FirstName	LastName	ProductID	QtyPurchased
Danny	Jones	37	4
Danny	Jones	38	3
Melissa	Jones	NULL	NULL
Scott	Smith	39	1
Alex	Riley	51	1
Chris	Avery	NULL	NULL
Jennifer	Avery	NULL	NULL
Bryan	Decker	NULL	NULL
Robin	Decker	NULL	NULL
Shelly	Alexander	37	10
Shelly	Alexander	38	5
NULL	NULL	41	6

Notice that you have examples where the data that comes from the Sales table (ProductID and QtyPurchased) is NULL, for Chris Avery and others, along with an example of ProductID of 41 and QtyPurchased of 6 that was purchased by someone not in the Person table.

Filtering with Outer Joins

One common use of an outer join is to find places where there aren't correlations in data. For example, if you wanted to find all the rows in the Person table that didn't have a corresponding row in `Sales`, which would mean a person who hadn't bought anything yet, you could run a query like this one:

```
SELECT FirstName, LastName, ProductID, QtyPurchased
FROM Person
        LEFT JOIN Sales
                ON Person.PersonID = Sales.PersonID
WHERE Sales.QtyPurchased IS NULL
```

This query exploits the fact that when you do a LEFT JOIN, the columns that are returned for the table on the right when there is no correlation are all NULL. The fact that the `QtyPurchased` column in the `Sales` table is used is just coincidence; any column in the `Sales` table that doesn't allow NULL values could be used. Whenever there is no correlation between the data rows, the columns for the table on the inside of the join are all set to NULL, making it a very easy target for filtering.

If you're using this data for a report, you probably don't want the word NULL showing up on the report. The managers and sales people who end up reading the report probably won't understand the word NULL. So, to steal some thunder from a bit later in the book, here's how you can get rid of those annoying NULLs:

```
SELECT FirstName, LastName, ISNULL(ProductID, 0),
➥ISNULL(QtyPurchased, 0)
FROM Person
        LEFT JOIN Sales
                ON Person.PersonID = Sales.PersonID
WHERE Sales.QtyPurchased IS NULL
```

The `ISNULL()` function returns the second argument if the first argument is NULL. So, for the cases where the `QtyPurchased` is NULL, it substitutes in a zero. `ISNULL()` is covered a bit later during the discussion about CASE expressions.

Cross Joins

Cross joins are joins that return all the rows from both tables associated with each other. For example, currently the `Person` table has 9 records and the `Product` table has 7 records. A CROSS JOIN of these two tables would return 63 rows: each of the 9 records in the `Person` table with each of the 7 records in the `Product` table. Whenever you use a CROSS JOIN, you should be aware that the returned resultset is likely to be very large. A CROSS JOIN does not have an ON clause; there is no correlation, so it's not needed.

Here's an example of using an ON clause to generate data for a custom order form:

```
SELECT FirstName, LastName, ProductDescription
FROM Person
        CROSS JOIN Product
ORDER BY FirstName, LastName, ProductDescription
```

The FROM clause of a SELECT statement is an incredibly complex piece of work. You have the different join types and their correlations all going on in there. So, how can you make it even more complex and harder to read?

Derived Tables

You can use derived tables to make your queries simpler to read, or at least simpler to write. To use a derived table, put a SELECT statement in parentheses in the FROM clause where you'd normally put a table name. An alias is required for a derived table.

Let's say that you have a query that looks something like this:

```
SELECT Person.PersonID, FirstName, LastName, ProductID,
➥QtyPurchased
FROM Sales
        RIGHT JOIN Person
                ON Person.PersonID = Sales.PersonID
```

And you'd like to get the address for the people returned as well. You've already done this once in the earlier examples, but here's another way to do it:

```
Select P.*, Address.StreetAddress, Address.City,
➥Address.ZipCode
        from
                (SELECT Person.PersonID, FirstName, LastName,
                ➥ProductID, QtyPurchased
                        FROM Sales
                        RIGHT JOIN Person
                                ON Person.PersonID = Sales.PersonID) P
                INNER JOIN PersonAddress
                        ON PersonAddress.PersonID = P.PersonID
                INNER JOIN Address
                        ON Address.AddressID = PersonAddress.
                        ➥AddressID
```

As you can see, there's a table here aliased to P that is actually a SELECT statement, and it's the same SELECT statement that was used earlier. So you can do some interesting things here with copy-and-paste: you can take a query and write another query around it.

The problem is, as you can see from the example, the resulting query can be very difficult to format or read. Things that are difficult to format and read also tend to be difficult to optimize, modify, and debug.

That's one example of using a query inside another query. Here's another.

The *IN* Operator

The IN clause can be used in comparisons inside nearly every SQL statement as an operator. The IN operator takes two arguments—a value and a set—and checks to see whether the value is part of the set. For example:

```
SELECT * FROM Person WHERE PersonID IN (1, 3, 5)
```

That's a good way to use the IN operator. It can also be used with select queries that return one and only one column, like this:

```
SELECT * FROM Person WHERE PersonID IN (Select PersonID
➥from PersonAddress)
```

In this case, the SQL statement returns every person who has an address, but it always returns each person only one time. If you run the same query with a join, you get back the same list, assuming each person has only one address. If some of the records in Person have more than one address, you end up with duplicates in the resultset.

```
SELECT Person.*
       from Person
              INNER JOIN PersonAddress
                  on PersonAddress.PersonID =
                  ➥Person.PersonID
```

This returns the same list, but SQL Server executes this differently. SQL Server is very efficient at processing joins, but it's not as efficient at processing IN clauses, so use IN clauses sparingly.

Sometimes you need a bit more flexibility in your queries to decide what data to include, based on the data in other fields.

CASE Expressions

A CASE expression works like an IF statement, but can be used in locations where an IF statement cannot. Specifically, a CASE expression returns one of a specific set of values based on the outcome of one or more expressions. Here's an example:

```
Select CASE datepart(weekday, getdate())
            WHEN 1 then 'Sunday'
            WHEN 2 then 'Monday'
            WHEN 3 then 'Tuesday'
            WHEN 4 then 'Wednesday'
            WHEN 5 then 'Thursday'
            WHEN 6 then 'Friday'
            WHEN 7 then 'Saturday'
            ELSE 'Unknown'
END
```

This example gets the day of week for today and turns it into a string that represents the text for the day of week. If, for some reason, the day of the week returned by the datepart function is invalid, it returns the string Unknown. The result is placed into the variable @Result. This is the proper syntax to use when the comparison you want to use is equality—in this situation, datepart(weekday, getdate()) = 1. Notice that the expression starts with the keyword CASE and ends with the keyword END. This is the only time you can use an END without a BEGIN. This is called a "simple" CASE statement, contrasted against the "searched" CASE statement, discussed later in this section.

Now, if you wanted to write code with a similar result, you can write this:

```
DECLARE @result varchar(30)
IF datepart(weekday, getdate()) = 1
        set @Result = 'Monday'
else if datepart(weekday, getdate()) = 2
        set @Result = 'Tuesday'
else if datepart(weekday, getdate()) = 3
        set @result = 'Wednesday'
else if datepart(weekday, getdate()) = 4
        set @result = 'Thursday'
else if datepart(weekday, getdate()) = 5
        set @result = 'Friday'
else if datepart(weekday, getdate()) = 6
        set @result = 'Saturday'
else if datepart(weekday, getdate()) = 7
        set @result = 'Sunday'
else set @result = 'Unknown'
PRINT @Result
```

Although that's certainly usable in this case, it's not usable if you want to embed the logic into an INSERT or UPDATE statement; plus the CASE involves a lot less typing. Here's another way to write the same code with a different syntax of CASE statement:

```
DECLARE @Result char(10)
SET @Result = CASE WHEN datepart(weekday, getdate()) = 1
➥THEN 'Sunday'
    WHEN datepart(weekday, getdate()) = 2 THEN 'Monday'
    WHEN datepart(weekday, getdate()) = 3 THEN 'Tuesday'
    WHEN datepart(weekday, getdate()) = 4 THEN 'Wednesday'
    WHEN datepart(weekday, getdate()) = 5 THEN 'Thursday'
    WHEN datepart(weekday, getdate()) = 6 THEN 'Friday'
    WHEN datepart(weekday, getdate()) = 7 THEN 'Saturday'
    ELSE 'Unknown'
END
```

This code will do the exact same thing, but notice that the expression isn't split up. That allows you to do something like this:

```
DECLARE @Result char(10)
SET @Result = CASE WHEN datepart(weekday, getdate()) in
➥(1,7) THEN 'Weekend'
                ELSE 'Weekday'
END
PRINT @Result
```

You couldn't use the IN clause with the simple case covered previously, but the searched form of the CASE statement is allowed to use IN along with the rest of the comparison operators.

The CASE expression is most often used in SELECT statements to modify data. For example, imagine that you want to find out which objects in your database were created on a weekend:

```
SELECT name,
        CASE WHEN datepart(weekday,crdate) in  (1,7) THEN
        ➥'Weekend'
                ELSE 'Weekday'
        END
FROM sysobjects
```

CASE statements can also be used in the WHERE clause, an ORDER BY clause, or anywhere else an expression is allowed, like this:

```
SELECT name
FROM sysobjects
WHERE CASE id % 2
            WHEN 1 THEN 1
            ELSE 0
    END = 1
```

The percent sign in this example is the modulo operator: it returns the remainder of the first number divided by the second number. Basically, what this SELECT statement does is return the names of all the odd-numbered (divisible by 2 with a remainder of 1) objects in the current database. When the ID modulo 2 is 1, then it's an odd number, and the CASE statement returns 1, which the WHERE clause then compares to the number 1, and the row is included in the resultset. Otherwise, the CASE statement returns 0, which does not equal one, so the row is not included in the resultset. The keen of wit will note that a better way to write this would be:

```
SELECT name
FROM sysobjects
WHERE id % 2 = 1
```

That, however, would not demonstrate the point of using CASE statements in a WHERE clause, nor would it be nearly as convoluted. It would, however, be readable and efficient.

You should be aware of a couple of shortcuts. The ISNULL function is a great way to handle NULL values without using a CASE statement. Instead of writing this:

```
SELECT CASE sid WHEN null THEN 0 ELSE sid END FROM sysusers
```

you could write this statement, which does the same thing:

```
SELECT isnull(sid, 0) FROM sysusers
```

Another statement that's a shortcut for a CASE statement is called COALESCE. It takes a series of values and returns the first one that's not null. You could rewrite the preceding statement with:

```
SELECT coalesce(sid, 0) FROM sysusers
```

and get the same results. Now that you've got the CASE statement down, you can learn how to join tables together end-to-end with the UNION operator.

The *UNION* Operator

The UNION operator is used to join two queries together end-to-end, instead of side-by-side. A UNION operator takes the output of two or more SELECT statements and creates one recordset. Each

SELECT statement in the list must return the same number of columns, and the columns must be of compatible types. So, if the first SELECT statement returns an int, a float, a varchar(15), and a char(6), the second has to contain two pieces of data that can be converted to numbers followed by two pieces of data that can be converted to characters.

So, what happens if the columns are different types? Well, if they are compatible, meaning that the types and data can be implicitly converted, then the output set will contain as close to the types of the first SELECT as possible, with the following rules for a given column:

◆ If any of the SELECT statements return a mix of variable-length and fixed-length fields, the output is variable length.

◆ If the SELECT statements contain columns of different lengths, the longest length is used for the output.

◆ If the two values are numerics, the value with the most precision is used.

So, if you have an integer and a float, the output is a float, because a float has the most precision. If you have an integer and a string that is a number (such as 42), then you will have an integer; but, if the string was 42.00, you'd have a numeric type that could contain two decimal places and a full integer. These are the "rules of thumb" that'll get you through most situations. If you want to see the entire set of data type precedence rules, it is available in Books Online. Search the index for "Precedence," and choose the article on "Data Type Precedence."

Here's an example of a UNION. This example uses a different set of sample data than the rest of the chapter, because of the type conversion topics:

```
CREATE TABLE Table1 (
        A int,
        B float,
        C varchar(15),
        D char(10)
)

CREATE TABLE Table2 (
        First numeric(5,2),
        Second int,
        Third int
)
```

```
INSERT INTO Table1 VALUES (1, 3.14, '42', 'Bogus')
INSERT INTO Table1 VALUES (2, 2.1828, '93', 'Data')
INSERT INTO Table2 VALUES (123.45, 3, 16)
INSERT INTO Table2 VALUES (456.78, 4, 29)

SELECT A, B, C FROM Table1
UNION
SELECT First, Second, Third FROM Table2
```

Notice that the column names are specified. If you use SELECT *
with both, they have an inconsistent number of columns, and you'll
get an error, All queries in an SQL statement containing a
UNION operator must have an equal number of expressions in
their target lists. This returns successfully, and the data types
are a numeric(5,2), a float, and an int. The numeric(5,2) is the
compromise between an int and a numeric(5,2); the float is the
compromise between a float and an int; and the data is converted
to int because all the varchar values in Table1 can convert to int. If
there had been a string that couldn't convert to an int, SQL Server
would have thrown an error message. If it can't convert a string to a
numeric value, it throws an error.

Three additional notes on UNION. First, if you want to sort a UNION,
you put the ORDER BY after the last SELECT statement, like this:

```
SELECT A, B, C FROM Table1
UNION
SELECT First, Second, Third FROM Table2
ORDER BY 1
```

Next, if you want to do a SELECT...INTO operation, you need to do
it as follows:

```
SELECT A, B, C
INTO #UnionOutput
FROM Table1
UNION
SELECT First, Second, Third FROM Table2
```

Finally, the column names returned are taken from the first query in
the set of UNION operators. So, in this example the columns would be
named A, B, and C.

IN THE FIELD

UNION OPERATORS AND DATABASE DESIGN

Recall for a moment Chapter 2, "Database Modeling." Remember that the elements that make up a database are called tables, and tables should classify entities. A person is an entity; a company is an entity; a sale of a product is another entity.

If you have one table for companies and a separate table for individual people, and you use those tables to track sales, it's pretty natural to write a query that would union the table of people with the table of companies to provide a summary report or even just a list of mailing addresses for a new company catalog.

On the other hand, if you have several different tables of company information, and you're joining the tables together with a UNION, you may have something wrong with your database design. Whenever you use a UNION, ask yourself why the tables on which you are using the UNION are separate tables. Is it because they represent distinct entities, or because the database isn't designed the way it should be?

In general, an overuse of the UNION operator is indicative of bad design. Objects that are so alike in structure that they can be joined with a UNION should in all probability be in the same table in the first place.

One unique feature of the UNION is that it automatically removes duplicates from the final resultset. So, if the Table1 and Table2 tables have rows that are identical, SQL Server automatically filters them all out. Of course, this does have a great deal of overhead associated with it. To avoid that overhead, if you don't care about duplicates, you can use the UNION ALL command, like this:

```
SELECT A, B, C FROM Table1
UNION ALL
SELECT First, Second, Third FROM Table2
```

You can now write queries that join data horizontally across columns with the various JOIN clauses and that join data vertically across rows with the UNION operator. You've also packed a few additional tools such as table aliases and derived tables into your toolbox. These are all foundational components for the next piece, grouping data.

GROUPING DATA WITH TRANSACT-SQL

▶ **Group data using Transact-SQL.**

SQL Server is all about reporting. If you think that the database you're designing is for storing data, you are looking at design from the wrong angle.

Reporting is typically how things come out of the database. If your database is for a payroll system, reporting is how it prints checks. If your database is for a cargo shipping application, then reporting is how it prints invoices and how many widgets the company will need to make next month if sales continue at the same rate. Reporting is what makes money for companies. Without effective ways of reading and presenting data, there are no payroll checks, shipping invoices, or sales projections.

Reporting is being able to count things, average things, find maximum values, and find minimum values, and do all that over different categories of data. If you've ever been involved in a report design, then you know that most reports are all about grouping different entities together and describing how those entities behave. How many widgets did we sell last month, what was the average cost to produce, and what was the average selling price? Those are the things that drive how business is done.

This section is going to cover big topics. It describes how to aggregate data, how to perform operations on those aggregates, and how to do computations across aggregates. Remember, it's all about the slice and dice.

Aggregate Functions

Aggregate functions are functions that provide summary data about sets. Questions like "How many rows are in that table?" "How many widgets did we sell last week?" and "What is the average price we charged for a widget?" are all answered with aggregate functions. Table 5.1 provides a list and a brief description of each aggregate function. This section also covers what they do and their syntax.

TABLE 5.1	

AGGREGATE FUNCTIONS

Function	Description
AVG()	Average value of the group.
BINARY_CHECKSUM(), CHECKSUM(), and CHECKSUM_AGG()	Return a number representing the value of the data in the group. Useful for detecting data changes.
COUNT(), COUNT_BIG()	Number of objects in the group.
MAX()	Maximum value of the group.
MIN()	Minimum value of the group.
SUM()	Sum of the values in the group.
STDEV(), STDEVP()	Standard deviation of values in the group.
VAR(), VARP()	Variance of the values in the group.

Aggregate functions take one of three types of arguments. Some take a simple wildcard (*). This means that the operation either doesn't apply to rows, or it should apply to all rows. Look at the following statement, for example:

```
SELECT COUNT(*) FROM Person
```

This example returns the number of rows in the Person table. The number of rows that are in the table is independent of any individual column. The COUNT() functions and the CHECKSUM() functions work this way. It applies the function across the entire group, regardless of the content of each row.

All the functions take a column name as an argument, and then the aggregate applies only to that column. You could have used this in the preceding query:

```
SELECT COUNT(PersonID) FROM Person
```

This example returns the number of not-null PersonIDs in the table.

Some functions enable you to apply the function to distinct values only. For example, if you want a count of the distinct values in a table, you can use COUNT (DISTINCT LastName), which provides a count of the number of distinct last names. The COUNT, AVG, and SUM functions support this and actually do something with it. MIN and MAX support it, but it doesn't mean anything; it is included only for SQL-92 compliance.

The following sections look at the functions by category: First the statistical aggregate functions, then the data management aggregate functions.

Statistical Aggregate Functions

Statistical aggregate functions perform various operations across their sets. The COUNT() function returns an integer representing the number of rows in the table. The COUNT_BIG() function does the same thing, but it returns a number of type bigint instead.

The AVG() function returns the average value for a given column. It requires a column name, and optionally you can use DISTINCT to get an average for just the distinct values in the table. Here's an example that determines the average size of an order from the sample Sales table:

```
SELECT AVG(QtyPurchased) FROM Sales
```

This returns a value of 3, which is the sum of the QtyPurchased (4 + 3 + 1 + 1 + 1 + 10 + 5 + 6, which is 31), divided by the number of records in the table (8). If you divide those two together and truncate the decimal places (because the example deals with integers), you get 3. If you execute this query:

```
SELECT AVG(DISTINCT QtyPurchased) FROM Sales
```

You get the value 4, which is the distinct QtyPurchased values (4 + 3 + 1 + 10 + 5 + 6, which is 29) divided by the number of distinct values (6). Truncate the decimal places and you get 4.

MAX() and MIN() are very simple. They return the maximum or the minimum value in the set. Here's an example:

```
SELECT MIN(QtyPurchased), MAX(QtyPurchased) FROM Sales
```

This returns a rowset with one record and two columns: 1 and 10. The SUM function is nearly as simple, it just returns the sum of all the values in the group:

```
SELECT SUM(QtyPurchased), SUM(DISTINCT QtyPurchased) FROM
➡Sales
```

As you can see, this is another one of the functions that can use the DISTINCT keyword. This returns 31 and 29. Finally, dust off your old statistics book, because the next two sets of functions are a bit advanced. The VAR() and VARP() functions calculate the variance of the group. The STDDEV() and STDDEVP() functions calculate the standard deviation of the group. Variance and standard deviation are used in statistics to determine the spread of a sample set. A sample set has a high variance and a high standard deviation if there is a wide range of values in the sample set. If there is a small range of values, then the variance and standard deviation is smaller. The STDEVP() and STDEV() functions differ in that the STDEV() determines the sample standard deviation, while STDEVP() returns the population standard deviation. VAR() and VARP() are similar. See the "Suggested Reading" section at the end of the chapter if you really want more information.

Data Management Aggregate Functions

Four functions specifically pertain to helping you manage data. Three of them revolve around checksums. A checksum is a number generated from a data value that essentially summarizes the data value. For example, if you have the string "This is a test", the checksum is 575031869. That doesn't mean much, but if you store that value, and then change the string to "The test is over", which has a checksum of 270787094, you can quickly tell by comparing the checksums that the value of the string changed. If you're working with large data sets, though, the ability to compare checksums saves an immense amount of time over comparing strings together.

The computer science folks call this a *hash function*. Basically, it's a way to compress your data for comparison purposes to make it easier to compare. There is a small chance that two pieces of data will have the same checksum. How small? Well, 2 in 4 billion. The checksums return some number that's an integer, and the chances that two pseudorandom integers will be the same are very small. So this is actually a very useful function for detecting changes in rows.

The CHECKSUM() and CHECKSUM_BINARY() functions aren't true aggregate functions. They return a checksum for whatever you ask them to—typically for a row. The difference between CHECKSUM() and CHECKSUM_BINARY() is that a CHECKSUM() checks data that's been localized for the server, whereas CHECKSUM_BINARY() checks raw data. In this case, "localized" means that the string is translated to how it would compare prior to computing the checksum. So, if you're on a server that's set up as not case sensitive, which is the default, the

CHECKSUM() for "Widget" and "widget" would be the same, whereas the BINARY_CHECKSUM() would be different.

The CHECKSUM_AGG() function is the aggregate function used to compute checksums over sets. This function enables you to get the aggregated checksum for an entire table. Look at some examples. First, here's an example of using just the CHECKSUM() function on a table:

```
SELECT CHECKSUM(*) FROM Sales
```

This returns 8 rows, each containing a checksum for the entire row. Now, if you want to use a checksum for the entire table, you can do this:

```
SELECT CHECKSUM_AGG(CHECKSUM(*)) FROM Sales
```

This gives you a checksum for the entire table. Now, look at a way to use this information. The key thing to remember about using a checksum is that it's a snapshot. To find differences, you've got to have a checksum before and a checksum after the changes occur. One way to do this is to create a table that contains the name and checksum of each other table in your database, like this:

```
Create Table ChecksumTracker (
        TableName sysname,
        Checksum int
)
```

Then populate the table with the checksum from each table. Then you can re-run the checksum query periodically and compare the results to see whether the table changed.

So far, every aggregate function you've seen has operated on a set that has been the entire table. So, how can you create several subsets out of a table and get aggregate information for those subsets?

Using *GROUP BY* to Aggregate Data

The GROUP BY operator creates subgroups within a query that can be used by aggregate functions. For example, look at the Sales table. Right now, the Sales table has one record for each sale, but you really want to know how many total items each person bought. Here's how GROUP BY solves that problem:

```
SELECT PersonID, sum(QtyPurchased) as TotalQtyPurchased
FROM Sales
GROUP BY PersonID
```

Here's the resultset:

```
PersonID    TotalQtyPurchased
----------- -----------------
1           7
3           1
4           2
9           15
10          6

(5 row(s) affected)
```

Each person is listed once, and the sum(QtyPurchased) is computed for each person across the aggregate.

There are, of course, some rules. (There are always rules, or what would the test cover?)

◆ The items in the SELECT statement that are not part of an aggregate function have to appear in the GROUP BY clause, and they probably should appear in the same order as they do in the SELECT statement.

◆ You can have multiple aggregates in one SELECT statement. For example, you can find MIN and MAX values for a particular column in one SELECT statement.

◆ The items in aggregate functions in the SELECT statement cannot appear outside aggregate functions in the SELECT statement. So although you can do SELECT MIN(value), MAX(value), you can't do SELECT value, MIN(value), MAX(value), even if you use the appropriate GROUP BY.

Here's another example. Imagine that you want to find out how many records each person has in the Sales table. You could do something like this:

```
SELECT PersonID, count(*)
FROM Sales
GROUP BY PersonID
```

This returns each person's PersonID and the number of records they have in the Sales table. You can include multiple columns in the SELECT list and get a different aggregate:

```
SELECT PersonID, ProductID, count(*)
FROM Sales
GROUP BY PersonID, ProductID
```

This returns each person and product, and the number of different purchases a person made for each product. You can also include an ORDER BY for sorting:

```
SELECT PersonID, ProductID, count(*)
FROM Sales
GROUP BY PersonID, ProductID
ORDER BY PersonID, ProductID
```

You could also order by count(*) and you'd get the expected results. It works just like any other returned column. You can do the normal filtering with a WHERE clause, also, as follows:

```
SELECT PersonID, count(*)
FROM Sales
WHERE DatePurchased > '11/1/2000'
GROUP BY PersonID
```

This filters out any sale with a DatePurchased after 11/1/2000, so the count reflects only sales since that time. So how can you find the people who purchased more than one item? To do that, you need to filter on the results from the aggregate function, which is something you cannot do in the WHERE clause. You need to use something a little different.

Using *GROUP BY* and *HAVING* to Filter Data

The HAVING keyword appears after GROUP BY in a SELECT statement, and it is used to filter data after the GROUP BY. You can actually use HAVING without using GROUP BY, in which case HAVING acts like a part of the WHERE clause. The HAVING operator is typically used with aggregate functions to filter out rows that don't meet certain criteria. For example:

```
SELECT PersonID, count(*)
FROM Sales
GROUP BY PersonID
HAVING count(*) > 1
```

This filters out all the records from the result of the aggregate that don't meet the criteria of COUNT(*) > 1, so you end up with:

```
PersonID
----------- -----------
1           2
4           2
9           2

(3 row(s) affected)
```

This leaves out all the rows with COUNT(*) equal to 1. A HAVING clause can be more complex and contain expressions separated by AND and OR as appropriate:

```
SELECT PersonID, count(*)
FROM Sales
GROUP BY PersonID
HAVING count(*) > 1 AND PersonID > 4
```

Notice that the HAVING in this case doesn't care about the fact that PersonID isn't an aggregate function; it just filters out everyone who is less than or equal to 4 and has had fewer than 2 sales.

Creating Breaks with *COMPUTE* and *COMPUTE BY*

So far, the operators you've looked at do not ever create data rows. That changes now. The COMPUTE and COMPUTE BY operators create summary data across your aggregates and add it into your rowset. Here's an example:

```
SELECT PersonID, QtyPurchased
FROM Sales
COMPUTE sum(QtyPurchased)
```

What does this code do? Well, it creates the sum of the QtyPurchased field, like this:

```
PersonID     QtyPurchased
-----------  -----------
1            4
1            3
3            1
4            1
4            1
9            10
9            5
10           6

             sum
             ===========
             31


(9 row(s) affected)
```

In addition, you can also find the summary information for each person by using this query:

```
SELECT PersonID, QtyPurchased
FROM Sales
```

```
ORDER BY personid
COMPUTE sum(QtyPurchased)
BY PersonID
```

Which yields these results:

```
PersonID     QtyPurchased DatePurchased
-----------  ------------ ------------------------
1            4            2001-07-22 16:50:38.257
1            3            2001-07-22 16:50:38.257

             sum
             ===========
             7


PersonID     QtyPurchased DatePurchased
-----------  ------------ ------------------------
3            1            2001-07-22 16:50:38.257

             sum
             ===========
             1
```

For the sake of brevity, the entire resultset is not shown, but you get the idea. It shows how many items each person purchased and when, and a summary of the total items purchased. Inevitably, there are rules about these sorts of things:

◆ If you use COMPUTE without using BY, you can use the COUNT aggregate. Otherwise, you can't.

◆ If you use COMPUTE with BY, you need to have an ORDER BY, with the same columns in the same order. You can have additional things in the ORDER BY, but you've at least got to have what is specified in the COMPUTE BY.

◆ You can't use COMPUTE or COMPUTE BY with SELECT INTO.

◆ You can't use COMPUTE or COMPUTE BY as the SELECT statement that feeds a cursor. (Cursors are covered in Chapter 6.)

If you look at the structure for the rowsets, you'll notice that the rowsets aren't consistent—they have the extra "stuff" in them for the aggregate. This "stuff" doesn't fit into a table very well; that's why it doesn't work with SELECT INTO. It also doesn't work with cursors for the same reason.

The only real difference between COMPUTE and COMPUTE BY is that a COMPUTE BY does an aggregation with each computation it splits the rowset up with whatever you've specified to break it up by and creates those extra columns once for each aggregate.

WARNING **Rowsets and Compute By**   When you're writing an application using ADO or OLE-DB, you may have some serious issues with COMPUTE and COMPUTE BY, along with anything else that returns irregular rowsets. This happens for the same reason that cursors and SELECT INTO aren't valid for these operators: the rowsets are irregular.

Now that you've seen how GROUP BY and COMPUTE BY work, you can apply this knowledge to some other summarization tools: CUBE and ROLLUP specifically. As you'll discover, the shortcomings of COMPUTE and COMPUTE BY can sometimes be overcome with these two operators.

SUMMARIZING DATA WITH TRANSACT-SQL

▶ **Summarize data using Transact-SQL.**

As humans, we have a finite attention span and finite capabilities for digesting large quantities of data. To deal with that, SQL Server provides several different ways to group and summarize data. You've seen some of the ways to group data and provide basic summary information, such as counts and average values; now you're going to see some other ways to count data and arrange aggregates to make the output easier to read and more palatable to outside applications.

In addition to the COMPUTE and COMPUTE BY operators, you can also use the CUBE and ROLLUP operators to summarize your data. Take a look at the CUBE operator first.

The *CUBE* Operator

CUBE works in conjunction with a GROUP BY to provide summary data. The CUBE operator puts this data directly into the rowset. Here's an example:

```
SELECT PersonID, ProductID, count(*) as Ct
FROM Sales
WHERE personID > 4
GROUP BY PersonID, ProductID
WITH CUBE
```

This produces the following output:

```
PersonID     ProductID    Ct
-----------  -----------  -----------
9            37           1
9            38           1
9            NULL         2
10           41           1
10           NULL         1
NULL         NULL         3
```

```
NULL        37          1
NULL        38          1
NULL        41          1

(9 row(s) affected)
```

The biggest question with a CUBE operator is not how to use it—because the syntax of WITH CUBE really is all there is to it—but instead, how do you interpret the output? It's pretty simple if you look at it like this: anywhere there is a NULL, it is a summary. So, the third value in the preceding resultset is PersonID 9, and ProductID NULL had a count of 2. This means that PersonID 9 across all products had 2 sales. The row that starts NULL NULL is the total summary, which means there were a total of 3 sales covered by the resultset. The row that starts NULL 41 means there was 1 sale of the product with ID 41.

In the case of a count, if you just want to mentally substitute the word "count" where you see NULL, it might make more sense—at least if you don't have any NULL values that you're counting. You'll see in a couple of sections how to do this programmatically.

So, what CUBE does, in effect, is provide total summary information for a query for a given GROUP BY. It shows the information cut across all possible dimensions, with each part of the GROUP BY returning NULL to expose the summary information for the remaining fields. If CUBE does the summary for the entire query for every combination of columns, is there a way to just get the totals for one column?

Summarizing Data with *ROLLUP*

ROLLUP is similar to CUBE, but it returns fewer results. The CUBE operator returns summary information for each column mentioned in the GROUP BY list from right to left *and* left to right. The ROLLUP operator returns the summary information for the elements of the GROUP BY from only right to left. For example, if you had these two SELECT statements:

```
SELECT A, B, C, D
FROM MyTable
GROUP BY A, B, C, D
WITH ROLLUP

SELECT A, B, C, D
FROM MyTable
GROUP BY A, B, C, D
WITH CUBE
```

The first example would return summary information for all combinations of C and D, combinations of B, C, and D, and combinations of A, B, C, and D. The second SELECT would return the same as the first, but would also return results for A and B, as well as A, B, and C.

The example given in the CUBE section received all the combinations of summaries for people who bought things and products that were purchased. Sometimes, though, you want to know only who bought things and the total number of things sold. That's what ROLLUP does:

```
SELECT PersonID, ProductID, count(*) as Ct
FROM Sales
WHERE personID > 4
GROUP BY PersonID, ProductID
WITH ROLLUP
```

Which yields this resultset:

```
PersonID    ProductID    Ct
----------  ----------   ----------

9           37           1
9           38           1
9           NULL         2
10          41           1
10          NULL         1
NULL        NULL         3

(6 row(s) affected)
```

In the third row, you can see the ProductID is NULL, and the count is 2, which is the total for PersonID 9. The ROLLUP operator works just like the CUBE operator, except that there's no per-product totals, only per-person totals.

You use both CUBE and ROLLUP with aggregates other than just COUNT(). For example:

```
SELECT PersonID, ProductID, sum(QtyPurchased) as
➥QtyPurchased
FROM Sales
WHERE personID > 4
GROUP BY PersonID, ProductID
WITH ROLLUP
```

Which returns the resultset:

```
PersonID    ProductID    QtyPurchased
----------  ----------   ----------
9           37           10
9           38           5
```

```
9          NULL       15
10         41         6
10         NULL       6
NULL       NULL       21
```

```
(6 row(s) affected)
```

As promised, now it's time to see how to get rid of those darn NULLs everywhere.

The *GROUPING* Keyword

The GROUPING keyword is used to clean up the output of CUBE and ROLLUP to make the output look nicer. It provides you with a programmatic way to identify where CUBE and ROLLUP are putting NULLs, as opposed to where the NULLs are in the data being queried. It goes like this:

```
SELECT CASE WHEN GROUPING(PersonID) = 1
            THEN '(Total)'
            ELSE CONVERT(varchar(10), PersonID)
        END PersonID,
        CASE WHEN GROUPING(ProductID) = 1
            THEN '(Total)'
            ELSE CONVERT(varchar(10), ProductID)
        END ProductID, SUM(QtyPurchased) as QtyPurchased
FROM Sales
WHERE personID > 4
GROUP BY PersonID, ProductID
WITH ROLLUP
```

Which yields the somewhat nicer looking resultset:

```
PersonID   ProductID  QtyPurchased
---------- ---------- ------------
9          37         10
9          38         5
9          (Total)    15
10         41         6
10         (Total)    6
(Total)    (Total)    21
```

```
(6 row(s) affected)
```

Now you don't have to mentally think "Total"; you can actually put it into the output. The GROUPING function returns a 1 whenever the column is NULL because of a grouping summarization found in a CUBE or ROLLUP. Otherwise, it returns 0.

When to Use *CUBE* and *ROLLUP*

CUBE and ROLLUP should be used instead of COMPUTE and COMPUTE BY whenever possible. Why? Well, SQL Server's internal mechanics are better at figuring out how to optimize CUBE and ROLLUP because the syntax is simpler. Of course, it's hard to beat a WITH ROLLUP or WITH CUBE as far as simplicity of syntax. Also, CUBE and ROLLUP return a simple single resultset, instead of the extra "stuff" returned by COMPUTE and COMPUTE BY.

In addition, in most cases a CUBE or ROLLUP provides you with the output you need, and the queries are shorter and simpler, making them easier to debug.

So, now you know how to query data on a local server using different types of joins and how to summarize the data. What happens if the data isn't on just one server, but is on several servers, in several formats? The rest of this chapter is dedicated to talking to other servers, importing and exporting data, and dealing with XML to conduct business.

R E V I E W   B R E A K

Review of Advanced Query Techniques

So far, we've covered a lot of material, from completing the SELECT statement to aggregating and summarizing data. We're about to move on to something completely different, so here's a review of what we've done so far.

- ▶ The JOIN operator, part of the FROM clause in a SELECT statement, is used to combine two related tables.

- ▶ The UNION operator is used to combine the output from two SELECT statements into one rowset.

- ▶ GROUP BY is used to create aggregates, which can then be analyzed with aggregate functions.

- ▶ COMPUTE and COMPUTE BY are used to generate subtotals, and they create odd breaks in a SELECT statement.

- ▶ CUBE and ROLLUP provide similar functionality to COMPUTE and COMPUTE BY, but SQL Server can do more optimization with them.

Well, you now know all the parts of a SELECT statement that you'll need to know for the exam. SELECT is the backbone of SQL; it's how things get queried in the Structured Query Language. The structures you've learned, especially the JOIN syntax, are used in the other main SQL statements—INSERT, UPDATE, and DELETE—and the syntax is the same as with SELECT. You'll find that CUBE and ROLLUP are useful, especially if you get into writing queries for reporting systems.

MANIPULATING HETEROGENEOUS DATA WITH *OPENQUERY, OPENROWSET,* AND LINKED SERVERS

▶ **Manipulate heterogeneous data. Methods include linked servers, OPENQUERY, and OPENROWSET.**

So far, all the data you've been able to access has been stored in databases on one SQL Server. This section talks about how to query data that's on other SQL Servers and in other systems without importing the data. Later sections in this chapter deal with how to import and export data with SQL Server.

You can use three different types of syntax to access data; each one serves a different purpose. First, you're going to see OPENROWSET, which is the most flexible but hardest to use of the three. Then OPENQUERY, which is easier to use but requires a bit more setup. Then you'll see how linked servers are set up and used.

Each of the three methods—OPENROWSET, OPENQUERY, and linked servers—relies on having an operable OLE-DB driver for the system you're trying to talk to. SQL Server 2000 ships with OLE DB drivers for SQL Server, text files, Oracle, IBM's DB/2, and others. To understand how to use each of these methods, you need to understand how to talk to an OLE-DB provider.

A Brief Discussion on OLE-DB

OLE-DB is a low-level database access protocol that is designed to enable a client to access different systems without having to under-

NOTE

Which OLE-DB Providers Are Installed? You can find a list of the OLE-DB providers that you have installed in the Registry at HKEY_LOCAL_MACHINE\Software\ Microsoft\MSSQLServer\Providers\ SQLOLEDB.

stand how each different system works. The foundation of OLE-DB is the OLE-DB provider, which has to implement certain methods. At this level, an OLE-DB provider needs to know certain things to make a connection to the system.

In the case of another SQL Server, the OLE-DB provider needs to know the name of the server and how to log into the server. In the case of a text file, the OLE-DB provider needs to know where the file is and what format the file is in, as well as other properties about the file, such as delimiters, whether the first row contains column names, and so on. The point here is that different providers have different requirements, but that after you get past those requirements they all work the same way as far as retrieving data.

The only way to understand how to use the provider is to consult the documentation for that provider and for that version of the provider. That's not a very good answer—it's not an answer that is going to make your life easier. Unfortunately, it's the only answer you're going to get.

Using *OPENROWSET*

The OPENROWSET function returns a rowset to SQL Server. It's used in a SELECT statement in the same place as a table. Here's the syntax of the OPENROWSET function:

```
OPENROWSET('provider_name', {'datasource';'userid';
➡'password'} or 'provider_string',
        {catalog.schema.object} or 'query')
```

The exact definitions of the different arguments are in the list that follows, but here's the general idea of how the syntax works. You have to use a provider_name. You can either use datasource, userid, and password, *or* you can use a provider_string. You can also specify a catalog.schema.object or use a query. Notice that the datasource, userid, and password are delimited by semicolons. The reason for this is simple: to give the people who write the MCP exams something to trick you with. Here are the parameters for the OPENROWSET function.

◆ provider_name. This is the name of the provider, as specified in the Registry. It is not optional.

◆ `datasource`. This is the name of the file, server, or whatever the OLE-DB provider needs to figure out what it should be talking to.

◆ `user_id`. This is the user name that the provider understands. Some providers may not need a user name, so this could be blank.

◆ `password`. This is the password that the provider understands. Some providers may not need a password, so this could be blank also.

◆ `provider_string`. This is a free text field that has everything else that the provider needs to initiate the connection. Only the provider knows for sure what this is; you'll have to dig through piles of documentation.

◆ `catalog`. This is the name of the database, catalog, or whatever the provider understands. It's the top level of the hierarchy of object names. It's also likely to be blank if the provider doesn't use it.

◆ `schema`. This is the name of the owner of the object. It also may be blank if the provider doesn't use it.

◆ `object`. This is the name of the object being manipulated. Believe it or not, this may be blank if there's only one object in the datasource, such as a text file.

◆ `query`. This is a string that's provider-specific, and it's passed directly to the provider as a query. It may be a SQL query; it may be something else. It's also not processed by SQL Server, so you should make sure that the syntax is valid before you send it, otherwise you'll get a very incomprehensible error message.

If you are somehow missing the point, nearly every single argument in the entire OPENROWSET function is optional, and it's use or lack thereof depends on the provider you are using. Experience dictates that the documentation and examples for how to use the particular provider in which you are interested will be either non-existent or inaccurate. In other words, good luck.

Actually, OPENROWSET is a very useful function; it's just complicated and difficult to set up. After you have it figured out for a particular provider, it works very well. You should plan on spending several hours with a new OLE-DB provider to figure out how it works. Here's an example of OPENROWSET in use:

```
SELECT * FROM openrowset('sqloledb',
      'SQLTest1';'sa';'',
      'SELECT * FROM master.dbo.sysobjects'
)
```

This example is a fairly simple case; it just returns a rowset from another SQL Server—in this case a SQL Server running on a box named SQLTest1, which has a blank SA password. You can tell it's a request to another SQL Server because 'sqloledb' is the provider, and that's the name of the provider used to talk to other SQL Servers. It runs a simple SELECT statement and returns a simple rowset. Notice that it uses a full three-part name for the table. This isn't required, but it is good practice for doing remote queries. You can then use the results just as you would any other table: You can join them to other local tables, filter them, or whatever you like:

```
SELECT SQLTest1sysobjects.name FROM openrowset('sqloledb',
      'SQLTest1';'sa';'',
      'SELECT * FROM sysobjects'
) SqlTest1sysobjects
INNER JOIN sysobjects
      ON sysobjects.name = SQLTest1sysobjects.name
WHERE SQLTest1sysobjects.type = 'u'
```

Notice that this uses a table alias to reference the OPENROWSET return values; it filters on the object type from the remote table and does a join. So it really does work as a table does. But the syntax is incredibly cumbersome. You're probably hoping there's some shortcut you can use to avoid all the complexity. Well, read ahead to see how that can happen.

Creating a Linked Server

You can think of a *linked server* as a prebuilt set of arguments for OPENROWSET stored in a database object. You can just create an object called a linked server, and create it with all the attributes that you'd normally use in a call to OPENROWSET. Then, rather than having to type all those parameters in over and over again, you can just use the linked server.

There are two ways to create a linked server: Using the Query Analyzer and using Enterprise Manager. Which one is easier? Well, the explanation for using Query Analyzer is going to take a paragraph, and the explanation for using Enterprise Manager is going to use an involved Step by Step. You be the judge.

In Query Analyzer, you create the linked server using the sp_addlinkedserver system stored procedure:

```
sp_addlinkedserver [ @server = ] 'server'
    [ , [ @srvproduct = ] 'product_name' ]
    [ , [ @provider = ] 'provider_name' ]
    [ , [ @datasrc = ] 'data_source' ]
    [ , [ @location = ] 'location ]
    [ , [ @provstr = ] 'provider_string' ]
    [ , [ @catalog = ] 'catalog' ]
```

Does that look familiar? The only parameters that aren't part of the OPENROWSET you've already learned about are server and provider; the rest are just bad names on the same parameters. Server is the name of the linked server you are creating. Any SQL Server-approved object name works; it doesn't necessarily have to be the name of the server, but it probably should be. The srvproduct argument is the name of the OLE-DB data source. The provider argument specifies the same thing as the srvproduct, but does it with an OLE-DB PROGID, which is a long identifier. The rest of the options are from OPEN-ROWSET. If you're linking to another Microsoft SQL Server, you can specify a @srvproduct of SQL Server only, and the @server argument must be the server's name. None of the other arguments are required or allowed. Here's a linked server definition for the server you saw used in the previous section:

```
sp_addlinkedserver @Server = 'OpenRowsetTest',
        @SrvProduct = 'sqloledb',
        @Provider = 'sqloledb',
        @DataSrc = 'SQLTest1'
```

Then—and this is the really great part—you can query it like this:

```
SELECT * FROM openrowsettest.master.dbo.sysobjects
```

That's a four-part name. They are required when using linked servers. You can't shortcut the object owner part either; you have to fully specify the entire thing. You could, of course, alias it, join it, or whatever you want to do; it's going to act just like a normal table.

Step by Step 9.1 takes you through one command operation done in full color in Enterprise Manager.

STEP BY STEP

9.1 Creating a Linked Server in Enterprise Manager

1. Open SQL Server Enterprise Manager. If you don't have the server you want to work with registered yet, you should do that now.

2. Expand the server you want to work with, then expand the Security container, and then click on the Linked Server container.

3. In the right side of the window, right-click in an empty spot and choose New Linked Server from the context menu. The Linked Server Properties - New Linked Server window appears, as seen in Figure 5.1.

4. There are a few boxes to fill in here. Fill in the Linked Server box with the name of the linked server you want to use. If the linked server is a SQL Server, you need to use the real name of the server in the Linked Server check box.

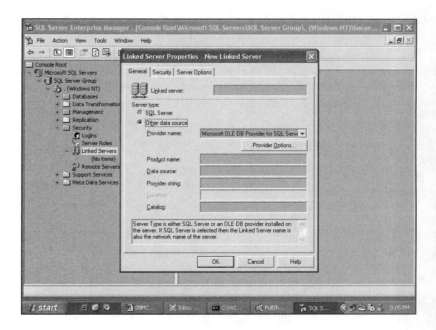

FIGURE 5.1
Window used to define a linked server.

5. If it is a SQL Server, choose the SQL Server radio button. This disables the rest of the input on the screen, and you can continue on with the next step. Otherwise, choose the Provider Name from the drop-down box, then fill in the product name, data source, and provider name as appropriate for the provider you are using. If you're using SQL Server, you have to put in the server's real name.

6. On the Security tab, shown in Figure 5.2, you can choose how users will log in to the linked server. A discussion on this tab follows these instructions.

7. The Server Options tab, shown in Figure 5.3, includes various options you can use to change the status of the connection. The Collation Compatible option specifies whether the remote server uses the same collation as the local server. The next three options, Data Access, RPC, and RPC Out, define how the connection can be used. A Data Access connection allows tables to be queried, whereas an RPC connection allows only stored procedures to be called. The RPC Out option enables the server to call remote stored procedures on the local machine. The Use Remote Collation options specifies that the linked server's collation order is to be used to run the query. Collation Name is the name of the collation to be used if the server is not collation compatible or if the Use Remote Collation option is off. Connection Timeout is the length of time a query should wait for the server to respond to a connection request, and a Query Timeout is the length of time a query should wait for a response.

8. Click OK to create the linked server.

The Security tab, mentioned in Step 6 in the Step by Step, needs a little more elaboration on a couple of fronts. First of all, in Figure 5.2 you'll notice that there are two different parts to the window. In the top part you can specify local logins and map them to logins on the remote server. In the bottom part you can specify what happens to local logins who aren't in the list. You can specify that users who are

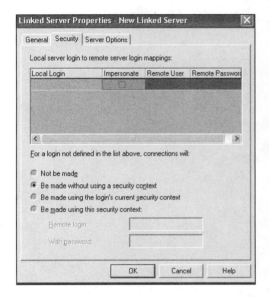

FIGURE 5.2
Window used to set the security options for the linked server.

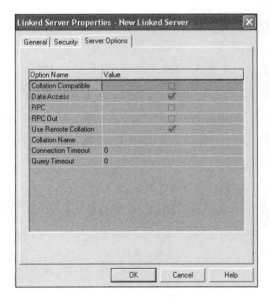

FIGURE 5.3
Other options for the linked server.

not on the list will not be allowed to use the remote server by choosing the Not Be Made option. You can choose that the users not on the list be forced into "guest" status, if available, on the remote server by choosing the Be Made Without Using a Security Context option. You can choose to attempt to pass through the authentication that the user has on the local server by choosing the Be Made Using the Login's Current Security Context item, or you can force everyone who isn't on the list in the top part of the window to use a specific login and password with the Be Made Using This Security Context option.

Now that you know how to create linked servers, it's time to look at using them in a little more detail.

Using Linked Servers

There are two ways to use an established linked server. The first—and easiest to understand—method is to use the four-part name as shown in the Step By Step 9.1. As you remember, a three-part name is *database.owner.object*, so for the sysobjects table in the Master database, you can reference it as *master.dbo.sysobjects*. For a linked server, you can use a four-part name, which is *server.database.owner.object*, or, in the example above, sqltest1.master.dbo.sysobjects.

The four-part name works great when you're using other SQL Servers as the remotes. What happens when you want to use something other than SQL Server on the other side? Then you need to use the OPENQUERY function. OPENQUERY looks suspiciously similar to OPENROWSET, but it takes only two arguments: the linked server name and a query. So you could run this:

```
SELECT * FROM  openrowsettest.master.dbo.sysobjects
```

or you could run this:

```
SELECT * from OPENQUERY(OpenRowsetTest, 'SELECT * FROM
➥master.dbo.sysobjects')
```

Notice that the linked server name does not have quotation marks around it. SQL Server doesn't like quotation marks there. Both these queries return the same resultset.

These linked servers are really great, but don't get any ideas about using them to import data. Although it works well for smaller datasets (less than a few hundred thousand rows), there are significantly more efficient ways to handle data imports, which is what is covered in a few sections. Next up, however, is a discussion on the cutting edge of Internet technology: Using XML.

EXTRACTING DATA INTO XML

▶ **Extract data in XML format. Considerations include output format and XML schema structure.**

XML, the eXtensible Markup Language, is an offshoot of HTML that is designed to provide an application-independent, character-set-independent method of transferring data, especially transaction-oriented data, across systems. If you're familiar with EDI (Electronic Document Interchange), then the concept behind XML should be pretty familiar to you, but the implementation is completely different. In this section, you'll see what XML is, and how to format and extract query results into XML.

If you feel the need to ask what XML is, the best answer is "Go get an XML book." (Look at the "Suggested Reading" section at the end of the chapter.) Basically, though, XML is a subset of SGML, which is a huge standard that is so complex nobody has ever completely implemented it. HTML is also a subset of SGML, but is quite limited; XML is less limited (and more complex) than HTML, but is still far less complex than SGML.

An XML document consists of one or more elements, which are bound between angle brackets <>. The first word that appears inside the angle brackets is the name of the element. The rest of the element consists of element attributes. For example, here's an element:

```
<row xmlns="x-schema:#Schema1" QtyPurchased="5"
➥PersonID="9" FirstName="Shelly"
          LastName="Alexander"/>
```

The name of the element, or the element type, is `row`. The `xmlns` property specifies the name of the schema, which is the format that the element will take. The element then has other attributes, such as `QtyPurchased`, `PersonID`, `FirstName`, and `LastName`, which all have values. The element ends with a forward slash and an angle bracket, indicating the end of the element.

An element can also contain other elements, like this:

```
<Person PersonID="1" FirstName="Danny">
        <Sales QtyPurchased="4"/>
   <Sales QtyPurchased="3"/>
</Person>
```

In this case, the `Person` element contains two `Sales` elements. Notice that on the first line, there isn't a slash before the ending bracket; the slash is actually down on the last line. This is how objects are nested in XML.

To put data into XML format, the `SELECT` statement includes an operator called `FOR XML`. This specifies to SQL Server that instead of returning a rowset, it should return an XML document. There are three different options for generating the XML: `RAW`, `AUTO`, and `EXPLICIT`.

Automatic XML Formatting

In `AUTO` mode, SQL Server returns the rowset in an automatically generated nested XML format. If the query has no joins, it doesn't have a nesting at all. If the query has joins, then it returns the first row from the first table, then all the correlated rows from each joined table as a nested level. For example, this query:

```
SELECT Person.PersonID, Person.FirstName, Person.LastName,
➡Sales.QtyPurchased
FROM Person
        INNER JOIN Sales
                ON Sales.PersonID = Person.PersonID
FOR XML AUTO
```

returns this XML:

```
<Person PersonID="1" FirstName="Danny" LastName="Jones">
        <Sales QtyPurchased="4"/>
        <Sales QtyPurchased="3"/>
</Person>
<Person PersonID="3" FirstName="Scott" LastName="Smith">
        <Sales QtyPurchased="1"/>
</Person>
<Person PersonID="4" FirstName="Alex" LastName="Riley">
        <Sales QtyPurchased="1"/>
        <Sales QtyPurchased="1"/>
</Person>
<Person PersonID="9" FirstName="Shelly"
➡LastName="Alexander">
        <Sales QtyPurchased="10"/>
        <Sales QtyPurchased="5"/>
</Person>
```

The actual XML, if you run the query, comes out all on one line as a stream of data. This is what it looks like if you format it to actually be readable. XML, however, doesn't know about linefeeds or making things readable; remember, it's designed for system-to-system traffic without people intervening.

As you add other joined tables, the nesting level increases. To figure out how to nest the different fields, SQL Server uses the order in which the columns appear in the SELECT statement. So if you rewrite the preceding SELECT statement as follows:

```
SELECT Sales.QtyPurchased, Person.PersonID,
➥Person.FirstName, Person.LastName
FROM Person
        INNER JOIN Sales
                ON Sales.PersonID = Person.PersonID
FOR XML AUTO
```

You end up with XML that looks like this:

```
<Sales QtyPurchased="4">
        <Person PersonID="1" FirstName="Danny"
        ➥LastName="Jones"/>
</Sales>
<Sales QtyPurchased="3">
        <Person PersonID="1" FirstName="Danny"
        ➥LastName="Jones"/>
</Sales>
<Sales QtyPurchased="1">
        <Person PersonID="3" FirstName="Scott"
        ➥LastName="Smith"/>
        <Person PersonID="4" FirstName="Alex"
        ➥LastName="Riley"/>
        <Person PersonID="4" FirstName="Alex"
        ➥LastName="Riley"/>
</Sales>
<Sales QtyPurchased="10">
        <Person PersonID="9" FirstName="Shelly"
        ➥LastName="Alexander"/>
</Sales>
<Sales QtyPurchased="5">
        <Person PersonID="9" FirstName="Shelly"
        ➥LastName="Alexander"/>
</Sales>
```

Notice that the nesting here is totally reversed. The easiest way to write queries for XML is to write them with the FOR XML clause left off, make sure that they are returning the data you want, and then add the FOR XML back onto the end of the query. That eliminates the need for a lot of extra formatting.

NOTE

Where's the XML? Unfortunately, Query Analyzer by default shows only the first 256 characters of a string that's returned. That's not going to work for most of the examples in this chapter, because they're larger than 256 characters. To fix Query Analyzer, go to the Tools menu, choose Options, click on the Results tab, and in the Maximum Characters per Column box enter some larger number, like 4096.

Minimal Formatting with the *RAW* Option

What if you don't want XML that is elaborately formatted? Then you can use the RAW mode. RAW mode returns each row as an element with the identifier row. Here's an example of the same query as you just saw, returned in RAW mode:

```
<row QtyPurchased="4" PersonID="1" FirstName="Danny"
➥LastName="Jones"/>
<row QtyPurchased="3" PersonID="1" FirstName="Danny"
➥LastName="Jones"/>
<row QtyPurchased="1" PersonID="3" FirstName="Scott"
➥LastName="Smith"/>
<row QtyPurchased="1" PersonID="4" FirstName="Alex"
➥LastName="Riley"/>
<row QtyPurchased="1" PersonID="4" FirstName="Alex"
➥LastName="Riley"/>
<row QtyPurchased="10" PersonID="9" FirstName="Shelly"
➥LastName="Alexander"/>
<row QtyPurchased="5" PersonID="9" FirstName="Shelly"
➥LastName="Alexander"/>
```

The query is written like the one discussed in the section "Automatic XML formatting", but it uses the RAW keyword instead of the AUTO keyword:

```
SELECT Sales.QtyPurchased, Person.PersonID,
➥Person.FirstName, Person.LastName
FROM Person
        INNER JOIN Sales
                ON Sales.PersonID = Person.PersonID
FOR XML RAW
```

If you have data that's stored in text or image format, SQL Server assumes that you don't want it in the XML file. If you do want to put the data into the XML file, you can use the BINARY BASE64 option, like this:

```
SELECT Sales.QtyPurchased, Person.PersonID,
➥Person.FirstName, Person.LastName
FROM Person
        INNER JOIN Sales
                ON Sales.PersonID = Person.PersonID
FOR XML RAW, BINARY BASE64
```

Explicitly Creating an XML Format

Another way to extract data with the FOR XML clause is to use the option EXPLICIT. The EXPLICIT option enables you to specify the format of the XML that will be created. To define the format, you have to alias the first column of output to the name Tag, name the second column Parent, and then each consecutive column has to be aliased to relate it to a specific Tag. The column names after Parent are named like this: [*ElementName!TagNumber!AttributeName! Directive*], complete with the square brackets around the alias. So, as an example:

```
SELECT 1 as TAG,
       NULL as Parent,
       Sales.QtyPurchased as [Sales!1!QtyPurchased],
       Person.PersonID as [Sales!1!PersonID],
       Person.FirstName as [Sales!1!FirstName],
       Person.LastName as [Sales!1!LastName]
FROM Person
       INNER JOIN Sales
              ON Sales.PersonID = Person.PersonID
FOR XML EXPLICIT
```

This returns this XML:

```
<Sales QtyPurchased="4" PersonID="1" FirstName="Danny"
➥LastName="Jones"/>
<Sales QtyPurchased="3" PersonID="1" FirstName="Danny"
➥LastName="Jones"/>
<Sales QtyPurchased="1" PersonID="3" FirstName="Scott"
➥LastName="Smith"/>
<Sales QtyPurchased="1" PersonID="4" FirstName="Alex"
➥LastName="Riley"/>
<Sales QtyPurchased="1" PersonID="4" FirstName="Alex"
➥LastName="Riley"/>
<Sales QtyPurchased="10" PersonID="9" FirstName="Shelly"
➥LastName="Alexander"/>
<Sales QtyPurchased="5" PersonID="9" FirstName="Shelly"
➥LastName="Alexander"/>
```

To do a nested element, you need to write two queries joined together with a UNION. The first query has a Tag of 1 and a Parent of NULL; the second has a Tag of 2 and a Parent of 1. The second query's Parent value relates to the first query's Tag value. So, to nest the preceding query, you do this:

```
SELECT 1 as Tag,
       NULL as Parent,
       Person.PersonID      as [Person!1!PersonID],
       Person.FirstName      as [Person!1!FirstName],
       Person.LastName      as [Person!1!LastName],
       NULL              AS [Sales!2!QtyPurchased]
FROM Person
UNION
SELECT 2 as Tag,
       1 as Parent,
       Person.PersonID      AS [Person!1!PersonID],
       Person.FirstName      as [Person!1!FirstName],
       Person.LastName      as [Person!1!LastName],
       Sales.QtyPurchased      as [Sales!1!QtyPurchased]
```

```
FROM Person
        INNER JOIN Sales
                ON Sales.PersonID = Person.PersonID
ORDER BY [Person!1!PersonID], [Person!1!FirstName],
➥[Person!1!LastName]
FOR XML EXPLICIT
```

There are a lot of necessary details in this query. First of all, notice that because this is a UNION query, each query has to have the same number of columns. Second, notice that there is an ORDER BY. This is required, or the objects do not nest properly. Here's the result XML:

```
<Person PersonID="1" FirstName="Danny" LastName="Jones">
        <Sales QtyPurchased="3"/>
        <Sales QtyPurchased="4"/>
</Person>
<Person PersonID="2" FirstName="Melissa" LastName="Jones"/>
<Person PersonID="3" FirstName="Scott" LastName="Smith">
        <Sales QtyPurchased="1"/>
</Person>
<Person PersonID="4" FirstName="Alex" LastName="Riley">
        <Sales QtyPurchased="1"/>
</Person>
<Person PersonID="5" FirstName="Chris" LastName="Avery"/>
<Person PersonID="6" FirstName="Jennifer"
➥LastName="Avery"/>
<Person PersonID="7" FirstName="Bryan" LastName="Decker"/>
<Person PersonID="8" FirstName="Robin" LastName="Decker"/>
<Person PersonID="9" FirstName="Shelly"
➥LastName="Alexander">
        <Sales QtyPurchased="5"/>
        <Sales QtyPurchased="10"/>
</Person>
```

Notice that the result gives all the people, not just the ones with Sales, because there isn't a join in the first SELECT in the union. If you want to have only people who had purchased things in the output, you can restrict the first query to dump those folks out.

Table 5.2 shows the syntax of the directives you can use as the fourth part of a column alias. The directives help you handle data in different ways, and they are optional.

TABLE 5.2

DIRECTIVES FOR USE IN XML COLUMN ALIASES

Directive	Description
ID	This is used to define an element as an anchor for a referral; other objects can then refer back to this one with IDREF and IDREFS. If you're not using the XMLDATA option, this option doesn't do anything.

Directive	*Description*
IDREF	This links the element with another element that is specified with the ID directive. Once again, if you're not using the XMLDATA option, this doesn't do anything.
IDREFS	Same thing as IDREF.
hide	This specifies that the attribute should not be displayed. This is handy for creating an element that you want to sort on, but you don't necessarily want to have in the resultset.
element	This forces the creation of a new element with the name specified in the alias and the data coming from the column data.
xml	This directive specifies that the data in the column is already XML, and shouldn't be parsed. It can only be used with the hide directive.
xmltext	The column is wrapped up into a tag that is stuck into the document. It also can only be used with the hide directive.
cdata	This wraps the column data in a CDATA section with no encoding at all. Can be used with only string and text types, and it can be used with only the hide directive.

The EXPLICIT option, as you can see, has a lot of rules and formatting constraints. It's going to be interesting to see how data is read in from the detailed and possibly convoluted structures.

USING OPENXML TO READ XML DATA

▶ **Import and manipulate data using OPENXML.**

The OPENXML function works similarly to the way OPENROWSET and OPENQUERY work, in that it returns a rowset that can be used in a SELECT statement. However, there is some additional up-front work you need to do to set it up. Here's an overview of how the process works:

1. Use the sp_xml_preparedocument system stored procedure to create a document handle.

2. Use the OPENXML statement to define the format of the XML document and return the rowset.

3. Use the sp_xml_removedocument system stored procedure to destroy the document handle.

The first thing to do is look at what `sp_xml_preparedocument` and `sp_xml_removedocument` do. A discussion on the OPENXML statement then follows.

Preparing and Removing an XML Document

To prepare an XML document, you need to read the document into a variable and call the `sp_xml_preparedocument` stored procedure. First, you somehow need to get the document into a T-SQL variable. Then you call the stored procedure, which returns a handle to the parsed document, which can be used by the OPENXML function. Here's an example.

```
DECLARE @hdoc INT
EXEC sp_xml_preparedocument @hdoc OUTPUT, '<Person
➡PersonID="9" FirstName="Shelly" LastName="Alexander">
     <Sales QtyPurchased="5"/>
     <Sales QtyPurchased="10"/>
</Person>'

EXEC sp_xml_removedocument @hdoc
```

The first thing you'll notice is a DECLARE statement. This is a variable declaration, and it's covered in more depth in Chapter 6. The `@hdoc` is a variable that holds a temporary value so you can use it later, in the `sp_xml_removedocument` as well as in the OPENXML that's coming up.

The next thing to note is that an `sp_xml_preparedocument` and `sp_xml_removedocument` are paired up. This is critical. Whenever you prepare a document, it takes up memory resources in SQL Server's cache memory, up to one eighth of the total memory available (12.5 percent, exactly). So, if you prepare documents and don't remove them, you'll end up with a memory leak—memory that you can't access but that is in use. This is known as a "bad thing" in computer science circles. The only way to recover the memory without the original handle is to restart SQL Server.

The `sp_xml_preparedocument` stored procedure has one optional argument: the `xpath_namespace` argument, which is used to specify an alternate namespace for the document. By default, the system uses the default namespace `<root xmlns:mp="urn:schemas-microsoft-com:xml-metaprop">`. If you specify an alternate namespace string, it replaces the `"run:schemas-microsoft-com:xml-metaprop"` with whatever you specify.

Using *OPENXML*

The OPENXML function has three parameters and an optional WITH clause. It takes the document handle, which is returned by the sp_xml_preparedocument procedure, the rowpattern, which specifies which rows to return, and a single byte value that can specify flags.

Here's an expansion of the preceding example:

```
DECLARE @hdoc INT
EXEC sp_xml_preparedocument @hdoc OUTPUT, '<Person PersonID="9"

FirstName="Shelly" LastName="Alexander">
        <Sales QtyPurchased="5"/>
        <Sales QtyPurchased="10"/>
</Person>'

select * from openxml(@hdoc, '*')

EXEC sp_xml_removedocument @hdoc
```

This returns a nearly useless recordset, because it isn't formatted. Here's a little bit of the recordset:

id	parentid	nodetype	localname	prefix	namespaceuri	datatype	prev	text
0	NULL	1	Person	NULL	NULL	NULL	NULL	NULL
2	0	2	PersonID	NULL	NULL	NULL	NULL	NULL
9	2	3	#text	NULL	NULL	NULL	NULL	9

Not very easy to work with. That's why there's a rowset filter, like this:

```
SELECT * FROM openxml(@hdoc, '/Person', 1)
```

This rowset filter returns another nearly useless rowset, but at least it's a shorter, nearly useless rowset; it contains only the attributes about the person. Now, if you could just put the rows where they need to be, you'd have it made:

```
SELECT * FROM openxml(@hdoc, '/Person', 1)
            WITH (FirstName varchar(30),
                 LastName varchar(30))
```

That WITH clause does the trick, and you finally get decent output.

```
FirstName                   LastName
--------------------------- ---------------------------
Shelly                      Alexander

(1 row(s) affected)
```

So, now you have the data you want, extracted from an XML rowset. Using the WITH clause is basically the same syntax as laying out the columns in a table: the column name, some space, the data type, a comma, and then the next column name.

IN THE FIELD

XML PARSERS

If the OPENXML stuff looks like it's extremely cumbersome to deal with, there's a good reason for it. It *is* extremely cumbersome. You can't read the XML in from a file very easily; you have to spend a huge amount of time fighting with arcane bit-field flags, and you get to completely reformat your data using a WITH option. And you do all that just to get a few rows out, because you can't declare a variable of type TEXT, so you can hold only about 8KB of XML in SQL Server at a time.

Learn this stuff for the test. If you are ever involved in a project that requires you to import XML, use any of about five readily available scripting languages (Perl, VBScript, Java, Python, and C# come to mind, and there are probably dozens more), parse the XML using the already written, elegant, and useful tools in those languages—tools that are specifically designed to parse XML—and have the scripts write out nice, comma- (or something) delimited text. You'll learn how to import that in the next section. That way, you don't have to worry about getting memory leaks in SQL Server, and you don't need to be concerned about running this a thousand times to get all your data in 8KB at a time.

Well, the syntax stays the same until you decide you don't *want* a column called FirstName; you'd rather have columns called FName and LName. So, now what?

```
SELECT * FROM openxml(@hdoc, '/Person', 1)
        WITH (FName varchar(30)   '@FirstName',
              LName varchar(30)   '@LastName'
        )
```

Now you end up with a nice, clean rowset. You need to look at one more thing for the exam. Imagine that you want to output something farther up the tree from where you specify the rowpattern.

You can enter the following if you want to use the rowpattern
'/Person/Sales' to return sales information, and show the first
name and last name for each sale:

```
SELECT * FROM openxml(@hdoc, '/Person/Sales', 1)
             WITH (FName varchar(30)  '../@FirstName',
                   LName varchar(30)  '../@LastName',
                   QtyPurchased int '@QtyPurchased'
             )
```

Notice the use of the ".." syntax in specifying the output of the
XML file. This SELECT statement uses the /Person/Sales as the
default level, so any value that exists at that level can be specified by
just the name of the value. Here's the output:

```
FName                        LName                        QtyPurchased
---------------------------- ---------------------------- --------------
Shelly                       Alexander                    5
Shelly                       Alexander                    10
```

Anything above or below the default level, /Person/Sales, has to be
qualified with a path, which is what the ".." syntax represents: a
path representing the level above the default, in this case /Person.
Here's another example:

```
select * from openxml(@hdoc, '/Person', 1)
             WITH (FName varchar(30)  '@FirstName',
                   LName varchar(30)  '@LastName',
                   QtyPurchased int 'Sales/@QtyPurchased'
             )
```

This shows a different syntax, and provides a different result. The
preceding example returned every person and sale. This example
returns only the first sale:

```
FName                        LName                        QtyPurchased
---------------------------- ---------------------------- ------------
Shelly                       Alexander                    5
```

It returns only the first sale because it's returning one row for each
default level, which is the /Person level in this case.

So, now you know how to export data to XML format, which is a
pretty useful thing. You also should have a good handle on how to
translate data from XML into a rowset, which is marginally useful.
So now it's time to move *real* data in and out of SQL Server.

> **EXAM TIP**
>
> **Pathing XML** Pathing XML is very
> likely to be on your exam because
> it's important to understand how it
> works if you're going to use
> OPENXML(), and because Microsoft
> is very proud of the new XML fea-
> tures in SQL Server 2000.

XML in Review

XML is a feature that is very well covered by the exam, so be sure to use the examples here and get a good understanding of OPENXML and how the path syntax works.

▶ XML is a document format that can be used to transfer hierarchical data between systems.

▶ XML documents can be created with the FOR XML clause of the SELECT statement. This clause provides several options for formatting XML output.

▶ You can create rowsets from XML documents using the OPENXML statement.

Spend some time typing in the examples from this chapter, or use the slightly more complex examples found in Books Online to get a complete idea of how the OPENXML and FOR XML ideas really work.

IMPORTING AND EXPORTING DATA

▶ **Import and export data. Methods include the bulk copy program, the Bulk Insert Task, and Data Transformation Services (DTS).**

Outside of XML-land, moving data around is pretty simple. There are three major ways to do import/export tasks in SQL Server. They all have strengths and weaknesses. The Bulk Copy Program (BCP) is probably the hardest to learn, but it is also extremely capable and almost ludicrously fast. The BULK INSERT statement implements part of BCP inside SQL Server, so it has all the speed of BCP with an easier-to-use interface. Finally, the Data Transformation Services, or DTS, provide a lot of flexibility and capabilities in a very graphically intensive, point-and-click environment.

Importing and Exporting Data with BCP

The first thing to understand about BCP, the Bulk Copy Program, is that it's not a SQL Server command. It's not part of T-SQL. If you attempt to use BCP in Query Analyzer, it does everything it can to just laugh at you. Don't do it; it doesn't work. BCP is a command-line tool. That's right: the big, black empty window with the blinking cursor command line. So fire up a command prompt and dig in.

BCP is ancient, in computer years anyway. It's part of the wild history of SQL Server, and has been part of SQL Server since at least version 4.21, back when it was still a joint development effort between Microsoft and Sybase. The reason it's still around is that it's an extremely useful tool for loading data into a database quickly. The reason it's a command-line tool is all about overhead. Keep in mind that you can run BCP across the network; it doesn't have to run on a server. You can have a bunch of servers all across your network using BCP at once, and, assuming you have enough disk speed, SQL Server just sits there and soaks up data.

BCP has lots of command-line options. The basic syntax is:

```
bcp <table> <in or out> <file> <security information>
➥<format information>
```

The `<table>` is the destination table, usually specified as a three-part name, like `Chapter5.dbo.sales`. The `<in or out>` is what direction. Telling BCP to go `IN` tells BCP to read from the file and put data `IN` SQL Server. Telling BCP to go `OUT` pulls data `OUT` of SQL Server and writes it to a file. The `<file>` is the name of the file that you want to use. If it's an `IN` operation, then the file should exist and have data in it. If it's an `OUT` operation and the file exists, the file gets overwritten by the data coming out; otherwise, the file is created.

The `<security information>` is the name of the server that you're trying to use, and either username and password or a note to use your Windows authentication to handle it.

Finally, `<format information>` tells BCP what kind of format the data is in. BCP can deal with three data formats: native, character-delimited, and column-delimited. Native format works only when you're moving data from one SQL Server to another, and the servers have to use the same collation and character set for it to work. It's

N O T E

BCP Speed and File Format What makes one method of BCP faster than another? Native format files are the smallest; character-delimited files are the next smallest; and column-delimited files are the largest. BCP is so fast and well optimized that it is bound by how fast it can read or write data to or from the file.

also the fastest format, so use it whenever you can. The second fastest format is character-delimited. Character-delimited formats use some character, typically a comma, space, or a vertical bar, to separate the data columns. Finally, there is column-delimited data, which means the columns within the data file start and end at specific positions in the file. This is also called "fixed column width" or just "fixed column" data format. This tends to be the slowest way to BCP data around.

BCP does not create tables. You have to have a table set up and waiting for BCP before you run BCP. So, how do you run BCP? Here's an example of reading data from a comma-delimited text file into a database table:

```
bcp chapter5.dbo.sales in sales.csv -T -c -r\n -t,
```

The -T tells BCP to use a trusted connection. There is no server specified; it would be specified with the -S option, so the data goes to the local server. The -c tells BCP that it's supposed to use a character-delimited copy; the -r says that each row will be delimited with a newline character; and the -t says that each column will be delimited with a comma.

BCP has a bunch of command-line parameters. Table 5.3 lists the ones that are used for determining the file format.

TABLE 5.3

BCP COMMAND-LINE PARAMETERS—FORMAT PARAMETERS

Parameter	Function
-c	Specifies a character-delimited file is to be used.
-r r\n,	Specifies the end-of-line character. Usually this is specified as -r\n, which specifies that there is a new line at the end of each line
-t	Specifies the end-of-field character, typically a comma, vertical bar, or sometimes a space. Commas can be specified as -t, but any delimiter can be specified in double-quotes, such as -t"|"
-f	Specifies a format file to use. This is typically used to handle delimited data.
-n	Specifies that BCP should use native mode for copying. This parameter will copy all normal character data and non-character data okay, but will destroy any Unicode values.

Parameter	*Function*
-N	Specifies a native mode that is slower than the -n, but that doesn't destroy Unicode.
-w	Specifies a native mode that's even slower than -N, because it also specifies a tab-delimited file with a newline character. The other native modes can store numbers in binary format, so they are faster.
-V	Tells BCP to use one of the old SQL Server versions' data types for import and export. For an export, this also translates null bit fields to zero, because previous versions didn't handle that. This has no effect on date fields, which are always copied out however ODBC wants to do it.

Notice that there is a command-line option -n and another one that's -N. All BCP command-line options are case sensitive.

If you don't specify one of -c, -f, -n, -N, or -w, BCP assumes that you don't have a format file, you don't want to use any of the predefined formats, and that you want to make one. It reads the layout of the table you're using and then walks you through a prompted one-column-at-a-time process, and then you can save the file as a format file. Here's an example of a BCP session where BCP is prompting for information:

```
C:\Documents and Settings\MILLCS>bcp Chapter5..Sales out
➥sales.dat -T

Enter the file storage type of field PersonID [int-null]:
Enter prefix-length of field PersonID [1]:
Enter field terminator [none]:

Enter the file storage type of field ProductID [int-null]:
Enter prefix-length of field ProductID [1]:
Enter field terminator [none]:

Enter the file storage type of field QtyPurchased [int-null]:
Enter prefix-length of field QtyPurchased [1]:
Enter field terminator [none]:

Enter the file storage type of field DatePurchased [datetime-null]:
Enter prefix-length of field DatePurchased [1]:
Enter field terminator [none]:

Do you want to save this format information in a file? [Y/n]
Host filename [bcp.fmt]:

Starting copy...
```

```
8 rows copied.
Network packet size (bytes): 4096
Clock Time (ms.): total          1
```

In this example, all the defaults were used by just pressing the Enter key. This session of BCP results in two files being created: one is the output file, and the other is the format file, which in this case was named bcp.fmt. The data file that is created is the same you'd get if you'd used the -n for native format. Here's a format file:

```
8.0
4
1       SQLINT        1     4      " "              1      PersonID        " "
2       SQLINT        1     4      " "              2      ProductID       " "
3       SQLINT        1     4      " "              3      QtyPurchased    " "
4       SQLDATETIME   1     8      " "              4      DatePurchased   " "
```

The first row of the format file is the version number of BCP. (If you want to see just the version number, by the way, you can use BCP -v at the command line.) The second row is the number of data rows that are in the file. The third row on to the end of the file is the actual layout of the file. The first column is the file column number. The second column is the data type. The third column is the prefix length, which is the number of bytes in the file that tell BCP how long the data field is, and is used only in native-format BCP. The fourth column is the number of bytes wide the data column is. The fifth column is the delimiter, which is what separates this column from the next column. Next is the server column order. Finally, the row ends up with the field name and the collation for the column.

The file column number and server column number fields are used to do a couple of interesting things. First of all, if the table has columns that are in a different order than the file, you can manipulate the server column number to make it correct. Second, if you set the server column number to zero, then the column from the file gets skipped.

Prefix length is used when copying data in SQL Server native mode. If the format file weren't native mode, then it would have SQLCHAR as the type for each column, rather than SQLINT or SQLDATETIME. The type is the type that is written (or read) from the file, not the database type. So if the type is SQLINT, then BCP is going to write out the actual 4-byte integer for the value 42, not the 2-byte character for 42. Here's an example of a session to create a character-based file:

```
C:\Documents and Settings\MILLCS>bcp Chapter5..Sales out
➥saleschar.dat -T

Enter the file storage type of field PersonID [int-null]: char
Enter prefix-length of field PersonID [1]: 0
Enter length of field PersonID [12]:
Enter field terminator [none]:

Enter the file storage type of field ProductID [int-null]: char
Enter prefix-length of field ProductID [1]: 0
Enter length of field ProductID [12]:
Enter field terminator [none]:

Enter the file storage type of field QtyPurchased [int-null]: char
Enter prefix-length of field QtyPurchased [1]: 0
Enter length of field QtyPurchased [12]: 12
Enter field terminator [none]:

Enter the file storage type of field DatePurchased [datetime-null]: char
Enter prefix-length of field DatePurchased [1]  0
Enter length of field DatePurchased [26]:
Enter field terminator [none]: \n

Do you want to save this format information in a file? [Y/n] y
Host filename [bcp.fmt]: bcpchar.fmt

Starting copy...

8 rows copied.
Network packet size (bytes): 4096
Clock Time (ms.): total        1
```

This creates the same output as if you'd specified just -c on the BCP command line. Notice that the field storage type and prefix length had to be changed for each row, and the last row had to have a field terminator of \n. The \n puts each record on a new line. The resulting output file is a nice, column-delimited file:

```
C:\Documents and Settings\MILLCS>type saleschar.dat
1       37      4       2001-07-22 16:50:38.257
1       38      3       2001-07-22 16:50:38.257
3       39      1       2001-07-22 16:50:38.257
4       51      1       2001-07-22 16:50:38.257
4       47      1       2001-07-22 16:50:38.257
9       37      10      2001-07-22 16:50:38.257
9       38      5       2001-07-22 16:50:38.257
10      41      6       2001-07-22 17:53:51.793
```

So far, all the examples have involved exporting data from SQL Server. Now it's time to take a look at importing data. The BCP command works the same both ways: you should specify IN instead of OUT to import data into SQL Server.

For large files, with more than a couple thousand rows perhaps, you should turn on the Select Into/Bulkcopy option for the database, or set the database recovery mode to BULK_LOGGED or SIMPLE. These options disable all transaction log backups while they are turned on, and you must do a full backup to get transaction log backups to work afterwards. What the option does is for certain operations, namely those involving SELECT INTO and BULK COPY; it changes how transaction logging works.

Typically, whenever you insert a row, SQL Server logs the row being inserted into the transaction log. This prevents data loss in case of power outage and enables you to do point-in-time database recovery. This also significantly slows down the process of inserting huge numbers of records. Switching to BULK_LOGGED or SIMPLE changes the behavior so that rather than logging the entire row insert, SQL Server just logs the page allocations, which involves a lot less overhead. Basically, when you do a BCP and the database is set for BULK_LOGGED or SIMPLE recovery, all the data goes into allocated space in the database; and when the copy commits, it attaches the allocated space to the table. It's really fast, and it's still very safe because all the page allocations are logged, and if the transaction fails and has to roll back, the pages are deallocated. This process is called *Fast Bulk Copy*.

In addition to having the BULK LOGGED or SIMPLE recovery option selected, you need to do a few other things to get fast bulk copy to work.

- ◆ The target table can't be involved in replication.
- ◆ The target table can't have any triggers.
- ◆ The target table either has zero rows or has no indexes.
- ◆ The TABLOCK hint is specified. This is covered in more detail later in the section; for now, the TABLOCK hint is another parameter you can give BCP to make it acquire a table lock before it begins writing data.

NOTE

What About SELECT INTO/BULKCOPY?
If you're used to using SQL Server 7.0 or previous versions, you're probably wondering what happened to the SELECT INTO/BULKCOPY option. It's been replaced by a Recover Mode option. You can choose one of three recovery modes: FULL, BULK_LOGGED, or SIMPLE. FULL mode is the default for everything except Desktop and the Data Engine versions of SQL Server. BULK_LOGGED is similar to the old SELECT INTO/BULKCOPY option, in that any bulk row operations have only allocations logged, not the data. FULL mode is the normal mode for most operations; it offers the widest variety of recovery options.

Typically, if you're adding more than 50% of the current table count or more into the table, you should drop the indexes first because they slow down the inserts, and the indexes will be better if you rebuild them after adding that much data anyway. Regardless, fast bulk copy doesn't work if there are indexes on the table unless the table is empty to begin with.

Another option for large bulk inserts sets the batch size. *Batch size* is the number of rows that will be inserted as part of a transaction. If the batch size is large, then the transaction that is generated will be large, and it may cause your transaction log to fill up. If the transaction is too small, SQL Server spends too much time committing transactions rather than writing your data, and performance suffers. Typically, a batch size between 1,000 and 10,000 is used. Files with lots of rows and very few columns tend to benefit from higher batch sizes. By default, BCP does the entire operation in one batch, but it lets you know when it finishes sending each 1,000 rows to SQL Server.

You should be aware of a few special options, as shown in Table 5.3, that are used for importing data into SQL Server.

TABLE 5.3

BCP DATA IMPORT PARAMETERS

Parameter	Function
-k	Tells SQL Server that if some of the data coming in has nulls in it, it shouldn't apply the default values; it should just leave the column null.
-E	If the table being imported into has an identity column, this option tells SQL Server to use the values in the file rather than the automatically created values from the IDENTITY property.
-R	Tells BCP to use the regional time, date, and currency settings rather than the default, which is to ignore any regional settings.
-b	Gives batch size, number of rows in each batch. Defaults to all of the rows in one batch.
-h	Gives Bulk Insert Hints (see Table 5.4)

The -h option enables you to specify one or more different hints to SQL Server about how to process the bulk copy. These options enable you to fine-tune BCP performance, and are listed in Table 5.4.

TABLE 5.4	

BCP Bulk Insert Hints

Hint	*Description*
ORDER (column ASC|DESC, column...)	This hint enables you to tell SQL Server in what order the data is coming through. If the data is in a specific order and clustered indexes are on the table, this option makes the inserts go faster.
ROWS_PER_BATCH=bb	This is the number of rows per batch. You can also specify this using the -b option. Don't use both.
KILOBYTES_PER_BATCH=cc	This is the number of kilobytes to put into each batch. Similar to rows per batch, but you can specify the amount of data to put into each batch.
TABLOCK	This causes SQL Server to put an exclusive lock on the entire table for the duration of the load. This significantly increases performance. You can turn on the Table Lock On Bulk Load option for a given table using sp_tableoption and get the same effect.
CHECK_CONSTRAINTS	This tells SQL Server to apply CHECK constraints as it inserts data. Causes a huge performance hit, but this is not the default, so if you need to check your constraints as you go, use this.
FIRE_TRIGGERS	This tells SQL Server to fire any triggers that are created for INSERT. By default, INSERT triggers are ignored for bulk copy.

Here is an example of using BCP to put data into a database:

```
C:\Documents and Settings\MILLCS>bcp Chapter5..Sales in
➥salesnative.dat -n -T

Starting copy...

8 rows copied.
Network packet size (bytes): 4096
Clock Time (ms.): total       1122

C:\Documents and Settings\MILLCS>
```

If more than 1000 rows were being copied, BCP would supply a running count of the number of rows inserted.

So, you keep seeing that -T option on the BCP examples and you want to know what it means? Table 5.5 shows you the rest of the BCP command-line switches:

TABLE 5.5

OTHER BCP COMMAND-LINE SWITCHES

Switch	Description
-m	Maximum number of errors allowed before BCP will terminate itself. Defaults to 10. This usually applies to data errors and data conversion errors.
-e	Error file. This is where error messages get written if there are any. Defaults to the command shell.
-F	First row. Enables you to skip rows at the beginning of the file for BCP IN.
-L	Last row. Enables you to limit the number of rows copied in. Very handy for testing out an import on a few rows before importing a large file.
-q	Sets quoted identifiers on, so that if you have table names with spaces or other characters, you can put them in double quotes on the BCP command line.
-i	This is an alternative to a format file; it's a file that contains just the responses to the BCP prompts, and BCP can read it and use it to form the responses.
-o	Specifies where the output of the BCP should go. This is the "8 rows copied" message, along with startup and statistics.
-a	Packet size. Number of bytes to put in a network packet. You can increase this and you might get better performance. If you put it too high, you'll cause degradation. Defaults to 4KB.
-S	Server name. In this chapter, all the copies in the example have been going to a local server. If you want to copy data to another server, use -S.
-U	Login ID, used if you don't use -T.
-P	Password. Used if you don't use -T.
-T	Specifies trusted connection (Windows authentication) should be used.
-v	Reports version information.

There are two other things to be covered with BCP, then you can move on. First of all, in addition to just pulling the data for a given table, you can use the QUERYOUT option in place of IN or OUT, and specify a query rather than a table name. The rest of the options work the same way. This works for output only. Here's an example:

```
C:\Documents and Settings\MILLCS>bcp "SELECT * FROM Chapter5..Sales S INNER JOIN
Chapter5..Person P on S.PersonID = P.Personid" queryout qo.txt -c -T

Starting copy...

14 rows copied.
Network packet size (bytes): 4096
Clock Time (ms.): total        1

C:\Documents and Settings\MILLCS>type qo.txt
1       37      4       2001-07-22 16:50:38.257 1       Danny   Jones
1       38      3       2001-07-22 16:50:38.257 1       Danny   Jones
3       39      1       2001-07-22 16:50:38.257 3       Scott   Smith
4       51      1       2001-07-22 16:50:38.257 4       Alex    Riley
4       47      1       2001-07-22 16:50:38.257 4       Alex    Riley
9       37      10      2001-07-22 16:50:38.257 9       Shelly  Alexander
9       38      5       2001-07-22 16:50:38.257 9       Shelly  Alexander
1       37      4       2001-07-22 16:50:38.257 1       Danny   Jones
1       38      3       2001-07-22 16:50:38.257 1       Danny   Jones
3       39      1       2001-07-22 16:50:38.257 3       Scott   Smith
4       51      1       2001-07-22 16:50:38.257 4       Alex    Riley
4       47      1       2001-07-22 16:50:38.257 4       Alex    Riley
9       37      10      2001-07-22 16:50:38.257 9       Shelly  Alexander
9       38      5       2001-07-22 16:50:38.257 9       Shelly  Alexander
```

Another option is the FORMAT option, which can be used in place of IN, OUT, or QUERYOUT. It produces a format file based on the specified options. If you use the FORMAT option, you must specify a value for the -f parameter. Here's an example call:

```
C:\Documents and Settings\MILLCS>bcp Chapter5..Sales FORMAT qo.txt -c -T -f
➡format.out

C:\Documents and Settings\MILLCS>type format.out
8.0
4
1       SQLCHAR         0       12      "\t"    1       PersonID              ""
2       SQLCHAR         0       12      "\t"    2       ProductID             ""
3       SQLCHAR         0       12      "\t"    3       QtyPurchased          ""
4       SQLCHAR         0       24      "\r\n"  4       DatePurchased         ""
```

This is a pretty powerful tool, but it's kind of difficult to use when you need to just read a file from within SQL Server as part of a script or scheduled job. It sure would be nice if there were a T-SQL equivalent.

Using the *BULK INSERT* Statement

The BULK INSERT statement is a lot like BCP, but inside T-SQL. It uses most of the same options, but it doesn't need to know which server to use or what security to use because you use it from within T-SQL, so it runs on that server with the security context with which you logged in.

The basic syntax goes something like this:

```
BULK INSERT table_name
FROM 'data file'
WITH ( operational and format options>
```

The table name is a table name or three-part name to use. You can actually use this statement to bulk copy into views as well as tables, which is a handy option. The data file is a data file as read from the server. Keep in mind that if you specify a data file like c:\myfile while talking to a remote server, it's going to try and read data from the c:\ drive on the server, not the one on your workstation.

Table 5.6 provides a list of all the operational and format parameters you can use. As mentioned, they're all fairly similar to the ones used by BCP.

TABLE 5.6

OPTIONS FOR THE *BULK INSERT* COMMAND

Option	Description
BATCHSIZE	Same as BCP option -b.
CHECK_CONSTRAINTS	Same as using the CHECK CONSTRAINTS hint in BCP.

continues

| TABLE 5.6 | *continued* |

OPTIONS FOR THE *BULK INSERT* COMMAND

Option	Description
CODEPAGE	Specifies which code page to use: ACP, which is the standard Windows code page; OEM, which is the default and contains all the regional characters the server can display; and RAW, which specifies that no code page translation should happen. You can also specify a code page name.
DATAFILETYPE	This specifies the type of data in the file. There are four options. The char option specifies that normal characters are used. The native option specifies that the data types used in the tables should be used. The widechar option specifies that the file is Unicode, and widenative specifies that all the results should be Unicode.
FIELDTERMINATOR	Specifies the field terminator, just like -t in BCP.
FIRSTROW	Same as -F in BCP.
FIRE_TRIGGERS	Same as the FIRE_TRIGGERS hint in BCP.
FORMATFILE	Path to the format file, same as -f in BCP.
KEEPIDENTITY	Same as -E in BCP.
KEEPNULLS	Same as -k option in BCP.
KILOBYTES_PER_BATCH	Same as KILOBYTES_PER_BATCH hint in BCP.
LASTROW	Same as -L in BCP.
MAXERRORS	Same as -m in BCP.
ORDER	Same as ORDER hint in BCP.
ROWS_PER_BATCH	Same as ROWS_PER_BATCH hint in BCP.
ROWTERMINATOR	Same as -r in BCP.
TABLOCK	Same as TABLOCK hint in BCP.

Here's an example, using the same bulk copy operation you used before. Remember, this runs in Query Analyzer, not on the command line:

```
BULK INSERT Sales
FROM 'C:\salesnative.dat'
WITH ( DATAFILETYPE = 'native'
)
```

This performs a standard native-mode insert of a file created earlier using BCP. The DATAFILETYPE='native' tells SQL Server that the file is stored in native mode.

Command line really got you down? Tired of all of this typing stuff? Take a look now at how to import and export data using the graphical tools.

Importing and Exporting Data with Data Transformation Services

SQL Server 2000 provides a great tool that imports and exports data for you called the Data Transformation Services (DTS) Import/Export Wizard. This tool uses SQL Server DTS to copy data into and out of SQL Server using nice, easy-to-understand graphical tools. Step by Step 5.2 provides an explanation of how to copy data out of SQL Server.

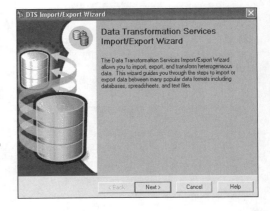

FIGURE 5.4
The startup screen for the Import/Export wizard.

STEP BY STEP

5.2 Importing Data with the Import and Export Application

1. Start the Import and Export application by going to Start, clicking on Microsoft SQL Server, and then clicking on Import and Export Data. The DTS Import/Export Wizard opening screen appears as shown in Figure 5.4. Click the Next button.

2. Next up is the Choose a Data Source window, shown in Figure 5.5. This is where you get to choose where the data will be coming from for your copies. Click the drop-down box labeled Data Source and choose a data source type. For this example, choose Microsoft OLE DB Provider for SQL Server, but notice you can choose a lot of different data sources.

3. After you choose the data source, you need to pick a server. In the example shown in Figure 5.5, the local server is shown, with Windows Authentication. Change the database to Pubs and click the Next button.

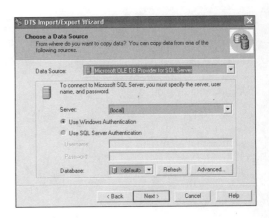

FIGURE 5.5
The window where you can choose from which data source to read data.

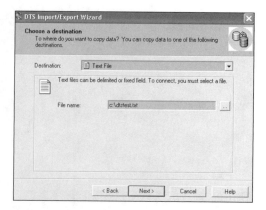

FIGURE 5.6
The window you can use to specify where to put your exported data.

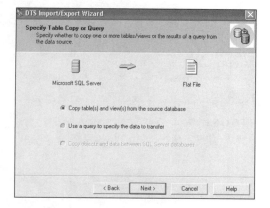

FIGURE 5.7
Where you tell the wizard what it's going to copy: a table or a query.

4. Next is the Choose a Destination window, shown in Figure 5.6. This looks very similar to the Choose a Data Source window. Just choose the destination source, which should be a text file. For a file name, use **C:\DTSTEST.TXT**.

5. Next is the Specify Table Copy or Query window, which is shown in Figure 5.7. If you choose Copy Table(s) and Views from the Source Database, you can copy an entire table; if you choose "Use a Query to Specify the Data to Transfer," you'll get to enter a query to run. If you chose SQL Server as the source and destination, you can choose the third option, which is to copy an entire database or at least a subset of database objects. Click on Next.

6. Almost done! Now you just need to tell the wizard specifically what you want to copy and what format you want it to land in, using the Select Destination File Format window, shown in Figure 5.8. Choose the `[pubs].[dbo].[titles]` table as the source. Do a delimited file, with a tab delimiter and no text qualifier. Also, check the First Row Has Column Names check box. This puts the column names in the first row, which will be handy when you copy the table back in later. This is also where you can specify a transformation to use, which is discussed in the text. Click on Next after you have the column delimiter set to Tab and the First Row Has Column Names check box is checked.

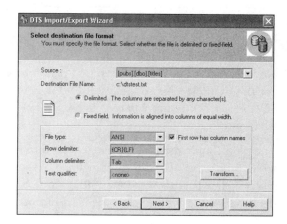

FIGURE 5.8
Window used to specify the file type, delimiters, and what table is going to be copied.

7. Next is the Save, Schedule and Replicate Package window, which you can see in Figure 5.9. This window enables you to run the package immediately, and/or schedule it to run periodically. You can also save the package to SQL Server, a Meta Data Services store, a Visual Basic file, or a Structured Storage file. For now, just run the package by clicking on Next.

8. The Summary window, shown in Figure 5.10, shows you all the options you've chosen for your export. Make sure everything is correct and click on Finish.

9. Then the Executing Package window appears, and it shows you what's going on. It counts rows—up to 18—and then pops up a window telling you it's all done, as shown in Figure 5.11.

The only really tricky part of the entire wizard is the transformations. DTS enables you to write transformations in VBScript that can make simple changes to data, such as formatting or localizing. By clicking on the Transform window, you can go into the transformation and change the VBScript so it changes the data format.

That's all there is for import and export. You've now finished quite a long chapter that covers everything from complex queries to the DTS Import/Export Wizard. Next up is a lesson on scripting, so you can find out what that @ was doing in the section on OPENXML.

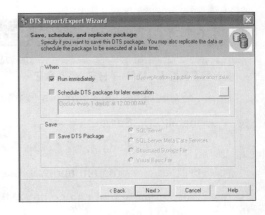

FIGURE 5.9

Save packages or even replicate them to other servers.

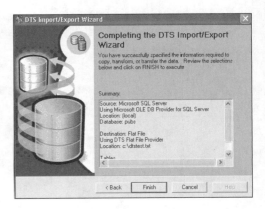

FIGURE 5.10

The summary screen for the wizard. Just click Finish to create your text file.

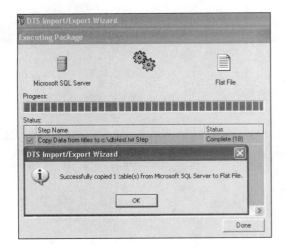

FIGURE 5.11

The window shows you the number of rows exported, where the rows were exported from, and shows completion status.

CASE STUDY: PORTER STEAK COMPANY

ESSENCE OF THE CASE

Here are the essential elements in this case:

- Install SQL Server.
- Move existing data.
- Fix the user program and web site.
- Write a query that can create XML to send to vendors.

SCENARIO

The Porter Steak Company is a nationwide gourmet foods distributor with offices in Des Moines, Iowa. They ship frozen gourmet steaks, fish, and some side dishes across the country and around the world. Their business is booming thanks to their new web site, so they need to move up to something a little faster than the FoxPro application they are currently using. They'd also like to be able to send XML transaction streams to Super Parcel USA, their shipping vendor, and to other vendors.

ANALYSIS

The first step is to get SQL Server up and running, then use the Import/Export wizard in DTS to copy all the data over into SQL Server. Fix up the web site so it can talk to SQL Server via ODBC instead of using FoxPro via ODBC, and the user interface should be ready. Then schedule a query to run periodically to create an XML document that can be sent to vendors.

CHAPTER SUMMARY

One of the fundamental capabilities SQL Server has is as a reporting platform. You have learned how to write some advanced queries, perform aggregate operations, create groups, and subtotal reports. This all builds on the basic SELECT statement from Chapter 3, filling in the gaps of querying multiple tables and showing correlations. Reporting is crucial to survival, and being able to create aggregated summary reports using COMPUTE and COMPUTE BY, along with the other aggregate functions, enables you to create great reports with useful summaries.

In addition, you've also learned how BCP, DTS, and possibly even XML work with SQL Server to provide a wide range of import and export functionality. These are important tasks because a database without data is just, well, base.

The next chapter covers script writing and programming techniques. All the JOIN and aggregate material in this chapter is used in Chapter 6 for writing scripts, and it's also used in Chapter 9 on writing stored procedures. Writing joins is fundamental to understanding SQL Server; it's used by nearly every command, so you'll end up using it a lot in the rest of this book, and you'll see it on the exam as well.

KEY TERMS

- JOIN
- derived tables
- IN operator
- CASE expression
- UNION operator
- aggregate functions
- GROUP BY operator
- linked server
- XML

APPLY YOUR KNOWLEDGE

Exercises

5.1   Writing Queries with Joins

This exercise demonstrates how to create a query with Query Analyzer to pull information from several tables in the Pubs database.

Estimated Time: 5 minutes.

1. Open SQL Server Query Analyzer, and log into a SQL Server.

2. Switch to the Pubs database using the Database drop-down in the Query window.

3. Find all the authors in the database with this query: "SELECT * from Authors". Notice there is a field called au_id.

4. Find all the book titles in the database with this query: "SELECT * FROM Titles". Notice there is a field called title_id.

5. To join the tables, you also need to use the TitleAuthor table. To find the structure of this table, use this query: "SELECT * FROM TitleAuthor". Notice that this table has both an au_id and a title_id field.

6. Use the following query to join the three tables together and find the author names and titles:

```
SELECT au_fname, au_lname, title
FROM Authors A
     INNER JOIN TitleAuthor TA
        ON TA.au_id = A.au_id
     INNER JOIN Titles T
        ON TA.title_id = T.title_id
```

5.2   Writing Queries with *GROUP BY*

This exercise demonstrates how to create a query with a GROUP BY and an aggregate function. This query finds

which authors have written more than one book, and how many books they have written.

Estimated Time: 5 minutes.

1. Open SQL Server Query Analyzer, and log into a SQL Server.

2. Switch to the Pubs database using the Database drop-down in the Query window.

3. Use the following query to join the two tables together and find the author names and the number of books written.

```
SELECT au_fname, au_lname, count(*)
FROM Authors A
     INNER JOIN TitleAuthor TA
        ON TA.au_id = A.au_id
GROUP BY au_fname, au_lname
HAVING count(*) > 1
```

5.3   Exporting Data with BCP

This exercise demonstrates how to export data from the Pubs database using BCP and the QUERYOUT option.

Estimated Time: 5 minutes.

1. Open a command prompt by clicking on Start, choosing Run, and typing **cmd**.

2. Type in the following at the command prompt, all on one line:

```
bcp "SELECT * FROM pubs..authors a INNER JOIN
➡pubs..titleauthor ta on ta.au_id = a.au_id
➡INNER JOIN pubs..titles t on t.title_id =
➡ta.title_id" QUERYOUT TitlesAuthors.txt -c
➡-U<user> -P<password> -S<server>
```

3. Be sure to substitute a valid username, password, and servername where appropriate in Step 2.

4. After running the BCP, use the command type titleauthors.txt to view the results.

Review Questions

1. What are the restrictions on the SELECT clause if a GROUP BY clause is present?

2. What are the restrictions on an ORDER BY clause if a COMPUTE BY clause is present?

3. What are the requirements to achieve fast bulk copy?

4. What is the difference between WHERE and HAVING in a SELECT statement?

5. Which of the following will generally return the fewest or largest number of rows: CROSS JOIN, LEFT JOIN, RIGHT JOIN, INNER JOIN?

6. What is the difference between a character-mode BCP and a native-mode BCP in terms of making the file readable by other systems? How about in terms of speed of import and export?

7. Explain the purpose of the Batch Size argument in BCP.

Exam Questions

1. The EconoVan Corporation is trying to figure out how many vans they have sold. They currently have a table that contains a sales record for each van by type that was created with this script:

```
create table VanSales (
VIN varchar(50),
SalePrice float,
Cost float,
Type int,
SaleDate datetime
)
```

Which of the following queries will show them the number of vans they have sold?

A. `select * from vansales order by 1`

B. `select cnt(*) from VanSales order by 1`

C. `SELECT count(*) FROM VanSales`

D. `SELECT COUNT(*) FROM VANSALES WHERE TYPE = "YEAR"`

2. The EconoVan Corporation is trying to figure out how many vans of each type they have sold. They currently have a table that contains a sales record for each van by type that was created with this script:

```
create table VanSales (
VIN varchar(50),
SalePrice float,
Cost float,
Type int,
SaleDate datetime
)
```

Which of the following queries will show them the number of vans they have sold by type?

A. `SELECT COUNT(*) FROM VanSales ORDER BY Type`

B. `SELECT Type, COUNT(*) From VanSales GROUP BY 1`

C. `SELECT Type, COUNT(*) From VanSales GROUP BY Type ORDER BY Type`

D. `SELECT COUNT(*) from VanSales GROUP BY Type`

3. You have two tables that were created like this:

```
create table birds (
BirdID int IDENTITY(1,1),
BirdName varchar(30)
)

create table BirdFeathers (
BirdID int,
FeatherID int
)
```

APPLY YOUR KNOWLEDGE

You need to find all the FeatherIDs for each BirdName. Which of the following queries will do the job?

A.
```
select BirdName, FeatherID from birds b
inner join birdfeathers bf on b.BirdID =
bf.birdid
```

B.
```
select BirdName, FeatherID from birds b
left join birdfeathers bf on b.BirdID =
bf.birdid
```

C.
```
select BirdName, FeatherID from birds b
right join birdfeathers bf on b.BirdID =
bf.birdid
```

D.
```
select BirdName, FeatherID from birds b
cross join birdfeathers bf on b.BirdID =
bf.birdid
```

4. You're doing asset management for a small business. You need to figure out how many laptops, how many desktops, and the total number of computers in the company. Here's the table where the data is stored:

```
create table PCAsset (
AssetID int,
PCType char(1), -- L or D, Laptop or Desktop
AcquireDate datetime
)
```

Which of the following queries will do the job?

A.
```
select AssetID, PCType from PCAsset group
by AssetID
```

B.
```
select PCType, Count(*) from PCAsset
group by PCType with rollup
```

C.
```
Select PCType, count(*) from PCAsset
compute by PCType
```

D.
```
Select PCType, count(*) from PCAsset
compute group by pctype with rollup
```

5. You need to query some data on a temporary remote server for a one-time report. Which of the following functions is the best to use?

A. OPENQUERY()

B. OPENROWSET()

C. Linked Servers

D. OPENXML()

6. You need to send an XML rowset to a parts supplier for your business that produces radio kits. The rowset should contain a parts list for your order for next week. The supplier has provided you with a schema you must use. Which of the following FOR XML options will enable you to conform to his schema?

A. FOR XML RAW, XMLDATA

B. FOR XML AUTO, BINARY BASE64

C. FOR XML EXPLICIT

D. FOR XML AUTO

7. There's a performance problem on one of your SQL Servers that you use to process XML. After a period of time processing XML data, the server's memory utilization is very high and the server won't allow any more XML statements to be prepared. Which of the following is the most likely cause for the problem?

A. There are cursors in the Transact-SQL batches that aren't deallocating properly.

B. The XML that is being parsed is not well formed.

C. The server has a hardware problem.

D. The XML strings are not being properly removed after preparation and use.

8. Leeks Unlimited has just acquired another company, the Garlic Crock. They're trying to import the several million rows of data from the Garlic Crock's databases by exporting the data from Garlic Crock's mainframe into text files and then using BCP to bulk copy the data into the Leeks Unlimited database server. The problem is that they keep filling up the transaction log of their database. Which of the following options would *not* help alleviate the problem?

   A. Rather than using BCP, use the same options with BULK INSERT.

   B. Use the batch size limiter on the BCP command line.

   C. Use the batch size limitation as a bulk copy hint.

   D. Make sure that the database's SELECT INTO/BULKCOPY option is turned on.

9. After importing all the Garlic Crock data from their mainframe, Leeks Unlimited needs to read a bunch of Garlic Crock's data from their Web server database back ends, which are currently using Microsoft Access. Which of the following tools would be the best for the job?

   A. The Bulk Copy Program

   B. OPENXML

   C. The BULK INSERT command

   D. The DTS Import/Export Wizard

10. Peekaboo needs to write a query that will help her understand how many toys are in her toy box. Here's the table she created to track her toys:

```
create table woof (
ToyID int,
ToyType char(1), --B for ball, S for squeaky
ToyName varchar(15)
)
```

   Which of the following queries will give Peekaboo a report complete with subtotals of each toy she has with subtotals for types?

   A. select ToyType, Count(*) from woof compute count(*) by toytype

   B. select toytype from woof compute count(toytype) by toytype

   C. select toyname, toytype from woof order by toytype compute count(ToyName) by Toytype

   D. select toyname, toytype from woof with cube

11. Eric has a couple of fairly large tables that handle the food inventory for his snack smuggling operation. He wants to cause a problem for his system administrator, preferably by just using up resources unnecessarily. What's the best way to do this?

   A. Cross-join the two tables.

   B. Left-join the two tables and union them together.

   C. Inner-join the tables and union them together.

   D. Right-join the tables and union them together.

12. Gordon is trying to get access to a server on the other side of the Black Mesa facility to complete his research. He just got access to the server, and is having problems running even simple queries. What's the problem with this query:

```
select count(*) from LambdaSQL.
➥BadThings.Creepy
```

APPLY YOUR KNOWLEDGE

His colleagues seem to be having no problems.

A. You can't run an aggregate function across a remote server.

B. You should use OPENROWSET for this kind of an operation.

C. You should use OPENXML for this.

D. He left the owner name out of the object specification.

13. Things have been pretty boring lately, so Barney the security guard wants to put some random top secret data on a laptop and then throw it over the wall at the local embassy. He wants to make sure the data is nice, complete, and easy-to-read XML. Which of the following should he use?

A. Use FOR XML AUTO, XMLDATA

B. Use FOR XML RAW

C. Use FOR XML BASE BINARY64

D. Use FOR XML BASE PORTABLE

14. Peekaboo is at it again. This time, she just wants a quick list of all of her toy names and types, but she'd like the types to be spelled out with Ball for B and Squeaky for S. How can you make that happen? Here's the table again:

```
create table woof (
ToyID int,
ToyType char(1), --B for ball, S for squeaky
ToyName varchar(15)
)
```

A. select ToyType, ToyName from woof

B.
```
select ToyName, case ToyType
    when 'B' then 'Ball'
    When 'S' then 'Squeaky'
    else 'broken'
end
from woof
```

C.
```
Select ToyName, case ToyType
    if 'B' then 'Ball'
    if 'S' then 'Squeaky'
    else 'broken'
end
from woof
```

D.
```
Select ToyName, case ToyType
    when 'B' then 'Ball'
    When 'S' then 'Squeaky'
    else 'broken'
from woof
```

15. Which of the following provides the slowest data throughput for BCP?

A. Native mode

B. Native mode with Unicode support

C. Wide native mode

D. Comma-delimited text

Answers to Review Questions

1. If there is a GROUP BY, the SELECT must contain all of the columns contained in the GROUP BY, and the columns can't be part of an aggregate function.

2. The ORDER BY must be present if the COMPUTE BY is there, and it must contain at least all the columns in the COMPUTE BY in the same order. The ORDER BY can have additional columns, however.

3. To achieve fast bulk copy, you have to have the recovery mode properly set, no triggers on the target table, no replication of the target table, and either no indexes or an empty target.

4. If there is no GROUP BY, there is no effective difference between WHERE and HAVING in a SELECT statement. If there is a GROUP BY, then HAVING can

be used to filter output from aggregate functions, whereas the WHERE clause even filters what gets processed by the aggregate function.

5. The most rows will be returned by the CROSS JOIN, which returns the number of rows in the first table times the number of rows in the second table. The fewest are returned by an INNER JOIN.

6. Character-mode BCP puts out files that are easy to read by other systems, but the files tend to be larger and slow the system.

7. The Batch Size argument determines the number of rows that are to be copied in each transaction. Smaller batch sizes tend to take more SQL Server time at the benefit of using less transaction log space.

Answers to Exam Questions

1. **C.** The other close answer is A, but that shows you all the records, and not necessarily the count. Option B is wrong because CNT() is not an aggregate function. COUNT(*) is an aggregate function, covered in the aptly named "Aggregate Functions" section.

2. **C.** Option A would work if you could find someone who wanted to sit and count through the output. Options B and D are invalid syntax: B because you have to name fields in a GROUP BY, and D because the Type field isn't in the SELECT list. There's a whole section on using the GROUP BY syntax called "Using GROUP BY to Aggregate Data" in this chapter.

3. **A.** They're all valid syntax except for the ON clause in the CROSS JOIN (option D), but only option A

returns the correct rowset. This is all about structuring joins, which is covered in the "Join Mechanics" section.

4. **B.** Only B uses correct syntax. Option A doesn't have everything in the select list it needs, and doesn't count anything, Option C should read COMPUTE COUNT(*) BY PCType and it would work, but it still wouldn't be as efficient as B. Option D is just a mess syntactically. COMPUTE and COMPUTE BY are discussed in the "Creating Breaks with COMPUTE and COMPUTE BY" section.

5. **B.** Either Option A or C would work, too, but they'd involve creating a linked server, and for a one-time report it's more efficient to just use OPENROWSET. There's a whole section on OPENROWSET called "Using OPENROWSET".

6. **C.** To successfully exchange data in a provided schema, you're going to have to dig through the documentation and figure out how to do explicit XML. If you need help on creating XML files from rowsets, check out the section on "Extracting Data into XML".

7. **D.** The sp_xml_removedocument stored procedure must be called to free memory by deallocating the memory for the XML strings, and if you lose the handles, the resulting memory leak will eventually cause SQL Server to be unable to process more XML. The section titled "Preparing and Removing an XML Document" goes into great detail about how all this works.

8. **A.** The BULK INSERT statement with the same parameters will fill up the logs just as fast as BCP. Any of the other options will help, though. There are two great sections—"Using the BULK INSERT Statement" and "Importing and Exporting Data with BCP"—in this chapter.

APPLY YOUR KNOWLEDGE

9. **D.** The only tool that can directly read Microsoft Access databases and import them is the DTS Import Export wizard. Any of the other tools listed require either exporting the data to text files or exporting it to XML. The DTS Import/Export wizard is covered in the "Importing and Exporting Data with Data Transformation Services" section.

10. **C.** (It took me three tries to get this one right, the first two options are actually things I tried on the way.) Option A is not correct because you can't use COUNT(*) with COMPUTE BY. Option B is not correct because it's missing the ORDER BY. The fourth one is totally fictitious. (Peekaboo is a dog, by the way, and she wandered into the office just in time to get famous.) Yet another question on COMPUTE BY calls for another wonderful referral back to the "Creating Breaks with COMPUTE and COMPUTE BY" section.

11. **A.** Cross-joins consume the most resources because they have the largest rowset, which is the size of table 1 times table 2. None of the other queries can come even close. A quick jump back to the "Join Mechanics" section would be in order if that one tripped you up.

12. **D.** All cross-server activity has to be done with four-part names. The correct name is probably something like LambdaSQL.BadThings.dbo.Creepy. Cross-server joins were all covered in the sections "Creating a Linked Server" and "Using Linked Servers".

13. **A.** The XMLData flag puts the schema, including all the data types, into the XML document for easy viewing. Putting data into XML files is covered by the "Extracting Data into XML" section in this chapter.

14. **B.** Option A doesn't fit the requirements; Option C uses if rather than when, and option D is missing an end. They're all about the CASE expression, which is covered in the section titled "CASE Expressions."

15. **D.** Option A is the fastest, and they get slower as you go down the list. BCP performance is covered in the "Importing and Exporting Data with BCP" section.

Suggested Readings and Resources

- For information about standard deviation and variance, try the Internet Statistics Glossary, located at http://www.animatedsoftware.com/statglos/statglos.htm

- New Riders publishes a book called *XML and SQL Server 2000*, the ISBN is 0735711127, and the author is John Griffin.

- SQL Server Books Online, the Overview articles on OPENXML, OPENROWSET, and OPENQUERY.

- SQL Server Books Online, the syntax for sp_addlinkedserver, sp_serveroption, and sp_dropserver.

- SQL Server Books Online, the overview page for BCP.

Manage result sets by using cursors and Transact-SQL. Considerations include locking models and appropriate usage.

▶ This objective requires you to understand how cursors work, including how the different types of cursors affect concurrency and performance. This objective also requires you to understand when to use cursors and when to use other statements.

Enforce procedural business logic by using transactions.

- **Design and manage transactions.**

- **Manage control of flow.**

▶ This objective requires you to know how transactions relate to business processes and why transactions are used at all.

Manage data manipulation by using transactions.

- **Implement error handling in transactions.**

▶ This objective requires you to understand how to manipulate data in a transaction model. This includes explicitly starting, committing, and rolling back transactions, how transactions relate to locking and concurrency issues, and how to raise errors within a transaction.

CHAPTER 6

Programming SQL Server 2000

▶ With SQL Server, the best way to learn is by doing. Write scripts and use the samples in this chapter to get started.

▶ Literally hundreds of different functions can be used in a script. Use SQL Server Books Online to learn some of them, paying particular attention to important ones, such as SUBSTRING, CONVERT, and the date and time functions.

▶ Pay close attention to the section on transactions. The exam will ask a lot of questions about how transactions roll back, commit, and save.

INTRODUCTION

One of the powerful features of Microsoft SQL Server 2000 is that it enables you to write scripts and batches to manipulate data. The aspect of SQL Server that provides this functionality is the Transact-SQL language. Transact-SQL (T-SQL) is an extension of ANSI standard SQL, and includes features like conditional execution constructs (IF...THEN), looping constructs (WHILE), and cursor functionality. These features combine to make T-SQL a limited yet fairly powerful tool. This chapter covers the features found in T-SQL that make it a true scripting language. Only a few exam objectives are directly related to this chapter, but the chapter covers a lot of foundational material that you need if you're going to understand the objectives here and the objectives in later chapters, especially Chapter 9, "Stored Procedures and User-Defined Functions."

SCRIPTS, BATCHES, AND TRANSACTIONS

T-SQL programs are technically called *scripts*. A script is usually contained within a text file on disk, which is then loaded into some tool (the Query Analyzer, or the command-line equivalent called OSQL) and can be executed. A script is made of one or more *batches*. Each batch is made up of zero, one, or more transactions. The following sections look at each of these entities.

Scripts

A script is made up of one or more batches. To separate one batch from another, put the word GO on a line by itself between the batches, like this:

```
SELECT * FROM sysobjects WHERE type = 'u'
go
SELECT COUNT(*) FROM sysobjects
```

This script contains two batches, one from the beginning of the file to the word GO, and another from the word GO to the end of the file.

Batches

Knowing how batches work is important for several reasons. Batches determine variable scope. This is covered again later, but you should always remember that a variable can only be used within the batch where it is declared.

SQL Server compiles and runs scripts batch by batch. If you have a script with several batches in it, and one of the batches contains a syntax error, the rest of the batches do execute, but the statement in the batch that had an error does not execute. If one of the statements would cause a constraint violation, then that statement doesn't execute, but all the other statements in the batch do execute.

Other runtime errors, such as arithmetic overflow errors, cause the batch to stop executing at that point, with all the preceding commands executed and none of the following commands executed.

When you use tools such as Query Analyzer or the command-line equivalent, ISQL, the tools themselves send the statements to SQL Server in batches, one batch at a time. SQL Server then compiles the single batch, processes it, and returns for the next batch as necessary. The keyword GO, then, isn't a keyword used by SQL Server; it is actually used by the various tools to determine when batches start and stop.

Batches control how certain statements execute. When you learn more about stored procedures later, in Chapter 9, you'll find that a stored procedure definition has to be in its own batch, and the stored procedure includes everything in the batch. This is an example of some rules you should know about batches:

- ◆ You can't add columns to a table and then reference the new columns with an UPDATE or INSERT within the same batch.

- ◆ The EXECUTE (or EXEC) statement isn't required if it's on the first executable line of the batch.

- ◆ You can't combine CREATE VIEW, CREATE PROCEDURE, CREATE RULE, CREATE TRIGGER, or CREATE DEFAULT statements in a batch.

Now it's time to add a little flexibility to how you work inside batches. How can you handle counting rows or storing intermediate values? You can't. Yet.

> **NOTE**
>
> **Working with System Tables** This chapter makes heavy use of the sysobjects system table in examples of selecting data. Remember that this is a system table. You can select out of it all if you want, but don't insert or update any system table without a note from your mother. Doing so is a very good way to corrupt a database. So, using SELECT is okay, but nothing else.

WORKING WITH VARIABLES

A *variable* is a temporary place to put pieces of data that you're working with. This can include things such as dates, numbers for counting with, or strings that you need to manipulate. SQL Server is a language that could be termed "strongly typed"; that is, it has several different types of variables, and there are certain restrictions on converting from one type to another. With respect to variables, you need to understand six topics:

◆ Naming variables

◆ Declaring variables

◆ Variable types

◆ Variable scope

◆ Setting and using variables

◆ Global variables

The first thing to understand is how variables are named.

Naming Variables

A variable follows the same naming scheme as a column name, with one slight addition. One of the big problems that SQL Server has is determining which part of a statement is a variable and which is a column name. If, for example, you have a variable that contains an object ID, and you want to find the name of the object, things might get very confusing:

```
SELECT name FROM sysobjects WHERE id = id
```

That statement returns all the rows in the sysobjects table (id is always equal to id, after all). That's probably not what you intended to do, but it's a common mistake. So, to allow SQL Server to make the connection between ID the column and ID the variable, you always have to put an at sign (@) in front of a variable name. So, the preceding statement becomes

```
SELECT name FROM sysobjects WHERE id = @ID
```

Now SQL Server can tell that what you really want is one specific row from the sysobjects table. This is, of course, assuming you declared the @ID variable. You didn't do that because you're not sure how to declare a variable? Well, it's time to learn.

Declaring Variables

A variable is declared using the handily named DECLARE statement. So, to declare a single variable with a type of int, you use something like this:

```
DECLARE @id int
```

That's pretty simple, so now try the advanced version:

```
DECLARE @id int,
        @foo int,
        @fee varchar(30
```

The comma separating each of the variables is required by SQL Server. The fact that they're all on new lines and tabbed in is just for the sake of style. The following is an equivalent statement:

```
DECLARE @id int, @foo int, @fee varchar(30)
```

So, it's important to note that you can take any statement and break it onto multiple lines. Don't overdo it, but use this feature to make your scripts easier to read and maintain. In addition, it's easier to draw conclusions about what a variable does by what kind of data is in the variable, or what type the variable has, and putting the variables on different lines helps to emphasize their types.

Variable Types

You can create variables of nearly any type that you can store in a table, with the restriction that you can't create variables of type TEXT, NTEXT, or IMAGE. So, you can create int, tinyint, smallint, datetime, smalldatetime, uniqueidentifier, varchar, nvarchar, char, nchar, and so on. You can (and should) specify lengths where appropriate, such as varchar(30) or nchar(15). You can create a string variable that holds up to 8,000 bytes, so you can build a varchar(8000) or an nvarchar(4000) in a variable. (Remember that the nchar and nvarchar types are double-wide characters, so they take up twice as much room as a varchar.)

There is also a special variable type called TABLE that can be used to store a recordset. For example, you can declare something like this:

```
DECLARE @tmp TABLE (id int,
                        tablename varchar(50)
            )
INSERT INTO @tmp SELECT id, name FROM sysobjects WHERE
➡ type = 'u'
```

That creates a table similar to a temporary table that is available only within the current batch. This is faster and requires fewer resources than a temp table, but with a more limited scope. Be aware, however, that this consumes SQL Server memory, so don't put exceptionally large tables into these structures. You also cannot use a local variable of type table as the target for something like this:

```
INSERT INTO @tmp EXEC sp_foo
```

You cannot use a variable of type table as the target of a SELECT..into statement, either. You can populate the table using only INSERT..SELECT, INSERT..VALUES, and UPDATE. The table automatically "goes away" at the end of the batch, which is the end of its scope.

Variable Scope

All variables cease to exist at the end of their scope. To keep things simple, SQL Server has only one scope for a variable, which is the local scope. (Yes, there is a section called "Global Variables." They don't count; you'll see why later in this chapter.) That means that when your script has a GO in it, any variables you have need to be redeclared and reset.

So, you now know how to create variables using the DECLARE statement, how to put different types of data into variables using variable types, and how variables get destroyed. Now it's time to learn how to use the variables.

Setting and Using Variables

There are four ways to put a value into a variable. If you need to put data into a variable that comes out of a SELECT statement, you can do something like this:

```
SELECT @id = id FROM sysobjects WHERE name = 'syscolumns'
```

NOTE

Picking Up the Trash "Garbage Collection" is the term computer science folks use to describe what happens to variables after they die. In many languages (C, C++, and others), the programmer has to deal with issues, such as heap fragmentation and memory management from creating and disposing of variables. SQL Server handles all these mechanics internally, so you don't have to worry about them.

After executing this, and assuming the variables are all declared properly, you'll end up with some number in the @id variable. That's one way to put a value into a variable. What's another way?

```
SET @id = 42
```

If the value you're putting into the variable does not come from a table, you can use the SET statement to put the value in. That includes things like this:

```
DECLARE @today datetime
SET @today=getdate()
```

The getdate() function is one of the built-in SQL server functions; it returns the current date and time, which the SET statement places into the variable @today. You can set a variable to the value of any SQL Server function, provided the data returned by the function will fit into the variable you declare. So, although it's appropriate to do something like the datetime example above, doing something like this

```
DECLARE @today datetime
SET @today=substring('hello', 1, 3)
```

doesn't work, because the substring function returns a string, not a date. The exact error message you get is Syntax error converting datetime from character string.

Another way to put a value into a variable is with the EXEC statement, like this:

```
DECLARE @ReturnCode int
EXEC @ReturnCode = sp_who
```

This executes the sp_who stored procedure, which returns a result set, which is displayed, and a return code, which is not the result set. A return code is a status code that the stored procedure can use to describe whether there were any errors. Return codes are limited to datatype int, so you can also use return codes to return integer data. Chapter 9 covers this topic in detail. The final way to set a variable is also to use an EXEC, but with an output parameter. That's covered in Chapter 9 as well.

You need to know a few other things about setting and using variables. First of all, setting a variable to an arithmetic expression follows the classic arithmetic orders of operation. So, to set the variable @value to 14, use this:

```
SET @value = 2 + 3 * 4
```

How does that work? T-SQL, and most programming languages, use what's called the *standard order of operations*, which is as follows: Any operations in parenthesis are done first, from the innermost set of parenthesis working outward. Then, any functions are evaluated. After that, multiplication and division are carried out, then addition and subtraction. So, to get a different result for the preceding expression, add parentheses:

```
SET @value = (2 + 3) * 4
```

This sets the variable @value to 20.

Similar to the way a DECLARE statement works, you can create statements like this by delimiting the values in the SELECT:

```
DECLARE @id int,
        @name varchar(30)
SELECT @id = id, @name = name FROM sysobjects WHERE
➥sysstat = 113
```

You should note three things here. First, both variables do get populated. Second, that result set contains multiple values (several records in sysobjects have a sysstat of 113). Which record puts values into the variables? It's non-deterministic. In other words, the values come out of one of the records, but there's no way to predict which record. So, writing code like that is probably a bad idea. Finally, the SELECT statement can do this multiple-assignment-in-one-statement trick, but the SET statement cannot.

Now, you've been setting these variables everywhere, but how do you know what's in them? There are two ways to display the contents of a variable. First, you can use the print statement, like this:

```
DECLARE @id int,
        @name varchar(30)
SELECT @id = id, @name = name FROM sysobjects WHERE
➥sysstat = 113
PRINT @id
PRINT @name
```

Or, you can do this:

```
DECLARE @id int,
        @name varchar(30)
SELECT @id = id, @name = name FROM sysobjects WHERE
➥sysstat = 113
SELECT @id, @name
```

What's the difference? There are three major differences. First, the SELECT statement returns a rowset, whereas the PRINT statement just prints out a string. So, the PRINT statement can just put the string into the output stream, but the SELECT statement can be used by applications. Second, a PRINT statement doesn't necessarily happen in sequence with the rest of a batch, and actually, PRINT statements usually aren't executed until the end of the batch or if there's a PRINT statement pending and the value needs to be changed. This happens only with very long and complicated batches, but can make debugging difficult. Finally, a SELECT statement returns any data you want, whereas a PRINT can return only the data that can be converted into strings directly. You cannot use PRINT with a function call or with anything else that cannot be implicitly converted to a string type.

So, say that you have a variable with the string "42" in it. Not the number 42, but the string "42". Here's an example:

```
DECLARE @TestValue varchar(30),
        @TestResult int
SET @TestValue = '42'
SET @TestResult = @TestValue + 3
PRINT @TestResult
```

This code will print the value 45, because it automatically converted the string value 42 to the integer value 42 and then added 3. Now look at this example:

```
DECLARE @TestValue varchar(30),
        @TestResult int
SET @TestValue = '42'
SET @TestResult = @TestValue + '3'
PRINT @TestResult
```

This prints out the value 423, because it takes the string 42 and adds the character 3 onto the end. To prevent confusion from these situations, it's best to use the convert function to convert values to the type for their result. In other words, do something like this:

```
DECLARE @TestValue varchar(30),
        @TestResult int
SET @TestValue = '42'
SET @TestResult = convert(int, @TestValue) + 3
PRINT @TestResult
```

This produces the same result, but it's easier to figure out exactly what's going on because there's no ambiguity that it might return 423 or the number 45. The plus sign is used for both string concatenation and addition.

Global Variables

Global variables are not variables. They are actually system functions that return various pieces of information about the current user environment for SQL Server. They are just called "functions" now, but we aren't going to do that here because the syntax is different, and it would be confusing to call two completely different constructs the same name. A global variable looks like a variable with two at-signs in front of it, as in @@CONNECTIONS, which returns the current number of user connections. You cannot declare global variables and you cannot directly change them with a SET or SELECT statement. So, if you use one of these special functions somewhere, realize that although it looks like a variable and can act like one, you can't assign any data to it; you can only read data from it. Table 6.1 provides a list of the global variables in SQL Server 2000:

TABLE 6.1

GLOBAL VARIABLES IN SQL SERVER 2000

Global Variable	Function
@@CONNECTIONS	Returns the current number of connections that applications currently have open to SQL Server.
@@CPU_BUSY	The time, in milliseconds, that SQL Server has been busy since the last time it was restarted.
@@CURSOR_ROWS	The number of rows that are in the previously opened cursor. If no cursor has been opened, it returns 0; if the cursor is asynchronous, it returns a negative number representing the number of rows that have been used so far; if the number is positive, it's the number of rows in the cursor; and if the value is -1, the cursor is dynamic, so there's no telling how many rows are in it. Cursors are covered in more detail later in this chapter.
@@DATEFIRST	Returns the number of the first day of the week. For example, if the first day of the week is set to Sunday, it returns 1, if it's set to Monday, it returns 2, and so on.
@@DBTS	Returns the current value of the timestamp for the database. This has absolutely no relation to system time, and is only used to manage certain inserts.
@@ERROR	Returns the error number for the last SQL statement executed.
@@FETCH_STATUS	Returns the status of the last cursor fetch operation: 0 for success, -1 for failure, or -2 for missing record.

Global Variable	*Function*
@@IDENTITY	Returns the value used for the last INSERT INTO an identity column for the current connection.
@@IDLE	Returns the time in milliseconds that SQL Server has been idle since the last restart.
@@IO_BUSY	Returns the time in milliseconds that SQL Server has spent waiting for IO to return from a read or write request.
@@LANGID	Returns the language identifier of the current language in use.
@@LANGUAGE	Returns the name of the language currently in use, which is probably more useful than the ID number.
@@LOCK_TIMEOUT	Returns the number of milliseconds that the current connection will wait for a lock to clear to complete its work.
@@MAX_CONNECTIONS	The maximum number of simultaneous user connections allowed on the current SQL Server.
@@MAX_PRECISION	The precision used by the DECIMAL and NUMERIC data types on the server. By default, this is 38.
@@NESTLEVEL	The current nesting level during stored procedure execution. (See Chapter 9.)
@@OPTIONS	Returns an integer representing the settings of the user options for the current connection. (See "User Options," later in this chapter.)
@@PACK_RECEIVED	The number of network packets received by the SQL Server since it was last restarted.
@@PACK_SENT	The number of packets sent by the SQL Server since it was last restarted.
@@PACKET_ERRORS	The number of packet errors that the SQL Server has seen since it was last restarted.
@@PROCID	The stored procedure identifier of the currently executing stored procedure.
@@REMSERVER	Returns the name of the SQL Server running the remote stored procedure.
@@ROWCOUNT	Returns the number of rows returned by the last statement. (See "Using @@ROWCOUNT," later in this chapter.)
@@SERVERNAME	Returns the name of the current server.

continues

TABLE 6.1	*continued*

GLOBAL VARIABLES IN SQL SERVER 2000

Global Variable	Function
@@SERVICENAME	Returns the name of the service under which SQL Server is running.
@@SPID	Returns the current process identifier used by SQL Server.
@@TEXTSIZE	The maximum number of bytes that will be returned in a result set to the current connection from selecting from a TEXT or IMAGE column.
@@TIMETICKS	The number of microseconds that occur in one tick of the computer's clock.
@@TOTAL_ERRORS	The total number of disk read/write errors that SQL Server has had since its last restart.
@@TOTAL_READ	The total number of physical disk reads that SQL Server has done since it was last started.
@@TOTAL_WRITE	The total number of physical disk writes that SQL Server has done since it was last started.
@@TRANCOUNT	This returns the number of transactions "deep" the current statement is in a nested transaction.
@@VERSION	Returns the version string (date, version, and processor type) for the SQL Server.

User Options

The @@OPTIONS variable uses a technique called bitmasking to return data. It's a good exercise in batch programming technique to see how to return specific data from the @@OPTIONS variable, because columns in some system tables use the same technique to store data.

To retrieve data from a bitmasked value, you need to have the map for how the value is laid out. The complete map for the value returned by the @@OPTIONS variable is found in SQL Server Books Online under the topic "User Options Option." In the table within that topic, the user option for ARITHIGNORE is 128. So, to check whether the ARITHIGNORE flag is turned on, take the options variable and use the logical AND function to see whether the flag is set:

```
DECLARE @UserOption int
SET @UserOption = @@OPTIONS
PRINT @UserOption & 128
```

If this value returns 128, then the flag was previously set, and
ARITHIGNORE is turned on. If the value returns 0, then the flag was
not set, and ARITHIGNORE is turned off. Other values that use this are
the status value in the sysdatabases table and the status value in
the sysobjects table.

Using @@ROWCOUNT

What's the fuss with @@ROWCOUNT? It just returns the number of rows
affected by the previous statement. Well, it can be a bit more complex than that. What would this do?

```
UPDATE mytable SET emptype = 'manager'
PRINT 'all done'
PRINT @@ROWCOUNT
```

This returns 0. Why? The PRINT statement does not change any
rows. As a matter of fact, PRINT statements never return rows. If you
want to use a rowcount, you must use it immediately after the row
from which you want to pull the data. The following code doesn't
work the way you'd expect, either:

```
BEGIN TRANSACTION
    UPDATE mytable SET emptype = 'manager'
COMMIT TRANSACTION
print @@ROWCOUNT
```

The COMMIT TRANSACTION does not change or select any rows, so
there's a zero value in @@ROWCOUNT. You'll learn more about BEGIN
TRANSACTION and COMMIT TRANSACTION a little later in this chapter.

Now imagine that you are working on finishing your great master-
piece batch, but you need to go home and get some sleep. How are
you going to remember where you left off when you come back in
the morning?

COMMENTS

Comments have two entirely different purposes within a T-SQL
batch or stored procedure. First, they can be used to document code,
to make it easier for folks who have to maintain software in the
future. Second, they can be used to temporarily disable lines of code
within your batch when you're trying to get it working.

If you've ever had a programming class, or ever read a programming book, the teacher or author has probably emphasized the use of comments over and over again. It bears repeating.

Using comments is the most reliable way of ensuring that you or anyone else can figure out what your code does. Comments are the most important part of the legacy you leave behind as a programmer. If you get hit by a truck, and don't leave any (or enough) comments in your code, it is probably going to be faster for someone to rewrite all of your code than to try and decipher what made perfect sense to you at the time.

SQL Server has two methods for putting comments in your code. The first is to start the comment with a double dash (--). The double dash can appear anywhere on the line, and anything between the double dash and the end of the line is a comment and will not be executed. For example:

```
--this is a comment on the whole line
SET @i = 42 --this is a comment, but the preceding code
➡will execute
--Nothing on this line executes SET @i = 21
```

The other style of comment, which is not seen as often anymore, is the slash-star comment. It works like this:

```
/* This is a multi-line, slash-star style comment.
note that this line is also part of the comment.
This type of comment can end in the middle
of a line */ SET @i = 42
```

In that case, the SET statement would be executed because it's outside the comment. One thing to watch for is that the string "GO" within a comment on a line by itself causes an error. So don't use the string "GO" in the comment. The more common convention by far is to use the double-dash style comment, and the new Query Analyzer for SQL Server 2000 provides you with an easy tool to create multi-line comments quickly and easily. Just highlight the lines you want to comment and press Control+Shift+C. This adds a double-dash to the beginning of each highlighted line. To uncomment the text, just use Control+Shift+R. This is a quick, easy, and painless way to comment out large chunks of code for testing and put them back later. There aren't any restrictions on any special words in the double-dash comment.

That's how you make a bunch of statements look like none: by commenting statements out. But how can you make a bunch of statements look like one statement?

STATEMENT BLOCKS WITH *BEGIN...END*

The BEGIN and END keywords work together to group statements together. This is used in later constructs for loops and conditional statements, so although it may not make a lot of sense now, after the next three sections it will make more sense.

BEGIN and END are used to create something called a *statement block*. A statement block is a group of statements that can be used anywhere one statement can be used. For example, you could write this:

```
UPDATE mytable SET emptype = 'manager' WHERE name = 'fred'
UPDATE mytable SET name = 'george' WHERE id = 42
```

Or, if you wanted to, this would work:

```
BEGIN
        UPDATE mytable SET emptype = 'manager' WHERE name =
        ➥'fred'
        UPDATE mytable SET name = 'george' WHERE id = 42
END
```

Note that traditionally the indentation is the preferred style, and is not required, but the person who has to modify your code a few weeks after you write it will hunt you down and torture you if you don't indent properly. BEGIN and END must occur as a pair. That's why they are indented as they are: it makes it easy to spot if one of them is missing, and it makes it easy to tell where the statement block ends. You can nest statement blocks as follows:

```
BEGIN
        UPDATE mytable SET emptype = 'manager' WHERE name =
        ➥'fred'
        BEGIN
                PRINT 'Whoopee, a nested statement block!'
        END
        UPDATE mytable SET name = 'george' WHERE id = 42
END
```

But there's no good reason to do that. There is no limit to the nesting, except that eventually you will run out of room to indent, and although that's not a technical limitation (SQL Server doesn't care) it's going to make it very hard to read the batch.

There's one other thing to mention about the BEGIN...END statement. There's a special keyword called RETURN. The RETURN statement is very flexible—you'll be using it in a lot of different ways here and later in Chapter 9 when you learn about user-defined functions and stored procedures. For now, you need to know what a RETURN does within a statement block. You can use it like this:

```
BEGIN
        UPDATE mytable SET emptype = 'manager' WHERE name =
        ➥'fred'
        RETURN
        UPDATE mytable SET name = 'george' WHERE id = 42
END
```

If you do that, the second UPDATE never runs. Not very useful now, but when you read through the next section on IF...THEN...ELSE, you'll understand.

CONDITIONAL STATEMENTS AND BRANCHING WITH *IF...THEN...ELSE*

So far, all the scripts you've seen start at the top and go to the bottom. There's no way of conditionally executing any statements; all the statements execute, top down. That's not good. So SQL Server provides you with a couple of different ways to do something just in case something else is true.

So, you want to actually write a batch that does something now? Need to insert a piece of data, but don't want to insert a duplicate? How about wanting to make sure that the data you're about to insert follows the rules for that type of data? Well, now you need to understand conditional execution and the IF...ELSE construct.

In T-SQL, an IF statement looks like this:

```
IF <expression>
        <statement>
ELSE
        <statement>
```

The expression has to be an expression that evaluates to a true or false condition, unlike some languages that use zero and non-zero. To evaluate something to true or false, you need to use the comparison operators—the same comparison operators you used to compare things in SELECT statements from Chapter 4, "Querying and Modifying Data." So, if you want to see whether your UPDATE statement actually changed any data, you could write something like this:

```
UPDATE mytable SET emptype = 'manager' WHERE name = 'fred'
IF @@ROWCOUNT > 0
      PRINT 'There were rows changed'
```

But what if no rows changed? How can you print a message for that? Use the ELSE part of the logic:

```
UPDATE mytable SET emptype = 'manager' WHERE name = 'fred'
IF @@ROWCOUNT > 0
      PRINT 'There were rows changed'
ELSE
      PRINT 'There were no rows changed'
```

Note once again the use of indentation. This is another example of optional, traditional indentation that you should do to make your code more readable.

Now imagine that you want to run the UPDATE statement only if Fred is already not a manager. You could write something like this:

```
IF (SELECT emptype FROM mytable WHERE name = 'fred') <>
➥'manager'
      UPDATE mytable SET emptype = 'manager' WHERE name =
      ➥'fred'
ELSE
      PRINT 'There were no rows changed'
```

It would be helpful if you could put more than one statement in there, to put that PRINT statement back. But unfortunately, the IF statement can take only one statement. The solution is to make several statements look like just one statement.

```
IF (SELECT emptype FROM mytable WHERE name = 'fred') <>
➥'manager'
BEGIN
      UPDATE mytable SET emptype = 'manager' WHERE name =
      ➥'fred'
      PRINT "There were rows changed"
END
ELSE
      PRINT 'There were no rows changed'
```

That's better. Note the use of BEGIN and END. An IF statement, like the WHILE statement that will be covered shortly, can operate on only one statement, so you need to use the BEGIN and END constructs to make it all look like one statement.

A few more examples are probably in order. Imagine that you want to insert a new record only if there aren't any existing records that match certain criteria. You could write something like this:

```
if NOT exists (SELECT * FROM mytable WHERE emptype =
➥'manager')
```

continues

continued

```
BEGIN
      UPDATE mytable SET emptype = 'manager' WHERE name =
      ➡'fred'
      PRINT 'There were rows changed'
END
ELSE
      PRINT 'There were no rows changed'
```

The EXISTS() function returns true if even one row in the enclosed select statement returns rows. This type of logic provides a lot of flexibility in script writing by making it easy to check that data meets certain criteria before you perform an insert.

IF constructs can also be nested in a couple of different ways. First, you can create scripts that chain together several constructs:

```
IF (SELECT emptype FROM mytable WHERE name = 'fred') <>
➡'manager'
BEGIN
      UPDATE mytable SET emptype = 'manager' WHERE name =
      ➡'fred'
      PRINT 'There were rows changed'
END
ELSE
BEGIN
      IF (SELECT emptype FROM mytable WHERE name = 'wilma')
      ➡<> 'manager'
            BEGIN
                  UPDATE mytable SET emptype = 'manager'
                  ➡WHERE name = 'wilma'
            END
END
```

Notice two significant things in that example. First, the statement has a fallback, if 'fred' is already a manager, it sets 'wilma' to manager also. An ELSE statement could be put into the bottom IF statement to print out the No records changed messages also. Another thing to notice is that the BEGIN-END pairs in the ELSE clause of the construct are optional and, in this case, not required. It could be rewritten like this:

```
IF (SELECT emptype FROM mytable WHERE name = 'fred') <>
➡'manager'
BEGIN
      UPDATE mytable SET emptype = 'manager' WHERE name =
      ➡'fred'
      PRINT 'There were rows changed'
END
ELSE
      IF (SELECT emptype FROM mytable WHERE name = 'wilma')
      ➡<> 'manager'
                  UPDATE mytable SET emptype = 'manager'
                  ➡WHERE name = 'wilma'
```

The argument could be made that the first example is more readable, but both are correct. You can also nest an IF statement this way:

```
IF (SELECT emptype FROM mytable WHERE name = 'fred') <>
➥'manager'
BEGIN
        UPDATE mytable SET emptype = 'manager' WHERE name =
        ➥'fred'
        PRINT 'There were rows changed'
        IF (SELECT emptype FROM mytable WHERE name = 'wilma')
        ➥<> 'manager'
                     UPDATE mytable SET emptype = 'manager'
                     ➥WHERE name = 'wilma'

END
```

This code behaves differently. It sets 'wilma' to be a manager if 'fred' is not a manager after setting 'fred' to be a manager also.

Next, you need to learn how to loop in T-SQL. That is done using the WHILE construct.

WHILE LOOPS

A WHILE loop is similar to an IF statement, but after executing the statement, it goes back up to the top and starts over. It has the same basic structure as an IF statement without the option of an ELSE clause:

```
while <expression>
        <statement>
```

A WHILE loop keeps executing the statement until the expression becomes false. If the expression never becomes false, you have a problem, also known as an *infinite loop*. So, the statement needs to do something useful, and it also needs to change one of the values involved in the expression so that eventually, when the time is right, the expression will evaluate to false and the looping will end.

A classic looping structure has three steps. The *initialization* step sets up the variables and populates them to initial values. The *test* step evaluates the expression and determines whether the loop should be repeated. The *incrementation* step performs useful work, usually changes the expression somehow, and returns to the test step. Just to help you see this structure, the upcoming examples point out where each of these steps occur in the while statement.

A simple WHILE loop that counts to 100 would look like this:

```
DECLARE @i int
SET @i = 1  --initialization
WHILE @i <= 100 --test
BEGIN
        PRINT @i
        SET @i = @i + 1  --incrementation
END
```

So, what happens if you leave out one of the steps? If you don't initialize the loop, then the test step becomes (NULL <= 100), which evaluates to false for the purposes of the loop, so the loop never executes. If you leave out the test, perhaps by putting in a test that always evaluates to false (1=0) or true (1=1), then you either have a loop that never executes or a loop that executes forever. If you leave out the intermediate step, which is the most common error of all, you end up with a loop that does the same thing over and over, in this case, printing the number 1.

Two special keywords can be used to change how a WHILE loop operates. The CONTINUE keyword short-circuits the statement being executed and immediately goes back up to the loop test, ignoring the rest of the statement block. The BREAK keyword exits the while loop and starts executing the statement after the end of the statement block. Here's an example of the BREAK keyword:

```
DECLARE @i int
SET @i = 1  --initialization
WHILE @i <= 100 --test
BEGIN
        PRINT @i
        SET @i = @i + 1  --incrementation
        IF @i = 42
                break
END
```

This causes the loop to stop counting when it reaches the number 42, but after it has printed 41. The number 42 will not be printed. Here's an example of using a CONTINUE keyword:

```
DECLARE @i int
SET @i = 1  --initialization
WHILE @i <= 100 --test
BEGIN
        PRINT @i
        SET @i = @i + 1  --incrementation
        IF @i = 42
        BEGIN
```

```
            SET @i = @i + 1
            continue
        END
    END
```

This skips printing the number 42 and goes straight on to printing 43 and up to 100. Why does it increment the variable before using CONTINUE? If it didn't, then the statement would actually print the number 42 and continue along, just like the very first WHILE loop.

Although loops are great, how often do you need to count things in T-SQL? It would be great if you could use this structure to work on one row from a table and then loop to perform the same operation with data from the next row. How would you do that? Read on.

MANAGING RESULT SETS BY USING CURSORS AND TRANSACT-SQL

▶ **Manage result sets by using cursors and T-SQL. Considerations include locking models and appropriate usage.**

Cursors are used to take the results of a SELECT statement and assign the output from the recordset to a set of variables, one at a time. This enables you to walk through the recordset one record at a time and use the information in the recordset to do interesting things.

Creating a cursor has five steps. First, you have to DECLARE the cursor with the DECLARE CURSOR statement. Next, open the cursor with the OPEN statement. After that, you have to FETCH rows from the cursor, and when you're done, you have to CLOSE the cursor and DEALLOCATE it.

Here's an example:

```
DECLARE @Name sysname
DECLARE SysObj cursor for SELECT name FROM sysobjects
OPEN SysObj
FETCH NEXT FROM SysObj INTO @Name
WHILE @@FETCH_STATUS = 0
BEGIN
      PRINT @Name
      FETCH NEXT FROM SysObj INTO @Name
END
CLOSE SysObj
DEALLOCATE sysobj
```

The first line declares a variable called @Name of type sysname. The sysname data type is a special nvarchar data type that is used to hold the names of different system objects. If you're putting system names into a variable, it's the correct type to use because if the length of names changes from this version of SQL Server to the next, your code will still work.

The DECLARE CURSOR line declares what the cursor is going to do. In this case, the cursor is going to return one value from the Name column in sysobjects. You can return multiple fields, and you can filter with a WHERE clause. You can do anything in the SELECT statement that you can do in any other SELECT statement, including joins.

The OPEN line opens the cursor for business. Until that OPEN is executed, the cursor is just an idea; the OPEN actually makes the cursor usable by allocating resources for it.

The FETCH NEXT fetches the next row from the cursor. Because you haven't fetched any rows from the cursor yet, it fetches the first one. It takes the value returned and places it into the @Name variable. Note that the returned data and the variable have to be the same type, or if they are two different types, they have to convert implicitly. If the cursor specified multiple return values, the additional variables would just be tacked onto the end with commas to separate the variable names. FETCH NEXT automatically sets the global variable @@FETCH_STATUS to 0 if the fetch was successful, and to other values (refer to Table 6.1) for other results.

Next up is the WHILE loop. Looking at it from a loop point of view, the preceding FETCH NEXT is the initialization for the loop; the @@FETCH_STATUS = 0 is the test; and the FETCH NEXT that's inside the loop is the iteration.

The PRINT statement prints out the value. Normally, you'd want to do a bit more with the value than just print it; you'll see other examples of things to do later in this section. This is just a warmup.

After printing, there's another FETCH. Why are there two fetches? Well, the first one initializes the @@FETCH_STATUS variable, so the loop will execute, and this one iterates the loop by changing the @@FETCH_STATUS when the loop is done. This is a technique called a *priming read*, and it's frequently used to solve the problem of initializing loops. If you didn't do a priming read, you may have some leftover value in there from a previous cursor. Even if you don't have any other cursors, however, you have no guarantee that the value of @@FETCH_STATUS is valid until you set it with a FETCH.

After the FETCH is the end of the loop, which then returns up to the test. Although @@FETCH_STATUS doesn't change every time, it changes when the end of the cursor is reached, so the loop doesn't go on forever.

The CLOSE and DEALLOCATE are what you use to tell SQL Server that you're finished with the cursor. This closes the cursor, which releases any locks you have, and deallocates the cursor, freeing the memory resources used by the cursor.

Now, this was just a basic example. Here's a more real example of what cursors can do:

```
DECLARE @CommaList varchar(8000),
      @Name sysname
SET @CommaList = ''
DECLARE SysObj CURSOR FOR SELECT name FROM sysobjects
OPEN SysObj
FETCH NEXT FROM SysObj INTO @Name
WHILE @@FETCH_STATUS = 0
BEGIN
      SET @CommaList = @CommaList + quotename(@Name) + ', '
      FETCH NEXT FROM SysObj INTO @Name
END
CLOSE SysObj
DEALLOCATE sysobj
SET @CommaList = SUBSTRING(@CommaList, 1,
➥datalength(@CommaList) - 2)
PRINT @CommaList
```

This creates a comma-delimited list out of your SELECT statement. This is a useful thing to do if you are trying to piece together an IN clause.

What else can cursors do? You can update data through a cursor. First, you need to create a table to play with:

```
CREATE TABLE foo ( ID int,
                   value varchar(30)
      )
INSERT INTO foo VALUES (1, 'Fred')
INSERT INTO foo VALUES (2, 'Barney')
INSERT INTO foo VALUES (3, 'Wilma')
INSERT INTO foo VALUES (4, 'Betty')
```

Using that as a basis, there are a few options that you can use in the DECLARE CURSOR statement. First of all, the cursor you've been using so far is the plain, default cursor. It puts a shared lock on rows in the cursor for the duration of the cursor, so they cannot be modified while the cursor is reading them. That's why it is important to close cursors when you are finished with them; otherwise you are holding locks you probably don't need to. To avoid the locking problem, tell SQL Server to make a copy of the data and run the cursor from the copy by using the INSENSITIVE keyword. The cursor takes longer to open because SQL Server actually copies all the data to run the cursor into a temporary table.

Another thing you can do with cursors is scroll back and forth through them. This is done by using the SCROLL keyword. Here's an example of both the INSENSITIVE and SCROLL keywords:

```
DECLARE @id int,
        @Value varchar(30)
DECLARE Flintstone INSENSITIVE SCROLL CURSOR
        FOR SELECT id, value FROM foo ORDER BY 1
OPEN Flintstone
FETCH FIRST FROM Flintstone INTO @ID, @Value
SELECT @ID ID, @Value Value
FETCH LAST FROM Flintstone INTO @ID, @Value
SELECT @ID ID, @Value Value
FETCH PRIOR FROM Flintstone INTO @ID, @Value
SELECT @ID ID, @Value Value
FETCH RELATIVE -2 FROM Flintstone INTO @ID, @Value
SELECT @ID ID, @Value Value
FETCH ABSOLUTE 3 FROM Flintstone INTO @ID, @Value
SELECT @ID ID, @Value Value
FETCH NEXT FROM Flintstone INTO @ID, @Value
SELECT @ID ID, @Value Value
CLOSE Flintstone
DEALLOCATE flintstone
```

This demonstrates some of the features of scrollable cursors. The first FETCH returns the first row, which is Fred. Then the last row, Betty, is returned. Then the row before the previously fetched row (Wilma) is returned. Then the row two rows before the Wilma row is returned, which is back to Fred. Then the third row in the cursor is fetched, which is Wilma again, then the row after that one is returned, which is Betty.

Those are the options for scrolling and fetching. Now see what things look like for inserts and updates through a cursor. By default, a cursor is updateable. To prevent updates to a cursor, use the FOR READ ONLY clause, which goes after the SELECT statement in the DECLARE cursor, like this:

```
DECLARE Flintstone SCROLL CURSOR
        FOR SELECT id, value FROM foo ORDER BY 1
        FOR READ ONLY
```

To update through a cursor, you need to tell SQL Server that you're going to update the cursor using the FOR UPDATE clause, which goes in the same place as the FOR READ ONLY in the preceding code sample. To actually update the data, a special form of the UPDATE statement is used, UPDATE WHERE CURRENT OF. It works like this:

```
DECLARE @id int,
        @Value varchar(30)

DECLARE Flintstone cursor
        for SELECT id, value FROM foo
        for UPDATE

OPEN Flintstone

FETCH NEXT FROM Flintstone INTO @ID, @Value

UPDATE foo SET Value = 'Fredrick'
        WHERE CURRENT OF Flintstone

CLOSE Flintstone
DEALLOCATE flintstone
```

Several rules have to be followed to update through a cursor. First, the cursor cannot be read-only. That's fairly obvious, but it implies that the cursor does not have the INSENSITIVE or SCROLL options turned on, in addition to having the READ ONLY option turned on. Many other options (which are discussed later) cause a cursor to be read-only. The FOR UPDATE in the cursor declaration is optional, but suggested. A cursor defaults to an updateable state, but if you explicitly state that the cursor is going to be updated, your code will be easier to read. It would be even better if the update specified FOR UPDATE OF columnname, because that's the only column that is updated.

Everything that has been discussed so far about cursors is part of the ANSI SQL-92 standard, so it's fairly generic and should be portable to any other database management system that is SQL-92-compliant. Table 6.2 lists some Transact-SQL-specific extensions to the cursor syntax that enable you to make performance enhancements for your cursor operations.

TABLE 6.2	

TRANSACT-SQL CURSOR EXTENSIONS

Extension	Description
LOCAL	This is the optional state for a cursor. It means the cursor is available for only the current batch and the current connection. To change the default behavior, set the Default to Local Cursor database option.
GLOBAL	"Global" in this case means "Global to the current connection." Declaring a cursor as global makes it available to subsequent batches or stored procedures that are run by the connection. The cursor is not available to other connections, even if the connection is from the same user.
FORWARD_ONLY	This tells SQL Server that the cursor is going to run only from the beginning of the recordset to the end of the recordset. The cursor is not allowed to go backward or skip around. The only fetch that works is FETCH NEXT. This is an optimization; it allows SQL Server to consume less overhead for the cursor.
STATIC	This does the same thing as the INSENSITIVE keyword in the SQL-92 syntax.
KEYSET	If you use this, your cursor will not be able to access data inserted by other users after the cursor is opened, and if a row is deleted by another user, an @@FETCH_STATUS of -2 (row is missing) will be returned if you attempt to fetch a deleted row. This type of cursor has less overhead than a DYNAMIC cursor, but (unless FORWARD_ONLY is also specified) all the different FETCH options are available.
DYNAMIC	A DYNAMIC cursor is the opposite of a KEYSET cursor. All inserts and deletes done by users are immediately available to the cursor. However, FETCH ABSOLUTE does not work with a dynamic cursor because the underlying data may change the position of the records.
FAST_FORWARD	This is a cursor that has all the properties of a FORWARD ONLY and READ_ONLY cursor, and is designed to go forward quickly with little overhead.
READ_ONLY	Does not allow updates to the cursor.
SCROLL_LOCKS	This causes SQL Server to exclusively lock each row that is touched by the cursor as they are read in, to prevent other users from updating the record.

Extension	Description
OPTIMISTIC	This causes SQL Server to not lock any rows during the scrolling of the cursor, and you have to just hope that none of the rows being changed by the cursor is simultaneously being changed by somebody else. Attempting to change a row through the cursor results in an error.
TYPE_WARNING	If somehow your cursor changes type implicitly, a warning is issued.

A few notes on the table. First, the default LOCAL or GLOBAL status of a cursor can be changed by changing the server-wide Default To Local Cursor configuration setting with sp_configure. Next, if you specify FORWARD_ONLY, and don't specify STATIC or KEYSET, the cursor behaves as a DYNAMIC cursor. In other words, the cursor sees any records inserted by other connections while the cursor is open. In addition, if you don't use the SCROLL, STATIC, KEYSET, or DYNAMIC options to specify that a cursor should scroll, the cursor will be FORWARD_ONLY. Also, you cannot use FORWARD_ONLY and FAST_FORWARD together.

All that said, it pays to specifically spell everything out in your DECLARE statement to make it very obvious what you are attempting to do with your cursor. In other words, if you're doing a forward-only, updateable cursor, you could just use the normal "DECLARE cursor foo for <select>", but it is better to do something like "DECLARE cursor foo forward_only for <SELECT statement> for UPDATE of <value>". That way, it is easy to tell exactly what that cursor is going to be used for and what restrictions there are on the use of the cursor.

So, when is it proper to use cursors? You should never use a cursor when you can write a better UPDATE statement to avoid using a cursor altogether. Cursors consume a lot of SQL Server resources, and they are nowhere near as fast as just running a single UPDATE statement, or even multiple UPDATE statements. Avoid using cursors. If you use cursors only when you absolutely have to, then you'll be using them properly.

IN THE FIELD

THE PROPER USE OF CURSORS

We tend not to be very nice to the people we are interviewing for a database administrator position. One of the things that happens during the process is having the candidate stand up at the whiteboard and tell the interviewers how he'd approach different database problems. One favorite is to ask the candidate to write the syntax for using a cursor on the board.

If they get it right it's a big negative mark. We don't want to hire someone who is too good with cursors, because that means that they use them too much.

If you approach every single problem with the attitude that it can be solved without a cursor, you will find a way to solve it without a cursor, and it will probably run faster and cause fewer problems than a solution that uses a cursor.

Use a cursor like a carpenter uses a sledgehammer. It's out in his truck, it's really heavy, and if there's any other way to solve the problem that doesn't involve walking all the way out to the truck and lugging a 20-pound hammer up into a house, he'll use that instead.

Sometimes a sledgehammer is the right tool for the job. But not very often.

Table 6.3 lists some interesting stored procedures that can be used to find out what cursors are available to the current connection and describes some of their properties.

TABLE 6.3

CURSOR STORED PROCEDURES

Procedure	Description
sp_cursor_list	Returns a list of all the declared cursors available to the current connection with some of their properties.
sp_describe_cursor	Returns the properties of the cursor, such as FORWARD ONLY and READ_ONLY.
sp_describe_cursor_columns	Returns the columns that are found in a cursor and their data types.

Procedure	Description
sp_describe_cursor_tables	Returns the tables used by a cursor, which you'll need to have for an UPDATE WHERE CURRENT OF statement.

These stored procedures can help you debug your cursor problems by enabling you to create the cursor and then track down what kind of cursor SQL Server is actually using. For example, if you declare a FORWARD_ONLY cursor, is it dynamic or static?

That's more than you'll ever need to know about cursors in real life, and enough to cover what you'll need to know for the exam.

Writing Scripts Using Statements, Comments, and More

We're about halfway through the chapter, so it's time for a quick review of some of the key points we've covered.

▶ Programming in SQL Server is done in the T-SQL language by writing scripts that are made up of batches, which are groups of statements.

▶ Variables are local objects that can be used to store temporary values, such as counters.

▶ Comments are used to make T-SQL batches easier to understand and to temporarily disable statements for debugging.

▶ The IF...ELSE construct can be used to conditionally execute statements, and the WHILE construct can be used to repeat statements.

▶ Cursors are used to work on rowsets one row at a time. They are useful, but not as efficient as direct statements on sets.

That's quite a bit of hands-on material, from writing scripts to managing loops and cursors. We still have more to cover in this chapter, including theory on locking and important points about transactions.

CONCURRENCY AND LOCKING

One of the hallmarks of a true database management system is whether it has the capability to handle more than one user performing simultaneous data modifications. The problem is that when several users in a database make changes, it's likely that they eventually will all want to update the same record at the same time. To avoid the problems that this would cause, SQL Server and most database management systems provide a locking mechanism.

A locking mechanism provides a way to "check out" a particular row or set of rows from the database, marking them so they cannot be changed by another user until the connection is finished and the changes are made. For connections that are reading data, locking provides a mechanism to prevent other connections from changing the data for the duration of the read or longer. There are two basic types of locks: shared locks and exclusive locks. A *shared lock* happens when a user is trying to read a row of data; for some duration, depending on the transaction isolation level (which is covered later in this chapter), the user owns a shared lock on the table. Because the user is just trying to read the record, there can be several shared locks on the row, so many people can read the same record at the same time.

Users obtain *exclusive locks* when the user needs to change the row. Exclusive locks are not shared; there can be only one user with an exclusive lock on a row at any given time.

Lock Contention

If a user needs to acquire an exclusive lock to a row that is already locked by another user, the result is *lock contention*. Some level of contention is normal in a database that is being frequently updated. Typically, an application waits for some arbitrary amount of time for the locks to clear and the transaction to complete. This results in an apparent slowdown of the application and the server, and excessive amounts of contention lead to performance degradation and possibly user complaints.

There are a few things you can do to reduce lock contention.

◆ Make transactions as simple as possible, but no simpler. Keep extraneous logic out of the transaction. The best case is when you do all the gathering of data and validation of that data outside of the transaction, and the transaction is used only to update and insert rows.

◆ Make sure that the application does not have any transactions that wait for user input. A transaction should be able to complete from beginning to end without waiting for a user to enter any data. What's the big deal? Users tend to do things like go to lunch, usually while they have windows open, waiting for them to enter data to complete their transactions. Collect all the data at once, then start the transaction, make the changes, and commit.

◆ Design applications and databases with concurrency in mind. Keep tables that are frequently updated small by moving columns that don't belong in the table or that aren't changed as often into another table.

◆ If a table is going to be updated frequently, make sure it isn't indexed more than necessary. Data modification statements, such as INSERT, UPDATE, and DELETE have to change the indexes as they go, so having too many indexes on a table requires them to modify several indexes.

Deadlocks

Deadlocks occur when two or more transactions cannot complete because of mutual locks. For example, if User A needs to update a row in the Deposit table and then a row in the Withdrawal table, whereas User B needs to update the Withdrawal table and then the Deposit table, there will be an instant in time when User A has an exclusive lock on the Deposit table and to complete his transaction he needs a lock on the Withdrawal table. Contrarily, User B has a lock on the record that User A needs in the Withdrawal table and needs a lock on the record in the Deposit table that User A already has locked. In this case, SQL Server detects the deadlock and more or less randomly kills one of the user processes.

Deadlocking is very important, so the next few paragraphs repeat a lot of what you just read, but from a different angle, just to make sure you've got it down.

NOTE **Who Lives and Who Dies?** Which process is killed in a deadlock isn't exactly random. If one user is the System Administrator and the other one is just a normal user, the normal user's process is terminated. Otherwise, SQL Server picks the user that has the least to lose from having its transaction terminated. If they're both equal, then SQL Server picks one at random. It's also possible to set a connection-level parameter with SET DEADLOCK_PRIORITY LOW to tell SQL Server that the transaction can be terminated if it is involved in a deadlock.

In Figure 6.1, you can see that there are two users: User 1 and User 2. User 1 wants to do two things: read a record from the Parts table and write a record to the Sales table. User 2 wants to do two similar things, but he's going to read from the Sales table and write to the Parts table.

Now, step through what happens if both transactions start at the same time:

1. Both users execute a BEGIN TRANSACTION statement.

2. User 1 executes a SELECT, which results in a lock on one or possibly several pages in the Parts table. User 2 executes a SELECT, which results in a lock on one or possibly several pages in the Sales table.

3. To continue, User 1 needs a lock on some of the pages in the Sales table. Unfortunately, User 2 has the pages locked already, so User 1 goes into a state of waiting for the lock to be resolved. At the same time, User 2 needs a lock on some pages in the Parts table, which User 1 already has a lock on, so he goes into a waiting state for the lock to be resolved.

4. The SQL Server lock manager process is watching the locks, and notices that neither of these processes can proceed, because they both have something the other needs exclusive control of to proceed. SQL Server then (according to the rules in the note) terminates one of the transactions. The other process runs to completion; the process that was killed receives an error (Error 1205) and terminates.

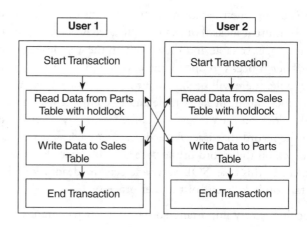

FIGURE 6.1
This is an example of a set of transactions that could cause a deadlock.

To avoid deadlocks, make sure that all the objects are always accessed in the same order. Make sure that in cases where a series of updates to different tables are done, they are always done in the same order. Keep transactions as short as possible, prevent user interaction within transactions, and set a low isolation level. What's an isolation level? Good question.

Isolation Levels

SQL Server knows that sometimes it's critical that the data you are reading from the database is absolutely one hundred percent committed data, whereas at other times you want the data to be read quickly, and incomplete or uncommitted transactions just don't matter.

To accommodate this, SQL Server supports four different transaction isolation levels:

◆ **Read Uncommitted.** This isolation level shows you all the data without getting a shared lock first. Another connection may change the data while it is being read. This can be great for applications that are doing system monitoring or reporting, where minimal impact to the rest of the system is desired. This is also called "dirty reads."

◆ **Read Committed.** This isolation level acquires a shared lock during the read of the data, but doesn't keep the shared lock for the entire transaction. The resulting data is complete, but may change after successive reads, showing new data or indicating missing data with each successive read. This is the default transaction isolation level, and is generally an acceptable tradeoff between reading dirty data and minimizing contention.

◆ **Repeatable Read.** This isolation level acquires a shared lock on the rows for the duration of the transaction, but still allows other users to add rows into the result set. That means that later reads may contain more data, but they won't contain any less.

◆ **Serializable.** This isolation level acquires a shared lock on the entire range of data that is being queried, preventing inserts or updates from happening for the duration of the transaction. This is a very dangerous thing to do from a concurrency perspective, because it generates a lot of locks and can more easily result in deadlock problems.

There is one more aspect of locking to discuss. SQL Server also has the capability to lock objects at different levels to increase performance. This is called *lock granularity*.

Lock Granularity

In addition to shared and exclusive locks, SQL Server also locks objects at different levels. SQL Server can lock a single row of a table, a single data page, or an entire table.

Typically, SQL Server operates in the page lock mode, where it locks the data pages being requested. After a certain amount of blocking is noticed, SQL Server slips into a row locking mode, where single rows are locked. On the other end of the scale, when a connection attempts to update a certain percentage of a table, SQL Server automatically escalates to a table lock, where it automatically locks the entire table either exclusively (in the case of a full table update), or shared (in the case of a full table read). SQL Server also determines lock escalation based on the activity occurring in the table at the time of the lock request. If the activity level is low, it saves itself some time by just escalating the lock sooner because it will have less effect on other users.

That means there are shared page locks, shared row locks, and shared table locks for reads, along with exclusive page locks, exclusive row locks, and exclusive table locks for writes.

ENFORCING PROCEDURAL BUSINESS LOGIC USING TRANSACTIONS

▶ **Enforce procedural business logic by using transactions.**

• **Design and manage transactions.**

• **Manage control of flow.**

Each statement that accesses a database is enclosed in a transaction. A transaction implies several things:

◆ **Atomicity.** A transaction cannot be broken up into smaller units; either the entire transaction happens or none of it happens.

◆ **Consistency.** A completed transaction leaves the database in a consistent state.

◆ **Isolation.** A transaction is isolated from other transactions in the database, so transactions can't overwrite each other's data. Transactions, in other words, can't interfere with other transactions that are running concurrently.

◆ **Durability.** A transaction, after it has been applied, sticks in the database.

These qualities are easy to recall by remembering the word "ACID": Atomicity, Consistency, Isolation, and Durability. SQL Server provides the atomicity, isolation, and durability for you, but it's up to you to make sure that a transaction leaves the database in a consistent state. Atomicity and durability are handled by the transaction logging system and, to an extent, by the lazy writer, which was covered back in Chapter 2, "Data Modeling." Isolation is handled by the lock manager, which is covered in this chapter.

Designing and Managing Transactions

▶ **Design and manage transactions.**

If you don't explicitly tell SQL Server to treat a group of statements as a transaction, it implicitly puts each statement in its own transaction. For the purposes of an implicit transaction, the only statements that really count are the statements that interact with a database: SELECT, INSERT, UPDATE, and DELETE.

To explicitly put a group of statements into a transaction, you can use the BEGIN TRANSACTION command. This command tells SQL Server all commands that follow up until the end of the transaction, which is noted with an COMMIT TRANSACTION. In the event of a problem with the data being manipulated, you can also call ROLLBACK TRANSACTION. If there is an error during the execution of the transaction, such as a server shutdown, a disk error of some type, or lock contention, then the transaction automatically rolls back.

Here's an example to help you understand why transactions need to be used. Let's say you have a bank database, and it has a Deposit table and a Withdrawal table. Somebody wants to transfer funds from one account, account number 42, into another account, account number 64. So here's how that would look:

```
INSERT INTO Deposit VALUES (64, 100.00)
INSERT INTO Withdrawal VALUES (42, 100.00)
```

That looks fine. However, the server crashed between the two INSERT statements. When the administrator brings it back up, there's been a deposit for $100.00 into one account, but no withdrawal to match, so the SQL Server just invented $100.00.

To do this correctly, these statements should be enclosed in an explicit transaction, like this:

```
BEGIN TRANSACTION
        INSERT INTO Deposit VALUES (64, 100.00)
        INSERT INTO Withdrawal VALUES (42, 100.00)
COMMIT TRANSACTION
```

Now if the server crashes when the transaction is halfway complete, SQL Server rolls back the transaction automatically so that no money is created out of thin air and you may not lose your job as quickly.

Managing Control of Flow with Transactions

▶ **Manage control of flow.**

SQL Server also has the capability to create nested transactions, where transactions are inside other transactions. In that case, the global function @@TRANCOUNT contains the current nesting level of transactions, which is basically the number of times you've executed a BEGIN TRANSACTION statement. You'll cover that a bit more later in this chapter in the section, "Raising Errors."

You need to be aware of a few rules about transactions.

◆ Some statements are not allowed inside an explicit transaction. These are CREATE DATABASE, ALTER DATABASE, DROP DATABASE, BACKUP DATABASE, RESTORE DATABASE, BACKUP LOG, RESTORE LOG, RECONFIGURE, and UPDATE STATISTICS.

◆ If you have nested transactions (transactions started within other transactions) and you call ROLLBACK TRANSACTION, it rolls back *all* the transactions currently pending.

◆ The COMMMIT WORK statement is functionally equivalent to the COMMIT TRANSACTION statement. The ROLLBACK WORK statement is functionally equivalent to the ROLLBACK TRANSACTION statement. These can all be abbreviated down to just COMMIT and ROLLBACK. You can also just abbreviate the word TRANSACTION to TRAN, such as COMMIT TRAN, and so on.

Two other complications need to be thrown into this already semi-confusing pile: naming transactions and savepoints. Any time you execute a BEGIN TRANSACTION, you can tell SQL Server to assign a name to the transaction. The name for a BEGIN TRANSACTION is fairly superfluous, however, because any rollback still rolls back all pending transactions. For example:

```
BEGIN TRANSACTION OuterTransaction
        INSERT INTO Deposit VALUES (42, 100.00)
        BEGIN TRANSACTION InnerTransaction
        INSERT INTO Withdrawal VALUES (100, 37.50)
        ROLLBACK TRANSACTION
```

The final ROLLBACK TRANSACTION is still going to roll back all the way to OuterTransaction. As mentioned, this just adds to the complication.

You can create a savepoint within a transaction and roll back to that savepoint without rolling back the entire transaction. To create a savepoint within a transaction, use the SAVE TRANSACTION command and name the savepoint. Then when you want to roll back to the savepoint, you can name the savepoint. The syntax is identical to a named transaction, just in case you weren't stupefied by the complexity yet. Here's an example:

```
BEGIN TRANSACTION OuterTransaction
        INSERT INTO Deposit VALUES (42, 100.00)
        SAVE TRANSACTION SavePoint1
        INSERT INTO Withdrawal VALUES (100, 37.50)
        ROLLBACK TRANSACTION SavePoint1 --rolls back to the
        ➥save point
```

If that ROLLBACK TRANSACTION didn't have the savepoint name out there, it would roll back to the beginning of the transaction, just as you'd expect.

EXAM TIP

Test Question There's almost guaranteed to be a question on your test about a rollback with a named transaction and how much does it roll back. Just remember: Unless there's a savepoint involved, a rollback goes all the way back to the first BEGIN TRANSACTION that wasn't followed by a COMMIT TRANSACTION.

> **IN THE FIELD**
>
> ### SCARED OF TRANSACTIONS?
>
> This can all be a bit overwhelming. Just to lower the fear factor a little bit, outside of this exam, it's extremely unlikely you'll ever see a named transaction or a savepoint. That's because just as it looks really complicated, it's also actually really complicated. Nobody, including experienced SQL Server administrators, uses savepoints except when those experienced administrators try to trip up other administrators over minutiae while hanging out at the local drinking establishment.
>
> You've got to learn it for the exam, because as that exam tip said, there's almost certain to be at least one question on it. Other than that, don't let it get you concerned that you're going to be consumed by some huge, ugly 30-nesting-levels-deep transaction with fourteen distinct savepoints. At least, not on one of this author's databases.

> **NOTE**
>
> **A Little Spelling Issue** Note the lack of two e's in the middle of RAISERROR. That's not a typographical error; it's the designers of Transact-SQL being cute. Don't let that trip you up as you work through the examples in this chapter.

Raising User-Defined Errors

This section concentrates on one statement: RAISERROR. This is the statement you can use in your batches, and later in your stored procedures, to handle things such as data exceptions.

System and User Error Messages

This section talks about what error messages really are, how to use them, and how to apply error handling in your transactions.

An error message has three distinct properties: an error number, an error severity, and the message text. The *error number* is a number that identifies the error message, specifically in the sysmessages table. The *error severity* is the status of the server during the error message. A user can raise errors with severities ranging from 1 to 16, and system administrators and the system itself can raise error messages from 17 to 25. The higher the severity level, the more severe the problem. Severity codes up to 10 are for informational messages; codes from 11 through 16 are error messages for users, such as "invalid object name" or "incorrect syntax near ','". The higher severity codes are for things such as data corruption and hardware failure.

There's also a fourth element that goes with error messages, and it's the mystical and strange *state parameter*. It's not used by SQL Server any more, but it's required whenever you raise an error. Just think of it as a free way to put information into the error log. It's just some number, ranging from 1 to 127. It doesn't matter which one you use—by convention it's generally left at 1. You do, however, have to have a state.

If you are writing an application or a script that needs to raise certain exceptions periodically, such as a data integrity problem, you can actually add a message into the sysmessages table to standardize the error. This is a great way to handle internationalization problems, because you can enter the same message with the same message number in several different languages, and SQL Server automatically picks the correct language for the user. This can be done using the sp_addmessage system-stored procedure.

The sysmessages table and the error handling facilities in SQL Server are very versatile. They enable you to insert tags into the message that can be replaced with specific information, such as table names and variable names, so that the error message can be customized to fit the specific situation.

Here's an example error message that could be created: "Data Error: Attempt to remove manager from group %s would leave the group without a manager." The %s in there should look familiar to C programmers; it's the tag used to denote that a string will be entered in that place. Later, when you write code that raises the error, you can specify the text to be added into the message.

Now, how do you raise an error?

Raising Errors

Raising an error involves using the aforementioned RAISERROR statement. Here's an example of that statement:

```
RAISERROR ('Unable to continue processing, insufficient
➥data', 10, 1) with log
```

Now you have the error message itself, the state (which is required in the command but is just an arbitrarily chosen number), and the phrase "with log," which tells SQL Server to put an event into the SQL Server error log as well as the Windows NT Event Log. Note the location of the parentheses in the statement. They are required. If you execute that, and then check your Windows NT event log, you'll see an informational message in the log from MSSQLSERVER.

Here's how you do one of those snazzy inline-replacement error messages described earlier:

```
RAISERROR ('Unable to continue processing, insufficient
data
➥in %s.', 10, 1, 'Job Table')
```

This prints out the error message "Unable to continue processing, insufficient data in Job table." You can add that into your sysmessages table this way:

```
sp_addmessage 50001, 10, 'Unable to continue processing,
➥insufficient data in %s.'
```

And then you can execute something like this:

```
RAISERROR (50001, 10, 1, 'Job Table') with log
```

This returns the same message as before. You could then add the message in a few different languages, and SQL Server would automatically respond back to the user in the language requested. You do that with the @lang parameter to sp_addmessage, which works like this:

```
sp_addmessage 50001, 10, 'Something bad happened in Spanish
➥%s.', 'Spanish'
```

MANAGING DATA MANIPULATION USING TRANSACTIONS

▶ **Manage data manipulation by using transactions.**

• **Implement error handling in transactions.**

Now that you know how to raise error messages to the user and the operating system, it's time to learn how to handle the error internally, so your data integrity is preserved. Basically, you use a combination of the material you've already examined in this chapter: the global variable @@TRANCOUNT, the ROLLBACK TRANSACTION statement, and RAISERROR.

Consider the scenario described earlier to explain why transactions are important: the bank transaction. This time, there's an Account Balance table, which contains the account number and the balance.

Here's the same transaction to move $100 from account 64 into account 42. (This block also builds the tables for you, to help you follow along.)

```
CREATE TABLE AccountBalance (
        AccountID int,
        Balance float
)
go
INSERT INTO AccountBalance VALUES (64, 500.00)
INSERT INTO AccountBalance VALUES (42, 500.00)
go

BEGIN TRANSACTION
UPDATE AccountBalance SET balance = balance + 100 WHERE
➥AccountID = 42
UPDATE AccountBalance SET balance = balance - 100 WHERE
➥AccountID = 64
COMMIT TRANSACTION
```

Now, this looks fine, but how can we check the account balance to make sure we haven't overdrawn account 64? One approach would be

```
BEGIN TRANSACTION
UPDATE AccountBalance SET balance = balance + 100 WHERE
➥AccountID = 42
UPDATE AccountBalance SET balance = balance - 100 WHERE
➥AccountID = 64
IF (SELECT Balance FROM AccountBalance WHERE AccountID =
➥64) < 0
        BEGIN
                RAISERROR ('Account Overdrawn for %s,
                ➥transaction cancelled.', 10, 1, '64')
                ROLLBACK TRANSACTION
        END
COMMIT TRANSACTION
```

The problem with this code is that eventually it causes an error because there's an attempt to commit the transaction after it's been rolled back. When the account balance in AccountID 64 falls to zero, the error is raised, and then the transaction is rolled back. The problem is that the script continues on and attempts to commit, but there is no transaction in progress, because it's been rolled back. There are two ways to fix this problem. You could simply put the COMMIT TRANSACTION into an ELSE clause, but what if there were more tests than this one? It would be nice to know whether a transaction is pending before the attempt to commit the transaction is made—something like this:

```
BEGIN TRANSACTION
UPDATE AccountBalance SET balance = balance + 100 WHERE
```

continues

continued

```
➡AccountID = 42
if @@ERROR <> 0
        BEGIN
                RAISERROR('Unable to credit account', 16,
                ➡1)
                ROLLBACK TRANSACTION
                RETURN
        END
UPDATE AccountBalance SET balance = balance - 100 WHERE
➡AccountID = 64
if @@ERROR <> 0
        BEGIN
                RAISERROR('Unable to debit account', 16, 1)
                ROLLBACK TRANSACTION
                RETURN
        END

IF (SELECT Balance FROM AccountBalance WHERE AccountID =
➡64) < 0
BEGIN
        RAISERROR ('Account Overdrawn for %s, transaction
        ➡cancelled.', 10, 1, '64')
        ROLLBACK TRANSACTION
END

IF @@TRANCOUNT > 0
COMMIT TRANSACTION
```

That way, if more complex operations needed to take place inside the transaction, there's an easy way to check to see whether a commit needs to happen when it's all over.

So, now you can write transactions that move millions of dollars around inside your database safely. How do you make sure that the other people who are using your database are moving money around properly?

IMPLEMENTING SECURITY

SQL Server has a built-in object security model that enables you as the system administrator to grant certain other individuals the rights to read and make changes to your databases. After all, you're a programmer or a system administrator—do you want to be doing all the data entry and reporting for your database? Probably not. Other people are going to have access to your data, and this section looks at how to keep those folks from inadvertently or maliciously messing things up.

The SQL Server Login/User Model

You need to learn some very strict terminology before you'll understand what's going on with security. This chapter uses terms, such as "individual" or "person," to describe an actual bipedal carbon-based life form. The term "login" describes a SQL Server login, whereas the term "NT Login" describes an operating system login. Finally, the word "user" relates to how a specific login interacts inside a database.

In SQL Server, there are two security modes. In Integrated security mode, each NT Login is mapped to exactly one SQL Server login. No passwords are stored in SQL Server in this case; instead, SQL Server accepts a token from the operating system, which basically says that the operating system trusts that the login is valid.

Mixed security mode includes Integrated security mode and what used to be called Standard security mode. With Standard mode, each login is created in SQL Server; SQL Server retains passwords for all the logins; and SQL Server is responsible for authenticating users. Microsoft keeps trying to bump off Standard security, but it's the only way that people using other operating systems or certain types of applications can use SQL Server.

Logins are stored in the Master database, complete with their passwords, which are stored encrypted. Each login is associated with one or more users. The user is associated with one database, and you must give each login access to each database it needs access to by creating a user in the database and linking it back to the login.

To add a login for a SQL Server user who has a Windows NT account, you use the sp_grantlogin command, like this:

```
sp_grantlogin 'MYDOMAIN\Doug'
```

This creates a login for the NT user for integrated security. To add a user who doesn't have a user account, use this:

```
sp_addlogin 'doug', 'dougspassword'
```

To add a user to a database, you can use the sp_adduser command, or the newer sp_grantdbaccess command:

```
sp_grantdbaccess 'doug'
go  --or
sp_adduser 'doug'  -but not both!
```

> **NOTE**
>
> **Operating System Security**   This section makes the somewhat large assumption that you or someone in your organization has gone about the task of securing the operating system on the computer your database is on—simple things, such as putting it behind a firewall, ensuring that the administrator account has a password, and so on. There are a lot of really great books on how to do this; check the "Suggested Reading" section at the end of the chapter.

If you do run both commands you'll get an error, because they both do the same thing. They both add a user linked to the login specified as the parameter to the current database. That's important: The user is added to the current database, so you need to make sure you know what database you are in before you execute those commands. Performing these operations in Enterprise Manager is the task of one of the end-of-chapter exercises.

SQL Server implements two types of permissions: the Statement permission and the Object permission. Statement permissions are permissions to execute certain statements, whereas Object permissions are permissions to access certain objects in specified ways.

Statement Permissions

Statement permissions are assigned to users to enable them to do things, such as create databases, define user-defined functions and stored procedures, and back up the database or transaction log. Statement permissions are assigned by using the GRANT statement, like this:

```
GRANT <statement> TO <account list>
```

The <statement> includes statements that create or destroy objects, such as CREATE DATABASE, DROP DATABASE, CREATE DEFAULT, DROP DEFAULT, CREATE FUNCTION, and so on, along with statements that perform other tasks, such as BACKUP DATABASE and BACKUP LOG. The <account list> is a comma-delimited list of security accounts or roles that you want to grant access to.

Object Permissions

Object permissions are permissions granted to access objects in certain ways. For tables and views, you can grant SELECT, DELETE, UPDATE, and INSERT permissions, and for stored procedure and function objects you can grant EXECUTE permissions. Permissions are granted to users, so the user must exist in the database before you grant permission. To give a user permission to access certain database objects, use the GRANT command, but with a different syntax:

```
GRANT <permission> ON <object> TO <account list>
```

So, to grant a particular user permissions to read a table called `MyTable`, you'd execute:

```
GRANT SELECT ON MyTable TO Doug
```

This grants Doug permission to select data from your table. If you wanted to give Doug permissions to do anything to your table short of dropping it, you could run either of these two statements:

```
GRANT ALL ON MyTable TO Doug
GRANT SELECT, INSERT, UPDATE, DELETE ON MyTable TO Doug
```

That's nice, but you also want to let Doug give other people permissions on the table, because you've gotten too busy. So, do something like this:

```
GRANT ALL ON MyTable TO Doug WITH GRANT OPTION
```

This enables Doug to grant permissions to other users on that object, up to the level of permissions that Doug has. So, if you give Doug only `SELECT` permissions, he can grant only `SELECT` permissions.

Now you've given Doug permission to change your table. That's probably not good given that Doug's boss fired him yesterday. Now what are you going to do? Good thing there's that `REVOKE` command.

```
REVOKE ALL ON MyTable FROM Doug
```

The `REVOKE` command works for statement permissions and object permissions, and it looks just like the `GRANT` statement in that you can revoke `SELECT`, `INSERT`, `UPDATE`, `DELETE`, or any combination thereof. What about revoking just the ability to grant permissions to other users?

```
REVOKE GRANT OPTION FOR ALL ON MyTable FROM Doug
```

That's only necessary if Doug still has permissions to access the table. But what if Doug had been giving people access to a bunch of tables he shouldn't have? You can revoke all the permissions that Doug ever granted on the table by using the CASCADE option.

```
REVOKE GRANT OPTION FOR ALL ON MyTable FROM Doug CASCADE
```

That's easy enough. But it would be nice to manage all these users as a group, wouldn't it?

NOTE

Where Have the Groups Gone? If you came up through an older version of SQL Server, such as SQL Server 7.0 or earlier, you're probably wondering where the groups are. Groups are now called roles. If you use one of the old-style group commands, such as sp_changegroup, you'll actually be changing the user's role. Roles have a lot more functionality than groups, such as enabling a user to belong to several roles.

User Roles

To provide the capability to grant multiple users access to the same objects the same way, SQL Server provides a mechanism for creating collections of users, called *roles*.

Fixed Roles

SQL Server provides you with a set of roles you can use to assign different levels of permission to users. There are two types of fixed roles. Fixed server roles are server-wide permissions that can be used regardless of the database you are in. Then there are fixed database roles, which apply to only one database.

There is very little you need to know about the fixed roles for the exam; that is all relegated to the SQL Server Administration exam. For more information about the fixed server roles, you can look in SQL Server Books Online at the overview topic under "Roles."

Defining Your Own Roles

You can also define your own role. To create a new role, use the sp_addrole system-stored procedure, like this:

    sp_addrole 'rolename'

The rolename is the name of the role, which of course has to meet all of the other restrictions for naming objects in SQL Server, except that roles cannot contain backslash characters. Backslash characters create an empty role with no permissions. To add users to a role, use the sp_addrolemember stored procedure:

    sp_addrolemember 'rolename', 'security_account'

The 'security account' parameter is the name of the security account that should be added to the role. A security account could include a user, a Windows NT account that has a user associated with it, or a Windows NT group. If a group is specified, then all the members of the Windows NT group who have associated users in the current database are added to the role.

To give the role access to other objects, use the GRANT statement, as described earlier, and use the name of the role in place of the username.

Application Roles

One of the handy features of this security model is the *application role*. An application role is similar to other roles, but the role has no members associated with it. The GRANT and REVOKE statements work the same way with an application role as with any other role. To create an application role, use the sp_addapprole system-stored procedure:

```
sp_addapprole 'AppRoleName', 'Password'
```

Yes, there is a password. To activate the application role for a given connection, the connection must execute another stored procedure, sp_setapprole, this way:

```
sp_setapprole 'AppRoleName', 'Password'
```

This stored procedure causes the connection executing the stored procedure to acquire the permissions granted to the application. In other words, the application has to run that stored procedure and send the password to invoke the correct permissions. At the point that sp_setapprole is used, any roles, permissions, or users associated with the connection are gone, and only the permissions assigned to the application role are valid.

An encryption option can be specified with the sp_addapprole command, which encrypts the password before it is sent across your network. To do this, use sp_setapprole as follows:

```
sp_setapprole 'AppRoleName', {Encrypt N'Password'}, 'odbc'
```

The little 'odbc' at the end specifies that the password should be encrypted using the standard ODBC encryption function. Otherwise, no encryption will be used.

Why all the bother with application roles? There are two reasons. First of all, you can set up an application role for a user application, and give the role access to all the tables and other objects it needs to access, but users who try to log in to SQL Server with Query Analyzer do not necessarily have a valid password to use to get the same level of access, which prevents them from modifying data incorrectly or running queries that may impede overall server performance.

CASE STUDY: DOUG'S CAR WASH AND DONUTS

ESSENCE OF THE CASE

Here are the essential elements of the case:

▶ Create a robust SQL batch that can insert the data into the database, so it doesn't get in there in little pieces that don't link together.

▶ Design the inserts and updates to avoid contention with the reporting that Doug is trying to run.

SCENARIO

Doug is starting a new career with a great business idea: a car wash and donut stand, so people can stop in on their way to work, get some donuts, and get their car washed at the same time. He's using some little wireless gadgets to have the attendants put in the name and address of his customers, so they can win free donuts. The problem is that the wireless connections seem to drop a lot, probably due to all the electrical motors in the car wash, and he's getting partial information into his database. He's also having problems with deadlock errors, between the attendants at the donut stand and the ones at the car wash entrance. What can Doug do to keep his dreams alive?

ANALYSIS

First, build a transaction that encapsulates all the inserts and updates; that way if the connection fails mid-stream, the data updates automatically roll back. Write the application, so that the transactions encapsulate only the UPDATE and INSERT statements. That way the critical time—the time when the application is transmitting the statements that change data—is kept to a minimum.

Then, make sure that all the different transaction types access tables in the same order. This prevents deadlocks and helps the customers get out the door quickly.

CHAPTER SUMMARY

This chapter has covered a significant amount of what it takes to be a real SQL Server programmer. You should now have an understanding of how basic looping and conditional statements can be used within a batch and how SQL Server handles locks. You have also seen how transactions and locks fit together to provide a robust environment for making changes to your data. The information covered about transactions, locks, and batches carries forward to Chapter 9 and its discussion on stored procedures, which are used in a similar way to batches and are also very useful for encapsulating transactions.

KEY TERMS

- Transact-SQL (T-SQL)
- script
- batch
- variable
- scope
- comment
- cursor
- lock
- deadlock
- login
- user
- role

APPLY YOUR KNOWLEDGE

Exercises

6.1   Writing a Batch That Uses a Cursor

This exercise demonstrates how to write a script in SQL Server, and also demonstrates how cursors can be used to access data.

Estimated time: 5 minutes

1. Open SQL Server Query Analyzer. Log in to the database you want to work with.

2. Type in the following text:

```
DECLARE  SI_Cursor CURSOR FORWARD_ONLY STATIC
➥FOR SELECT DISTINCT id, name FROM
➥sysindexes

DECLARE @IndexName sysname,
        @ID int

OPEN SI_Cursor

FETCH NEXT from SI_Cursor INTO @ID,
➥@IndexName

WHILE @@FETCH_STATUS = 0
BEGIN
        print 'Table ' + object_name(@id) + '
➥has an index named ' + @IndexName + '.'
        FETCH NEXT FROM SI_Cursor INTO @ID,
➥@IndexName
END

CLOSE SI_Cursor
DEALLOCATE SI_Cursor
```

3. Run the query by clicking the Play button.

6.2   Creating and Managing a Login

In this exercise, you'll see how to create and manage a login in SQL Server Enterprise Manager.

Estimated Time: 15 minutes

1. Open SQL Server Enterprise Manager, connect to your SQL Server, and open the Security container. Click on the Logins container.

2. Right-click in the list of logins and choose New Login. The SQL Server Login Properties—New Login dialog box should appear.

3. Enter the name Doug for the login.

4. Choose SQL Server Authentication. This sets up an account that doesn't require Windows authentication. Type in a password for Doug.

5. Choose a default database for Doug. This should be the database he will use most often. Choose the Pubs database.

6. On the Server Roles tab, verify that nothing is checked. This is the list of server-fixed roles that are available.

7. Click on Database Access. On this tab, you grant Doug access to the databases he's going to be able to use. Grant Doug access to the Pubs database by clicking in the empty check box to the left of the database name.

8. After you choose Pubs, you're given the option of adding Doug to several database roles. Add Doug to the db_datareader role. This enables him to read data, but he can't change any data, and can't execute any stored procedures.

9. Click OK to create the user. Notice that Doug now shows up in the Login list.

10. Open the Databases container, open the Pubs database, and click on the Users container. Notice that Doug is a user in the database. That's what you did in step 7.

APPLY YOUR KNOWLEDGE

11. Go back to the Logins container and delete Doug by right-clicking his login and choosing Delete. Notice that the error message says it will also remove all the database users for you. Click OK.

6.3 Monitoring Contention

In this exercise, you'll see how to use SQL Server Enterprise Manager to monitor what locks are present on a SQL Server.

Estimated Time: 5 minutes

1. Open SQL Server Enterprise Manager, connect to your SQL Server, and open the Management container, then open the Current Activity container. Click on the Locks / Process ID container.

2. Click on the various connections, which are referenced here as Process ID's, or SPID's. You'll see what objects a specific connection has open.

3. Click on the Locks / Object container. Click on the various objects listed to find out what users are accessing the objects and what kind of locks they have. See whether you can find a user with a lock on both the master.dbo.spt_values table and a table called ##lockinfo in TempDB. This is your SQL Server Enterprise Manager session and the locks that it is using to find information to display for you.

Review Questions

1. Explain the hierarchy of a script, a batch, and a transaction.

2. Why is locking important to provide concurrency in a database management system?

3. Why should most SELECT statements be done outside a transaction?

4. When should you use a cursor?

5. What can you do to avoid deadlocking in a database?

6. Explain the difference between a static and a dynamic cursor.

7. Explain the difference between a FORWARD_ONLY and SCROLLABLE cursor.

Exam Questions

1. Eric is a database developer at the Acme Widget corporation. He's working on setting up a new product application.

   Eric runs the following two queries:

   ```
   SELECT * FROM Sales1
   UPDATE Products SET price= price * 2
   GO
   ```

   When Eric runs the batch, he receives an error message stating that the table Sales1 was not found and figures out he should have been updating the table Products. He also notices that the UPDATE statement didn't run. How could the batch be rewritten so the update statement runs?

   A. GO

   ```
   SELECT * FROM Sales1
   UPDATE Products SET price= price * 2
   ```

   GO

   B.
   ```
   SELECT * FROM Sales1
   UPDATE Products SET price= price * 2 AS
   ➡INDEPENDENT
   ```

   GO

APPLY YOUR KNOWLEDGE

C.
```
SELECT * FROM Sales1
GO

UPDATE Products SET price= price * 2
GO
```

D.
```
SELECT * FROM Sales1
UPDATE Products SET price= price * 2
```

2. You are a database administrator at a small web development shop in south central Wisconsin. Your boss is an idiot. He has been trying to write SQL Scripts again. He's given you this script to run, but you want to make sure it doesn't block all the users out of the server and set all the pricing information to zero, like last time. So, given the following script:

```
DECLARE @Var int
SET @var = 1
GO

WHILE @Var < 11
BEGIN
PRINT @Var * 2
SET @Var= @Var + 1
END
```

What will be printed on the output screen?

A. A line of zeros.

B. A line of ones.

C. The multiples of two.

D. An error will occur.

3. You are a SQL Developer working on an Internet application in SQL Server 2000. You need to write a batch that prints the first ten multiples of 5. Which of the following gets the job done?

A.
```
DECLARE @MyVar int
SET @MyVar =1

WHILE @MyVar < 11
BEGIN
PRINT @MyVar *5
SET @MyVar = @MyVar +1
END
```

B.
```
DECLARE @MyVar int
SET @MyVar =1

WHILE @MyVar < 10

BEGIN
PRINT @MyVar *5
SET @MyVar = @MyVar +1
END
```

C.
```
DECLARE @MyVar int
SET @MyVar =1

WHILE @MyVar < 11

BEGIN
PRINT @MyVar *5
SET @MyVar = 5
END
```

D.
```
DECLARE @MyVar int
SET @MyVar =1
GO

WHILE @MyVar < 11

BEGIN
PRINT @MyVar *5
SET @MyVar = @MyVar +1
END
```

4. When using a cursor, which of the following statements cause the data to be returned to the batch?

A. DECLARE

B. OPEN

C. RETRIEVE

D. FETCH

5. Paul has a 5-batch script, and is creating a T-SQL cursor in batch one. He wants to use the cursor in batches two, three, and four. What must Paul do to access the cursor from any batch?

A. Use the DECLARE CURSOR statement in every batch and then re-populate it.

APPLY YOUR KNOWLEDGE

B. Creating this type of cursor is not possible in SQL Server 2000.

C. Create the cursor using the GLOBAL keyword.

D. Create the cursor using the PUBLIC keyword.

6. Bob has just finished using his cursor and will not need it for the rest of the time he is connected. What can Bob use to fully release all system resources held up by the cursor?

   A. Run DBCC_CURSOR_PERFORMANCE.

   B. Run the DEALLOCATE command.

   C. Run the CLOSE CURSOR command.

   D. Run the ALL SYSTEMS statement with the CURSOR argument.

7. Paul needs to create a cursor that is sensitive to data updates and deletes. He knows that the number of rows in the query he's using should be around 50. Paul subsequently uses the @@CURSOR_ROWS global variable to check for the number of rows in the cursor, which apparently should be around 50. To his surprise, he notices another value. What is this value?

   A. 0

   B. 1

   C. -1

   D. NULL

8. Stan runs a query and receives an error message with a severity level of 17. How serious is this error?

   A. The error was not that serious; the user should rerun the query.

B. The query contained one or more typographical errors.

C. The query was severe and most probably caused by a fault in hardware or software.

D. The severity level has nothing to do with how serious the error was.

9. What is the value of the @@TRANCOUNT function when this code is finished executing?

```
declare @Counter int
begin transaction
        update mytable set value = 42
        save transaction Point1
        while @Counter < 19
        begin
                begin transaction
                insert into MyTable values
                ➥(2, 3, 42, 'hello')
                set @Counter = 1
                commit transaction
        end
        rollback Point1
        begin transaction Point2
                insert into mytable (2, 3,
                ➥42, 'goodbye')
        rollback
```

   A. -1

   B. 0

   C. 1

   D. 2

10. Carl needs to write a SQL Script that will change everyone's pay status from part-time to full-time. Which of the following is the best way to accomplish the task?

   A.
```
declare cursor FixStatus for SELECT ID,
➥Status from employees for update of
➥status
declare @ID int, @Status varchar(4)
fetch next from FixStatus into @ID,
➥@Status
while @@FETCH_STATUS = 0
```

APPLY YOUR KNOWLEDGE

```
begin
        update Employees set Status
        ➥= 'Part'
                where current of FixStatus
        fetch next from FixStatus into @ID,
        ➥@Status
end
```

B.
```
declare cursor FixStatus for SELECT ID,
➥Status from employees for update of
➥status
declare @ID int, @Status varchar(4)
fetch next from FixStatus into @ID,
➥@Status
while @@FETCH_STATUS = 0
        begin
                update Employees set
                ➥Status = 'Part'
                        where
                        ➥current of
                        ➥FixStatus
                fetch next from
                ➥FixStatus into
                ➥@ID, @Status
        end
close FixStatus
Deallocate FixStatus
```

C.
```
begin transaction
declare cursor FixStatus for SELECT ID,
➥Status from employees for update of
➥status
declare @ID int, @Status varchar(4)
fetch next from FixStatus into @ID,
➥@Status
while @@FETCH_STATUS = 0
        begin
                update Employees set
                ➥Status = 'Part'
                        where
                        ➥current of
                        ➥FixStatus
                fetch next from
                ➥FixStatus into
                ➥@ID, @Status
        end
close FixStatus
Deallocate FixStatus
commit transaction
```

D. `update employee set status = 'full'`

11. What is the value of @@TRANCOUNT after this code is run?

```
begin transaction OuterTransaction
        insert into MyTable (2, 3, 19,
        ➥'hello')
        save transaction innertransaction
                insert into MyTable (2, 3,
                ➥37, 'goodbye')
        rollback transaction innertransaction
```

A. -1

B. 0

C. 1

D. 2

12. You are a database administrator at a small corporation. You've just been asked to run a stored procedure, but you're wary because the last time someone did this, it caused massive lock contention and forced a system shutdown. What is printed by the following stored procedure?

```
begin transaction
        declare @foo int
        select @foo = id from mytable
 print @foo
rollback transaction
```

A. Nothing.

B. There are no database changes to the database, so this causes an error.

C. It prints the value of @Foo.

D. It prints the value of @Foo twice because of the rollback.

13. You're an administrator of a SQL Server 2000 server. You're hearing complaints from users about their applications hanging, occasionally receiving error messages. You've found a couple of

batches that are being run at the time that the users are getting errors. Here are the batches:

Batch 1:

```
SET TRANSACTION ISOLATION LEVEL SERIALIZABLE
BEGIN TRANSACTION
Declare @ProductID int
Select @ProductID = ProdCode From Product
➥where ProductName like 'Deluxe Widget'
Update SalesTracker Set ProdCode = @ProductID
        where SalesID = 19
Commit Transaction
```

Batch 2:

```
SET TRANSACTION ISOLATION LEVEL SERIALIZABLE
BEGIN TRANSACTION
Declare @SalesID int
Select @SalesID from SalesTracker where
➥ProductCode = 42
Update Product Set SalesCode = @SalesID
        where ProductCode = 42
Commit Transaction
```

What's a likely cause of the problem?

A. Lock contention in the Product table.

B. Lock contention in the SalesTracker table.

C. A deadlock between the Product table and the SalesTracker table.

D. All of the above.

Answers to Review Questions

1. A script contains one or more batches. A batch contains zero or more statements. A transaction contains zero or more statements. A batch has no relation to a transaction.

2. Locking is important because it enables multiple users to access the database at the same time without having the users tromp on each other's data. Without locking, users could not manipulate data without partially overwriting each other.

3. Most SELECT statements should be done outside a transaction to keep the transactions shorter. To make transactions run quickly and reduce lock contention, you need to make sure the statements between BEGIN TRANS and COMMIT TRANS are the ones that need to be there. The exception is when you need to pull the most recent value possible from a table, and there is a chance it may change from outside the transaction to inside the transaction.

4. Generally, you shouldn't use a cursor. But you will have to when the operation you want to perform on each row is dependent upon the operations you've performed on previous rows. For example, if you want to write an algorithm to find a statistical median, you have to use a cursor. Statistical mean, however, is a built-in function, and you can get a statistical MODE with a count(*) and GROUP BY.

5. You can do two common things to reduce deadlocking in a database. First, always access objects in the same order. It doesn't matter what order—alphabetical order is fine—it just has to be the same order all the time. Second, keep transactions as short as possible to reduce lock contention. Generally, anything that you can do to reduce lock contention also reduces deadlocking.

6. Static cursors are created from a copy of the data set, and do not reflect changes made to the underlying data after the initial instantiation, which occurs at the OPEN statement. Dynamic cursors always reflect changes in the underlying data.

7. A FORWARD_ONLY cursor can only be used with FETCH NEXT; it cannot be used with FETCH FIRST, FETCH LAST, and so on. It also cannot go backward through the rowset.

APPLY YOUR KNOWLEDGE

ANSWERS TO EXAM QUESTIONS

1. **C.** The GO delimiter separates one batch from another. The syntax error in the batch prevented the entire batch from running, so to make the UPDATE statement run, put it into a different batch. For more on this, refer to the section titled "Scripts, Batches, and Transactions".

2. **D.** An error will occur because the variable @Var does not exist when the second batch of the script runs. See the section, "Variable Scope" to find out why.

3. **A.** Batch A works correctly and prints the multiples of 5 from 5 to 50. Batch B prints the multiples of 5 from 5 to 45, so it prints only nine of them. Batch C is an infinite loop because it doesn't increment its loop counter, and Batch D has a GO in the middle of it, so the variables aren't defined when they're being used. Check out the section "*WHILE* Loops" to see why it works that way.

4. **D.** The FETCH statement is used to retrieve data from a cursor. DECLARE and OPEN initialize the cursor, and RETRIEVE isn't a command. Cursors are covered in the section titled "Managing Result Sets by using Cursors and Transact-SQL."

5. **C.** Global cursors are available to later batches from the same connection. By the way, there is no such thing as a public cursor. This is a good example of an exam question because none of the answers look quite right and you'll spend way too much time trying to figure it out. Remember, the instructions are to pick the *best* answer. There's some information on cursor scope in the section

"Managing Result Sets by Using Cursors and Transact-SQL" that may help if you had trouble with this question.

6. **B.** The DEALLOCATE command releases all the resources used by a cursor. This information is covered in the "Managing Result Sets by Using Cursors and Transact-SQL" section.

7. **C.** The value of the @@CURSOR_ROWS global variable is -1 only when the cursor is declared as dynamic, and Paul's cursor was declared as dynamic. Information about using global variables is located in the "Global Variables" section, and how cursor status works is in the section titled "Managing Result Sets by Using Cursors and Transact-SQL."

8. **C.** The severity levels from 17 to 19 designate hardware and/or software problems. Subsequent processing may be stopped. For more information, check out the section titled "Raising Errors."

9. **B.** The value of the @@TRANCOUNT variable increases by one when a BEGIN TRAN statement is encountered, and decreases to 0 when the ROLLBACK happens. The last transaction statement run was a ROLLBACK, which leaves @@TRANCOUNT set to 0. For more fun with transactions and using @@TRANCOUNT, see the section, "Managing Control of Flow with Transactions."

10. **D.** To some extent, all the answers work. The only differences between the first three are minor tweaks to the cursor operation. The best answer is to not use a cursor, though, which is usually the right answer anyway. "Managing Data Manipulation Using Transactions" is the section that covered this particular question.

APPLY YOUR KNOWLEDGE

11. **C.** The rollback, in this case, rolls back to the savepoint, so it leaves the transaction count alone with just the initial BEGIN TRANSACTION having taken effect, so the answer is 1. If you need some more information, see "Managing Data Manipulation Using Transactions."

12. **C.** It will print the value of @Foo. Rollbacks do not change how print statements work. A print happens immediately. Also, it's not an error to have an empty transaction or a transaction that just doesn't do any database updates. It's unwise,

but not an error. The "Managing Data Manipulation Using Transactions" section covers what you need to know for this question.

13. **D.** Any and all of the options could cause the symptoms described. A deadlock is probably the best explanation, but with that high a transaction isolation level, you're going to have lock contention in any busy database. The section on "Concurrency and Locking" discusses deadlocks and isolation levels.

Suggested Readings and Resources

SQL Server 2000 Books Online

- Batches, especially the Overview and Processing topics.

- DECLARE. The article that shows you the syntax for DECLARE has a lot of rich detail about some useful, but seldom used options.

- Comments, the overview topic.

- The syntax page for BEGIN...END has a lot of information about nesting BEGIN...END blocks and some interesting samples.

- IF...ELSE in the Transact-SQL reference.

- If you look up the topic "Lock Granules" in the index, you'll get a very interesting page called "Understanding Locking in SQL Server," which goes into an unreasonable amount of detail about lock mechanics.

- For security, check the articles on GRANT and REVOKE, in addition to the articles on sp_grantdbaccess.

- The "Roles—SQL Server" overview topic is excellent for finding out about fixed system roles and fixed database roles.

This chapter meets the Views objectives for Microsoft's Designing and Implementing Databases with Microsoft SQL Server 2000 Enterprise Edition exam. These objectives include:

Create and alter database objects. Objects include views.

• **Specify schema binding and encryption for stored procedures, triggers, user-defined functions, and views.**

▶ The purpose of this objective is to test your knowledge of how to create and alter views in SQL Server 2000. You have to know how and when to alter views and what options to change. You also need to know when to create views in a given situation. This chapter covers the different considerations that arise when creating and altering views.

Manage data manipulation by using views.

▶ This objective deals with data modification on a base table via a view. Even if you have no knowledge of views, you probably guessed that they can be used to view information from the database. However, not only can they act as data retrieval centers, but they can also be used to modify data residing on underlying base tables, and that's what this objective deals with.

Alter database objects to support partitioned views.

• **Design a partitioning strategy.**

• **Design and create views.**

▶ This objective looks at the implementation of partitioned views in SQL Server 2000. Partitioned views include distributed partitioned and locally partitioned data, which are covered near the end of the chapter.

CHAPTER 7

Working with Views

Control data access by using views.

• Apply ownership chains.

• Use programming logic and objects. Considerations include implementing row-level security and restricting direct access to tables.

• Troubleshoot and optimize programming objects. Objects include views.

▶ This objective teaches you how to access data by using a view. This objective includes creating a view in such a way so that users actually benefit from its existence. Security mechanisms can be obtained by controlling data access, which is done by granting users access to a view but not granting them direct access to underlying tables. Many of the restrictions that apply to views deal with data manipulation, and these restrictions can prevent your views from operating as expected.

▶ This chapter contains pure objective-related information, making the entire chapter important, but focuses on the main elements of the view statement, including the WITH ENCRYPTION and WITH CHECK options. Also, make sure you have a good understanding of ownership chains.

▶ Indexed views are without doubt going to show up on the exam. However, they are examined in Chapter 3, "Physical Database Design," and Chapter 10, "Boosting Performance with Indexes." This chapter mentions view components that affect the creation of index views.

▶ Test out several types of views on a SQL Server. The more practical work you do, the more likely it is that you will remember the facts.

INTRODUCTION

This chapter takes an in-depth look at views. Views were introduced in Chapter 3, "Physical Database Design," as a component that makes up part of the physical design of the database. Chapter 3 only introduced views as one of the many components that can make up a database, and this chapter follows up on the topics that were introduced there and expands on them.

Before beginning this chapter, you should have a good understanding of Chapter 4, "Querying and Modifying Data," which deals with data retrieval and the SELECT statement. Views are based on the SELECT statement, but have some restrictions, which are also covered in this chapter.

In simple terms, a view is a predefined SELECT statement that creates a dynamic virtual table. Although not a real table, a view can be used for many tasks for which an actual table can be used and is often referenced in the same way as a table. You will see a view based on the SELECT statement when the CREATE VIEW statement is covered.

Views can be used to define numerous combinations of rows and columns from one or more tables. When views use only a few of the columns in a table, then the table data is referred to as being *vertically filtered*; and when views use only a portion of the rows in a table, then the table data is referred to as being *horizontally filtered*. The capability to filter data is a great advantage of using views. For example, if you need only a subset of data from a table, then a view prevents users from accidentally (or intentionally) seeing too much data, because the most that can be seen is what is contained in the view. The next few sections describe how to design and create views in SQL Server 2000.

Views can also be used with horizontally or vertically partitioned data through a partitioned view. This is where data that could have been put into one table is split into several tables to improve performance. A view can then be used to join all this data together. If the data is on different servers, then you are working with a *distributed partitioned view*.

NOTE

Server Federation   With horizontal and vertical partitioning of data across several servers, the servers that are working together to provide the data are referred to as a *federation of servers*.

UNDERSTANDING VIEWS

You can think of a view as a virtual table, similar to an ordinary table and capable of performing tasks like an ordinary table. This virtual information includes all parameters and other SQL Server-specific information used in executing your query.

A view is a stored definition of a SELECT statement that specifies the rows and columns SQL Server retrieves when the view is opened. A view can contain 1024 columns that are extracted from a single table or multiple tables. A view can return an unlimited number of rows, so the number of rows is dependent on the number of rows in the table or tables referenced.

As a matter of fact, views are named "views" because they enable you view the contents of selected columns or rows in a table. They enable you to perform numerous operations that are similar to those you can perform with tables, such as updating, deleting, and querying data, but have some restrictions that tables do not have. These restrictions are explored later in this chapter. Many people mistakenly think that a view actually stores the data. This is not true; the view merely provides access to the data in the underlying tables. The difference between a view and a table can be shown when a column is added to a referenced table: the column does not automatically appear in the view definition until the view is refreshed after it is either altered or re-created. If the referenced table is modified, you can check on the validity of the view by using the sp_refreshview stored procedure. The view is no longer valid if referenced columns no longer exist or have been renamed.

Information in views can define a filtering strategy. However, it is not a mandatory task. You could have a view that defines a SELECT statement for a whole table. Or, you could vertically filter them by selecting specific columns. You could also horizontally filter them by selecting certain rows. Filtering strategies enable you to increase the level of protection for confidential data.

View access permission can also be granted to specific users throughout your database, which produces a flexible security management plan.

NOTE

Where is the Data? Remember that the data referenced through a view is always coming from its underlying table. The view is actually a SELECT statement against other views or tables.

View Benefits

Views provide many benefits and, because of this, are very common throughout an enterprise database environment. The number one reason a view is created is to protect data from inquisitive eyes. This means that the developer has to worry only about allowing access to the view and further restricting the rows that are returned. Views provide many other benefits, which are as follows:

- **Make querying easier**. Views enable users to execute specific SELECT statements, without requiring the user to provide the entire SELECT statement each time it executes. For example, if the following view exists:

```
CREATE VIEW PriceList AS
  SELECT TOP 100 PERCENT
    ProductID, ProductName, UnitPrice
    FROM NorthWind..Products
    ORDER BY ProductName
```

  Then users can retrieve the data by using

```
SELECT * FROM NorthWind..PriceList
```

  Without the view, they would have had to type

```
SELECT ProductID, ProductName, UnitPrice
  FROM NorthWind..Products
  ORDER BY ProductName
```

- **Hide irrelevant data**. Views enable you to SELECT only the data that is needed or of interest.

- **Enforce security**. Users can view only what you let them see. This may be a set of rows or columns or both. This is especially important when sensitive information is involved, such as salary and credit card information. This information can also be blocked by implementing column-level permissions on the table. Views provide a more efficient data retrieval process and easier security management because permissions are checked and maintained at only one level.

- **Export data easily**. Views can gather data from different views and tables, thus making it easy to export data. This data can be exported using the Bulk Copy Program (BCP) or Data Transformation Services (DTS). Regardless of the tool that you are using, it is easier to create an export statement if you can tell it to take all the data in a specific table. The view can be used to consolidate this data for this purpose.

The greatest benefits that views provide relate to their role as predefined SELECT statements. This enables them to consolidate relevant information into convenient locations. There are some restrictions on what data can be combined in a view, and the following section covers some of those guidelines.

View Creation Guidelines

Views offer some great advantages, but have several restrictions that do not exist in normal SELECT statements. Before examining the view creation process, you should review some facts and restrictions that deal with views. SQL Server will not let you forget these facts when you are creating your views; it throws up an error, usually detailing what you are missing or doing wrong. The most important of these facts are the following:

◆ A view is nothing more than a SELECT statement that has been given a name and saved in the database. The view does not contain the data, but defines where the data comes from. The view can often be treated like a table.

◆ Because a view is only a SELECT statement, you can filter the data that is returned to include some or all of a table's rows or columns. You can stick to the important data.

◆ The view's definition can comprise of rows and columns from one or more tables in the current or other databases.

◆ A view can contain a maximum of 1024 columns.

◆ Defaults, triggers, and rules are not allowed to be associated with a view. The only exception to this rule is the new INSTEAD OF trigger.

◆ A view can use data that may be anywhere (such as another database) as long as the view is created in the current database.

◆ View names must follow the rules for identifiers.

◆ Views cannot be created using the ORDER BY clause unless they use the TOP clause (as in TOP 100 PERCENT).

◆ Views cannot be created using the COMPUTE BY or SELECT INTO clauses.

◆ View names must adhere to uniqueness rules. Two users may create a view named MyView because the object owner makes the fully qualified names unique.

◆ Views cannot be created on temporary tables.

◆ Temporary views cannot be created.

◆ Views can be nested up to 32 levels.

By now you should have a general feel for what a view is. You should also be aware of the benefits derived from and the restrictions that apply to views. With that knowledge, you can begin the next section. The next section looks at creating the view and the syntax required.

CREATE AND ALTER VIEWS

▶ **Create and alter database objects. Objects include views.**

This section looks at creating views, including how to restrict the data that is returned through the view, and how to enhance these views by using aggregates and joins. Finally, it explains how to modify views and remove views. Because it is best to start at the beginning, the first thing to study is how to create views.

Creating Views

Views can be created using the Enterprise Manager, the Create View Wizard, or using T-SQL within the SQL Query Analyzer. When you use the Query Analyzer, you use the CREATE VIEW statement to create your virtual table. When creating a view, remember these guidelines. The following shows the syntax for the CREATE VIEW statement.

```
CREATE VIEW [ < database_name > . ] [ < owner > . ]
➡view_name [ ( column [ ,...n ] ) ]
  [ WITH < view_attribute > [ ,...n ] ]
  AS
  < SELECT_statement >
    [ WITH CHECK OPTION ]

< view_attribute > ::=
  { ENCRYPTION | SCHEMABINDING | VIEW_METADATA }
```

◆ `view_name` is the name of the view and must adhere to the rules for identifiers.

◆ `column` is the name to be used for the columns that are returned from the select statement. This is useful when you want to change the name of the column identifier.

◆ `WITH ENCRYPTION` encrypts the syscomments columns that contain the text of the `CREATE VIEW` statement. Encryption prevents people from being able to see the view definition, replicate the view, or generate a complete database creation script. If you attempt to view the properties of the view through Enterprise Manage or `sp_helptext`, you see a comment telling you that the view is encrypted. If you query `sys_comments` directly, you see an encrypted string or gibberish.

◆ `WITH SCHEMABINDING` specifies that the view be bound to the schema. Visually this means that tables, views, and functions that the view refers to must contain the owner name in the reference (for example, `dbo.sales`). Schema binding is designed to prevent objects from being dropped or modified while the view still refers to them, because that would cause the view to cease functioning.

> **NOTE**
>
> **Indexed Views and `SCHEMABINDING`**
> Note that `SCHEMABINDING` has to be specified when you create indexed views. Also, when `SCHEMABINDING` is specified, you have to adhere to the owner.object syntax when referencing tables or views in the creation of your view. Indexed views are covered in Chapter 10, "Boosting Performance with Indexes."

When creating a view, you may want to name an alias for a certain column to make a better user interface for your users. However, it is not obligatory. If a column alias is not specified, the view refers to the column name in the underlying table or view referenced. You must assign a column alias when joining two tables that have the same column names.

Selecting Specific Columns and Rows

As you have noted in previous sections, views are effective for securing data and reducing the display of non-relevant data. Views can help in showing your users only what you want them to see. This may be a set of rows or columns or both. This is especially important when sensitive information is involved, such as salary and credit card information. Views allow you to retrieve only the data that is needed or relevant.

At a particular point in time, you may want to limit your view data to specific rows or columns of data. The following two sections look at selecting columns for your view and selecting rows for your view. The actual requirement for which data should be shown depends on your specific circumstances.

Selecting Specific Columns

You can define a view that is made up of some, or all, of the columns of a table. This process is sometimes known as vertically filtering a table (see Figure 7.1). Selecting certain columns is useful when you want to protect data from prying eyes. A good example of this might be when you want to hide a salary column of a table, and therefore create a view that references all columns except the salary column. Step by Step 7.1 shows you how to specify columns with the Enterprise Manager.

Base Table

	emp_id	fname	minit	lname	job_id	job_lvl	pub_id
1	PMA42628M	Paolo	M	Accorti	13	35	877
2	PSA89086M	Pedro	S	Afonso	14	89	1389
3	VPA30890F	Victoria	P	Ashworth	6	140	877
4	H-B39728F	Helen		Bennett	12	35	877
5	L-B31947F	Lesley		Brown	7	120	877
6	F-C16315M	Francisco		Chang	4	227	9952
7	PTC11962M	Philip	T	Cramer	2	215	9952
8	A-C71970F	Aria		Cruz	10	87	1389
9	AMD15433F	Ann	M	Devon	3	200	9952

View 1

	emp_id	fname	minit	lname
1	PMA42628M	Paolo	M	Accorti
2	PSA89086M	Pedro	S	Afonso
3	VPA30890F	Victoria	P	Ashworth
4	H-B39728F	Helen		Bennett
5	L-B31947F	Lesley		Brown
6	F-C16315M	Francisco		Chang
7	PTC11962M	Philip	T	Cramer
8	A-C71970F	Aria		Cruz
9	AMD15433F	Ann	M	Devon

View 2

	job_id	job_lvl	pub_id
1	13	35	877
2	14	89	1389
3	6	140	877
4	12	35	877
5	7	120	877
6	4	227	9952
7	2	215	9952
8	10	87	1389
9	3	200	9952

FIGURE 7.1
A sample view filtered by column.

STEP BY STEP

7.1 Creating Views by Selecting Specific Columns Using the Enterprise Manager

1. Open the Enterprise Manager from the Start menu and connect to the default instance of SQL Server.

2. To create a new view in the Pubs database, expand Pubs from the right pane and then right-click the Views icon. Select New View to start designing a new view.

3. This example uses the Sales table as a base table for the new view and you will design it so that it selects all columns from the Sales table except for the Payterms column. To do this, right-click in the topmost pane and select Add Table; this initializes the Add Table dialog box. Scroll down the list to find Sales; click Add, and then click Close to close the Add Table dialog box. Notice that the table was added graphically on the top-most pane.

4. To add a new column to the view definition, select the check box next to it. For this example, select all columns except Payterms. Adding a column using this graphical method automates coding (see for yourself by looking at the code pane) and, thus, is a good solution for a user who is an SQL programming novice. This is shown in Figure 7.2.

5. After you have selected the desired columns to be referenced in your view, you can take it on a test run by clicking on the red exclamation mark on the toolbar.

6. You can now save your view by clicking on the disk button in the toolbar. Save the view with an appropriate name, such as SalesViews, and then you are finished.

You can also specify desired columns using the Query Analyzer. Examine the following code:

```
CREATE VIEW SelectedColumns AS
    SELECT Type, Price
        FROM Titles
```

FIGURE 7.2
Automated coding using the View Designer.

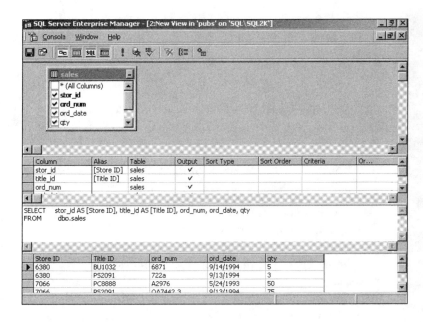

Now that you have seen how to restrict data in a view by columns, you now see how to limit the number of rows that are returned.

Selecting Specific Rows

You can also define a view that references some, or all, of the rows of a table. Selecting certain rows involves the help of the WHERE clause. This filters out all entries that do not match the conditions defined in a WHERE clause (see Figure 7.3), and is known as horizontal filtration. Using the WHERE clause returns only relevant data and forces data security through the restricting of the returned data.

With horizontal filtration, the types of attributes (or columns) returned in the view remains constant, but you can see the difference in the number of rows returned. This is like pulling out a few pages of a phone book. Each entry in a phone book has a name, address, and phone number (the columns), but the few pages that were pulled out represent the portion of the data that you are going to use. This is how a horizontally filtered view behaves, with all the columns, but not all the rows. To create a view based on horizontal filtration, see this code:

```
CREATE VIEW SelectedRows AS
  SELECT Au_ID, State, au_FName
    FROM Authors
      WHERE State = 'CA'
```

Base Table

	emp_id	fname	minit	lname	job_id	job_lvl	pub_id
1	PMA42628M	Paolo	M	Accorti	13	35	877
2	PSA89086M	Pedro	S	Afonso	14	89	1389
3	VPA30890F	Victoria	P	Ashworth	6	140	877
4	H-B39728F	Helen		Bennett	12	35	877
5	L-B31947F	Lesley		Brown	7	120	877
6	F-C16315M	Francisco		Chang	4	227	9952
7	PTC11962M	Philip	T	Cramer	2	215	9952
8	A-C71970F	Aria		Cruz	10	87	1389
9	AMD15433F	Ann	M	Devon	3	200	9952

FIGURE 7.3
A sample view filtered by row.

View 1 (WHERE lname LIKE 'A%' or lname LIKE 'B%')

	emp_id	fname	minit	lname	job_id	job_lvl	pub_id
1	PMA42628M	Paolo	M	Accorti	13	35	877
2	PSA89086M	Pedro	S	Afonso	14	89	1389
3	VPA30890F	Victoria	P	Ashworth	6	140	877
4	H-B39728F	Helen		Bennett	12	35	877
5	L-B31947F	Lesley		Brown	7	120	877

View 2 (WHERE lname LIKE 'C%' or lname LIKE 'D%')

	emp_id	fname	minit	lname	job_id	job_lvl	pub_id
6	F-C16315M	Francisco		Chang	4	227	9952
7	PTC11962M	Philip	T	Cramer	2	215	9952
8	A-C71970F	Aria		Cruz	10	87	1389
9	AMD15433F	Ann	M	Devon	3	200	9952

The following query shows you what horizontal filtering looks like:

```
SELECT * FROM SelectedRows
```

After executing this statement, you should notice that the State, FirstName, and Au_ID columns are shown WHERE the State is CA. This is shown in Figure 7.4.

You should now have a good grasp of the basics of a view. You know how to restrict the amount of data that is returned through the selection of columns and rows. The next section looks at further controlling the data that is returned through the view.

Accessing Views

Displaying the definition of a view may need to be done at some time. To access the exact definition of the view you created, use the sp_helptext system stored procedure. The actual definition of a view is stored in the syscomments system table. The sp_help-text procedure queries the syscomments, organizes the information required, and displays the view definition. As you've already seen, protecting a view definition is possible if you use the WITH ENCRYPTION option. sp_helptext lets you know what tables and views your view references. This information is helpful if you are having trouble figuring out why your view does not work because you will see what tables or views your malfunctioning view uses.

Knowing the actual structure of the tables that your view references is useful when troubleshooting or redesigning your view; but knowing what views or stored procedures reference your view is useful when you plan to make alterations to or drop a view. If you do not check on known dependencies, then you risk making other views or stored procedures unusable. To see what objects reference a view, use the sp_depends stored procedure. View dependencies are stored in the sysdepends system table. When the sp_depends stored procedure is executed, it queries the sysdepends table and summarizes the final result. Step by Step 7.2 shows you how to access views.

FIGURE 7.4

Creating a row-based filtration on a view.

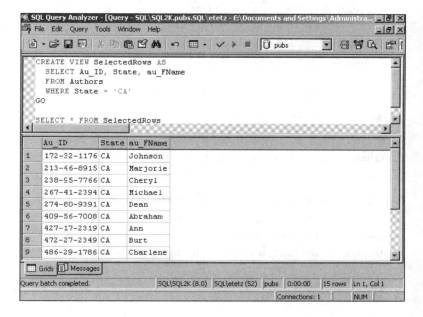

STEP BY STEP

7.2 Accessing Views

1. Open the Query Analyzer by selecting it from the Start menu and logging in.

2. To view the definition of `titleview` from the `Pubs` database (see Figure 7.5), execute the following:

   ```
   USE pubs
   GO
   EXEC sp_helptext titleview
   ```

3. To display the view's associated tables, execute the following query. This process is shown in Figure 7.6.

   ```
   EXEC sp_depends titleview
   ```

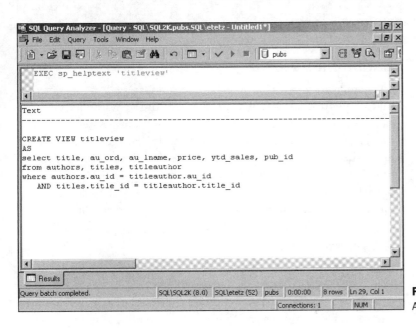

FIGURE 7.5
Accessing the definition of a view.

FIGURE 7.6
Accessing the dependencies of a view.

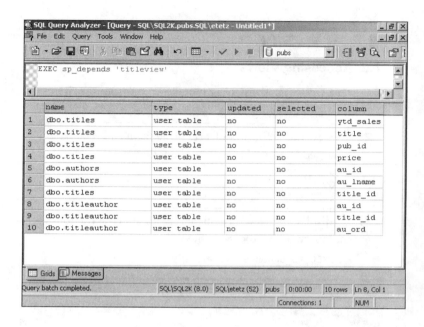

Enhancing Views

You can create view definitions beyond mundane SELECT statements that simply place data statements into a resultset. With views, you can use joins to get data from multiple tables. This is useful because the desired data is not always stored on a single table (in fact, this is rarely the case). You can also leverage the complexity of aggregate functions in your views in the same way you would use them on a normal table. You can further refine data retrieval by building views on views, so that data is filtered on the appropriate conditions.

Aggregates and Views

Aggregates offer a great deal of calculation power and views can make use of them. These aggregates include AVG, COUNT, DISTINCT, and similar functions. Leveraging the power of aggregates enables you to create useful reports that can be produced based on data in a table.

The following example outlines the importance of aggregates with the example of a user who requests to see a report on the minimum, maximum, average and total values of the Quantity column (grouped by orderID) from the Order Details table in the

`Northwind` database. Running the following code produces a view named `QuantityAnalysis`:

```
CREATE VIEW QuantityAnalysis AS
  SELECT OrderID, MIN (Quantity) AS minimum, MAX (Quantity)
  ➥AS maximum,
        AVG (Quantity) as Average, SUM (Quantity) AS Total
  FROM [Order Details]
  GROUP BY Order_ID
```

Now, to see the results that this query produces, find out what the view will produce. To do this, execute the following query, as shown in Figure 7.7:

```
SELECT *
  FROM QuantityAnalysis
```

The summary or statistical features of aggregates are not the only way to enhance a view; you can also join tables to consolidate information.

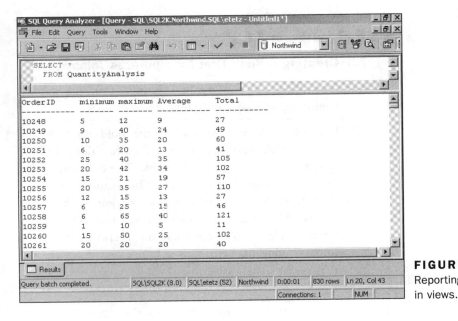

FIGURE 7.7

Reporting summary data using aggregates in views.

Joins and Views

Ever wondered how to gather information from multiple tables to form a view definition? This can be accomplished with a join.

Implementing joins within your views enables you to consolidate related data that may be scattered around your database. When you incorporate joins into your view, you are literally assembling information from diverse tables, but not actually storing data on the view, because the view does not contain the actual data. Joins are used to display data from multiple tables in a single resultset. They help in the management of your data by saving the join definition, thereby releasing the user from needing to know how to construct the join.

A resultset may use joins to gather data from a number of tables—say two, three, or four. You can reference up to 256 tables in a single SELECT statement or view. Take the Pubs database, for instance. To find out the royalty rate of an author, you can't just query the Authors table, because it doesn't store adequate information; you have to join two tables. The purpose of a resultset is to gather information into a single pot. To create a view that joins data, follow Step by Step 7.3.

STEP BY STEP

7.3 Creating a View That Incorporates Joins

1. Open the Query Analyzer by selecting it from the Start menu. Log in with the appropriate credentials.

2. In this example, you create a view that holds the author's name from the Authors table as well as the titles written by that author from the Titles table. The only way to do this is by creating a multi-join, first by creating a join to the TitleAuthor table and then a second join to the Titles table. To create a multi-join view that joins the Authors table, TitleAuthor table, and Titles table, execute the following:

```
CREATE VIEW AuthorSummaryInfo AS
  SELECT Authors.au_fname, Authors.State, title
    FROM Authors
    JOIN titleauthor ON Authors.au_ID =
    ➥TitleAuthor.Au_ID
    JOIN titles on titleauthor. Title_ID =
    ➥Titles.Title_ID
```

3. To see the view you created, run the following as shown here and in Figure 7.8:

```
SELECT * FROM AuthorSummaryInfo
```

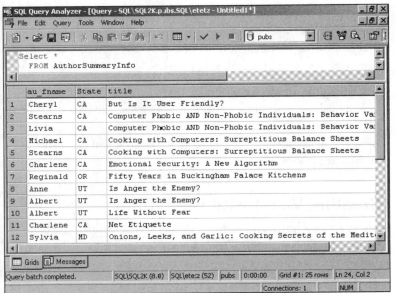

FIGURE 7.8
Incorporating joins in views.

Joins enable views to act as data consolidation points. Next, you see how to re-filter the data by creating a view based on another view.

Views on Views

Similar to the way a table serves as the base for a view, a view can gather its information from another view. Creating a view using an existing view as the underlying information source helps when you want to further refine criteria on an existing view. To create a view referencing a base view, examine the following code listing. This creates a view called `AuthorsView` that includes information on all authors, regardless of the states they live in. The next view, `AuthorsCA`, creates a view that references `AuthorsView` and selects only those authors from California:

```
CREATE VIEW AuthorsView AS
  SELECT Au_fname, State, Au_lname
    FROM Authors
GO

CREATE VIEW AuthorsCA AS
  SELECT Au_fname, State
    FROM AuthorsView
    WHERE State = 'CA
```

To display the newly created view, query it using

```
SELECT *
  FROM AuthorsCA
```

You should notice that only the authors living in California are listed. If the authors in California represent a piece of information that is regularly required, you now have an easy way to extract that data from a view that was already useful.

You should now have a clear understanding of how to enhance a view by using the summary power of aggregates, the data consolidation of joins, and the refined filtering of basing a view on another view. If you do not need advanced view features, you can make use of the Create View Wizard.

Creating Views with the Wizard

If you are in a hurry and just want a quick view with all the basic elements, you can use the Create View Wizard. This is a five-step process that takes only a few seconds to complete.

Before you can use the wizard, you have to open it. You will find all the wizards in Enterprise Manager in the Tools Menu. The Create View Wizard is in the Database section, as shown in Figure 7.9. Select it and choose OK.

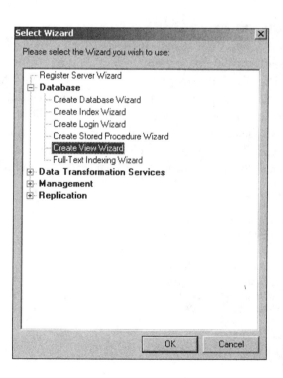

FIGURE 7.9
The Create View Wizard is accessible through the Wizards dialog.

The Welcome screen for the wizard shows you what to expect during the wizard. This welcome screen is shown in Figure 7.10.

The five steps to the Create View Wizard are

1. Select the database that will be used for the view.

2. Select one or more tables for use in the view.

3. Select one or more columns from the selected tables.

4. Type a WHERE clause to restrict the returned rows.

5. Name the new view.

The wizard provides a way of specifying advanced options, such as ENCRYPTION or SCHEMABINDING, but does simplify the view creation process.

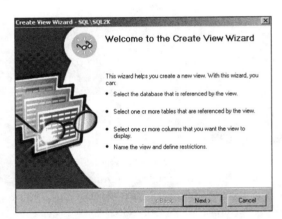

FIGURE 7.10
The Create View Wizard is a simple five-step wizard.

Altering Views

SQL Server accommodates the need to adjust a view, whether it is renaming or completely changing a view definition. This flexibility is provided via the sp_rename stored procedure and the ALTER VIEW statement. The following sections describe these two in greater depth.

> **NOTE**
>
> **Changing Object Names** The sp_rename system procedure is used to rename any database object in your database, so it's one you should remember.

Renaming a View

Renaming a view, or any object for that matter, is done with the sp_rename system stored procedure.

```
sp_rename [ @objname = ] 'object_name' ,
    [ @newname = ] 'new_name'
    [ , [ @objtype = ] 'object_type' ]
```

NOTE

The Missing 'OBJECT' In most cases, you can omit the @objtype if it is going to be 'OBJECT'.

To use this procedure, first supply the original name followed by a comma and then type in the new name of the view. Because this system stored procedure is extremely generic and used for a lot of objects, you have to specifically specify OBJECT as object_type. Views, triggers, constraints, and stored procedures all belong in the category OBJECT. Renaming views and stored procedures causes the sysobjects system table to be updated. For example, to rename a view in the Pubs database you could use:

```
use pubs
GO
sp_rename 'titleview','oldtitleview', 'OBJECT'
```

Use a great deal of care when renaming objects because any scripts, stored procedures, or objects that refer to the renamed object by its old name will fail to work.

Editing a View

You may need to change the way a view accesses data, known as the *view definition*. When doing this, there must already be a previously created view using only the CREATE VIEW statement. You can also drop and re-create the view, but doing so resets previously granted permissions. Using the ALTER VIEW statement, you can easily reshape the definition of a view without affecting permissions granted. The syntax for ALTER VIEW is as follows:

```
ALTER VIEW [ < database_name > . ] [ < owner > . ]
➥view_name [ ( column [ ,...n ] ) ]
[ WITH < view_attribute > [ ,...n ] ]
AS
    < select_statement >
[ WITH CHECK OPTION ]

< view_attribute > ::=
    { ENCRYPTION | SCHEMABINDING | VIEW_METADATA }
```

The syntax is relatively similar to CREATE VIEW. view_name is the name of the view being altered. The WITH ENCRYPTION clause protects the definition of your view. You encrypt the definition of your view because you may not want users to display it, to protect your design from duplication. Encrypting your view using WITH ENCRYPTION ensures that no one can display your view, whether using sp_helptext, viewing it through the Enterprise Manager, or generating it through a Database Creation Script.

If your original view was created with WITH ENCRYPTION or WITH SCHEMABINDING, then your ALTER VIEW statement must include the same options. To alter a view using ALTER VIEW, see Step by Step 7.4

STEP BY STEP

7.4 Altering a View Using the ALTER VIEW Statement

1. Open the SQL Server Query Analyzer by selecting it from the Start menu.

2. Before altering the definition of a view, there must already be an existing view. Run the following query to create a new view for the purposes of this example:

```
USE pubs
GO
CREATE VIEW EmployeeView AS
  SELECT emp_id, fname, lname, job_lvl
    FROM Employee
    WHERE fname LIKE ' p%'
```

3. To change the definition of the view you created in Step 2, you need the help of the ALTER VIEW statement. Run the following query:

```
ALTER VIEW EmployeeView AS
  SELECT emp_id, fname, lname, job_lvl
    FROM Employee
    WHERE job_lvl <150
```

WARNING

Don't Be Careless with Changes Altering views or tables that are used by views may cause the dependent views to stop working. SQL Server does not back-check all table or view alterations to ensure they do not create errors. This is where the SCHEMABINDING option helps out. If you have SCHEMA-bound objects, then you cannot ALTER the source objects at all. It may be preferable to drop and recreate a series of objects, rather than have objects that do not function. This means more planning.

You may find that SQL Server does not allow you to perform tasks because of one dependency or another. For instance, all objects are dependent on their owner, so you are not able to drop a user from the database if they own objects. The number of database objects that the server checks for dependencies is very large, but it is easy to find out what objects they are. A quick query of sysobjects can reveal any object ownership dependencies.

Scripts, stored procedures, and views can exist anywhere, and refer to tables or views in your database. There is no easy location that can be checked that tells SQL Server who is referencing your table or view. Another user can reference your view from an entirely different server, without your knowledge, if that user has been granted the SELECT permission to it. Therefore, there is no back-checking of integrity when you change the structure of tables or views—who knows who might be using it? When examining the situation from this perspective, it is easy to see why SQL Server does not check; but it is still surprising that it does not check. Take for example the following script:

```
USE pubs
GO
CREATE VIEW AuthorInfo AS
  SELECT au_id, au_fname, au_lname, city, zip
    FROM dbo.Authors
GO
CREATE VIEW AuthorShortInfo AS
  SELECT au_id, au_fname, city
    FROM dbo.AuthorInfo
GO
ALTER VIEW AuthorInfo AS
  SELECT au_id, au_fname, au_lname, zip
    FROM dbo.Authors
GO
SELECT * FROM AuthorShortInfo
```

Running this script would yield the following error messages in Query Analyzer:

```
Server: Msg 207, Level 16, State 3, Procedure
➥AuthorShortInfo, Line 2
Invalid column name 'city'.
Server: Msg 4413, Level 16, State 1, Line 1
Could not use view or function 'AuthorShortInfo' because of
binding errors.
```

This error states that a required object (the 'city' column) no longer exists. This problem is possible, and can easily occur, because of the lack of checking on changes to source objects. This same error message would result if you execute sp_refreshview on AuthorShortInfo, and sp_refreshview would return a non-zero value because of the failure. It is possible to create a small procedure to query sysobjects for views, loop them through them, and refresh each view to ensure that they are all still valid.

Dropping Views

To remove a view from a database, use the DROP VIEW statement.
Dropping a view removes the definition of the view from the database and an entry in the sysobjects while not affecting the underlying tables and views.

The DROP VIEW command is relatively simple as shown here:

```
DROP VIEW { view } [ ,...n ]
```

To drop a view named my_view, you simply have to execute DROP
VIEW 'my_view'. With the DROP VIEW command you may also choose
to remove a number of views at the same time. To do this, specify
each view in a comma-delimited list. Dropping an indexed view leads
to the removal of all indexes associated with that view. To drop the
view created in Step by Step 7.4, enter and run the following code:

> **WARNING**
>
> **Dropping Used Views** Dropping
> views that are used by other views
> causes the dependent views to
> stop working, because the object
> that they refer to no longer exists.

```
DROP VIEW EmployeeView
GO
```

If you drop a view that is used by another object, such as a view, you
cause problems with the dependent view. For example, examine the
following code:

```
CREATE VIEW auth1 AS
  SELECT au_fname, au_lname, city, state
    FROM pubs.dbo.authors
GO

CREATE VIEW auth2 AS
  SELECT au_fname, au_lname
    FROM pubs.dbo.auth1
GO

DROP VIEW auth1
GO

SELECT * FROM auth2
GO
```

When this code is executed, you get the following error message:

```
Server: Msg 208, Level 16, State 1, Procedure auth2, Line 3
Invalid object name 'pubs.dbo.auth1'.
Server: Msg 4413, Level 16, State 1, Line 1
Could not use view or function 'auth2' because of binding
errors.
```

This error message lets you know that the dependent view
'pubs.dbo.auth1' is not present in the database.

Modifying Data Through Views

▶ **Manage data manipulation by using views.**

Not only can you retrieve data by using a view, you can also modify the data. Modification includes all inserts, deletes, and updates. When you modify, delete, and update data, the data definition in the view does not change; the data modification is aimed at the underlying referenced tables associated with the view. A view does not in any way lose its definition; therefore it is not affected in any way when modification queries are executed.

You can easily modify the data through a view, as long as the view has been based on at least one table, and it does not SELECT aggregate functions. In addition, if you need to perform additional data modification through the view, you can use the INSTEAD OF triggers. INSTEAD OF triggers exist for UPDATE, DELETE, and INSERT statements. For the time being, we'll stick with modifying data through a view without the help of the INSTEAD OF trigger, which is covered in greater detail in Chapter 8, " Triggers."

Inserting Rows Through Views

In addition to retrieving rows, you can use views to insert data into an underlying base table. Adding data through a view is extremely similar to adding data directly to a normal table. Therefore, you can still use the INSERT statement in the same way. After you've created the view, you reference the view in an INSERT statement to add rows just as if you've referenced a table in the INSERT statement.

Adding data through a view is as easy as adding data to a regular table. However, you must adhere to a number of conditions. The most important of these conditions are the following:

◆ INSERT and UPDATE statements must modify only one of the underlying tables at a time. If you want to UPDATE data that resides in more than one table, you have to perform the UPDATE in two or more statements.

◆ Inserts against the underlying table must provide values for all NOT NULL columns, unless DEFAULT values are declared for those columns.

◆ Inserted data must conform to the view definition when WITH CHECK is specified on the view.

If you are not sure whether your INSERT will be valid, you may want to use sp_helptext to check the SELECT statement that creates the view.

A view is not a table, even though it an often be treated like one. If a view displays columns from only one table, then you do not have to worry about inserts and updates affecting more than one table. If, however, your view is used to consolidate data from many tables, you have to be careful when you UPDATE columns in more than one table. When you INSERT data through the view, you may find that the view actually makes the process difficult. For example, if you create the following view in the Pubs database:

```
CREATE VIEW TitleAuthors AS
   SELECT dbo.Authors.au_id, dbo.Authors.au_lname,
          ➥dbo.Authors.au_fname, dbo.Authors.phone,
          ➥dbo.Authors.contract, dbo.Titles.title,
          ➥dbo.Titles.type
     FROM dbo.Authors INNER JOIN
          ➥dbo.TitleAuthor ON dbo.Authors.au_id =
          ➥dbo.TitleAuthor.au_id INNER JOIN
          ➥dbo.Titles ON dbo.TitleAuthor.title_id =
dbo.Titles.title_id
```

You can then add an author record with the following statement:

```
INSERT INTO TitleAuthors
   (au_id, au_lname, au_fname, phone, contract)
   VALUES ('212-55-1212', 'Burns', 'Bobby', '212 555-1212', 1)
```

After this, however, the Bobby Burns record will not be visible to the view. To then associate the new (non-visible) author with a book, you have to UPDATE the TitleAuthor table, which cannot be done through the view, because those columns are not present in the view. References to the TitleAuthor table are used to create the view, but are not part of the column structure in the view.

To properly satisfy the INSERT requirement for the Author table, the previous UPDATE to the TitleAuthors view had to UPDATE at least the au_id, au_lname, au_fname, phone, and contract columns because these columns are all set to not allow NULL values. The only piece of information that could have been left out of the INSERT would have been the phone column, because that defaults to ('UNKNOWN').

If you examine the view definition that was used in the TitleAuthor view, you will notice that it is a result of an INNER JOIN between three tables. This implements a restriction on the visible data. Other restrictions on the visible data may be the result of the WHERE clause. In the previous Bobby Burns INSERT, you were able to INSERT data that was then no longer visible to the view. You can confirm that Bobby Burns is in the Authors table by using SELECT * FROM Authors WHERE au_lname = 'Burns'. The current view definition enables you to INSERT data that is not actually visible through the view. If you want to prevent this from happening, you can use the WITH CHECK OPTION when creating your view. Here is an example of the TitleAuthors view using the WITH CHECK OPTION:

```
CREATE VIEW TitleAuthors AS
    SELECT dbo.authors.au_id, dbo.authors.au_lname,
        ➥dbo.authors.au_fname, dbo.authors.phone,
        ➥dbo.authors.contract, dbo.titles.title,
        ➥dbo.titles.type
    FROM dbo.authors INNER JOIN
        dbo.titleauthor ON dbo.authors.au_id =
        ➥dbo.titleauthor.au_id INNER JOIN
        dbo.titles ON dbo.titleauthor.title_id =
        ➥dbo.titles.title_id
    WITH CHECK OPTION
```

Now if a similar data INSERT is attempted, you will receive the following error message:

```
Server: Msg 550, Level 16, State 1, Line 1
The attempted insert or update failed because the target
view either specifies WITH CHECK OPTION or spans a view
that specifies WITH CHECK OPTION and one or more rows
resulting from the operation did not qualify under the
CHECK OPTION constraint.
The statement has been terminated.
```

Because this INSERT results in data that was not visible through the view, it is not allowed. This may be advantageous for some databases if you want to restrict what values are inserted into the view. In this particular case, it prevents the addition of both Authors and Titles, because you can't use a single statement to INSERT into both tables, and either INSERT creates data that is not visible through the view. Data updates, other than inserts, are still allowed, as long as the resulting data is still visible through the view.

Enabling users to add data to a view that will not then be visible leaves two problems. After the INSERT has been carried out, the data will not be visible, which causes some users to attempt additional updates (thinking the previous one failed). If the users are aware that the data INSERT did succeed, they are still unable to check the accuracy of the UPDATE, because the data is not visible. You should consider using the WITH CHECK OPTION with all views to limit data inserts and avoid user confusion.

To add data through a view, follow Step by Step 7.5.

STEP BY STEP

7.5 Adding Data Through a View

1. Open the Query Analyzer by selecting it from the Start menu.

2. You are going to add data through EmployeeView, which was the view you created in Step by Step 7.4. To avoid adding a row that will conflict with the WHERE clause condition, you need to see the definition of the view. Use sp_helptext to display the definition of the view, as shown in Figure 7.11:

   ```
   Sp_helptext EmployeeView
   ```

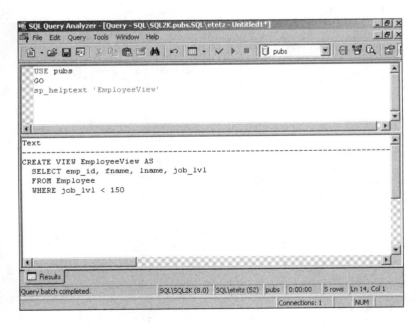

FIGURE 7.11
The definition of EmployeeView.

3. Now, INSERT a record into the base table, making sure the new record does not conflict with the condition specified in the WHERE clause of the view definition:

```
INSERT INTO EmployeeView
    (emp_id, fname, lname, job_lvl)
    VALUES ('AEE21349M', 'John', 'Mathew', 10)
```

4. To display the view with the updated record, enter and run the following:

```
SELECT *
    FROM EmployeeView
    WHERE emp_id = 'AEE21349M'
```

5. To see that the record has been added to the base table, Employee, run the following. The results of both of these SELECT statements are shown in Figure 7.12:

```
SELECT *
    FROM Employee
    WHERE emp_id = 'AEE21349M'
```

Now that you have seen how to put data into a table through a view, you should also know how to get the data back out of the database through a view.

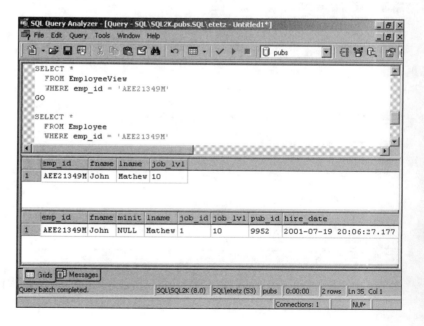

FIGURE 7.12
Inserting data through a view.

Deleting Rows Through Views

In the same way data can be retrieved and inserted through a view, it can also be removed. Rows can be removed through a view in almost the same fashion that they can be inserted. In fact, deleting rows from a view is as easy as knowing how to DELETE rows from a regular table.

The biggest rule that can never be broken when you DELETE a row through a view is that the affected row can reference only one table. In other words, the view can be based on only one table. If the view referred to or was based on more than one table, then every row would reference more than one table and could not be deleted. If you attempt to DELETE a row that is based on more than one table, then you receive an error message. Here is an attempted deletion and subsequent error message:

```
DELETE FROM TitleAuthors WHERE au_id = '213-46-8915'
GO

Server: Msg 4405, Level 16, State 1, Line 1
View or function 'TitleAuthors' is not updatable because
the modification affects multiple base tables.
```

Another requirement for deleting data through a view is that the data specified in the DELETE statement must actually be visible in the view. For example, the following shows the creation of a view, and an attempted data deletion using state as part of the deletion criteria while it is not part of the view. This fails with the specified error.

```
CREATE VIEW AuthorsInCA AS
  SELECT au_id, au_lname, au_fname
    FROM authors
    WHERE state = 'CA'
GO

DELETE FROM AuthorsInCA WHERE au_lname = 'Burns' and state
➥= 'CA'
GO

Server: Msg 207, Level 16, State 3, Line 1
Invalid column name 'state'.
```

If the view was created with the state column visible, then the DELETE statement would have succeeded. All components of the DELETE statement must be defined in the view.

The last requirement for deletion of data through a view is that the deletion of the record may not cause any foreign key violations. This type of deletion would not have been allowed outside the view, so it is not allowed through the view either. For example, in the Pubs database, you are not allowed to DELETE an author record if that author is assigned to a book, because the FK_Constraints are declared on the TitleAuthor table with the Authors table.

To DELETE a row through a view, go through the Step by Step 7.6.

STEP BY STEP

7.6 Deleting a Row via a View

1. Open the Query Analyzer by selecting it from the Start menu.

2. You will DELETE data through the view you created in the EmployeeView example. To avoid deleting a row that will conflict with the WHERE clause condition, you need to see the definition of the view by running the following:

```
SP_Helptext EmployeeView
```

3. Now, DELETE the row you added by running the following code:

```
DELETE EmployeeView
    WHERE emp_id =  'AEE21349M'
```

4. To make sure the record was deleted, try to query it using the following code. This process is shown in Figure 7.13.

```
SELECT *
    FROM EmployeeView
    WHERE emp_id = 'AEE21349M'
```

You will often want to UPDATE data, rather than DELETE it and re-create it. The next section leads you through the requirements for updating data through a view.

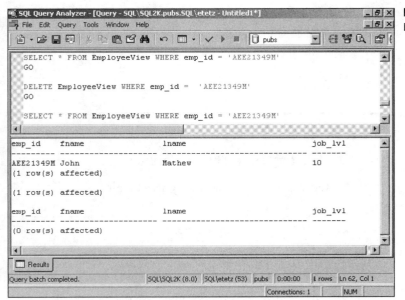

FIGURE 7.13
Deleting data via a view.

Updating Rows Through Views

You can use an UPDATE statement to change one or more rows that a view references. Any changes that are undertaken through the view are actually applied to the underlying table in which the view is defined. The restrictions that applied to INSERT statements used with views also apply to UPDATE statements. These restrictions include the following:

◆ UPDATE statements must modify only one of the underlying tables at a time. If you want to UPDATE data that resides in more than one table, you have to perform the UPDATE in two or more statements.

◆ Updated data must conform to the view definition when WITH CHECK is specified on the view.

◆ Updated data cannot create FOREIGN KEY constraint violations.

When updating a view, you may want to use the WITH CHECK OPTION to force all data modifications executed to be constrained by the view definition. This is important for the same reasons that were important when dealing with inserts: it reduces user confusion with disappearing data, and it enables users to always confirm the accuracy of their data UPDATE.

To UPDATE a record, follow Step by Step 7.7.

STEP BY STEP

7.7 Updating Data Through a View

1. Open the Query Analyzer by selecting it from the Start menu.

2. INSERT a record into the view:

```
INSERT INTO EmployeeView
    (emp_id, fname, lname, job_lvl)
    VALUES ('ARP21349M', 'Frandos', 'Fung', 10)
```

3. Assume that you mistook Frandos's last name with another name. To UPDATE the lname column on this record to his real last name, Thatch, run the following query:

```
UPDATE EmployeeView
    SET lname = 'Thatch'
    WHERE emp_id = 'ARP21349M'
```

4. To see the updated record, run the following code. This process is shown in Figure 7.14.

```
SELECT *
    FROM EmployeeView
    WHERE emp_id = 'ARP21349M'
```

With this discussion of the UPDATE statement, you have now examined all the different options for data modifications: Inserts, Updates, and Deletes, and how these are accomplished through the use of a view. You have seen what can be done, and what cannot be done because of the restrictions that are placed on data modifications through a view. Some of these restrictions are annoying, but most help you develop applications that maintain a higher quality of data.

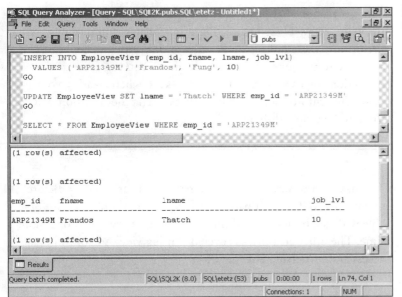

FIGURE 7.14
Updating data through a view.

Coming to Terms with Views

A view offers several benefits to both a database programmer and a database user. One benefit is ease of use, which comes from the view definition. The view definition may be based on a complex SELECT statement, and the view reduces the definition to a virtual table or record set. The created record set can be used in many areas where normal tables are.

When working with a view definition, use standard commands that would be used with a table: CREATE, to create a view; ALTER, to change the view's definition; and DROP, to delete the view from the database. These commands are similar to the table commands of the same name, and serve the same function. The biggest difference is with the CREATE command, which references columns in a table, rather than storing the definition of each column.

Because the view is based on the SELECT statement, you saw that options that can enhance SELECT statements can also enhance views. These options include aggregates, joins, and views based on views.

The last section that you examined was on data manipulation through a view. These included inserts, updates, and deletes. Performing these tasks is similar to working with a table, but there are some restrictions on what can be done. You can increase these restrictions by using the WITH CHECK OPTION when creating your view. This enforces a requirement that all data modification will continue to be visible through the view.

The next sections examine two more major areas of views. Before attempting to deal with partitioned views, you should be comfortable with the topics covered thus far. If not, review them one more time. The other area that is covered is using views to control data access and ownership chains.

ALTER DATABASE OBJECTS TO SUPPORT PARTITIONED VIEWS

▶ **Alter database objects to support partitioned views.**

> **NOTE**
>
> **Server Federations** With a distributed partitioned view, the data resides on several servers that work together to maintain and display the data. These servers may be called *federated database servers*. This term is used to refer to these servers that share the data-hosting job, but are independently administered.

A partitioned view combines horizontally partitioned data from *member tables* across one or more servers (distributed partitioned views). A member table can be thought of as a segment from a larger table. There are two types of partitioned views in SQL Server: a *local partitioned view* and a *distributed partitioned view*. A local partitioned view is a partitioned view where all member tables reside on the local instance of SQL Server. Distributed partitioned views are new to SQL Server 2000 and are a bit more advanced than local partitioned views. The key difference between a distributed partitioned view and a local partitioned view is that in a local partitioned view, the data is collected from a single server alone. In contrast, a distributed partitioned view collects data from two or more instances of SQL Server, hence the name "distributed." Distributed partitioned views are used when processing needs to be spread throughout a group of servers, as shown in Figure 7.15.

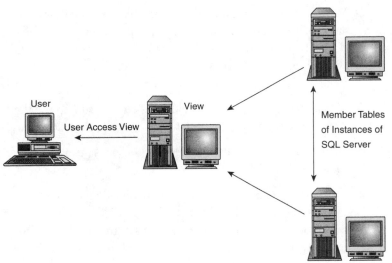

FIGURE 7.15
An illustration of a how a distributed partitioned view works.

User

User Access View

View

Member Tables
of Instances of
SQL Server

In simple words, with partitioned views, tables that store large amounts of data can be split up (using horizontal partitioning) into smaller member tables. This data in the member table holds the same number of columns as the original table; it is only the number of rows that is decreased. After the data is broken down into smaller member tables, a view defined with UNION ALL is used to bring all member tables together. This view looks like a single large resultset. When a SELECT query is run against the partitioned view, SQL Server uses CHECK constraints in determining which member table the data is from. The CHECK constraint is usually created on the Primary Key column.

> **NOTE**
>
> **Defining Union All** UNION ALL specifies that multiple queries are to be combined into a single resultset. The ALL argument specifies that all rows be incorporated, even duplicate value rows. If ALL isn't specified, duplicate values are removed.

Partitioned View Considerations and Guidelines

When creating partitioned views, you should give careful thought to a few considerations:

◆ Local partitioned views do not need to use CHECK constraints. Not using CHECK constraints also provides the same results as using a CHECK constraint, except that the Query Optimizer has to perform a lengthy search against all member tables meeting the query search condition. Using CHECK constraints reduces the cost of queries.

◆ When creating partitioned views, be sure that all columns of each member table are included in the partitioned view definition. Also, make sure that the same column is not referenced twice in the SELECT list. Make sure that all identical columns in all tables are of the same data type.

◆ When referencing member tables in a view, be sure to use the FROM clause to specifically declare a reference each table will use.

◆ Be sure that Primary Keys are defined on the same column for each member table.

◆ It is possible to create updateable partitioned views. This requires that each table's SELECT statement refers to only one base table, the UNION ALL operator is used to join the resultsets together, and non-local tables use the full four-part identifier in their names.

To decide whether you should create a partitioned view or not, you have to examine the data you will be working with, and consider how it is used. If you have a table that is used by many different department or regions (each with its own server), then you can look at partitioning the database along those lines.

For example, a company sells five major product lines. Each product line is managed by a department and each department has its own SQL Server for its specific data. All customers in the organization buy products from only one department, and there is no crossover between product lines, but all customers are stored in one table, which is stored on a central server. When looking for its own customers, each department must then SELECT against the central table, sifting through the entire customer base. Thought has been given to splitting the data into separate customer tables, but the central billing application requires that all the data be stored in one table.

In this scenario, you have an ideal candidate for a distributed (updateable) partitioned view. The customer table can be divided into tables based on product line, and joined together by a partitioned view. This enables each table to be queried individually or through the view. The CHECK constraint can be based on the product line that the customer purchases, enforcing which server is to hold the data. Even if the view is queried, the CHECK constraint is used to determine which servers and tables actually have to be queried. If the SELECT against the view uses a WHERE clause to specify product1 and `product2`, then only the servers that contain those products are queried. This reduces the volume of data that is actually queried against. In this scenario, the central billing application can make use of the partitioned view, and it appears that all the data still resides in one table. Now you have enough knowledge of partitioned views to actually implement them, which you will do in the next section.

Creating Partitioned Views

After reviewing all the guidelines for creating partitioned views, you are ready to implement them in SQL Server. When creating partitioned views, as noted earlier, the first step is cutting the table into horizontal sections, each section being called a member table and having the same number of columns and same attributes as the original table. To create a partitioned view, follow Step by Step 7.8.

STEP BY STEP

7.8 Creating a Partitioned View

1. Initiate the SQL Query Analyzer by selecting Query Analyzer from the Start menu.

2. You need the member tables to exist before you can gather the partitioned data. For this example, you will create three member tables to hold products for a multi-national food company. This company makes products to be sold in several different countries, and the products have been separated into tables related to their regions or countries. The following code creates the three tables:

```
CREATE TABLE Product1
(
   Product_ID INT PRIMARY KEY CHECK (Product_ID
   ➥BETWEEN 1 and 50),
   Product CHAR(30)
)
CREATE TABLE Product2
(
   Product_ID INT PRIMARY KEY CHECK (Product_ID
   ➥BETWEEN 51 and 100),
   Product CHAR(30)
)
```

continues

continued

```
CREATE TABLE Product3
 (
   Product_ID INT PRIMARY KEY CHECK (Product_ID
   ➡BETWEEN 101 and 150),
   Product CHAR(30)
 )
```

3. These tables have to have some data before you can combine them into a view. INSERT two records for each as follows and as shown in Figure 7.16.

```
INSERT Product1
  (Product_ID, Product)
  VALUES ('1', 'Zcheese')
INSERT Product1
  (Product_ID, Product)
  VALUES ('5', 'AustralianJam')

INSERT Product2
  (Product_ID, Product)
  VALUES ('60', 'SpicyDelights')
INSERT Product2
  (Product_ID, Product)
  VALUES ('69', 'FarEastSpecialty')

INSERT Product3
  (Product_ID, Product)
  VALUES ('120', 'DelicateClam')
INSERT Product3
  (Product_ID, Product)
  VALUES ('140', 'FishNChips')
```

4. Now, to create a partitioned view that collects all this information, execute the following code as shown in Figure 7.16.

```
CREATE VIEW AllProducts AS
  SELECT *
    FROM Product1
    UNION ALL
  SELECT *
    FROM Product2
    UNION ALL
  SELECT *
    FROM Product3
```

NOTE

Using WHERE with Your Partitioned View   When you query a distributed partitioned view based on the partitioning criteria in the WHERE clause, you are querying against only the servers that fall within the scope of the WHERE clause. This yields a performance increase for you because of the way the distributed partitioned view uses the mandatory CHECK constraint. You receive the same advantage if you use CHECK constraints on local partitioned views.

If you perform a SELECT against this view, you will find that it returns the entire resultset. This complete resultset is achieved by selecting against each individual table.

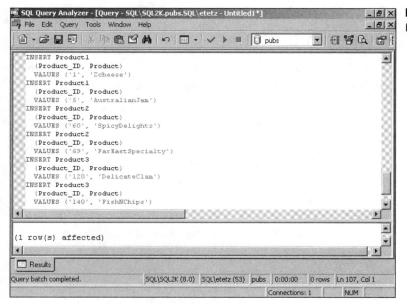

FIGURE 7.16
Inserting sample data into the member tables.

With the completion of this section, you should be able to explain what a partitioned view is and differentiate between local partitioned views and distributed partitioned views. You should also be aware that the UNION ALL operator is used to consolidate the different tables into a single view. Lastly, you should know that the table structure for each table used in the view must be identical. If you feel comfortable with this information, then move on to the next section, which covers application security through views and ownership chains.

CONTROL DATA ACCESS BY USING VIEWS

▶ **Control data access by using views.**

So far, we've looked at most of the aspects of views and data modifications. What we have not examined yet is security and permissions. The next section explains how to apply permissions through several layers of views, and ownership chains.

Granting Permissions and Ownership Chains

Views help you apply security to your database applications by how permissions are checked in your view and underlying tables. Views make it easy to control access to this data. Managing permission for views is similar to managing permissions for tables.

There are three basic commands to set permissions and five different actions that they can control. The commands are GRANT, REVOKE, and DENY. The actions are SELECT, INSERT, UPDATE, DELETE, and DRI. GRANT and DENY allow or disallow access to the view, whereas REVOKE removes a previous GRANT or DENY. SELECT, INSERT, UPDATE, and DELETE should be self-explanatory, whereas DRI enables users to create references to the view, which would be required to create an object that refers to the view with the WITH SCHEMABINDING clause. For complete information about these statements and applying permissions, refer back to Chapter 6, "Programming SQL Server 2000."

If you use the following script to create a new table and view,

```
CREATE TABLE dbo.DBOPermsTable
(
  id int,
  name varchar(20),
  description varchar(20),
  address varchar(20)
)
GO

CREATE VIEW dbo.DBOPermsView AS
  SELECT id, name
    FROM DBOPermsTable
```

then you can set permissions with the following statements:

```
REVOKE all ON DBOPermsTable TO public
DENY all ON DBOPermsTable TO Mary
REVOKE all ON DBOPermsView TO public

GRANT SELECT ON DBOPermsView to Mary
```

Even though you have not granted permissions to the underlying table, Mary still has permissions to the view, and that gives her access to the requested data. In this way, views provided additional data security because users do not need to be granted access to the source tables, and in this example, can actually be denied access to the base tables. This magic is accomplished through the *ownership chain*.

Ownership chains were designed to make it easier for you to assign permissions, and to enhance security by requiring users to have permissions to only the upper-level objects, such as views or stored procedures. As long as the same person owns all the objects in the chain, permission is only checked at the first object that she accesses. In this case, Mary was granted permission to the view (`DBOPermsView`), but was denied access to the table (`DBOPermsTable`). Because the dbo owns both objects, as access moves from the view to the table, the permissions are not checked, and Mary has access to the data. However, if Mary attempts to access the table directly, the permissions are checked at the table, and she is denied access. The reasoning behind the ownership chain works like this: If I own a table and I own the view, then when I grant permissions to the view, I obviously want the user to have access to the table. By not granting specific permissions to the table, you also restrict access to the data because this data is accessible only through the view.

Dealing with Broken Ownership Chains

One problem that can arise when you are using views occurs when you have different owners for objects in your database. Whenever there is a change in ownership, the owner of each object has to grant permissions to the object. When the ownership of objects in a chain is changed, there is a break in ownership or you have a broken ownership chain.

The following script creates tables and views for a database. It then applies permissions to the upper-layer objects. This script creates a broken ownership and illustrates the issues that you should be aware of with different object owners.

```
CREATE TABLE dbo.DBOTable1 ( id int, name varchar(20) )
CREATE TABLE bob.BobTable1 ( id int, description
➥varchar(20) )
CREATE TABLE jane.JaneTable1 ( id int, address varchar(20) )
GO

INSERT INTO dbo.DBOTable1 VALUES (1, 'Buddy')
INSERT INTO Jane.JaneTable1 VALUES (1, '123 Some Street')
INSERT INTO Bob.BobTable1 VALUES (1, 'What was his name?')
GO

CREATE VIEW Jane.JaneView1 AS
  SELECT dbo.DBOTable1.id, name, address
```

continues

continued

```
      FROM dbo.DBOTable1
      INNER JOIN Jane.JaneTable1
      ON dbo.DBOTable1.id = Jane.JaneTable1.id
GO

CREATE VIEW Jane.JaneView2 AS
  SELECT id, description
    FROM Bob.BobTable1
GO

CREATE VIEW Bob.BobView1 AS
  SELECT Jane.JaneView1.id, name, address, description
    FROM Jane.JaneView1
    INNER JOIN Jane.JaneView2
    ON Jane.JaneView1.id = Jane.JaneView2.id
GO

REVOKE all ON dbo.DBOTable1 TO public
REVOKE all ON Jane.JaneTable1 TO public
REVOKE all ON Bob.BobTable1 TO public

GRANT SELECT ON Bob.BobView1 to Mary
```

The hierarchy of data access can be seen in Figure 7.17. With the current permissions, Mary cannot access the upper-level view (BobView1), even though Bob has granted her SELECT permissions to BobView1. Mary's error message from SELECT * FROM Bob.BobView1 would look like this:

```
Server: Msg 229, Level 14, State 5, Line 1
SELECT permission denied on object 'DBOTable1', database
➡'pubs', owner 'dbo'.
Server: Msg 229, Level 14, State 1, Line 1
SELECT permission denied on object 'BobTable1', database
➡'pubs', owner 'Bob'.
Server: Msg 229, Level 14, State 1, Line 1
SELECT permission denied on object 'JaneView1', database
➡'pubs', owner 'Jane'.
Server: Msg 229, Level 14, State 1, Line 1
SELECT permission denied on object 'JaneView2', database
➡'pubs', owner 'Jane'.
```

To gain access to the view, Jane has to grant SELECT on JaneView1. This additional grant automatically gives Mary access to JaneTable1, but not DBOTable1. With the dbo providing a grant, the last holdout would be Bob to grant SELECT on BobTable1. Even though Bob created the top-level view, there is an ownership chain between his view and his table. Each time the owner changes, permissions have to be re-granted. It makes sense that if I have created a view based on your table, that does not mean you want people who access my view to have access to your table.

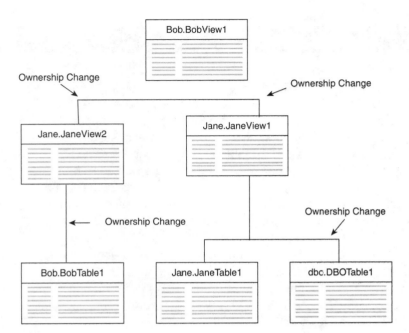

FIGURE 7.17
The data access hierarchy can lead to broken ownership chains.

When dealing with ownership chains, the single point that will reduce permission management for you is to have a single owner for the entire chain. The dbo makes a nice owner for all objects in the database. This means that you have to apply permissions only once—to the upper-level objects. If you have a broken ownership chain, then you may have to apply permissions to objects along the entire chain, which makes it more difficult to implement permissions and you will have reduced security. The reduced security is caused by the additional permissions granted to subsequent objects, which may create holes in your data security.

To assign dbo as the owner of objects you are creating, you have to specify dbo in the object name your are creating. For example, to create a view for dbo, you could use CREATE VIEW dbo.NewView AS . . . . You must be a member of the role.

CASE STUDY: BOSS NEEDS TO SCREEN DATA

ESSENCE OF THE CASE

- ▶ A new table is launched onto the database and is accessed by many users.

- ▶ The table contains private information about employees.

- ▶ Your boss needs you to restrict access to some of the data in this table, without changing the structure of the table. This needs to be fixed before he starts getting complaints about the private information becoming public information.

SCENARIO

Entering your office room, you find a note from your boss concerning confidential and private information given out to users accessing the newly set up table Employees, and he states that he urgently needs you to find a solution. With the number of users accessing your database, it is likely that many will pry into the leaked information, so you must finish this task at the earliest possible time. Your boss states that he may receive objections from employees about disclosed personal information, such as salary, from the newly created Employees table. You know your boss is waiting for an answer so you quickly look for a solution.

ANALYSIS

You quickly investigate the SQL Server Books Online and seem to find a solution. You are astonished to find such a simple solution that can be applied in less than five minutes. The solution is the view. Because you have a stronger background in the administration of SQL Server, you may have not known how to implement a view, which is often considered to be a design topic. Then you scroll down to the bottom of the article and find that a view may also be implemented with the easy-to-use interface of the SQL Server Enterprise Manager. Relieved, you read on to learn how to actually limit the rows and columns using the apparent power of the view. You come across a term called "filtering" and learn that it means selecting or deselecting columns (vertical) or rows (horizontal). You implement a filtering view strategy, so that users see only what they need to see, and decide to learn more about the development side of SQL Server 2000.

CHAPTER SUMMARY

This chapter covered a lot of material related to implementing views. To ensure that you picked up on the most important points, take a quick look at them.

You saw that views resemble tables in concept and many operations that you execute against tables can also be executed against views. These include SELECT, INSERT, UPDATE, and DELETE statements. The one major difference between views and tables was that views refer to tables, and do not actually contain their own data. A view could be related to a television set; it doesn't actually store movies but makes it possible for you to view them remotely.

You saw that the CREATE VIEW statement defines the view, and saw that it is based on a SELECT statement, with some restrictions. The basic function of the statement is to define the range of data (columns and rows) that should be displayed from the table or tables used in the view. You also saw that many advanced features of the SELECT statement, such as joins and aggregates, carry over to views.

Data modification with views introduced several restrictions that prevent many types of modifications (INSERT, UPDATE, and DELETE) from happening. You were introduced to the WITH CHECK OPTION, which further restricts what you can do. These restrictions serve two purposes: they enable you to validate the data you enter and to make restrictions to prevent unwanted data modifications.

The next topic was ownership chains. You learned that if the same person owns a series of objects, such as views and the base tables, then she has to grant permissions to only the upper-layer objects or views. This is designed to make administration easier. You also learned what happens if you don't own all the objects, and what is required to grant access to the data. Object ownership should be limited to a single user: dbo.

Data access performance was dealt with when you examined what partitioned views are. You learned that partitioned views can be local to one server or distributed across many servers. Two main items you had to remember about partitioned views were the use of CHECK constraints (to define what data is found in what table) and the view (which is created using the UNION ALL operator).

KEY TERMS

- ALTER VIEW
- distributed partitioned view
- DROP VIEW
- local partitioned view
- partitioned view
- CREATE VIEW
- WITH ENCRYPTION
- WITH SCHEMABINDING

APPLY YOUR KNOWLEDGE

Exercises

Exercise 7.1   Creating a Filtered View

This exercise demonstrates how to create two different views. These views implement vertical and horizontal filters. Many of the views that you will implement on databases will utilize some type of filtering.

Estimated Time: 10 minutes.

1. Open the Query Analyzer from the Start menu.

2. To create a new view using vertical filtering, select the Pubs database and enter the following query:

```
CREATE VIEW SelectedColumns AS
  SELECT Au_ID, State, au_FName
    FROM Authors
```

3. Step 2 creates a view that includes only the State and Au_fname columns. To create a view that includes only rows where the first name has the letter *J* as the first letter, enter the following code:

```
CREATE VIEW SelectedRows AS
  SELECT  *
    FROM Authors
    WHERE au_fname LIKE 'J%'
```

4. Test your view by running a SELECT against the view. Your SELECT statement should return all columns and rows so that you can see how much data is now available through the view. If you have not already done so, you should also SELECT the entire Authors table, in order to see how much data is in the base table.

Exercise 7.2   Renaming and Dropping Views

This example demonstrates renaming and dropping views using sp_rename and DROP VIEW. Any job that is done can either be done better or becomes obsolete.

This exercise shows you how to change an established view's name, as well as remove an obsolete view.

Estimated Time: 10 minutes.

1. Open the SQL Server Query Analyzer by selecting it from the Start menu. Connect to your server, and change to the Pubs database.

2. Examine the contents of the Titles table by selecting the entire contents.

3. You first have to create a view. To do this, enter the following code:

```
CREATE VIEW ExampleView AS
  SELECT  *
    FROM titles
    WHERE type = 'business'
```

4. Test your new view by selecting against it.

5. To change the previously created view's name to TestView, enter the following code:

```
sp_rename 'ExampleView', 'TestView', OBJECT
```

6. Examine what views exist in the Pubs database using the following statement:

```
SELECT name
  FROM sysobjects
  WHERE type='V'
```

7. To delete TestView (formerly ExampleView), enter the following query:

```
DROP VIEW TestView
```

8. Re-examine the views that exist in the Pubs database using the same command that you used in Step 6.

APPLY YOUR KNOWLEDGE

Exercise 7.3 Creating a Partitioned View

This exercise demonstrates creating a partitioned view from member tables. You start by creating two base tables, and then you join them through the creation of a view.

Estimated Time: 15 minutes.

1. Open the SQL Server Query Analyzer by selecting it from the Start menu. Connect to your server, and change to the Pubs database.

2. To begin, you will need to create two tables that act as members—the tables that will be joined together. To do this, follow this code:

```
CREATE TABLE member1
(
    Identification INT
      PRIMARY KEY
      CHECK (Identification BETWEEN 1 and 20),
    Name varchar(20)
)

CREATE TABLE member2
(
    Identification INT
      PRIMARY KEY
      CHECK (Identification BETWEEN 21 and
40),
    Name varchar(20)
)
```

3. Now INSERT some example data into the member tables you created in Step 1. To do this, execute the following queries:

```
INSERT member1
  (Identification, Name)
  VALUES ('7', 'Abraham')
INSERT member1
  (Identification, Name)
  VALUES ('18', 'Jauna')

INSERT member2
  (Identification, Name)
  VALUES ('23', 'John )
INSERT member2
  (Identification, Name)
```

```
  VALUES ('36', 'Dennis')
```

4. To create a view that combines these two member tables, execute the following:

```
CREATE VIEW AllProducts AS
  SELECT *
    FROM member1
    UNION ALL
  SELECT *
    FROM member2
```

5. Test your new view by running a SELECT against it. You should have a complete listing of all four records.

Exercise 7.4 Accessing a View

This exercise shows you how to access a view by displaying its definition and dependencies. Being able to research a view's definition and dependencies is useful when trying to find out why a view may not be working.

Estimated Time: 10 minutes.

1. Open the SQL Server Query Analyzer by selecting it from the Start menu. Log in and select the Pubs database.

2. Create a new view by executing the following query:

```
CREATE VIEW BusinessTitleView AS
  SELECT *
    FROM titles
    WHERE type = 'business'
```

3. To access the definition of this view, execute the following:

```
EXEC sp_helptext TitleView
```

4. To display any view dependencies, use the following query:

```
sp_depends TitleView
```

APPLY YOUR KNOWLEDGE

Review Questions

1. Describe in relative terms how much data a view is capable of containing and the storage requirements that may be necessary for a view.

2. How does the CHECK constraint help in the implementation of partitioned views?

3. What is the advantage of creating a view that is based on a view, rather than on a table?

4. When would you want to use a partitioned view?

5. Generally speaking, when would you want to implement a view into your database?

6. Which objects are not allowed to be associated with a view?

7. When modifying data through a view, what are you actually modifying?

Exam Questions

1. Which of the following statements best describes a view?

    A. A table stored on physical memory whose contents are derived from a query

    B. A definition of what data should be extracted from a table or tables

    C. A normal table except that it can be partitioned

    D. The way a table is shown is SQL Server

2. Tom is interested in examining ways to improve his data access performance through view imple-mentations. He is currently managing a database that is replicated between five servers (for load balancing) and contains customer information for six sales divisions. The Customer table currently contains a consolidated list of 100,000 customer records. What could Tom try to implement to improve server performance?

    A. Aggregated views

    B. Partitioned views

    C. Complex views

    D. Full outer views

3. Which of the following is a benefit provided by a view? Choose all that apply.

    A. Minimize unneeded data.

    B. Security is enforced using views.

    C. Data is easily transformable.

    D. Data can be easily exported using tools, such as BCP.

4. Henry is the system administrator of the data-bases at his company. Users who access the data-base often query the Sales table, which has more than 50,000 rows and 15 columns. Most of the columns retrieved by users are unnecessarily retrieved. Henry needs to disallow the retrieval of the unnecessary columns and allow users to retrieve only the data that is needed. He decides to use a view. Which of the following tools can Henry use to create views? Choose all that apply.

    A. Query Analyzer

    B. SQL Server Enterprise Manager

C. View Edit Wizard (VEW)

D. None of the above

5. John works in a major telecom company. Each table in his central database has numerous columns and he wants to create a view by joining data from four tables. He does this, so that he can enable users to retrieve data efficiently from a view rather than retrieving the different columns manually by using JOIN statements. What is the maximum number of columns that can be joined by the view John is creating?

A. 250

B. 1024

C. It depends on the number of tables being referenced

D. An unlimited amount

6. Jauna works for a trading company and has a massive amount of data held in databases that are found on multiple servers. This was done because they thought that putting the tables on multiple servers would ensure more efficient data access. Which of the following would you use to gather all this data into a single unit?

A. Indexed view

B. Replication view

C. Distributed partitioned view

D. Extended partitioned view

7. Your company keeps track of all sales on a monthly basis. The company requires that the sales manager enter all sales that are greater than $20,000 into a database. They do not want the sales manager to be able to enter values that are less than $20,000 in the database. You are in charge of creating a view for the Sales table that includes the following columns: amount, date, and sales_person. You would like this view to enable the sales manager to enter the valid sales figures. Which of the following describes the view needed?

A.
```
CREATE VIEW ApprovedSales AS
SELECT date, Sales_Person, Amount
FROM Sales
WHERE Amount<=20000
```

B.
```
CREATE VIEW ApprovedSales AS
SELECT Number, SalesPerson, Amount
FROM Sales
HAVING Amount<=20000
```

C.
```
CREATE VIEW ApprovedSales AS
SELECT date, SalesPerson, Amount
FROM Sales
WHERE Amount<=20000
WITH CHECK OPTION
```

D.
```
CREATE VIEW ApprovedSales AS
SELECT Number, SalesPerson, Amount
FROM Sales
HAVING Amount<=20000
WITH CHECK OPTION
```

8. Chris works as a SQL Server database developer in the technical department of a nationwide bookstore. Chris needs to create a view by filtering data for the 50 customers having greatest payments due from the Customers table. Which strategy would be the best for him to use?

A. Retrieve slices of the Customers table horizontally

B. Retrieve slices of the Customers table vertically

C. Both A and B

D. Use the filtered view, new to SQL Server 2000

APPLY YOUR KNOWLEDGE

9. You are working on your new view called `SummaryData`, which uses complex aggregates and joins for a company database. The view `SummaryData` you have just created took you a good amount of time and effort. You don't want other users to see how you created your view. What is the best and easiest way to implement this type of security?

    A. Create it with the `WITH ENCRYPTION` option.

    B. Create it with the `WITH CHECK` option.

    C. Create it in Enterprise Manager and select Hidden Definition

    D. Create it with the `HIDDEN DEFINITION` option.

10. You work with several developers who regularly `CREATE`, `DROP`, and `ALTER` views within your database. These actions have been causing many views to malfunction when dependent objects are altered. What option can you use to prevent some of your problems?

    A. `CREATE INDEXED VIEW`

    B. The `WITH SCHEMABINDING` option

    C. The `WITH ENCRYPTION` option

    D. The `WITH CHECK` option

11. Jeffery has just created a view to enforce data security on the `Sales` table. You are an assistant developer and are receiving complaints relating to the view Jeffery created some time ago. You assume that he made mistakes when creating the view and so in an attempt to do some cleanup, you try to access the view definition. When trying to access the definition of the view, you find that you are not able to. What is the most common reason to not be able to access a view definition?

    A. Jeffery specified the Encrypt On View option when he created the view.

    B. Jeffery specified `SECURE DEFINITION` when he created the view.

    C. Jeffery did not repair the view since the first time it was created three months ago.

    D. Jeffery used WITH ENCYPTION when he created the view.

12. You are troubleshooting an access problem with a view. Mary is having problems using Bob's new view, `Bob.BobView1`. Examine the following exhibits to figure out what is causing Mary's access problem. Exhibit 1 contains the tables that are in the database, Exhibit 2 contains the definitions of the views that are in the database, and Exhibit 3 are the permissions that were assigned to each object. After examining the exhibits, choose the best answer to explain Mary's access problem.

    Exhibit 1: Create Tables

    ```
    CREATE TABLE dbo.DBOTable1
    (
      id int,
      name varchar(20)
    )

    CREATE TABLE bob.BobTable1
    (
      id int,
      description varchar(20)
    )

    CREATE TABLE jane.JaneTable1
    (
      id int,
      address varchar(20)
    )
    GO

    INSERT INTO dbo.DBOTable1 VALUES (1, 'Buddy')
    INSERT INTO Jane.JaneTable1 VALUES (1, '123
    ➥Some Street')
    INSERT INTO Bob.BobTable1 VALUES (1, 'What
    ➥was his name?')
    ```

APPLY YOUR KNOWLEDGE

Exhibit 2: Create Views

```
CREATE VIEW Jane.JaneView1 AS
  SELECT dbo.DBOTable1.id, name, address
    FROM dbo.DBOTable1
    INNER JOIN Jane.JaneTable1
    ON dbo.DBOTable1.id = Jane.JaneTable1.id
GO

CREATE VIEW Jane.JaneView2
  WITH ENCRYPTION AS
  SELECT id, description
    FROM Bob.BobTable1
GO


CREATE VIEW Bob.BobView1 AS
  SELECT Jane.JaneView1.id, name, address,
➥description
    FROM Jane.JaneView1
    INNER JOIN Jane.JaneView2
    ON Jane.JaneView1.id = Jane.JaneView2.id
```

Exhibit 3: Assign Permissions

```
REVOKE all ON dbo.DBOTable1 TO public
REVOKE all ON Jane.JaneTable1 TO public
REVOKE all ON Bob.BobTable1 TO public

GRANT SELECT ON Bob.BobView1 TO Jane, Mary
GRANT SELECT ON Jane.JaneView1 TO Mary, Bob,
➥dbo
GRANT SELECT ON dbo.DBOTable1 TO Jane
GRANT SELECT ON Bob.BobTable1 TO Mary, Jane
GRANT SELECT ON Jane.JaneTable1 TO Bob, dbo
GRANT SELECT ON Jane.JaneView2 TO Mary
```

A. When you create a view using WITH ENCRYPTION, you must use GRANT WITH DECRYPTION.

B. One GRANT is missing for Mary.

C. Two GRANTs are missing for Mary.

D. There is nothing wrong with the code in the exhibits; the problem is likely with Mary's network connection.

13. Mary has created a view that is going to be used to create an employee phone list. She would like to sort the new view by the employees' last names. She has tried to create the view using the ORDER BY clause, but it always fails. What can Mary do to create her view?

A. Order the base table using a clustered index, then the required data will already be in the correct order.

B. Use the TOP clause rather than the ORDER BY clause.

C. Use the TOP clause in addition to the ORDER BY clause.

D. This clause cannot be used.

Answers to Review Questions

1. A view refers to data that is found in a table. The view does not actually contain any data. Although it takes up some space in the sysobjects and syscomments tables, in relative terms, the storage requirements are very small.

2. The CHECK constraint is used to identify which portion of the data can be found in which table. This published division speeds up searches for data through the view.

3. If you base a view on an existing view, you can further restrict, filter, or merge data that is currently defined through the existing view or views.

4. Generally, you would want to use a partitioned view when you want to gather information from many tables and make them appear as a single table. You may need to do this if you have split your data across several servers. This is done in some circumstances to improve data access performance.

APPLY YOUR KNOWLEDGE

5. You should implement a view in your database when you would like to disallow redundant data, enforce security, or export data easily.

6. Defaults, triggers and rules are not allowed to be associated with a view. INSTEAD OF triggers may be defined on a view. Even though a view is defined by a SELECT statement, it is not allowed to use the COMPUTE BY or SELECT INTO clauses. The ORDER BY clause may only be used in conjunction with the TOP clause. Finally, views cannot be based on temporary tables.

7. When data is being modified, deleted, and updated through a view, the data definition in the view does not change; the data modification is aimed at the underlying referenced tables associated with the view.

Answers to Exam Questions

1. **B.** A view does not contain data as a table does. It is often accessed with methods that are similar to those you use with a table, but the view is a definition or description of data that should be retrieved from a table or tables. For more information about view basics, see the section "Understanding Views."

2. **B.** Partitioned views, and specifically distributed partitioned views, may improve the data access for Tom's database. Because a large number of rows could be separated by sales division per server (with one server maintaining information for two divisions), his database tables may be ideal candidates for distributed partitioned views. For more information about partitioned views, see the section "Creating Partitioned Views."

3. **A, B, D.** The main benefits of views are that they disallow unneeded data, improve security enforcement, ease data exporting and generally make querying easier. For more information about the benefits for views, see the section "View Benefits."

4. **A, B.** Both the Query Analyzer and the SQL Server Enterprise Manager can create views. For more information about creating views, see the section "Creating Views."

5. **B.** A total of 1024 columns can be referenced in a view definition. For more information about what a view is and some of its restrictions, see the section "Understanding Views."

6. **C.** A distributed partitioned view collects data from two or more instances of SQL Server, hence the name "distributed." Essentially, distributed partitioned views are used when you want to spread processing out over a group of servers, but want the data to be treated as a single unit. For more information about partitioned views, see the section "Alter Database Objects to Support Partitioned Views."

7. **C.** The WITH CHECK OPTION forces all data modification statements executed against the view to adhere to the criteria set within the view definition. When a row is modified through a view, the WITH CHECK OPTION guarantees that the data remains visible through the view after the modification has been committed. For more information about restrictions on data modifications, see the section "Updating Rows Through Views."

8. **A.** Horizontally filtering the table will work because he can use a WHERE clause to query for the 50 customers having the greatest due payments.

APPLY YOUR KNOWLEDGE

For more information about filtering data, see the section "Selecting Specific Columns and Rows.'

9. **A.** The WITH ENCRYPTION option protects the definition of your view. When you specify this, you encrypt the definition of your view because you may not want users to display it. Encrypting using WITH ENCRYPTION disallows users from seeing your view, whether they use sp_helptext or view it through the Enterprise Manager. For more information about encrypting your views, see the section "Accessing Views."

10. **B.** WITH SCHEMABINDING specifies that the view be bound to the schema. When this is done, objects with dependent objects cannot be modified. For more information about options that are available when creating views, see the section "Creating Views."

11. **D.** When Jeffery created the view for security reasons, he used the WITH ENCRYPTION option to secure his definition. Any user who tries to view the view definition will see encrypted lines of code, impossible to understand. For more information about options that are available when creating views, see the section "Creating Views."

12. **B.** Although Mary has not been granted the SELECT permission to DBOTable1 or JaneTable1, she requires only a GRANT for SELECT on DBOTable1. She will be automatically allowed to use JaneTable1 because it will be through Jane's view. For more information about permissions and ownership chains, see the section "Control Data Access by Using Views."

13. **C.** If you need to use the ORDER BY clause, then you also have to specify the TOP clause, such as TOP 100 PERCENT. For more information about restrictions on creating views, see the section "View Creation Guidelines."

Suggested Readings and Resources

1. Inside SQL Server 2000 – Kalen Delaney (www.insidesqlserver.com)

   This is not a beginner book, but it fills in many of the gaps left out of the SQL Server Books Online documentation. Explains fully how SQL Server stores and processes data internally.

2. SQL Server 2000 Books Online

   • SQL Server Architecture: Database Architecture: Logical Database Components: SQL Views. This contains basic information about the creation and definition of views.

   • Creating and Maintaining Databases: Views: Creating a View: Creating a Partitioned View. This document introduces you to partitioned views.

   • Administering SQL Server: Managing Security: Managing Permissions: Using Ownership Chains. These documents cover how ownership chains work and how to manage security with them.

Create and alter database objects. Objects include triggers, and how to specify schema binding and encryption settings.

▶ This objective in general requires you to know how to create triggers using the CREATE TRIGGER statement. When creating triggers, you also need to know how to set properties such as definition encryption.

Manage data manipulation by using triggers including validate data.

▶ This objective deals with controlling what goes in and what gets deleted in your table. You need to know how to create UPDATE, DELETE, and INSERT triggers and when to use them.

Control data access by using triggers.

▶ This objective is linked to the previous objective on managing data manipulation. This objective looks specifically at how triggers can be used to restrict which users are able to modify the data protected by a trigger.

Enforce procedural business logic by using triggers.

- **Specify trigger actions.**

- **Filter data by using triggers.**

▶ This objective looks at creating the actual contents of the trigger. This includes writing procedural code to fire when an UPDATE, DELETE, or INSERT statement is executed. Take a look at Chapter 6, "Programming SQL Server 2000," to see how to create professional triggers.

Troubleshoot and optimize programming objects. Objects include triggers.

▶ This objective deals with altering and viewing triggers to make them more efficient. This chapter includes lots of tips to help you create efficient, working triggers.

CHAPTER 8

Triggers

▶ Be prepared to deal with questions that test your knowledge of the options that are used with the CREATE TRIGGER and ALTER TRIGGER statements. Make sure you know what options such as NOT FOR REPLICATION and WITH ENCRYPTION do, because these are the two main options that can be used with triggers. The WITH ENCRYPTION option should be easy to remember, because it prevents viewing the definition of the object, which is the same thing that it does for views and stored procedures.

▶ Understand how INSTEAD OF triggers work. They are new and have a high chance of being on the exam. You should know how to implement these triggers on a view, because they are the only triggers that can be applied to a view. Views have specific requirements to allow updates to be carried out, and INSTEAD OF triggers can be used to allow updates on views that might not normally allow updates.

▶ Be able to create professional triggers. Professional triggers should handle error trapping and single or multi-row operations. In addition to following the Step by Steps and exercises in this chapter, create triggers on your own. For information on error handling and trapping, read Chapter 9, "Stored Procedures and User-Defined Functions."

▶ Finally, know what actions can cause a trigger to execute. There are only three: UPDATE, DELETE and INSERT. A single trigger can be tied to one or more of these actions. There can be multiple AFTER triggers for each action, but only a single INSTEAD OF trigger per action.

INTRODUCTION

This chapter takes a close look at triggers. Triggers are sections of SQL Server programming code that execute when data modification is performed on a table in the database.

Triggers offer a method of constraining data input and performing other tasks when data is added, deleted, or updated in the database. Other methods of constraining data include using constraints and rules. Constraints and defaults are covered in Chapter 3, "Physical Database Design." To learn more about writing programming code that can be implemented by a trigger, see Chapter 9, "Stored Procedures and User-Defined Functions."

Triggers perform an important role in SQL Server 2000: They enable you to control what happens when a user inserts, deletes, or updates data in the tables or views in your database. This control can be used to restrict the values that are inserted, prevent deletion of records, update related tables, store denormalized data, or log actions. Triggers might be used for these reasons and others, but many triggers are used to restrict or constrain data input when traditional constraints are not capable enough. A trigger contains code that is similar to a stored procedure, but it is automatically executed when an INSERT, DELETE, or UPDATE statement is invoked. Triggers are often used to help enforce and follow business logic for your organization.

For instance, imagine a company that has a sales database that records invoice line items in a table. If they decide to implement a minimum sales value for each line item on the invoice, they can use a CHECK constraint to enforce this setting. If they want to create custom minimum value for individual products, then a constraint will not do; they must use a trigger. They can create a new table or add a minimum sales value column to their existing Products table. Because each product can have a different minimum sales value, a trigger can query the table to locate the minimum value and ensure that the current value is above the minimum.

CONSTRAINING DATA MODIFICATIONS

Triggers play a role in the database environment in constraining data that is modified in the database. Some other techniques that are used for constraining data include views, stored procedures, defaults, rules, and constraints. The data constraining method that is best for you at any given time depends on a number of variables, such as permissions on tables, the number of tables tested against, and desired performance or CPU cost.

Views

Views can be used to restrict what data is visible in a database. Because you can restrict what is visible in the view, you can restrict what data can be deleted. Views can also be created with the WITH CHECK OPTION. When the view is created using WITH CHECK OPTION, the view enables data to be added to the database only if the resulting data will be visible in the view.

If you compare views to triggers, triggers offer much greater flexibility in controlling what can be added, deleted, or modified in the database. Although views are very restricted in their power, they also have a very low processor cost. Views can restrict inserts into the database, but their main function is to restrict visibility of data.

For more information about views, consult Chapter 7, "Working with Views."

Stored Procedures

Stored procedures can be used to modify data rather than allowing users to access that data tables directly. When using stored procedures, you are able to write simple or complex logic that is performed when the stored procedure executes. Rather than the user issuing the statements manually, the stored procedure is used to make the modification based on parameters passed to the procedure. Stored procedures can impose rules and policies on the modification, and can perform complex procedures without the possibility of user-induced errors.

When comparing stored procedures to triggers, and assuming that the code used in each is of similar complexity, both offer some advantages. Stored procedures might be less CPU-intensive on data failures than AFTER triggers, because an AFTER trigger reverses the data modifications, whereas a stored procedure just doesn't make the data modification. Stored procedures follow the same ownership chain rules as views do. For example, if you own a table, and you own the stored procedure that performs an action on the table (such as a DELETE), then you only need to grant the EXECUTE permission to the stored procedure and do not need to grant the DELETE permission to the table. In this way, the stored procedures can offer greater data security; but when you implement a trigger, the code will be executed when the data is modified in the table, regardless of whether the stored procedure is used or not. This function of triggers is useful, because some people are granted access directly to the table and the code will still be executed.

For more information about stored procedures, consult Chapter 9.

Defaults

Defaults do not restrict what data is put into a table, but rather are used to provide values for columns into which you are not inserting data. An example of a default would be a company that is based in the United States with 80% of its client base in the U.S. This company might decide to place a default on the country field in its customer table, because in most cases it will be correct. This default is used only if the INSERT statement does not provide a country value.

A trigger can be used to provide default values when values are missing on an insert, but at a higher cost than defaults. Defaults are a lower-level option, so they can be applied more efficiently; however, triggers are able to make decisions on what values should be applied based on other criteria. Whenever possible, keep it simple by using defaults, and only resort to triggers if you need to make a choice between values.

For more information about defaults, consult Chapter 3.

Rules

Rules have been implemented in SQL Server 2000 for backward compatibility. They operate in a fashion similar to CHECK constraints—which are now preferred—with the exception that only one rule can be bound to a column of a table, whereas there can be multiple CHECK constraints on a single column. The following code shows how to implement a rule to restrict the guess column in the guesses table to a number between 1 and 10.

```
CREATE RULE guess_check AS @gu BETWEEN 1 and 10
GO
CREATE TABLE guesses
   (
   user_id   int
   PRIMARY KEY,
   guess   int,
   )
GO
sp_bindrule guess_check, 'guesses.guess'
GO
```

Rules offer very basic tests for valid data. Rules apply only to inserted and modified data, but perform no actions on deleted rows. Rules operate with a very low processor cost.

For more information about rules, consult Chapter 3.

Constraints

There are five basic constraints that can be used to restrict inserts and updates: NOT NULL, CHECK, UNIQUE, PRIMARY KEY, and FOREIGN KEY. These constraints place restrictions on what data can be inserted or updated in the database. FOREIGN KEY constraints can also be used to restrict what data can be deleted from the database.

Constraints offer a fair amount of flexibility, but do not possess the level of code or logic that is present in a trigger. Triggers can reference columns in other tables, and can evaluate the change in the data because they can examine the data both before and after modification. In general, constraints should be used when possible because they are more efficient and cost less on the CPU, and triggers should be used whenever constraints are not powerful enough to perform the job. Constraints are executed after INSTEAD OF triggers, but before AFTER triggers.

The following code tests for valid data by means of a constraint, which was discussed earlier:

```
CREATE TABLE guesses
    (
    user_id  int  PRIMARY KEY,
    guess  int,
    CONSTRAINT check_guess CHECK (guess BETWEEN 1 and 10 )
    )
```

The following would be an AFTER trigger method of implementing the same task:

```
CREATE TABLE guesses
    (
    user_id  int  PRIMARY KEY,
    guess  int
    )
GO
CREATE TRIGGER guess_trigger
    ON guesses
    FOR INSERT, UPDATE
    AS
      IF UPDATE (guess)
        IF NOT ((SELECT guess FROM inserted) BETWEEN 1 AND
        ➡10)
          BEGIN
            ROLLBACK TRAN
            RAISERROR ('Guesses must be between 1 and 10.',
            ➡16, 1)
          END
```

In this example, the trigger is performing only a rudimentary task, but does enable you to create a custom error message. You will see how triggers are created later in this chapter.

For a quick comparison of the difference between the different types of constraint methods, see Table 8.1.

TABLE 8.1

COMPARING CONSTRAINTS, TRIGGERS, AND STORED PROCEDURES

Constraining Method	Description	Benefit	Drawback
NOT NULL	Forces a column to not accept NULL values.	Offers the most efficient way to prevent NULL columns.	It only verifies that the column is not NULL, it cannot test for specific values.
CHECK	Performs a Boolean test on simple conditions, such as entered value was BETWEEN 1 AND 10.	This offers a quick test to ensure that the value entered is valid. This constraint does not use a high level of processor activity.	The types of test are very rudimentary. When test fails the transaction is rolled back, there is no other error handling that can perform additional actions.

| TABLE 8.1 | *continued* |

COMPARING CONSTRAINTS, TRIGGERS, AND STORED PROCEDURES

Constraining Method	*Description*	*Benefit*	*Drawback*
UNIQUE	Ensures that all values entered in the column or set of columns are unique from each other. NULL values are allowed.	UNIQUE constraints are more efficient than unique indexes.	Like CHECK constraints, when the constraint fails, the only action that is performed is a rollback of the transaction.
PRIMARY KEY	Ensures that all values entered in the column or set of columns are unique. NULL values are not allowed.	Every table should have a PRIMARY KEY, since a unique column will ensure a unique record, and may improve the speed of sorting and searching.	Like CHECK constraints, when the constraint fails, the only action that is performed is a rollback of the transaction.
FOREIGN KEY	References values that are stored in another table. This constraint can also force entered values to exist in the referenced table.	FOREIGN KEY constraints can support an ON DELETE action, as well as ON UPDATE action. Either of these actions can fail the transaction with NO ACTION or CASCADE, which will fail the command and rollback the transaction, or update or delete the referenced information.	FOREIGN KEY constraints can only rollback transactions, and cannot perform more complex actions when data fails the constraint.
TRIGGER	Automatically execute SQL scripts when data update events occur. Events include INSERT, UPDATE, and DELETE statements. INSTEAD OF triggers fire before constraints are checked, while AFTER triggers are fired after the constraints are checked.	Triggers are capable of performing a complex sequence of commands that can carry out tests and actions on the data. These tests and actions can be more in-depth than CHECK, PRIMARY KEY, and FOREIGN KEY constraints.	Triggers are more processor intensive than constraint actions, and should only be used when constraints will not satisfy the requirements of the data.
STORED PROCEDURE	An SQL script that can carry out an action.	Stored procedures can be executed instead of INSERT, UPDATE, and DELETE commands. They can then perform a complex sequence of tests and actions prior to issuing the INSERT, UPDATE, and DELETE commands.	Stored procedures do not execute automatically with data modifications, and must be specifically called.

For more information about constraints, consult Chapter 3. The next section examines the creation and management of triggers, and later in the chapter you will learn the differences between different types of triggers.

TRIGGERS

> ▶ **Create and alter database objects. Objects include triggers, and how to specify schema binding and encryption settings.**

This section begins with an overview of triggers, followed by an examination of how to create and manage triggers. Later, this chapter goes into depth with AFTER and INSTEAD OF triggers, but this section discusses triggers in general. When points that are specific to one type of trigger or another are discussed, we identify which type of trigger (AFTER or INSTEAD OF) they apply to. This section comes full circle, from the creation of a trigger, through altering and renaming the trigger, and finally dropping the trigger.

Overview of Triggers

SQL Server's capability in managing data extends to controlling data as it is manipulated in the table. There are two main types of triggers: AFTER and INSTEAD OF triggers. Triggers can be used for a number of tasks, including data validation. Triggers are pieces of T-SQL programming code (like stored procedures are) that execute when data is manipulated within a table. The data manipulation could be an INSERT, DELETE, or UPDATE. There is no way to force a trigger to execute without performing the associated data modification on the table. Triggers can be used to enforce the business rules in a database when constraints are not sufficient. Typically, triggers are a more CPU-intensive way to implement tasks, and you are usually better off to implement restrictions through constraints, such as FOREIGN KEY or CHECK constraints, because they do not cause performance to suffer as much. Most of the performance impact that triggers suffer from occurs when they reference tables that are not in memory.

Triggers provide many advantages and benefits. The following list sums them up:

◆ Triggers are capable of enforcing complex restrictions as opposed to CHECK constraints, such as raising a user-defined error using the RAISERROR() command.

◆ Triggers can be used to track or log changes to a table.

◆ More than one AFTER trigger can be created on a table. With INSTEAD OF triggers, only one trigger of each type (INSERT, UPDATE, or DELETE) can be created on a table.

◆ Triggers consume relatively more performance than FOREIGN KEY constraints. If the trigger references only tables that are in memory, then performance is similar.

◆ Stored procedures, both local and remote, might be executed from triggers.

When working with triggers, it is important to remember the order in which they execute. INSTEAD OF triggers execute instead of the attempted data modification (INSERT, UPDATE, or DELETE). The INSTEAD OF trigger could actually proceed to perform the modification to the table itself. Constraints are applied after the INSTEAD OF trigger, and AFTER triggers are executed after the constraints and data modification takes place.

Creating Triggers

Before you look at the syntax of the CREATE TRIGGER statement, you should be aware of a few facts about triggers. Then after you study the syntax of the CREATE TRIGGER statement, you can look at creating a trigger in both Query Analyzer and Enterprise Manager.

◆ Triggers can process all three actions: UPDATE, DELETE and INSERT.

◆ AFTER triggers apply to a single table and can be made column-level.

◆ AFTER triggers cannot be created on views or temporary tables.

◆ INSTEAD OF triggers are the only triggers that can be created on views.

◆ Triggers can be created with the SQL Server Enterprise Manager, the Query Analyzer, and programmatically through SQL-DMO.

◆ Triggers are database objects and follow object-naming conventions.

◆ Triggers can be created and altered by the sysadmin, db_owner and db_ddladmin roles, as well as the table owner.

◆ Triggers cannot use any of the following statements:

```
CREATE
DROP
ALTER TABLE
GRANT
REVOKE
DISK
ALTER DATABASE
LOAD DATABASE
RESTORE DATABASE
UPDATE STATISTICS
SELECT INTO
LOAD TRANSACTION
RECONFIGURE
```

Now it's time to examine the CREATE TRIGGER statement. The following lists the basic syntax of the CREATE TRIGGER and then gives an explanation to each argument:

```
CREATE TRIGGER [owner.]trigger_name
  ON [owner.]{table_name | view_name}
  [WITH ENCRYPTION]
  {FOR | AFTER | INSTEAD OF} {INSERT, UPDATE, DELETE}
  [NOT FOR REPLICATION]
    AS
      [IF UPDATE (column)]
      [{AND | OR} UPDATE (column)]
        sql_statements
```

◆ Trigger_name. The name of the new trigger; most follow the naming rules for identifiers.

◆ Table_name. The name of the table on which the trigger is executed.

◆ WITH ENCRYPTION. Encrypts the contents or description of the trigger by encrypting the record in the syscomments table. This prevents anyone (including you) from being able to read the

trigger definition and seeing what the trigger does. As with
views, this might be done for security or to protect your development investment or intellectual property.

◆ AFTER. Specifies that the trigger be executed after all operations
specified in the triggered SQL statement have executed in success. This trigger fires after any constraints or rules that are on
the table. FOR might also be used to create an AFTER trigger. FOR
is supported for backward compatibility.

◆ INSTEAD OF. Specifies that the trigger is fired rather than the
triggering SQL statements. This allows the trigger to execute
prior to constraints and rules that might be on the table.

◆ {INSERT, UPDATE, DELETE}. Specifies which actions invoke
the trigger.

◆ [NOT FOR REPLICATION]. Specifies that the trigger should not
fire when a replication process changes the underlying table.

◆ IF UPDATE (*column*). Specifies that the trigger applies to
updates in only certain columns. AND operators and OR operators can be used to have these statements apply to updates in
multiple columns. This statement applies only to AFTER triggers because there can be only one INSTEAD OF trigger for the
UPDATE action.

◆ AS *SQL Statements*. Specifies the course of action, such as
rejecting the values being entered, for example. Here you
might need to use some programming logic, which is
explained in Chapter 6. In many cases you might have to
create two sections of code in your trigger: one to handle
single record inserts, updates, or deletes, and one to handle
multi-record modifications. This chapter shows this type of
code to let you see what might be necessary when creating
your own triggers.

Because triggers are an important tool for validating input, and
because practice makes perfect, follow Step by Step 8.1 to see how
to create an INSERT trigger using Query Analyzer. The differences
between INSERT, UPDATE, and DELETE triggers are covered later in
this chapter.

STEP BY STEP

8.1 Creating an *INSERT* Trigger Using Query Analyzer

1. Open the SQL Server Query Analyzer by selecting it from the SQL Server 2000 group under Programs on the Start menu.

2. You will create a trigger on the Order Details table in the Northwind database. To create a new trigger, enter and execute the following code:

```
USE Northwind
GO
CREATE TRIGGER PriceCheck
  ON [Order Details]
  FOR INSERT
  AS
DECLARE @counter int
    SET @counter = @@ROWCOUNT
    DECLARE @unitprice money
    DECLARE order_details_insert_cursor CURSOR FOR
      SELECT UnitPrice
        FROM inserted

    IF @counter = 1
      BEGIN
        IF(SELECT UnitPrice FROM inserted)> 300
        --If the price entered is greater than 300
          BEGIN
            -- print a warning
            PRINT 'Cannot Enter Price Greater Than 300
            --Take back the command
            ROLLBACK TRANSACTION
          END
      END
    ELSE
      BEGIN
        OPEN order_details_insert_cursor
        FETCH NEXT FROM order_details_insert_cursor
        ➡INTO @unitprice
        WHILE @@FETCH_STATUS = 0
          BEGIN
            IF @unitprice > 300
            --If the price entered is greater than 300
              BEGIN
                -- print a warning
                PRINT 'Cannot Enter Price Greater
                ➡Than 300'
                --Take back the command
                ROLLBACK TRANSACTION
                RETURN
                --Exit trigger immediately
              END
```

```
            FETCH NEXT FROM
            ➥order_details_insert_cursor INTO @unitprice
          END
        CLOSE order_details_insert_cursor
      END
    DEALLOCATE order_details_insert_cursor
```

3. To see that the trigger was created, enter the following query as displayed in Figure 8.1, which purposely defies the trigger:

```
INSERT INTO [Order Details]
    VALUES (11076, 32, 320, 12, 0)
```

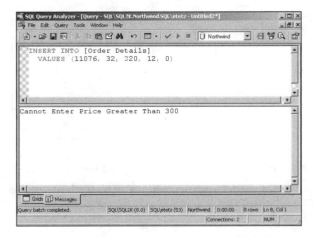

FIGURE 8.1
Seeing an INSERT trigger in action.

Having a clear understanding of how to create an UPDATE trigger is important when you want to control what takes place as data is updated. Step by Step 8.2 takes you through the process of creating an UPDATE trigger using Enterprise Manager.

STEP BY STEP

8.2 Creating an *UPDATE* Trigger Using Enterprise Manager

1. Open the SQL Server Enterprise Manager by selecting it from the SQL Server 2000 group under Programs on the Start menu.

continues

continued

2. To create an UPDATE trigger on the Jobs table, expand the Console Root through your SQL Server Group, your Server Instance, Databases folder, Pubs database, and select Tables. Right-click on the Jobs table and select All Tasks, Manage Triggers, as seen in Figure 8.2.

FIGURE 8.2
Trigger management with Enterprise Manager.

3. After you have found the Trigger Properties dialog box (see Figure 8.3), enter the following code under the name of <new>:

```
CREATE TRIGGER LevelCheck
  ON Jobs
  FOR UPDATE
  AS
    DECLARE @counter int
    SET @counter = @@ROWCOUNT
    DECLARE @maxlevel tinyint
    DECLARE @minlevel tinyint
    DECLARE jobs_update_cursor CURSOR FOR
      SELECT max_lvl, min_lvl
        FROM inserted

    IF @counter = 1
    --If only one record was inserted, then run this
    ➡code block
      BEGIN
        IF(SELECT max_lvl FROM inserted) < (SELECT
        ➡min_lvl from inserted)
        --If the maximum level is smaller than the
        ➡minimum level
          BEGIN
            --Print a warning
```

```
            RAISERROR ('How can the maximum level be
            ➥smaller than the minimum level?', 16, 1)
              WITH LOG, NOWAIT
            PRINT 'Correct your mistake!'
            --Take back the command
            ROLLBACK TRANSACTION
            PRINT 'Transaction Cancelled'
          END
      END
  ELSE
  --If more than one record was inserted, then
  ➥work with the cursor
    BEGIN
      OPEN jobs_update_cursor
      FETCH NEXT FROM jobs_update_cursor INTO
      ➥@maxlevel, @minlevel
      WHILE @@FETCH_STATUS = 0
        BEGIN
          IF @maxlevel < @minlevel
            BEGIN
              --Print a warning
              RAISERROR ('How can the maximum
              ➥level be smaller than the minimum
              ➥level?', 16, 1)
                WITH LOG, NOWAIT
              PRINT 'Correct your mistake!'
              --Take back the command
              ROLLBACK TRANSACTION
              PRINT 'Transaction Cancelled'
              RETURN
              --Exit trigger rather than
continuing
            END
          FETCH NEXT FROM jobs_update_cursor INTO
          ➥@maxlevel, @minlevel
        END
      CLOSE jobs_update_cursor
    END
  DEALLOCATE jobs_update_cursor
```

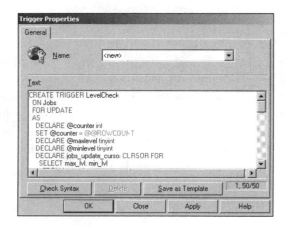

FIGURE 8.3
Creating an UPDATE trigger in Enterprise Manager.

FIGURE 8.4
The UPDATE trigger not allowing the update.

4. To ensure the syntax is correct, use the Check Syntax button. If it is successful, then use the OK button to create the trigger. To test the new trigger, enter the following query in Query Analyzer as displayed in Figure 8.4, which purposely defies the trigger:

```
UPDATE Jobs
  SET min_lvl=100, max_lvl=20
  WHERE job_id=1
```

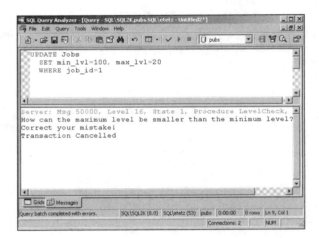

Now that you know how to create a trigger, you can examine how to modify or alter the trigger to meet your ever-changing needs.

Altering Triggers

You might need to make slight changes to the way a trigger processes because policies or procedures change in your organization. This is not a problem. You can easily change the way a trigger processes by either deleting and then re-creating the trigger, or by altering the trigger via a one-step process using ALTER TRIGGER. ALTER TRIGGER is the preferred method because the ID in the syscomments table remains the same. If you have other scripts on your server that have been coded to look for the trigger by its object_ID, then these scripts fail if the object_ID is changed; coding your scripts with these types of dependencies is generally a bad practice. The syntax for ALTER TRIGGER is:

```
ALTER TRIGGER [owner.]trigger_name
  ON [owner.]{table_name | view_name}
  [WITH ENCRYPTION]
  {FOR | AFTER | INSTEAD OF}{INSERT, UPDATE, DELETE}
  [NOT FOR REPLICATION]
    AS
      [IF UPDATE (column)]
      [{AND | OR} UPDATE (column)]
        sql_statements
```

The syntax for ALTER TRIGGER is comparable to the CREATE TRIGGER
statement and has all the same arguments, so refer to the syntax of
the CREATE TRIGGER statement earlier in this chapter to find out what
each option does.

To edit a trigger with Query Analyzer, see Step by Step 8.3.

STEP BY STEP

8.3 Editing a Trigger Using ALTER TRIGGER in Query Analyzer

1. Open the SQL Server Query Analyzer by selecting it
from the SQL Server 2000 group under Programs on
the Start menu.

2. For this example, you will edit the trigger you created in
Step by Step 8.1. Type the following into Query Analyzer:

```
USE Northwind
GO
ALTER  TRIGGER PriceCheck
  ON [Order Details]
  FOR INSERT
  AS
DECLARE @counter int
    SET @counter = @@ROWCOUNT
    DECLARE @unitprice money
    DECLARE order_details_insert_cursor CURSOR FOR
      SELECT UnitPrice
        FROM inserted

    IF @counter = 1
      BEGIN
        IF(SELECT UnitPrice FROM inserted)> 500
        --If the price entered is greater than 500
          BEGIN
            -- print a warning
            RAISERROR ('ERROR: PRICE CANNOT EXCEED
            ➡500', 16,1) WITH LOG
```

continues

continued

```
                                    --Take back the command
                                    ROLLBACK TRANSACTION
                                    PRINT 'TRANSACTION CANCELLED'
                                END
                        END
                    ELSE
                      BEGIN
                        OPEN order_details_insert_cursor
                        FETCH NEXT FROM order_details_insert_cursor
                        ➥INTO @unitprice
                        WHILE @@FETCH_STATUS = 0
                          BEGIN
                            IF @unitprice > 500
                            --If the price entered is greater than 500
                              BEGIN
                                -- print a warning
                                RAISERROR ('ERROR: PRICE CANNOT
                                ➥EXCEED 500', 16,1) WITH LOG
                                --Take back the command
                                ROLLBACK TRANSACTION
                                RETURN
                                --Exit trigger immediately
                              END
                            FETCH NEXT FROM
                            ➥order_details_insert_cursor INTO
                            ➥@unitprice
                          END
                        CLOSE order_details_insert_cursor
                      END
                    DEALLOCATE order_details_insert_cursor
```

3. Run the command.

To edit the same trigger with Enterprise Manager, follow Step by Step 8.4.

STEP BY STEP

8.4 Alter a Trigger Using Enterprise Manager

1. Open the SQL Server Enterprise Manager by selecting it from the SQL Server 2000 group under Programs on the Start menu.

2. To edit a trigger on the Order Details table, expand the Console Root through your SQL Server Group, your Server Instance, Databases folder, Northwind database, and select Tables. Right-click on the Order Details table and select All Tasks, Manage Triggers.

3. After you have found the Trigger Properties dialog box, select PriceCheck from the Name drop-down menu, and alter the text to resemble the following (if you have completed Step by Step 8.3, use this as an opportunity to confirm that the trigger was altered):

```
CREATE TRIGGER PriceCheck
  ON [Order Details]
  FOR INSERT
  AS
DECLARE @counter int
    SET @counter = @@ROWCOUNT
    DECLARE @unitprice money
    DECLARE order_details_insert_cursor CURSOR FOR
      SELECT UnitPrice
        FROM inserted

    IF @counter = 1
      BEGIN
        IF(SELECT UnitPrice FROM inserted)> 500
        --If the price entered is greater than 500
        BEGIN
          -- print a warning
          RAISERROR ('ERROR: PRICE CANNOT EXCEED
          ➡500', 16,1) WITH LOG
          --Take back the command
          ROLLBACK TRANSACTION
          PRINT 'TRANSACTION CANCELLED'
        END
END
    ELSE
      BEGIN
        OPEN order_details_insert_cursor
        FETCH NEXT FROM order_details_insert_cursor
        ➡INTO @unitprice
        WHILE @@FETCH_STATUS = 0
          BEGIN
            IF @unitprice > 500
            --If the price entered is greater than 500
              BEGIN
```

continues

continued

```
                            -- print a warning
                            RAISERROR ('ERROR: PRICE CANNOT
                            ➡EXCEED 500', 16,1) WITH LOG
                        --Take back the command
                        ROLLBACK TRANSACTION
                        RETURN
                        --Exit trigger immediately
                    END
                FETCH NEXT FROM
                ➡order_details_insert_cursor INTO
                ➡@unitprice
            END
        CLOSE order_details_insert_cursor
    END
DEALLOCATE order_details_insert_cursor
```

4. To save your changes, press the OK button and exit Enterprise Manager.

In addition to modifying triggers by altering the content, there might be times that you will have to change the name of the trigger to better reflect its purpose.

Renaming Triggers

Triggers might also be renamed by any user who has the correct permission and by the database owner. Triggers must follow the rules for naming identifiers. You are not likely to have to rename a trigger very often, but you might end up with a naming conflict with another item you want to add to the database. If policy or procedures prevents you from being able to rename the new item, you might have to rename your trigger.

To rename a trigger, use the sp_rename system stored procedure. The syntax for sp_rename is as follows:

```
sp_rename [ @objname = ] 'object_name' ,
    [ @newname = ] 'new_name'
    [ , [ @objtype = ] 'object_type' ]
```

In this example, 'object_name' is the original name of the trigger, 'new_name' is the new name given to the trigger, and 'object_type' is the object being renamed. A trigger comes into the OBJECT value, so it is adequate to specify OBJECT as the value for 'object_type' when renaming triggers.

> **WARNING**
>
> **Careful Renaming**   When renaming a trigger, any references to the trigger name inside of the trigger or on dependent objects are not updated, and have to be updated manually or they will not work. You should run sp_depends 'trigger_name' to find out where the trigger is referenced before you rename the trigger.

Rather than renaming a trigger, you might want to delete it and re-create the trigger with a new name. The next topic is deleting or dropping triggers.

Dropping Triggers

Deleting triggers is as easy as renaming them. Deleting a trigger does not affect the underlying table or data contained in the table. To remove triggers using the SQL Server Query Analyzer, you have to use the DROP TRIGGER statement. The syntax is as follows:

```
DROP TRIGGER { trigger_name } [ ,...n ]
```

The only argument you must specify is *trigger_name*, which is the trigger or triggers to delete. Deleting many triggers at a time is possible when a comma is used to separate trigger names.

To drop and rename a trigger, follow Step by Step 8.5.

STEP BY STEP

8.5 Renaming and Dropping Triggers

1. Open the SQL Server Query Analyzer by selecting it from the SQL Server 2000 group under Programs on the Start menu.

2. To rename the trigger you created in Step by Step 8.2, enter the following:

```
sp_rename 'LevelCheck', 'RT', OBJECT
```

3. To drop the renamed trigger, enter the following:

```
DROP TRIGGER RT
```

4. Execute the statements as displayed in Figure 8.5.

WARNING

Careful Trigger Deletion When dropping a trigger, you should first find out whether any tables or objects reference it. To find out what objects reference a trigger, run sp_depends *'trigger_name'* before you drop the trigger. If you do not check to see what objects reference the trigger, then you risk having those objects fail to function. After you have deleted the trigger, then you cannot perform this check.

You have now seen the mechanics of creating and managing triggers. The next things to look at are the actions that triggers can be associated with and why you might want to use them.

FIGURE 8.5
Renaming and dropping a trigger.

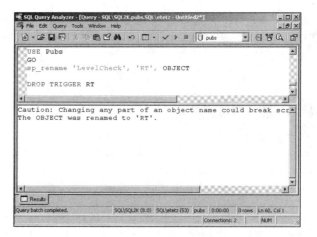

TRIGGER ACTIONS AND ORDER

▶ **Manage data manipulation by using triggers, including validate data.**

• **Specify trigger actions.**

This section examines the two major type of triggers, which are AFTER triggers and INSTEAD OF triggers. Each of these triggers can be associated with INSERT, DELETE, and UPDATE actions. Because the actions for both triggers are similar, you will see most of the issues dealt with in the AFTER trigger section, and only exceptions listed in the INSTEAD OF trigger section. At the end of this discussion is an explanation of the order of triggers and how you can modify it.

AFTER Triggers

AFTER triggers are the most common type of triggers that you will find being implemented on systems today. This is primarily because they were the only type of trigger that existed prior to Windows 2000. Because they were the only trigger type, the FOR keyword was used in place of the AFTER keyword. In either case, these triggers fire after the data modification (INSERT, DELETE, or UPDATE) is carried out.

The following sections look at each type of AFTER trigger that can be created. If you refer back to the CREATE TRIGGER statement, you will notice that rather than creating individual triggers, you can actually create one trigger that applies to all three actions using syntax like the following:

```
USE Pubs
GO
CREATE TRIGGER ModifiedDataTrigger
  ON dbo.authors
  FOR INSERT, UPDATE, DELETE
  AS
    PRINT 'You changed something!'
```

To make it easier to keep each action straight, look at each trigger action separately.

INSERT Triggers

INSERT triggers are used to modify and disallow data at the attempted change of a record. As you saw in a previous example, an INSERT trigger might be used on a sales table, approving insertions of only those records where the sales amount is greater than $50,000. INSERT triggers are not restricted to approving or rejecting inserts, but can also be used to perform additional actions during the data insert. Additional actions could include recording information about the insert (such as the time) in a log or alternate table. Complex business logic can be easily implemented through a trigger.

When an INSERT is made to a database, constraints are applied to the data. Any INSERT statements that satisfy the constraints are accepted into the table. Before completing the statement, any INSERT triggers are fired sequentially. If you want to know what data is being inserted into the table, you can query the Inserted table. This table has the same data structure as the table that the INSERT statement applies to, and it can be used to find out what data was entered into the table. You can refer to this table only from within the trigger code. When you reference this table, its name is Inserted.

The Inserted table might contain one or more rows. Your trigger code has to accommodate the difference between statements that apply to multiple rows and statements that apply to a single row. When possible, rowset commands rather than cursors should be used, because cursors might have a negative impact or performance.

> **NOTE**
>
> **Logging and Triggers** You are not able to reference text, ntext, or image columns in an AFTER trigger because this data is not actually stored in the same data structures as the rest of the table. You can, however, reference this data when using an INSTEAD OF trigger. With non-logged operations, triggers do not fire or execute. Non-logged operations include bulk copy operations and TRUNCATE TABLE statements.

DELETE Triggers

DELETE triggers control what happens after a DELETE is carried out. You can use this trigger to restrict what data is deleted from your database or to perform any other action you want when the data is deleted. A developer might want to restrict the deletion of data because of the data integrity problems that might be caused, or might want to cascade delete child records in other tables. Another use of the trigger might be to log the deletion, or copy deleted data to another table. For example, a developer might allow database users to delete customers who have been inactive for more than 300 days (tested with a trigger), but might use the trigger to copy the customer data to a Past_Customers table.

When a DELETE statement is executed against a table having a DELETE trigger, the record(s) being deleted are copied to the Deleted table. During the execution of the DELETE trigger, you can refer to the data in the Deleted table. Having this data available enables you to perform tasks such as archive the data or log what data was deleted. When all triggers have completed, the data in the Deleted table is flushed. During the execution of the trigger, you can reverse the deletion by issuing a ROLLBACK TRANSACTION statement, which rolls back to the beginning of the transaction that initiated the trigger. If you are not using transactions, then the statement that initiated the trigger is its own implicit transaction.

UPDATE Triggers

In the same way that INSERT triggers are used to control what actions take place after an INSERT, UPDATE triggers can control what actions take place after an UPDATE. These actions can include restricting or allowing update modifications to be performed on one or more tables, logging the update, or any other action you can think of. Updating data means to modify existing data, which means that some data is lost or deleted and replaced with new data that is inserted.

An example of when an UPDATE trigger might be used is when you are the DBA of a trading company, XYZ, and the company's policy is to take sales figures only during a certain period—for instance, from May to June. These sales figures might need to be changed once in a while because of miscalculations. The DBA might want to implement a trigger on the Sales table that allows updates only when the UPDATE statement includes in the Date column any date value between May and June.

UPDATE triggers are not always used to restrict data modifications, but can also perform other actions when the update occurs. For example, a developer might program an UPDATE trigger on a table so that each time someone changes that table, the change and the user are recorded in a special table and the RAISERROR statement is used to generate an alert. The developer might perform these actions because of the type of data that exists in the table.

Similar to an INSERT statement, when an UPDATE statement is executed, SQL Server creates an identical copy of the data that is being inserted into the database. This data is found in the Inserted table. Because this inserted record is actually modifying an existing record, you technically end up with data being deleted from the database as well. The original record, prior to the update, can be found in the Deleted table. By using the Inserted and Deleted tables, SQL Server 2000 is able to retain what the data looked like before the update and how it looks after the update. In your trigger code, then, you can perform actions on either or both of these tables. One possible action is to take a copy of the original data (Deleted table) and store it in another table (Old_Records) so that the data can be referred to if an error is discovered at a later date. The Inserted and Deleted tables are both special tables stored in memory that are automatically created and managed by SQL Server.

In addition to these three types of AFTER triggers, you can also work with INSTEAD OF triggers.

INSTEAD OF Triggers

Before SQL Server 2000, the only type of trigger available was an AFTER trigger—a trigger that contains a set of statements that fire *after* a modification to a table, after any applicable constraints have been applied. INSTEAD OF triggers are new to SQL Server 2000 and execute *instead of* the triggering action. In other words, INSTEAD OF triggers can change any data-modification statement into a customized action. INSTEAD OF triggers place all the rows of a DELETE statement that *would* have taken place into the Deleted table, and all the rows that *would* have been inserted into the Inserted table. You can then script an appropriate set of steps to validate the proposed action, before the application or violation of any constraints that might be implemented. Constraint violations roll back your last statement, whereas the INSTEAD OF trigger can test for violations and then modify the proposed action to avoid the constraint violation. If an INSTEAD OF trigger has already been executed, and the constraints are still violated, then any actions taken in the INSTEAD OF trigger are rolled back.

As an example, imagine that you have an Employees table that contains a DeptID for the employee, and the DeptID is referenced in the Department table. When using constraints, you find that when people attempt to add employees with invalid department codes, the statement fails the constraints on the tables, and the statement is not committed or cancelled. This cancel occurs before the AFTER trigger fires, so you do not know who attempted the update. With the INSTEAD OF INSERT trigger, the proposed update (including who attempted it) can be logged, and you can issue a rollback before the constraints are applied. You might also decide that all invalid DeptIDs should be replaced with a generic DeptID, and the insert should be allowed to complete. This can be accomplished in the INSTEAD OF trigger by re-issuing the INSERT statement from within the INSTEAD OF trigger.

In this example, the INSTEAD OF INSERT trigger now tests for invalid DeptIDs. If they are found, it replaces the DeptID with a generic DeptID, and then re-issues the INSERT statement. Because the INSERT statement is re-issued, you might think that the INSTEAD OF INSERT trigger fires again, but it does not. This trigger cannot cause itself to be called again. After the correct INSERT statement is executed, the INSTEAD OF trigger is skipped, and the rest of the statement is carried out.

Just to stress this point because it is important, INSTEAD OF triggers are not fired recursively. If the INSTEAD OF INSERT trigger fires, and then proceeds to issue the INSERT on the table, the INSTEAD OF trigger would be skipped, constraints would be checked, and the AFTER trigger would fire. Failure at the constraints would cause the statement to be cancelled, and a rollback could be issued if the AFTER trigger fails. A rollback would reverse all actions performed since the original statement was issued, so any actions performed by the INSTEAD OF trigger would also be rolled back.

One of the great benefits of INSTEAD OF triggers is that they can be added to views. The INSTEAD OF trigger is the only type of trigger that can be placed on a view. Normally, views that reference multiple tables are not updateable because changes can be made to only one table at a time. With the help of an INSTEAD OF trigger, these views can be made to appear to update multiple tables at once. Also, views based on multiple tables using joins cannot normally have data deleted, but with an INSTEAD OF trigger, this too can be accomplished. An INSTEAD OF trigger has access to the deleted table, so it can use this deleted information to find which underlying base table needs to have data deleted.

The following are some guidelines that should be observed when INSTEAD OF triggers are created:

◆ There can be only one INSTEAD OF trigger for each action on a table.

◆ AFTER triggers execute after the triggering statement completes, so other constraints have already been applied. All triggers in SQL Server 7.0 and earlier were AFTER triggers. INSTEAD OF triggers are new to SQL Server 2000 and execute prior to the triggering statement. INSTEAD OF triggers are the only triggers that can be implemented on a view.

◆ INSTEAD OF triggers are never recursively fired. That is, if an INSTEAD OF trigger fires a custom INSERT statement to the same triggered table, the INSTEAD OF trigger will not fire again.

◆ INSTEAD OF triggers cannot be used on tables that have cascaded updates.

◆ INSTEAD OF triggers can reference text, ntext, and image columns in their Inserted and Deleted tables.

Trigger Order

Only a few options allow you to change when a trigger is executed. One is when the trigger is created, and the other is with the sp_settriggerorder procedure. Recursion can also play a role in how triggers are fired or executed. The first thing to look at is the different types of triggers.

Trigger Type Order

When you create a trigger, you create an INSTEAD OF, AFTER, or FOR trigger. Depending on the type of trigger, your trigger will execute at a different time. This is an issue that has been previously discussed in this chapter, but it is important, and it's worth covering again.

When creating a trigger, you use one of the following statements:

◆ CREATE TRIGGER <name> ON <table> INSTEAD OF <action>. Trigger fires before constraints are checked and before that data modification is processed.

◆ `CREATE TRIGGER <name> ON <table> AFTER <action>`. Trigger fires after the data modification and after constraints are checked. Constraints can cancel the statement, causing the trigger to never fire.

◆ `CREATE TRIGGER <name> ON <table> FOR <action>`. Trigger fires after data modification and after constraints are checked. There is no difference between `FOR` or `AFTER`. Microsoft's SQL Server includes both `FOR` and `AFTER` for backward compatibility, but treats both these triggers the same way. Before SQL Server 2000, all triggers were `FOR` triggers.

In addition to the type of trigger you are working with, you can set a first and last trigger when you are working with `AFTER` triggers.

First and Last

Because there can be only one `INSTEAD OF` trigger of each type on a table, there is no need or reason to attempt to set the fire order of `INSTEAD OF` triggers. However, there can be many `AFTER` triggers of each type set on a single table.

You might have multiple triggers so that you can define multiple actions to take when data in a table is modified. Rather than having multiple triggers, you can alter a trigger, making it larger and larger to accommodate all the logic. In many cases, smaller, more specific triggers can be easier to manage, code, and troubleshoot. Because there are multiple triggers of each type, you might have a reason to want one to fire before the others, and therefore want to set the order of triggers.

To change the fire order of triggers, you can use the `sp_settriggerorder` stored procedure. The syntax of the command is

```
sp_settriggerorder 'triggername', 'value', 'statement_type'
```

where

◆ *Triggername* is the name of the trigger for which you are setting the order.

◆ *Value* is trigger order for the trigger, and it can be either `FIRST`, `LAST`, or `NONE`.

◆ *Statement type* is the statement type being modified, such as `INSERT`, `UPDATE`, or `DELETE`.

Outside of FIRST and LAST, you have no control over how triggers will fire. If you have already specified a FIRST or LAST trigger, you cannot specify another trigger as FIRST or LAST. If you want to remove a FIRST or LAST option, the ALTER TRIGGER statement always removes this setting when it is executed. If you alter a trigger and want to leave it as FIRST or LAST, then you will have to re-execute the sp_settriggerorder statement.

The sp_settriggerorder statement requires a statement_type value such as INSERT, UPDATE, or DELETE. If you have a trigger that executes for all these actions, and you want it to be the FIRST trigger, you have to execute sp_settriggerorder three times: once for each statement type.

Recursive Triggers

Triggers are used to keep the flow of data within the boundaries of proper business logic, and this is why they are so widely used. Their capability is equal to stored procedures, and they are able to change records in *other* tables. There are two types of recursion, and each type of recursion has a solution within the SQL Server. The two types of recursion are *direct* and *indirect*. Before any recursion takes place, the database option of recursive triggers must be set to ON. This option can be set with sp_dboption and defaults to OFF.

With direct recursion, an update causes a trigger to execute, which attempts to perform an update to the original table, causing the trigger to execute again, and updating the table again. If not checked, this would continue an infinite number of times, but the default setting for the database disables recursive triggers. For example, take the following trigger created on the Northwind.dbo.Products table:

```
CREATE TRIGGER update_stock
  ON Products
  FOR insert, update
  AS
    DECLARE @counter int
    SET @counter = @@ROWCOUNT
    DECLARE @ProductID int
    DECLARE @InStock smallint
    DECLARE @ReOrder smallint
    DECLARE @OnOrder smallint
    DECLARE @ReOrderQty smallint
    DECLARE stock_update_cursor CURSOR FOR
      SELECT ProductID, UnitsInStock, ReorderLevel,
      ➥UnitsOnOrder
        FROM inserted
```

```
            IF @counter = 1
              BEGIN
                SELECT @InStock = UnitsInStock,
                       @ReOrder = ReorderLevel,
                       @OnOrder = UnitsOnOrder
                  FROM inserted
                SET @ReOrderQty = 5
                IF (@InStock + @OnOrder) < @ReOrder
                  BEGIN
                    UPDATE Products
                      SET UnitsOnOrder = @OnOrder + @ReOrderQty
                      WHERE ProductID = (SELECT ProductID FROM
                      ➥inserted)
                    PRINT 'Order for ' + RTRIM(@ReOrderQTY) + '
                    ➥units has been placed.'
                  END
              END
            ELSE
              BEGIN
                OPEN stock_update_cursor
                SET @ReOrderQty = 5
                FETCH NEXT FROM stock_update_cursor INTO
                ➥@ProductID, @InStock, @ReOrder, @OnOrder
                WHILE @@FETCH_STATUS = 0
                  BEGIN
                    IF (@InStock + @OnOrder) < @ReOrder
                      BEGIN
                        UPDATE Products
                          SET UnitsOnOrder = @OnOrder + @ReOrderQty
                          WHERE ProductID = @ProductID
                        PRINT 'Order for ' + RTRIM(@ReOrderQTY) + '
                        ➥units has been placed.'
                      END
                    FETCH NEXT FROM stock_update_cursor INTO
                    ➥@ProductID, @InStock, @ReOrder, @OnOrder
                  END
                CLOSE stock_update_cursor
              END
            DEALLOCATE stock_update_cursor
```

When there is an insert or update to the table, the trigger fires and places an order of five units of the product if the UnitsInStock + UnitsOnOrder are less than the ReOrderLevel. This order actually updates the same record in the Products table. With the default database options, an insert like the one in Figure 8.6 would only result in one firing of the trigger, which is evident because only one order was processed and the UnitsOnOrder are set to only five units.

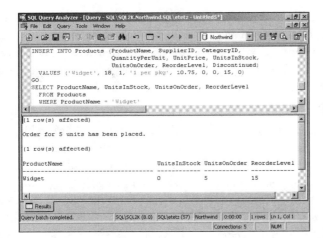

FIGURE 8.6
Direct recursive triggers fire only once if
`recursive triggers` are turned off.

If you enable `recursive triggers` for your database, this trigger fires
multiple times—up to 32 times. You can use either of the following
commands to enable `recursive triggers`:

```
sp_dboption 'Northwind', 'recursive triggers', TRUE

ALTER DATABASE Northwind
   SET RECURSIVE_TRIGGERS ON
```

When you are using the `recursive triggers` option, the same insert
will have very different results. In this case the trigger fires as many
times as necessary to bring the `UnitsOnOrder` to a level that `Reorders`
are not required. This is done in steps of five units, and can be seen
in Figure 8.7.

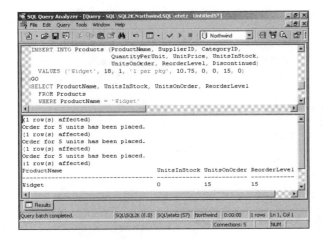

FIGURE 8.7
Direct recursive triggers might fire up to
32 times.

With indirect recursion, an update causes a trigger to execute, which attempts to perform an update to another table, and the other table has a trigger that attempts to update the original table, which completes a circle of triggers. This circle of triggers would continue infinitely, unless checked.

For an example of indirect recursion, add a new table to the Northwind database called ProductReplenishment. This table will actually hold the ReOrder orders. When a sale updates the Products table, the Update_Stock trigger will fire and possibly create a new ProductReplenishment order. The New_Order trigger on the ProductReplenishment table then completes the order by updating the Products table, thus firing the Update_Stock trigger again. This type of recursion occurs even if recursive triggers is set to false. The recursive triggers option only applies to direct recursion. The following script creates the new table and the triggers. Review it, and see the results in Figure 8.8. (Some of the results were deleted for readability.)

FIGURE 8.8
Indirect recursion is not affected by the recursive trigger option.

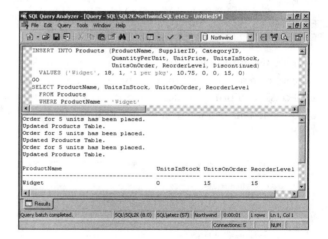

```
CREATE TABLE ProductReplenishment
  (OrderID       smallint
     IDENTITY(1,1)
     PRIMARY KEY CLUSTERED,
   ProductName nvarchar(40),
   SupplierID    int,
   Quantity      smallint)
GO
```

```
CREATE TRIGGER new_order
  ON ProductReplenishment
  FOR insert
  AS
    DECLARE @counter int
    SET @counter = @@ROWCOUNT
    DECLARE @ProductName nvarchar(40)
    DECLARE @Quantity smallint
    DECLARE @InStock smallint
    DECLARE @ReOrder smallint
    DECLARE @OnOrder smallint
    DECLARE @ReOrderQty smallint
    DECLARE Prod_Replenish_Cursor CURSOR FOR
      SELECT ProductName, Quantity
        FROM inserted

    IF @counter = 1
      BEGIN
        SELECT @InStock = UnitsInStock,
               @ReOrder = ReorderLevel,
               @OnOrder = UnitsOnOrder
          FROM Products
          WHERE ProductName = (SELECT ProductName FROM
          ➥inserted)
        SET @ReOrderQty = (SELECT Quantity FROM inserted)
        IF (@InStock + @OnOrder) < @ReOrder
          BEGIN
            UPDATE Products
              SET UnitsOnOrder = @OnOrder + @ReOrderQty
              WHERE ProductName = (SELECT ProductName FROM
              ➥inserted)
            PRINT 'Order for ' + RTRIM(@ReOrderQTY) + '
            ➥units has been placed.'
          END
      END
    ELSE
      BEGIN
        OPEN Prod_Replenish_Cursor
        FETCH NEXT FROM Prod_Replenish_Cursor INTO
        ➥@ProductName, @Quantity
        WHILE @@FETCH_STATUS = 0
          BEGIN
            SELECT @InStock = UnitsInStock,
                   @ReOrder = ReorderLevel,
                   @OnOrder = UnitsOnOrder
              FROM Products
              WHERE ProductName = @ProductName
            SET @ReOrderQty = @Quantity
            IF (@InStock + @OnOrder) < @ReOrder
              BEGIN
                UPDATE Products
                  SET UnitsOnOrder = @OnOrder + @ReOrderQty
                  WHERE ProductName = @ProductName
                PRINT 'Order for ' + RTRIM(@ReOrderQTY) + '
                ➥units has been placed.'
              END
            FETCH NEXT FROM Prod_Replenish_Cursor INTO
```

```
                                              ➥@ProductName, @Quantity
                                        END
                                  CLOSE Prod_Replenish_Cursor
                              END
                        DEALLOCATE Prod_Replenish_Cursor
GO

CREATE TRIGGER update_stock
  ON Products
  FOR insert,update
  AS
     DECLARE @counter int
     SET @counter = @@ROWCOUNT
     DECLARE @InStock smallint
     DECLARE @ReOrder smallint
     DECLARE @OnOrder smallint
     DECLARE @ReOrderQty smallint
     DECLARE Prod_Update_Cursor CURSOR FOR
        SELECT UnitsInStock, ReorderLevel, UnitsOnOrder
          FROM inserted

     IF @counter = 1
       BEGIN
         SELECT @InStock = UnitsInStock,
                @ReOrder = ReorderLevel
                @OnOrder = UnitsOnOrder
           FROM inserted
         SET @ReOrderQty = 5
         IF (@InStock + @OnOrder) < @ReOrder
           BEGIN
             INSERT INTO ProductReplenishment (ProductName,
             ➥SupplierID, Quantity)
               VALUES ('Widget', 18, @ReOrderQty)
             PRINT 'Updated Products Table.'
           END
         ELSE
           BEGIN
             OPEN Prod_Update_Cursor
             FETCH NEXT FROM Prod_Update_Cursor INTO
             ➥@InStock, @ReOrder, @OnOrder
             WHILE @@FETCH_STATUS = 0
               BEGIN
                 SET @ReOrderQty = 5
                 IF (@InStock + @OnOrder) < @ReOrder
                   BEGIN
                     INSERT INTO ProductReplenishment
                     ➥(ProductName, SupplierID, Quantity)
                       VALUES ('Widget', 18, @ReOrderQty)
                   END
                 FETCH NEXT FROM Prod_Update_Cursor INTC
                 ➥@InStock, @ReOrder, @OnOrder
               END
             PRINT 'Updated Products Table.'
           END
         CLOSE Prod_Update_Cursor
       END
```

```
      DEALLOCATE Prod_Update_Cursor
GO

ALTER DATABASE Northwind
   SET RECURSIVE_TRIGGERS OFF
GO
```

Notice that recursive triggers were disabled for the previous example, but the triggers still functioned with the required recursion. That was because of the indirect recursion. If you want to disable this default feature of SQL Server 2000, then you have to change the server configuration option for 'nested triggers'.

If the nested triggers option is set to '0', then trigger nesting (a trigger that causes another trigger to fire) is disabled. A nested triggers setting of '1' enables trigger nesting for up to 32 levels. The level of 32 was an arbitrary value assigned by Microsoft, because there was a chance that poor loop structure could cause this to continue infinitely. If the 32-level limit is hit, then the transaction is rolled back to the original calling transaction. Figure 8.9 shows an insert of a product that will exceed this limit with a ReOrderLevel of 160 units. If it is allowed to continue, this will hit 32 levels of recursion; but after 32 levels, the entire transaction is rolled back. The rollback is evident by 0 rows being returned from the select of the inserted product. One recursion counter is shared between stored procedures, functions, triggers, and views, so if a stored procedure performs an insert that fires a trigger, which executes the stored procedure, then this cycle continues for only 16 cycles, setting the recursion counter to 32.

To see whether nested triggers are enabled on your server, you can use the following command:

```
USE Master
GO
sp_configure 'nested triggers'
```

which returns the following:

name	minimum	maximum	config_value	run_value
nested triggers	0	1	1	1

If you want to change the setting and put it into effect immediately, you can use the following command:

```
sp_configure 'nested triggers', '0'
RECONFIGURE
```

FIGURE 8.9
Transactions are rolled back after 32 recursion levels.

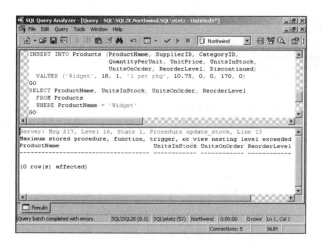

If you don't use the `RECONFIGURE` command, you have to re-start the SQL Server service before the `sp_configure` command takes effect.

If you disable nested triggers, then you might find that you do not get the results that you are hoping for. In the example with the `ProductReplenishment` table, disabling nested triggers would be very noticeable. Figure 8.10 shows the results. The first trigger is allowed to fire, which creates the order in the `ProductReplenishment` table—evident by the Updated Products Table message that is generated by the `Update_Stock` trigger. The second trigger that should have fired was the trigger on the `ProductReplenishment` table, which would have updated the `UnitsOnOrder` value in the `Products` table. This value is still at 0, so the trigger never fired.

If you want to see the level of nesting in the current trigger chain, you can use `TRIGGER_NESTLEVEL`. This command might look like this:

```
IF ((SELECT TRIGGER_NESTLEVEL() ) > 10 )
   PRINT 'This statement nested over 10 levels of
   ➥triggers.'
```

This command returns the total number recursion levels in the current trigger chain, but not the total level of recursion for non-trigger recursion. If non-trigger items are in the chain, then `TRIGGER_NESTLEVEL` will return the number of triggers that executed, although the recursion level could be much higher. If you specify a trigger `object_ID` as a parameter, then it tells you how many times that specific trigger fired.

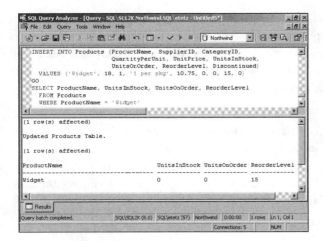

FIGURE 8.10
Disabling nested triggers could have unwanted consequences.

The next section looks at security implications with triggers, such as using triggers to control data modifications.

SECURITY IMPLICATIONS WITH TRIGGERS

- ▶ Control data access by using triggers.
- ▶ Enforce procedural business logic by using triggers.
- ▶ Filter data by using triggers.

This section revisits information covered earlier in this chapter to ensure that you have properly absorbed the material. These topics include controlling data access and enforcing business logic, as well as using triggers to implement referential integrity and filtering data.

Controlling, Filtering, and Enforcing Data Access

The discussion of AFTER triggers earlier in this chapter included several examples given that showed you when and how you might want to implement triggers.

Triggers are capable of performing any action you want during their execution, and they execute based on data modification in a table. One task that can be given to triggers is controlling what modifications might be made to the data in a table. This could include restrictions like the following:

◆ We would like only one customer/contact record for each company to exist. When a second customer/contact is added in the form of a new customer record, an INSERT trigger can check for the existence of that company in the Customer table. If the record exists, it can take the new contact and add it to an Alternate Contact column.

◆ From the deletion perspective, you might allow multiple contact records to exist for each company in the Customer table. When a contact record is deleted, a DELETE trigger can confirm that this is not the last record for that company. If it is, you can have the deletion cancelled and simply remove the contact name from the record.

These are just two examples of how triggers can control what is done to the data in a table. Triggers can be used to restrict or log any and all data modifications made to a table in your database.

Enforcing Referential and Data Integrity

Referential integrity requires that every FOREIGN KEY value map to a PRIMARY KEY value. To get a full appreciation of how FOREIGN KEY constraints and referential integrity work, consult Chapter 3. Triggers can be used to provide the same services as FOREIGN KEY constraints if you make sure each related table is updated in respect to the originally updated table. For example, an UPDATE trigger can be placed on a primary table so that it automatically performs data modifications to other related tables after changes are made to the primary table. This would mean the trigger could cascade changes to all associated tables to ensure that no orphaned or irrelevant rows exist.

Data integrity involves keeping consistent and correct data stored in a database. Methods of ensuring data integrity include validating individual columns and verifying that data in one table maps to data in another table. Triggers enable you to create custom error messages for referential and data integrity functions.

Most FOREIGN KEY constraints would be used to provide referential integrity, such as preventing the deletion of referenced rows or providing cascading deletes. For example, you might want to deal with the deletion of a row in one table, but do not want any FOREIGN KEY constraints to have an effect. If you use an INSTEAD OF trigger, then your code can execute before the FOREIGN KEY constraints, but these constraints still apply. INTEAD OF triggers do not fire if cascading FOREIGN KEY constraints are on the table, which could prevent your code from executing. You want to create your own custom handler for the deletion event that will be used in place of the FOREIGN KEY constraint.

In the following example, the FOREIGN KEY constraint—which could have prevented you from being able to delete a ship that has assigned crew—is removed. The problem that arises with the lack of this constraint is that you can now have crew assigned to ships that have been deleted and are now non-existent. Normally the constraint would prevent the deletion of the ship, or would delete the associated crew records. Because of the requirements, neither of these events is desirable, and instead you want to simply record the unassigned crew members. To deal with this problem, you can create an AFTER trigger to handle the situation. This custom trigger tracks the deleted ship, locates the crew from the ship, and sets their ShipAssigned value to NULL.

For this to work, you have to create a table that does not use FOREIGN KEY constraints. A sample database is defined in the following:

```
CREATE DATABASE CrewAssignmentDB
  ON
    ( NAME = 'CrewAssignmentDB_dat',
      FILENAME = 'c:\program files\microsoft sql
      ➥server\mssql\data\crewdb.mdf',
      SIZE = 1MB,
      MAXSIZE = 1MB,
      FILEGROWTH = 0MB )
  LOG ON
    ( NAME = 'CrewAssignmentDB_log',
      FILENAME = 'c:\program files\microsoft sql
      ➥server\mssql\data\crewdblog.ldf',
      SIZE = 1MB,
      MAXSIZE = 1MB,
      FILEGROWTH = 0MB )
GO

USE CrewAssignmentDB
GO

CREATE TABLE dbo.Ship
  (ShipID          smallint
```

```
            IDENTITY(1,1),
   ShipName        nvarchar(20))
GO
CREATE TABLE dbo.Crew
  (CrewID        smallint
      IDENTITY(1,1),
   CrewName      nvarchar(20),
   ShipAssigned  smallint   NULL)
GO

INSERT INTO Ship (ShipName) VALUES ('Enterprise')
INSERT INTO Ship (ShipName) VALUES ('Voyager')
INSERT INTO Ship (ShipName) VALUES ('Defiant')
GO
```

```
INSERT INTO Crew (CrewName, ShipAssigned) VALUES ('Kirk',1)
INSERT INTO Crew (CrewName, ShipAssigned) VALUES ('Spock',1)
INSERT INTO Crew (CrewName, ShipAssigned) VALUES ('McCoy',1)
INSERT INTO Crew (CrewName, ShipAssigned) VALUES ('Janeway',2)
INSERT INTO Crew (CrewName, ShipAssigned) VALUES ('Seven-of-nine',2)
INSERT INTO Crew (CrewName, ShipAssigned) VALUES ('Torres',2)
INSERT INTO Crew (CrewName, ShipAssigned) VALUES ('Sisko',3)
INSERT INTO Crew (CrewName, ShipAssigned) VALUES ('Worf',3)
GO
```

Now that there are no constraints to interfere with data modifications, you can create a trigger to handle deletion of ships from the database. The following trigger serves that function:

```
CREATE TRIGGER ref_delete_ship
  ON Ship FOR delete AS
    DECLARE @row_count int
    SET @row_count = @@ROWCOUNT
    DECLARE @DeletedShip nvarchar(20)

    IF @row_count = 1
      BEGIN
        UPDATE Crew
          SET ShipAssigned = NULL
          FROM Crew INNER JOIN deleted
            ON Crew.ShipAssigned = deleted.ShipID
          WHERE Crew.ShipAssigned = deleted.ShipID
        SET @row_count = @@ROWCOUNT
        SET @DeletedShip = (SELECT ShipName FROM deleted)
        PRINT 'Ship named ' + RTRIM(@DeletedShip) + ' has been deleted.'
        PRINT 'There are ' + LTRIM(@row_count) + ' new crew without a ship.'
        PRINT 'The crew without ships are:'
        SELECT CrewName FROM Crew WHERE ShipAssigned IS NULL
      END
    ELSE
      BEGIN
        -- Flag the multirow deletion, and let the user
        ➥know it is not allowed.
        RAISERROR ('You are only able to delete one ship at
        ➥a time',16,1)
      END
```

This trigger sets all ShipAssigned fields to NULL, and then displays a list of all crew that are currently unassigned. This trigger could have also deleted the crew members that were affected or rolled back the entire transaction. This method leaves them in the database, deals with the ship deletion, and provides a custom message. The result of a ship deletion is shown in Figure 8.11.

Triggers, however, aren't your best bet when it comes to enforcing data integrity. Many simpler methods, such as constraints, operate with less processor overhead. Nonetheless, triggers can be used to program business logic and heavy error trapping.

As you have seen in this section and chapter, triggers are capable of restricting and controlling what data modifications are allowed to take place in the database.

NOTE

Trigger Syntax The error handling in the ship/crew trigger example has been deleted for brevity in the example. This should not be deleted from your production triggers. Additionally, this trigger returns a result set, in the form of a crew list. Triggers do not return a result set, whereas this trigger creates a result set as part of its operation.

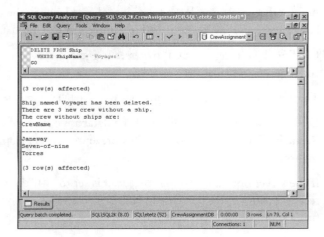

FIGURE 8.11
Triggers can serve the same function as most constraints.

TROUBLESHOOTING TRIGGERS

▶ **Troubleshoot and optimize programming objects. Objects include triggers.**

When working with triggers, you might find from time to time that they appear to stop functioning. This section provides you with guidance on where to start your troubleshooting efforts. It includes information on what can cause your triggers to not execute, and then moves into viewing the trigger definition. The trigger definition is useful when you want to know what the trigger was supposed to do in the first place.

Most problems that arise from triggers have to do with either execution being prevented or improper code or logic within the trigger. If the problem has to do with the code, you have to examine the trigger code and correct the problem. This section shows you how to access the code. To solve problems with the code, read Chapter 9, which was devoted to SQL Server programming techniques.

What Prevents Triggers from Executing

Triggers might not execute for a number of reasons. Here is a list of some of the common reasons and things that you might do to avoid problems and ensure that your triggers function properly:

◆ Actions that insert non-logged data into the table when the database is set to use the Bulk-Logged or Simple recovery model.

◆ Loading data using the BCP bypasses triggers, CHECK constraints, and rules.

◆ The TRUNCATE TABLE command does not fire DELETE triggers.

◆ Direct recursion does not occur if the database option of Recursive Triggers is set to OFF. This prevents triggers from firing multiple times.

◆ If the server option of Nested Triggers is set to '0', then indirect recursion is also prevented. This prevents triggers from firing multiple times.

If you avoid the items on this list, then your triggers should fire when you want them to. If the trigger fires, and just does not do what you want it to, then you have to examine the actual code.

Viewing a Trigger

Viewing the definition of a trigger is not a difficult task in SQL Server 2000. You can view the name, date created, and the types of triggers on a table. You might also want to know the complete definition of a trigger to help implement a new trigger design. You might also want to view the definition to find out why the trigger is not functioning properly. It might be that the wrong type of trigger was created, or there is a flaw in the programming logic.

Viewing the definition is possible, provided that the definition was not encrypted with the WITH ENCRYPTION option. Use the sp_helptrigger, sp_helptext, and sp_help stored procedures to view information about the trigger. You can use sp_helptrigger to view the types of triggers on a table, sp_help to see information about a trigger such as date created, and sp_helptext to view the trigger definition itself. The syntax for all three is as follows:

```
sp_helptrigger [ @tabname = ] 'table'
    [ , [ @triggertype = ] 'type' ]

sp_help [ [ @objname = ] 'name' ]

sp_helptext [ @objname = ] 'name'
```

For sp_helptrigger, 'table' is the name of the table on which the triggers are set, and 'type' specifies the type of trigger to return information about and is either INSERT, DELETE, or UPDATE. For the other two stored procedures, 'name' is the name of the trigger that you want to view. To view trigger-specific information, follow Step by Step 8.6.

STEP BY STEP

8.6 Viewing Trigger Information with Both Query Analyzer and Enterprise Manager

1. Open the SQL Server Query Analyzer by selecting it from the SQL Server 2000 group under Programs on the Start menu. Open a connection to your server and select the Northwind database.

2. To view a specific type of trigger on a table, such as UPDATE, use sp_helptrigger, as follows:

```
sp_helptrigger 'Order Details', 'INSERT'
GO
```

3. To view trigger information, use the sp_help stored procedure, as follows:

```
sp_help 'PriceCheck'
GO
```

4. To view the trigger definition, use the sp_helptext stored procedure, as follows:

```
sp_helptext 'PriceCheck'
GO
```

continues

continued

5. Execute these stored procedures and you should get something looking like Figure 8.12.

6. Close the Query Analyzer and open Enterprise Manager from the SQL Server 2000 group under Programs on the Start menu.

7. To view a trigger on the Order Details table, expand the Console Root through your SQL Server Group, your Server Instance, Databases folder, Northwind database, and select Tables. Right-click on the Order Details table and select All Tasks, Manage Triggers.

8. After you have found the Manage Trigger dialog box, select PriceCheck from the Name drop-down menu. You can now see the contents of this trigger in the open dialog window.

9. Close the dialog box using the Cancel button, and then exit Enterprise Manager.

After viewing the definition of the trigger, as long as it was not encrypted, you should be able to review it and identify any errors that are related to the trigger. If there are problems with the trigger, you might then have to issue an ALTER TRIGGER statement.

You should now have a good feeling about what can prevent triggers from firing and how to deal with those issues by examining the trigger definition, and then making any necessary corrections to its syntax.

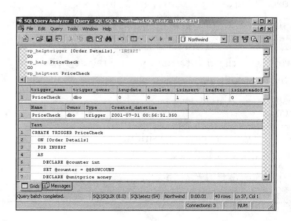

FIGURE 8.12
Viewing trigger-specific information.

CASE STUDY: EMERALD SHARP

ESSENCE OF THE CASE

- ▶ All new data that is entered in the main tables should automatically update pricing information in the foreign tables.

- ▶ Foreign pricing should be 10% less than domestic pricing.

- ▶ Like all organizations, they would like to have the prices synchronized with a minimum cost, effort, and time.

SCENARIO

Emerald Sharp is a large manufacturer of high-quality cut-glassware products. It enjoys a national reputation for its products, but until now has not exported any goods. Emerald Sharp manufactures cut-glassware products in both mass production and careful customized production, for those willing to pay additional fees. Now Emerald Sharp is running at a profit with its 300 highly skilled employees. The company has 30 factories located around the nation, all in remote areas. Emerald Sharp has out-competed all its rivals who manufacture similar products, which are in great demand because of their quality. Emerald Sharp wants to reach out to the world with its quality products by dedicating ten more factories as export manufacturers to locations around the world. The company therefore needs to somewhat alter its existing data model to accommodate the needs of the factories abroad. After altering the data model, its employees will start to enter the new data into the database. Emerald Sharp has set the international price for its products as 10% less than their domestic price on all models created after May 15th, 2001. Emerald Sharp sells identical products both domestically and internationally, and creates almost 25 new models of glassware each month.

You work as a contractor and are hired to construct and implement this scenario Emerald Sharp is in.

CASE STUDY: EMERALD SHARP

ANALYSIS

You investigate the current scenario at Emerald Sharp and notice that Emerald Sharp sells to foreign countries at a discounted price of 10% less than the domestic price of goods on all models created after May 15, 2001. You have thought of a way to automate the process, so that Emerald Sharp will not have to manually create and populate a new table named ForeignPrice. You can create a trigger on the Product table and then write code to insert values into a new column or table named ForeignPrice. You decide to create

an INSERT trigger on the Products table. The INSERT trigger fires when products are added into the table. The trigger verifies that the Manufacture_Date column of the record added is greater than May 15th, 2001. If it passes, it is entered into the table with an entry in the ForeignPrice column of 10% less than the domestic price. If the manufactured date of the product is not greater than May 15th, 2001, it is still entered into the table and has an entry in the ForeignPrice column that is equal to the domestic price.

CHAPTER SUMMARY

KEY TERMS

- Trigger
- INSERT trigger
- DELETE trigger
- UPDATE trigger
- INSTEAD OF trigger
- Recursive trigger
- ALTER TRIGGER
- CREATE TRIGGER

This chapter examined triggers. You saw that there are three basic types of triggers (INSERT, UPDATE, and DELETE), as well as two firing modes (INSTEAD OF and AFTER). Triggers are used to coordinate and manage the INSERT, UPDATE, and DELETE of data within your database. INSTEAD OF triggers execute before the update and are the only types of triggers that might be implemented on a view, whereas AFTER triggers are implemented after the update and any constraints have been completed.

Triggers can be used to modify the basic INSERT, UPDATE, and DELETE actions by following steps that are similar to those of constraints, but triggers are also capable of much more. Triggers can be used to execute custom constraints on the data modification action, to log the action, to modify the action, or to prevent or reverse the action.

You saw that triggers might cause other triggers to fire. If a trigger forces itself to fire, such as an UPDATE trigger, updating the same table that caused it fire in the first place, then it is directly recursive; if it updates another table or calls a stored procedure, the trigger is indirectly recursive.

CHAPTER SUMMARY

Trigger management is similar to many other components in SQL Server, through the use of the CREATE TRIGGER, ALTER TRIGGER, and DROP TRIGGER statements.

This chapter gave you a good grasp of how to implement a trigger, but you won't see much of the basic programming that is covered in this book until you read the following chapter, Chapter 9, "Stored Procedures and User-Defined Functions."

APPLY YOUR KNOWLEDGE

EXERCISES

8.1   Creating an INSERT Trigger

This exercise demonstrates how to create an INSERT trigger on the Sales table in the Pubs database. It will disallow a record with a quantity greater than 500 from being entered into the Sales table of the Pubs database.

Estimated Time: 10 minutes

1. Open the SQL Server Query Analyzer by selecting it from the SQL Server 2000 group under Programs on the Start menu.

2. Type the following code to create the trigger:

```
USE Pubs
GO

CREATE TRIGGER QuantityVerify
  ON Sales
  FOR INSERT
  AS
    IF @@ROWCOUNT > 1
    BEGIN
       --Print warning message
       PRINT 'Please only add one record at
       ➥a time.'
       ROLLBACK TRANSACTION
    END
  ELSE
    BEGIN
       IF(SELECT qty FROM inserted)> 500
       --If the quantity entered is greater
       ➥than 500
         BEGIN
           --Print a warning
           PRINT 'Cannot Enter Quantity
           ➥Greater Than 500'
           ROLLBACK TRANSACTION
         END
    END
```

3. Now execute the command and then attempt to insert a record that defies the trigger to see the result.

8.2   Creating a DELETE Trigger

This exercise demonstrates how to stop removal of certain records using the DELETE trigger.

Estimated Time: 10 minutes

1. Open the SQL Server Query Analyzer by selecting it from the SQL Server 2000 group under Programs on the Start menu.

2. To create the DELETE trigger, enter the following code. This trigger does not allow removal of stores within California.

```
USE Pubs
GO

CREATE TRIGGER StateCheck
  ON Stores
  FOR DELETE
  AS
    DECLARE @counter int
    SET @counter = @@ROWCOUNT
    DECLARE @state char(2)
    DECLARE stores_delete_cursor CURSOR FOR
      SELECT state FROM deleted

    IF @counter = 1
    BEGIN
      IF(SELECT state FROM deleted) =
'California'
        BEGIN
          PRINT 'CANNOT REMOVE STORES IN
          ➥CALIFORNIA'
          --Take back the command
          ROLLBACK TRANSACTION
        END
    END
  ELSE
    BEGIN
      OPEN stores_delete_cursor
      FETCH NEXT FROM stores_delete_cursor
      ➥INTO @state
      WHILE
        BEGIN
          IF @state = 'California'
            BEGIN
              PRINT 'CANNOT REMOVE STORES
              ➥IN CALIFORNIA'
```

APPLY YOUR KNOWLEDGE

```
                        --Take back the command
                        PRINT 'Transaction Cancelled'
                        ROLLBACK TRANSACTION
                        RETURN
                        --Exit trigger
                    END
                FETCH NEXT FROM
                ➥stores_delete_cursor INTO
                ➥@state
            END
        CLOSE stores_delete_cursor
    END
DEALLOCATE stores_delete_cursor
```

3. Now create a DELETE statement to test this trigger by attempting to delete a record for a store that is in California. Remember to use the WHERE clause to limit the delete.

8.3 Viewing and Deleting a Trigger

This exercise demonstrates how to view trigger information and delete triggers. You must complete Exercise 8.2 before performing this exercise.

Estimated Time: 10 minutes

1. Open the SQL Server Query Analyzer by selecting it from the SQL Server 2000 group under Programs on the Start menu.

2. To view trigger information about the trigger created in Exercise 8.2, StateCheck, execute the following:

```
USE Pubs
GO

sp_help StateCheck
GO
sp_helptext StateCheck
GO
```

3. To delete the StateCheck trigger, execute the following:

```
DROP TRIGGER StateCheck
```

8.4 Managing Data by Using Triggers

This exercise is designed to tie together all the concepts that were dealt with in this chapter. You will create a database with two tables (Customers and OldCustomers). You will then create and test a series of triggers to handle inputs and deletions of data in the tables. This exercise will perform all of its work from Query Analyzer.

To make the coding of your triggers easier to read, you are going to eliminate most error handling and support only single record updates. You should not do this when working on your production databases.

Estimated Time: 30 minutes

1. This exercise starts with creating a database and its associated tables. Use the following code:

```
USE Master
GO

CREATE DATABASE TriggerTest
  ON
    ( Name = 'TrigTestDat',
      Filename = 'C:\Program Files\Microsoft
      ➥SQL Server\MSSQL\Data\TrigTest.mdf',
      Size = 1MB,
      MaxSize = 1MB,
      FileGrowth = 0MB)
  LOG ON
    ( Name = 'TrigTestLog',
      Filename = 'C:\Program Files\Microsoft
      ➥SQL Server\MSSQL\Data\TrigTest.ldf',
      Size = 1MB,
      MaxSize = 1MB,
      FileGrowth = 0MB)
GO

USE TriggerTest
GO

CREATE TABLE Customers
  ( CustID    smallint IDENTITY (1,1),
    Name      nvarchar (20),
    Balance   money
        CONSTRAINT CK_Cust_Balance CHECK
        ➥(Balance >= 0))
GO
```

APPLY YOUR KNOWLEDGE

2. Execute the script and then attempt to insert data into the table using the following commands:

```
INSERT INTO Customers (Name, Balance)
  VALUES ('Bob', 75.30)
INSERT INTO Customers (Name, Balance)
  VALUES ('Mary', -35)
GO

SELECT * FROM Customers
```

3. Execute the preceding script. You should notice that there is only one record in the Customers table. You are going to add an AFTER trigger that tests for a negative balance and sets the balance to zero in those cases. Create your trigger with the following code:

```
CREATE TRIGGER Neg_Balance
  ON Customers
  AFTER INSERT
  AS
    DECLARE @varName nvarchar (20)
    DECLARE @varBalance money
    SELECT @varName = Name,
           @varBalance = Balance
      FROM Inserted
    IF @varBalance < 0
      BEGIN
        INSERT INTO Customers (Name, Balance)
          VALUES (@varName, 0)
      END
    ELSE
      BEGIN
        INSERT INTO Customers (Name, Balance)
          VALUES (@varName, @varBalance)
      END
```

4. Execute the code and then attempt to add the record for Mary from Step 2. You should find that you have the same conflict with the CHECK constraint CK_Cust_Balance as you did in Step 2. That happens because you created an AFTER trigger, and it is executed after the INSERT and after the constraints are checked. Confirm that Neg_Balance is an AFTER trigger by using the following:

```
sp_helptext 'Neg_Balance'
```

5. Because Neg_Balance is an AFTER trigger, you have to drop the Neg_Balance trigger and re-create it as an INSTEAD OF trigger. Use the following code:

```
DROP TRIGGER Neg_Balance
GO
CREATE TRIGGER Neg_Balance
  ON Customers
  INSTEAD OF INSERT
  AS
    DECLARE @varName nvarchar (20)
    DECLARE @varBalance money
    SELECT @varName = Name,
           @varBalance = Balance
      FROM Inserted
    IF @varBalance < 0
      BEGIN
        INSERT INTO Customers (Name, Balance)
          VALUES (@varName, 0)
      END
    ELSE
      BEGIN
        INSERT INTO Customers (Name, Balance)
          VALUES (@varName, @varBalance)
      END
```

6. Execute the code, and attempt to add Mary's record. This time, it should work. Notice that the trigger actually had to issue the INSERT statement again. If the trigger did not issue the insert, then the insert would not have taken place. The second issue of the INSERT (from within the INSTEAD OF trigger) forces the INSTEAD OF trigger to be skipped; the constraints are checked and any AFTER trigger then fires. Also, note Mary's CustID is set to 4. The two times that the constraints failed were after the insert, and the IDENTITY value was incremented.

The next piece of code creates an AFTER trigger that lists the users in the table that currently have a $0 balance. This is done after any INSERT, UPDATE, or DELETE. Type and execute the following:

```
CREATE TRIGGER Current_Zero_Balance
  ON Customers
  AFTER INSERT, UPDATE, DELETE
```

APPLY YOUR KNOWLEDGE

```
AS
  PRINT 'The following customers have a $0
  ➥balance:'
  SELECT Name, Balance
    FROM Customers
    WHERE Balance = 0
GO
INSERT INTO Customers (Name, Balance)
  VALUES ('Bill', -10)
GO
```

7. Test the AFTER trigger again, but with a positive balance insert and then an update. Execute the following two statements to test the triggers:

```
INSERT INTO Customers (Name, Balance)
  VALUES ('Tom', -10)
GO

UPDATE Customers
  SET Balance = 75
  WHERE Name = 'Mary'
GO
```

8. The last major step is to create a DELETE trigger that copies deleted customers to an OldCustomers table. Create the OldCustomers table and the DELETE trigger on the Customers table with the following:

```
CREATE TABLE OldCustomers
  ( CustID    smallint,
    Name      nvarchar (20),
    Balance   money)
GO

CREATE TRIGGER Archive_Deleted_Customer
  ON Customers
  AFTER DELETE
  AS
    DECLARE @varCustID    smallint
    DECLARE @varName      nvarchar (20)
    DECLARE @varBalance   money

    SELECT @varCustID = CustID,
           @varName = Name,
           @varBalance = Balance
      FROM Deleted
    INSERT INTO OldCustomers (CustID, Name,
    ➥Balance)
      VALUES (@varCustID, @varName,
      ➥@varBalance)
    PRINT 'Customer Archived: ' + @varName
GO
```

9. To test the final trigger, type and execute the following:

```
DELETE FROM Customers
  WHERE Name = 'Mary'
GO
SELECT * FROM OldCustomers
```

10. The last statement should see both AFTER DELETE triggers fire on the Customers table. The first one was the Current_Zero_Balance trigger, and the second was the Archive_Deleted_Customer trigger. If you want to change the order of execution, because you have a requirement for reporting purposes, type and execute the following:

```
sp_settriggerorder
➥'Archive_Deleted_Customer', 'FIRST', 'DELETE'
GO
DELETE FROM Customers
  WHERE Name = 'Tom'
```

The final output that you should see should now have the triggers executing in reverse order. This exercise should have given you a good overview of all of the topics that were covered in the chapter.

Review Questions

1. Why would a developer want to use an INSTEAD OF trigger rather than an AFTER trigger?

2. What can be done to change the order in which trigger code is executed, and why would you want to change the order of execution?

3. What is indirect recursion, what is the maximum level of it, and what can be done to prevent it within SQL Server 2000?

4. What problems can arise from disabling all recursion and nesting of triggers?

5. How are the Inserted and Deleted tables used when a user invokes an UPDATE?

APPLY YOUR KNOWLEDGE

6. What steps can be taken to protect trigger code from being reused, and what are the disadvantages of protecting the code?

7. What tools can be used to create a trigger, and what are the benefits of each?

Exam Questions

1. You have an accounting SQL Server database application that is accessed by 50 users on your company network. When a user inserts or updates a record, you want to make sure that all the required columns have appropriate values. Which of the following would be best for this situation?

   A. A stored procedure and a trigger

   B. A batch and a trigger

   C. An UPDATE trigger and an INSERT trigger

   D. One trigger

2. You are a developer for a database. Currently the structure of data and the usage have been causing high CPU utilization on the server. You have decided that you must add several triggers to your database to validate data and generate alerts based on data modifications. You are worried about the impact of the triggers on your already heavily utilized server. Generally, how will triggers affect the performance of your server?

   A. Relatively low performance overhead, most of it involved in referencing tables.

   B. Severely impacts database performance.

   C. Does not impact performance whatsoever.

   D. Triggers consume less performance than any other type of resource in SQL Server;

execution of programming logic uses most of the performance.

3. You have a database that contains several FOREIGN KEY and CHECK constraints. Users are having problems with data entry on the database, because the data that they are adding is constantly in violation of the CHECK constraints. Corporate policy regarding database design prevents you from modifying the current constraints, so you decide to implement your changes via a trigger. Which types of triggers would be best suited for this task? Select the best answer.

   A. UPDATE, DELETE, and INSERT triggers.

   B. Just UPDATE and INSERT triggers.

   C. INSTEAD OF triggers.

   D. Triggers cannot be used in this circumstance.

4. You are working for a medical agency that tracks statistics for doctors throughout the country; these statistics are later involved in economic decisions. This year, the medical agency plans on creating statistics for the salaries of doctors and storing them in a SalarySurvey table. To get more accurate statistics, the agency does not include values of salaries that are greater than $200,000 or smaller than $10,000. Which of the following is the best way to implement this? All these examples are set to support only single row inserts, which would not be typical on a production database.

   A. The following code:

```
CREATE TRIGGER SalaryCheck
  ON SalarySurvey
  FOR INSERT
  AS
    IF (SELECT MonthlySalary FROM inserted)>
    ➥200,000 or
      (SELECT MonthlySalary FROM inserted)<
      ➥10,000
```

APPLY YOUR KNOWLEDGE

```
BEGIN
   RAISERROR (  Cannot Enter Salary -
   out of range', 16, 1) WITH LOG
   ROLLBACK TRANSACTION
END
```

B. The following code:

```
CREATE TRIGGER SalaryCheck
  ON SalarySurvey
  FOR INSERT
  AS
    IF (SELECT MonthlySalary FROM updated)>
    200,000 or
       (SELECT MonthlySalary FROM updated)<
       10,000
      BEGIN
         RAISERROR ( 'Cannot Enter Salary -
         out of range', 16, 1) WITH LOG
         REVERSE TRANSACTION
      END
```

C. The following code

```
CREATE TRIGGER SalaryCheck
  ON SalarySurvey
  AFTER UPDATE
  AS
    IF (SELECT MonthlySalary FROM inserted)>
    200,000 or
       (SELECT MonthlySalary FROM inserted)<
       10,000
      BEGIN
         RAISERROR ( 'Cannot Enter Salary -
         out of range', 16, 1) WITH LOG
         ROLLBACK TRANSACTION
      END
```

D. The following code:

```
CREATE TRIGGER SalaryCheck
  ON SalarySurvey
  FOR INSERT
  AS
    IF (SELECT MonthlySalary FROM inserted)>
    200,000 or
       (SELECT MonthlySalary FROM inserted)>
       10,000
      BEGIN
         RAISERROR ( 'Cannot Enter Salary -
         out of range', 16, 1) WITH LOG
         ROLLBACK TRANSACTION
      END
```

5. In what order do these events happen?

   A. Constraints, BEFORE triggers, INSTEAD OF triggers.

   B. INSTEAD OF triggers, constraints, BEFORE triggers, AFTER triggers.

   C. INSTEAD OF triggers, constraints, AFTER triggers.

   D. Constraints, INSTEAD OF triggers, AFTER triggers.

   E. None of the above.

6. Which of the following statements cannot be used within a trigger? Select all that apply.

   A. CREATE TABLE

   B. ROLLBACK TRANSACTION

   C. LOAD TRANSACTION

   D. RECONFIGURE

7. You are a senior developer working at a consulting firm. You have to make sure that a user does not enter an alphabetical character in the Telephone, Date, and SSN columns of the Client table. What is the best way to implement this type of validation?

   A. Create an INSERT trigger.

   B. Create an INSTEAD OF trigger.

   C. Use CHECK constraints.

   D. There is no way to implement this.

8. You plan on implementing a simple triggering strategy for a large college located in the heart of New York. The college has planned a 30-day trip to Paris for those interested. The college enters the names of those desiring to go and then checks to see whether they have paid the fees. If they have not paid the required fees, their names

APPLY YOUR KNOWLEDGE

do not get entered in; otherwise, they should be entered. Which type of trigger should the school implement?

A. Indirect recursion trigger (IRT)

B. Direct recursion trigger (DRT)

C. INSERT trigger

D. UPDATE trigger

9. Which of the following statements are not true for all types of triggers?

A. Triggers can fire on all three events—UPDATE, DELETE, and INSERT.

B. Only one trigger per table is allowed.

C. Triggers can execute stored procedures.

D. Triggers can be used to validate the data being entered into a table.

10. Which of the following methods can be used to create a trigger and then later modify its definition?

A. Sp_createtrigger and sp_altertrigger

B. CREATE TRIGGER and MODIFY TRIGGER

C. CREATE TRIGGER and ALTER TRIGGER

D. Both A and C

11. What should you do before renaming or dropping a trigger?

A. Use sp_freename to ensure the name of your trigger can be reused.

B. Use sp_helpdependants to check for dependent objects.

C. Use sp_depends to examine dependencies.

D. No additional steps are required.

12. Non-updateable views can be made to accept updates by doing which of the following?

A. Executing sp_makeupdatableview.

B. Creating an AFTER trigger.

C. Creating a DELETE trigger.

D. Creating an INSTEAD OF trigger.

13. Which of the following commands would enable you to read a trigger definition?

A. sp_helptext

B. sp_helptrigger

C. sp_displaydef

D. sp_help

Answers to Review Questions

1. When considering the difference in triggers, remember that there can be only one INSTEAD OF trigger per action. This means that the single INSTEAD OF trigger might end up being large and unruly with all the logic that must go into it. Each INSTEAD OF trigger also executes only once per update, so there is no direct recursion.

   On the plus side of INSTEAD OF triggers, they execute instead of the attempted update. This means that they execute before the data modification and constraints are checked, so they can change the way the data modification is made and avoid constraint violations.

   INSTEAD OF triggers are also the only types of triggers that can be applied to a view, so that they can modify how updates are performed in a view and allow INSERT, UPDATE, and DELETE support for views that normally would not have allowed these actions.

APPLY YOUR KNOWLEDGE

These are two of the most of the most compelling reasons to use an INSTEAD OF trigger. An AFTER trigger is not capable of performing these tasks. In many cases you will implement both types of triggers on a table, each performing the duties that it is best suited for.

2. You can change the order of trigger code by using INSTEAD OF triggers rather than AFTER triggers. When working with AFTER triggers, you can set a FIRST and LAST trigger by using the sp_settriggerorder stored procedure. You might want to use INSTEAD OF triggers so that the data modifications can be examined and changed before the firing of table constraints. Setting the order of AFTER triggers (FIRST and LAST) enables you to have specific actions performed in a certain order. You might have two separate triggers firing on an action: One generates a text file report based on the update, and another attaches the report to an email message. It would be important to have these triggers execute in a specific order.

3. Indirect recursion occurs when a trigger performs an action such as updating a remote table or calling a stored procedure, and that action eventually causes its own table to be modified and it executes again. This is different from direct recursion, where the trigger initiates the action that causes itself to execute again. A DELETE trigger that causes the deletion of similar records in its own table would be an example of direct recursion. To prevent all recursion, you can disable the server option of nested triggers. When nested triggers are enabled, there is a general recursion level of 32 steps that is shared between views, stored procedures, and triggers.

4. If you disable the nested triggers server option, then no trigger recursion happens on your server. This can actually cause procedures to produce results that you do not expect. This issue is illustrated in the "Recursive Trigger" section of this chapter.

5. When an UPDATE trigger is fired, it sends a copy of the value being modified to the Deleted table and then sends the desired record to the Inserted table. These two tables can then be queried to find out what is being changed during the update.

6. You can protect your trigger code by using the WITH ENCRYPTION option when you create the trigger. This prevents anyone (including yourself) from being able to read the trigger definition. The potential problem with this is that you are not able to read the trigger definition. If you have not recorded the trigger elsewhere, you cannot easily recreate or alter it.

7. You can create triggers using Query Analyzer, Enterprise Manager, or SQL-DMO. Query Analyzer offers the advantage of being able to execute pre-made script files that might already contain your trigger definitions. Script files offer an excellent way to copy or apply the same triggers to multiple servers. Enterprise Manager has the benefit of being a graphical tool and allows for easier editing or altering of a trigger. SQL-DMO provides another scripting alternative: this time VBScript rather than T-SQL. SQL-DMO can also be used from within a programming language such as Visual Basic or Visual C++. SQL-DMO enables you to add trigger creation features to other applications that you might be creating. Because the SQL-DMO interface will not be focused on for the exam, this chapter only mentioned it as a method in passing.

APPLY YOUR KNOWLEDGE

Answers to Exam Questions

1. **D.** A single trigger can be used to perform validation on more than one event, such as an INSERT and an UPDATE. For more information about the differences between trigger types, see the "Overview of Triggers" section of this chapter.

2. **A.** Triggers usually require very little CPU time. Most of the time involved in executing a trigger deals with referencing tables, which might have to be read from the disk.

   Execution time is usually low, but actual impact can be hampered depending on what is done in the programming code of the trigger. You might code CPU-intensive tasks into your trigger by calling on certain stored procedures or commands. These commands might not be typical in a trigger. For more information about triggers, see the "Triggers" section at the beginning of this chapter.

3. **C.** INSTEAD OF triggers would be required for this task, because you must check for constraint violations before the update occurs. If there are constraint violations, then AFTER triggers will not fire. Most likely you will be implementing INSTEAD OF INSERT or INSTEAD OF INSERT, UPDATE triggers. When trigger actions are listed, such as an INSERT trigger, you cannot know for sure whether it is an INSTEAD OF or AFTER trigger, but you should assume that it is a FOR or AFTER trigger if not specifically mentioned. For more information about the order that triggers and constraints are applied, see the "Trigger Actions and Order" section of this chapter.

4. **A.** This is the only answer choice that is implemented as an INSERT trigger and has correct use of ROLLBACK TRANSACTION. For more information about INSERT, UPDATE, and DELETE triggers, see the "AFTER Triggers" section of this chapter.

5. **C.** The correct order for the events are INSTEAD OF triggers, constraints, AFTER triggers. For more information about triggers and trigger order, see the "Trigger Order" section of this chapter.

6. **A, C, D.** CREATE TABLE, DROP TABLE, ALTER TABLE, GRANT, REVOKE, DISK, ALTER DATABASE, LOAD DATABASE, RESTORE DATABASE, UPDATE STATISTICS, SELECT INTO, LOAD TRANSACTION, and RECONFIGURE are all commands that cannot be used within a trigger. For more information about creating triggers, see the "Creating Triggers" section of this chapter.

7. **C.** Making sure a user does not enter data of a different type is not best done with a trigger because the same can be done with a CHECK constraint, which processes faster and with less overhead than a trigger. For more information about different ways to constrain data input, see the "Constraining Data Modifications" section of this chapter.

8. **C.** An INSERT trigger is the best choice because data is validated as it is *inserted*. Second, there are no such things as direct and indirect recursion triggers; recursion is something the triggers might do. For more information about the types of triggers that exist, see the "Trigger Actions and Order" section of this chapter.

9. **B.** More than one trigger may be placed on a table; however, only one INSTEAD OF trigger, per trigger action, may be placed on a table. For more information about restrictions on triggers and trigger functions, see the "Trigger Actions and Order" section of this chapter.

10. **C.** The CREATE TRIGGER statement is used to create a trigger, and the ALTER TRIGGER statement is used to later modify the trigger. For more information about the CREATE TRIGGER and ALTER TRIGGER statements, see the "Triggers" section of this chapter.

APPLY YOUR KNOWLEDGE

11. **C.** You should check for dependent objects when renaming or deleting a trigger. For more information about checking for dependencies, see the "Renaming Triggers" and "Dropping Triggers" sections of this chapter.

12. **D.** INSTEAD OF triggers can be used to make non-updateable views capable of supporting updates.

For more information about functions offered by INSTEAD OF triggers, see the "INSTEAD OF Triggers" section of this chapter.

13. **A.** The sp_helptext stored procedure can be used to read the trigger definition. For more information about working with trigger definitions, see the "Viewing a Trigger" section of this chapter.

Suggested Readings and Resources

1. *Inside SQL Server 2000*, by Kalen Delaney (www.insidesqlserver.com)

   Not a beginner book, but fills in many of the gaps left out of the SQL Server Books Online documentation. Explains fully how SQL Server stores and processes data internally.

2. SQL Server 2000 Books Online

   • Creating and Maintaining Databases: Enforcing Business Rules with Triggers.

   • Accessing and Changing Relational Data: Cursors

3. SQL Server Magazine (www.sqlmag.com)

   The magazine is a great source of current discussions and tips on how to use and implement Microsoft SQL Server. You are able to read current and archived issues, and search across the magazine archives. At the time of writing, a search for "Triggers" yielded 361 hits.

This chapter is split into two major topics. First, it covers stored procedures and then user-defined functions. This means the five objectives are split up into ten smaller pieces, half for stored procedures and half for user-defined functions. It's a good logical break, but it doesn't necessarily get along with how the objectives are laid out. This chapter isn't ordered the way the objectives are written, but by how you need to learn the material.

Enforce procedural business logic using stored procedures and user-defined functions.

▶ Playing the role of the middle tiers in n-tier architecture, stored procedures and user-defined functions provide facilities for validating and modifying data to conform to business rules.

Pass and return parameters to and from stored procedures and user-defined functions.

▶ To control what your stored procedures and functions do, you can pass them different values that control how they work, called parameters. In addition, parameters provide a way to retrieve the data found by your stored procedures and user-defined functions.

Manage data manipulation by using stored procedures and user-defined functions

▶ Stored procedures and user-defined functions can be used to manipulate and store data by encapsulating SELECT, INSERT, UPDATE, and DELETE functionality.

Filter data by using stored procedures and user-defined functions.

▶ Web-based applications commonly use stored procedures and user-defined functions to determine which data will be displayed, taking advantage of the cached plans and easier management found in stored procedures.

CHAPTER 9

Stored Procedures and User-Defined Functions

Implement error handling in stored procedures and user-defined functions.

▶ Error handling is very important if you want to achieve true data integrity and provide feedback to the user. Stored procedures and user-defined functions provide capabilities to handle many errors and provide this feedback.

STUDY STRATEGIES

▶ As in Chapter 6, "Programming SQL Server 2000," practicing the techniques shown in this chapter will help you understand the material.

▶ If available, find stored procedures from peers and coworkers that operate on a database you have some familiarity with and review those stored procedures and functions.

▶ Spend some time looking at the different ways to pass parameters into stored procedures and how optional parameters work. You're almost guaranteed to have one exam question that revolves around positional and named parameters and default values.

INTRODUCTION

Stored procedures are the mainstay of application programming with SQL Server. Typically, applications that perform well and that are easily managed employ stored procedures exclusively for their data retrieval and update needs. This helps facilitate centralized management of queries, the ability to change data models and tune queries without rewriting code, and the ability to manage transactions without user intervention. User-defined functions, a new feature for SQL Server 2000, provide further encapsulation of logic into highly reusable and efficient components. This chapter combines what you learned in Chapter 5, "Advanced Data Retrieval and Modification," about writing queries and in Chapter 6 about writing batches and scripts to show you the logical extension of those things: writing reusable queries and batches that can be accessed from applications to provide consistent output and central change control.

MANAGING DATA MANIPULATION USING STORED PROCEDURES

▶ **Manage data manipulation by using stored procedures.**

The first half of this chapter is devoted to understanding how stored procedures work. You'll learn what stored procedures are, how they are created and managed, how they are executed, why they are so important, and finally some error handling strategies for stored procedures.

What Is a Stored Procedure?

According to SQL Server Books Online, a stored procedure is "a group of Transact-SQL statements compiled into a single execution plan." What does that mean? Well, it's a group of Transact-SQL statements, which is similar in nature to the idea of a batch discussed in Chapter 6. It's compiled into an execution plan, which means it can be compiled once and the execution plan may be reused, which reduces overhead somewhat.

Guessing from the name, a stored procedure is probably, well, *stored* somewhere. In this case, a stored procedure is actually stored in a database—any database you want. Specifically, if you're really interested, stored procedures are stored in the syscomments system table in each database. This table contains the source code—the T-SQL—that you write to create the stored procedure.

A stored procedure can have input parameters, which make it possible to tell the stored procedure things, such as the parameters for the queries it should run. A stored procedure can return results in several ways: with an integer return code, with one or more resultsets, and with output parameters.

This is all very abstract. Take a look at how stored procedures are created; that should make things a bit more solid.

Creating and Managing Stored Procedures

Stored procedures are created using the aptly named CREATE PROCEDURE statement. The CREATE PROCEDURE statement has to be the first executable line in a batch, and the stored procedure continues until the end of the batch, which is until the end of the file or until the word GO. You can abbreviate the word PROCEDURE to just PROC. Here's an example:

```
CREATE PROCEDURE TableList AS
SELECT name FROM sysobjects WHERE type = 'u'
GO
```

This stored procedure returns the same thing all the time: the list of tables, which includes the objects of type 'u', in the database in which the stored procedure was created. The name of the stored procedure is TableList. Stored procedure names follow the same rules as other object names. The keyword AS marks the beginning of the actual code to be executed. The end, of course, is marked with GO, which tells SQL Server that the batch is at a close and the stored procedure should be compiled.

That's not particularly a useful or helpful stored procedure; it's almost faster to type the entire query than it is to try and remember the stored procedure name. How about something a bit more interesting:

```
CREATE PROCEDURE TableList2
@NamePattern sysname = null
AS
if @NamePattern is null
```

```
SELECT name FROM sysobjects WHERE type = 'u'
else
SELECT name FROM sysobjects WHERE type = 'u' and name like
➡'%' + @NamePattern + '%'
GO
```

Now you have a stored procedure that can do something almost helpful. The @NamePattern sysname = null looks like a variable declaration, but it's actually a parameter declaration. A *parameter* is a variable that is passed in to a stored procedure to give the stored procedure a little guidance on how to get things done.

In this case, it's a parameter of type sysname. The = null part means that the parameter is optional, and if it's not specified it should be null. It's just as proper to do "= ''" to default it to an empty string, or any other arbitrary string that makes sense as a default. The only rule is that the default has to be the correct datatype and length to fit into the parameter. Notice that the AS keyword goes before the code starts, but after the parameter declarations. A stored procedure can have up to 2,100 parameters. A default can be any value, including NULL. It can contain the wildcards and pattern matching characters, such as asterisks and square brackets. All the parameters can have defaults, so you can call the stored procedure with no parameters if you want just the defaults.

The code in the example is fairly straightforward, if the @NamePattern is null, the stored procedure returns all the tables in the database; if the parameter has a value, it returns tables that contain the string that is contained in @NamePattern. Step by Step 9.1 shows you how to create the same stored procedure with Enterprise Manager:

> **NOTE**
>
> **Variables and Datatypes**   The sysname variable type is frequently used when you're going to be handling object names, such as table names, column names, or database names, because it's the data type that SQL Server uses in system tables. It's the preferred type to use for this type of information because as Microsoft changes the specifications for what an object name can and cannot be, the sysname type changes also, which should cause fewer coding revisions if you move to a different version of SQL Server.

STEP BY STEP

9.1 Creating a New Stored Procedure with Enterprise Manager

1. Open SQL Server Enterprise Manager and connect to the server to which you want to add a stored procedure. If you need to, you can register the server now.

2. View the containers inside the server by clicking the plus sign to the left of the server, as shown in Figure 9.1.

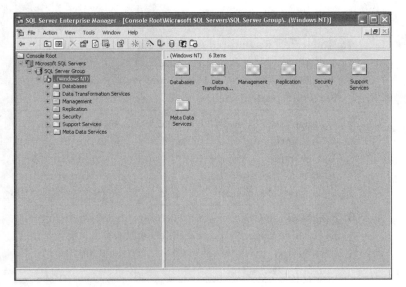

FIGURE 9.1
These are the objects within the server in SQL Server Enterprise Manager.

3. Open the Databases container, again by clicking the plus sign to the left of the word Databases. Choose a database from the list and view its containers by clicking the plus sign to the left of the database you want to work with. If you're just playing with the examples in the book, use the Pubs database. Click the Stored Procedures container, as shown in Figure 9.2.

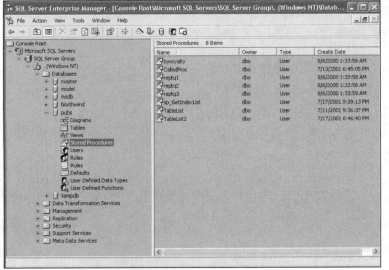

FIGURE 9.2
These are stored procedures within the Pubs database.

continues

continued

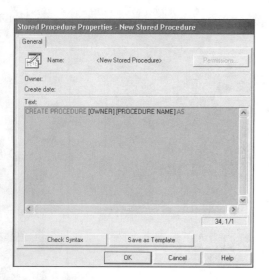

FIGURE 9.3

This is the window you use to create new stored procedures.

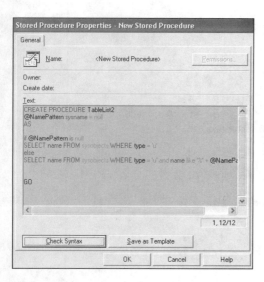

FIGURE 9.4

This is an example stored procedure typed into the Stored Procedure Properties window.

4. To create a new procedure, right-click in the right pane and choose New Stored Procedure. The Stored Procedure Properties - New Stored Procedure window appears, as shown in Figure 9.3.

5. Change [OWNER] and [PROCEDURE NAME] to the correct owner and name of the procedure. If you're unsure of the owner name, delete the [OWNER] and the period that follows it. Then, after the AS keyword, type in your stored procedure. An example is shown in Figure 9.4.

6. Click on the Check Syntax button to make sure you typed everything properly. This should pop up a dialog box that says Syntax check successful!. Clear the dialog box by clicking OK.

7. Click OK to save your stored procedure.

8. To edit an existing stored procedure, just double-click on it. You'll have the same option to check syntax as before.

The stored procedures you've seen in this chapter so far provide output by creating an output record set. Stored procedures can also pass back return values—integers that usually relay status information to the caller. To pass back a number to the caller, use the RETURN statement. The RETURN statement immediately exits the stored procedure, so don't use it until the stored procedure is all done, like this:

```
CREATE PROCEDURE TableList3
       @NamePattern sysname = null
AS
if @NamePattern is null
begin
       SELECT name FROM sysobjects WHERE type = 'u'
       RETURN 1
end
else
begin
       SELECT name FROM sysobjects WHERE type = 'u' and
➥name like '%' + @NamePattern + '%'
       RETURN 0
end
GO
```

This returns a value of 1 if the resultset contains all the tables, or a zero if it is returning a filtered set. Provided that the calling application is expecting the return value and knows how to decipher it, return values can be very helpful for returning record counts, error messages, or anything else meaningful back to the calling application. All the system stored procedures, for example, return a value of 0 for success and some non-zero result for failure. The RETURN statement can be used only to return integers.

In addition to return codes, stored procedures can also pass data to the calling application by using output parameters. Output parameters are declared like other parameters in the CREATE PROCEDURE statement with the word OUTPUT after them, like this:

```
CREATE PROCEDURE TableList4
      @NamePattern sysname = null,
      @RowCT int OUTPUT
AS
if @NamePattern is null
begin
      SELECT name FROM sysobjects WHERE type = 'u'
      SET @RowCT = @@ROWCOUNT
      RETURN 1
end
else
begin
      SELECT name FROM sysobjects WHERE type = 'u' and
      ➥name like '%' + @NamePattern + '%'
      SET @RowCT = @@ROWCOUNT
      RETURN 0
end
GO
```

This enables the calling program to accept the number of rows returned in a variable. You can also use an output parameter of type cursor to return the rowset, like this:

```
CREATE PROCEDURE TableList5
@NamePattern sysname = null,
@RowCT int OUTPUT,
@OutputCursor CURSOR VARYING OUTPUT
AS
if @NamePattern is null
begin
SET @OutputCursor = CURSOR FORWARD_ONLY STATIC FOR
SELECT name FROM sysobjects WHERE type = 'u'
SET @RowCT = @@ROWCOUNT
OPEN @OutputCursor
```

```
RETURN 1
end
else
begin
SET @OutputCursor = CURSOR FORWARD_ONLY STATIC FOR
SELECT name FROM sysobjects WHERE type = 'u' and name like
➡'%' + @NamePattern + '%'
SET @RowCT = @@ROWCOUNT
OPEN @OutputCursor
RETURN 0
end
GO
```

Notice that the OPEN statement absolutely has to be in the procedure, or the cursor does not return properly. There are a few additional rules with using cursors for output:

◆ If the cursor is declared as FORWARD_ONLY and opened, but none of the rows are fetched, the entire resultset will be returned.

◆ If the cursor is declared as FORWARD_ONLY, and rows are fetched, then the cursor will only contain unaccessed rows.

◆ If the cursor is declared as FORWARD_ONLY, and all the rows in the cursor are fetched, but the cursor is not closed, then the cursor will contain an empty recordset.

◆ If the cursor is closed, or if the cursor isn't opened in the first place, the cursor variable won't contain a cursor; it will be NULL.

◆ If the cursor is scrollable, all the rows in the resultset are returned.

If you're in doubt about the validity of the cursor variable, you can use the CURSOR_STATUS() function. This function returns different values depending on the condition of the cursor, provided that you know the type of cursor (local, global, or variable). The syntax is CURSOR_STATUS('<type>', '<variable>'). The single ticks are mandatory. For example, to diagnose the preceding cursor, you could use CURSOR_STATUS('variable', '@OutputCursor'). Table 9.1 shows what the CURSOR_STATUS function returns:

TABLE 9.1

CURSOR_STATUS Return Values

Return Value	Explanation
1	The cursor is allocated, open, and valid, and has at least one row if it is a static cursor, or it may have zero rows if it is dynamic.
0	The cursor is allocated and open, but it is empty. This can happen only on static cursors.
-1	The cursor is closed.
-2	An error occurred, because the variable wasn't assigned or the cursor was closed and de-allocated.
-3	The cursor doesn't exist.

IN THE FIELD

USING CURSORS AS RETURNS

Cursors are not used as returns very often because there are better ways of dealing with returning rowsets, such as just returning the rowset or the temporary table method discussed in the section titled, "Stored Procedures and Temporary Tables." Even the new table data type as an output parameter is more likely to get used than a cursor as an output parameter.

If you go back and read the service pack notes for past versions of SQL Server, you'll notice that nearly every one references bugs that can cause access violations related to cursors. Also, cursor performance tends to be about an order of magnitude below that of set operations, because SQL Server was built from the ground up to handle sets, and it handles row-by-row operations with some hesitation. Finally, there are very few operations that you cannot do without using a cursor. Cursors are the last resort, to be used sparingly, if at all.

Stored Procedure Groups

When you create a set of stored procedures, you can also add them all into a group by specifying a number after the stored procedure name—for example:

```
CREATE PROCEDURE TableList;1
```

You can then create a whole bunch of procedures with the same name and different numbers. This is called a stored procedure group. For example, if you have several applications that all run in one database, you can assign them all the same name and different numbers. That way when the application is removed from the database, it's easy to remove the associated stored procedures.

Stored procedure groups is a feature that is not used very often because it hides the functionality of the stored procedure by keeping it out of the name of the stored procedure. However, it's part of the syntax for CREATE PROCEDURE, so you should know what it does.

> **WARNING**
>
> **Don't Use Stored Procedure Groups!** Some features discussed in this chapter aren't widely used, but have to be discussed because they may be on the test. Stored procedure groups are one of them. Don't use stored procedure groups in real life because you may drop procedures inadvertently and it hides the true nature of a stored procedure by forcing it to have an artificial name.

CALLING STORED PROCEDURES; PASSING AND RETURNING PARAMETERS TO AND FROM STORED PROCEDURES

▶ Pass and return parameters to and from stored procedures.

Stored procedures are called using the EXEC statement, or, if the call to the stored procedure is the first statement in a batch, just by using the stored procedure name. For the system stored procedure sp_who, for example:

```
sp_who --valid, first line of a batch
go
sp_who  --still valid, first line of a batch after a GO
go
exec sp_who  --valid, the exec is optional
go
print 'Going to run sp_who now'
sp_who  --not valid, bad syntax, exec required here
go
```

Yes, the preceding code is kind of strange and perhaps a bit confusing. It's a shortcut for administrators who tend to spend a lot of time running one stored procedure in a batch, and it saves them from typing a lot. That's a pretty simple stored procedure call; what about calling a stored procedure with a return value? That's fairly simple also. It goes something like this:

```
DECLARE @Status int
EXEC @Status=TableList3 'spt'
print @Status
```

This calls the stored procedure that was written earlier in this chapter, and shows you the names of all of the tables that contain 'spt'. The return code, in this case, is just a status number. So, how about output parameters?

```
DECLARE @Status int,
@LocalRowCount int
EXEC @Status=TableList4 'spt', @LocalRowCount OUTPUT
print @Status
print @LocalRowCount
```

Notice the keyword OUTPUT in the EXEC line. If you don't put that keyword in there, the batch runs without error, but it also doesn't put a value into @LocalRowCount, which remains NULL in this case. That's a very common error that takes a long time to track down. Now, how about that returned cursor?

```
DECLARE @Status int,
@LocalCursor cursor,
@LocalCount int,
@TableName sysname

EXEC @Status = TableList5 null, @LocalCount OUTPUT,
➥@LocalCursor OUTPUT
PRINT @LocalCount
PRINT @Status
SELECT CURSOR_STATUS('variable', '@LocalCursor')
FETCH NEXT FROM @LocalCursor INTO @TableName
WHILE @@FETCH_STATUS = 0
BEGIN
PRINT @TableName
FETCH NEXT FROM @LocalCursor INTO @TableName
END
CLOSE @LocalCursor
DEALLOCATE @LocalCursor
```

Notice the SELECT CURSOR_STATUS line actually just prints the status. It would be more effective to make that statement an IF statement that would avoid error messages if something happened and the cursor didn't return properly.

There's another way to use the EXEC statement. So far, when there have been multiple parameters to pass, you've just passed the first parameter first, the second parameter second, and so on, like this:

```
EXEC @Status = TableList5 null, @LocalCount OUTPUT,
➥@LocalCursor OUTPUT
```

That is called using *positional parameter passing*, because the first parameter in the EXEC matches up with the first parameter in the CREATE PROCEDURE, and the second matches up with the second, and so on. There's another way to call stored procedures: using named parameters, which looks like this:

```
EXEC @Status = TableList5 @NamePattern=null, @RowCT =
➥@LocalCount OUTPUT,
        @OutputCursor = @LocalCursor OUTPUT
```

You don't have to put them in the same order, either:

```
EXEC @Status = TableList5 @RowCT = @LocalCount OUTPUT,
        @OutputCursor = @LocalCursor OUTPUT,
        ➥@NamePattern=null,
```

There are some rules about how this all works, of course. The main rule is that if you start with named parameters, you have to use named parameters all the way through. If you start with positional parameters, you can use positional parameters until the first named parameter, then you have to use named parameters for all the rest of the parameters. For example:

```
EXEC @Status = TableList5 @RowCT = @LocalCount OUTPUT,
➥@OutputCursor = @LocalCursor OUTPUT  --valid
EXEC @Status = TableList5 null, @RowCT OUTPUT,
➥@OutputCursor = @LocalCursor OUTPUT  --valid
EXEC @Status = TableList5 @RowCT = @LocalCount OUTPUT,
➥@LocalCursor OUTPUT  --NOT valid
```

Notice that in the first statement, the @NamePattern variable was completely left out, which will cause it to default to null. This is one of the strengths of using named parameters: it lets you leave out the optional parameters you don't use, and the default values are used in their place.

So, how does EXEC know from which database to pull the stored procedure? That's a very good question.

Stored Procedure Scoping

System stored procedures are stored in the Master database. When you execute a stored procedure, such as sp_who in a database other than Master, how does SQL Server know where to look for the stored procedure? The set of rules that determine where stored procedures will be executed are called the *scoping* rules. For example:

```
use pubs
go
sp_who   --why does this work?
go
```

One of the scoping rules is being used in that code block. The sp_who stored procedure is not in the Pubs database, but it can be executed from any database because it is stored in the Master database, and it's name starts with "sp_". So, if you need to write a stored procedure that can be accessed from any database, you can follow this convention and you'll be in good shape.

When you execute a stored procedure that resides in Master, where does it look to find tables and other objects that it is looking for? For example, if you run something like this:

```
use pubs
go
sp_help sysobjects
```

Which of the sysobjects tables will be examined and have its column list returned: the one in Master or the one in Pubs? Obviously, it's the one in Pubs. But what happens if you run this:

```
use pubs
go
master..sp_help sysobjects
```

The preceding code returns the column list in the Master database. Confused yet? If you specify a database name (such as master..sp_help) in the exec statement, then it's like performing a "use" statement to move over to the Master database before executing the stored procedure, and then another "use" statement to move back to the original database after the stored procedure is done. The stored procedure runs in the context of the exec statement, not the current database. If you do not specify a database name, then SQL Server runs the stored procedure in the current database. Here's another example:

```
USE master
go
CREATE TABLE ScopeTest ( i int)
go
sp_help scopetest
go
USE pubs
go
sp_help ScopeTest
go
master..sp_help ScopeTest
go
```

So, what happens if you create a procedure in a local database with the same name as a stored procedure named sp_ in Master? The stored procedure that's local is ignored. It cannot be run, even by specifying the database name. If you name a stored procedure sp_something in a database other than Master, and there is a procedure with that name already in Master, then your non-Master stored procedure cannot be run until you give it a new name. Here's an example:

```
USE pubs
go
CREATE PROCEDURE sp_who as
begin
print 'the fake sp_who is here'
end
go
sp_who          --runs the real sp_who
go
pubs..sp_who  --once again, the real sp_who
```

Stored Procedures and Temporary Tables

Temporary tables are tables created in Tempdb that exist only inside a given connection. They are created with the Create Table statement, but they are all named with a single pound sign (#) at the beginning. Typically, they're given names such #tmp or something similar, but this is just convention—and not a very good one because it doesn't give you any information on what the temporary table is used for.

A temporary table lasts the duration of its connection, but across several batches. So, if you create a temporary table inside a stored procedure, the temporary table goes away at the end of the stored procedure, just like the variables do.

However, if you create a temporary table in one batch and call a stored procedure inside a later batch, the stored procedure has access to the temporary table. For example:

```
create table #tmp(id int)
go
create proc GetIDs
as
insert into #tmp
select id from sysobjects
go
```

If you run the stored procedure, you end up with a temporary table full of ID numbers. Now, what happens if you drop the #tmp table and attempt to run the stored procedure? You get a message something like this: Invalid object name '#tmp'.

The problem here is that when you create a stored procedure, all the objects that the stored procedure needs to access must be present when the stored procedure is created. In addition, if the stored procedure creates objects, including temporary tables, then the temporary tables can't exist when you create the stored procedure.

When you create a temporary table inside a stored procedure, the stored procedure automatically recompiles itself. This can cause performance problems, but there are things you can do to avoid serious slowdowns. First, avoid the use of temporary tables when you can; use local variables of type table as appropriate. Second, put all your CREATE TABLE statements at the beginning of the stored procedure. If you need to put data into a temporary table and then share the data with other sessions, you can create a global temporary table by naming the table with two pound signs (##) rather than one. A global temporary table can be accessed by all connections on the server, but is destroyed when the connection that created it ends.

If you need a bit more persistence than that, you can actually directly create tables in Tempdb. These tables persist until the server is restarted. The Tempdb database, the database that holds all temporary tables, is rebuilt every time the server starts, so the table is destroyed when the server starts, along with the rest of the objects in Tempdb.

> **IN THE FIELD**
>
> ---
>
> ### USING TEMP TABLES AND VARIABLES OF TYPE Table
>
> You should use variables of type `table` and temporary tables in the appropriate places. Temporary tables can be populated using an `EXEC` statement, which, from a practical standpoint, is the only thing you can't do with a variable of type `table`. There are other restrictions, but that's the one you'll run into most often.
>
> Use temporary tables when you need to store huge amounts of temporary information, as well as variables of type `table` for smaller rowsets.
>
> Now, on the performance front, you should always make sure that f you have a temporary table storing a huge amount of information, there is a good reason for it. Generally, an appropriately sized yet large temporary table is probably on the order of a few thousand rows—any more than that and you probably are doing something wrong from a query design standpoint.
>
> ---

You can now create stored procedures. You have a pretty good handle on how to run them and where they are going to run from, but how do you change or drop a stored procedure?

Dropping Stored Procedures

To drop a stored procedure, use the DROP PROCEDURE statement, as follows:

```
DROP PROCEDURE tablelist3
```

Surprisingly, this has nowhere near the rules and obligations as creating a stored procedure. You can drop stored procedures in only the current database, so something like the following is *not* valid:

```
DROP PROCEDURE master..tablelist3
```

You can put as many DROP PROCEDURE statements in a batch as you'd like. If the stored procedure is in use when you issue the DROP PROCEDURE command, the connection running the stored procedure continues to execute the stored procedure, but it won't exist after the stored procedure finishes executing.

Altering a Stored Procedure

To alter a stored procedure, use the ALTER PROCEDURE command. It looks nearly identical to the CREATE PROCEDURE command, but it has the word ALTER in it rather than CREATE. If the stored procedure you are trying to alter does not exist, you get an error.

Typically, there are two ways to change a stored procedure. The way SQL Server's scripting engine does it is to drop the original stored procedure and then create the new one. The problem with this technique is that it removes all the security settings from the stored procedure. If you use ALTER, then the stored procedure changes, but the security doesn't.

Stored Procedure Text

Getting stored procedure text from within Enterprise Manager is very straightforward. Basically, you just hunt through the tree view, right-click on the stored procedure, choose All Tasks and Generate Script from the context menus, click the Preview button, and that's it. Getting them from within Query Analyzer is a nice shortcut, and not much more complex. Use the sp_helptext command, like this:

```
USE master
go
sp_helptext sp_who
```

This displays all the text for the stored procedure that is passed in as the parameter, in the CREATE PROCEDURE format. So, all you have to do to make a change is a little copy-and-paste, change the CREATE to ALTER, and make your functional changes.

Nested Stored Procedures

Stored procedures can call other stored procedures. One restriction, however, should be mentioned. If the called stored procedure uses an INSERT with an EXEC statement, the calling stored procedure cannot use the output of the called stored procedure as an INSERT with an EXEC. For example:

```
CREATE  PROCEDURE CalledProc
as
CREATE TABLE #tmp (
```

```
spid int,
ecid int,
status varchar(30),
loginname sysname,
hostname sysname,
blk int,
dbname sysname,
cmd varchar(30)
)

INSERT INTO #tmp
EXEC sp_who
go
CREATE TABLE #localtmp (
spid int,
ecid int,
status varchar(30),
loginname sysname,
hostname sysname,
blk int,
dbname sysname,
cmd varchar(30)
)

INSERT INTO #localtmp
EXEC calledProc
```

This looks like a fairly innocent bit of code, but it results in an error: An INSERT EXEC statement cannot be nested. So, if you call one stored procedure from another stored procedure, you can use a cursor to pass back the results, but don't use a temporary table like this one.

ENFORCING PROCEDURAL BUSINESS LOGIC WITH STORED PROCEDURES

▶ **Enforce procedural business logic using stored procedures.**

Why use stored procedures at all? They do look like a lot of work, and there are many restrictions to keep in mind. However, there are several benefits to using stored procedures that far outweigh the costs.

◆ **n-Tier Architecture**. SQL Server can provide both the bottom tier (data storage) and middle tier (business logic) parts of a large-scale, client-server application. With judicious use of stored procedures and triggers, data integrity and business rules can be enforced.

◆ **Speed**. Stored procedures can be faster than equivalent "dynamic" batches because SQL Server can cache the query plan and reuse the query plan. So, the code is pre-parsed, pre-planned, and ready to run, eliminating some of the startup time for running a batch, especially a significantly large batch.

◆ **Code Control**. Typically, programmers write programs and database administrators spend most of their time either writing queries for the programmers or fixing broken queries from the programmers. If the queries are encapsulated into stored procedures, the queries can be changed by the database administrator easily, and the database administrator just has to keep the incoming parameters and outgoing data formatted the same, but can make other changes inside the stored procedure without changing the application code.

◆ **Reducing Round Trips**. Typically, applications that do not use stored procedures for handling data make repeated trips to the database to get little pieces of information, which are then correlated and usually applied to the database. This involves data making several trips across the network, and sometimes involves making and breaking several database connections. This is a lot less efficient than simply telling SQL Server how to handle your data and letting the stored procedure process the data without it leaving the server.

The stored procedures mentioned in this chapter are fairly simple. It is common in systems that use stored procedures extensively to have stored procedures that are hundreds or thousands of lines long, making them extremely complex. Having this type of logic in a language (T-SQL) that is designed to manipulate data in tables provides centralized management and efficiency improvements.

Stored procedures are used extensively to encapsulate business logic, especially by implementing transactions. Remember from Chapter 6 that one of the hallmarks of a good transaction processing system is that the transactions are isolated and do not require user input to proceed from beginning to end. Using stored procedures is an effective way to encapsulate an entire transaction into one line of execution: the stored procedure call. Using parameters to pass in data and result-sets to return output is a very common way to make sure that the data that comes in is validated and correct and that the correlations between the data being returned conform to established business rules.

Where's the Rest of the Structure?
There are a lot of partial database designs from here out. These are not intended to be fully designed databases, and you should be thinking to yourself that the author should be storing first and last name separately. You're right. He should. But the names aren't an important part of the example; they're just present to flesh out the structure.

For example, say that you have a system that needs to handle some business rules about sales representatives and their territories. Each sales rep has a territory made up of one or more zip codes, and is given credit for sales made within his or her zip codes only. You would build a table like this for the sales reps:

```
CREATE TABLE SalesRep (
SalesRepID int IDENTITY(1,1),
SalesRepName varchar(75),
)
```

Then you'd have a related table to track zip codes for each sales rep, which would look like this:

```
CREATE TABLE SalesRepZipCode (
SalesRepID int not null,
ZipCode varchar(6) not null
)
```

You need a table that contains customer records:

```
CREATE TABLE Customer (
CustomerID int,
CustomerName varchar(50),
CustomerZip varchar(6)
)
```

And finally, a table that contains sales records:

```
CREATE TABLE Sales (
SalesID int identity(1,1),
SalesRepID int,
ProductID int,
CustomerID int,
QtySold int,
Price float
)
```

Jim the salesman sells 42 widgets to the customer with ID number 27. An application that logs this type of transaction would do something like this:

```
create procedure LogSale
@SalesRepID int,
@ProductID int,
@CustomerID int,
@QtySold int,
@Price float
as
begin
declare @SoldInZipCode varchar(6)
SELECT @SoldInZipCode = ZipCode
        FROM Customer
    WHERE CustomerID = @CustomerID
```

```
if (SELECT count(*)
            FROM SalesRepZipCode
            WHERE SalesRepID = @SalesRepID
                    and ZipCode = @ZipCode) = 0
begin
RAISERROR("Unable to insert sale-Customer out of Sales Rep
➥Territory", 16, 1)
return 0
end
else
INSERT Sales VALUES (@SalesRepID, @ProductID, @CustomerID,
➥@QtySold, @Price)
return 1
end
```

This is a fairly simple example. A more complete procedure would also check to make sure that the price the sales rep sold at was a valid price, that the quantity was valid, and so on. Using this technique, you can validate data before it enters your database, and ensure that it doesn't violate business rules.

FILTERING DATA USING STORED PROCEDURES

▶ **Filter data using stored procedures.**

Stored procedures can also be used to filter data. This is critical in web-based applications, where you tend to present a lot more data than you receive. For example, say that you're designing a web site for an auto insurance company. You want to provide a page that shows customers a list of claims centers in their city that they are eligible to use based on the insurance plan they have. So you need a table of customers, like this:

```
CREATE TABLE Customer (
CustomerID int IDENTITY(1,1),
CustomerName varchar(100),
PlanID int
)
```

And you also need to have a table of claim centers:

```
CREATE TABLE ClaimCenter(
ClaimCenterID int IDENTITY (1,1),
ClaimCenterAddress varchar(100),
ClaimCenterCity varchar(100),
ClaimCenterState varchar(2)
)
```

Finally, you need to know which claim centers can be used with which insurance plans:

```
CREATE TABLE ClaimCenterPlan (
ClaimCenterID int,
PlanID int
)
```

Now, when a customer comes to a web site, you want to write a stored procedure that returns all the claim centers within the customer's city that uses his or her plan. In addition, if the customer doesn't have a plan, you want to show all the claim centers.

```
CREATE PROC GetClaimCenterList
        @City varchar(100),
@State varchar(2),
@CustomerID int=NULL

AS
BEGIN
IF @CustomerID IS NULL
SELECT * FROM ClaimCenter WHERE ClaimCenterCity = @City
ELSE
SELECT CC.*
FROM Customer C
INNER JOIN ClaimCenterPlan CCP
ON CC.PlanID = CCP.PlanID
INNER JOIN ClaimCenter CC
on CC.ClaimCenterID = CCP.ClaimCenterID
WHERE C.CustomerID = @CustomerID
AND C.CustomerCity = @City
END
```

This provides the web page with a resultset that includes all the relevant claim center information, which is helpful for the user, and reduces the chance that customers will show up at a claim center that can't help them.

IN THE FIELD

WEB APPLICATIONS AND STORED PROCEDURES

If you've worked on web applications before, you've probably realized that most web programmers weren't hired to write good queries; they were hired to write good web pages. By encouraging, or perhaps mandating, the use of stored procedures, you can encapsulate all the queries that the web programmers write into one place with a consistent interface. Then, as the SQL guru you will be when you finish reading this book, you can go through and tweak their queries, make them more efficient, and leave the rowsets that get sent to their application and the parameter list the same. That way, you can rewrite the queries and leave the web pages completely alone.

IMPLEMENTING ERROR HANDLING IN STORED PROCEDURES

▶ **Implement error handling in stored procedures.**

Stored procedures can also manage some error conditions, whether caused by data exceptions or by problems with SQL Server. There are ways to handle errors inside a stored procedure.

First of all, judicious use of return codes is recommended to ensure that the applications upstream understand the execution status of the stored procedure. Within SQL Server, using the integer return codes is a good way to make sure that calling stored procedures understand how called stored procedures completed their tasks. It is important to create written standards on how return codes should be used, such as whether the return value 0 is a "success" value or a "failed" value. Some systems use 0 as success, so that the other numbers are available to denote specific types of errors.

Next, make sure you are using transactions, @@TRANCOUNT, and ROLL-BACK correctly within the stored procedure. That's all covered back in Chapter 6.

Some T-SQL statements are more likely to cause errors than others, such as statements that perform BULK INSERT operations or that interact with other servers using the Distributed Transaction Coordinator. To discover whether a particular T-SQL statement was successful, you can check the value of the @@ERROR global variable. This variable is set similar to how @@ROWCOUNT is set in that it is valid only if you check it immediately following the statement that caused the error. If the @@ERROR variable is set to zero, then no error occurred during execution of the preceding statement. If @@ERROR is set to something other than zero, then an error occurred during the attempt to run the statement. The @@ERROR variable can be used to handle errors that won't stop a batch (or a stored procedure) from running, such as constraint violations or problems with aggregate functions that don't have enough data.

Here's an example of what error handling in a stored procedure might look like:

```
CREATE PROC errhandler AS
BEGIN
DECLARE @ErrorCollector int
BEGIN TRANSACTION
INSERT INTO mytable VALUES (1, 4, 3, 19)
        SET @ErrorCollector = @@ERROR
IF @ErrorCollector <> 0
begin
ROLLBACK TRANSACTION
RETURN @ERRORCOLLECTOR
end
else
COMMIT TRANSACTION
return 0
END
```

A few notes on this. First of all, using BEGIN and END to wrap the whole thing up is not required; it's just another style you can use. The @ErrorCollector variable is used to hold the @@ERROR value for the return code, if needed. The function also uses transactions to handle data integrity, and returns a non-zero number if the stored procedure fails, which represents the error code.

Stored procedures have two options that can be set when they are being created or altered: ENCRYPTION and RECOMPILE. The ENCRYPTION option specifies that the text of the stored procedure should not be available in syscomments or to the sp_helptext stored procedure. This is typically done when you are distributing proprietary code to customers and you don't want them to be able to see your code. It also typically has to be removed before you install version upgrades and some service pack upgrades for SQL Server, which is a good reason to *not* use it, because removing the encryption means re-creating all the stored procedures.

The RECOMPILE option specifies that the stored procedure's execution plan should be recompiled before it is executed. This is used when the queries in the stored procedure change significantly based on incoming parameters—changes that would change the indexes or join strategies SQL Server uses. To use either of these options, the syntax is:

```
create procedure myproc
@MyParameter int
```

```
with recompile
as
      do stuff here
go
```

Whenever a user executes a stored procedure, SQL Server checks the stored procedure cache, which is a part of the memory that SQL Server uses for disk cache, to see whether the stored procedure execution plan is present in the cache. If it is, then SQL Server uses the cache to avoid having to figure out the execution plan again. The problem is that sometimes you *want* SQL Server to re-figure the execution plan. For example, if the stored procedure references tables that have indexes that change, or if the stored procedure just has an extremely convoluted plan, you may want to force a recompile by creating the stored procedure with the RECOMPILE option. If the stored procedure has already been created without the RECOMPILE option, you can change it to recompile on execution by using the sp_recompile system stored procedure. If you want to recompile the plan just once, you can use the WITH RECOMPILE option for the EXEC statement to execute the stored procedure—just tack WITH RECOMPILE onto the end of the EXEC.

REVIEW BREAK

- ▶ Stored procedures are objects stored in the database that contain code similar to batches.

- ▶ Stored procedures can return data as a rowset, an output parameter, a cursor, or by populating a temporary table.

- ▶ Stored procedures can be used to encapsulate business processes by validating data and controlling transactions.

- ▶ Stored procedures can also be used to filter data sent to applications.

Stored procedures are vitally important for applications that use SQL Server, and you'll run into them constantly. The next section is going to cover very similar objectives, but the "user-defined function" part of the objective is structured similarly to what you've been doing on stored procedures. User-defined functions are very useful and have a lot of useful applications.

MANAGING DATA MANIPULATION WITH USER-DEFINED FUNCTIONS

▶ **Managing data manipulation with user-defined functions.**

User-defined functions have been on the most-requested-feature list of most SQL Server programmers for a very long time. The system-defined functions, such as USER_NAME(), SERVER_NAME, CONVERT(), and GETDATE(), are used constantly; they provide the functionality that makes T-SQL useful in many respects. By passing back basic values, user-defined functions can be used in many places where stored procedures just wouldn't work.

Types of User-Defined Functions

There are three types of functions. *Scalar functions* are functions that return a single scalar data value. The word *scalar* in this context means "single value," and includes variables of the type int, bigint, varchar, and so on. Scalar functions cannot return data of a user-defined data type, a table type, a cursor, or the usual exceptions to most rules: text, ntext, timestamp, and image.

Table-valued functions return variables of type table, which were discussed in Chapter 6. These are essentially variables that are accessed like tables, with rows and columns. There are two types of table-valued functions: inline and multi-statement. An *inline table-valued function* is one statement long, it has no BEGIN or END, and the table that results is from one SELECT statement. A *multi-statement table-valued function* has a BEGIN and an END, and returns a table.

Restrictions on User-Defined Functions

User-defined functions have a whole list of things that they cannot do, which can be summed up with one term: *side effects*. In classic computer science jargon, a side effect is something that a function does that changes something outside the function. In general, functions are allowed to look at anything they want, but they cannot change anything except the variables that are declared inside the function. Any changes made to objects outside the function are called side effects, and are at least bad form, and, in this instance, are just downright not allowed. Functions are not allowed to change data in any databases except for incidental changes to Tempdb. They are not allowed to send email, to change objects, or to return a resultset to the user. They are also not allowed to call any of the following system-defined functions:

@@CONNECTIONS	@@PACK_SENT	GETDATE()
@@CPU_BUSY	@@PACKET_ERRORS	GETUTCDATE()
@@IDLE	@@TIMETICKS	NEWID()
@@IO_BUSY	@@TOTAL_ERRORS	RAND()
@@MAX_CONNECTIONS	@@TOTAL_READ	TEXTPTR
@@PACK_RECEIVED	@@TOTAL_WRITE	

Now look at what user-defined functions actually can do.

Creating User-Defined Functions

You may have guessed that the statement used to create your own user-defined function is CREATE FUNCTION. To create a scalar function, you just do something like this:

```
CREATE FUNCTION <function name>
(<parameter list>)
RETURNS <data type>
[WITH <options>]
AS
BEGIN
<function stuff>
RETURN <value>
END
```

Looks a lot like the CREATE PROCEDURE syntax, doesn't it? The parameter list is just like the one for CREATE PROCEDURE, except this one doesn't allow OUTPUT parameters and has to have parentheses around it. The RETURNS keyword is new; that's where you put the data type of the data you want to send back. You're allowed to send only one value back. The keyword AS is optional. The WITH <options> part is, well, also optional.

Only two options are allowed, and they're allowed for all three function types: ENCRYPTION and SCHEMABINDING. The ENCRYPTION option encrypts the function's code, so users can't see what's going on inside and the actual inner workings are kept secret. This is similar to how the ENCRYPTION option works for stored procedures.

The SCHEMABINDING option ties the function to database objects and doesn't allow the database objects to be altered or dropped as long as the function exists. This prevents any objects from being dropped that would impair the function of the function, if you will. You can remove the binding by dropping the function or altering the function to remove the SCHEMABINDING option. You can use this option only when all the following apply:

◆ Any views or other user-defined functions used by this function also have SCHEMABINDING turned on.

◆ The objects are all local to the same database and not referenced by a two-part name.

◆ The user creating the function has REFERENCES permission on all the objects used in the function.

Here's a simple, yet useful, function:

```
CREATE FUNCTION distance (
@x1 int = 0,
@y1 int = 0,
@x2 int = 0,
@y2 int = 0
)
returns float
as
begin
declare @distance float
set @distance = sqrt ( power(@y1 - @y2, 2) + power(@x1 -
➥@x2, 2) )
return @distance
end
```

You may remember this function from your high school algebra class: It finds the distance between two points on a square grid. So, how can you create these user-defined functions with Enterprise Manager? See Step by Step 9.2.

STEP BY STEP

9.2 Creating User-Defined Functions with SQL Server Enterprise Manager

To create a user-defined function using SQL Server Enterprise Manager, follow these steps:

1. Open SQL Server Enterprise Manager and connect to the server to which you want to add a stored procedure. If you need to, you can register the server now.

2. View the containers inside the server by clicking the plus sign to the left of the server, as shown in Figure 9.5.

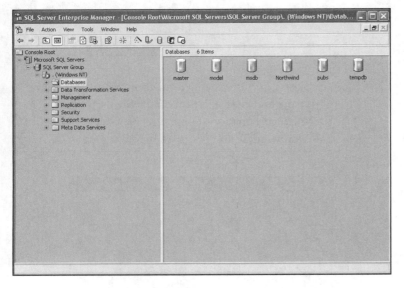

FIGURE 9.5

These are the objects within the server in SQL Server Enterprise Manager.

3. Open the Databases container, again by clicking the plus sign to the left of the word Databases. Choose a database from the list and view its containers by clicking the plus sign to the left of the database you want to work with. If you're just playing with the examples in the book, use the Pubs database. Click the User Defined Functions container, as shown in Figure 9.6.

continues

continued

FIGURE 9.6
These are User-Defined Functions within the Pubs database.

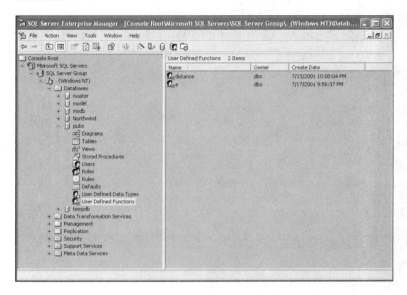

4. To create a new user-defined function, right-click in the right pane and choose New User-Defined Function. The User-defined Function Properties - New User-Defined Function window appears, as shown in Figure 9.7.

FIGURE 9.7
This is the window you use to create new user-defined functions.

5. Change the [OWNER] and [FUNCTION NAME] to the correct owner and name of the function. If you're unsure of the owner name, delete the [OWNER] and the period that follows it. Fill in the PARAMETER LIST, return_type_spec, and FUNCTION BODY. An example is shown in Figure 9.8.

FIGURE 9.8
This is an example user-defined function typed into the Stored Procedures Properties window.

6. Click the Check Syntax button to make sure you've typed everything in properly. This should pop up a message box that says Syntax Check Successful!. Clear the box by clicking OK.

7. Click OK to save your user-defined function.

8. To edit an existing user-defined function, just double-click it. You'll have the same option to check syntax as before.

Scalar functions, like the following, have to be fully qualified with at least a two-part name when you call them:

```
print dbo.distance(1, 1, 2, 2)
```

If you create that function in the Pubs database, that's how you'd call it. It returns a floating point number, 1.41421. That's a pretty simple call, though. Now look at something a bit more complex:

```
use pubs
go

create table coords (x int, y int)
go

insert into coords values (1, 1)
insert into coords values (1, 2)
insert into coords values (1, 3)
insert into coords values (4, 1)
insert into coords values (4, 2)
insert into coords values (4, 3)
insert into coords values (4, 4)

select *
from coords Point1
cross join coords Point2
where pubs.dbo.distance(Point1.x, Point1.y, Point2.x,
➥Point2.y) > 4.0
```

This is an example of how you use a function to filter data. The SELECT statement returns only rows that are a minimum of 4 units apart, which in this case is the points (1,1) to (4,4) only. You can use a user-defined function anywhere you can use an expression or a system function, such as in a column list or an order by.

For an inline user-defined function, the entire function can consist of only one SELECT statement. The returned recordset is then placed into the variable of type table, which is returned back to the caller. Here's an example of an inline user-defined function:

```
CREATE FUNCTION ObjectList (@ObjectType char(1))
RETURNS table
AS
RETURN (SELCT name
FROM sysobjects
WHERE type = @ObjectType
)
go
```

Here's an example of how that function would be called:

```
SELECT * FROM master.dbo.ObjectList('u')
```

Why is this better than just using a view? Well, you can't pass parameters to a view, so you're stuck with the WHERE clause specified in the view. An inline function provides a lot more flexibility than a view. Also, if you create function like this on top of an indexed view, and the parameters that you use for the function are part of the index, then you can dramatically improve performance because you've created a parameterized, indexed view.

The third type of function is the multi-line table-valued function. Basically, this just combines the scalar function's capability to do more complex logic and functions, and the capability of an inline function to return a table. The layout of the table being returned is specified in the RETURNS clause, like this:

```
CREATE FUNCTION TableDistance (@x1 int,
      @y1 int,
      @MaxDistance int
)
RETURNS @DistanceTable TABLE (
ID int,
Dist float
)
AS
BEGIN
INSERT @DistanceTable
SELECT ID, sqrt ( power(@y1 - y, 2) + power(@x1 - x, 2) )
FROM location
WHERE sqrt ( power(@y1 - y, 2) + power(@x1 - x, 2) ) <=
➥@MaxDistance
RETURN
END
```

This particular function scans a table called location and finds all the points within a radius of @MaxDistance of the point (@x1, @y1). Here's how to call it:

```
CREATE TABLE location (
ID int IDENTITY(1,1),
X int,
Y int
)
GO
INSERT INTO location VALUES (1, 1)
INSERT INTO location VALUES (2, 1)
INSERT INTO location VALUES (2, 2)
INSERT INTO location VALUES (3, 1)
INSERT INTO location VALUES (3, 2)
INSERT INTO location VALUES (3, 3)
SELECT * FROM dbo.TableDistance(4, 3, 1)
```

If you've been following along so far, you've probably created a whole bunch of functions all over the place. So, how do you get rid of them?

Dropping and Altering User-Defined Functions

User-defined functions can be dropped with the DROP FUNCTION statement. Just do DROP FUNCTION and the name of the function. You probably already figured that out, though.

The ALTER FUNCTION statement affects functions similarly to how the ALTER PROCEDURE statement changes stored procedures. It does not create a new function for you, but it does change the function without changing the permissions on the function.

Determinism and Functions

Functions can be placed into two different categories: deterministic and non-deterministic. A *deterministic function* is a function that always returns the same output with the same input. For example, the DATALENGTH() function always returns the same value if you pass it the same string; the ABS() function always returns the same value if you pass it the same number; and the distance user-defined function you just saw always returns the same distance value when passed the same set of coordinates, but it is not deterministic because it does not have the SCHEMABINDING option set.

For a user-defined function to be deterministic, it has to pass a four-part test:

◆ The function must be schema bound.

◆ Any function called by the user-defined function must be deterministic.

◆ The function cannot reference database objects outside of its scope—it cannot contain select statements that reference a database.

◆ The function cannot call any extended stored procedures.

There are also many non-deterministic functions. These are functions that don't return the same output for the same input. For example, GETDATE() never returns the same output twice: unless you monkey around with your system clock, it always returns the current date. The NEWID() function is extremely non-deterministic: it always returns a unique value.

Why is this important? First of all, non-deterministic system functions are not allowed in a user-defined function. Remember the list that laid out which functions you can't use in a user-defined function? Well, those are all non-deterministic system functions. Also, if you use an expression to define a computed column, and if the expression relies on a non-deterministic function, you cannot index the computed column. Also, you cannot create a clustered index on a view that relies on a non-deterministic function.

<table>
<tr><td>EXAM TIP</td><td>**Is "Deterministic Function" on the Test?**   Probably not, as such. But you need to understand what a deterministic function is so that you can understand what functions cannot do and how the SCHEMABINDING works, because those *will* be on the test.</td></tr>
</table>

When to Use Functions or Stored Procedures

When do you use stored procedures and when do you use functions? Here's the general rule: Use a stored procedure whenever you need to return output to an application. Use a function whenever you need to return the output to a query or other T-SQL statement.

If you need to return a rowset that you're going to use in the FROM clause, use a function. If you're going to return a rowset that you want to use in an application, use a stored procedure.

PASSING AND RETURNING PARAMETERS TO AND FROM USER-DEFINED FUNCTIONS

▶ **Pass and return parameters to and from user-defined functions.**

Parameters for user-defined functions are passed positionally in a comma-delimited list. There is nothing analogous to named-variable passing for user-defined functions; the arguments must be passed positionally. So, this works:

```
print pubs.dbo.distance(1, 1, 2, 2)
```

And this does not:

```
print pubs.dbo.distance(@x1=1, @y1=1, @x2=2, @y2=2)   --BAD
➥CODE doesn't work
```

The preceding code shows you how to print out the results, but what if you want to put the results into a variable? That would go something like this:

```
declare @Distance float
set @Float = pubs.dbo.distance(1,1,2,2)
```

You can handle returned tables with an insert statement into a permanent table, a temporary table, or, in the following example, a variable of type `table`:

```
declare @Distance table (
ID int,
Dist float
)

insert into @Distance
select * from master.dbo.TableDistance(4, 3, 1)
```

Calling user-defined functions is much less cumbersome and perhaps less confusing than calling stored procedures because there are no output parameters to deal with, no named parameters are possible, and there is only one output value.

ENFORCING PROCEDURAL BUSINESS LOGIC USING USER-DEFINED FUNCTIONS

▶ **Enforce procedural business logic using user-defined functions.**

User-defined functions are useful for modularizing code. The previous examples that determine distances on a grid show how a messy formula can be shortened down to a simple function call, resulting in a more readable query. In addition, if you needed to change the distance formula to determine distance over a sphere instead of a flat grid, you could do that by changing the internal workings of the function without changing the interface to the function. User-defined functions can also encapsulate business rules, especially rules that involve complex formulas, making the overall application maintenance easier.

User-defined functions can and should be used to encapsulate business functions. To extend one of the earlier examples, the following examples examine how the salesman is paid, based on the purchase price, quantity sold, and his commission rate. First, modify the `SalesRep` table like this:

```
alter table SalesRep add ComissionRate float
```

You need to populate it with some data, and then you can calculate commissions for a given rep like this:

```
CREATE FUNCTION GetCommission (
@SalesRepID int
)
RETURNS float
AS
BEGIN
DECLARE @ComissionAmount float
SELECT @ComissionAmount = SUM(QtySold * price*
➥CommissionRate)
FROM Sales
INNER JOIN SalesRep
ON Sales.SalesRepID = SalesRep.SalesRepID
RETURN @ComissionAmount
END
```

Calling this function provides the commission for the sales rep. This provides a simple and accurate way to encapsulate and document how this calculation is done, so that it's always done the same way, which is just good business procedure.

FILTERING DATA WITH USER-DEFINED FUNCTIONS

▶ **Filter data using user-defined functions.**

User-defined functions can be very handy to have around for use in a WHERE clause or ORDER BY clause in a select statement to limit the number of returned rows. Extending the sales rep example, what would happen if the sales manager wanted to find out how his salespeople ranked by the amount of commission that they earn? A query could be written like this:

```
SELECT SalesRepName, master.dbo.GetCommission(SalesrepID)
FROM SalesRep
ORDER BY 2
```

Another example would be to write the same thing, but only for sales reps with more than $50,000 in sales, which would be done like this:

```
SELECT SalesRepName, master.dbo.GetCommission(SalesrepID)
FROM SalesRep
WHERE dbo.GetCommission(SalesrepID) > 50000
ORDER BY 2
```

That's how you can use user-defined functions to filter data—the same way you use system functions to filter data, and the same way you use a WHERE clause to filter data. Just plug in the user-defined function and you're ready to go.

You've already seen how table-valued, user-defined functions can be used to filter data. Look again at the preceding TableDistance function, which returns a filtered data set. An extension to that would be to use it in the FROM clause to restrict how data is returned. If you have a set of points you are interested in keeping track of, like this:

```
CREATE TABLE PointsOfInterest(
PointID int IDENTITY(1,1),
LocationID int,
PointDescription varchar(100)
)
insert into PointsOfInterest values (4, 'Times Square')
```

Then you can populate the PointsOfInterest table, and each location can have several points of interest associated with it. Then you can use the TableDistance function to filter the data, like this:

```
SELECT POI.PointDescription
FROM PointsOfInterest POI
INNER JOIN dbo.TableDistance(4,1,1) TD
on TD.ID = POI.LocationID
```

This finds all the points of interest that are within one unit of the coordinate (4,1), which is Times Square.

IMPLEMENTING ERROR HANDLING IN USER-DEFINED FUNCTIONS

▶ **Implement error handling in user-defined functions.**

Implementing error handling in user-defined functions is different from doing so with stored procedures or transactions because of the complication of side effects. You see, a RAISERROR statement isn't allowed inside a user-defined function because it has side effects, such as the possibility of logging the error into the Windows NT event log or the SQL Server error log. The only way to really return an error from a user-defined function is to have a specified, agreed-upon return code that means "The function didn't work." For a table-valued function, this could mean returning an empty table; for a scalar function, it could mean returning a zero, an empty string, or a NULL.

It's also not possible to detect errors the same way in a user-defined function because the @@ERROR variable isn't available. Remember back in Chapter 6 when you learned that the global variables (the variables that start with two at-signs) are actually system functions? Well, they're also non-deterministic system functions. @@ERROR is not guaranteed to return the same thing if you call it twice. So, there really isn't a good way to find out you've had an error, and there's not a good way to handle it even if you could find out that it happened.

The good news is that you can't really cause errors in a user-defined function that easily. Typically, the errors that you handle using the traditional @@ERROR and RAISERROR techniques are problems with constraint violations and out-of-bounds data going into a table. Because you can't really insert data into a permanent table or a temporary table, the only way you can create an error is to insert a bad value into a variable of type table. And if you do that, your stored procedure is going to stop executing, the batch or stored procedure that called it is going to abort, and you're off to the next statement.

Here's an example. Say that you have a function and a call like this:

```
CREATE FUNCTION CauseError(
@InsertValue int
)
returns int
as
begin
declare @LocalTable table (
Value int
        )

insert into @LocalTable values (4 / @InsertValue)
return 1
end
go
print master.dbo.CauseError(0)
```

This is going to cause a divide-by-zero error: `Divide by zero error encountered. The statement has been terminated.` So, in the grand tradition of structured programming, you're going to need to handle the error before it arises, like this:

```
CREATE FUNCTION CauseError2(
@InsertValue int
)
returns int
as
begin
declare @LocalTable table (
Value int
        )

        IF @InsertValue = 0 Return 0
insert into @LocalTable values (4 / @InsertValue)
return 1
end
go
print master.dbo.CauseError2(0)
```

So, basically, the only way to handle errors in your code is to be aware of what values can cause errors to occur and to make sure the values are properly handled.

CASE STUDY: JOE'S BURGER AND MALT SHOP

ESSENCE OF THE CASE

Here are the essential elements in this case:

- ▶ Gather location information.
- ▶ Build a table for the location information.
- ▶ Write a function to calculate the distance.
- ▶ Write a query, or a stored procedure, to find the appropriate locations.

SCENARIO

Joe, the owner of Joe's Burger and Malt Shop, has a full SQL Server database system that he uses to track store performance, payroll, accounting, and human resources. He's looking for a way to figure out where to build the next store, so that it's not too close to the other stores. He's already worked to find a list of all the current store locations, and a list of about 50 locations in the city to put his new store. How can Joe figure out where to put his new store?

ANALYSIS

The first thing to do is put the stores all on a big map. Then lay a grid on top of the map and assign each store a coordinate pair. Then create

CASE STUDY: JOE'S BURGER AND MALT SHOP

a location table, with each store's ID number and its coordinates, like this:

```
create table Location (
id int,
xcoord int,
ycorrd int
)
```

Put all the existing stores into this location table. Then create another table with the same layout, called `ProspectiveLocations`, and populate it with the data on the prospective locations. Then write a stored procedure that uses the `Distance` function defined earlier to find the prospective store location that is farthest away from the other stores:

```
CREATE PROCEDURE FindNewStoreLocations
AS
BEGIN
    Populate table of prospective-to-
➡existing distances
SELECT PL.ID AS PLID, L.ID AS LID,
➡master.dbo.distance(PL.Xcoord, PL.Ycoord,
➡L.XCoord, L.Ycoord) AS Distance

INTO #Distances
FROM ProspectiveLocation PL, Location L
```

```
SELECT PLID, MIN(distance)
FROM #Distance
GROUP BY PLID
ORDER BY 2 DESC
END
```

This gives Joe a list of all the prospective locations with the distance to the closest store, so Joe can look at the list and make his decision.

If you take a close look at the second SELECT statement in that stored procedure, you'll notice it uses a GROUP BY statement to find the closest distance. If you just did something like this:

```
SELECT PLID, Distance
from #Distance
order by 2 desc
```

This wouldn't properly filter the list. For example, if there was a store in the middle of town, a store in the northeast corner of town, and a prospective store in the southwest corner of town, you'd end up with the prospect in the southwest corner of town rated fairly highly, even though there are stores fairly close to it, like the one in the middle of town.

CHAPTER SUMMARY

This chapter has covered two critical concepts for creating efficient database applications: stored procedures and user-defined functions. Stored procedures enable you to modularize frequently used queries and complex logic into an easy-to-manage database object. User-defined functions provide similar functionality, but with the additional capability to return single values or tables to the caller, which provides a great deal of flexibility.

KEY TERMS

- ALTER
- CREATE
- deterministic
- DROP

CHAPTER SUMMARY

- non-deterministic
- SCHEMABINDING
- stored procedure
- user-defined function

Stored procedures and user-defined functions are critical to the success of any application from a management and performance perspective. They provide a clear line between what the application is responsible for and what the database is responsible for, with the capability to provide a clearly defined interface between application and data.

Both stored procedures and user-defined functions are used to filter data, enforce business rules, and manage how data is changed in a database. These are exam objectives, but they are also important concepts to understand if you are going to successfully write applications that use SQL Server. The philosophy behind both is simple: modularize code to reduce programming mistakes that result from having similar code repeated throughout an application. Stored procedures and user-defined functions are the building blocks of good, stable applications. That is why stored procedures and user-defined functions are on this exam.

The previous chapters all lead up to this chapter. The chapters on database design, query writing, and script writing all tie together here. Without an understanding of database design, you can't write good queries. Without an understanding of how queries and scripts are written, you can't write good stored procedures or user-defined functions.

APPLY YOUR KNOWLEDGE

Exercises

9.1   Creating a Stored Procedure

This exercise demonstrates how to create a new stored procedure to select the names of all of the indexes for a given table in alphabetical order.

Estimated Time: 10 minutes

1. Open SQL Server Enterprise Manager, connect to your SQL Server, and open the Databases container.

2. Open the Master database and click on the Stored Procedures container.

3. Right-click under the stored procedures listed on the right and choose New Stored Procedure.

4. Enter the following text:

```
create procedure sp_GetIndexList
@TableName sysname
as
select name from sysindexes where id =
➥object_id(@TableName) order by name
```

5. Click the Check Syntax button. If you don't receive the Syntax Check Successful! dialog box, you need to check your typing.

6. Click OK to clear the dialog box, and OK again to save your stored procedure.

9.2   Executing a Stored Procedure

This exercise demonstrates how to run a stored procedure. It assumes you've already completed Exercise 9.1. If you skipped it, shame on you—go back.

Estimated Time: 5 minutes

1. Open SQL Server Query Analyzer and log into the server used in Exercise 9.1.

2. Enter use pubs to use the Pubs database.

3. Enter exec sp_GetIndexList 'authors'.

4. Run the query.

9.3   Creating a User-Defined Function

This exercise demonstrates how to create a user-defined function by creating a function that returns the mathematical constant e, the base for natural logarithms.

Estimated Time: 5 minutes

1. Open SQL Server Enterprise Manager, connect to your SQL Server, and open the Databases container.

2. Open the Pubs database and click on the Use Defined Functions container.

3. Right-click under any user-defined functions in the right pane and choose New User Defined Function.

4. Enter this text into the window:

```
create function e ()
returns float
begin
return exp(1)
end
```

5. Click the Check Syntax button. If you don't receive the Syntax Check Successful! dialog box, you need to check your typing.

6. Click OK to clear the dialog box, and OK again to save your user-defined function.

9.4   Calling a User-Defined Function

This exercise shows how to call a user-defined function. It relies on Exercise 9.3 being completed, so if you didn't do that yet, go stand in a corner for a bit, and then do it.

APPLY YOUR KNOWLEDGE

Estimated Time: 5 minutes

1. Open SQL Server Query Analyzer and log into the server used in Exercise 9.3.

2. Enter `use pubs` to use the `Pubs` database.

3. Enter `select dbo.e()`.

4. Run the query.

Review Questions

1. What are the differences between a stored procedure and a user-defined function?

2. Why are stored procedures faster than just re-running the same batch over and over again?

3. What is the difference between a multi-statement table-valued function and an inline table-valued function?

4. Why would you use an inline function rather than a view?

5. Why is an `EXEC` not required on the first line of a batch?

Exam Questions

1. Which of the following problems would be appropriately implemented with a scalar user-defined function?

    A. Returning a list of customer names.

    B. Updating a customer name to upper case.

    C. Getting the absolute value of a number.

    D. Calculating a customer's outstanding account balance.

2. Which of the following is *not* a valid reason to use a view rather than an inline user-defined function?

    A. Need to update the recordset directly.

    B. Need to return a recordset with a consistent set of parameters.

    C. Need to combine data from several tables into one resultset.

    D. Need to be able to change the filter on the recordset.

3. Eric is having a problem getting his stored procedure to run with acceptable performance with all the different parameters he can use. Basically, the parameters specify whether a search should be done on last name, first name, or address, or some other parameter in his customer table. What can Eric do that may improve performance?

    A. Use views rather than stored procedures.

    B. Create the procedure using the `WITH RECOMPILE` option to avoid using the cached query plan.

    C. Create the procedure in Enterprise Manager rather than Query Analyzer.

    D. Use more user-defined functions to handle the parameter input.

4. Kyle is writing a system that will monitor the number of customer accounts in the database and, when an account representative has exceeded the number of accounts he is allowed to manage, send an email to the sales manager. He's going to use the SQL Server Agent to schedule the job to run nightly. Which of the following tools can he use to send the email?

A. A stored procedure.

B. A table-valued user-defined function.

C. A scalar user-defined function.

D. An inline user-defined function.

5. Stan is trying to figure out why his user-defined function isn't working properly. He keeps getting an "incorrect syntax near the keyword 'return'" error. What's wrong?

```
create FUNCTION distance (
        @x1 int = 0,
        @y1 int = 0,
        @x2 int = 0,
        @y2 int = 0
)
return float
as
begin
        declare @distance float
        set @distance = sqrt ( power(@y1 -
        ⇒@y2, 2) + power(@x1 - @x2, 2) )
        return @distance
end
```

A. Side effects are caused by returning a value of type `float`.

B. A comma is missing after the `@y2` parameter.

C. The `return float` should be `returns float`.

D. A parenthesis is missing on the `SET @distance` statement.

6. Kenny is trying to pass values into a stored procedure. Here's what the CREATE PROCEDURE statement looks like:

```
create Procedure CalculateSalesTax
        @ItemPrice float,
        @Qty int,
        @TaxRate float,
        @SalesTax float OUTPUT
```

Which of the following EXEC statements return the sales tax into the `@SalesTax` variable?

A. `EXEC CalculateSalesTax 2.39, 1, 4,`
   ⇒`@SalesTax`

B. `EXEC @SalesTax = CalculateSalesTax 2.39,`
   ⇒`1, 4, 0`

C. `EXEC CalculateSalesTax @ItemPrice = 2.39,`
   ⇒`1, 4, @SalesTax OUTPUT`

D. `EXEC CalculateSalesTax @ItemPrice = 2.39,`
   ⇒`@Qty = 1, @TaxRate = .04, @SalesTax =`
   ⇒`@SalesTax OUTPUT`

7. Wendy has created a stored procedure to insert new values into her database:

```
create procedure InsertPlayer
        @PlayerID int,
        @Comment varchar(2000)
as
begin
        insert into CommentTracker values
        ⇒(@PlayerID, @Comment)
        exec xp_sendmail @message = @Comment,
                        @recipients =
                        ⇒'WendyT',
                        @subject = 'Comment
                        ⇒Activity'
end
```

The problem is that sometimes the insert fails with a constraint violation, and she'd like an email when those fail also. Which of the following approaches would enable this to happen?

A. Capture the value of @@ERROR and use an IF statement to send an email if the INSERT statement fails.

B. Capture the value of @@ERROR and use a WHILE loop to retry the insert in the event of an error.

C. Combine the INSERT and the xp_sendmail into a transaction.

D. Capture the value of @@LAST_ERROR and use an IF statement to send an email if the INSERT statement fails.

8. What's wrong with this user-defined function?

```
create function InsertPlayer
     (@PlayerID int,
     @Comment varchar(2000))
returns int
begin
        insert into CommentTracker values
     ➥(@PlayerID, @Comment)
        return 1
end
```

A. It's poorly formatted.

B. It's missing the keyword AS before the BEGIN.

C. It has a side effect.

D. It is table-valued.

9. BeBe is trying to write a stored procedure that will return a subset of a table back to her script. Which of the following methods *will not* work?

A. Use a temporary table defined inside the stored procedure.

B. Use a static cursor as an output parameter.

C. Insert data into a temporary table that's defined before calling the stored procedure.

D. Use a variable of type table as an output parameter.

10. Given the following stored procedure declaration:

```
CREATE PROC Test2
     @I int,
     @J float,
     @K varchar(2000)
```

Which of the following EXEC statements will work?

A. EXEC Test2 4.3, 19, 27

B. EXEC Test2 @J=4.3, @I = 20, @K = 'value'

C. EXEC Test2 20, @J=4.3, 'value'

D. EXEC Test2 20, @J=4.3, @K = 'value'
➥OUTPUT

11. To properly process an insurance claim, Esther has to have a client ID number and a claim amount. On claims over a certain amount of money, she has to have the name of the adjuster. Which of the following would be the best way to make sure that Esther had entered all the information properly before trying to process the claim?

A. A multi-line table-valued stored procedure.

B. An inline function

C. A cursor

D. A stored procedure

12. Which of the following accepts the return value from the stored procedure CheckInsuranceClaim?

A. declare @RetVal float =
➥CheckInsuranceClaim @ClaimID = 41400

B. declare @RetVal int
exec CheckInsuranceClaim @ClaimID =
➥41400, @RetVal OUTPUT

C. declare @RetVal int
exec CheckInsuranceClaim @ClaimID = 41400

D. declare @RetVal int
exec @RetVal = CheckInsuranceClaim
➥@ClaimID = 41400

APPLY YOUR KNOWLEDGE

13. Which of the following inline function definitions would correctly return the information for the customer with CustomerID 42?

    A. ```
    Create Function GetCustomerInfo
           @CustomerID int = 42
       returns select * from customer where
       ↪customerid = @CustomerID
    ```

    B. ```
    Create Function GetCustomerInfo (
           @CustomerID int = 42
           )
       returns table
       as return (select * from customer where
       ↪customerid = 42)
    ```

    C. ```
    Create Inline Function GetCustomerInfo (
           @CustomerID int = 42)
       returns (select * from customer where
       ↪customerid = 42)
    ```

    D. ```
    Create Function GetCustomerInfo (
           @CustomerID int = 42)
       returns @ReturnTable table (CustomerID
       ↪int, CustomerName varchar(50))
       as begin
           insert into @ReturnTable
           select * from customer where
           ↪customerid = @CustomerID
           return
       end
    ```

14. Which of the following is true?

    A. A stored procedure must have a return statement.

    B. A function must have a return statement.

    C. A stored procedure must have output parameters.

    D. A stored procedure cannot return a table.

15. After examining his stored procedure that runs one statement, an INSERT, Larry determines that he's going to have a problem with users passing in bad data, which will cause inserts to fail because of constraints. Which of the following is the best approach to handling the situation?

    A. Use an inline function to check the constraint first.

    B. Check all the applicable constraints with SELECT statements before performing the insert.

    C. Attempt the insert and check the @@ERROR variable after the insert.

    D. Remove the constraints.

Answers to Review Questions

1. The principal differences are side effects and output. A stored procedure is allowed to change data values in tables, change table schemas, and generally write any data anywhere within the permissions of the creator of the stored procedure. A user-defined function cannot directly change data. Also, a stored procedure has many different options for output: return value, resultset, output parameters, and any combination thereof. A function can return only one of two things: a scalar value or a table.

2. Stored procedures can be faster because they have pre-cached execution plans, so SQL Server doesn't have to recompile the T-SQL every time it runs, which it does have to do for batches and scripts.

3. Inline table-valued functions consist of one select statement. Multi-statement table-valued functions can contain additional logic.

APPLY YOUR KNOWLEDGE

4. You would use an inline function rather than a view to provide increased flexibility. A view cannot take a parameter, so its output is fairly fixed, whereas an inline function can filter output based on input parameters.

5. EXEC is not required on the first line of a batch, so lazy system administrators can type **sp_who** as the only thing in a batch. After all, EXEC sp_who is a lot more typing.

Answers to Exam Questions

1. **D.** Option A needs to return a list, not a single value; Option B would change data, which is not allowed; Option C is already implemented through a system-defined function. Option D needs to return only a single number, the value of the bill, so it's the best answer. You can find more information in the section titled, "Types of User Defined Functions".

2. **D.** Options A, B, and C are all possible using a view. Option A is not possible with a user-defined function. Option D is not possible with a view; a view has a static filter on the output. The section titled "When to Use Functions or Stored Procedures" covers this in some detail.

3. **B.** Option A doesn't allow enough flexibility in the resultset; Options C and D would make absolutely no difference at all. The "Implementing Error Handling in Stored Procedures" section talks about how to effectively handle these situations.

4. **A.** User-defined functions cannot send email; sending email is a side effect, and user-defined functions are not allowed to have side effects.

This is also mentioned in the "When to use Functions or Stored Procedures" section.

5. **C.** The return and returns do different things, but that's a very common typographical error to make. It's all covered in the "Creating User-Defined Functions" section.

6. **D.** Option A will run without an error, and won't return the result. Option B will run without an error, and capture the return code into the @SalesTax variable, which can't handle the floating point number that is the @SalesTax. Option C won't work because the first parameter is specified by name, but the rest are specified positionally, which is a syntax error. This is covered in the "Calling Stored Procedures, Passing and Returning Parameters to and from Stored Procedures" section.

7. **A.** Using an IF statement with @@ERROR sends the email. Option B won't send an email, and will probably result in a particularly nasty infinite loop; Option C won't work because it doesn't send the email on failure, and Option D won't work because @@LAST_ERROR isn't a valid system function. The section on "Implementing Error Handling in Stored Procedures" talks about the correct ways to handle errors in stored procedures.

8. **C.** INSERT statements into local tables are not allowed within functions because they have the side effect of changing data in a table somewhere. Formatting is not relevant to how well the function operates; the keyword AS is optional in a CREATE FUNCTION statement (but required in a CREATE PROCEDURE); and the function is scalar, not table valued, but that doesn't even matter. The "Creating User-Defined Functions" section examines this in some detail.

APPLY YOUR KNOWLEDGE

9. **A.** If a temporary table is created inside a stored procedure, it is dropped when the stored procedure terminates, so this won't work to get tabular data outside the stored procedure. To find out how to pass data into and out of stored procedures, check out the section called "Calling Stored Procedures; Passing and Returning Parameters to and from Stored Procedures".

10. **B.** Option A is a type mismatch because trying to put the value 4.3 into an integer doesn't work. Option C has a positional parameter after a named parameter, which won't work, and Option D has something as OUTPUT which isn't declared that way. The section on "Calling Stored Procedures; Passing and Returning Parameters to and from Stored Procedures" has a lot of information about how to declare parameters.

11. **D.** Option A is nonsense. Option B won't work, because functions can't actually record anything. Option C won't work because cursors aren't used to validate data. The "When to Use Functions or Stored Procedures" section talks about how this works.

12. **D.** Option A is an incorrect declare statement; Option B would be valid for an output parameter, but not a return value; and Option C just ignores the whole return value issue altogether. The "Calling Stored Procedures; Passing and Returning Parameters to and from Stored

Procedures" section covers how to declare stored procedures properly.

13. **B.** Option A is missing a lot of parentheses; Option C is wrong because there isn't a CREATE INLINE FUNCTION statement; and Option D is a multi-line table-valued function, not an inline. Using user-defined functions in this manner is covered in the "Filtering Data with User-Defined Functions" section.

14. **B.** Functions must have return statements. Stored procedures are not required to, but are allowed to, and can return only integers. Stored procedures can return variables of type table, and they don't have to have an OUTPUT parameter. The sections titled "Creating User-Defined Functions" and "Creating and Managing Stored Procedures" cover how the two different types of objects are created.

15. **C.** Options A and B are going to have the same problem: If the constraints on the tables change, the user-defined function or the stored procedure will need to be rewritten. Option D would be nice, but the constraints are probably there for a reason, and removing them just so an INSERT can put suspect data into a table is not the correct approach. If you're in doubt about whether it's appropriate to use a stored procedure or a user-defined function, read the section on "When to Use Functions or Stored Procedures".

Suggested Readings and Resources

SQL Server Books Online

- CREATE PROCEDURE

- CREATE FUNCTION

- SQL Server Architecture: SQL User-Defined Functions

This chapter covers the following Microsoft-specified objectives for the Indexing section of the Database Development SQL Server 2000 exam:

Implement indexing strategies.

▶ An indexing strategy involves your decisions on how to implement indexes, which columns you choose to index, and how you decide one index is better than another. SQL Server supports two kinds of indexes: clustered and nonclustered. Depending upon the underlying circumstances present in your table structure and your needs, you will have to decide upon one or the other.

Create indexes including clustered and non-clustered, covering index, indexed views.

- **Specify index characteristics. Characteristics include clustered, FILLFACTOR, nonclustered, and uniqueness.**

▶ This objective looks at the different characteristics an index can take. Some of these are the index's fill factor, the type of index, and the uniqueness of the index.

Improve index use by using the Index Tuning Wizard, index placement and statistics.

▶ This objective looks at how to use the Index Tuning Wizard to improve and design accurate, efficient, and proficient indexes on the fly with fascinating results. The Index Tuning Wizard enables you to select and create powerful indexes and statistics for a Microsoft SQL Server 2000 database without prior knowledge of index and database structural designs. The Index Tuning Wizard simplifies one of the tasks that weigh down on DBAs' backs: choosing the correct column to index.

CHAPTER 10

Boosting Performance with Indexes

Implementing Indexed Views

▶ Creating indexes against a view is new to SQL Server 2000. With this functionality comes a few advanced implementations. Pay particular attention to restrictions and required settings, because they are sure to be needed on the exam.

STUDY STRATEGIES

▶ Choosing an indexing strategy can be an extremely hard decision. Know when to implement certain indexes and where to put them. Index choice is definitely going to be questioned on the exam.

▶ Have a good understanding of indexed views because they are new to SQL Server 2000.

▶ The indexed view can significantly cut down the time-consuming process of choosing an indexing strategy. Learn how to use it well because it covers a whole objective itself.

▶ Full-text searches and full-text indexing are topics that might show up on the exam. Because they're not one of the current objectives of the exam, I wouldn't suggest that you concentrate too much study time on them. Always check Microsoft's web site every now and then because objectives are subject to change at any time.

▶ And finally, practice function syntaxes over and over again and to some extent memorize them.

INTRODUCTION

A lot of factors affect SQL Server and the applications that use its data resources. Gaining performance and response time from a server is a primary concern for database developers and administrators. One key element in obtaining the utmost from a database is an indexing strategy that helps to achieve the business needs of the enterprise, in part by returning data from queries in a responsive fashion.

The query optimizer in SQL Server reliably chooses the most effective index for use with any given query, which helps considerably if indexes have been created to choose from. In the majority of cases the optimizer provides the best performance from the index choices provided. The overall index design strategy should provide a good selection of indexes for the optimizer to use.

You can't just start putting a lot of indexes throughout your table structures until you understand the implications of indexes. Though indexes provide good query performance, they can also take away from other processes. Indexes consume hardware resources and processing cycles; memory overhead is associated with their use; regular maintenance is required to keep them at optimum levels; and many database processes have to work within the presence of the index.

This chapter covers SQL Server indexing strategies from the most basic starting points to advanced tuning and design considerations. The exam covers indexing in many categories, including index selection, tuning, maintenance, and specialty implementations.

OVERVIEW OF INDEXING

▶ **Implement indexing strategies.**

One of the most difficult database tasks to be performed is choosing a working indexing strategy to accompany the system's business's needs. This chapter gives you the detailed insight you need to understand indexes and how to create them for high-power applications and databases. This chapter will acquaint you with the types of indexes available in SQL Server 2000, and how to create and alter them. You will discover a strategy for selecting appropriate columns to include in an index. You will also look at tools that you can use to analyze and improve on existing index strategies.

Simply put, indexes are database objects that provide efficient access to data in rows in tables. Indexes may also function to provide uniqueness throughout certain rows in your table. Through SQL Server's built-in query optimizer, SQL Server is able to select from a table's many indexes and choose a few of them that will execute a query the fastest.

Indexes can significantly boost performance in your database. In fact, after database design, the next thing you'll want to consider for improving the performance of database searches should be indexes. Fortunately, indexes are not hard to implement.

To understand indexing and apply appropriate indexes to any project, it is necessary to have an understanding of the physical storage constructs SQL Server uses. Data and index storage concepts are discussed in the following section.

Indexing and Data Storage

You can compare indexing and data storage in SQL server to the same material in a book. Pages, data sequencing, topic pointers, and additional descriptive data can be found in SQL Server storage, and you can understand them if you understand the principles at work in a book.

In both SQL Server and in a book, the physical data and indexes are stored on pages. The pages of the book store data in the form of topics and descriptions. In SQL Server, pages are also the fundamental unit of data storage. Data pages contain all the data in data rows except `text`, `ntext`, and `image` data, which is stored in separate pages. Data rows are placed on the page starting after a page header.

There are many types of pages in SQL Server used to store data in a variety of ways. The list that follows shows the eight types of pages in the data files of a SQL Server 2000 database:

◆ **Data.** Stores data rows with all data except `text`, `ntext`, and `image` data.

◆ **Index.** Stores index entries.

◆ **Text/Image.** Stores data for `text`, `ntext`, and `image` data types.

◆ **Global Allocation Map.** Information about allocated extents.

◆ **Page Free Space.** Information about free space available on pages.

◆ **Index Allocation Map.** Information about extents used by a table or index.

◆ **Bulk Changed Map.** Information about extents modified by bulk operations since the last BACKUP LOG statement.

◆ **Differential Changed Map.** Information about extents that have changed since the last BACKUP DATABASE statement.

Each page used to store data in SQL Server contains a number of separate elements. Data, freespace, page header, and row offsets all make up a portion of a page, as illustrated in Figure 10.1.

Pages represent the elementary structure for storing all SQL Server object information and data. Pages also represent the basis for all index and data interactions. In the table of contents and topical index at the back of a book, you have numerical pointers to the pages where the data is actually located. SQL Server indexes serve a similar purpose, pointing to the location of the data on specific data pages.

Indexing Architecture

Indexes in databases are similar to indexes in books. In a book, an index enables you to find information quickly without reading the entire book. In a database, an index enables the database program to find data in a table without scanning all the data in the entire table. An index in a book is a list of words with the page numbers that contain each word. An index in a database is a list of values in a table with the storage locations of rows in the table.

Indexes act as very flexible mechanisms for providing order and structure to a table. An index can be created on either a single column or a combination of columns in a table. Indexes can provide the physical order of data storage or can simply allow for alternate methods of sequencing data. Indexes also can enable faster searching of data to improve user response time and general system performance.

SQL Server supports indexes defined on any column in a table, including computed columns. If a table is created with no clustered

N
O
T
E

Extent Storage Extents are the basic unit in which space is allocated to tables and indexes. An extent is 8 contiguous pages, or 64KB. This means SQL Server 2000 databases have 16 extents per megabyte.

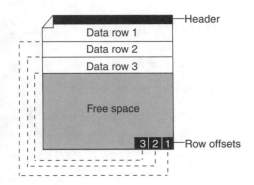

FIGURE 10.1
Layout of a data page.

index, the data rows are not stored in any particular order. This structure is called a *heap*. If order is supplied by a clustered index, then heap storage is not used. In this case, the data is stored in a given sequence based on the clustered index.

SQL Server supports indexing of two basic types, although there are many variations of those types. The two types of SQL Server indexes are *clustered* and *nonclustered* indexes. Clustered indexes are implemented so that the logical order of the key values determines the physical order of the corresponding rows in a table. Nonclustered indexes are indexes in which the logical order of the index is different than the physical, stored order of the rows on disk. The following sections examine them both.

Clustered Indexes

As seen in the previous sections, a clustered index is a type of index in which the logical order of the key values determines the physical order of the data stored on disk. Because a clustered index shows how the physical data of a table is stored, there can be only one clustered index per table.

The selection of appropriate column(s) on which to base a clustered index is particularly important. Column(s) should be chosen where range searches are frequently performed or based upon the expected order of the majority of reports printed from the data. A range search occurs within a WHERE conditional operation, as in selecting the range of all authors who have an advance greater than $500 but less than $4000. With this type of range search, the index, if present, first locates the smallest value (500), and then it locates the other values alongside that value until the last value is reached (4000).

IN THE FIELD

PRIMARY KEY CONSIDERATION

The clustered index is defined by default for the Primary Key when you define a table. However, you may often want to have a column other than the Primary Key be the basis for the physical order of the data. To accommodate this design, you may want to create a nonclustered Primary Key. This is beneficial where surrogate keys are used, because reports are rarely going to be placed in order of the surrogate.

Clustered indexes also save time in searches for a specific row when the values on a column are unique. For example, if you have an SSN column on an `Employees` table and you place a clustered index on this column, you should notice an increase in data retrieval speed when performing searches on SSN. Naturally, the index on SSN does no good when searching for `last name = "Doe"`.

Candidates for clustered indexes have the following characteristics:

◆ A column queried using range operators such as `BETWEEN`, `<`, or `>`.

◆ Columns that are grouped using the `GROUP BY` clause or that involve joins or that represent the `ORDER` of displayed or printed output.

◆ Queries and reporting that access sequential data.

◆ Operations that result in large resultsets.

◆ Columns that don't have incremented values; for example, an ID column has incremented values.

◆ Columns with many duplicate values.

◆ Columns that don't have incremented values; for example an ID column has incremented values.

◆ On the PK when there are many inserts causing all records to be inserted on the same page, which can remain in memory.

In SQL Server 2000, clustered indexes are implemented as b-trees, as shown in Figure 10.2. Each index page holds a header that is followed by index rows. Each of these rows contains a pointer value to another sub-page or a row of data. The lowest level of implementation in clustered indexes is known as the *leaf page* or *node* and contains data rows and pages. The first level of implementation is known as the *root node*. Anything between the root node and leaf node is referred to as *intermediate-level pages*.

Because you can create only one clustered index, the majority of indexes created are nonclustered indexes. A nonclustered index can operate over an existing clustered index or over a data heap.

NOTE

Clustering versus Heap The only time the data rows in a table are stored in sorted order is when the table contains a clustered index. If a table has no clustered index, its data rows are stored in a heap.

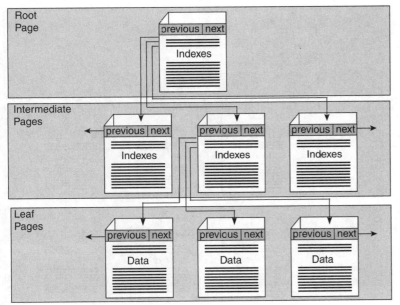

FIGURE 10.2
Clustered indexes are implemented in a b-tree structure.

Examining Nonclustered Indexes

Nonclustered indexes are indexes in which the logical order of the key values in the index is different than the physical order of the rows in the indexed table. Nonclustered indexes are also implemented as b-tree structures, as shown in Figure 10.3. There are two major differences that distinguish them from clustered indexes. First, the leaf node of the nonclustered index does not contain the concrete data. It contains index rows having a nonclustered key value that point to a data row. Second, as already noted, nonclustered indexes do not physically rearrange the data.

When you query data on a column with a nonclustered index, SQL Server 2000 first tries to find a record containing your table object ID and a value in the indid column from the sysindexes table that is >= 1 and < 255, because a 0 implies there is no index at all, and 255 implies that the table has Text/Image pages. After it finds the record, SQL Server examines the root column to find the root page of the index. After SQL Server finds the root page, it can begin a search for your data.

FIGURE 10.3
Nonclustered indexes are also structured in b-tree format.

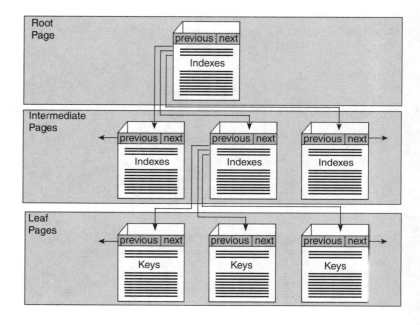

The SQL Server 2000 optimizer chooses an index to use for the search. The Keys column in sysindexes lists what columns are involved in each index. If the optimizer knows this and knows what columns you are searching on, it can use index statistics to determine which index to use. In the simplest case, if you are searching on only one column, A, and only one index exists on column A, then it uses that index. When searching on multiple columns, and many or all of these columns are indexed, it uses statistical methods to determine the index.

It's important to understand the following guidelines before you create nonclustered indexes:

◆ Nonclustered indexes are good when queries don't return large resultsets.

◆ Columns that are used in a SELECT list or the WHERE clause are good candidates for nonclustered indexes.

◆ A nonclustered index is the default index in SQL Server.

◆ There can be up to 249 nonclustered indexes on a single table.

◆ Nonclustered indexes generally take more overhead than clustered indexes, so you should create them only when it is absolutely necessary.

> **Index Default** Nonclustered index is the default index created if no particular type is specified.
>
> — NOTE

◆ Nonclustered indexes make a good choice for use as a covering index.

SQL Server searches through the index to find a particular value and then follows that pointer to the row containing that value. An index implemented in a SQL Server database is an internal table structure that holds a list of ordered values from one or more columns of a table. Column selection should be made carefully.

What to Index?

So, which columns do you really need to index? Column selectivity is a major step in the process of indexing. In general, columns that are frequently accessed by the WHERE or the ORDER BY clauses should be considered. Indexes should never be added to a column unless you know they actually will help.

When you build indexes, try to narrow indexes down to the minimum number of columns needed. Multicolumn indexes act negatively on performance. Columns with unique values serving as Primary Keys are also good candidates. The more unique rows there are in a column, the more ideal it is for an index. If a column has 50 rows, 25 of which have distinct unique values in one column, then you have a column that has 40 distinct values. The former serves as a better candidate because there are more unique values based on the number of rows.

The challenge for the database designer is to build a physical data model that provides efficient data access. This can be done by minimizing I/O processing time. The following types of columns are good ones to index:

◆ A column that acts as the table's Primary or Foreign Key.

◆ Columns that are regularly sorted by the ORDER BY clause.

◆ Columns that are filtered on an exact condition using the WHERE clause. For instance, WHERE state= 'Ca'.

◆ Columns that are queried on joins.

◆ Columns that hold integer values rather than character values.

◆ Searches for rows with search key values in a range of values. For example, WHERE Royalty BETWEEN 1000 and 4000.

◆ Queries that use the like clause may only benefit if they start with character data. Examine the following: WHERE au_fname LIKE 'sm%'.

Indexes may also be chosen by a factor known as *index selectivity*. The *selectivity* is the percentage of rows accessed by an UPDATE, SELECT, or DELETE statement. A query has high selectivity when it is filtered on exact criteria, where all values are unique. For example, a user may execute a query that selects the emp_id of an employee from the Employees table where emp_id equals 112.

A query characterized by low selectivity is one in which the searched column has few unique values, such as a search against the contract column (having values of 0 and 1) in the authors table. Indexes placed on columns having high selectivity can make searches significantly more efficient. The classic scenario of a low selectivity column is gender. You should never build an index on gender because there are only two possibilities.

To find the selectivity of a query, use the following formula:

```
Selectivity ratio = [100 * (Total number of distinct index
➥rows)] / (Total number of rows in the table)]
```

Formulas may help in making a selection in very large database scenarios. The true test of any index strategy occurs when queries are processed during day-to-day operations. Strong guidelines also exist on things that should not be indexed.

What Not to Index?

You really can't and shouldn't index all the columns in your table. Doing so would significantly drop performance on inserts and deletes, even though most queries would run fast. When determining whether to index a small table, look to see whether it requires more page reads to scan the index than there are pages in the table. In this case an index will hurt performance, not help it. Therefore, a table with less than three pages is not helped by any index. Learn to use the SQL Server Query Analyzer tool as a guide for whether an index is useful or not. Recognize table scans; the process of reading all records from a table in sequence may take fewer cycles than accessing an index first—particularly on small tables.

Here are some conditions that would indicate you should not index a column:

◆ If the index is never used by the query optimizer.

◆ If the column values exhibit low selectivity, often greater than 95% for nonclustered indexes.

◆ If the column(s) to be indexed are very wide.

◆ If the table is rarely queried.

◆ Do not index columns that are not used in where clauses, aggregated, or used in sorting.

Indexes provide many trade-offs. Although queries may show a performance improvement, INSERT, UPDATE, and DELETE operations could see a decline in performance. You may not know the power of indexes until you perform large searches on tables having tens of thousands of rows. Implementing an indexing strategy would not be proper for a small database with a few tables containing no more than 50 rows. Tables are benefited by indexing for the following reasons:

◆ As many as 249 nonclustered indexes can be created on a single table.

◆ Indexes help increase efficiency on complex searches on large tables.

◆ Indexes are easy to implement.

◆ Sixteen columns can comprise the same composite index, as long as the total key length is less than 900 bytes.

◆ Indexes may be used to enforce uniqueness throughout rows in tables.

Nonclustered Covering Indexes

A covering index is a nonclustered index that is built upon all the columns needed to satisfy a SQL query, both in the selection criteria and the WHERE clause. Covering indexes save a huge amount of I/O and build a lot of efficiency in a query. For instance, if you query SQL Server with the following statement:

```
SELECT au_fname, au_lname FROM authors
WHERE state= 'ca'
```

NOTE **What's New in Indexes** New to SQL Server 2000 is the power to index on computed columns and the capability to create indexes on views. You can specify whether indexes are created in ascending or descending order. Also, the CREATE INDEX statement can now use the Tempdb database as a work area for the sorts required to create an index. This results in improved disk read and write patterns for the index creation step.

You can run the following to create in index:

```
CREATE NONCLUSTERED INDEX MyIndex
ON Authors(state, au_fname, au_lname)
```

MyIndex would be considered a covering index because a composite index is built on all columns specified in the SELECT statement and WHERE clause.

Covering indexes significantly boost performance because all the data for the query is contained within the index; only the index pages, not the data pages, of the table must be referenced to retrieve the data.

If your query plan shows a bookmark lookup, that is always a sign that a covering index should be considered. Bookmark lookups indicate that the query plan has located the rows needed in an index, but it then has to jump to the datapages to get information from additional columns outside the index. Adding the additional rows to the index eliminates the bookmark lookups, which are often expensive operations. Of course, in some cases the additional columns make the index so inefficient you loose out on the deal, but nonetheless bookmark lookups always indicate a location where a covering index should be considered.

Covering indexes don't work for clustered indexes because the leaf pages are the datapages themselves, and all columns are already there.

An indexing strategy will undergo many changes as the life cycle of the database system continues. Close monitoring of performance and application activity, as well as other significant database events, will help you decide on appropriate changes to be made in the future.

REVIEW BREAK

Indexing Strategies

An indexing strategy is an integral part of a database system implementation. Appropriate design increases query performance and reduces user response times. Inappropriate design unnecessarily slows down data additions, modifications, and deletions. A balance between the two that meets business needs is essential.

One clustered index per table can be used and, if implemented, it determines the physical order of the data. Nonclustered indexes act like those in the back of a book—pointing out the physical location of the data. Nonclustered covering indexes can be created in cases where the exact query content is known.

Keys, ranges, and unique values are strong selections for index candidates. Seldom-used data, binary data, and repeating values are poor index candidates. After index candidates have been selected, monitor application usage. Adjust the indexing strategy on a regular basis to provide reliably high performance.

CREATING AND ALTERING INDEXES

▶ **Create indexes, including clustered and nonclustered, covering index, indexed views.**

Before you can implement an indexing strategy, you must know how to create indexes. Indexes can be created using both the Enterprise Manager or through T-SQL code. The syntax of the CREATE INDEX statement is as follows:

```
CREATE [UNIQUE][CLUSTERED|NONCLUSTERED] INDEX index_name
    ON {table|view}(column[ASC|DESC][,...n])
    [WITH<index_option>|,...n]]
    [ON filegroup]

<index_option >::={PAD_INDEX|FILLFACTOR = fillfactor|
                    IGNORE_DUP_KEY|DROP_EXISTING|
                    STATISTICS_NORECOMPUTE|SORT_IN_TEMPDB}
```

The CREATE INDEX command has a variety of options that can be used to define the particulars of the index. Those options are as follows:

◆ UNIQUE. Specifies that the index created is a unique index; that is, two rows may not have the same index value. If UNIQUE is not specified, then duplicate key values are allowed.

◆ CLUSTERED. Creates an object where the physical order of rows is the same as the indexed order of the rows. It creates a clustered index.

◆ NONCLUSTERED. Creates an object that specifies the logical order of a table. It specifies a nonclustered index is to be made.

◆ Index name. The name you want to refer to the index you create. This name must be locally distinct throughout the table.

◆ Table name. The table that contains the column or columns to be indexed.

◆ View name. The name of the view to be indexed. The creation of a nonclustered index on a view is prohibited without the prior creation of unique clustered index.

◆ `Column name`. Is the column or columns to which the index applies. Specify two or more column names to create a composite index. Columns holding `text`, `ntext`, and `image` data are prohibited from being indexed.

◆ `ASC/DESC`. Determines the ascending or descending sort direction for the particular index column. The default is `ASC`.

◆ `FILLFACTOR`. Specifies how full SQL Server should make each page and is expressed as a percentage from 0 to 100, inclusive. When an index page fills up, SQL Server must take time to split the index page to make room for new rows. 0, although the system default, is not allowed in a `CREATE INDEX` statement.

◆ `IGNORE_DUP_KEY`. Controls what happens when an attempt is made to insert a duplicate key value into a column that is part of a unique clustered index. If `IGNORE_DUP_KEY` is specified for the index and an `INSERT` statement that creates a duplicate key is executed, SQL Server issues a warning and ignores the duplicate row.

◆ `DROP_EXISTING`. This is specified when there is already a preexisting index name identical to yours. When the `DROP_EXISTING` statement is thrown, SQL Server drops the old index before creating the new one.

◆ `ON filegroup`. The index is created on the supplied filegroup.

When you create a clustered index, an identical copy of the original table is taken, and then rows from that table are sorted. SQL Server then takes the original table and deletes it. The index created in Step by Step 10.1 will be used throughout the chapter.

STEP BY STEP

10.1 Creating a Clustered Index Using Code

1. Open the Query Analyzer by selecting Query Analyzer from the Start menu.

2. Create a new index on a new table. To do this, first create a new table in the Pubs database. In the code pane, type in the following:

```
use Pubs
go

CREATE TABLE IndexPractice
( YourName   char(32)  NULL,
  Age        integer   NULL,
  BirthDate  integer   NULL )
```

3. After creating a new table, create a new clustered index. To do this, code in the following:

```
CREATE CLUSTERED INDEX age_index
    ON IndexPractice (age)
```

4. To see your new index, open the Query Analyzer, expand the Pubs database in the Object Browser, and then expand User Tables. Expand IndexPractice and then expand Indexes. If you followed the steps properly, you should see age_index listed below Indexes.

You can also create indexes on the fly using the Enterprise Manager. A general summary of steps involved in doing this is outlined in Step by Step 10.2.

STEP BY STEP

10.2 Creating Indexes Using the Enterprise Manager

1. Open the SQL Server Enterprise Manager; expand a server group and then expand a server.

2. Expand Databases; expand the database in which you want to create your table.

3. Right-click Tables, and then click New Table.

4. In the Choose Name dialog box, enter a name for the table.

continues

continued

5. Fill in the columns as appropriate. Each row represents one column in the table.

6. Right-click any row; then click Properties.

7. On the Indexes/Keys tab, click New.

8. In the Column Name list, click the columns that are part of the index.

9. In the Index Name text box, enter a name for the index.

10. In Index file group, select a file group on which to create the index.

11. Select Create UNIQUE to make this index a unique constraint. Or click Index to make this index unique.

12. Select Create As CLUSTERED to make this index clustered.

13. In Fillfactor, specify how full SQL Server should make the leaf level of each index page during index creation. Fillfactor is covered later in the chapter.

Creating nonclustered indexes is pretty much similar to the creation of clustered ones. To create a nonclustered index, follow Step by Step 10.3.

STEP BY STEP

10.3 Creating a Nonclustered Index in Code

1. Open the Query Analyzer by selecting Query Analyzer from the Start menu.

2. Create a new index on a new table. To do this, first create a new table in the Pubs database. In the code pane, type in the following:

```
use Pubs
CREATE TABLE IndexPractice2
( Student_ID  char(32)  NULL,
  Height      integer   NULL,
  Weight      integer   NULL )
```

3. After creating a new table, create a new clustered index as shown in Figure 10.4. To do this, code in the following:

```
Use Pubs
CREATE CLUSTERED INDEX Weight_index
ON IndexPractice2 (Weight)
```

4. To see your new index, open the Query Analyzer, expand the Pubs database in the Object Browser, and then expand User Tables. Expand IndexPractice2, and then expand Indexes. If you followed the steps properly, you should see Weight_index listed underneath Indexes. If you still have Query Analyzer open, you may need to right-click User Tables under the Pubs database and choose Refresh before the new table will appear.

Composite indexes can be created on two or more columns. To create a composite index, specify two or more column names in the CREATE INDEX statement. The columns listed for composite indexes should be listed in sort-priority order. Composite indexes are best utilized when two or more columns are searched on a single unit. Columns involved in a composite index must be in the same table. A composite index can include 16 separate columns, up to a 900-byte limit.

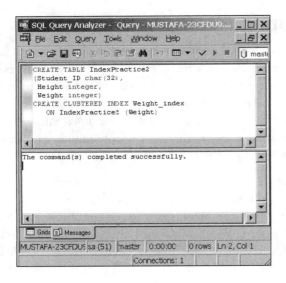

FIGURE 10.4
Creating the IndexPractice2 table and then a clustered index.

NOTE

Finding Special Index Information
Information on indexes is located in every database in the sysindexes system table. To find more information about indexes in your database, query the sysindexes table using SELECT * from sysindexes. For instance, the indid column in the resultset tells whether the index is clustered, nonclustered, or the columns contain image or text data. A value of indid >1 means that the index is nonclustered; indid=1 means that the index is clustered; indid=255 means that the table contains image or text data.

The dpages column is the count of the data pages used for the index if the indid value is 0 or 1. If the indid value is 255, dpages = 0. If the value of indid is not 0, 1, or 255, then dpages is the count of the nonclustered index pages used by the index. Between 2 – 249 is nonclustered, 1 = clustered, 0 = heap.

Automatically Maintained Statistics Remember that statistics are automatically maintained on only the first column of a compound index, and in these cases the creation of addition statistics on all columns may give improved queries.

Automatically Created Clustered Index Creating a PRIMARY KEY or UNIQUE constraint automatically creates a unique clustered index on the specified columns in the table. The PRIMARY KEY constraint defaults to clustered unique; UNIQUE constraint defaults to nonclustered unique.

Unique Indexes It is better—and a more efficient process—to create unique indexes rather than non-unique indexes, because all rows in a unique index are distinct. When SQL Server finds a row, it can stop the search (because there can never be two rows of the same value).

Setting the Fillfactor One topic that is sure to appear on the exam is setting the fillfactor for a page. Simply put, the FILLFACTOR option specifies how full SQL Server should make each page when it creates a new index using existing data. The FILLFACTOR option does not hold empty space over time, and the space will be taken up as data is inserted.

With so many options available, SQL Server indexing is flexible yet intricate to manage. Indexes need to be designed using the most appropriate indexing mechanisms required by an application.

UNIQUE Indexing

A unique index ensures that the indexed column does not contain duplicate values. Unique is not actually a type of index but rather a property; thus, both clustered and nonclustered indexes can be defined as Unique. It only makes sense to use a unique index when the data on a column is to be unique, as in a Social Security Number (SSN) column. If you create an index on the SSN column of an Employee table, and a user types in an indistinct value for SSN, the table does not save the value and an error is generated.

Creating unique indexes is as simple as adding an extra word to the normal CREATE INDEX statement. After you have decided on creating a unique index, you can set the option IGNORE_DUP_KEY when calling the CREATE INDEX statement. If IGNORE_DUP_KEY was specified for the index and an INSERT statement that creates a duplicate key is executed, SQL Server issues a warning and ignores the duplicate row. IGNORE_DUP_KEY can be set for only unique clustered or unique nonclustered indexes.

Exploring *FILLFACTOR*

Simply put, the FILLFACTOR option specifies how full SQL Server should make each page when it creates a new index using existing data. The FILLFACTOR option is applied only when an index is being created or when maintenance activities reset the fill factor. Specify FILLFACTOR to leave extra space and reserve a percentage of free space on each leaf-level page of the index to accommodate future expansion in the storage of the table's data.

Values can be set from 1–100, expressed as a percent of the page to fill. The default value is 0; however, this does not mean SQL Server fills the page 0% full. With a value set to 0, SQL Server allows for a clustered index in which all data pages are full and for a nonclustered index in which all leaf pages are full. If 100 is specified as the fillfactor, SQL Server creates the indexes with each page 100% full, allowing minimal amount of storage space.

Information concerning indexes can be viewed by using the sp_helpindex stored procedure. You may need to find out which columns are indexed on a particular table or how much database space indexes are taking. Step by Step 10.4 shows you how to do this.

```
sp_helpindex 'objectname'
```

Where 'objectname' is the name of the object (view or table) from which you want to find index information.

STEP BY STEP

10.4 Viewing Index Information Using sp_helpindex

1. Open the Query Analyzer by selecting Query Analyzer from the Start menu.

2. To see the index-specific information about the indexes on the previously created table, IndexPractice, execute the following:

   ```
   EXEC sp_helpindex IndexPractice
   ```

3. Alternatively, you can query the sysindexes table to find more information about the index you created in Step by Step 10.3. To do so, execute the following:

   ```
   Use Pubs
   Select * from sysindexes
   where name = 'age_index'
   ```

> **NOTE**
>
> **Setting the FILLFACTOR Option** The reason FILLFACTOR is specified is to increase performance. A smaller value for the FILLFACTOR means that the data pages will take more storage space and page splits will be minimized. On the other hand, a large value is suitable for read-only tables only, because low amounts of additional storage is consumed. SQL Server is more likely to perform page splits, firing back on performance. Page splits are shown in Figure 10.5. In deciding on an appropriate FILLFACTOR, you have to look for a balance between the needs of the users rendering data versus the needs of those making insertions.

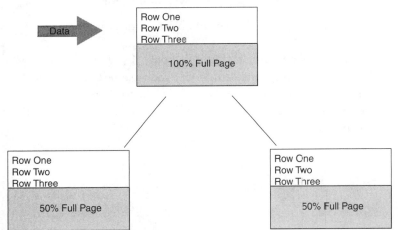

FIGURE 10.5
How a page split due to excessive inserts occurs.

Many commands assist in providing information about SQL Server objects. Other commands are covered later in the chapter during the discussion of index maintenance. After indexes are created, alterations may need to be made to have the index better suit needs.

Altering Existing Indexes

Periodically, for maintenance reasons or to change some of the index properties, you are going to want to rebuild your indexes. In SQL Server 2000, rebuilding an index using the DROP_EXISTING clause of the CREATE INDEX statement can be efficient if you want to re-create the index in a single step, rather than delete the old index and then create the same index again. This is useful for both clustered and nonclustered indexes.

Indexes can be created and altered through the Enterprise Manager, through CREATE INDEX operations, or through CREATE TABLE or ALTER TABLE statements.

If you ever need to rename indexes, you can accomplish this by using the sp_rename stored procedure, as follows:

```
sp_rename [ @objname = ] 'object_name' ,
   [@Newname = ] 'New_name'
   [, [@Objtype =] 'object_type']
```

Where

◆ 'Object_name' is the original name of the index

◆ 'New_name' is the new name given to the index.

◆ 'Object_type' is the type of object (in this case INDEX).

Creation of tables is often performed through T-SQL using the CREATE TABLE statement with a full definition. A fully defined table would normally have entries included for Primary Key as well as other potential entries for UNIQUE constraints. Both these options create accompanying indexes.

Index Drawbacks

With all the talk about indexes, you may think that indexes are virtually flawless. Nevertheless, this is not the case; improper use of indexes may result in excessive memory usage and hard disk space consumption, which cause undesirable results.

Indexes have to be balanced; too many indexes may very well make processing slow; too few indexes may make database searches a time-killing process that is hard on you and your organization.

It is a little tricky, at best, to select an appropriate indexing strategy, and maintaining it in the face of ongoing changes inherent in a database life cycle is even more of a challenge. Index maintainance over time is the next consideration.

Review of Creating and Altering Indexes

Index creation and alteration are two necessary mechanisms in any indexing strategy. A database goes through a life cycle and will undergo size changes, application uses, and other growth. Any database system is in a constant state of flux as data is always being added, changed, removed, or otherwise affected by change.

A solid indexing strategy is the first step in achieving success. Appropriate creation of indexes without using unnecessary additional ones is an involved process. Often other activities, such as table creations and other schema alterations, can also affect the number and types of indexes used.

After the initial indexes are created and modifications have been made in testing, it is time for the real test: the end user. Indexing needs to be monitored to ensure that goals set for performance and response time are being met. Other system activity may also need to be monitored because indexing isn't the only technology affecting performance. Chapter 12, "Monitoring SQL Server," looks further into other performance tuning activity.

INDEX MAINTENANCE

▶ **Improve index use by using the Index Tuning Wizard, index placement, and statistics.**

Sometimes indexes need to be rebuilt because of changes in data that occurred after it was built. Rebuilding indexes helps in collecting the scattered information and bringing index data back to its original form. This increases the overall performance by making it easier for SQL Server to read pages to get data. You can re-create an index in three ways:

◆ Deleting the original index and then re-creating it

◆ Specifying DROP_EXISTING in the CREATE INDEX clause

◆ Using the Database Console Command (DBCC), DBCC DBREINDEX

The first option is highly unfavorable for clustered indexes because other levels of indexes use the same index's cluster key as a pointer to data rows. When a clustered index is defined on a table, this dictates the physical order of the data. The clustered index key values are used as data pointers for all other nonclustered keys. Deleting a clustered index and then re-creating it means deleting and re-creating all nonclustered indexes.

The second option is rebuilding the index. The method reduces unnecessary work and is advantageous both to clustered and nonclustered indexes in that it significantly reduces the overhead of rebuilding the index.

The third option is the preferred out of the three, because it enables you to rebuild multiple indexes in a single shot, without rebuilding indexes individually. It is demonstrated in Step by Step 10.5. It also enables you to rebuild indexes on tables that use PRIMARY and UNIQUE constraints without requiring you to delete and rebuild each constraint.

SQL Server enables you to rebuild one or more indexes on a table by using the DBCC DBREINDEX statement, without having to rebuild each index separately. DBCC DBREINDEX is also useful if you want to rebuild indexes that enforce PRIMARY KEY or UNIQUE constraints without having to delete and re-create the constraints. For example, you may want to rebuild an index on a PRIMARY KEY constraint to reestablish a given FILLFACTOR for the index. If simple defragmentation of index space is desired, use the INDEXDEFRAG option.

Unlike DBCC DBREINDEX, DBCC INDEXDEFRAG is an online operation. It does not hold locks long term, and thus does not block running queries or updates. A relatively unfragmented index can be defragmented faster than a new index can be built because the time to defragment is related to the amount of fragmentation. A very fragmented index might take considerably longer to defragment than to rebuild. In addition, the defragmentation is always fully logged, regardless of the database recovery model setting. The defragmentation of a very fragmented index can generate more log entries than even a fully logged index creation. The defragmentation, however, is performed as a series of short transactions, and thus does not require a large log if log backups are taken frequently or if the recovery model setting is SIMPLE.

> **A Note on Syntax** When specifying any of the optional parameters—FILLFACTOR or index_name—you have to specify all parameters preceding it.

The syntax for DBCC DBREINDEX is as follows:

```
DBCC DBREINDEX
    (    [ 'database.owner.table_name'
          [ , index_name
              [ , fillfactor ]
          ]
      ]
    )    [ WITH NO_INFOMSGS ]
```

Where

◆ 'Table_name' is the name of the table for which to rebuild indexes.

◆ 'Index_name' is the name of the desired index to rebuild. If 'index_name' is not specified, all indexes on 'table_name' are rebuilt.

◆ 'Fillfactor' specifies the percentage of space on each index page to be used for storing data when the index is rebuilt. The new fillfactor overwrites the original. However, if the new fillfactor is 0, the old fillfactor is used.

◆ WITH NO INFOMSGS, as the name suggests, disallows printing of informational messages.

STEP BY STEP

10.5 Rebuilding All Indexes Using DBCC DBREINDEX

1. Open the Query Analyzer by selecting Query Analyzer from the Start menu.

---

2. To rebuild all indexes on the previously created IndexPractice table with a FILLFACTOR of 54, execute the following query:

   ```
   DBCC DBREINDEX (IndexPractice,' ', 54)
   ```

Rebuilding indexes represents only one activity that should be considered in attempting to improve database performance.

Indexing to Improve Performance

You should not always assume that index usage means improved performance, and vice versa. If using an index always produced the best performance, the job of the query optimizer would be simple. In reality, incorrect choice of indexed retrieval can result in less than optimal performance. Therefore, the task of the query optimizer is to select indexed retrieval only when it will improve performance and to avoid indexed retrieval when it will negatively affect performance.

If you expect indexes to produce a performance gain, you need to be aware that a number of factors contribute to the performance achieved. You should write queries that update as many rows as possible in a single statement, rather than using multiple queries to update the same rows. By using only one statement, optimized index maintenance can be exploited. Of course, other aspects of the system can be affected by long-running transactions, and therefore some compromise is needed.

When creating indexes, use integer keys where possible for clustered indexes. Additionally, clustered indexes benefit from being created on unique, non-null, or IDENTITY columns.

Create nonclustered indexes on all columns frequently used in queries. This can maximize the use of covered queries.

The time taken to physically create an index is largely dependent on the disk subsystem. Important factors to consider are:

◆ RAID level used to store the database and transaction log files.

◆ Number of disks in the RAID disk array.

◆ Size of each data row and the number of rows per page. This determines the number of data pages that must be read to create the index.

◆ The columns in the index and the data types used. This determines the number of index pages that have to be written.

Often, a long-running query is caused by indexing a column with few unique values, or by performing a join on such a column. This is a fundamental problem with the data and query, and usually cannot be resolved without identifying this situation. Creating an index never makes a query slow; however, if the index is not useful, a table scan or use of another less useful index could result in a long-running query.

Indexing and Statistics

The SQL Server query optimizer chooses the index that accesses data fastest. To choose the right course of action, the query optimizer is dependent on indexes' statistical figures. SQL Server keeps statistics about the distribution of the key values in each index and uses these statistics to determine which index(es) to use in query processing.

Index statistics need to be up to date for the optimizer to decide upon the fastest route of access. As data is modified in rows of a table, or when indexes on tables change, index statistics are not automatically updated. When this happens, the statistics become somewhat out of date because now the optimizer can't properly decide on an optimum index. Index statistics need to be frequently updated so that the optimizer can have full power on its search. An index's statistics are first automatically created when the index is first created.

> **NOTE**
>
> **Update with Backup** You should always update index statistics before performing database backups. This will ensure the statistics are up to date and accurate in the event a restore operation is needed.

After the index is created, it is up to an SQL Designer to frequently make use of the UPDATE STATISTICS to manually update index information.

SQL Server 2000 provides two commands that can help you as a SQL Server designer maintain index statistics. These are

◆ The STATS_DATE or DBCC SHOW_STATISTICS command, used to show the last time statistics were updated for a particular index.

◆ The UPDATE STATISTICS command, which updates statistical information for an index.

Users can create statistics on nonindexed columns by using the CREATE STATISTICS statement. But it is recommended that this be used with extreme caution and only by an experienced database administrator. The option Auto Create Statistics is on by default. SQL Server automatically creates statistics on columns if the statistics might be useful.

Querying an Index's Statistics

As noted above, an index's statistics can be viewed by the DBCC SHOW_STATISTICS command or the STATS_DATE function. The two major differences are that STATS_DATE is a function (it returns a date-time value that tells the last time an index was updated) and that STATS_DATE queries only the last time an index was updated. The syntaxes for both are as follows:

```
STATS_DATE ( table_id , index_id )
```

Where

◆ Table_id is the ID of the table.

◆ Index_id is the index's ID.

```
DBCC SHOW_STATISTICS ( table , target )
```

Where

◆ 'table' is the name of the table from which to display statistical information.

◆ 'target' is the name of the index to which to show the statistical information.

Looking at statistics in this manner or through execution plans in the Query Analyzer will help you diagnose and catch potential problems before they can cause more serious problems.

The *UPDATE STATISTICS* Statement

A shortened syntax of the UPDATE STATISTICS statement is as follows:

```
UPDATE STATISTICS table | view
        Index_name

[ ALL | COLUMNS | INDEX ]
   ]
```

Where

◆ 'Table | view' is the name of the table or view on which statistical updating needs to be performed.

◆ 'Index_name' is the name of the index for which statistics are being updated. If index_name is not specified, all indexes in the table or view are updated.

◆ 'ALL | COLUMN | INDEX' specifies whether all indexes are updated, only column indexes are updated, or only index statistics are updated. The default value is ALL.

STEP BY STEP

10.6 Querying and Updating Index Statistics

1. Open the Query Analyzer from the Start menu.

2. To see the statistics for the titleind index in the Titles table, use the following:

```
USE pubs
GO
DBCC SHOW_STATISTICS (titles, titleind)
```

3. To update its statistics, run the following:

```
UPDATE STATISTICS titles titleind
```

If the system is already set to automatically update statistics through the database properties, then this will minimize the need for manual updates.

NOTE

Deleting an Index Used by a Constraint To delete an index used by a PRIMARY or UNIQUE constraint, you must delete the constraint causing the associated index to then be deleted automatically.

Dropping Unwanted Indexes

If an index isn't in use any longer, you may wish to delete it. Deleting an index means freeing all storage space the index was previously holding. It also results in more efficient INSERT, UPDATE, and DELETE operations. Only a table owner is granted permission to delete indexes. To delete an index or indexes, run the DROP INDEX statement.

```
DROP INDEX 'table.index | view.index' [ ,...n ]
```

Where

- ◆ 'table | view' is the name of a table or view in which the index resides.

- ◆ 'Index' is the name of the index being dropped.

Dropping an index may require the removal of constraints if those constraints are directly related to the index. In other instances, you may just want to remove an index that has outlived its usefulness. To help determine index validity, the Index Tuning Wizard is provided as an assistant in index analysis. You can't drop an index created with a PRIMARY KEY or UNIQUE constraint; the alter table command *must* be used.

The Index Tuning Wizard

The Index Tuning Wizard is a graphical tool that enables you to select and create powerful indexes and statistics for Microsoft SQL Server 2000 databases. The Index Tuning Wizard simplifies the task of choosing which indexes to create in a table. As you've seen previously, one of the most difficult tasks for a DBA is determining which columns get indexed. Fortunately, Microsoft has shipped a wizard that identifies the best clustered and nonclustered indexes for a table and the indexes that are most likely to improve query performance.

The Index Tuning Wizard is used to find the most efficient path of execution in a set of input. This input is a table or file, namely a workload. To make workloads, use the SQL Profiler to set a trace. The SQL Profiler enables you to monitor and record activity events in a file or table. SQL Profiler traces enable the Index Tuning Wizard to make accurate decisions. Traces of the different events that happen while work is performed can be recorded for hours or even days, depending on the period of time desired to be monitored. After the events are recorded, the Index Tuning Wizard then works with the query processor to establish the viability of a configuration.

Before you learn to use the powerful features of the Index Tuning Wizard, be sure to examine some guidelines, benefits, and limitations that are included in the following list:

◆ Make sure there are enough rows of data in the sample tables you use for the SQL Profiler. The Index Tuning Wizard may not make accurate decisions or decisions at all if there is not enough data in the tables being sampled.

◆ In SQL Server 2000, index tuning can also be invoked from a command-line utility called `itwiz`.

◆ The Index Tuning wizard may not offer suggestions. This could be because indexes would most likely not increase performance.

◆ The Index Tuning Wizard consumes excessive CPU overhead. Decreasing the size of the workload can assist this. So, you shouldn't capture an excessive workload in order to do index tuning.

◆ The Index Tuning Wizard does not support backward compatibility with creating and selecting indexes on databases made in SQL Server 6.5 and earlier.

Examining the Index Tuning Wizard

Before creating indexes using Index Tuning Wizard, you have to create a load trace file to monitor average activity. Subsequently, you can start Index Tuning Wizard by selecting it from the Tools menu.

Step by Step 10.7 guides you using Index Tuning Wizard to create indexes from scratch.

The Index Tuning Wizard is an extremely powerful tool that makes automatic and efficient decisions on clustered and nonclustered table and view indexes. This Step by Step covers using this marvelous tool to create indexes. Before using Index Tuning Wizard, you have to open a trace file by creating and running a trace. (For more information on the SQL Profiler, see Chapter 12.)

STEP BY STEP

10.7 Creating a Trace

1. Open the profiler by selecting SQL Enterprise Manager (found in Programs, SQL Server 2000) from the Start menu, and then selecting Tools, Profiler.

2. Click on File, New Trace, provide login information if necessary, and then type **MyTrace** in the Trace Name text box. Check Save to File; this saves the workload file onto disk for future use. Save the trace as C:\MyTrace.trc, and then execute the trace by selecting Run in the Trace Properties dialog box, as shown in Figure 10.6.

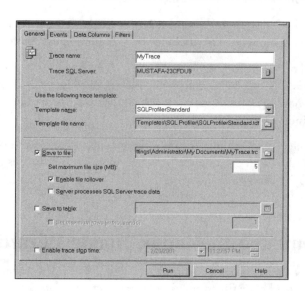

FIGURE 10.6
Creating a trace in the SQL Profiler.

3. Now you have to manually make SQL Server process queries so that the trace you just set up may be able to monitor the events configured. To do this, switch to the SQL Query Analyzer and execute the following query:

```
SELECT *
FROM Authors
WHERE au_fname LIKE 'C%'
GO

SELECT *
FROM titles
```

4. Now end the trace by going back to the Profiler and clicking the Stop button or selecting File, Stop Trace from the menu.

Step by Step 10.8 shows you how to use Index Tuning Wizard to create indexes.

STEP BY STEP

10.8 Creating an Index with Index Tuning Wizard

1. Open the Index Tuning Wizard by selecting it from the menu, Tools, Wizards, Management, Index Tuning Wizard.

2. When you start the Index Tuning Wizard, a screen displays the goals and aims that you can accomplish through using the Index Tuning Wizard. Click Next.

3. This will lead to the opening of the second screen, which is used to select the server and database. Type in the name of your server and then select Pubs as the database (this is the database you are interested in tuning). Select Thorough for the tuning mode. Choosing Thorough processes a thorough, but time-taking analysis of the current situation and provides best results (see Figure 10.7). Click Next to proceed.

4. This screen is where you choose workload-specific information. As the workload file, choose C:\MyTrace.trc.

continues

continued

FIGURE 10.7
Selecting a database and tuning mode.

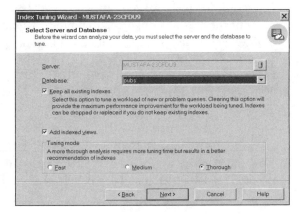

5. Now you have a selection screen that asks which tables you want to tune. Select Dbo.Authors as the table and click Next.

6. This screen processes workload information and gives advice as to which indexes should be placed on which columns. Click Next to continue.

7. This is the last screen of Index Tuning Wizard. Click Finish.

For the Index Tuning Wizard to really be useful, it must be executed during production use of the database, or at least under circumstances where a sufficient query load will produce meaningful results.

REVIEW BREAK

Indexing Review

Here are some points that recap the concepts you have come across in this chapter:

▶ Information concerning indexes can be viewed by using the sp_helpindex stored procedure. To rename or delete an index, use the sp_rename stored procedure and DROP INDEX statement, respectively.

▶ When information that affects data is modified, index information can go loose throughout the database. Rebuilding indexes helps in collecting the scattered information and bringing data back to its original form. Use the DBCC DBREINDEX to re-index a single or all indexes in a table.

▶ Defining clustered indexes on views enables you to store the resultsets of the view in the database, thereby reducing the overhead of dynamically building the resultset.

▶ Index statistics need to be up to date for the optimizer to decide upon the fastest route of access. You can use the UPDATE STATISTICS command, which updates statistical information for an index.

▶ The Index Tuning Wizard enables you to select and create powerful indexes and statistics for a Microsoft SQL Server 2000 database without prior knowledge of index and database structural designs.

INDEXED VIEWS

▶ **Implementing indexed views.**

Indexed views are a new concept introduced in SQL Server 2000. They allow view resultsets to be stored in the database's physical storage after an index is created. In contrast to this, in a non-indexed view, the view is activated at run time and the resultset is dynamically built based on logic needed to create output from the underlying base tables. Any computations, such as joins or aggregations, are done during query execution for each query referencing the view, ultimately leading in degraded performance. Indexed views and other views are covered in full in Chapter 10.

A view can be thought of as a virtual table or a stored query. The results of using a view are not permanently stored in the database. Defining clustered indexes on views enables the resultsets of the view to be stored in the database, thereby reducing the overhead of dynamically building the resultset. This means that indexed views can be treated like any other table because additional nonclustered indexes can be added. An indexed view can be created using the CREATE INDEX or CREATE VIEW statements, which is done when data is occasionally updated. Some of the benefits of indexed views are as follows:

◆ They increase performance of queries that use joins and aggregates to process numerous rows.

◆ Data residing in an indexed view is automatically updated when a base table gets modified.

◆ Views that aggregate and join data are improved because when an index is created on a view, the view is executed and the resultset is stored in the database.

◆ The first time you create an index on a view, it has to be of type unique clustered. After this has been created, additional nonclustered indexes can be created.

Although benefits can be had from applying an index to a view, there are many considerations to be made that may affect other applications as well.

Indexed View Requirements and Restrictions

Some prerequisites need to be met before you create an indexed view, as follows:

◆ The first index on a view must be a clustered index.

◆ Non-deterministic functions are not allowed in the view's definition.

◆ The view must be created using the WITH SCHEMABINDING (which prevents the dropping and altering of tables partic_pating in the indexed view).

◆ Session-level settings must be modified as shown in Table 10.1.

TABLE 10.1

MANDATORY SETTINGS

Session Level Setting	Value
ANSI_NULLS	ON
ANSI_WARNINGS	ON
ARITHABORT	ON
CONCAT_NULL_YEILDS_NULL	ON
QUOTED_IDENTIFIERS	ON
ANSI_PADDING	ON
NUMERIC_ROUNDABORT	OFF

◆ Indexed Views' definitions cannot use the following:

ORDER BY

COMPUTE or COMPUTE BY

TOP

Text, ntext, or image columns

DISTINCT

MIN, MAX, COUNT, STDEV, VARIANCE, AVG

A derived table

A rowset function

Another view

UNION

Sub-queries, outer joins, self joins

Full-text predicates such as CONTAIN or FREETEXT

> **NOTE**
>
> **Switching Session-Level Settings**
> One way of turning session settings on or off is to use the session property statement. For example, to switch the ANSI_WARNINGS setting on, you can run the following query
>
> ```
> IF sessionproperty
> ('ANSI_WARNINGS') =
> 0 SET ANSI WARNINGS ON
> ```
>
> These session settings must be on during the creation of the indexed view, as well as for the clients who wish to use the indexed view.

To avoid having problems with indexed views, keep the restrictions in mind, but also be aware that options must also be in place at the time the indexed view is created. When creating indexed views, keep the following points in mind:

◆ Extra data storage will be needed. The data in the view is permanently stored both in its base table and in the clustered index of the indexed view.

◆ Keep indexes on view as small as possible. Doing so enables the SQL optimizer to quickly locate row data.

◆ Indexed views can increase query speed substantially.

◆ Applications that run repeated queries benefit from indexed views.

◆ At times, view indexes would be inconvenient because they restrict you from using non-deterministic functions and other important aggregates.

With all this in mind, there is a lot to consider about the specifics of an implementation of indexed views.

Creating Indexed Views

Creating an indexed view is as simple as altering the CREATE INDEX statement. Use the same syntax used in creating table indexes except that the table name is replaced with the view name. Also, some session-level options must be toggled (see the preceding section). Keep in mind that only the view owner is allowed to execute a CREATE INDEX statement on a view. To create an indexed view, go through Step by Step 10.9.

STEP BY STEP

10.9 Creating an Indexed View

1. Open the Query Analyzer by selecting Query Analyzer from the Start menu.

2. Type in the following in the code pane. The first part of the code configures session-level settings. Remember, some settings need to be enabled and disabled before you can create an indexed view. The second part creates a view so that you can create an index. The last part creates a unique clustered index on the view as shown in Figure 10.8. Notice that WITH SCHEMABINDING option has to be specified.

```
Use Pubs
SET ANSI_PADDING,CONCAT_NULL_YIELDS_NULL,
➥ANSI_WARNINGS,ARITHABORT,ANSI_NULLS,
➥QUOTED_IDENTIFIER ON
SET NUMERIC_ROUNDABORT OFF

GO

CREATE   VIEW IndexView WITH SCHEMABINDING
AS
SELECT Au_Fname + ' ' + Au_Lname,  Au_id
FROM Authors
WHERE Contract = 1
GO

CREATE UNIQUE CLUSTERED Index MyINDEX ON IndexView
➥(au_id)
Go
```

3. To see your index view, open the Query Analyzer and the Object browser.

4. Expand Pubs and then expand views.

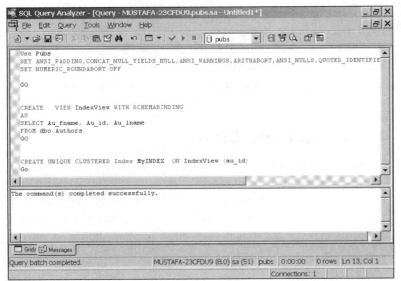

FIGURE 10.8
Creating an indexed view.

5. Click IndexView and then expand indexes. You should see
the index you created listed under Indexes as shown in
Figure 10.9.

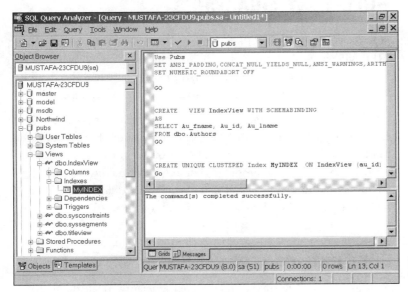

FIGURE 10.9
The newly created index on the view.

All indexes on a view are dropped if the view is dropped. All nonclustered indexes on the view are dropped if the clustered index is dropped. Nonclustered indexes can be dropped individually. Dropping the clustered index on the view removes the stored result set, and the optimizer returns to processing the view like a standard view.

Using Indexed Views

Indexed views work best when the underlying data is static or infrequently updated. The maintenance of an indexed view can be higher than the cost of maintaining a table index. If the underlying data is updated frequently, then the cost of maintaining the indexed view data may outweigh the performance benefits of using the indexed view.

Indexed views are best used in reporting systems with many joins, functions, aggregations, and other calculations. Any time data is to be summarized, grouped, or otherwise analyzed, indexed views will be of benefit. Indexed views are best when there are many or very expensive selects compared to the number of inserts, updates, and deletes.

FULL-TEXT SEARCHES

SQL Server and other relational database management systems (RDBMS) have always had the capability to search data stored as text using basic search criteria, but have never really had the capability to search data using more sophisticated forms of search criteria.

Full-Text Search is a completely separate program that runs as a service, namely Microsoft Search Service or MSSearch. Full-Text Search can be used in conjunction with all sorts of information from all the various MS BackOffice products. The full-text catalogs and indexes are not stored in a SQL Server database. They are stored in separate files managed by the Microsoft Search service.

Full-Text Indexes

Full-text indexes are special indexes that efficiently track the words you're looking for in a table. They help in enabling special searching functions that differ from regular indexes. Full-text indexes are not automatically updated, and they reside in a storage space called the full-text catalog.

When a full-text index is created, you can perform wildcard searches (full-text search) that locate words in close proximity. All full-text indexes are by default placed in a single full-text catalog. Each SQL Server at its apex can store 256 full-text catalogs.

The full-text catalog files are not recovered during a SQL Server recovery. They also cannot be backed up and restored using the T-SQL BACKUP and RESTORE statements. The full-text catalogs must be resynchronized separately after a recovery or restore operation. The full-text catalog files are accessible only to the Microsoft Search service and the Windows NT or Windows 2000 system administrator.

To enable full-text searches, you can run the Full-Text Indexing Wizard, which enables you to manage and create full-text indexes. Note that full-text indexes may be created only on columns that contain only text. Full-text indexes are not automatically updated, thereby bringing up the need to automate the process of updating by setting a job or performing a manual administrative task.

Administering Full-Text Features

SQL Server enables you to easily manage full-text features with the Enterprise Manager and many stored procedures. These are summarized in Table 10.2.

TABLE 10.2

FULL-TEXT STORED PROCEDURES

Stored Procedure	Brief Description
sp_fulltext_database	Initializes full-text indexing or removes all full-text catalogs from the current database.
sp_fulltext_table	Marks or unmarks a table for full-text indexing.
sp_fulltext_column	Specifies whether a particular column of a table participates in full-text indexing.
sp_fulltext_catalog	Creates or drops a full-text catalog.
sp_fulltext_service	Changes Microsoft Search Service properties.

To find syntaxes for these stored procedures, look through the index in Books Online. If you noticed, each one of the stored procedures' syntaxes has an Action argument that determines what action the procedure performs.

Creating Full-Text Indexes

An easy way to add full-text indexes is to use the Full-Text Indexing Wizard. Step by Step 10.10 shows you how to add full-text index functionality on the pub_info table in the Pubs database. In Step by Step 10.10, you are going to create a full-text index and full-text catalog, and then populate that catalog.

STEP BY STEP

10.10 Using the Full-Text Wizard

1. Initiate the Full-Text Wizard by selecting the Pubs database on the left pane and then selecting Full-Text Indexing from the Tools menu.

2. The first screen describes the aims of the wizard. Having read them, click Next to enter the Database Selection screen. In this, you select the table you want to index. The table that you select can be among the tables found in the Pubs database. In this case, select the dbo.pub_info table and click Next.

3. This screen advises you that there must already be a unique index associated with the table if you are going to continue. The wizard locates one for you, UPKC_pubinfo. This index is the unique Primary Key for the pub_info table.

4. After clicking Next, you can choose the columns on which you want full-text indexing to be enabled. In this case, select the check box next to pr_info (because it is a column that contains text data) and click Next.

5. Before using full-text searches, you must make a full-text catalog or choose from an existing one listed. You don't have any existing catalogs, so type **Catalog Pubs** in the New Catalog Name box as shown in Figure 10.10, and click Next to proceed.

6. This screen enables you to choose the population schedule type. You can schedule repopulation for a whole catalog at once or a table at a time. Choose New Catalog Schedule to repopulate this catalog.

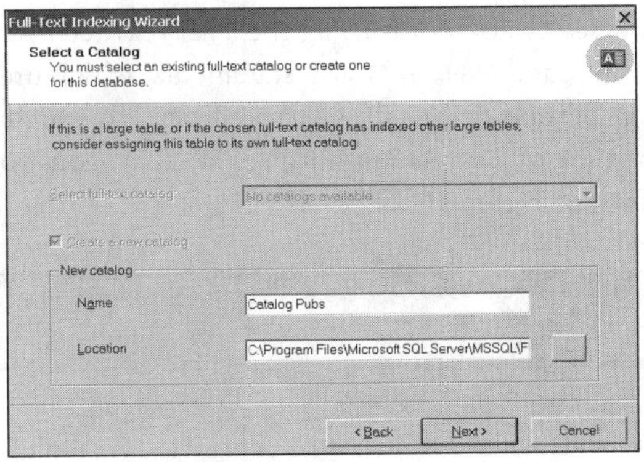

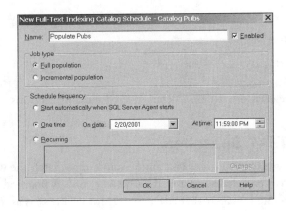

FIGURE 10.10
Creating a new catalog.

7. The next screen enables you to specify options to populate the new catalog. You can choose the time when SQL Server repopulates the new catalog you have created: either when the Server agent starts or at a time specified. Type **Populate Pubs** as the name and leave all other settings with their defaults as shown in Figure 10.11. Click OK and then Next.

8. The final screen shows you a summary of the decisions you made. Click Finish to end the wizard.

After completing Step by Step 10.10, you have to populate your full-text catalog. To do this, open SQL Server Enterprise Manager from the Start menu.

Expand Server Group, expand your server, expand databases, and then expand Pubs. Click Full-Text Catalogs, and then right-click Catalog Pubs. Select Start Full Population.

FIGURE 10.11
Scheduling population of Catalog Pubs.

You can now search for words using the FREETEXT, CONTAINS, CONSTAINSTABLE, and FREETEXTTABLE statements, which unleash search power beyond that of the LIKE predicate. To search for the word *Book* in the pr_info column using FREETEXT, you would enter code as shown in Figure 10.12.

FIGURE 10.12
Making sure full-text indexing succeeded.

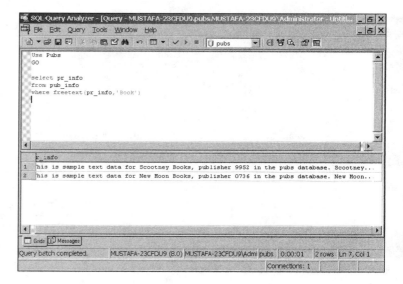

Executing Full-Text Searches

After full-text indexes have been created and a catalog is populated, you can proceed with actually performing a search. A full-text search is nothing more than a SELECT statement, in the WHERE clause, with the optional addition of four useful operators:

- ◆ FREETEXT
- ◆ FREETEXTTABLE
- ◆ CONTAINS
- ◆ CONTAINSTABLE

These are each discussed in detail in the following sections.

FREETEXT Searches

FREETEXT searches columns containing values that match the words given. It is somewhat similar to the LIKE keyword. A practical example is given in Step by Step 10.11. The syntax for FREETEXT is as follows:

```
FREETEXT ( { column | * } , 'freetext_string' )
```

Where

◆ `column` is a full-text index-enabled column, to which the search is directed.

◆ `*` specifies that all columns are enabled for full-text search and that the search is directed to these columns.

◆ `'freetext_string'` specifies the search criteria. This has to be data of type `char`, `varchar`, `nchar`, `nvarchar`, or any other character data. This argument is required.

STEP BY STEP

10.11 Executing Full-Text Searches Using FREETEXT

1. Open the Query Analyzer from the Start menu in Programs, SQL Server 2000.

2. To search for all records that contain the word *publishing* in the `pr_info` column, regardless of case, execute the following:

```
USE Pubs
GO

SELECT pr_info
FROM pub_info
WHERE FREETEXT (pr_info, 'PuBLiShInG')
```

FREETEXTTABLE Searches

`FREETEXTTABLE` searches columns based on a search condition and returns a resultset. Unlike the `FREETEXT` search statement, `FREETEXTTABLE` can be specified in the `FROM` clause of a `SELECT` statement. Additionally, if rows with highest occurrences of related words are to be chosen, the `FREETEXTTABLE` supplies an additional argument `top_N_by_Rank`. The syntax for `FREETEXTTABLE` is as follows.

```
FREETEXTTABLE ( table , { column | * } , 'freetext_string'
➥[ , top_n_by_rank ] )
```

Where

◆ `Table` is the name of the table enabled for full-text searching.

◆ `Column` is a full-text index-enabled column, to which the search is directed.

◆ `*` specifies that all columns are enabled for full-text search and that the search is directed to these columns.

◆ `'Freetext_string'` specifies the search condition, a character string, phrase, or even sentence.

◆ `Top_n_by_rank` specifies that only the *n* number of rows having the most occurrences of words from the search condition are to be returned.

◆ Word values in searches may *not* be variables.

CONTAINS Searches

`CONTAINS` is a statement that is similar to both the `LIKE` and `FREETEXT` predicates. Its purpose is to search for strings, phrases, or even sentences that occur throughout records. It provides extreme flexibility for accurate searching, hence its favor over the `LIKE` and `FREETEXT` keywords. The full syntax of `CONTAINS` predicate is as follows:

```
( { column | * } , '< contains_search_condition >'
)
```

Where

◆ `Column` is a full-text index-enabled column, to which the search is directed.

◆ `*` specifies that all columns are enabled for full-text search and that the search is directed to these columns.

◆ `'< contains_search_condition >'` specifies how to filter the data, and is similar to the `'freetext_string'` of the `FREETEXT` predicate. This argument can further be subdivided into smaller syntaxes, listed in the syntax that follows.

The preceding explanation is the general outline of the `CONTAINS` predicate. The `Contains_Search_Condition` argument has its own querying structure, as follows:

```
< contains_search_condition > ::=
      { < simple_term >
```

```
        | < prefix_term >
        | < generation_term >
        | < proximity_term >
        | < weighted_term >
        }
        | { ( < contains_search_condition > )
        { AND | AND NOT | OR } < contains_search_condition > [ ...n ]
        }
```

And each one of these sub-arguments can be broken down into their most basic form:

```
< simple_term > ::=
    word | " phrase "

< prefix term > ::=
    { "word * " | "phrase * " }

< generation_term > ::=
    FORMSOF ( INFLECTIONAL , < simple_term > [ ,...n ] )

< proximity_term > ::=
    { < simple_term > | < prefix_term > }
    { { NEAR | ~ } { < simple_term > | < prefix_term > } } [ ...n ]

< weighted_term > ::=
    ISABOUT
        ( { {
                < simple_term >
                | < prefix_term >
                | < generation_term >
                | < proximity_term >
                }
            [ WEIGHT ( weight_value ) ]
            } [ ,...n ]
        )
```

Where

◆ Simple_term searches for an exact match for a word or phrase.
   If a word is given with the exclusion of spaces (database, for
   example), it can be written without quotation marks. A word
   specified with the inclusion of spaces (as in "SQL Server
   Database") needs to be written with the inclusion of double
   quotation marks (" ").

◆ Prefix term is used to specify a root word—a prefix—that
   returns all words beginning with it. To signify this, use an
   asterisk (*), which acts as zero, one, or more characters. If a
   phrase is specified, it considers each word a root declaration.
   Therefore, executing the following query lists titles containing
   "computer", "complete" and "comparison", and so on.

```
SELECT * FROM titles
    WHERE CONTAINS (title, '"comp*"')
```

◆ Generation_term is used when forms of simple_term may vary. INFLECTIONAL is used alongside generation_term when inflectional forms of words are to be returned. To distinguish that you are specifying an argument for generation_form, use the FORMSOF keyword.

◆ Proximity_term specifies that words in proximity to each other should be returned. You accomplish this with the help of the NEAR keyword, using NEAR as an operator similar to AND. For example, the following query searches and returns results only when the words IBM and Aptiva are close to one another.

```
SELECT * FROM computer_names
 WHERE CONTAINS (computer_names, 'IBM NEAR Aptiva')
```

◆ 'Weighted_term' specifies different words or phrases that are to be matched to return a resultset. Each of these can be referred by a weighted value that gives a sort of "rank" to each word.

```
WEIGHT ( weight_value )
```

This optionally gives each term mentioned in the weighted_term argument a decimal value between 0 and 1 inclusive to show the importance of each word. To distinguish WEIGHT from other arguments, use the ISABOUT keyword.

Therefore, to return all rows in the ProductName column (in the Products table of the Northwind database) that have Hot (first priority), Sauce (second priority), and Cranberry (third priority), execute the following:

```
SELECT * FROM Products
WHERE CONTAINS (ProductName, 'ISABOUT (Hot WEIGHT (0.9),
➡Sauce WEIGHT (0.5), CRANBERRY WEIGHT (0.2))'
```

Step By Step 10.12 illustrates the ability to search through text with the CONTAINS option.

STEP BY STEP

10.12 Searching Using CONTAINS

1. Open the Query Analyzer from the Start menu.

2. To search for different forms of the word *Publish* in the
pr_info column, execute the following:

```
USE Pubs
GO
SELECT pr_info
FROM pub_info
WHERE CONTAINS(pr_info , ' FORMSOF (INFLECTIONAL, publish) ')
```

CONTAINSTABLE Searches

CONTAINSTABLE works much the same as FREETEXTTABLE works and
has similar arguments to that of the CONTAINS statement. The syntax
for CONTAINSTABLE is as follows:

```
CONTAINSTABLE ( table , { column | * } , '
➥< contains_search_condition > '
    [ , top_n_by_rank ] )
```

Where

◆ 'table' is the name of the table that has been set for full-text
searching.

◆ Column is a full-text index-enabled column, to which the search
is directed.

◆ * Specifies that all columns are enabled for full-text search and
that the search is directed to these columns.

◆ ' < contains_search_condition > ' is what you want to
search for. The ' < contains_search_condition > ' argument
regulates the same rules as the ' < contains_search_condition
> ' argument in the CONTAINS statement.

◆ top_n_by_rank specifies that the *n* number of matches, in
descending order, are to be returned.

Internally, SQL Server sends the search condition to the Microsoft
Search service. The Microsoft Search service finds all the keys that
match the full-text search condition and returns them to SQL
Server. SQL Server, and then uses the list of keys to determine which
table rows are to be processed.

CASE STUDY: WESTERN FURNITURE LTD.

ESSENCE OF THE CASE:

▶ Western Furniture wants to increase business by adding more users and importing more furniture.

▶ All imported furniture is recorded in the Products table in the central database. Each table in this database stores over 50,000 records.

▶ Database users report slow response times when querying columns on the Products table after the recent upgrade.

SCENARIO

Your company, named Western Furniture, imports furniture from different parts of the world, with twenty sales offices around the nation. This company is well known for the quality furniture it provides. Company officers want to increase their supply by increasing the amount of imported furniture by four times and creating four new sales offices in Washington, Chicago, Toronto, and New York. They also want to increase the number of users accessing their database from 50 to 150.

All imported furniture is recorded in the Products table in the central database. Each table in this database stores over 50,000 records. Sales and supply information is updated daily in the Sales table. The users of the database report slow response times when querying columns on the Products table after the recent upgrade. The workforce does not currently have employees specializing in database performance tuning but are planning to hire in the near future.

ANALYSIS

The best solution for this type of situation would be to index the Products table. This would provide faster access to data, especially when querying with the SELECT statement, because the number of rows is more then 50,000. But the hard decision would be which column or columns should be indexed. Your SQL Server administrators know very little about database performance. In this case, Index Tuning Wizard comes in. The Index Tuning Wizard chooses the best course of action for your index. It determines which column or columns need to be indexed and which type of index needs to be used. Also, the Index Tuning Wizard does not require anyone to know about index internals, which makes it a perfect solution for the SQL Administrators. Also consider whether there is a blocking problem.

CHAPTER SUMMARY

You've seen what indexes are and their internal structures. There are two types of indexes: clustered and nonclustered. Clustered indexes sort and store the data rows in the table based on their key values. Clustered indexes are efficient for finding rows because the rows are kept in sorted order on the clustered index key.

Nonclustered indexes have a design entirely separate from the data rows. Rows of nonclustered indexes contain index key values with each index key holding a pointer mapping to a data row containing that index key. The data rows themselves are not stored in the order specified by the nonclustered index definition.

We've also learned about index considerations and how to implement them into your application with the CREATE INDEX statement. The FILLFACTOR argument specifies how full SQL Server should make each page and can be expressed as a percentage from 1 to 100, inclusive. You also learned about the functions involved in renaming and deleting indexes.

We looked at rebuilding indexes to reorganize scattered or fragmented pages. One way of doing this is to delete the original index and then re-create it. This is not favored because it is a two-way process and consumes overhead. Deleting a clustered index and then recreating it means deleting and recreating all nonclustered indexes. The other, one-shot method is to use the DBCC_DBREINDEX statement.

Then we learned about index statistics and how to manage them. Index statistics need to be up to date for the optimizer to decide upon the fastest route of access. Updating statistics involves the use of the UPDATE STATISTICS statement.

We examined the Index Tuning Wizard, a tool that reduces index-tension for many beginners and even professional DBAs. To use Index Tuning Wizard, you have to monitor the default environment by setting up a trace.

Full-text searching was discussed next. Full-text search leverages the power of flexible searches. To set up full-text searches, you first have to run a custom setup and install the Full-Text Search service. (Full-Text Search Service is a program separate from SQL Server 2000.)

KEY TERMS

- index
- clustered index
- nonclustered index
- FILLFACTOR
- rebuilding indexes
- DBCC DBREINDEX
- UPDATE STATISTICS
- indexed view
- Index Tuning Wizard (ITW)
- full-text index
- full-text catalog

APPLY YOUR KNOWLEDGE

Exercises

10.1 Creating a Nonclustered Index on a New Column with the Enterprise Manager

This exercise offers practice in creating a nonclustered index using the SQL Server Enterprise Manager. Before creating an index, an existing table has to be available. This exercise uses the Authors table.

Estimated Time: 10 Minutes

1. Open the SQL Server Enterprise Manager; expand a server group and then expand a server.

2. Expand Databases, expand the Pubs database, and then select Tables.

3. Right-click Authors; click on Design Table.

4. On the toolbar, click the Table and Index Properties button, which has a picture of a hand pointing to a table.

5. Select the Indexes/Keys table to change specific properties pertaining to indexes.

6. On the Indexes/Keys tab, click New.

7. In the Column Name list, you have to click the column or columns that are part of the index. For this exercise, select au_id for the column name.

8. Select the Create UNIQUE check box to make this index a unique constraint.

9. In Fillfactor, you have to specify how full SQL Server should make the leaf level of each index page during index creation. For this exercise, specify 60%.

10. To save changes, click the Save button on the toolbar.

11. Close the dialog box.

10.2 Creating a Clustered Index Using Code

You saw in Exercise 10.1 just how simple it was to create an index using the Enterprise Manager. In this exercise, you will also examine index creation, this time using code.

Estimated Time: 10 Minutes

1. Open the Query Analyzer by selecting Query Analyzer from the Start menu.

2. Create a new index on a new table. To do this, first create a new table in the Pubs database. In the code pane, type in the following:

```
use Pubs
CREATE TABLE IndexPractice
(YourName char(32),
 Age integer,
 BirthDate integer)
```

3. After creating a new table, you have to create a new clustered index. To do this, code in the following:

```
Use Pubs
CREATE CLUSTERED INDEX age_index
    ON IndexPractice (age)
```

4. To see your new index, open the Query Analyzer, expand the Pubs database in the Object Browser, and then expand User Tables. Expand IndexPractice and then expand Indexes. If you followed the steps properly, you should see age_index listed below Indexes.

APPLY YOUR KNOWLEDGE

10.3 Creating an Indexed View

This exercise requires you to optimize a view by creating an index on it.

Estimated Time: 10 Minutes

1. Open the Query Analyzer. To do this, select the Query Analyzer from the Start menu.

2. Type the following in the code pane to configure session-level settings needed when creating an indexed view:

```
Use Pubs
SET ANSI_PADDING,CONCAT_NULL_YIELDS_NULL,
➥ANSI_WARNINGS,
ARITHABORT,ANSI_NULLS,QUOTED_IDENTIFIER ON
SET NUMERIC_ROUNDABORT OFF

GO
```

3. Now you actually create the view. To create the view with the WITH SCHEMABINDING option set, copy out the following code:

```
CREATE VIEW ExerciseView WITH SCHEMABINDING
AS
SELECT Au_fname, Au_id, Au_lname
FROM dbo.Authors
GO
```

4. Now you have to create a unique clustered index on the view. To do this, copy out the following code snippet:

```
CREATE UNIQUE CLUSTERED Index ExerciseIndex
ON ExerciseView (au_id)
Go
```

5. To see the indexed view you have just created, open the Query Analyzer and then the Object browser.

6. Expand Pubs and then expand Views.

7. Click ExerciseView and then expand Indexes. You should see ExerciseIndex listed under Indexes.

Review Questions

1. Briefly describe clustered and nonclustered indexes.

2. What does FILLFACTOR specify? In what cases would an implementation benefit from its use?

3. What is a nonclustered covering index?

4. How would you go about rebuilding indexes?

5. What are indexed views?

6. Why do index statistics need to be updated? How do you update them?

Exam Questions

1. You are working for a small manufacturing company that has been operating well for some time. Lately the end users have been reporting that when performing queries against information on customers, the system is growing increasingly slow. After examining the system, you determine that the table definition has recently been altered. You want the response time to improve and be similar to what it was before the change. How would you fix the problem?

   A. Run a DBCC DBREINDEX.

   B. Drop and re-create the table's clustered index.

   C. Drop and re-create all indexes.

   D. Update the index statistics.

   E. Stop and restart the server.

APPLY YOUR KNOWLEDGE

2. Your company has a table named `Products` that is dedicated to its goods. A month ago, you added three nonclustered indexes to the table named `NC1_Pro`, `NC2_Pro`, and `NC3_Pro`. You also added a clustered index named `C1_Pro` on the Primary Key named `Prod_ID`. You monitor the performance on the indexes and notice that the indexes are not as efficient as before. You decide to rebuild each index in the table. Which method should you use to rebuild all indexes in the fastest and most efficient way?

   A. `DBCC DBREINDEX` (Products).

   B. Create clustered index with drop-existing; create nonclustered index with drop-existing.

   C. Delete all indexes and then re-create them.

   D. `DBCC DBREINDEX` (NC1_Pro, NC2_Pro, NC3_Pro, C1_Pro).

   E. Update the index statistics.

3. You have a SQL Server database implemented in a library that stores library-specific information. The description of each title that is present in the library is stored in the `Titles` table. The `Description` column is implemented as data type `text`. A full-text index exists for all columns in the `Titles` table. You want to search for a title that includes the phrase *Programming SQL*. Which query should you execute to return the required results?

   A. `SELECT * FROM Titles WHERE Description like '_Programming SQL_%'`

   B. `SELECT * FROM Titles WHERE Description like '%Programming SQL%'`

   C. `SELECT * FROM Titles WHERE CONTAINS (Titles, Description, 'Programming SQL')`

   D. `SELECT * FROM Titles WHERE FREETEXT (Description, 'Programming SQL')`

4. You have a table that is defined as follows:

   ```
   CREATE TABLE Books ( Book_ID char,
   ➥Description Text, Price Integer, Author
   ➥char(32))
   ```

   You write the following:

   ```
   SELECT * FROM Books WHERE CONTAINS
   ➥(Description, 'Server')
   ```

   You know for a fact that there are matching rows, but you receive an empty resultset when you try to execute the query. What should you do?

   A. Ensure that there is a nonunique index on `Description` column.

   B. Create a unique clustered index on the `Description` column.

   C. Create a `FULLTEXT` catalog for the `Books` table and then populate it.

   D. Use the `sp_fulltext_populate` stored procedure.

5. You have 50,000 records in a database file, and you know you want to add another 25,000 records in the next month. What `FILLFACTOR` should you specify to maximize performance? It should be mentioned that a new index is to be created and that you will change your `FILLFACTOR`; you also want fast `INPUT` into the tables.

   A. 0 (default setting)

   B. 100

   C. 70

   D. 50

APPLY YOUR KNOWLEDGE

6. You have a table named Products that holds information pertaining to the products your company trades. You need to perform quality searches on the Description column so that you can find products needed using diverse methods. You decide using full-text searches is the best method and so enable full-text indexing in your table. You want to keep performance consistent with the full-text indexes so that they do not degrade, and you want to minimize overhead associated with their maintenance. What should you do?

   A. Expand the database to accommodate future growth of the full-text indexes.

   B. Use the Index Tuning Wizard.

   C. Repopulate using the Full-Text Indexing Wizard and specify Keep Performance Consistency.

   D. Schedule regular repopulates of the full-text indexes.

7. You are a database developer for a computer manufacturing company named Optima. For a limited time, Optima ships free software with the purchase of any desktop computer or notebook. The software titles, descriptions, values, and other information are located in the Software table. You configure full-text indexing on the Software_Description column that contains over 2000 rows and is located in the Software table. After executing a search using FREETEXT for the word *Windows*, you notice an empty resultset in the results pane. Why is this happening?

   A. The catalog is not populated.

   B. FREETEXT is not a valid keyword recognized by SQL Server 2000.

   C. FREETEXT is not allowed for columns that contain 2000 or more rows.

   D. You didn't create a nonclustered index.

8. Which statements show the maximum number of clustered and nonclustered indexes allowed in a single table?

   A. Clustered 249 and nonclustered 149

   B. Clustered 249 and nonclustered 249

   C. Clustered 1 and nonclustered 249

   D. Clustered 1 and nonclustered unlimited

9. What is true about the WITH SCHEMABINDING argument of the CREATE INDEX statement? Choose all that apply.

   A. It must be specified to create an indexed view.

   B. It allows a view's name and other properties to be changed dynamically.

   C. It prevents the dropping and altering of tables participating in the indexed view.

   D. It has to be specified only when you are creating a unique clustered index on a text column.

APPLY YOUR KNOWLEDGE

10. John has just been impressed with the power full-text searches can provide and how easy they are to implement. Before John actually upgrades to a full-text search, John wants to try out the full-text searching "dream" capabilities by just testing them on the `Products` table of his company's database. John would like to perform flexible searches on a text column in the `Products` table. Which tool helps him accomplish his task?

    A. Index Tuning Wizard

    B. Full-Text Searching Wizard

    C. Full-Text Indexing Wizard

    D. MSSearch Index Wizard

11. Jauna is a DBA who has received complaints from many users concerning the data retrieval and modification times on the `Sales` table. She knows that you are a developer and asks you to figure out a way to resolve the problem she is facing. Because you are a new developer, you happen to know indexes increase performance, and that's just about all you know about indexes. You imprudently index all twelve columns in the `Sales` table. Which of the following statements outline the consequence of using the numerous indexes you have just done?

    A. Numerous indexes make it difficult to modify data.

    B. Numerous indexes are not allowed to be built; indexes can be used only in smaller quantities.

    C. Numerous indexes result in a very short index lifespan.

    D. Numerous indexes decrease performance on queries that select data with the `SELECT` clause.

12. David is a database implementer who works for a major car retailer that tracks information on the latest car models available by the various car manufacturers. The company currently searches for the latest car model description using a regular search engine that is not capable of performing such complex searches as full-text searches can perform. David needs to upgrade the company's searches to full-text searches. What must he do before creating a full-text index?

    A. End all wizards and programs using the MSSearch utility.

    B. Create an index using the Index Tuning Wizard.

    C. Run a custom setup to install Microsoft Full-Text Search Engine.

    D. He doesn't have to do anything.

13. Which of the following statements is true when using full-text indexing? Choose all that apply.

    A. The column that you plan on indexing must not contain text if at all possible.

    B. The column that you index has to be made up of text data.

    C. Full-text indexes are not automatically updated and they reside in a storage space called a full-text catalog.

    D. There can be up to 200 catalogs and not more in a single server.

    E. Full-text searches are best performed on columns that hold integer values.

APPLY YOUR KNOWLEDGE

14. You are designing a database that will serve as a back end for several large web sites. The web sites themselves will communicate with each other and pass data back and forth using XML. You would like to control the data displayed on the user browser based on interactions with the user. In many cases columns and rows need to be eliminated based on the criteria supplied. You would like to minimize round trips to the server for data exchange purposes. What technology is the best to apply?

    A. Use a user-defined function with SCHEMABINDING set to the XML recordsets.

    B. Create an Indexed View of the XML recordset specifying only the columns needed and supply a WHERE condition based on the rows selected.

    C. Create standard views of SQL Server data and export the requested data using XML.

    D. Send data requests and updates directly from the client machine to the SQL Server using FOR XML and OPENXML options.

    E. Use HTML and an XML schema to provide the necessary view of the data.

Answers to Review Questions

1. Clustered indexes are implemented so that the logical order of the key values determines the physical order of the corresponding rows in a table. Nonclustered indexes are indexes, similar to those in the back of a book, in which the logical order of the index is different than the physical, stored order of the rows on disk. See "Clustered Indexes" and "Examining Nonclustered Indexes."

2. The FILLFACTOR option specifies how full SQL Server should make each page when it creates a new index using existing data. See "Exploring FILLFACTOR."

3. A covering index is a nonclustered index that is built upon all the columns needed to satisfy a SQL query, both in the selection criteria and the WHERE clause. See "Nonclustered Covering Indexes." It must cover *all* columns referred to in the query from that table, including group by, having, compute, compute by, and so on.

4. To rebuild indexes, you should use DBCC DBREINDEX because it allows all indexes to be rebuilt in a single shot. See "Rebuilding Indexes" for further explanation.

5. Indexed views enable views to be stored in a database's physical storage after an index is created. See "Indexed Views" for further study.

6. Index statistics need to be up to date for the optimizer to decide upon the fastest route of access. To update them, use the UPDATE STATISTICS statement. See "Updating Statistics" for more detail.

Answers to Exam Questions

1. **D.** Because the table structure has recently been altered, it is a good possibility that this change has caused the indexing information to become unstable or that statistics affecting the index have not been updated. If you restart the service, SQL Server should then update the statistical information accordingly. After the restart, you may want to ensure that all statistics are intact. Also consider index fragmentation as a possible source to the problem. For more information, see the section "Indexing and Statistics."

APPLY YOUR KNOWLEDGE

2. **A.** DBCC DBREINDEX. Answer B is wrong because this would be more time-consuming than DBCC DBREINDEX. You would have to individually rebuild all indexes. Answer C is not correct because deleting a clustered index and then re-creating it means deleting and re-creating all nonclustered indexes. Also, the process would have to involve two separate steps. For more details, refer to the section titled "Index Maintenance."

3. **D.** Answer A is incorrect because the LIKE keyword cannot search on text-based columns. Answer B is wrong for the same reason. Answer C is wrong because the syntax for CONTAINS is wrong. Answer D is correct because it uses the correct method of searching, using FREETEXT. See the section "Creating Full Text Indexes" for more information.

4. **C.** To enable full-text searching, you must create a catalog for a table and then populate manually or schedule a job. Answer A is incorrect because creating a nonunique index does not help in any way whatsoever. B is incorrect because creating a unique clustered index does not enable full-text searching. D is incorrect because there is no such procedure as sp_fulltext_populate (but there is a stored procedure named sp_fulltext_catalog). For more information, see "Creating Full Text Indexes."

5. **D.** You know exactly how many new records are coming in. 25,000 is 50% of 50,000, so filling the page by 50% and leaving 50% free space for the remaining 50,000 records seems logical. For more details, see the section "Exploring FILLFACTOR."

6. **D.** Unlike regular SQL indexes, full-text indexes are not automatically kept up to date as data is modified in the associated tables. Full-text indexes should be frequently updated to maintain performance. For more information, see "Creating Full Text Indexes."

7. **A.** Before executing full-text searches, you must create and populate a full-text catalog. A full-text catalog is the basis of the storage used for the indexes. Periodically these catalogs should be repopulated to ensure usefulness. Repopulation can be done by schedule or by administrative task. For more details, see "Creating Full Text Indexes."

8. **C.** There can be only one clustered index per table and as many as 249 nonclustered indexes. For more details, refer to SQL Server Books OnLine.

9. **A, C.** The WITH SCHEMABINDING argument of the CREATE INDEX statement is needed when creating an indexed view. When WITH SCHEMABINDING is specified, tables participating in the indexed view are prevented from alteration and deletion. "Indexed View Requirements and Restrictions" provides additional information on use of the WITH SCHEMABINDING option.

10. **C.** The Full-Text Indexing Wizard is a graphical tool that enables full-text searches on columns by easily and quickly creating full-text indexes and full-text catalogs. For more details, see "Creating Full Text Indexes."

11. **A.** Indexes used in larger quantities often degrade the rate at which insertions, deletions, and some modifications to data occur. Nevertheless, indexes generally speed up data access in cases where the data in the table is sufficient to warrant indexing. For more information, see "Indexing to Improve Performance."

APPLY YOUR KNOWLEDGE

12. **A.** Before creating a full-text index, it is required that you close all applications and wizards running or using the MSSearch utility. For more details, see "Creating Full Text Indexes."

13. **B, C.** The column that you plan to index has to be made up of text data. After you create a full-text index, it is not automatically updated and it resides in a storage space called a full-text catalog. For more details, see "Creating Full Text Indexes."

14. **E.** SCHEMABINDING refers only to SQL Server objects—specifically tables, views, and user-defined functions. An XML schema cannot be bound in this manner. XML resides in memory and is processed against its own internal set of rules, referred to as a schema. An XML schema interacts directly with the data to supply logic and display attributes on the user's browser. HTML does not have the required functionality. For more information, see the "Indexed View Requirements and Restrictions."

Suggested Readings and Resources

1. SQL Server Books Online

   - Index Tuning Recommendations

   - Placing Indexes on Filegroups

   - Database Design Considerations

   - Creating and Maintaining Databases: Indexes

The Microsoft-specified objectives for the Replication section of the Database Development SQL Server 2000 exam are as follows:

Alter database objects to support replication

- **Support merge, snapshot, and transactional replication models.**

- **Resolve replication conflicts.**

▶ This objective looks at the different replication model types available. The replication types are merge, transactional, and snapshot; each of these models is covered in detail. This objective also requires that you be able to troubleshoot the different replication processes. To have a thorough understanding of replication, as well as the ability to make appropriate implementations, you need to study replication internals and physical models in more detail than you did in Chapter 3, "Physical Database Design."

CHAPTER 11

Implementing and Understanding Replication Methodologies

▶ Make sure you have a solid understanding of the Publisher/Subscriber Metaphor.

▶ Go through the Step by Step so you become familiar with how to implement replication. The exam will not require you to know every step, so you should not spend your time memorizing all the different screens of the wizard. The concept of replication and its effect on the database and front-end applications will be the exam focus.

▶ Make sure you understand how replication works. Understanding the process and components eliminates the need for memorization, which don't provide you with the skills necessary to implement a strategy in the real world.

▶ There are not any functions, statements, or stored procedures that need to be learned in this chapter pertaining to the exam. In some real-world scenarios, however, you may want to be able to access the processes that will permit you to use replication-related stored procedures to automate a complex configuration.

INTRODUCTION

This chapter covers the Microsoft-specified objectives with regard to the design and development of applications that involve replication. Many scenarios on the exam will relate to the efficient, appropriate design of a database for replicating data from one server to another. This was touched on in the replication overview provided in Chapter 3, "Physical Database Design."

The exam requires you to choose the appropriate technology and also asks about particular aspects of replication. It is imperative, therefore, that you have a complete understanding of what replication offers in contrast to other aspects of SQL Server.

You need to fully understand three separate areas of replication: physical replication models, types of replication, and replication processing. Each topic is covered in detail in this chapter so that you can understand the replication process completely.

Replication is the process by which data and database objects are distributed from SQL Server to other database engines that reside across your enterprise; this data can be distributed to other SQL Server databases or even non-SQL Server databases such as Oracle and others. To help you become more acquainted with the general format of replication, this chapter looks at SQL Server's implementation of the *Publisher/Subscriber metaphor*, which is a metaphor consisting of a Publisher, Subscriber, and Distributor that forms the basis of replication. The various types of replication available, and how to implement them in SQL Server, are covered later in this chapter.

REPLICATION

Has data ever been placed on different servers throughout your business? How was that data transferred from one source to another in a safe, efficient, and reliable manner? Now, imagine that you have two production sites located across the world from each other: How are they going to collaborate and share information? Many corporations distribute information from remote sales locations to central order processing locations. Other organizations operate distributed warehouses, with each individual location needing knowledge of the others' inventories. The problems are many. One of the potential solutions is the implementation of a replication strategy.

Replication is the process of carrying, modifying, and distributing data and database objects (stored procedures, extended properties, views, tables, user-defined functions, triggers, and indexes) from one source server to another, in a consistent fashion, independent of location. Replication is a huge topic. Any implementation can use multiple types and an endless number of forms. The following section describes just why replication is implemented.

BENEFITS OF REPLICATION

Replication, with its many benefits, serves as a backbone for many businesses. Without replication, businesses would be incapable of carrying out robust branch operations across the globe. DBAs favor replication for the following reasons:

◆ The primary and most certainly obvious reason for implementing replication is that businesses are capable of having data copied from server to server in a multi-site enterprise, which provides flexibility and more efficient use of networking resources.

◆ Replication allows for a greater concurrent use of data. That is, more people can work with copies of data at the same time. Also, with copies of the database distributed, users can benefit from multiple machines providing a form of load balancing.

◆ Replication is perfect for the traveling salesman or roaming disconnected user. It enables mobile users who work on laptops to be updated with current database information when they do connect.

Replication clearly provides numerous benefits. The next section starts you off with a foundation on replication: the Publisher/Subscriber metaphor. This concept encompasses the main replication components that are needed in even the most basic replication: the Publisher, Subscriber, and Distributor.

Understanding Replication Components: The Publisher/Subscriber Metaphor

Before you get involved in a deeper discussion on replication, it's important that you become familiar with the basic concept of the Publisher/Subscriber metaphor. The Publisher/Subscriber metaphor defines the different roles SQL Server can play throughout the replication process. Frankly speaking, SQL server can also play a third role: the Distributor. Each role provides functionality that aids in the replication process. In simple terms, the *Publisher* is the server that makes the data available so that it can be sent to the Subscriber. The *Distributor* is the intermediary that collects the data from the Publisher and transports it to the Subscriber. The *Subscriber* is the server that ends up receiving the data.

This metaphor is analogous to the processing of a monthly magazine subscription or other periodical. In the case of a magazine, the magazine company produces copies of the magazine that they then send to a distributor to be circulated to individual customers. As you will see, this is similar to the roles of the Publisher and Distributor in a replication scenario. The Publisher makes the data available to be dispersed to the subscribing machines through a Distributor. The magazine distributor (courier or mailman), like the Distributor, is used as an intermediary between the magazine company and the customer. The replication Distributor is responsible for the delivery of the data to all subscribers. Finally, the individual customer who receives the magazine copy through the mail can be thought of as the Subscriber in SQL Server, with one important difference: In some SQL Server replication scenarios, the Subscriber can change the content and send updates back to the publisher (which I'm sure would not be desirable in the case of most magazine subscriptions). This process is represented in Figure 11.1. Each role is discussed in more detail in the following sections.

EXAM TIP

The Publisher/Subscriber Metaphor on the Exam   Obviously, the exam will not ask you such direct questions as, "What is the Publisher/Subscriber metaphor?" Nevertheless, understanding the Publisher/Subscriber metaphor is vital in understanding how replication is implemented, which may very well be a question on the exam.

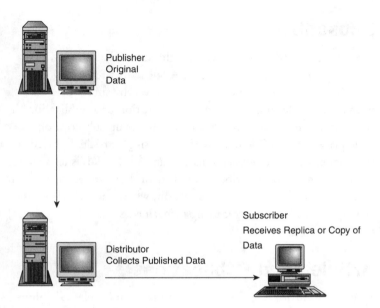

FIGURE 11.1
The Publisher/Subscriber metaphor.

Publisher

In replication terminology, the Publisher is the server that produces the original data for the use of the replication process. The Publisher can produce many *publications* or sets of data to be distributed to other subscribing machines. One Publisher can produce data to be replicated to many Subscribers. Also, many Publishers may produce data to be distributed to just a single, central Subscriber. The former is implemented as a standard Central Publisher/Distributor/Subscriber replication model, and the latter is referred to as a Central Subscriber replication.

Distributor

In SQL Server terminology, the Distributor is the server that contains the distribution database, data history, and transactions; as its name implies, it sends data to Subscribers. The Distributor may be implemented on the same physical server as the Publisher or Subscriber, though it doesn't need to be. It can reside on a separate server across the world connected via a network. The placement of the Distributor and its characteristics depends on the type of replication used.

Subscriber

A Subscriber in SQL Server terms is the server that receives replicated data through the Distributor. A Subscriber receives publications by subscribing to them—not, however, by subscribing to individual articles that represent only a portion of a publication. It is also possible to use stored procedures to set up subscriptions, in which case it is possible to subscribe to a single article. Subscribers can choose from the publications available at the Publisher and don't necessarily need to subscribe to all of them. Remember the magazine example at the beginning of this section, where the Subscriber is analogous to a customer receiving magazine issues.

Articles and Publications

Simply put, *articles* are data structures made up of selected columns and/or rows from a table. An article could also be the entire table, although it is recommended that the content of an article be kept to just the minimum amount of data needed for the specifics of an implementation. One or more articles are bundled into a *publication* to be used for replication. Selecting subsets of tables (certain rows or certain columns) is known as *partitioning*, which is discussed in more detail later in this chapter.

Articles must be grouped into a publication before they are ready to be replicated. In other words, a publication is a collection of one or more articles and is capable of being replicated.

Horizontal and Vertical Partitions

Horizontal partitioning is the breaking down of tables into smaller subsets based on the selection of rows. Row selections are made using a standard condition that would be provided as a WHERE clause for a SELECT statement. *Vertical partitioning* is the segmenting of tables into a subset based on the selection of only the columns that are needed as opposed to all columns in the table.

You can, however, choose not to use either form of partitioning and publish the entire table, if this is what is needed to meet the goals of the implementation. Partitions are used when a business does not need to replicate all the information contained in a table; they also make the replication process more efficient by minimizing the amount of data being sent over a network. Partitions are also used when you do not want confidential information to be sent to users, and when the storage space on the Subscriber is a consideration. Vertical and horizontal partitioning are supported by all three types of replication (merge, snapshot, and transactional, covered later in this chapter).

IN THE FIELD

ARTICLE COMPOSITION

A single article may take advantage of both vertical and horizontal partitioning at the same time. In fact, because doing so produces the smallest amount of data to be transferred, it is considered the desired technique.

Vertical partitioning, also known as vertical filtering, provides a good solution when a business needs to replicate only a subset of data, which is produced by a few columns segmented from a table.

For example, imagine a food manufacturing business called Purls that keeps a table called "Products" residing in their headquarters, which lists detailed information for each product they have. Columns included in the Products table might be Product_Id, Product, Price, and Description. Eight branch offices located in different areas throughout the country need a copy of the Price column from the Products table as soon as possible.

In this case, Purls decides to vertically partition their article by selecting only the columns that are needed (that is, the Price column and Product_Id column), and then replicating them to all branch offices. This increases the efficiency with which the data is sent to the different branch offices, because Purls avoids sending unnecessary information held on the Description and Product columns, and sends only what is required: the Price column.

Horizontal partitioning is used in similar ways. In another example, there might be a major ISP (Internet Service Provider) business called PrimeNet that tracks information on clients in a Customer table. PrimeNet maintains data for both active and inactive clients. It is probably desirable to replicate only the active customer information to sales representatives. A condition such as WHERE Status = ACTIVE can be applied to eliminate inactive clients and create a much smaller amount of information to be transmitted.

Subscriptions

Subscriptions are requests from the Subscriber for data or data objects to be sent. A subscription depends upon three factors: when publications will be received, what publications will be received, and where the publications will be received.

There are two types of subscriptions: a push subscription and a pull subscription. A *push* subscription is one where the Publisher initiates a subscription and provides the basis for scheduling the replication process. The *pull* subscription is one where the Subscriber initiates the subscription and provides the basis and timing on which data is to be obtained. In either case, whoever initiates a subscription selects the appropriate articles to be transmitted.

REPLICATION CONFIGURATIONS

Replication can be set up in a number of ways. The different scenarios in which replication is set up each provide specific benefits and qualities. SQL Server can serve as Publisher, Subscriber, or Distributor. The individual roles can all be set up on a single machine, although in most implementations there is at least a separation between a Publisher/Distributor and the subscribing machine(s). In some other scenarios, the subscriber of the data from one machine may re-publish the data to still other subscribers. The possibilities are endless. You can choose to implement any of the following common scenarios, which cover the basics of a physical replication model. In real-world scenarios, however, the actual physical model used could have any combination of these elements, based on a business's individual needs.

- ◆ Central Publisher, multiple Subscribers
- ◆ Multiple Publishers, multiple Subscribers
- ◆ Multiple Publishers, single Subscriber
- ◆ Single Publisher, remote Distributor

Central Publisher, Multiple Subscribers

In this form of replication, the data originates at the publishing server, and that original data is sent to multiple Subscribers via the Distributor. Depending on the form of replication used, changes to the data at the destination servers can enable updates to be propagated back to the Publisher and other Subscribers or can be treated as read-only data, where updates occur only at the Publisher. Later, this chapter looks at the specifics of the different forms of replication, because the physical model chosen does not affect the capability of the server to accept updates on the data received.

This type of scenario is typically used when a company has a master catalog at the headquarters and has many different Subscribers located elsewhere. This configuration is shown in Figure 11.2.

For example, a chemical manufacturing company named Fronted Chemicals has headquarters located in Geneva, Switzerland, that keeps a list of the chemicals they produce in a table named `Chemicals`. This table holds specific information about each chemical such as `DangerLevel`, `UnitPrice`, `TotalQuantity`, and so forth. What they want to do is send this list of chemicals to 25 international sales offices located in North America and Europe. They can use replication based on a multiple Subscribers, with the central Publisher in Geneva sending the chemical list to all offices.

An advantage of this configuration is that multiple copies of the data from a central server are available for user processing on multiple machines. Data can be distributed to the locations where it is needed. With this form of replication, data can be brought closer to the user, and the load on a single server can be reduced. Expensive bandwidth can also be utilized in an improved manner.

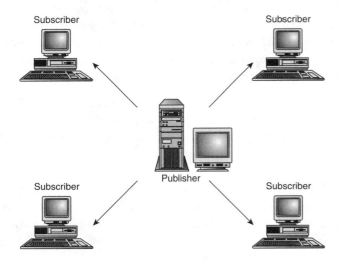

FIGURE 11.2
The Central Publisher, Multiple Subscribers configuration.

The location of the subscribing servers is not really relevant to the model, although variations on the model may be necessary to minimize costs and decrease the time needed to synchronize data at all locations. The Subscribers receiving the data can be within the same building or city where there are a large number of users within a very close proximity who need access to the data. It might be necessary to locate Subscribers throughout separate regions of the country so that the data can be brought closer to the end user, thereby minimizing communications over a WAN link. A different implementation may have a global corporation with Subscribers located around the world.

Although it is a common solution for copying data from one server to many others servers, the single, central Publisher with multiple Subscribers is only one of many basic configurations. The next few sections examine a number of other configurations that are used in some different situations.

Multiple Publishers, Multiple Subscribers

In the Multiple Publishers, Multiple Subscribers scenario, each server involved in the replication process acts as both a Publisher and a Subscriber. In this replication, every server publishes a particular set of rows that relate to it and subscribes to the publications that all the other servers are publishing, so that each of them receive data and send data.

Multiple Publishers, Multiple Subscribers is typically used in a distributed warehouse environment with inventory spread out among different locations, or any other situation in which the data being held at each location-specific server needs to be delivered to the other servers so that each location has a complete set of data.

You might have this type of replication set up in chained public libraries. When a reader comes to request a particular book, the librarian checks the book inventory table and finds it is not available in this local branch. The replicated data she gets from all other Publishers' book inventories is combined with her results to show which library currently holds the desired book. This is not only the case with her library, but all the other libraries in the chain. (This configuration is shown in Figure 11.3.) If data were replicated to only a single library, it would have been a Multiple Publisher, Single Subscriber model, which is what the next section covers.

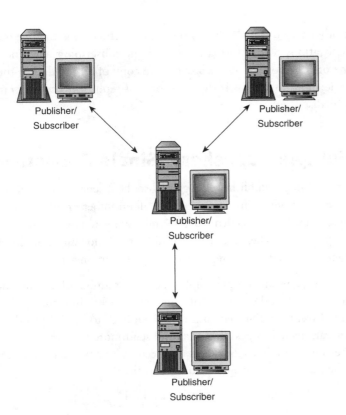

FIGURE 11.3
The Multiple Publisher, Multiple Subscribers configuration.

In the figure, the servers are acting as both Publishers and Subscribers of data, although not every server receives data from every other server. In some forms of this type of replication, all servers publish and subscribe to all other servers. For this form of replication, the correct database design is crucial to having each server publish and subscribe to the correct information. The table structure for the data involved in the publication is usually implemented with a compound Primary Key or unique index, although it is possible to use an Identity or other algorithm that enables each location to be uniquely identified within the entire table.

One portion of the key is an identifier for the location, whereas the second element is the data identifier. In the library example, the key would likely be made up of a library location identifier combined with an ISBN number or other distinguishing value that defines the individual book. Each library would publish a subset of the table based on its location identifier while subscribing to each other library's subset.

Another way to involve a compound key structure is to have multiple locations send information to a single subscribing machine. The only location that has a complete copy of all the data is the single subscriber. This is the next form of replication configuration to be discussed.

Multiple Publishers, Single Subscriber

In the Multiple Publishers, Single Subscriber scenario, a server subscribes to publications on some or all of a number of other publishing servers. This is needed when overall data is required at only one site, possibly the headquarters. Consider the following scenario where data need not be replicated to more than one site.

A car distribution company holds a diverse number of cars in stock, and they record the number of cars sold per week into the Sold Table Inventory. This data must be given back to the HQ so that they can make business decisions and send more cars when a certain type goes short. This data does not need to be replicated to other branches because it would be useless to them.

This configuration is shown in Figure 11.4.

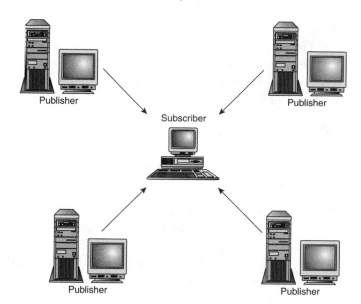

FIGURE 11.4
The Multiple Publisher, Single Subscriber configuration.

Single Publisher, Remote Distributor

Replication does not need to include a Distributor residing on the same server or even within close proximity to the Publisher. Instead, the machine handling the distribution can be implemented as a totally separate segment. This is practical when you need to free the publishing server from having to perform the distribution task and minimize costs that can be incurred over long distance or overseas network connections. Data can also be replicated faster and delivered to many Subscribers at a much lower cost while minimizing the load on the Publisher. This configuration is shown in Figure 11.5.

The individual roles of each server are implemented in all types of replication; the physical configuration does not dictate the type of replication used. The next section examines the types of replication and their implementation.

EXAM TIP

Slow Connections You may find this type of scenario on the exam: If the network connection is over a slow link or the links between the Publisher and Subscriber are over high-cost connections, then a remote Distributor should be used to lower the cost and increase data transfers rates.

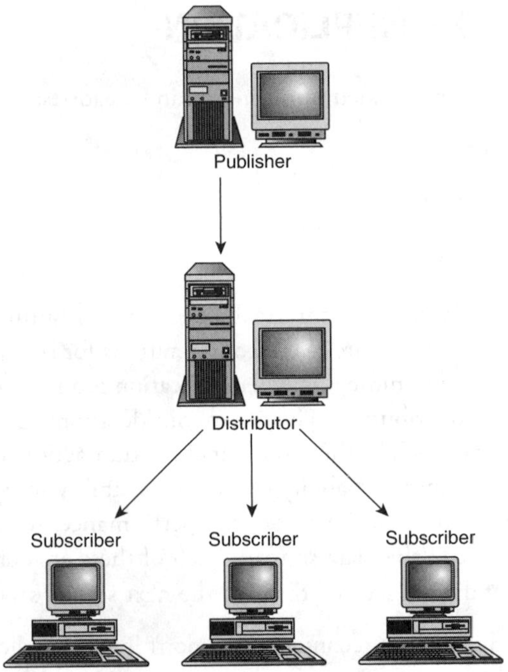

FIGURE 11.5
The Single Publisher, Remote Distributor configuration.

Publisher/Subscriber Metaphor and Replication Configurations

So far we have learned about the Publisher/Subscriber metaphor and the different replication configurations available. The Publisher/Subscriber metaphor is the basis of all replication processes and defines the data originator (Publisher), data sender (Distributor), and the data receiver (Subscriber). Replication configurations enable the Publisher, Distributor, and Subscriber to be arranged in a diverse number of ways, enough to meet all real-world situations. In any given replication scenario, the publishing server has the copy of the original data.

TYPES OF REPLICATION

Replication can be divided into three main categories:

◆ Snapshot

◆ Transactional

◆ Merge

Each model provides different capabilities for distributing data and database objects. There are many considerations for selecting a replication type or determining whether replication is a suitable technique for data distribution. The many considerations to determine the suitability of each of the models include transactional consistency, the subscriber's capability or lack of capability to update data, latency, administration, site autonomy, performance, security, update schedule, and available data sources. Each of these are defined as replication and are discussed through the next several sections.

Other data distribution techniques that don't involve replication can offer a different set of features but may not provide for the flexibility offered by replication. To determine which replication type is best suited to your needs, consider the three primary factors: site autonomy, transactional consistency, and latency. These three considerations are illustrated in Figure 11.6, which also compares and contrasts data distribution techniques.

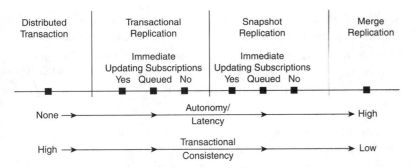

FIGURE 11.6
Site autonomy in replication.

Site autonomy refers to whether one site is independent from all other sites when processing modifications. Site autonomy measures the effect of your site's operation to another. A site having full autonomy is completely independent of all other sites, meaning it can function without even being connected to any other site; high site autonomy can be achieved in SQL Server replication where it would not be possible using other data distribution techniques. Not all replication configurations achieve autonomy; such high site autonomy can be seen best with merge replication, which is detailed later.

Site autonomy directly affects transactional consistency. To achieve an environment that is both autonomous and has a high degree of transactional consistency, the data definition must provide a mechanism to differentiate one site from the other. A compound Primary Key, for example, in a Central Subscriber or Multiple Publisher, Multiple Subscriber scenario allows autonomy while achieving transactional consistency. If an implementation enables each site to update the same data, then it will always have some degree of transaction inconsistency or at least a delay before consistency is achieved.

Transactional Consistency in Replication

Transactional consistency is a measure of changes made to data, specifically those changes that remain in place without being rolled back. Changes can get rolled back due to conflicts, and this will affect user changes and other user activities. In replication you have multiple distinct copies of your data, and if you allow updates to each copy, then it is possible for different copies of a piece of data to be changed differently. If this situation is allowed, as is the case in some forms of replication, you have imperfect (low) transactional consistency. If you prevent two copies from changing independently, as is the case with a distributed transaction, then you have the highest level of transactional consistency.

In a distributed transaction, the application and the controlling server work together to control updates to multiple sites. Two-phase commits implemented in some forms of replication also help. The two phases used are *preparation* and *committal*. Each server is prepared for the update to take place, and when all sites are ready the change is committed at the same time on all servers. After all sites have implemented the change, transactional consistency is restored.

Latency in Replication

Latency can be thought of as how long data in the Subscriber has to wait before being updated from the copy of the data on the Publisher. Several factors contribute to latency, but it is essentially the length of time it takes changes to travel from the Publisher to the Distributor and then from the Distributor to the Publisher. If there is no need for the data to be the same, at the same time, in all Publishers and Subscribers, then the latency resident within a replication strategy will not negatively affect an application. A two-phase commit, as SQL Server implements through the use of immediate updating, can minimize latency on updates coming from the Subscriber, but has no effect on updates sent from the Publisher.

Latency can be affected by the workload on the Publisher and Distributor, the speed and congestion of the network, and the size of the updates being transported.

Snapshot

Snapshot replication distributes data and database objects by copying the entire contents of the published items via the Distributor and passing them on to the Subscriber exactly as they appear at a specific moment in time, without monitoring updates. A snapshot is stored on the Distributor, which encapsulates data of published

---

NOTE

Non-Replicable Objects   In a replication process, system tables in any database cannot be replicated. The following databases also cannot be replicated:

- Model
- Msdb
- Master
- TempDb

tables and database objects; this snapshot is then taken to the Subscriber database via the Distribution Agent.

Snapshot replication is advantageous when replicated data is infrequently updated and modified. A snapshot strategy is preferable over others when data is to be updated in a batch. This does not mean that only a small amount of data is updated, but rather that data is updated in large quantities at distant intervals. Because data is replicated at a specific point in time and not replicated frequently, this type of replication is good for online catalogs, price lists, and the like, where the decision to implement replication is independent of how recent data is.

Snapshot replication offers high levels of site autonomy. It also offers a great degree of transactional consistency because transactions are enforced at the Publisher. Transactional consistency also depends on whether you are allowing updating Subscribers, and what type (immediate or queued).

Snapshot replication can be used alongside Immediate Updating Subscribers using two-phase commit (2PC). In this type of replication, the Subscriber needs to be in contact with the Publisher. Queued update, on the other hand, doesn't require constant connectivity. When you create a publication with queued updating, and a Subscriber performs INSERT, UPDATE, or DELETE statements on published data, the changes are stored in a queue. The queued transactions are applied at the Publisher when network connectivity is restored.

After the information is delivered (by either method), the Subscriber can change the replica on its local server; hence snapshot replication provides medium-to-high autonomy. When Updating Subscribers are used, a trigger is located at the Subscriber database that monitors for changes and sends those changes to the publishing server via the Microsoft Distributed Transaction Coordinator (MS DTC).

Snapshot replication is suited to situations where data is likely to remain unchanged, it is acceptable to have a higher degree of latency, and replication involves small volumes of data. It is preferred over Transaction replication when data changes are substantial but infrequent. Application of snapshots using native BCP or compression helps to improve performance.

> **NOTE**
>
> **What Exactly is 2PC?** 2PC, or Two-Phase Commit, is replication where modifications made at the Publisher are made *at exactly the same time* on the Subscriber. The two phases are "Prepare" and "Commit." All servers prepare for the changes and then, when ready, commit the changes at the same time.

There are some significant points to remember about snapshot replication and how it differs from the other types of replication:

◆ Snapshot replication is the simplest type of replication.

◆ Snapshot replication is most suitable when the Subscribers do not need to have the data kept up to date, because changes are made on the Publisher and it is acceptable for Subscribers to get their information refreshed (replaced) on a less frequent basis.

◆ Snapshot replication is not dependent on other sites when updates are not made to Subscriber data; in other words, it has strong site autonomy.

◆ Snapshot replication uses up little overhead resources on the server because data modifications are not monitored, unlike transactional replication.

◆ Snapshot information and objects are located on the Distributor in the Mssql\Repldata directory. (This is the default and can be changed.)

Network considerations include the application of the original data on the subscribing machines as well as ongoing operation of the replication processes. Transferring the initial data to a CD-ROM and shipping the CD to the Subscriber may be the best solution in the case of a slow or intermittent network link. Compression of the initial snapshot into .CAB files, as defined in the following process, can also preserve the network bandwidth.

Step by Step 11.1 shows you how to compress and send snapshots:

STEP BY STEP

11.1 Changing Snapshot Location

1. In Enterprise Manager, expand the Replication and Publications directories, right-click the desired publication, and select Properties.

2. On the Snapshot Location tab, select Generate Snapshots in the Following Location, provide a location for the files, and then select Compress the Snapshot Files in This Location.

3. Configure snapshot delivery on the Subscriber from the Enterprise Manager, expand the subscription database and the Subscriptions directory, right-click the desired subscription, and select Properties.

4. On the Snapshot File Location tab, select Get the Snapshot From the Following Folder.

5. Supply the path where you want snapshot files to be placed.

If you want to compress snapshots, an alternate snapshot location can be made, and *only* in the alternate location can the snapshot be compressed. The snapshots can then bet moved using FTP.

Transactional Replication

Transactional replication is defined as the moving of transactions captured from the transaction log of the publishing server database and applied to the Subscriber's database. The transactional replication process monitors data changes made on the Publisher.

Transactional replication captures incremental modifications that were made to data in the published table. The committed transactions do not directly change the data on the Subscriber but are instead stored on the Distributor. These transactions held in distribution tables on the Distributor are sent to the Subscriber. Because the transactions on the Distributor are stored in an orderly fashion, each Subscriber acquires data in the same order as is in the Publisher.

When replicating a publication using transactional replication, you can choose to replicate an entire table or just part of a table using a method referred to as *filtering*. You can also select all stored procedures on the database or just certain ones that are to be replicated as articles within the publication. Replication of stored procedures ensures that the definitions they provide are in each location where the data is located. Processes that are defined by the stored procedures can then be run at the Subscriber. Because the procedures are being replicated, any changes to these procedures are also replicated. Replication of a stored procedure makes the procedure available for execution on the local server.

In transactional replication, like snapshot replication, Updating Subscribers may be used with 2PC for the immediate update option. This enables the Subscriber to change the replica at his local server. Changes made to data at the Subscriber are applied both to the Subscriber and Publisher databases at the same moment, proving high transactional consistency and less latency.

It is possible to get a conflict when using the queued update option. No conflicts can occur with immediate updating of Subscribers because of the use of a 2PC that guarantees that a change is reflected on both the Publisher and the Subscriber, or neither.

A Primary Key must be defined on the published table, and a WRITETEXT or UPDATETEXT operation must supply the WITH LOG option.

Before implementing or going further into replication, you should be well acquainted with the preliminaries. Some transactional replication considerations are given in the following list:

- ◆ Data is replicated as read-only by default. To change this, you can set Updateable Subscriptions at the Publisher. The Subscriber can switch between Immediate to Queued and back *if* the Publisher has allowed Immediate with Failover for the publication.

- ◆ Changes can be set up to be propagated to other sites in a moment's time, thereby having a very short latency.

- ◆ Transactional replication is a good solution when you want updated changes at the server in almost real time.

- ◆ Transactional replication begins with a snapshot.

Merge Replication

Merge Replication is the process of transferring data from the Publisher to the Subscriber, enabling the Publisher and Subscriber to update data while they are connected or disconnected, and then merge the updates after they both are connected, providing virtual independence. Merge replication therefore allows the most flexibility and adds the most autonomy to the replication process. Merge replication is also the most complex replication because it enables the

Publisher and Subscriber to work virtually independently. The Publisher and Subscriber can combine their results at any certain time and combine or merge their updated results.

The Snapshot agent and the Merge agent help in carrying out the process of merge replication. The Snapshot agent is used for the initial synchronization of the databases. The Merge agent then applies the snapshot; after that, the job of the Merge agent is to increment the data changes and resolve any conflicts according to the rules configured.

Conflicts are likely to occur with merge replication. Conflicts occur when more than one site updates the same record. This happens when two users concurrently update or modify the same record with different values. When a conflict occurs, SQL Server has to choose a single value to use. It resolves the conflict based on either the site priority on the database site or a custom conflict resolver. You could give more priority to, for instance, a user in the HR department than one from the sales department. When a conflict is detected, it is resolved immediately after the conflict resolver is executed. A conflict occurs when the publisher and subscriber have *both* changed the record since they last shared a common version. Conflicts can be record based or column based. The default is column based.

Merge replication is well suited to scenarios where conflicts are less likely to occur. For instance, a site might make changes to its internal records only, possibly needing data from all other locations, but not changing any of it. A conflict occurs when the two participants have *both* changed a record (or column within a record) since they last shared the same version.

Merge replication offers site autonomy at its apex—because sites are virtually independent—and low transactional consistency. These sites, or Subscribers, can freely make modifications to their local copies of the replicated data. These modifications and updates made to data are combined with modifications made at the other Subscribers and also with the modifications at the Publisher. This process ultimately ensures that all Subscribers and Publishers receive modifications and updates from all other sites; it is better known as *convergence*. You may think right away that this type of replication lends itself to the Multiple Subscribers, Multiple Publishers configuration, but this is not always the case.

As mentioned earlier, transactional consistency is extremely low and can be a problem in merge replication because conflicts can occur when different sites change the same data. For instance, there may be users on two sites that modify the same record on their local copy of a database. If a user in Texas modifies record #5 of a table and a user in California modifies record #5 as well, a conflict will occur on record #5 when replication takes place because the same record has been modified at two different sites; thus, SQL Server has to determine which value to accept. One record has to overwrite another. There are ways to control this dilemma, the default rule being that site priority determines which record is accepted. You can also create custom stored procedures that verify which record is the correct record to use.

Whether this is a conflict or not depends on the situation. If the conflict is column-based and both sites change a different column in the same record, it is *not* a conflict. If one of these two sites is the Publisher and the conflict is record-based, then it would be a conflict.

There is a lot of activity occurring regardless of the type and model of replication being used. Management over this process requires that there be database server elements, executing on all participating machines, to perform the individual operations. In SQL Server these elements are referred to as *agents*. The agents involved in the process and a description of their roles is the next topic of discussion.

REPLICATION AGENTS

In a replication environment, there are seven replication agents that handle tasks such as moving data from the Publisher to the Distributor and then from the Distributor to the Subscriber. Replication agents are replication processes that enable SQL Server to perform the different types of replication processes talked about in the preceding section. Each replication process contains a minimum of three agents. These agents are used to move data along to the Publisher and Subscriber via the Distributor and keep the entire replication process running smoothly. The following list provides a summary of the agents:

◆ **SQL Server agent.** The SQL Server agent hosts and schedules all other agents used in a replication process as well as provides an easy way to run replication agents.

◆ **Log Reader agent**. Located on the Distributor, the Log Reader agent's job is to monitor the transactional logs of published databases and copy new transactions onto the Distributor.

◆ **Distribution agent.** The Distribution agent moves the transactions from the Distributor to the Subscriber.

◆ **Snapshot agent**. The Snapshot agent is responsible for creating the snapshot files on the Distributor.

◆ **Merge agent**. The Merge agent converges records from multiple sites and resolves any conflicts in merge replication.

◆ **Queue Reader agent**. The Queue Reader agent is used when "update queue" has been enabled and runs on the Distributor.

◆ **Miscellaneous agents**. Cleanup agents listed under the Miscellaneous Agents folder in Replication Monitor complete scheduled and on-demand maintenance of replication.

Each agent plays an important part in replication, although not every agent is used in all types of replication. Each of the agents involved directly in the replication process are discussed in more detail in the next several sections.

The Snapshot Agent

The Snapshot agent helps in preparation of the schema and initial data files of published tables and stored procedures. Not only does the Snapshot agent deal with snapshot replication, but it also helps in merge and transactional replication, as seen in Figure 11.7.

Note that before incremental changes can be sent to a Subscriber, tables need to be created on the Subscriber. This is done through the receiving of scripts, which are run at the Subscriber to create the necessary structure. The Snapshot agent also runs BCP to export the initial copy of the data and store this in files. All replication types begin with a snapshot. Each publication created has its own Snapshot agent, which runs at the Distributor. The Snapshot agent can be managed and configured easily using SQL Server Enterprise Manager.

FIGURE 11.7
Role of Snapshot agent.

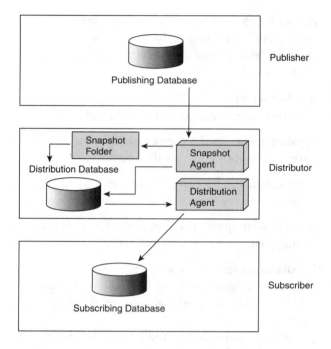

The Log Reader Agent

The Log Reader agent moves transactions from the transaction log of the published database on the Publisher to the distribution database or server, as shown in Figure 11.8.

The Log Reader agent is used only in transactional replication. The Log Reader agent moves transactions that are marked for replication.

The Distribution Agent

The Distribution agent moves transactions and snapshot jobs held in the distribution database out to the Subscribers; it can be administered using the SQL Server Enterprise Manager. The Distribution agent can run on either the Distributor's server or the Subscriber's server. It is not required to run on the Distributor only, which is new functionality in SQL 2000 called Remote Activation. Merge publications do not have a Distribution agent at all; rather, they rely on the Merge agent, which is discussed in the following section.

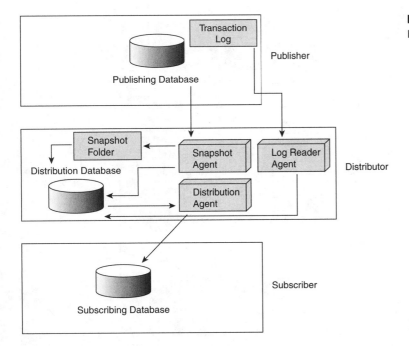

FIGURE 11.8
Log Reader agent.

The Merge Agent

The Merge agent moves the initial snapshot jobs found in the publication database tables to the Subscriber as seen in Figure 11.9. Each Merge publication has a Merge agent that connects to the publishing server and the subscribing server, updating both.

In a complete merge scenario, the Merge agent first uploads all changes from the Subscriber to the Publisher. Changes are then brought over from the subscribing machines and applied to the Publisher. The Merge agent is also responsible for resolving conflicts that can occur at the row or column level. Whether or not conflicts are diagnosed at the row/column level depends upon the configuration. In row conflicts, changes were made to the data for a single record. In a column configuration, the conflict does not occur unless the data changed is within the same field as well as the same data record. The agent resolves conflicts by reversing the process and downloading any changes needed back to the Subscribers. The Merge agent is used only in merge replication, so snapshot and transactional publications do not use them whatsoever.

FIGURE 11.9
Role of the Merge agent.

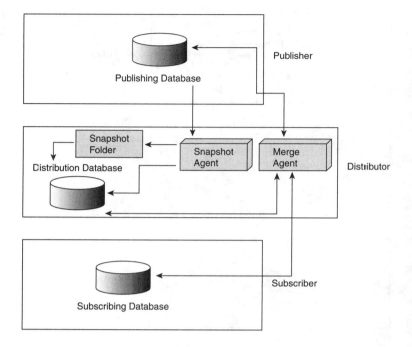

The Queue Reader Agent

The Queue Reader agent is responsible for taking messages from a queue and applying them to the appropriate publication. This agent is used only if Immediate Queued Update is defined as either a main or failover replication process.

Only one instance of the Queue Reader Agent exists to service all Publishers and publications for a given Distributor.

A lot of programmatic pieces all work together to form a replication scenario. Along with software, hardware and network infrastructure all participate in this activity. Each type of replication performs differently and provides different challenges. Now it's time to look into the specifics of implementation for each of the replication types.

REPLICATION INTERNALS

Now it's time to see how all of the types of replication are actually implemented: how they process their work, how they relate to one another in processing, and the events they undergo. Here you will find how each replication is implemented internally in SQL Server 2000 and what events fire in a given situation.

To support and configure snapshot, merge, and transactional replication (as in the sub-objective, "Support merge, snapshot, and transactional replication models"), you need to know the internals of these three models.

Inside Snapshot Replication

So, how does snapshot replication work? How does the publication get from the Publisher to the Subscriber in this model?

The Snapshot agent copies snapshot files (containing published tables and database objects such as stored procedures) into the Snapshot folders, which by default reside in the Distributor.

The following events take place in snapshot replication:

1. Snapshot replication is configured, and the Snapshot agent tries to connect to the publisher.

2. If the connection is successful, the Snapshot agent transfers snapshot files (containing published tables and database objects such as stored procedures) into the Snapshot folder.

3. The Distribution agent takes these database objects and schemas (found in the Snapshot folder) and rebuilds them in the Subscriber.

4. The Distribution agent tries to connect to both the Distribution database and the Subscriber's database.

5. If the connection succeeds, the Distribution agent reads the database objects and schema and copies them onto the Subscriber.

You know how snapshot replication works. What about transactional replication? How is it internally different? The next section describes it.

Inside Transactional Replication

As you learned in the preceding section, transactional replication differs from other types of replication in that it copies the transactions that occurred in the publishing database to the distribution database on the Distributor. The three agents involved in

Transactional replication are the Distribution, Log Reader, and Snapshot agents. As in snapshot replication, the Snapshot agent copies snapshot files (containing published tables and database objects such as stored procedures) into the Snapshot folder, which by default resides on the Distributor. (However, as in snapshot replication, it is possible to specify an alternate location for storage.) The Snapshot agent does this only to create the initial snapshot, which can then be propagated to the Subscriber.

The new agent used in transactional replication is the Log Reader agent. The Log Reader agent has a pretty straightforward job. Its job is to keep track of the Transaction log of the databases that are marked for Transactional replication and to copy those certain transactions (that are marked for replication) into the distribution database. It might be worth noting that the Log Reader agent examines only the transactional log of the Publisher.

Similar to the way the Distribution agent works in snapshot replication, the Distribution agent in transaction-based replication copies the tables containing the transactions from the Distributor onto the Subscriber. The snapshot transactions are held in a folder until the Distribution agent moves them to all Subscribers or a Distribution agent residing at the Subscriber calls for the transactions. The Snapshot folder contains schema and data of published tables; it is propagated to the Subscriber only once, to set up the replication for the first time. Copying the whole publication onto the Subscriber is called *applying the initial snapshot*. After the initial snapshot is applied at the Publisher, the Subscriber can then receive incremental changes made at the Publisher.

Transactional replication is best used in situations where you want changes to be delivered to Subscribers as they occur, when you need strict adherence to ACID properties (as defined in Chapter 2, "Data Modeling"), the network connection is reliable, or Subscribers connect frequently. This is usually the technique of choice because it requires little if any modification of the table structure and delivers changes with very little latency.

Another situation when transactional replication is useful is when the amount of data in the tables is huge and the number of changes, inserts, and deletes is relatively small. In this case it is faster and better to use transactional replication and simply replicate the changes than it is to use snapshot and resend the entire huge table on a scheduled basis.

The following events take place in transactional replication:

1. Snapshot or transactional replication is configured and the Snapshot agent tries to connect the Distributor with the Publisher.

2. If the connection is successful, the Snapshot agent transfers Snapshot files (containing published tables and database objects such as stored procedures) into the Snapshot folder.

3. The Distribution agent tries to connect the Distributor with the server on which it is located (either the Distributor or Subscriber).

4. If the connection succeeds, the Distribution agent reads the database objects and schema and copies them onto the Subscriber.

5. The Log Reader agent monitors the transaction log (hoping to find any UPDATE, INSERT, and/or DELETE statement) and when it finds modifications, it sends it to the distribution database. The scheduled basis at which the Log Reader agent monitors can be set to either continuous monitoring or monitoring after a custom time interval.

6. When the Distributor sends a push or the Subscriber calls a pull, the Distribution agent reads the files from the distribution folder, and the actions are applied at the Subscriber. When a Subscriber activates the agent through a pull, changes are propagated to all Subscribers.

Now you have seen how transactional replication works, and have learned that it is a good solution when data needs to be sent and received in real time. In other instances, however, transactional replication is not the best alternative. Many scenarios require more flexibility, such as that offered by merge replication. The next section describes merge replication and how it processes replication.

Inside Merge Replication

In SQL Server 2000, merge replication is made possible by using both the Snapshot and Merge agents. As in other types of replication, the Snapshot agent carries out the job of preparing initial Snapshot files (containing published tables and database objects such as stored procedures) and transfers them to the Snapshot folder.

As soon as you allow users in multiple locations to change their own copies of the data independently, data conflicts become inevitable. A conflict occurs when data has been changed at more than one location and then an attempt is made to synchronize the data. You have a choice whether to use row-level or column-level conflict tracking. In row-level tracking, a change to two separate columns still results in a conflict. For example, one person might change a person's name while another person changes the phone number.
In column-level tracking this is not an issue, but using row-level tracking results in a conflict.

Timestamp column values are regenerated when the data is copied to the Subscribers. Timestamps can be compared to determine when changes were made.

If you are replicating columns that are defined as Foreign Keys, make sure to include the reference table in the publication so that integrity can be maintained.

The Merge agent is responsible for the detection of all conflicts. Conflicts are resolved by priority, by first synchronization, or by a custom resolver as defined through a stored procedure or COM object. The default mechanism used by SQL Server is priority based, where priorities are assigned to each Subscriber.

The Merge agent transfers modifications from the Publisher and applies them at the Subscriber and then takes modifications made at the Subscriber and applies them at the Publisher. If conflicts occur during synchronization between the Publisher and Subscriber, the Merge agent gets notified and takes the proper course of action. Taking the proper course of action depends on how resolution has been set up.

Merge replication allows for the most flexibility of all the replication models, but latency is the highest of the three models. This form of replication is appropriate in situations where the Subscribers need to be able to update the data they receive, network connectivity is not consistent, and conflicts have been minimized by application design or are otherwise unlikely. Merge replication requires the highest degree of design planning in that merge replication requires a `uniqueidentifier` column with the `rowguidcol` attribute included. When applied, merge replication may have to alter the table structure and will require conflict resolution strategies to be applied.

Merge replication enables each copy of data to be changed independently, but it is not the only solution if data needs to be changed at the Subscriber. The alternative is to allow updating subscriptions with transactional and snapshot replication.

UPDATING SUBSCRIBERS

Updating Subscribers, as the name implies, gives the Subscriber the power to update or modify data after it is replicated. This option can be used with snapshot replication and transactional replication. Data by default is replicated in one direction from the Publisher to the Subscriber. Transactional and snapshot replication enables the power to update replicated data at the Subscriber level by using subscriptions that are updateable. You can use two configurations to enable Updateable Subscribers: immediate updating and queued updating. Data is *not* read-only on the Subscribers. In any form of replication there is nothing in the data or database or server that requires or enforces read-only; however, if you make local changes without choosing Updating Subscribers, they might be overwritten.

Immediate Updating

Immediate updating allows replication to send changes and updates from a Subscriber back to the Publisher and then on to other Subscribers. An immediate connection must be available to use this type of Updateable Subscriber. This update of data made by the Subscriber is reflected directly back to the Publisher through a two-phase commit (2PC). Immediate updating uses triggers, stored procedures, and the Microsoft Distributed Transaction Coordinator (MS DTC) to accomplish this task. A special trigger on the Subscriber monitors the changes made to the replica on the Subscriber. When a change is made, the trigger fires and the Subscriber uses a remote stored procedure to gather the transactions and send them to the Publisher.

The Microsoft Distributed Transaction Coordinator (MS DTC) maintains a two-phase commit execution between a Subscriber and Publisher inside a stored procedure call.

The following steps are involved when immediate updating takes place:

1. A publication is enabled to support the Immediate Updating Subscribers option, and the initial synchronization takes place.

2. The Subscriber server is allowed to modify replicated data only when the transaction is executed using two phase commit (2PC) controlled by the Publisher.

3. When the Subscriber modifies the data, a trigger is fired and two-phase commit transactions are automatically sent to the Publisher without the prior knowledge of the Subscriber.

4. After the change is made and sent to the Publisher automatically, it is ultimately published to all other Subscribers who subscribe to that particular publication through normal replication methods.

Immediate updates provide for tighter control over data. To gain this control, you need to have a reliable network connection between the Publishers and Subscribers. If that reliable connection does not exist and there is still a need for Subscribers to update the data, the alternative would be Queued Updating.

Queued Updating

Queued updating is similar to immediate updating in that they both allow data to be changed from the read-only default into a modifiable replica. The major difference is that in queued updating an active network connection is not absolutely necessary; it allows snapshot replication and transactional replication Subscribers to modify published data without an active network connection to the Publisher.

The following events take place when queued updating is involved:

1. A publication is enabled to support the Queued Updating Subscribers option.

2. When the Subscriber modifies the data, a trigger marked NOT FOR REPLICATION is fired and the updates and modifications are stored in a SQL Server queue.

3. These changes in the SQL Server queue are stored in a table dedicated for queue storing called the MSreplication queue table.

4. The Queue Reader agent reads the `MSreplication_queue` table and applies the queued transactions to the appropriate publication. Conflicts, if any, are resolved based on the conflicts policy.

5. The changes made at the Publisher are ultimately published to all other Subscribers who subscribe to that particular publication.

With queued updates you can set up replications that allow for dial-up connections or more appropriate use of resources. Another mechanism that can be used to provide for better resource utilization is remote agent activation.

Remote Agent Activation

In SQL Server 2000, Microsoft disconnected the "who controls the schedule" part of replication from "where the work is done." Although there are default locations where each of the agents run, you may find that altering these locations provides a better load balance. You may have a push subscription that has the Distribution agent run on either the Distributor or Subscriber. You may have a pull subscription in which the Distribution agent runs on either the Distributor or Subscriber. Although this is something you are unlikely to see on the exam, it is worth noting that this option is available as a final option in replication configuration.

With remote agent activation, you can reduce the amount of processing on the Distributor or Subscriber by running the Distribution agent or Merge agent on another computer and then activating that agent remotely. You should set up regular push or pull subscriptions before configuring remote agent activation. You are not able to configure remote agent activation on a local computer (for example, when the Subscriber and Distributor reside on the same computer).

You have seen a lot of aspects of SQL Server replication and it's time to sit back and take a look at everything that is involved. The following Review Break summarizes the key points involved in replication, but so far, this chapter has only talked about SQL Server. In a lot of environments you find third-party data sources that you may also want to replicate to and/or from. After reviewing replication, you will see how every source can easily participate.

R E V I E W   B R E A K

Aspects of Replication

You have seen a lot of the aspects of replication using Microsoft SQL Server. The different types of replication are merge, snapshot, and transactional, and you've seen what each has to offer. You have also seen several ways to make the data updateable at all servers and optimize the process through load distribution.

Merge replication is best suited to applications that need updateable information and the highest degree of site autonomy, such as in an environment that has only dial-up connectivity. Snapshot replication is more suited to situations that have relatively static data and require a periodic refresh of the data, such as with seasonal updates. Transactional replication is used in scenarios where data updates are more frequent, such as in a 24-hour order processing system.

Subscriptions can be made updateable through immediate, queued, or merge replication settings. Immediate is used in cases where the data needs to be as consistent as possible at all times and there is sufficient, reliable communication links to handle the process. The next few topics cover some of the remaining replication features that have not yet been discussed.

Several issues exist surrounding replication. Identities, constraints, available bandwidth, and conflict resolution strategies have to be thought out to provide for adequate resource utilization. Most of these issues are common to all models and are covered over the next several paragraphs; however, other issues specific to the model chosen are handled in the sections that follow.

HETEROGENEOUS INTEROPERABILITY

Replication can also be set up among database servers other than SQL Server. SQL Server is built upon OLE-DB, which enables data to be replicated from SQL Server to any other database server such Sybase or Oracle. There is only a single requirement: The foreign Subscriber must provide a 32-bit ODBC or OLE DB driver on Microsoft Windows 2000, Microsoft Windows NT Server 4.0, or the Windows 98 operating system. When the non-SQL Server database meets this requirement, it can receive using a push subscription. When you need to pull a subscription from SQL Server to a third-party database system such as Oracle, you need to create a custom program that accesses Distributed Management Objects (SQL-DMO).

Non-SQL Server database engines may also very well act as Publishers that replicate data and database objects to SQL Server Subscribers. The requirement mentioned in the preceding paragraph must also be met if you want to configure a publishing non-SQL Server database. SQL Server uses ODBC to make replication connections to other servers. That is, a foreign Subscriber must support transactions and be Level 1, ODBC compliant. When it meets this requirement, it can also receive data that is sent via a push subscription.

Replication can be performed across platforms, to and from virtually any data source. SQL Server provides for a very diverse strategy for implementing a replication strategy. After it is enabled, you can monitor the progress and quickly be alerted to any problem situations.

ENABLING REPLICATION IN YOUR APPLICATION

Replication can be implemented in many ways with SQL Server 2000. SQL Server 2000 provides many wizards, the Enterprise Manager, and even programming interfaces that enable you to implement diverse replication strategies for your business's needs. The SQL Server Enterprise Manager also enables you to monitor replication status. This is done through the Replication Monitor, which enables you to view and manage replication agents across your enterprise.

To enable replication, you need a Publisher, Distributor, and Subscriber. The first step is creating a Distributor. After that you can create a publication and set articles within that publication.

Finally, you need to define the various Subscribers who subscribe to a publication. The first thing to do is to install and create the Distributor. To do this, use a handy wizard called the Configure Publishing and Distribution wizard.

CONFIGURING THE DISTRIBUTION SERVER

Replicating a database is a long process. The first step is to set up the distribution server, which is described in this section. Step by Step 11.2 shows you how to implement replication:

STEP BY STEP

11.2 Configuring the Publishing and Distribution Mechanism

1. Open the Enterprise Manager from the Start menu in Programs, SQL Server 2000.

2. Select the default instance of SQL Server and on the Tools menu. Point to Replication and then select Configure Publishing, Subscribers and Distribution, which initiates the Configure Publishing and Distribution wizard.

3. On this screen, you are prompted to select a Distributor. Make sure that the Distribution working folder and Distribution database have enough hard disk space. Select the default setting and click Next. If you want to choose some other server as your Distributor, that Distributor must be configured as such.

4. The third screen asks you whether you want to customize your Distributor or you want to stick with the default settings provided by SQL Server. In this case, select the first option (Yes, Let Me . . .). Choosing this enables you to change Distributor-specific information; this is used for example purposes so that you may know how to configure all steps in the wizard.

5. Because you selected the option specifying that you would configure your Distributor, you are faced with the Provide Distribution Database Information selection screen as displayed in Figure 11.10. This screen enables you to name the Distribution database, set the folder of the distribution database, and set the folder of the distribution log. When placing the distribution database and log, make

sure you have enough hard disk space. In this case, leave the default settings as they are and click Next to continue.

6. This wizard also helps enable your Publishers, and this is the screen on which you do it. This screen lists all the registered SQL Servers. Only one listed registered server is on the list (to install a second server, you have to install another instance of SQL Server 2000; it is, however, not necessary to install a second server), so select it as the Publishing server and click Next to continue.

7. Use this screen to enable publication databases to be replicated. This screen lists the databases that can be replicated under Databases. You can select for merge or transactional replication. In this case, select the Pubs database and check the box under Trans, as shown in Figure 11.11, to set up transactional replication.

8. Similar to the selection screen in step 6, this screen enables you to select the Subscriber or Subscribers. Remember that this example uses a single instance of SQL Server 2000 so all three roles (Publisher, Distributor, and Subscriber) will be played by one server. Select the Subscriber, and click Next.

9. The final screen displays the configurations you have made throughout this wizard. If everything is correct, click Finish.

After you click finish, SQL Server has adequate information to implement the choices you have made.

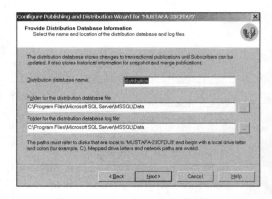

FIGURE 11.10
Distribution database information.

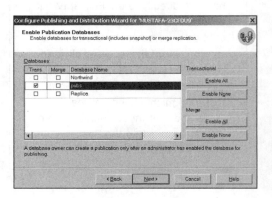

FIGURE 11.11
Setting up transactional replication.

You have now implemented the first part of replication. To see for yourself, expand your server in the left pane of the Enterprise Manager and then expand Databases. You can see a new Distribution database. Also, notice that the icon beside the Pubs database has a small hand beside it which shows that it is configured for replication. The Replication Monitor icon also signifies replication.

After you implement the Publisher, Subscriber, and Distributor, you have to implement a publication for the Subscriber to receive. When setting up a publication, you have to decide on the replication type you want to use. Step by Step 11.3 shows you how to add a publication.

Quick Recap on Immediate Updating
Immediate updating enables the Subscribers to change their local copies of data; these changes made by Subscribers are sent back to the Publisher (using MS DTC). Queued updating is when the Subscribers are enabled to change their local copy of replicated data. These changes are not sent directly to the Publisher but are stored at an intermediate state until they are sent. Therefore, if you select none of these, the replicated data is read-only. Also, if the Subscriber tries to change the data, that data might change at the Subscriber, but those changes are not propagated back to the Publisher and the other Subscribers.

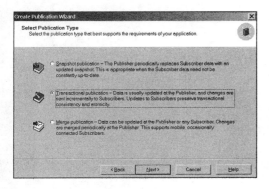

FIGURE 11.12
Setting the replication type.

STEP BY STEP

11.3 Setting Up a Publication

1. Open the Enterprise Manager from the Start menu in Programs, SQL Server 2000.

2. Select the current server and then choose Create and Manage Publications from the Tools menu. This initiates the Create and Manage Publications dialog box.

3. Select Pubs and then click on Create Publication. This starts the Create Publication Wizard.

4. If the Show Advanced Options check box is selected, you can choose whether Subscribers are updateable and data is transformable. Select Show Advanced Options and then click Next to continue.

5. On the second screen, you can choose the database you want to be published. Select Pubs and then click Next to proceed.

6. On the third screen, you are asked which type of publication you want to implement (transactional, merge, snapshot). In this case, select Transactional Publication, as shown in Figure 11.12, and click Next to proceed.

7. This screen asks whether you want queued updating, immediate updating, none, or both for your Subscribers.

8. This screen asks whether you want to send slightly different data to the Subscribers in your enterprise. This is used when slightly different data is needed at different Subscribers and when more than one Subscriber is involved. Transformable subscriptions can be enabled only in a snapshot or transactional replication strategy. Because you have only one Subscriber and don't need different data at the Subscriber, select the second radio button, to Bypass Selection, and click Next.

9. The next screen asks whether the Subscriber is running Microsoft SQL Server 2000, SQL Server 7, or a totally different Database Management System (DBMS) altogether. In this case, you run only SQL Server 2000, so select SQL Server 2000 and click Next.

10. From this screen, you choose what to publish as an Article, whether it is a table, a stored procedure, or a view, but in this case you will publish a table. Publishing a table requires that the table include a Primary Key.

On the right pane, select the Authors table and display its Properties page by clicking the ellipsis (. . .) button as shown in Figure 11.13. Some of the tables can't be replicated, because they probably don't include a Primary Key. This requirement is only for a transactional publication.

11. This opens the Table Article Properties dialog box. On the General tab, change the Destination Table name to rtblAuthors and Destination owner to Dbo. Because you are using the Publisher also as the Subscriber, naming the destination table with the prefix rtbl (rtblAuthors) is done to avoid confusion that could occur on the Subscriber with the existing Authors table.

The Snapshot tab is where the setting for the initial Snapshot is configured. Leave all properties to their default, and then click OK.

12. When you get back to the Specify Articles screen, click Next.

13. This leads to the Choose Publication Name screen. In the Publication Name box, enter Publishers Data. As the description, type an appropriate name for your publication and click Next to continue.

14. This screen asks whether you want to add more complexity to the publication. Selecting Yes enables data filters, anonymous subscriptions, and other properties to be set. Select Yes and then click Next.

15. The next screen asks whether you're going to filter data using vertical partitioning or horizontal partitioning. With vertical partitioning, also known as vertical filtering, you select only certain columns of the published data. With horizontal partitioning, a certain number of rows are selected from the published data.

Selecting Horizontal Partitioning produces one screen and selecting Vertical Partitioning results in another screen. Select Vertical Paritioning and click next.

NOTE **Selecting Subscriber Type** When you select SQL Server 7 as the subscription type, only Subscribers running version 7 of SQL Server may subscribe to it. Also, the options thereafter in the wizard are shaped so that they are compatible to SQL Server 7 Subscribers. If you select Heterogeneous Subscribers, you are specifying that the Subscriber is either Microsoft SQL Server 7 or earlier, or that the Subscriber is using a different DBMS. Subscribers classified as running heterogeneous data sources can subscribe to only transactional or snapshot publications.

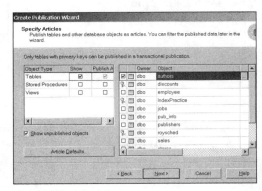

FIGURE 11.13
Article selection.

NOTE **Anonymous Subscription** An anonymous Subscriber is a type of pull Subscriber where the Subscriber and subscription information is not stored.

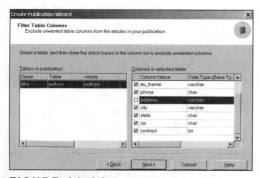

FIGURE 11.14
Column selection.

16. As shown in Figure 11.14, you can now select and deselect columns for your publication. For this example, deselect the Address column and click Next.

17. This screen asks whether you would like to allow anonymous Subscribers to access your publication. In a scenario where there are numerous Subscribers and pull subscriptions would be desired, a Yes choice would be appropriate. Select Yes and then click Next.

18. This is the last selection screen for the Create Publication Wizard. This screen is the Snapshot Agent Schedule screen. The Snapshot agent schedule determines when a snapshot is created to refresh the data at the Subscribers. Remember that before setting replication, a Subscriber must receive a Snapshot of your data. Select the Create the First Snapshot Immediately check box and click Next.

19. This is where the wizard ends. Click Finish to end the wizard. This leads back to the Create and Manage Publications dialog box.

After creating a publication, you have to pull or push it to the Subscriber. This example pulls it. Follow the steps in Step by Step 11.4 to do this.

REVIEW BREAK

Updating Subscribers

When a Subscriber is said to be updateable, it means that the Subscriber is able to make changes to the replica, as opposed to its read-only default. Updating Subscribers can be implemented when data is replicated with either transactional or snapshot replication. There are two types of updateable Subscribers: immediate updating and queued updating. The big difference in these two is that in queued updating an active network connection is not absolutely necessary; it allows snapshot replication and transactional replication Subscribers to modify published data without an active network connection to the Publisher.

STEP BY STEP

11.4 Pulling a Subscription

1. Open the SQL Server Enterprise Manager from the Start menu and connect to your default server.

2. Highlight your server and then select Replication, Pull Subscription to Your Server from the Tools menu. This initiates the Pull Subscription dialog box. Select Pubs and then click Pull New Subscription.

3. On the first screen, check the Show Advanced Options check box and then click Next.

4. The second screen offers you a choice to either search through registered servers or through the Active Directory for the publication you want to subscribe to. Select the Look at Publications from Registered Servers radio button and click Next.

5. Expand your server and then select Publishers Data: Pubs and then click Next. (You may have an extra screen to Specify Synchronization Agent Login.)

6. Now you choose where you want the replica to reside. Click New and then type **Replica** as the name of the new database. Leave all properties as they are and then click OK. Coming back to the wizard, select Replica and click Next to continue.

7. This screen asks whether the subscription is anonymous— extra information about the subscription and Subscriber is not needed; thus it can be used for Internet-based sites with FTP download involved. Select No, This Is a Named Subscription and click Next.

8. To initialize the subscription, select the default option, Yes, Initialize the Schema and Data. The Distribution Agent then runs and applies the snapshot files to the Subscriber.

   If you are planning to manually load the schema and data at the Subscriber, the subscription does not need to be initialized and you should select No. In this case, select Yes and then click Next.

NOTE

Active Directory Services Active Directory is a topic that can span a couple hundred pages; so, I'll try summing it up in a couple of sentences. The Active Directory is a central component found in Windows 2000 that provides storage for information about network-based entities, such as applications and files. With the Active Directory, you can view the different replication objects available, and also even subscribe to publications.

9. This screen asks you to specify where the snapshot folders reside at the time of subscription initialization. This can be the distribution working folder, an FTP server for downloading, or the Internet or any other media. Select the default option (which is the distribution folder) and then click Next.

10. This screen enables you to select the update frequency of the Distribution Agent. The first option specifies that it updates continuously, providing minimized latency in modifying at the Publisher. The second offers the choice of setting the updating time: after hours, days, or between certain times. The last option tells SQL Server that you will manually replicate changes (best suited for Merge Replication). Select the last option (On Demand Only), the type of replication that you are doing does not need continuous updating, and click Next.

IN THE FIELD

CONTINUOUS REPLICATION

Actually, in a real-world situation, transactional replication would most probably be implemented with continuous updating, but because we're just testing replication, we'll stick with On Demand.

11. Review the desired options on the finishing screen and then click Finish to end the wizard.

Now you have to start the replication process manually. First, synchronize your subscription. To do this, expand your default server and then click the Replication folder. Click the Subscriptions folder, then right-click your subscription, and then select Start Synchronizing.

Great! That was your final step in setting up a complete replication process. Now to convince yourself that the replication was successful, follow Step By Step 11.5.

After your replication process has been configured, you need to perform a few tasks to ensure that the replication has been set up and is ready for operation. To confirm replication success, you should perform the following check:

STEP BY STEP

11.5 Confirming Success of Replication

1. Open the SQL Server 2000 Enterprise Manager from the Start menu in Programs, Microsoft SQL Server.

2. Connect to your default server, expand it, and expand Databases.

3. Expand the Replica database and then click on Tables.

4. Locate RtblAuthors and then right-click it.

5. Point to Open Table and then select Return All Rows.

6. If you followed the steps correctly, you should see a result-set returning all columns from the replicated Authors table. Notice that the address column is not there. Vertical partitioning removed it.

CASE STUDY: DAVE'S VIDEO RENTAL CHAIN

ESSENCE OF THE CASE

- ▶ DRV is a video rental firm.

- ▶ They have multiple branches but have difficulty knowing which video is available at which store at any given time.

- ▶ They have to implement a solution soon, before they become extremely inefficient.

- ▶ The multiple branches need, but do not have access to, each other's inventory. Additionally, near real-time information is required. These two requirements are what lead to the decision to use transactional replication rather than the other types.

SCENARIO

Dave's Video Rental is a firm created and owned by Dave Stuart that rents and sells videos. Included in their rentals are video games, historical films, video accessories, and movies. Dave's Video Rental had been a single branch for almost two years. The company expanded business six months ago by creating three new branches located in different parts of the city. "The problem occurs when a certain video is not available, and we have to find out which of our stores currently has it," says one of the employees at DRV. Lengthy phone calls are made to each of the three other stores just to confirm the availability of a single item. "Our efficiency is decreasing and so are our sales. If we don't correct this

continues

CASE STUDY: DAVE'S VIDEO RENTAL CHAIN

continued

problem soon, we're going to go down real bad," says Dave, owner of DRV. He hires you to investigate the situation and come up with a solution.

ANALYSIS

A situation like this most obviously requires data to be put in a central location or that the same data be accessible to all the branches. This scenario is perfect for replication because the currently available videos need to be known by all branches so that they can save long time-consuming telephone calls and just locate the available titles in an online database. The recommended configuration would be Multiple Publishers/Multiple Subscribers because all machines need the same copy of the data. Transactional replication is a good solution when you want updated changes at the server in almost real-time.

CHAPTER SUMMARY

KEY TERMS

- Publisher
- Subscriber
- Distributor
- replication agents
- snapshot replication
- merge replication
- transactional replication
- Updateable Subscribers
- article
- publication
- replication configuration

This chapter has introduced you to practical replication. You learned what replication is, what requires replication, and how to implement it.

First, you saw the basic idea behind replication: the Publisher/Subscriber metaphor. Basically, the Publisher is the server that creates the original data and the Subscriber is the machine that receives it.

After that, you looked at data partitioning or filtering. This enables you to trim data down, either by column or row.

You also saw the different replication configurations a firm might decide to implement. These include Central Publisher/Multiple Subscribers, Multiple Publishers/Multiple Subscribers, Multiple Publishers/Single Subscriber, and Single Publisher/Remote Distributor.

You next studied the replication agents in SQL Server. These agents are used to move data along the Publisher and Subscriber via the Distributor and keep the replication process as a whole run smoothly. These agents include the Log Reader agent, Distribution agent, Snapshot agent, and Merge agent.

CHAPTER SUMMARY

Then you looked at the different types of replication. Replication can be divided into three main categories: snapshot, transactional, and merge. Each of these models provides different capabilities and levels of autonomy and Transactional consistency when used in an application on a site. To determine which replication is best suited for your needs, you need to consider three factors: site autonomy, transactional consistency, and latency.

This chapter also discussed some of the ideas behind Updating Subscribers. Using Updating Subscribers, as the name implies, gives the Subscriber the power to update or modify data when it is replicated. This option can be used with snapshot replication and transactional replication. You can use two configurations to enable Updateable Subscribers: immediate updating and queued updating.

You saw how to actually implement replication in your database. The first step is creating a Distributor and Publisher. Then you create a publication and set articles within that publication.

And finally you learned how to define the various Subscribers who subscribe to a publication. SQL Server 2000 makes implementing replication simpler with the easy-to-use wizards provided.

As you have seen, replication is quite an involved and diverse process that requires a lot of planning and careful consideration as well as ongoing monitoring. Monitoring replication as well as other database activity is an important aspect of working with SQL Server from day to day. It will also be a significant topic on the exam. The next chapter looks at all aspects of monitoring and fine-tuning SQL Server processes.

> **EXAM TIP**
>
> **Reviewing Replication** When reviewing this chapter before sitting the exam, be sure to know the different replication configurations available, the different types of replication, and the components in the Publisher/Subscriber metaphor, along with the description, uses, and benefits of each. Most questions on the exam relating to replication are scenario-based; a good example of this is the first exam question at the end of this chapter.

APPLY YOUR KNOWLEDGE

Exercises

11.1   Creating a Publication for Snapshot Replication

The purpose of this exercise is to create a snapshot publication in SQL Server.

Estimated Time: 15 minutes

1. Open the SQL Server Enterprise Manager from the Start menu and connect to your default instance of SQL Server.

2. Click on Tools, Replication, and then select Create and Manage Publications.

3. Select Northwind and then click Create Publication.

4. On the starting screen of the Create Publication Wizard, leave the Show Advanced Options check box unchecked and click Next. The next screen prompts you to select a database. Select Northwind and click Next.

5. You should be on the Publication Type screen. Select Snapshot Replication and click Next.

6. Now you have to choose what version of SQL Server (if they even use SQL Server) your Subscribers use. Selection screens vary depending on what you choose, so select SQL Server 2000, leaving the other two options blank, and click Next to continue.

7. You should be at the Specify Articles selection screen. Select the check box next to the Customers object and then click the ellipsis (. . .) to its right. Leave all settings as they are, except change the Destination Table Owner to Dbo and Destination Table Name to rtblCustomers and then close the dialog box. You are returned to the Article Selection screen, where you should click Next.

8. Arriving at the Publication Name selection screen, leave all defaults in place and click Next.

9. On Property Customization, select the option No, Create the Publication as Specified, and then click Next. This ends the wizard and completes the creation of a new publication.

After the creation of the publication, you can then allow the Subscribers to pull subscriptions. As an alternative, the Publisher can push the subscription out, but the following exercise shows a pull from the Subscriber's side.

It is worth noting that if this is the first time you have set up replication on any given installation, you will see additional configuration screens that were addressed in the Step by Step operations earlier in this chapter. Before Step 4 of this exercise, you would have three additional screens to provide the Distributor configuration, SQL Server startup options, and snapshot folder location.

11.2 Creating a Pull Subscription

The purpose of this exercise is to create a pull Subscription for the publication created previously in Step by Step 11.4.

Estimated Time: 15 minutes

1. Connect to your default instance of SQL Server.

2. Click on Tools, Replication, and Pull Subscription to initialize the Pull Subscription dialog box.

3. Click Pull New Subscription, which starts the Pull Subscription Wizard.

4. On the starting screen, leave Show Advanced Options unchecked and then click Next.

APPLY YOUR KNOWLEDGE

5. On the Look for Publications screen, select the first option that specifies it will search on registered servers for publications.

6. On the Choose Publication screen, expand the default server; you should find an entry named Northwind: Northwind. Select it and then click Next.

7. If you've already gone through the replication implementation in Step by Step 11.2, you should see a database called `Replica`. If you haven't, then create the database by clicking New and entering **Replica** as the database name. Leave all values except for Name to their defaults, and then click OK to complete the dialog. Click Next to continue.

8. Select Yes, because when you implement replication the first time an initial snapshot must already have been applied at the Subscriber; only then can the Subscriber receive incremental changes.

9. Select the Default Snapshot folder (MSSQL\ReplData) option and click Next.

10. On the next screen, select the last option (On Demand Only) and then click Next. Select On Demand Only because the data at the Subscriber does not need to be updated at all in this example or the examples to come.

11. You are at the final screen of the wizard. Click Finish to complete the wizard.

12. You now have to manually initiate the Snapshot agent. To do this, expand Replication Monitor, Agents, Snapshot Agents, and right-click Northwind. To initiate the Snapshot Agent, select Start Agent.

Now that you have tried a pull subscription, the following exercise shows you how to push a subscription from the Publisher's side of the operation.

11.3 Creating a Push Subscription

This exercise demonstrates how to push a subscription.

Estimated Time: 15 minutes

1. On the Tools menu, select Replication, Push Subscription to Others.

2. Expand Northwind, click on the Northwind publication, and then click Push New Subscription, which initiates the Push Subscription Wizard.

3. On the starting screen, click Next without selecting Advanced Options.

4. This screen inquires about the Subscriber you want to receive the publication. In this case, select your local instance of SQL Server and click Next.

5. In this screen you choose where the replica is placed; in this case create a new database called `replicaPush`. Click Browse or Create and then click the Create New button. As the database name, type **ReplicaPush**, and leave all settings on their default.

6. Determining the schedule for the Distribution Agent depends on how frequently you want updated data. Because you do not want updated data at all, select Using the Following Schedule and click Next.

7. Select Yes, Initialize Schema and Data because when you implement replication the first time, an initial snapshot must already have been applied at the Subscriber; only after this can the Subscriber receive incremental changes. Also select "Start the Snapshot..." to automatically start the Snapshot Agent.

APPLY YOUR KNOWLEDGE

8. You need the SQLServerAgent running for this subscription, which this screen corroborates.

9. This is the final screen of the Push Subscription wizard. Click Finish.

10. You have to start the Distribution Agent manually. To do this, select Replication Monitor, Agents, Distribution Agents, and then find the entry in the list of publications where the PublisherDB is Northwind and the type is Push.

11. After you have found it, right-click it and select Start Agent.

Review Questions

1. Generally, which is the most important consideration: transactional consistency, latency, or autonomy? Why?

2. According to what you have learned so far, what is the most common type of replication? Explain why it is so prominent.

3. Some suggest that merge replication might increase in popularity in the future. What's your opinion and why?

4. What is the Snapshot agent's role in the replication process?

5. How do Updating Subscribers work in SQL Server?

6. Why might you want heterogeneous interoperability?

7. When do you think snapshot replication would be a good type to implement? Why?

Exam Questions

1. You are the administrator of a SQL Server 2000 computer at your company's warehouse. All product orders are shipped out from this warehouse. Orders are received at 30 sales offices throughout the country. Each sales office offers a range of products specific to its own region.

   Each sales office contains one SQL Server 2000 computer. These servers connect to the warehouse through dial-up connections once a day. Each sales office needs data pertaining to only its own region.

   You need to replicate inventory data from the server at the warehouse to the servers at the sales offices. You have decided to use transactional replication. You want to minimize the amount of time needed to replicate the data.

   Which actions should you take? (Choose three.)

   A. Create one publication for each Subscriber.

   B. Create one publication for all Subscribers.

   C. Enable horizontal partitioning.

   D. Enable vertical partitioning.

   E. Use pull subscriptions.

   F. Use push subscriptions.

2. You are setting up a new snapshot replication environment for five large tables. To save disk space, you want to delete the data objects that are generated by snapshot replication. Where can you find these objects?

   A. Inside the MSSQL2000\Replication\Data directory on the Publisher.

B. In the sysArticles table in the database that is being published.

C. In the Mssql\Repldata directory in the Distributor.

D. In the Mssql\Repldata directory on the Subscriber.

3. The master price list for the shoes your company has in stock is maintained in SQL Server in the corporate office that is updated constantly. You want all your outlets to receive the updated prices as quickly as possible from the corporate office. Which sort of replication is best suited for a situation like this?

   A. Transactional replication

   B. Snapshot replication

   C. Merge replication

   D. Immediate replication

4. You configure transactional replication on the Headquarters server and make numerous publications available. Later, a member of the Sales department subscribes to one of the publications. However, the only article from the publication that he needs is MonthlyRevenue. He needs data quickly and needs to avoid receiving the redundant data that would come from subscribing to the whole publication. What can be done to solve this?

   A. Change the style of replication being used to snapshot replication.

   B. Filter the publication so that only MonthlyRevenues can be replicated; push this subscription to the Sales department.

   C. Create a new publication that containerizes only a single article, MonthlyRevenues.

   D. There is no way to solve this problem. He needs to subscribe to the whole publication.

5. Southwest Specialists is a firm dealing with the production of valuable ornamental goods. It is using merge replication to publish customer and order information to its infrequently connected sales representatives. The DBA does not, however, want sales representatives to see actual amounts paid, so it deselects the Amounts column and then replicates the data. This article is made so that it contains only selected columns from a table. What is this called?

   A. Horizontal partitioning

   B. Horizontal filtering

   C. Vertical partitioning

   D. Column Restriction Filtering (CRF)

6. What is the role of the Merge agent?

   A. Propagate updates and monitor and resolve conflicts on Publishers and Subscribers.

   B. Store records on the Distribution folder until needed and then merge them with transactions.

   C. Enable records to be broken down into smaller subsets.

   D. The Merge agent triggers when data modifications are made at the Subscriber after it has received a replica of data.

APPLY YOUR KNOWLEDGE

7. You have set up a replication process using the default locations for the agents. Your process involves data being replicated to 20 Subscribers using a transactional replication strategy. How are the replication agents configured in transactional replication that uses a push subscription?

   A. The Log Reader agent resides on the Subscriber and the Distribution agent is on the Subscriber.

   B. The Log Reader agent resides on the Distributor and the Distribution agent is on the Subscriber.

   C. The Log Reader agent resides on the Subscriber and the Distribution agent is on the Publisher.

   D. The Log Reader agent resides on the Distributor and the Distribution agent is also located on the Distributor.

8. Debra has just recently configured replication from the `Products` table to the `Analysis` table, located on the Headquarters and Research servers, respectively. Recently, Debra has noticed that replication failed for some unknown cause. Which of the following might be a likely cause of this problem? Choose all that apply.

   A. Replication requires three separate servers and Debra may not have implemented three servers.

   B. Replication cannot involve the `Master`, `Msdb`, `Tempdb`, and `Model` databases. Debra could have incorporated one of these databases with replication.

   C. Any replication process requires the use of at least two replication agents. Debra may have disabled one of the agents.

   D. Debra might have enabled Updating Subscribers, which is not allowed with any type of replication except for merge replication.

   E. The Transaction log of the Publisher may have been fully occupied, thus creating problem replication.

9. Which of the following statements describe the role of the Log Reader agent?

   A. The Log Reader agent moves transactions from the Transaction log of the published database on the Publisher to the Distribution database or server.

   B. The Log Reader agent moves transactions and snapshot jobs held in the Distribution database out to the Subscribers.

   C. The Log Reader agent gives you the ability to run transactions in a sequence.

   D. The Log Reader agent deletes transactions at the click of a button.

10. Transactional replication offers low site autonomy and merge replication offers high site autonomy. What is meant by "site autonomy"?

    A. The measuring of the consistency of transactions.

    B. How long data in the Subscriber can stay without being renewed.

    C. The independence of one site in relation to others.

    D. How many Subscribers and Publishers are involved in a replication process.

APPLY YOUR KNOWLEDGE

11. You work in a finance company where changes to the values in the Finance table are made quickly, and thus you want these incremental changes to be propagated to Subscribers as they occur. These Subscribers are frequently connected to the Publisher with a reliable connection. Which type of replication is used when you want updated changes at the server in almost real time?

    A. Snapshot replication

    B. Snapshot replication with Updating Subscribers

    C. Transactional replication

    D. Merge replication

12. You and Josh are replicating data to multiple Subscribers who need to update data at various times and propagate those changes to the Publisher and to other Subscribers. These Subscribers need to be able to make changes offline and later synchronize data; this means that they need a replication strategy that offers high autonomy. Which type of replication offers almost complete site autonomy?

    A. Snapshot replication

    B. Snapshot replication and transactional replication

    C. Merge replication

    D. Transactional replication

    E. Transactional replication with Updating Subscribers

13. Your company has just purchased an accounting application from a vendor. The application stores its data in a database named Accounting. The tables in this database contain columns that function as Primary Keys, but PRIMARY KEY and FOREIGN KEY constraints are not used.

    You need to replicate data from this database to another SQL Server computer. This server will use the replicated data to generate reports. Most reports will run each month, but the accounting department needs to have the ability to run reports at any time. Reports should be accurate through the last full working day.

    You cannot make any changes to the database, but you need to implement replication. Which two actions should you take? (Each correct answer represents part of the solution. Choose two.)

    A. Implement merge replication.

    B. Implement snapshot replication.

    C. Implement transactional replication.

    D. Schedule replication to run continuously.

    E. Schedule replication to run during off-peak hours.

14. Your company has just purchased an accounting application from a vendor. The application stores its data in a database named Accounting. The tables in this database contain columns that function as Primary Keys, but PRIMARY KEY and FOREIGN KEY constraints are not used.

    You need to replicate data from this database to another SQL Server computer. This server will use the replicated data to generate reports infrequently. Most reports will run each month, but the accounting department needs to have the ability to run reports at any time. Reports should be accurate through the last full working day.

APPLY YOUR KNOWLEDGE

Disk space is at a premium and you want to conserve space as much as possible. Which action should you take?

A. Use transactional replication.

B. Use snapshot replication.

C. Use a linked server for reporting.

D. Use DTS to the reporting server.

E. Use XML to the reporting server.

Answers to Review Questions

1. Generally, the most important consideration is transactional consistency; autonomy and latency considerations are usually up to you. Transactional consistency deals with the correctness of data, and this is a major factor. It is difficult to choose one factor as the most important, even generally speaking. For example, in merge replication poor transactional consistency is unavoidable, but the comparative level of transactional consistency is determined entirely by the latency. Latency in this case can be configured, but transactional consistency cannot be.

2. Transactional replication is by far the most common type of replication. It offers a bit of everything: transactional consistency, latency, and autonomy. With the use of Updating Subscribers, it supports transactional consistency, medium-to-high autonomy, and low latency.

3. Merge replication has a chance to increase popularity because an increasing number of remote users need replicated data. Nevertheless, it still has conflicts that throw it back to where it began. These conflicts can be avoided with the use of

region codes in tables that minimize the risk of same data being altered concurrently.

4. The Snapshot agent is responsible for preparing the schema and initial data files of published tables and stored procedures, storing the snapshot on the distribution server and recording information about the synchronization status in the Distribution database.

5. When Updating Subscribers are used, a trigger is located at the Subscriber database that monitors for changes and sends those changes to the publishing server.

6. SQL Server is built upon OLE-DB, which enables data to be replicated from SQL Server to any other database server, such as Sybase or Oracle. Using this feature is useful when one or more sites are not running simple SQL Server, but diverse database management systems instead.

7. Snapshot replication is exceptionally advantageous when replicated data is infrequently updated and modified. A snapshot strategy is preferable over others when data is to be updated in batches at distant intervals. Because data is replicated at a certain point in time and not replicated frequently, this type of replication is good for online catalogs, price lists, and so on.

Answers to Exam Questions

1. **A, C, E.** It is necessary to design the structure of the database so that the publications can include an article specific to each location. This will mean a compound Primary Key containing regional information and an article for each Subscriber that is horizontally partitioned based

APPLY YOUR KNOWLEDGE

on the region. Because the connection is initiated by the Subscriber dial-up, you must also set up pull subscriptions. For more information, see the "Types of Replication" section.

2. **C.** The default location for the snapshot information is in the Distributor in the Mssql\Repldata folder. Using the publication properties, this location can be altered to a newly desired position. Be sure to enable FTP access to this new location if FTP is being used to transfer the snapshots. See "Configuring the Distribution Server" for more details.

3. **A.** To receive updated prices as quickly as possible, use transactional replication. Merge replication is not appropriate because of the timing considerations, and snapshot replication would be too intensive, slow down operations, and produce a lot of latency (delay). Immediate replication does not exist, though immediate Updating Subscriptions are an option of transactional and snapshot replication types. Often exam answers attempt to fool you by using wording that is purposefully confusing, so read carefully and make no assumptions. For more details, see the "Types of Replication" section.

4. **C.** Of the options offered, creating a new publication is the best choice because it is the only option that will work. Creating filters can only be done vertically (column) or horizontally (rows). A more experienced individual could use stored procedures to subscribe to a single article, but this option is not present in the answer choices. For more information, consult the "Horizontal and Vertical Partitioning" section of this chapter.

5. **C.** Vertical partitioning is the selection of some (but not all) columns in a table. Horizontal par-

titioning is the creation of an article based on some (but not all) rows in a table. Horizontal filtering is a term that is sometimes used as a synonym for horizontal partitioning. For additional details, consult the "Horizontal and Vertical Partitioning" section.

6. **A.** The Merge agent connects to the publishing server and the subscribing server and updates both as changes are made. The major role of the merge agent is to propagate the updates, and then monitor for conflicts. The agent is also responsible to apply the initial snapshot at the subscriber. See "Inside Merge Replication" for more information.

7. **D.** In transactional replication, the Log Reader agent, by default, resides on the Distributor. Because you are using a push subscription, the Distribution agent is also located on the Distributor, by default. If you were to use a pull subscription, the Distribution agent would by default be located on the Subscriber. You can alter the location on which the agent is run by using remote agent activation if the load would be better distributed by not using defaults. See "Inside Transactional Replication" for more details.

8. **B, C.** Out of the answer choices provided, only two were actually requirements: The Model, Master, Msdb, and TempDB databases cannot be replicated, and a replication process must contain at least two agents, depending on the replication options chosen. For more details, see the section titled "Publisher."

9. **A.** The Log Reader agent moves transactions from the transaction log of the published database on the Publisher to the distribution database or server. For more information, see the section on the "Log Reader Agent."

APPLY YOUR KNOWLEDGE

10. **C.** Site autonomy refers to one site's independence from all other sites for processing modifications. Autonomy measures the effect of your site's operation to another. A site that has full autonomy is completely independent of all other sites, meaning it can function without even being connected to another. See "Types of Replications" for more information on autonomy and other considerations.

11. **C.** Transactional replication is a good solution when you want updated changes at the server in almost real time. Because of the frequency of the changes, snapshot replication is not a good solution. Merge replication can be set up in a single direction but is generally used only when the Publisher and Subscribers make updates while connected or disconnected. See "Inside Transactional Replication" for more details.

12. **C.** Merge replication allows the most flexibility and adds the most autonomy to the replication process, enabling the Publisher and Subscriber to work virtually independently. The Publisher and Subscriber can combine their results and updates at any time. See "Inside Merge Replication" for more details.

13. **B, E.** Because there is no Primary Key and no other changes to the database can be performed, the only alternative that does not require either is snapshot replication. Because the data does not need to be up-to-the-minute, a scheduled data refresh occurring overnight or during other non-peak times is most appropriate. See "Inside Snapshot Replication" for more details.

14. **C.** Use of a linked server will allow for heterogeneous data access but does *not* take up any additional disk space. The other solutions use some disk space; without this restriction any of the other solutions are possible. See "Heterogeneous Interoperability" for more details.

Suggested Readings and Resources

1. *Microsoft SQL Server 2000 Administrator's Companion.* Marci Frohock Garcia, Jamie Reding, Edward Whalen, Steve Adrien DeLuca. Microsoft Press.

   An excellent book that covers all SQL Server administrative functions and their proper implementation.

2. SQL Server Books Online
   - Introducing Replication
   - Types Of Replication
   - Implementing Replication
   - Replication Options

3. MSDN Online Internet Reference (http://msdn.microsoft.com)
   - SQL Server Replication (/library/officedev/odeopg/deovrsqlserverreplication.htm)
   - Replication Between Different Versions of SQL Server (/library/psdk/sql/replimpl_4joy.htm)

This chapter covers the following Microsoft-specified objectives for aspects of troubleshooting, monitoring, and auditing SQL Server for the 70-229 Database Design SQL Server 2000 exam:

Troubleshoot programming objects. Objects include stored procedures, transactions, triggers, user-defined functions, and views.

▶ One of the primary jobs of any developer is that of troubleshooting and debugging. Troubleshooting is also a part of almost every IT job description. The appropriate use of all SQL Server tools is an important aspect in being able to troubleshoot effectively.

Optimize programming objects used in SQL Server 2000 including the interaction with the operating system.

▶ The SQL Server and operating system work together to provide a productive database management environment. There are many SQL Server hooks into the operating system and OS resources available to observe the database server as it operates. Other tools allow for quick diagnosis of problems that may be affecting the server.

Optimize programming objects. Objects include stored procedures, transactions, triggers, user-defined functions, and views.

▶ Any database implementation will need periodic adjustments or fine tuning. To achieve better performance, more throughput, faster response times, and periodic maintenance are necessary.

Monitor and troubleshoot database activity by using SQL Profiler.

▶ This is an extremely involved topic and one that has implications throughout multiple exam objectives and questions. This is also the area of premier importance when you are on the job.

CHAPTER 12

Monitoring and Tuning SQL Server Databases

Capture, analyze, and replay SQL Profiler traces. Considerations include lock detection, performance tuning, and trace flags.

▶ To really get inside the server and see all the interactions will require the use of the Profiler. With this tool all activity within the database environment can be viewed, reported, and replayed.

Analyze the query execution plan. Considerations include query processor operations and steps.

▶ Use of the Query Analyzer can help you obtain more efficient processes and procedures. It is an important element in the fine tuning of T-SQL processes.

Define object-level security, including column-level permissions, by using GRANT, REVOKE, and DENY.

▶ Who can create and use objects, and in what manner they can use them, are defined by SQL Server permissions. Permissions can be given on the objects or on the underlying data in the tables. Knowledge of statement and data permissions is important in the development of most business procedures.

STUDY STRATEGIES

▶ Practice with each tool using the Step by Step procedures, exercises, and experiments of your own. Try a variety of different options and variants with each tool.

▶ Note where each tool plays an important role and in what instances one tool is chosen over another.

▶ Experiment with settings in a controlled environment; the production environment is not the place to try playing trial and error. The information in this chapter will potentially be the hardest to master; because of that, extra time should be taken in observing the details of each operation before you take the exam.

INTRODUCTION

If you have progressed through the use of SQL Server and are looking toward optimization, you have seen a vast array of capabilities, applications, objects, and numerous interactions. All this functionality, of course, comes with a cost. A database server can and usually does service the largest load of all computerized processes in any corporation.

It would certainly be easy to resolve any problem that exists in a computer environment if the solution were only to provide more hardware. Many techniques are available to minimize the response time for each query and to maximize the throughput of the entire database server by reducing network traffic, disk I/O, and/or CPU time. Many factors affect performance, including the logical and physical structure of the data, as well as tradeoffs between conflicting uses of the database, such as online transaction processing and decision support.

Of course, maximizing the hardware is always important. With the price of RAM so low, you can bulk up your servers and desktops at a very reasonable cost (considering what I paid to maximize RAM in all my machines two years ago). Hard disk space and processor power is also relatively inexpensive in contrast to a few years ago. So the first consideration on obtaining the most from your machines is to spend the money where it will provide the best and fastest results. Put as much RAM in the machine as it can hold and look at the hard drive, processing ability, and network infrastructure for optimum storage, speed, and throughput.

On the database system and operating system software side of things, performance issues should be considered throughout the development cycle, not just at the end when the system is implemented. Ongoing adjustments are always a part of any complete solution, but you should still always design with performance issues in mind. Many significant performance issues are resolved through careful design from the outset. To most effectively optimize performance, you must identify the areas that utilize the most resources and then concentrate your efforts on those areas.

This chapter appears at the end of the book, but that is more because of the way Microsoft put together the exam study guide than anything else. Don't let the fact that this is the last chapter reduce its significance. The materials covered will not only be a major focus on the exam, but also on the job.

TOOLS AVAILABLE FOR MONITORING AND TUNING

▶ **Troubleshoot programming objects. Objects include stored procedures, transactions, triggers, user-defined functions, and views.**

IN THE FIELD

OPTIMUM HARDWARE

Computerization in every office has exploded. The average office has three heavily used servers: the email server, the Internet server, and the database server. These services each require specialized computer equipment that must address hard drive space, RAM requirements, and processing speed. Assume for all three servers that you are to use the highest available hardware in all categories. If choices must be made, then more thorough analysis of the complete automated business structure would be required.

There is a complete set of tools for monitoring events and troubleshooting objects within SQL Server. Your choice of tool depends on the type of monitoring and the events to be monitored. To be able to select any of these tools, you must understand where each tool is used and the process for analyzing the data. You must also determine a goal for the optimization. To best troubleshoot any object, you must first have some knowledge of the circumstances surrounding the system and make observations that will form the basis of the study. The following list represents the tools that are used to diagnose SQL Server Implementations:

◆ **Query Analyzer.** Used to diagnose T-SQL statements and activity and aid in application performance tuning and optimization tasks.

◆ **SQL Profiler.** Provides access to all SQL Server activity and objects. Used for detailed monitoring of selected server-wide events.

◆ **System Monitor.** Provides a broad spectrum of server analysis. Used primarily for hardware and operating system activity as well as interactions between the operating system and SQL Server.

◆ **Current activity window.** This is what's happening now. View user, process, and lock information based on the present utilization.

◆ **Transact-SQL.** Many commands are available that can be used from the Query Analyzer or other T-SQL connections.

◆ **Error logs.** This won't necessarily tell you all the "whys," but it is an excellent start to find out the "whats."

A lot of resources are also at your disposal to help provide answers to your questions and/or perform further research into a problem. These resources are also useful in preparing for the exam or researching specific technologies:

◆ **Web Resources.** Too many to mention here, though there is a complete list at the end of the chapter in the "Suggested Readings and Resources" section.

◆ **SQL Server Books OnLine.** As always, the first place to look for answers to any questions.

◆ **The Microsoft Public Newsgroups.** Find them at news.microsoft.com. Although there are many relevant groups, the microsoft.public.sqlserver.programming and microsoft.public.sqlserver.tools are particularly useful.

You began looking into the Query Analyzer way back in Chapter 1 and have been using the tool throughout the entire book. You were first given only a little bit of detail about a common SQL coding tool, but by now it has become probably your single most effective tool, and you have seen how SQL Server architects have come to depend on it. At the end of this chapter you will discover much more usefulness. The SQL Server Query Analyzer provides for very query-specific analysis. It is an important tool used in fine tuning any T-SQL application. The analyzer is most beneficial when you really want to drill down and focus in on detailed analysis and tuning.

Although the Query Analyzer is an excellent tool for looking into specific queries, the primary monitoring tool covering all aspects of the server applications is the SQL Server Profiler. This represents an important tool because of the vast amount of information it can provide. The SQL Server Profiler enables you to monitor server and database activity. You can capture SQL Profiler data to a table or a file for later analysis, and also replay the events captured on SQL Server. Arguably, if the Profiler is not set up properly, it can provide too much information to be useful. It is important, therefore, to learn the idiosyncrasies of the tool to make it as useful a tool as it can be.

Other tools used on the server for troubleshooting and other forms of analysis are available. To look at the hardware configuration, operating system and other analysis tools are available as part of the NT and Windows 2000 operating system. To monitor hardware and operating system events, you would use the System Monitor tool.

The System Monitor enables you to monitor server performance and activity using predefined objects and counters or user-defined counters to monitor events. System Monitor is referred to as Performance Monitor in Windows NT. Its role is to collect counts rather than data about the events. You can set thresholds on specific counters to generate alerts and notify the individuals who need to address the problem. Often the best place to start the troubleshooting process is to observe the current activity.

The Current Activity window is found in the SQL Server Enterprise Manager and graphically displays information about processes currently running. It also displays blocked processes, locks, user activity, and other useful information for ad hoc views of current activity. Equally helpful are the logs that SQL Server provides for the reporting of errors.

Error Logs contain additional information about events in SQL Server beyond what is available elsewhere. You can use the information in the error log to troubleshoot SQL Server-related problems. The Windows application event log provides an overall picture of events occurring on the Windows NT 4.0 and Windows 2000 system as a whole, as well as events in SQL Server, SQL Server Agent, and Full-Text Search. Several stored procedures have been built in to SQL Server to provide for specific benefits.

It probably goes without saying (but is worth a friendly reminder) that monitoring and troubleshooting have always played an important part in the activities performed on the job. Microsoft as well has always made this an exam focus. It is important to understand what each of the tools can do to aid in monitoring and troubleshooting. Knowing which tool to select based on symptoms of the problems is the focus of this chapter, as well, as you'll go into further depth within each of these areas.

Stored Procedures Used to Diagnose and Optimize

Many useful stored procedures are available for people who are a little more advanced with T-SQL and the design of system-level applications. Often a programmatic solution is desired over one that provides only visual feedback. In these instances the output from the stored procedures can be acted upon in an automated manner. (See the "Job, Operator, Alert Integration" section later in this chapter).

The sp_who stored procedure reports snapshot information about current SQL Server users and processes. This is a T-SQL alternative to viewing user activity in the current activity window in SQL Server Enterprise Manager. Similarly, sp_lock reports snapshot information about locks, including the object ID, index ID, type of lock, and type or resource to which the lock applies. The sp_lock procedure is also a Transact-SQL alternative used to view lock activity in the current activity window in SQL Server Enterprise Manager.

Other procedures also present alternative mechanisms to query for results normally displayed. The sp_spaceused procedure displays an estimate of the current amount of disk space used by a table or database. This is a T-SQL alternative to viewing database usage in the Enterprise Manager.

Still further procedures provide specific information that can be immediately acted upon. The sp_monitor statement displays statistics, including CPU usage, I/O usage, and the amount of time idle since last executed. This information can be used as an advanced mechanism for SQL Server monitoring.

Other information of interest to system developers is the availability of a wide variety of built-in system functions. Everything from the name of the server to the name of the user and beyond can be identified for a particular connection.

Built-in Functions

A number of built-in SQL Server functions are available to find out information about the server. This information can be used as an aid in troubleshooting, determining SQL Server utilization, and/or to provide for optimization and performance tuning.

Statistics about SQL Server activity since the server was started are stored in predefined SQL Server counters. Other information pertaining to the server is also stored in similar variables. Functions are all categorized by the type of information provided. The sets of functions discussed in this unit can be as well found in Books Online (BOL) under these categories:

◆ Configuration Functions

◆ Metadata Functions

◆ System Functions

◆ System Statistical Functions

Configuration functions are scalar functions that operate on a single value and then return a single value. Scalar functions can be used wherever an expression is valid. Use these functions to return information about current configuration option settings. All configuration functions are nondeterministic and will not always return the same results every time they are called.

Configuration Functions

Configuration functions return information about settings in the current configuration and allow for adjustments to be made where applicable (as with SET options) using the sp_configure stored procedure. The full list of these functions with a short description is as follows:

◆ @@DATEFIRST. Returns the current value of the SET DATEFIRST parameter, which indicates the specified first day of each week: 1 for Monday, 2 for Tuesday, and so on through 7 for Sunday.

◆ @@DBTS. Returns the value of the current timestamp data type for the current database.

◆ @@LANGID. Returns the local language identifier (ID) of the language currently in use.

◆ @@LANGUAGE. Returns the name of the language currently in use.

◆ @@LOCK_TIMEOUT. Returns the current lock timeout setting, in milliseconds, for the current session.

◆ @@MAX_CONNECTIONS. Returns the maximum number of simultaneous user connections allowed on a SQL Server.

◆ @@MAX_PRECISION. Returns the precision level used by decimal and numeric data types.

◆ @@NESTLEVEL. Returns the nesting level of the current stored procedure execution.

◆ @@OPTIONS. Returns information about current SET options.

◆ @@REMSERVER. Returns the name of the remote SQL Server as it appears in the login record.

◆ @@SERVERNAME. Returns the name of the local server running SQL Server.

◆ @@SERVICENAME. Returns the name of the Registry key under which SQL Server is running. @@SERVICENAME returns MSSQLServer if the current instance is the default instance; this function returns the instance name if the current instance is a named instance.

◆ @@SPID. Returns the server process identifier (ID) of the current user process.

◆ @@TEXTSIZE. Returns the current value of the TEXTSIZE option of the SET statement, which specifies the maximum length, in bytes, of text or image data that is returned by a query.

◆ @@VERSION. Returns the date, version, and processor type for the current installation.

As you can see, configuration functions are primarily used to determine the server properties for the current installation. There is little fine-tuning that can be performed using these functions. The SET parameters affect the user connection greatly and are discussed in full later in this chapter. These functions provide information about the server; other functions must be used to get information about the databases and their objects.

Meta Data Functions

Meta data functions are scalar functions that return information about the database and database objects. These functions are also nondeterministic and return results based on the current situation. The full list of these functions with a short description is as follows:

◆ COL_LENGTH. Returns the defined length (in bytes) of a column.

◆ COL_NAME. Returns the name of a database column given the corresponding table identification number and column identification number.

◆ COLUMNPROPERTY. Returns information about a column or procedure parameter.

◆ DATABASEPROPERTY. Returns the named database property value for the given database and property name.

◆ DATABASEPROPERTYEX. Returns the current setting of the specified database option or property for the specified database.

◆ DB_ID. Returns the database identification (ID) number.

◆ DB_NAME. Returns the database name.

◆ FILE_ID. Returns the file identification (ID) number for the given logical file name in the current database.

◆ FILE_NAME. Returns the logical file name for the given file identification (ID) number.

◆ FILEGROUP_ID. Returns the filegroup identification (ID) number for the given filegroup name.

◆ FILEGROUP_NAME. Returns the filegroup name for the given filegroup identification (ID) number.

◆ FILEGROUPPROPERTY. Returns the specified filegroup property value when given a filegroup and property name.

◆ FILEPROPERTY. Returns the specified file name property value when given a file name and property name.

◆ fn_listextendedproperty. Returns extended property values of database objects.

◆ FULLTEXTCATALOGPROPERTY. Returns information about full-text catalog properties.

◆ FULLTEXTSERVICEPROPERTY. Returns information about full-text service-level properties.

◆ INDEX_COL. Returns the indexed column name.

◆ INDEXKEY_PROPERTY. Returns information about the index key.

◆ INDEXPROPERTY. Returns the named index property value given a table identification number, index name, and property name.

> **NOTE**
>
> **DATABASEPROPERTY and DATABASEPROPERTYEX** The function DATABASEPROPERTYEX is used to obtain information about the current setting of database options or the properties of a specified database. The DATABASEPROPERTY function is provided for backward compatibility and should not be used with a 2000 installation.

◆ OBJECT_ID. Returns the object identification number.

◆ OBJECT_NAME. Returns the object name.

◆ OBJECTPROPERTY. Returns information about objects in the current database.

◆ @@PROCID. Returns the stored procedure identifier (ID) of the current procedure.

◆ SQL_VARIANT_PROPERTY. Returns the base data type and other information about a sql_variant value.

◆ TYPEPROPERTY. Returns information about a data type.

Meta data functions are usually used programmatically to determine information about the database and objects that are currently in use by the session. In the following example, the col_length function is used to determine the length of the Titles column within the Title table of the Pubs database.

```
Select col_length('Titles', 'Title') As 'Length In Bytes'
```

In the next example, the OBJECTPROPERTY function is used in conjunction with the object_id to determine the type of object.

```
IF OBJECTPROPERTY (object_id('titles'),'ISTABLE') = 1
    PRINT 'Titles is a table'
ELSE IF OBJECTPROPERTY (object_id('titles'),'ISTABLE') = 0
    PRINT 'Titles is not a table'
ELSE IF OBJECTPROPERTY (object_id('titles'),'ISTABLE')
  IS NULL
    PRINT 'ERROR: Titles is not a defined object'
```

System functions and system statistical functions enable you to perform operations and return information about values, objects, settings, and statistical information about the system. System functions are also available to find out more information pertaining to the server, databases, objects, and current session.

System and System Statistical Functions

Many of the system functions pertain more to the application development side than to the troubleshooting, optimizing, and performance-tuning topics, and those functions are not discussed in this chapter. Those functions that can provide useful information have been provided in the following list. Note that unlike the previous groups of functions discussed, some system functions are deterministic.

◆ APP_NAME. Returns the application name for the current session, if set by the application.

◆ COLLATIONPROPERTY. Returns the property of a given collation.

◆ CURRENT_TIMESTAMP. Returns the current date and time; equivalent to GETDATE().

◆ CURRENT_USER. Returns the current user; equivalent to USER_NAME().

◆ @@ERROR. Returns the error number for the last T-SQL statement executed.

◆ fn_helpcollations (Deterministic). Returns a list of all the collations supported.

◆ fn_servershareddrives. Returns the names of shared drives used by a clustered server.

◆ fn_virtualfilestats. Returns I/O statistics for database files, including log files.

◆ GETANSINULL. Returns the default nullability for the database for this session.

◆ HOST_ID. Returns the workstation identification number.

◆ HOST_NAME. Returns the workstation name.

◆ PARSENAME (Deterministic). Returns the specified part of an object name. Parts of an object that can be retrieved are the object name, owner name, database name, and server name.

◆ PERMISSIONS. Returns a value containing a bitmask that indicates the statement, object, or column permissions for the current user.

> **NOTE**
>
> **Existence Test** The PARSENAME function does not indicate whether an object exists. It just returns the specified piece of the given object name.

IN THE FIELD

PERMISSIONS

The PERMISSIONS function is particularly useful in testing real-world scenarios. Often the vast number of permission settings within an enterprise makes it difficult to obtain permission information about individual users. Because this function returns a value containing a bitmask that indicates the statement, object, or column permissions for the current user, diagnosis of security situations is simplified.

◆ SERVERPROPERTY. Returns property information about the server instance.

◆ SESSIONPROPERTY. Returns the SET options settings of a session. (SET is discussed in detail later in this chapter)

◆ SESSION_USER. Enables a system-supplied value for the current session's username to be inserted into a table when no default value is specified. Also enables the username to be used in queries, error messages, and so on.

◆ STATS_DATE. Returns the date that the statistics for the specified index were last updated.

IN THE FIELD

STATISTICAL UPDATES

Use the STATS_DATE function to test statistic update settings for any index. Often non-updated statistics cause a system to slow and become unresponsive over time. Periodic checking and UPDATE STATISTICS execution is warranted on most production systems.

◆ SYSTEM_USER. Enables a system-supplied value for the current system username to be inserted into a table when no default value is specified.

◆ USER_NAME. Returns a user database username from a given identification number.

What is probably one of the best function sets has been saved until last. Though all the functions mentioned in this unit are important and have their appropriate usage, the most useful set of functions for optimization purposes would be the system statistical functions.

For example, @@CPU_BUSY contains the amount of time the CPU has been executing SQL Server code. The full list of these functions with a short description is as follows:

◆ @@CONNECTIONS. Returns the number of connections, or attempted connections, the server last started.

◆ @@CPU_BUSY. Returns the time in milliseconds (based on the resolution of the system timer) that the CPU has spent working since the server was last started.

NOTE

@@CPU_BUSY This setting enables the database system team to see whether the current configuration is responding well to system stress or would benefit from the use of additional processor consideration. See also @@IDLE for related information.

◆ `fn_virtualfilestats`. Returns I/O statistics for database files, including log files.

◆ `@@IDLE`. Returns the time in milliseconds (based on the resolution of the system timer) that the server has been idle since last started.

◆ `@@IO_BUSY`. Returns the time in milliseconds (based on the resolution of the system timer) that the server has spent performing input and output operations since it was last started.

◆ `@@PACK_RECEIVED`. Returns the number of input packets read from the network by the server since last started.

◆ `@@PACK_SENT`. Returns the number of output packets written to the network by the server since last started.

◆ `@@PACKET_ERRORS`. Returns the number of network packet errors that have occurred on the server since it was last started.

◆ `@@TIMETICKS`. Returns the number of microseconds per tick.

◆ `@@TOTAL_ERRORS`. Returns the number of disk read/write errors encountered by the server since last started.

◆ `@@TOTAL_READ`. Returns the number of non-cache disk reads by the server since last started.

◆ `@@TOTAL_WRITE`. Returns the number of disk writes by the server since last started.

> NOTE
>
> `@@IO_BUSY` This setting enables the database system team to see whether the current file and disk storage configuration is responding well to system stress or would benefit from the use of additional disk storage consideration.

As you can see from the wide array of functions SQL Server provides, a lot of useful diagnostic information can be used to optimize throughput while providing maximum performance and user response time. One of the primary database administration tools to begin on this arduous journey is DBCC. You can use DBCC to diagnose and act upon some of the most frequent inadequacies of a server configuration.

Database Console Command (DBCC)

The Transact-SQL programming language provides DBCC statements that act as Database Console Commands. DBCC statements enable you to check performance statistics and the logical and physical consistency of a database system. Many DBCC statements can fix detected problems.

DBCC options provide techniques you can use to obtain server status, perform data and index validation, and provide maintenance services. Other miscellaneous options can also affect how an application responds. There are four major groupings of DBCC operations, which have each been addressed separately in the sections that follow.

Status DBCC Operations

Some DBCC operations provide useful information about the processes that have been performed most recently on the server. This type of information can be quite useful in pinpointing the source of SQL activities. Each of the options, presented in the following list, provides a small piece of a very large puzzle, but collectively they can provide a useful picture of the current server activity.

◆ DBCC INPUTBUFFER. Provides the last statement sent from a client to the server.

◆ DBCC OPENTRAN. Provides transaction information for the oldest active transaction, distributed transaction, and non-distributed replicated transaction.

◆ DBCC OUTPUTBUFFER. Returns the current output buffer in hexadecimal and ASCII format for the specified system process ID.

◆ DBCC PROCCACHE. Displays information about the procedure cache.

◆ DBCC SHOWCONTIG. Displays fragmentation information for the data and indexes.

NOTE

DBCC OPENTRAN Results are displayed only if there is an active transaction or if the database contains current replication information.

IN THE FIELD

DBCC OPERATIONS

One of the most frequently used DBCC status operations is the SHOWCONTIG. Because it can display information specific to data and index fragmentation, it is useful in determining when to carry out maintenance operations.

◆ DBCC SHOW_STATISTICS. Displays the current distribution statistics for the specified target on the specified table.

◆ DBCC SQLPERF. Provides statistics about the use of transaction log space in all databases.

◆ DBCC TRACESTATUS. Displays the status of trace flags.

◆ DBCC USEROPTIONS. Returns the SET options active (set) for the current connection. SET options are addressed in their entirety later in this chapter.

All these options can provide valuable data to help you determine how performance can be improved. After status information has been generated, the next task in information retrieval is obtaining validation data that can also give you insight into a server.

Validation DBCC Operations

The validation options represent tools available that can reveal database storage problems and also provide the mechanisms to modify and fine-tune the environment.

◆ DBCC CHECKALLOC. Checks the consistency of disk space.

◆ DBCC CHECKCATALOG. Checks for consistency in system tables.

◆ DBCC CHECKCONSTRAINTS. Checks the integrity of a constraint(s).

◆ DBCC CHECKDB. Checks the allocation and structural integrity of all the objects in the database.

◆ DBCC CHECKFILEGROUP. Checks the allocation and structural integrity of tables in a filegroup.

◆ DBCC CHECKIDENT. Checks the current identity value for a table and, if needed, corrects the value.

◆ DBCC CHECKTABLE. Checks the integrity of the data, index, text, ntext, and image pages.

◆ DBCC NEWALLOC. Checks the allocation of data and index pages. Equivalent to CHECKALLOC and used for backward compatibility only.

Some of these functions are very CPU- and disk-intensive. Caution should be exercised around the time of day a DBCC CHECKDB operation is performed. Other functions as well can impact the server and temporarily increase system overhead.

> **NOTE**
>
> **DBCC CHECKDB and DBCC CHECKALLOC** Use of CHECKALLOC is unnecessary if CHECKDB is used first. CHECKDB contains a superset of options that includes all the functionality provided by CHECKALLOC.

> **NOTE**
>
> **Version Improvement** Execution of DBCC CHECKDB can be performed with users connected to the database in the 2000 version, which improves upon the locking mechanisms used in SQL Server 7.0 and earlier versions.

Maintenance DBCC Operations

Regular maintenance is needed in all database environments. Data and index pages will become fragmented. Data may become corrupt, file sizes may need to be adjusted, and regular maintenance will help you optimize the server environment.

- ◆ DBCC DBREINDEX. Rebuilds one or more indexes.

- ◆ DBCC DBREPAIR. Drops a damaged database.

- ◆ DBCC INDEXDEFRAG. Defragments clustered and secondary indexes of the specified table or view.

- ◆ DBCC SHRINKDATABASE. Shrinks the size of the data files in the specified database.

- ◆ DBCC SHRINKFILE. Shrinks a specified data file or log file.

- ◆ DBCC UPDATEUSAGE. Reports and corrects inaccuracies in the sysindexes table, which may result in incorrect space use reported by sp_spaceused.

A group of DBCC options do not directly fit into any one of the aforementioned categories. Listed as miscellaneous options, these DBCC operations can provide assistance, help free and better use resources, and provide some tracking mechanisms.

Miscellaneous Operations

- ◆ DBCC dllname (FREE). Unloads the specified extended stored procedure DLL from memory.

- ◆ DBCC HELP. Returns syntax information for the specified DBCC statement.

- ◆ DBCC PINTABLE. Marks a table to be pinned, and does not flush the pages for the table from memory.

- ◆ DBCC ROWLOCK. Used for Microsoft SQL Server 6.5, enabling Insert Row Locking operations on tables.

- ◆ DBCC TRACEOFF. Disables trace flag(s). Trace flags are discussed in the next section.

- ◆ DBCC TRACEON. Enables trace flag(s). Trace flags are discussed completely in the next section.

NOTE **DBCC DBDEPAIR Compatibility** DBCC DBREPAIR is included for backward compatibility only. It is recommended that DROP DATABASE be used to drop damaged databases. DBCC DBREPAIR may not be supported in a future version of SQL Server.

NOTE **Row Lock Compatibility** Row-level locking is enabled by default in SQL Server version 2000. The locking strategy is row locking with possible promotion to page or table locking. DBCC ROWLOCK is included for backward compatibility. In a future version of SQL Server, DBCC ROWLOCK may not be supported.

◆ DBCC UNPINTABLE. Marks a table as unpinned. Table pages in the buffer cache can be flushed.

Although DBCC represents one of the premier Microsoft tools available to a SQL Server administrator, there are other alternatives for troubleshooting.

Alternative Mechanisms

A variety of tools from Microsoft, third parties, and industry standards are available for use in troubleshooting, optimization, and reporting of SQL Server information. The next two sections examine some more traditional troubleshooting tools historically used through many versions of SQL Server.

Trace Flags

Trace flags display information about a specific activity within the server and are used to diagnose problems or performance issues. They are particularly useful in deadlock analysis. Trace flags temporarily set specific server characteristics or switch off a particular behavior. Trace flags are often used to diagnose and debug stored procedures and analyze complex system elements.

Four common trace flags are used for troubleshooting different elements of SQL Server.

◆ 260. Determines DLL version information.

◆ 1204. Determines the command affected by a deadlock and the type of locks that are participating.

◆ 2528. Disables/enables parallel checking of objects during DBCC operations.

◆ 3205. Disables/enables tape drive compression support.

> **NOTE**
>
> **Future Compatibility** Trace flag usage has been a longstanding debugging tool that in the past has proven useful. However, with other graphic tools now available that are easier to use and decipher, the use of trace flags is decreasing. Microsoft has stated that behaviors available with these flags may not be supported in future releases of SQL

To determine dynamic link library version information, see the support for GetXPVersion() in SQL Server Books OnLine, but other utilities are available without the use of a flag. Parallel DBCC checking should not usually be disabled, and tape dumps and backups should usually be compressed. Also, the locking information provided can be obtained by viewing the information available through the Enterprise Manager, as shown in Step by Step 12.1.

STEP BY STEP

12.1 Viewing SQL Server Debugging Information Using the Enterprise Manager

1. Start the Enterprise Manager and expand your server, and then the Management folder.

2. Expand the Current Activity Store to view the current processes in use on the system and any locks currently in place because of server activity.

3. Click on Process Info and size the columns in the right pane so that you can simultaneously view Process ID, User, Database, and Status. Make a note of the highest process identification number. (A lot of other information is available for these processes, and you may want to scroll right to see the types of process information available.)

4. Start an instance of the Query Analyzer from the Windows Start menu and provide connection information if needed. Select the Northwind database from the drop-down menu at the top of the screen.

5. Return to the Enterprise Manager, leaving the Query Analyzer window open.

6. Right-click on Current Activity and select Refresh.

7. Click on Process Info and notice the new processes added and the databases in use for the instance of the Query Analyzer you have started.

8. Expand Locks/Process ID and locate the process identification number for the Query Analyzer.

9. Notice the lock in place for Northwind database. Also note that the type of lock is DB (database) and the mode of the lock is S (shared). This is the lowest locking level allowed.

SQL Server uses a number of different lock types and modes. You'll learn more about locking mechanisms later in this chapter, including full details of the implications of each of these mechanisms.

With TCP/IP protocol mechanisms, another form of troubleshooting often implemented is to use the inherent protocol suite properties. TCP/IP is a detailed set of protocols that enables a large amount of information to be passed back and forth within a variety of packet types. SNMP is one protocol within this suite that has a lot of troubleshooting capability.

Simple Network Management Protocol (SNMP)

SNMP is an application protocol that is part of the larger TCP/IP protocol suite. SNMP provides for network management services that report and diagnose operating system and protocol information. Using SNMP, you can monitor an instance of any server that has been configured to report its information. SQL Server can be monitored running on Windows NT 4.0, Windows 98, and UNIX, as well as other platforms.

SNMP requires that a service report information to an agent who can then send data to monitoring computers. Using different tools, an administrator can view and report on a variety of information from the operating system, SQL Server software, and database objects. SNMP uses management information databases (MIB) for each service that it diagnoses. This database provides the necessary hierarchy to enable an agent to query the server for the desired data.

With the Microsoft SQL Server Management Information Base (MSSQL-MIB), you can use SNMP applications to monitor SQL Server. You can monitor performance information, access databases, and view server and database configuration parameters. Monitoring tools are available from a variety of third-party vendors. Systems Management Server, NT, and Windows 2000 all have built-in tools that can be optionally installed to perform SNMP queries.

Optimizing Performance Using Views

To maximize performance in large applications, the design of partitioned views should be examined. Also, placing indexes on views will provide for faster searching and retrieval of data. In itself, a view generally provides for better performance because less data is involved. Always consider the use of views in situations where tables have an extremely large number of columns, application design is left to the user, and tables contain sensitive information.

SQL Server Tool Use

You have no doubt noticed that a great deal of functionality is available in SQL Server to provide information that can then be beneficially used. Having an enterprise-level database server such as SQL Server necessitates a wide knowledge base to get the best performance and efficiency from the product.

Repeated use of the tools will help you develop the skills necessary to troubleshoot the SQL Server environment and make recommendations on areas of improvement. Whether it be general maintenance, problem solving, or optimization, SQL Server administrators will spend a great deal of their time using these tools.

Over the remainder of the chapter, you will gain some valuable experience using the utilities available in SQL Server. In preparation for the exam, ensure that you have used each tool to the point where you can define its usage and use the tool as a problem-solving mechanism. You will find many exam questions surrounding the use of these tools in a number of the exams you take on your way to becoming an MCSE, MCSD, and/or MCDBA.

Your knowledge of the tools and their uses will be tested by giving you many sample outputs and scenarios that were in place when the output was taken. It will be your responsibility to absorb all the facts and recommend a solution to the problem based on the set of choices given in the answers.

OPTIMIZING THE OS CONFIGURATION

▶ **Optimize programming objects used in SQL Server 2000, including the interaction with the operating system.**

Much of the performance of any database system relies on the application and database designers. The use of the network, processor, memory, and disk storage can all be dictated by the type of database design and the use of the applications operating against the database server. For this reason, the operating system usually acts as only a starting point in any performance analysis testing. If the hardware configuration and operating system is not properly configured, however, the database engine won't be able to respond optimally.

The first task that the hardware and operating system serve in any database system is to provide a means to store and operate the database software and objects. The operating system is also responsible for reporting hardware and software problems, as well as making it possible for you to monitor everything executing on the machine.

NT Server and Windows 2000 Server offer some basic utilities and mechanisms for monitoring and viewing server activity. The System Monitor (Windows 2000) and Performance Monitor (NT Server) are tools provided by Microsoft to watch everything that is going on in the system. The operating system also offers other reporting mechanisms that you will also be exploring.

Using Performance/System Monitor

The monitoring tools that ship with Microsoft operating systems are built upon as you install individual application software packages. Each software package places additional information in the form of counters and interfaces into the available System Monitor tool. The following list represents the SQL Server objects that are installed for the use of the Windows 2000 System Monitor and NT Server Performance Monitor tools and what the counter provides:

- **Access Methods.** Allocation of SQL Server database objects.

- **Backup Device.** Information about backup devices.

- **Buffer Manager.** Information about the memory buffers used by SQL Server.

- **Cache Manager.** Information about the SQL Server cache.

- **Databases.** Information about a SQL Server database.

- **General Statistics.** Information about general server-wide activity.

- **Latches.** Information about the latches on internal resources.

- **Locks.** Information about the individual lock requests made by SQL Server.

- **Memory Manager.** Information about SQL Server memory usage.

- ◆ **Replication Agents.** Information about the SQL Server replication agents.

- ◆ **Replication Dist.** The number of commands and transactions read from the Distributor database and delivered to the Subscriber databases by the Distribution Agent.

- ◆ **Replication Logreader.** The number of commands and transactions read from the published databases and delivered to the distribution database by the Log Reader agent.

- ◆ **Replication Merge.** Information about SQL Server merge replication.

- ◆ **Replication Snapshot.** Information about SQL Server snapshot replication.

- ◆ **SQL Statistics.** Provides information about aspects of SQL queries.

- ◆ **User Settable Object.** Allows for custom monitoring. Each counter can be a custom-stored procedure or any T-SQL statement that returns a value to be monitored.

Each object contains a variety of counters, and there can be multiple instances for many of the objects. These aspects are important when it comes to determining what exactly to monitor. In addition, the operating system will only provide a higher level of information. If you need information like tracking the SQL Server objects and the events that they fire, you should be using one of the tools provided with SQL Server that will drill down into the specifics of any condition.

If you would like to monitor the basics of the system (disk, CPU, and memory), the set of counters provided by the operating system can be used without the specific SQL Server counters. An illustration of this is provided in SQL Server Books Online under "Monitoring with System Monitor."

To observe the true value of this tool, you will have to explore different combinations of counters to learn the causes and effects of particular server situations. Step by Step 12.2 uses a common set of counters that can be used as a starting point in monitoring performance.

STEP BY STEP

12.2 Using the Windows 2000 System Monitor.

1. From the Windows Start, Administrative Tools menu, select Performance to open the System Monitor.

2. Select the PLUS/Add button in the toolbar to bring up the Object/Counter selection interface.

3. Select the following counters by finding the object in the drop-down list box and selecting the counter from the list of available counters. Select the Add button. When you have finished, close the window.

- `SQLServer:Buffer Manager: Buffer cache hit ratio`

- `SQLServer:Buffer Manager:Page Reads/sec`

- `SQLServer:Buffer Manager:Page Writes/sec`

- `SQLServer:General Statistics:User Connections`

- `SQLServer:Memory Manager:Total Server Memory(KB)`

- `SQLServer:SQLStatistics:SQL Compilations/sec`

4. Note that if you are performing this exercise on a test machine, there will be little activity shown. To produce a load on the system, you have to start an instance of the Query Analyzer, provide the connection information if necessary, and enter some data queries.

In general, when you select an object the most frequently used counter comes up as the default for the object, although many other frequently used counters are also available.

It can be useful to monitor Windows 2000 and SQL Server counters at the same time. This can help you determine any relevance between the performance of SQL Server and Windows. Monitoring a computer using System Monitor can slightly impact the performance of the computer. Monitor only the counters that need monitoring; too many counters adds excessive overhead.

Counter Values

Disk, CPU, and memory utilization are some of the primary reasons for using the System Monitor. The exam will test by asking you to recognize when the counter values are too high. Two of the primary counters that can be monitored to determine disk activity are the `PhysicalDisk: % Disk Time` and `PhysicalDisk: Avg. Disk Queue Length`.

The `% Disk Time` counter monitors the percentage of time that the disk is busy reading or writing information. If the counter value is more than 90%, this would indicate abnormally high usage. The `Current Disk Queue Length` counter enables you to see how many system requests are waiting for the disk subsystem. The number of waiting requests should never be more than 1.5 to 2 times the number of spindles in the actual physical disk. Most disks have one spindle, although RAID volumes almost always have more.

CPU usage rates can be monitored to determine the processing use of the server. This could help you determine whether a server is trying to perform too much or whether the server could handle more duties. A continually high rate may indicate a CPU upgrade is needed or you need to provide for additional processors. Conversely, a high CPU usage rate may actually be an indication of a poorly tuned system or inefficient application design. A consistently low value could indicate that you have too much server for the task at hand (a rather nice situation to find yourself in).

A good way to determine CPU utilization is to monitor `Processor:% Processor Time` counter. The `% Processor Time` counter monitors the amount of time the CPU spends processing. A consistent state of 80–90% indicates problems. For multiprocessor systems, a separate instance of this counter should be monitored for each processor. This value represents the sum of processor time on a specific processor. To determine the average for all processors, use the `System: %Total Processor Time` counter instead.

Additionally, CPU counters that are valuable in the monitoring process are `Processor: % Privileged Time`, `Processor: %User Time`, and `System: Processor Queue Length`. The `% Privileged Time` counter represents the time the processor is spending executing operating system commands. If this counter is consistently high when the `Physical Disk` counter is high, consider a faster or more efficient disk subsystem. The `% User Time` counter measures the time the processor is spending executing user processes such as SQL Server and other applications. The "Processor: Queue Length" counter corresponds to the number of threads waiting for processor time.

When you examine processor usage, consider the type of work that SQL Server is performing and the period in time for which a sample was taken. You can help processor overuse by balancing the workload over several machines. Values around 100%, where many client requests are executing, may indicate that processes are queuing up. Resolve this type of problem by adding more powerful processors or simply more processors.

Monitoring memory usage involves considerations for RAM and Disk Subsystem (remember we are talking about a virtual memory operating system). In general, the `Memory: Available Bytes` and `Memory: Pages/sec` counters are quick indicators of potential problems. `Available Bytes` indicates how much memory is available for use. `Pages/sec` shows the number of pages either retrieved or written to disk.

Low values for the Available Bytes counter can indicate that there is an overall shortage of memory on the computer or that an application running on the server is not releasing memory. A high rate for the `Pages/sec` counter could indicate excessive paging. Monitor the `Memory: Page Faults/sec` when monitoring disk activity to make sure that the disk activity is not caused by paging.

A low rate of paging is typical, even if the computer has plenty of available memory. To determine whether SQL Server, rather than another process, is causing excessive paging, monitor the `Process: Page Faults/sec` counter for the SQL Server process instance.

To isolate the memory used by SQL Server over other applications and processes, you must consider the fact that normally SQL Server changes its memory requirements dynamically, based on available resources and actual needs. If SQL Server needs more memory, it queries the operating system and uses the memory if it is available. When a determination is made by SQL Server that it no longer needs the memory, it releases it back to the operating system. If this option has been overridden using the Min Server Memory, Max Server Memory, and Set Working Set Size server configuration options, then SQL Server may not be using memory as efficiently as it could. These options should be adjusted only when you have a dedicated SQL Server, and you also have knowledge of all application interactions.

To monitor the amount of memory being used by SQL Server you should refer to the `Process: Working Set`, `SQL Server: Buffer Manager: Buffer Cache Hit Ratio`, `SQL Server: Buffer Manager: Total Pages`, `SQL Server: Memory Manager: Total Server Memory (KB)` counters.

`Working Set` shows the amount of memory used by a process. If this number is consistently below the memory SQL Server is configured to use, SQL Server is configured for more memory than it needs. Buffer Cache Hit Ratio is application-specific. A rate of 90% or higher is desirable. Add more memory until the value is consistently greater than 90%. If the Total Server Memory (KB) counter is consistently high compared to the amount of physical memory in the computer, it may indicate that more memory is required.

The Event Viewer

The Microsoft Event Viewer tool is provided with all NT and Windows 2000 operating systems. This tool monitors events and records information in application, security, and system logs. It also categorizes and stores information pertaining to the networking security and application services. The application log contains events logged by application programs such as SQL Server. The security log (if events are being audited) contains valid and invalid logon attempts, as well as events related to resource use. The system log contains events logged by the operating system components.

From the Event Viewer you can quickly spot problems and diagnose the series of steps that led up to any given situation. The event viewer has options available for you to filter events to specific categories and severity. You can also select other computers to view and find out additional information about any event.

To see only the desired events, you need to configure a view for the log with the appropriate selections. If you view the properties of any of the logs, you can find general and filter information under the appropriate tabs. In the General tab you can see and set pertinent information for the log itself. The Filter tab, as displayed in Figure 12.1, can be used to view only the desired errors.

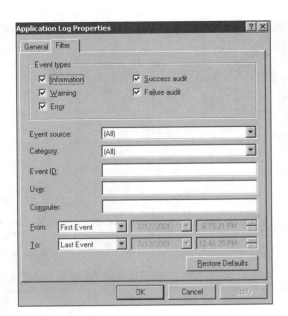

FIGURE 12.1
The Filter dialog box for event viewer logs.

Figure 12.2 represents a sample of the application log with only the MSSQLSERVER events that are non-informational.

Of course on every server the goal is to avoid the yellow yield sign and the red circular X flags. In any system these represent potential problems. A warning message indicates something went wrong but the system was able to work around it. A red flag indicates that administrative effort is needed to resolve a more serious problem.

Reporting to the Event Viewer by SQL Server is made to the application event log. Use this log when looking for messages sent by any of the SQL Server related services.

The Windows Application Log

The application log records events that pertain to SQL Server, using any of the following sources:

◆ MSSQLSERVER. This is the primary source for event information and, along with SQLSERVERAGENT, will be responsible for most of your diagnostic focus. The SQL Server service manages all the database files used by an instance of SQL Server. It is the component that processes all statements sent from client applications. The service allocates resources between users and enforces business rules as defined.

FIGURE 12.2
Application log with Warning and Error messages.

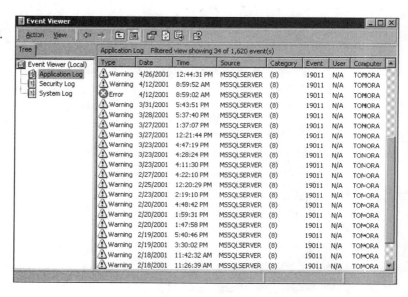

◆ **SQLSERVERAGENT.** The SQL Server agent supports the non-data-specific activity in an installation. It is involved in the scheduling of activities, notification of problems, and definition of important contact personnel. This is done in the form of Jobs, Schedules, Operators, and Alerts.

◆ **MSSQLServerOLAPService.** The primary service used in OLAP (OnLine Analytical Processing) to manage statistical operations between data cubes.

◆ **MSDTC.** The Microsoft Distributed Transaction Coordinator is an operating service accessed by SQL Server for coordinating transaction atomicity across multiple data resources using a two-phase commit. You can enable distributed transaction support in applications by using the appropriate distributed transaction identifiers around the block of code to be handled by MSDTC similar to the following:

```
BEGIN DISTRIBUTED TRANSACTION
        /* Commands used in the
           distributed transaction */
END DISTRIBUTED TRANSACTION
```

◆ **MSSQLServerADHelper.** The MSSQLServerADHelper service performs the two functions necessary for active directory integration. It adds and removes objects used in Active Directory, and it ensures that the Windows account under which a SQL Server service is running has permissions to update the Active Directory objects.

- ◆ `SQLServerProfiler`. SQL Server and Profiler interface operations.

- ◆ `SQLCTR`. Performance/System Monitor interface operations.

- ◆ `SQLFTHNDLR`. Full Text query handler.

Of course, if you are running multiple versions of SQL Server on the same machines, you will see these also represented as information sources. Some of these sources do not show up on all installations. If a server is not using an aspect of SQL Server, then that source does not report any information. Now that the hardware and operating system interactions have been addressed, it's time to move into the server itself to begin a more granular look.

Query Governor Cost Limit

The query governor cost limit is a configuration option available for limiting the length of time a query will be allowed to run. The option, when set, specifies an upper limit for the time in which a query can run based on a costs estimate. The option does not actually cancel a long running query, but it prevents a query from starting if the estimated elapsed time, in seconds, required to execute a query is larger than the setting allows.

The query estimate is based on the specific hardware configuration of the server. A query that is permitted on one machine may not be permitted on another, even though both machines have the same setting for this option.

If you specify any positive value for this setting, the query governor disallows execution of any query that has an estimated cost exceeding the configured value. If you leave the setting at the default value of 0 (zero) the query governor is disabled and all queries are permitted.

If you use `sp_configure` or the server properties of the Enterprise Manager to change the value of the query governor cost limit, the value affects all queries run on the server. It is possible to change the value on a session-by-session basis by using the `SET QUERY_GOVERNOR_COST_LIMIT` statement in a single connection.

OPTIMIZING SQL SERVER CONFIGURATION

▶ **Optimize programming objects. Objects include stored procedures, transactions, triggers, user-defined functions, and views.**

A number of tools, utilities, and information sources are built in to SQL Server to help you optimize SQL Server operations. These mechanisms can be used to diagnose, maintain, and optimize all operations.

To obtain immediate information about the server, you can observe the current activity using the Enterprise Manager or stored procedures. To observe information from a historical perspective, you can view the SQL Server Logs from the Enterprise Manager.

Current Server Activity

The SQL Server Enterprise Manager provides a facility where an administrator can go to find out pertinent information about what the server is currently doing. Use the Current Activity window to perform monitoring of SQL Server. This enables you to determine, at a glance, the volume and general types of activity on the system related to current blocked and blocking transactions in the system, connected users, the last statement executed, and locks that are currently in effect.

The Current Activity view provides a display of process information, locks broken down by process identification, and locks broken down by object.

Process Information

The process information provides information on all activity currently executing against the system. It also lists current connections that may not be active but are still using resources. Here are descriptions of the process information columns:

◆ **Process ID.** SQL Server Process Identifier.

◆ **Context ID.** Execution Context Identifier, used to uniquely identify the sub-threads operating on behalf of the process.

◆ **User.** Identifier of the user who executed the command.

◆ **Database.** Database currently being used by the process.

◆ **Status.** Status of the process.

◆ **Open Transactions.** Number of open transactions.

◆ **Command.** Command currently being executed.

◆ **Application.** Name of the application program being used.

◆ **Wait Time.** Current wait time in milliseconds. When the process is not waiting, the wait time is zero.

◆ **Wait Type.** Indicates the name of the last or current wait type.

◆ **Wait Resources.** Textual representation of a lock resource.

◆ **CPU.** Cumulative CPU time for the process.

◆ **Physical IO.** Cumulative disk reads and writes.

◆ **Memory Usage.** Number of pages in the procedure cache that are currently allocated. A negative number indicates that the process is freeing memory allocated by another process.

◆ **Login Time.** Time at which a client process logged in to the server.

◆ **Last Batch.** Last time a client process executed a remote stored procedure call or an EXECUTE statement.

◆ **Host.** Name of the workstation.

◆ **Network Library.** Column in which the client's network library is stored. Every client process comes in on a network connection. Network connections have a network library associated with them that enables them to make the connection.

◆ **Network Address.** Assigned unique identifier for the network interface card on each user's workstation.

◆ **Blocked By.** Process ID (SPID) of a blocking process.

◆ **Blocking.** Process ID (SPID) of processes that are blocked.

> **NOTE**
>
> **CPU Returning Zero** The CPU entry is updated only for processes performed on behalf of T-SQL statements executed when SET STATISTICS TIME ON has been activated in the same session. When zero is returned, SET STATISTICS TIME is OFF. CPU time for each process is accumulated regardless of the statistics setting.

A significant amount of information is available about each of the processes utilizing the SQL Server database system. Each process also controls SQL Server locking behavior.

Lock Information

Locking information provides information on all locks currently being used by SQL Server to protect the object and data integrity of all SQL Server objects. Here are descriptions of the lock information columns:

◆ `spid`. Server process ID of the current user process.

◆ `ecid`. Execution context ID. Represents the ID of a given thread associated with a specific spid.

◆ `Lock type`. Any of a number of available types. Lock types are listed and defined later in this unit.

◆ `Lock mode`. The level a lock has been given according to the needs of the process. Lock modes are defined later in this unit.

◆ `Status`. Whether or not a lock was obtained (`GRANT`) or is being blocked (`WAIT`) or converted (`CNVT`).

◆ `Owner`. The lock owner.

◆ `Index`. The index associated with the resource. If the index is clustered, you see the table name instead.

◆ `Resource`. Resource being locked.

There are several available lock types and lockable SQL Server resource:

◆ `RID`. Row identifier. Used to lock a single row individually within a table. This is identified by a `fileid:page:rid` combination, where `rid` is the row identifier on the page.

◆ `KEY`. Key; a row lock within an index. Used to protect key ranges in serializable transactions. This is represented as a hexadecimal number used internally by SQL Server.

◆ `PAG`. Data or index page. The page is identified by a `fileid:page` combination, where `fileid` is the file id in the `sysfiles` table, and `page` is the logical page number within that file.

◆ EXT. Contiguous group of eight data pages or index pages. The first page number in the extent being locked. The page is identified by a `fileid:page` combination.

◆ TAB. Entire table, including all data and indexes. The `ObjId` column contains the object ID of the table.

◆ DB. Database; the `dbid` column contains the database ID of the database.

Several lock modes control how SQL Server sets and recognizes locks, blocking, and user access. Lock modes represent levels of locking from the lowest level—shared—to the highest level—exclusive.

◆ Shared (S). Used for operations that do not change or update data.

◆ Update (U). Used on resources that can be updated.

◆ Exclusive (X). Used for data modification operations.

◆ Intent (I). Used to establish a lock hierarchy.

◆ Schema. Used when an operation dependent on the schema of a table is executing. There are two types of schema locks: schema stability (Sch-S) and schema modification (Sch-M).

◆ Bulk update (BU). Used when bulk copying data into a table and the TABLOCK hint is specified.

◆ RangeS_S. Shared range, shared resource lock; serializable range scan.

◆ RangeS_U. Shared range, update resource lock; serializable update scan.

◆ RangeI_N. Insert range, null resource lock. Used to test ranges before inserting a new key into an index.

◆ RangeX_X. Exclusive range, exclusive resource lock. Used when updating a key in a range.

Locks are set at different modes as needed to allow for data updates, index creation, and table redefinition. An example of locking used during an update process is shown in Step by Step 12.3.

continued

STEP BY STEP

12.3 Viewing Lock Behavior

1. Start the Enterprise Manager and expand your server and the Management folder.

2. Expand the Current Activity Store to view the current processes in use on the system and any locks currently in place because of server activity.

3. Click on Process Info and size the columns in the right pane so that you can simultaneously view Process ID, User, Database, and Status. Make a note of the highest process identification number.

4. Start an instance of the Query Analyzer from the Windows Start menu and provide connection information if needed. Select the Northwind database from the drop-down menu at the top of the screen.

5. Return to the Enterprise Manager, leaving the Query Analyzer window open, right-click on Current Activity, and select Refresh.

6. Click on Process Info and notice the new processes added and the databases in use for the instance of the Query Analyzer you have started.

7. Expand Locks/Process ID and locate the process identification number for the Query Analyzer.

8. Notice the lock in place for the Northwind database. Also note that the type of lock is DB (database) and the mode the lock is S (shared). This is the lowest locking level that allows other user activity to resume normally.

9. Return to the Query Analyzer and enter the following code to begin a transaction and hold a data update without committing it:

```
BEGIN TRANSACTION
UPDATE Customers
     SET ContactName = 'Maria Anderson'
     WHERE CustomerID = 'ALFKI'
```

continues

10. Return to the Enterprise Manager, leaving the Query Analyzer window open, right-click on Current Activity, and select Refresh.

11. Expand Locks/Process ID and locate the process identification number for the Query Analyzer.

12. Now notice the additional locks held until the update is committed. These locks will prevent any other process from updating the data until the current update is finished.

13. Return to the query analyzer and execute a COMMIT TRANSACION statement.

14. Refresh the locking information in the Enterprise Manager to ensure all locks are removed.

Only compatible lock types can be placed on a resource that is already locked. Table 12.1 provides a compatibility matrix for resource lock modes that shows which locks are compatible with other locks obtained on the same resource.

TABLE 12.1

LOCK COMPUTABILITY MATRIX

Requested Lock Mode	Existing Granted Lock Mode					
	IS	S	U	IX	SIX	X
Intent Shared (IS)	✓	✓	✓	✓	✓	X
Shared (S)	✓	✓	✓	X	X	X
Update (U)	✓	✓	X	X	X	X
Intent Exclusive (IX)	✓	X	X	✓	X	X
Shared with Intent Exclusive (SIX)	✓	X	X	X	X	X
Exclusive (X)	X	X	X	X	X	X

The compatibility matrix indicates whether a specific type of lock can be granted with another already in place.

Some of the same information seen in the Current Activity window can also be retrieved programmatically using stored procedures. Stored procedures play an important part in developing system code to aid in server management.

Stored Procedures

Stored procedures can be used to perform data gathering in much the same manner that the Enterprise Manager uses to gather its information to display to the user. By querying system objects, functions, and counters, the stored procedures produce output that can be used directly, or they can perform other conditional activity through the systematic use of the results. Much system level coding can be developed by leveraging the procedures that already exist.

Hundreds of available stored procedures are installed with SQL Server, as well as a few dozen extended stored procedures. Not all these procedures are used in data gathering, troubleshooting, and optimization, but many provide information that assists in these activities.

Stored procedures are stored in the Master and user databases, whereas extended stored procedures are found in only the Master database. Additional stored procedures can be created, and additional extended stored procedures can be installed. A selection of the more commonly used procedures is covered in this section. For more information on these and other procedures, refer to stored procedures coverage in SQL Server Books Online.

sp_who

This procedure reports current information about users and processes, including the executing statement and whether the statement is blocked. This is a T-SQL alternative to viewing user activity in the Enterprise Manager.

The resultset provided by this procedure provides user and process information, including the process identification and status information, as well as an ID for any blocking process. Also provided from the command is the database in use and the T-SQL command that is executing.

sp_lock

This procedure reports information about locks and the resources affected by locking. This is a T-SQL alternative to viewing lock activity in the Enterprise Manager.

It provides a resultset similar to the one displayed in the Enterprise Manager, listing all relevant locks, their status, mode, and resources being affected.

sp_monitor

This procedure displays statistics, including CPU usage, I/O usage, and the amount of time idle since the stored procedure was last executed.

A variety of information is produced in the resultset for this command. The time of execution of sp_monitor, the number of seconds that SQL Server has been working, the number of seconds that SQL Server has been performing input and output operations, and the number of seconds that SQL Server has been idle provide information that can be useful in determining whether processing resources are adequate.

The number of input packets read by SQL Server, output packets written by SQL Server, and errors encountered by SQL Server while reading and writing packets can help you determine SQL Server's network utilization.

The number of reads by SQL Server, number of writes, and the number of errors encountered by SQL Server while reading and writing can help you determine file storage interactions.

Knowing the number of logins or attempted logins to SQL Server can be useful in security information gathering or as an aid in determining SQL Server utilization.

sp_spaceused

This procedure displays an estimate of the current amount of disk space used by a table or database. This is a T-SQL alternative to viewing database usage in the Enterprise Manager. With sp_spaceused you can easily see the number of rows, disk space reserved, and disk space used by a table in the current database, or display the disk space reserved and used by the entire database.

xp_sqlmaint

This is an extended stored procedure that calls the SQL maintenance utility. Passed during the call to this utility is a string containing switches that indicate the tasks to be performed and other related details. The sqlmaint utility performs a set of maintenance operations on one or more databases, in a similar fashion as each operation's corresponding T-SQL functions.

The sqlmaint utility performs maintenance operations on one or more databases. Use sqlmaint to run DBCC checks, back up a database and its transaction log, update statistics, and rebuild indexes. The utility performs database maintenance activities and generates a report. The report can be sent to a designated text file, HTML file, or email account.

sp_configure

This stored procedure is used to display and/or alter global configuration settings for the server. When executed with no parameters, the stored procedure returns a resultset showing the current configuration options.

After you execute the procedure to change a configuration option, you should use the RECONFIGURE WITH OVERRIDE statement for the change to take immediate effect.

sp_dboption

This procedure is used to display and/or alter database options. It is supported for backward compatibility, and you should therefore use ALTER DATABASE to set database options.

sp_help

This procedure reports information about an object listed in the sysobjects table. In general, you can tack any object name to the end of help to receive help and information about a particular type of object, such as sp_helpalert, sp_helpfilegroup, sp_helpserver, and sp_helpuser. Over 100 stored procedures have the sp_help prefix.

SQL Profiler Stored Procedures and Functions

Use T-SQL stored procedures to gather SQL Profiler statistics. The SQL Profiler uses stored procedures to create traces and send the trace output to the appropriate location. These procedures can be used from within an application to create traces manually. This enables you to write custom applications specific to the needs of your business.

In SQL Server version 7.0, these procedures were all prefixed with xp_trace. The features of many of these procedures have been combined, and in the 2000 release there are fewer, more streamlined procedures, as summarized in the following list:

- ◆ fn_trace_geteventinfo. Returns information about the events traced.

- ◆ fn_trace_getfilterinfo. Returns information about the filters applied to a trace.

- ◆ fn_trace_getinfo. Returns information about a trace.

- ◆ sp_trace_create. Creates a trace definition. The new trace is created in a stopped state.

- ◆ sp_trace_generateevent. Creates a user-defined event.

- ◆ sp_trace_setevent. Adds or removes an event or event column. May be executed only on an existing stopped trace. SQL Server returns an error if this stored procedure is executed on a trace that does not exist or is not stopped.

- ◆ sp_trace_setfilter. Applies a filter to a trace. May only be executed on an existing stopped trace.

- ◆ sp_trace_setstatus. Modifies the current state of the specified trace. Stops, starts, or deletes the trace definition.

Using these stored procedures, you can configure and execute traces and forward trace events from one or more servers to a file.

Finding the Facts

Now you have examined everything in a SQL Server installation, using all but the two most diverse and granular tools, Query Analyzer and Profiler. Gathering information from the operating system tools and the server activity procedures and displays plays an important part in the initial fact-finding that must be performed to alter any of the properties of the server.

The processes discussed thus far are often used in an implementation as a starting point toward:

▶ Development of system documentation

▶ Establishing record keeping procedures

▶ Troubleshooting system problems

▶ Optimizing the database server

▶ Tracking data trends

As you begin any of these processes, begin with the hardware and operating system and then proceed into the application server. As you get further into data gathering and analysis, you should look into each database and the interactions between the data and user applications. To view SQL Server tasks in detail, after the initial data gathering processes, use the SQL Server Profiler to develop a more complete picture. When more granularity is desired and you want to look into the user applications, the functionality provided by the Query Analyzer can be used to obtain the most detailed and granular data.

MONITOR ACTIVITY WITH THE PROFILER

▶ **Monitor and troubleshoot database activity by using SQL Profiler.**

The SQL Profiler tool is a graphical mechanism that enables you to monitor SQL Server events. The tool enables you to capture and save data about every event on the server. The data can be stored to a file or SQL Server table. Stored data can then be analyzed and events can be replayed.

The SQL Profiler should be used to monitor only the events of interest. Monitoring all events on the server produces so much data that the data can become overwhelming. Large traces can be filtered so that you are viewing only the information you want to see. You can use filters to view a subset of the event data that was captured. Monitoring too many events also adds excessive amounts of overhead to the server. This overhead can slow the monitoring process and cause the large amounts of output from the trace to create a file or table that is very large. This is particularly important when you are going to be performing the monitoring over long periods.

SQL Profiler is a useful tool for a number of circumstances. Use SQL Profiler to:

◆ Monitor the performance of SQL Server.

◆ Debug T-SQL statements and stored procedures.

◆ Identify long-running queries.

◆ Step through procedures to ensure that they are working as expected.

◆ Capture events on a production system and replay them on a test system.

◆ Diagnose problem situations through the capturing of event data.

◆ Audit and review events.

In troubleshooting the SQL Server environment, you will typically use the SQL Profiler. The tool is best used to find queries that are not performing well or ones that are executing for long periods of time. It is also useful in identifying the cause of data blocking and deadlock situations. In monitoring a healthy server, the SQL Profiler is generally used to monitor performance and to audit application, user, database, and job activity.

> **NOTE**
>
> **A Monitoring Machine** Don't run the SQL Server 2000 Profiler on the same server you are monitoring. Running the Profiler uses considerable resources and this can noticeably affect the server's performance. Instead, run it on another server or workstation acting as a monitoring machine and have all data collected there.

Before you start using the Profiler, you should become familiar with profile templates. A *template* defines the criteria for each event you want to monitor with SQL Profiler. Predefined templates can be used for individual circumstances, and you can create your own template, as well, specifying which events, data columns, and filters to use. A template can be saved, and at any time a trace can be loaded and started with the template settings. To help identify long-running queries, use the Profiler's Create Trace Wizard to run the "TSQL by Duration" template. You can specify the length of the long-running queries you are trying to identify, and then have these recorded in a log.

The SQL Profiler captures data using a trace based upon the selected events, data columns, and filters. The trace is the basis for all data collected and can be defined on an ad hoc basis, drawn from a template, or a combination of the two. Even though you have defined the data collected, you may still apply filters to the data after it is captured to focus in on the type of information you want. For this reason you may want to save traces even after you are finished with the current activity. A past trace can possibly be used and applied to a number of circumstances.

At times, when monitoring with the Profiler, you will find the amount of data provided to be considerable and possibly overwhelming. It can be difficult to find what you are looking for within a trace that covers a broad range of events. A useful technique that can ease this process is to write the trace to a SQL Server table (see Step by Step 12.4), and then query the table from within the Query Analyzer. Assuming you know what you are looking for, this method can greatly speed up finding the data in the trace you need.

The Profiler can store captured data in a text file or in a table. If you decide to store the data in a SQL Server table, don't store it in a database you are profiling or, if possible, not even on the same server, because it could affect the performance of the server you are profiling. Instead, store the trace data in a database on another server.

After data is captured (which is the easy part of the process), you must sift through the data collected to draw some meaning from the results.

STEP BY STEP

12.4 Creating a Profile Trace

1. Start the SQL Server Profiler from the Start, Programs, Microsoft SQL Server shortcut menu.

2. From the File menu, select New Trace and provide connection information if necessary.

3. In the Trace Properties dialog box, provide a name for the trace, and select SQLProfilerStandard from the Template Name drop-down list box, as displayed in Figure 12.3.

4. Select the Save to File option and select a location in which to store your sample file. (The file can be stored in any location that has sufficient free space. There must always be at least 10MB of free space for storage for the Profiler to run, regardless of any size limits set.)

5. You can view the settings of this template by selecting the Events, Data Columns, and Filters tabs on the dialog box. Leave the remaining entries at their default settings and click Run.

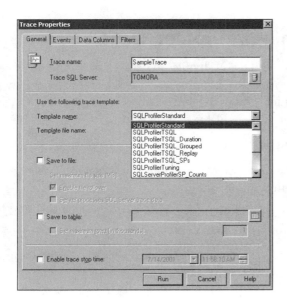

FIGURE 12.3
Trace Properties dialog box.

6. The trace begins to execute and collect data to your storage file. After a few seconds (15–20) stop the trace by selecting the Stop button at the top of the Trace window.

7. Notice that the default template, SQLProfilerStandard, gathered information on Existing Sessions, Stored Procedures, T-SQL Statements Completing, and Audit Logins/Logouts.

8. Close/Exit the Profiler window.

The Profiler can use many existing templates to gather information for a variety of types of circumstances. You may want to select some of these templates to see the actual information that is being gathered. After it has been created, the trace is permanently stored until it is deleted. The trace can be started again by name through the Profiler interface or via stored procedure.

To use the output generated by a trace, you must first determine what type of data you are most interested in from the trace. The next section illustrates how to get the most valuable information from the trace results.

Defining a Profiler Trace

When using the SQL Profiler to define a trace, you use event categories to select the events to monitor. Event categories have been grouped into classes of events. The following list of classes and their descriptions are available to be selected:

◆ **Cursors.** Events produced by use of cursors.

◆ **Database.** Events produced when data or log files grow or shrink automatically.

◆ **Errors and Warnings.** Events produced when a SQL Server error or warning occurs.

◆ **Locks.** Events produced when a lock is acquired, cancelled, released, or other lock activity.

◆ **Objects.** Events produced when database objects are created, opened, closed, dropped, or deleted.

◆ **Performance.** Events produced when SQL data manipulation operators execute.

◆ **Scans.** Events produced when tables and indexes are scanned.

◆ **Security Audit.** Events used to audit server activity.

◆ **Sessions.** Events produced by clients connecting and disconnecting.

◆ **Stored Procedures.** Events produced by the execution of stored procedures.

◆ **Transactions.** Events produced by the execution of Microsoft Distributed Transaction Coordinator transactions or by writing to the transaction log.

◆ **TSQL.** Events produced by the execution of T-SQL statements.

◆ **User Configurable.** User-configurable events.

Each event class has a number of different objects that can be monitored. To select any of the objects when defining a trace, use the Events tab of the Trace Properties dialog box as shown in Figure 12.4. You add and remove objects, not whole classes, although a whole class of objects can be traced, if desired.

<table>
<tr><td>EXAM TIP</td><td>**Event Classes** On the exam, you may be expected to select the correct event classes and objects given a specific scenario. Ensure that you are familiar with the classifications of the Profiler trace objects and under what circumstances you would select them. By viewing the objects selected for each of the default templates, you can familiarize yourself with these</td></tr>
</table>

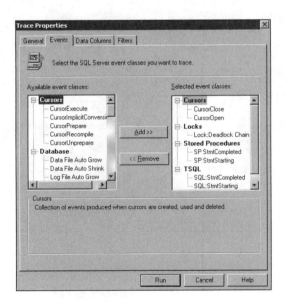

FIGURE 12.4
Trace Properties.

After the objects have been selected, two steps still remain to complete the trace definition: selection of data columns for the trace report and specification of filters to select appropriate data.

The Data Columns tab enables you to select the groupings and columns that will represent how a particular trace report is visually presented. Select the groups of objects that will best suit your needs when the time comes to decipher the output. The data columns selected will be the columns of the report grouped in the manner selected by Groups. A sample grouping and column list definition is illustrated in Figure 12.5.

Grouping by database and object names may not be the desired format for all situations. For example, you may want to group the report by duration to more easily find the statements that execute for the longest time.

The final step in the process of defining a trace is to filter out desired information or set up the filters to focus on only particular information. There are really two approaches to setting filters:

◆ See all information except particular types.

◆ See only information of a particular type.

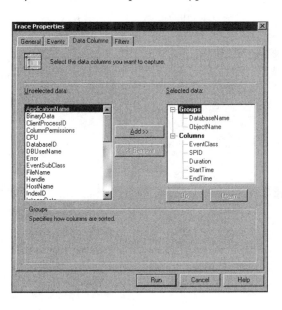

FIGURE 12.5
Trace group and column definition.

Filters can be set to ignore information or to specifically look at information of only a particular nature. By setting filters you can determine
which database(s) to capture, which application, whether system information is to be included in the trace, and so on. Figure 12.6 shows a
filter setting that will not show information for the Pubs database.

After it has been defined, the trace execution gathers results based on
the criteria you have selected. Depending on the amount of data that
has been collected, you will be adding some overhead to the machine
where the trace is executing. It is best, therefore, to select the time
you are going to run the trace, and don't allow it to run longer than
necessary. Also, if you are replaying the trace you should have a test
server available for that purpose.

Viewing the results, then, should bring light to the issues surrounding the reason you decided to trap the data in the first place.

FIGURE 12.6
Filtering out the Pubs database.

Profiler Traces to Diagnose Locking

SQL Profiler provides the Locks event classes to monitor locking
behavior during trace operations. Several of these classes are useful in
monitoring locking, blocking, and deadlocking situations on the
server. The following list represents the classes with a short narrative
description of what each class can be used for:

◆ Lock:Acquired. Shows the acquisition of a resource lock.

◆ `Lock:Cancel`. An event is fired when a lock on a resource has been cancelled. A lock can be cancelled by SQL Server because of a deadlock or by a programmatic cancellation by a process.

◆ `Lock:Deadlock`. A deadlock occurs if two concurrent transactions have deadlocked each other by trying to obtain locks on resources that the other owns.

◆ `Lock:Deadlock Chain`. The chain of events produced for each of the processes leading up to a deadlock situation.

◆ `Lock:Escalation`. An event fired when the server determines that a lock should be converted to a larger scope.

◆ `Lock:Released`. The event fires when a resource lock is released.

◆ `Lock:Timeout`. Fires when a lock request has timed out because another process is blocking a resource with its own lock.

`Lock:Acquired` and `Lock:Released` are used to monitor the timing of lock behavior. These events indicate the type of lock and the length of time the lock was held. Often a redesign of the application that is setting the locks in place can lessen the lock duration considerably.

The `Lock:Deadlock`, `Lock:Deadlock Chain`, and `Lock:Timeout` are used to monitor deadlock and timeout situations. This information is useful to determine whether deadlocks and timeouts are affecting the user and/or application.

Using Profiler Results

The Results window of the SQL Profiler is segmented into two view panes. If you have included `TextData` as one of the columns in your definition, then the bottom pane shows you SQL statement information. The top pane illustrates the current trace data view where event information is displayed based on current filter settings. A sample of trace output in Figure 12.7 illustrates the events from a simple query in the captured results.

After trace event data has been collected, you can save the trace to have it replayed later. The SQL Profiler Playback feature is powerful but carries a little overhead. It is well worth considering having a test machine available to act as a playback and troubleshooting server.

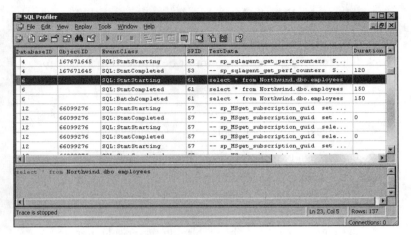

FIGURE 12.7
Sample of trace output in the Profiler window.

Playback of events is accomplished through the SQL Server multi-threaded playback engine. This engine can simulate user connections and SQL Server authentication. The event data can be played back to reproduce the activity captured in the trace. Replay can be very useful in troubleshooting an application or other process problem.

TRACE PLAYBACK AND DIAGNOSIS

▶ **Capture, analyze, and replay SQL Profiler traces. Considerations include lock detection, performance tuning, and trace flags.**

After you have identified the problem and implemented corrections, run the trace that was originally collected against the corrected application or process to see whether the proposed solution accomplishes the desired effect. The replay of the original trace can be a useful mechanism in designing solutions. The trace replay feature has advanced debugging support. You can make use of break points and run-to-cursor features.

To enable playback support for any particular trace, a considerable number of properties must be included in the trace definition.

Playback Requirements

A considerable number of classes must be captured to enable playback. The following event classes must be captured in a trace to allow for replay:

- ◆ Connect
- ◆ CursorExecute (when replaying server-side cursors)
- ◆ CursorOpen (when replaying server-side cursors)
- ◆ CursorPrepare (when replaying server-side cursors)
- ◆ Disconnect
- ◆ Exec Prepared SQL (when replaying server-side prepared SQL statements)
- ◆ ExistingConnection
- ◆ Prepare SQL (when replaying server-side prepared SQL statements)
- ◆ RPC:Starting
- ◆ SQL:BatchStarting

Many data column settings are also mandatory to enable playback capability. The following data columns must be captured in a trace to enable the trace to be replayed:

- ◆ Application Name
- ◆ Binary Data
- ◆ ClientProcessID or SPID
- ◆ Database ID
- ◆ Event Class
- ◆ Event Sub Class
- ◆ Host Name

◆ Integer Data

◆ Server Name

◆ SQL User Name

◆ Start Time

◆ Text

NOTE

Replay Template A trace template has already been prepared that can be used as a starting point for gathering traces to be replayed. The SQLProfilerTSQL_Replay trace has all required properties for traces capturing data for replay.

A variety of login requirements, described in the following list, must be in agreement between the source and target computers to enable the trace to be replayed:

◆ All logins and users contained in the trace must be present on the target.

◆ All logins and users must be in the same database as the source.

◆ All logins and users in the target must have the same permissions as they had in the source.

◆ All login passwords must be the same as the user executing the replay.

When the target computer is going to be other than the computer originally traced, you must ensure that the database IDs on the target are the same as those on the source. You can accomplish this by creating (from the source) a backup of the Master database, as well as any user databases referenced in the trace, and restoring them on the target. In this manner a test SQL Server can be used as a debugging server for any multiple-application environment.

The default database for each login contained in the trace must be set on the target. The default database of the trace activity login must be set to the database that matches that login name, even in cases where the database name might be different. To set the default database of the login, use the sp_defaultdb system stored procedure.

Traces cannot be replayed if the contents of the trace conflicts with security, file, and connection situations that may be specific to the source computer through network, interface, and other identifiers. The following trace content would not enable a trace to be replayed:

◆ Captured from connections using Windows Authentication Mode.

◆ Containing replication and other transaction log activity.

◆ Containing operations that involve globally unique identifiers.

◆ Containing operations on text, ntext, and image columns involving the bcp utility, BULK INSERT, READTEXT, WRITETEXT, and UPDATETEXT statements, and full-text operations.

◆ Containing session binding: sp_getbindtoken and sp_bindsession system stored procedures.

◆ Containing .log file operations that contain SQL Server 6.5 server-side cursor statements (sp_cursor).

Replays are rather involved to configure but are one of the most useful devices available to the administrator or the developer alike.

Performing the Replay

You have a lot of flexibility in playing back events from a captured trace. Replay options enable you to specify a server, output file name, and a variety of other options. Any server specified must meet the replay requirements. The output file will contain the result of replaying the trace. If Progress is selected for the output file, then the output file can also be replayed later.

You have the option of replaying the events in the order they were traced. If selected, this option enables debugging. This enables you to implement debugging techniques such as stepping through the trace. Replaying the events using multiple threads will optimize performance but will disable debugging. The default option is to display the results of the replay. If the trace you want to replay is a large capture, you may want to disable this option to save disk space.

SQL Profiler as an all-around tool is a fully functional system-debugging environment. Now it's time to look next at query analysis and optimizing.

Templates and Wizards for Specific Monitoring

The Profiler and accompanying wizard can be used to assist in index tuning. Use the Profiler's Create Trace Wizard to run the Identify Scans of Large Tables trace. This trace tells which tables are being scanned by queries as an alternative to using an index to seek the data. This should provide you with data you can use to identify which tables may need more or better indexes. Of course, the Index Tuning Wizard is also beneficial for this situation.

To help identify deadlock problems, use the Identify the Cause of a Deadlock trace from the Create Trace Wizard. Other locking problems, as well, can be identified using this trace. The data gathered provides you with the information you need to help isolate the causes of a deadlock.

If you are in need of a trace that focuses on performance problems with stored procedures, run the Profile the Performance of a Stored Procedure trace to provide you with the data you need to identify performance problems within stored procedures.

These and many other templates and wizard options are predefined and available for specific purposes. Often after tracing events, other tools can be used to provide assistance in tuning. Particularly useful for diagnosing and tuning long-running queries is the Query Analyzer. This tool interacts with the SQL Server Optimizer to assist in developing the most efficient means of query execution.

SQL SERVER OPTIMIZER

▶ **Analyze the query execution plan. Considerations include query processor operations and steps.**

The SQL Server Query Optimizer is the database engine component of SQL Server 2000. As the database engine, it oversees all data-related interaction. It is responsible for generating the execution plans for any SQL operation. In diagnosing a query, the Optimizer must decide upon the most efficient means of executing the query and interacting with the database objects.

SQL Server has a cost-based optimizer that can be extremely sensitive to the information provided by statistics. Without accurate and up-to-date statistical information, SQL Server has a great deal of difficulty in determining the best execution plan for a particular query.

Statistics maintained include the following:

◆ Number of rows in the table.

◆ Number of pages used by the table.

◆ Number of modifications made to the keys of the table since the last update of statistics.

◆ An equi-height histogram on the first column of an index.

◆ Densities on all column prefixes in an index.

◆ Average key length for an index.

SQL Server goes through a considerable process when it chooses one execution plan out of several possible methods of executing a given operation. This optimization is one of the most important components of a SQL Server database system. Although some overhead is incurred by the optimizer's analysis process, this overhead is saved in execution.

The optimizer uses a cost-based analysis procedure. Each possible method of execution has an associated cost. This cost is determined in terms of the approximated amount of computing resources used in execution. The query optimizer must analyze the possible plans and choose the one that has the lowest estimated cost.

It is not uncommon for some complex SELECT statements to have thousands of possible plans. Of course in this case, the optimizer does not analyze every possible combination. It uses a complex series of processes to find a plan that has a cost reasonably close to the minimum—a minimum that is only theoretical and unlikely to be achieved.

The query optimizer relies on up-to-date statistical information that is maintained within the meta data of a database system. This information is collected and updated based on changes to the index and data structure. Proper maintenance should ensure that the statistical data is maintained and accurately reflects the current database environment.

The primary tool available for the interaction with the query optimizer is the SQL Query Analyzer, which is an all-in-one T-SQL editor, debugging environment, and object viewer.

Query Analyzer

At this juncture in the book, and in your own experience with SQL Server, you should have begun to master using this tool to enter SQL. The object browser and templates, color-coded entry environment, variety of display formats, and powerful toolset all make the tool a mandatory element of an administrator's or programmer's toolset.

Now that you are familiar with the tool, it is time to turn it into one of the most important elements of the application diagnostic and performance-tuning framework. Capable of reaching into individual commands and objects, this tool provides for the finest level of granularity and deepest interaction with the SQL Server architecture.

SQL Query Analyzer can be used to gain access to SQL Server meta data and can tear a query down into its individual objects for analysis. For any given query, you can make a number of view changes to see the execution plan, server trace, and/or client statistics if desired. When these options are on, extra tabs are added to the output pane as illustrated in Figure 12.8.

The Grids tab displays the output of the statement(s) executed. The Execution Plan tab graphically illustrates the method used to execute the query. The Trace tab displays the processes needed on the server to perform the command. The Statistics tab displays the application, network, and time statistics. The Messages tab is used to display any user feedback from the command(s) executed.

When viewing an execution plan, you have the capability of representing the activity the optimizer needs to perform in a graphic set of icons. To accompany the graphic is a set of statistics that goes along with that portion of the operation.

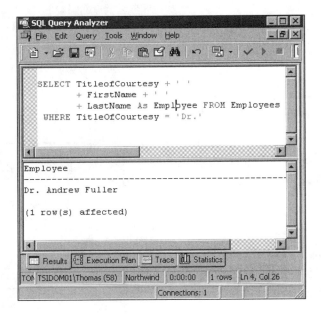

FIGURE 12.8
Query Analyzer—full tab display.

Query Execution Plans

The Execution Plan options graphically display the data retrieval methods chosen by the query optimizer. The graphical execution plan uses icons to represent the execution of specific statements and queries in SQL Server, rather than the tabular text representation produced by the SET SHOWPLAN_ALL or SET SHOWPLAN_TEXT statements. Analysis of a query plan is a very important process that helps you understand the performance characteristics of a query.

An execution plan is particularly useful in determining the steps a complex query needs to take. See Figure 12.9 for a sample query that displays invoice information from combining data from six separate tables.

The actual steps needed to solve the query aren't very obvious. It is easier to see the work involved by looking at the plan SQL Server uses to display the data as illustrated in Figure 12.10.

The graphical plan is read from right to left and from top to bottom. Each query in the batch that is analyzed is displayed, including the cost of each query as a percentage of the total cost of the batch.

```
SELECT O.ShipName, O.ShipAddress, O.ShipCity, O.ShipRegion, O.ShipPostalCode, O.ShipCountry,
       O.CustomerID, C.CompanyName, C.Address, C.City, C.Region, C.PostalCode, C.Country,
       (FirstName + ' ' + LastName) AS Salesperson, O.OrderID, O.OrderDate, O.RequiredDate,
       O.ShippedDate, S.CompanyName 'Shipper', OD.ProductID, P.ProductName, OD.UnitPrice,
       OD.Quantity, OD.Discount,
       (CONVERT(money,(OD.UnitPrice*Quantity*(1-Discount)/100))*100) AS Price, O.Freight
FROM Shippers S
    INNER JOIN (Products P
    INNER JOIN (Employees E
    INNER JOIN (Customers C
    INNER JOIN Orders O ON C.CustomerID = O.CustomerID)
    ON E.EmployeeID = O.EmployeeID)
    INNER JOIN "Order Details" OD ON O.OrderID = OD.OrderID)
    ON P.ProductID = OD.ProductID)
    ON S.ShipperID = O.ShipVia
```

FIGURE 12.9
Complex join operation to print invoice data.

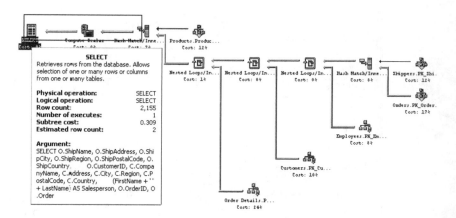

FIGURE 12.10
Execution Plan for Invoice Query.

Reading Execution Plans

The graphical execution represents an execution plan with icons, whereas the SET SHOWPLAN_ALL or SET SHOWPLAN_TEXT statements use a tabular representation. Each of these mechanisms enable you to look under the hood of the server to see what is actually occurring. The exam will expect you to be able to look at any of these outputs and decipher what is happening. You will also have to provide recommendations for improvement(s). Being able to see behind the scenes is very useful for understanding the performance characteristics of a query. The showplan icons are illustrated in Figure 12.11.

Many potential processes are represented in Figure 12.11. Some of these processes are discussed in full in this chapter because they pertain to material you are likely to find on the exam. For information on other processes, you should refer to SQL Server Books Online.

Each of the icons specifies a logical and physical operation. An execution plan will have any number of icons dependent upon the number of operations needed to perform the query. A single query—even a simple one—will have a number of icons, each used to represent a part of the query or statement.

Each node is related to a parent node. All nodes with the same parent are drawn in the same column. Rules with arrowheads connect each node to its parent. Recursive operations are shown with an iteration symbol, and operators are shown as symbols related to a specific parent. When the query contains multiple statements, multiple query execution plans are drawn.

Execution Plan Caching and Sharing

The memory used by SQL Server is divided among a number of processes. A pool of this memory is divided between the storage of execution plans and allocation of data buffers. The actual division between the two varies significantly depending on the system use. The portion of this memory pool that is used to store execution plans is referred to as the *procedure cache*. The data buffers are similarly called the *data cache*. In any given execution plan there are two main components: the plan itself and the context on which the query was executed.

The majority of the plan is a read-only structure that can be used by any number of applications, connections, and users. No actual user

FIGURE 12.11
Graphical showplan icons.

Bookmark Lookup Operation   One of the execution plan processes that you may run into on the exam is the Bookmark Lookup operation. This operation performs a data find operation using a bookmark (row ID or clustering key), and this value is used to look up the corresponding row in the table or clustered index.

context is stored within the plan itself. The execution context is a data structure stored for each user currently running the query associated with the plan. This area stores any data specific to a single use, such as parameter values.

When a query is executed, the server first looks through the procedure cache to verify that a plan already exists. If present, the plan is reused. This reuse of execution plans saves on the overhead associated with recompiling the query. If no plan exists, the server generates a new one. SQL Server 2000 has integrated logic that enables a plan to be shared between connections without requiring that an application prepare the statement.

In rare instances you may be able to apply index and other optimizer hints to change the way a query is performed. The optimizer in most cases produces the best plan, and attempts at bettering the plan don't usually provide any gains.

Optimizer Hints

A "hint" is a method of providing information in the SQL syntax that tells the query optimizer to use a specific plan rather than the one it may normally choose. Index, join, locking, query, table, and views all can be supplied with hint information to be passed to the query analyzer. Table 12.2 lists the options available for join, query, and table hints:

TABLE 12.2

SQL SERVER QUERY HINTS

Hint Type	Option	Description
Join	LOOP|HASH|MERGE|REMOTE	Provides joining strategy option.
Query	{HASH|ORDER}GROUP	Selects hashing or ordering to be used in a COMPUTE GROUP BY and COMPUTE aggregations functions.
Query	{MERGE|HASH|CONCAT}UNION	Provides strategy for method used to perform UNION operations.
Query	FAST *integer*	Optimizes for retrieval of a specific number of rows.
Query	FORCE ORDER	Mandates the joins in the order the tables appear in the query

continues

TABLE 12.2	*continued*

SQL SERVER QUERY HINTS

Hint Type	*Option*	*Description*
Query	ROBUST PLAN	Creates a plan that accommodates maximum potential row size in bytes.
Table	FASTFIRSTROW	Has the same effect as the FAST 1 query hint.
Table	INDEX =	Instructs SQL Server to use the specified index rather than select its own index.
Table	HOLDLOCK|SERIALIZABLE| REPEATABLEREAD|READCOMMITTED| READUNCOMMITTED|NOLOCK	Specifies the data isolation level used for a table locking and lock bypass purposes.
Table	ROWLOCK|PAGLOCK|TABLOCK| TABLOCKX|NOLOCK	Specifies locking granularity.
Table	READPAST	Skips locked rows altogether.
Table	UPDLOCK	Takes update locks rather than shared locks. Cannot be used with NOLOCK or XLOCK.
Table	XLOCK	Takes an exclusive lock held until the end of the transaction. Cannot be used with NOLOCK or UPDLOCK.

Hints can provide additional control over the individual operations performed by the optimizer in the act of retrieving data with a query. Though not necessarily used to improve performance, hints are used for changing the action that would normally be taken. Hints can provide additional functionality that enables system-level applications to be designed that may need access to data beyond the capabilities of a standard data read. In most cases, the use of hints is not recommended because the optimizer usually selects the best mechanism to retrieve the data from a given query.

SET Options

The SET command is used to alter the current session handling of specific information. Many different facilities are affected by the SET command. Each of the options provides a setting for the current session that changes that aspect of the interaction with the server.

SET options are grouped into many categories; each category has several statements that affect the format of the display to the user, the data that is actually displayed, and/or the interaction with the server. The categories covered by SET operations are as follows:

◆ **Date and Time.** Controls the format of the date and/or configures what is to be treated as the first day of the week.

◆ **Locking.** Controls the way the session reacts to a deadlock and/or the amount of wait time before a lock is released.

◆ **Query Execution.** Handles the treatment of errors in mathematical operations, the format, amount, and type of data returned to the client, and/or whether a query is to be parsed, compiled, or executed.

◆ **Statistics.** A group of debugging settings that determines whether to give the user execution plan information and statistics.

◆ **Transactions.** Controls the way transactions are treated.

◆ **SQL-92 Settings.** Determines whether settings are to be set to SQL-92 industry standard values.

◆ **Miscellaneous.** A grouping of functions that don't fit into any one of the previously mentioned categories, yet can enable you to alter the interaction with the server and current database.

Some SET options take effect at parse-time, whereas others affect the execute-time environment. Parse-time options take effect as the options are encountered in text, without recognizing the control of flow of the procedure. Execute-time options take effect during the execution of the code in which they are specified. Execute options that have been set at the time of a failure in a procedure remain set. The QUOTED_IDENTIFIER, PARSEONLY, OFFSETS, and FIPS_FLAGGER options are parse-time options. All other SET options are execute-time options.

Options set in a script apply until they are reset or until session termination. Options that are set in a stored procedure or trigger apply until reset inside that stored procedure or trigger, or until control returns to the code that called the procedure. Unless explicitly reset, option values from all higher-level code apply within any procedure. Unless reset, options set for a connection apply after a connection is made to a different database. Some values are stored within the stored procedure, and used during the execution of that stored procedure regardless of other higher-level settings. For monitoring, troubleshooting, and optimizing a server you will find the STATISTICS and SHOWPLAN options to be the most useful.

SET STATISTICS Evaluation

If any performance issue is related to a query, a database's performance can be determined by using the SET SHOWPLAN, STATISTICS IO, STATISTICS TIME, and STATISTICS PROFILE statement options. SHOWPLAN describes the method chosen by the optimizer to retrieve the data. STATISTICS IO reports information about the number of scans, logical reads (pages accessed in cache), and physical reads (number of times the disk was accessed) for each table. STATISTICS TIME displays the amount of time (in milliseconds) required to parse, compile, and execute a query. STATISTICS PROFILE displays a result-set after each executed query that represents a profile of the execution of the query.

Proactive/Automated Optimization

It is the role of the SQL Server Agent service running on the server to control a lot of mechanisms within an instance of SQL Server. The SQL Server Agent is responsible for running jobs and tasks scheduled to occur at specific times and/or intervals. The agent also helps detect conditions for which administrators have defined actions to be taken. The agent also runs replication tasks, and in general is responsible for handling repetitive tasks and exception handling conditions defined through the other SQL Server components.

The statistical maintenance functionality introduced in SQL Server 7 and expanded upon in SQL Server 2000 may generate unwanted overhead on a production system if it initiates statistical updates during heavy production periods or starts a high number of UPDATE STATISTICS processes. It may be worthwhile scheduling this type of maintenance to occur during idle time to prevent this behavior.

Using the SQL Server Agent to automate tasks involves scheduling periodic activities on the server. Jobs are defined for tasks that are to be scheduled. Jobs can also be defined to run on demand or during idle time on the server. Notification of completion, errors, or other defined conditions is performed through the definition of operators and the assignment of conditions under which the operator is to be contacted. The definition of alerts identifies circumstances that the agent will watch for and act upon when they occur.

Jobs are objects consisting of one or more steps to be performed. Each step can be an operating system activity or executable, a T-SQL operation, active-x script, or replication activity. Jobs are extremely flexible and powerful operations that can perform any activity from maintenance to reporting, backups, and/or application processes.

Alerts are actions to be taken when specific events occur, such as an error on the server, an application process call, or any other definable event. A *definable event* is any process that places information into the Windows 2000 application event log. Specific errors, errors of certain severity, or performance criteria can all have a corresponding alert defined. The alert can be defined to take such actions as sending an email notification, paging an operator through a paging service, or running a job to respond to the situation.

Operators are individuals or groups of individuals, who can be identified by a network account, email identifier, or computer identification, who can address problems with the database and other servers. An operator can be sent a message resulting from an alert, a job step, job completion, or other SQL Server processes. Messages can be sent through email, a pager, or a net send network command.

Job, Operator, Alert Integration

Jobs, alerts, and operators can be defined as a single step because the interface tools in the Enterprise Manager are linked together, and each portion of the definition allows for new entries.

An organized approach to automation, however, is recommended. Possibly the first step is to define the important individuals in the environment who could respond to potential problems. As you create the operators, you should as well accompany the operator definitions with short descriptions of the operator's purpose and function as it relates to the database system. Step by Step 12.5 shows you how to define a sample operator.

STEP BY STEP

12.5 Operator Definition

1. Start the Enterprise Manager and expand your server, the Management folder, the SQL Server Agent, and select the Operators icon.

2. Right-click Operators and select the New Operator option.

3. Enter **SalesPeople** for the name of the operator. (This operator will actually contain a group of individuals. Operators can be single users, groups of users, or a computer name.)

4. If your SQL Server is configured to use mail, you can add an email address. Any email address can be used for an operator. It is best to use a group alias for email messaging purposes.

5. Use your own computer name as the net send address. Use the test buttons on the right side of the interface to test any of the contact mechanisms specified.

6. Notice the listing of information on the Notifications tab. When you create an operator, you can at the same time indicate the alerts that this operator will respond to. For this example, leave this blank for now. Select OK to create the operator.

Any of the operators defined can be selected to receive notification by a number of SQL Server operations. Email and other message sending capabilities have been built into most of the features in SQL Server 2000. For this example, the operators are going to receive notification of a new customer. After they have been contacted, they can potentially contact the customer and perform an initial sales call.

As well as operator notification, you may want to execute tasks based on an alert condition. Step by Step 12.6 sets up a job that will initialize demographic information storage for each new customer that comes into the system.

STEP BY STEP

12.6 Initialize Demographics

1. Start the Enterprise Manager and expand your server and then the databases folder. Select the Tables icon and in the right pane select the CustomerDemographics table.

2. Right-click on the table, select Open Table, and select Return All Rows. This should open up a new window revealing no current records in the table.

3. Enter **Unknown** as the CustomerTypeID and **No Demographics** as the CustomerDesc.

4. Close the window to save the record and return to the Enterprise Manager.

This newly created record will act as a default for all new customers entering the system. Step by Step 12.7 now configures a job to be executed for each new customer that will initialize the new customer's demographic information.

STEP BY STEP

12.7 Job Description

1. Start the Enterprise Manager and expand your server, the Management folder, and the SQL Server Agent. Select the Jobs icon.

2. Right-click Jobs and select the New Job option.

3. Provide the name **InitializeCustomer** for the job and a description of **Start demographic data recording for the new customer.**

4. Select the Steps tab and then click the New button to define a new step for the job.

5. The job's single action is to insert a new record into the `CustomerCustomerDemo` table with a `CustomerTypeID` of Unknown. Use the following T-SQL command:

```
Declare @CustID nChar(5)
Select @CustID = CustomerID from Customers
INSERT Northwind.dbo.CustomerCustomerDemo
  VALUES(@CustID, 'Unknown')
```

You do not apply a schedule in this example because the intent for this job description is to have it run when a new customer is entered into the system. When a new customer is entered, a chain reaction starts where the operator is notified and the job is executed.

6. On the Notifications tab you would usually select Failure of Steps and/or Jobs to contact an administrator. For the purpose of this exercise, you can use the salesperson as the setup for that ID and that will signal the local computer. Select the `SalesPerson` operator as a `net send` operator and select when the job completes from the list of available options.

For the job or operator to serve any purpose, you must configure an alert (as shown in Step by Step 12.8) to recognize the condition you are looking for. In this case the condition is a new customer being entered into the system.

STEP BY STEP

12.8 Alert Definition

1. Start the Enterprise Manager and expand your server, the Management folder, and the SQL Server Agent. Select the Alerts icon.

2. Right-click Alerts and select New Alert.

3. Enter the name **NewCustomer** for the alert and select the `Northwind` database from the database selection drop-down list box.

continues

4. You need to define an event number to be used. SQL Server sees all event alert identifiers as error numbers, though you can define elements other than errors. Select error number and then select the ellipses to allow for your own definition.

5. On the Messages tab, select the New button, which should bring up the next available user-defined error number dialog.

6. Leave the severity on informational and select the Always Write to Windows event Log check box. For an alert to respond to any event, it must have been written to the Windows application event log first.

7. Add the following message text to the text box using the %s markers as a way of providing parameters to the message. Parameter information will be passed into the event when it is fired:

```
New customer in the system Customer ID: %s
                           Contact ID: %s
                           Phone No.: %s
```

(To insert a new line within the text box hold the Ctrl key while pressing Enter.)

8. Press OK to close the window and save the custom message. Press OK to close the Manage SQL Server Messages dialog box.

Note the error number that was given to you. Later you will need this number. 50001 would be used if this is the first user-defined alert in the system

9. On the Response tab, select the Execute Job check box and then select the previously created job. Select the Net Send check box of the `SalesPeople` operator and click OK to close and save the alert definition.

A new customer will be entered into the `Customers` table. This process must fire the alert provided in the preceding steps and pass the `CustomerID`, `ContactName`, and `Phone` to the alert so that this information can be placed into a message to the salespeople.

The whole chain reaction starts with an INSERT trigger on the Customers table. Because INSERT triggers are automatically fired by SQL Server when new data is entered, it is the perfect mechanism for this type of operation. The trigger must fire off an event to be recognized by SQL Server as the one being monitored by the alert definition. Step by Step 12.9 shows how to trigger the alert.

STEP BY STEP

12.9 Triggering the Alert

1. Start the Enterprise Manager and expand your server and the databases folder. Select the Tables icon and in the right pane select the Customers table.

2. Right-click on the table, select All Tasks, and select Manage Triggers. This should open up a new window that enables you to define the trigger.

3. Create the INPUT trigger using the following code:

```
CREATE TRIGGER NewCustomerEntry ON [dbo].[Customers]
FOR INSERT
AS
DECLARE @CustNo nchar(5)
DECLARE @Contact nvarchar(30)
DECLARE @PhoneNo nvarchar(24)
SELECT @CustNo = CustomerID, @PhoneNo = Phone,
            @Contact = ContactName FROM INSERTED
RAISERROR(50001, 1, 1, @CustNo, @Contact, @PhoneNo)
```

   50001 is based on the error number that was created earlier. If your error number was not 50001, then the code would need to be altered accordingly.

4. Right-click on the Customers table, select Open Table, and then select Return All Rows.

5. Scroll down to the bottom of the table and enter the information for a new customer.

A lot of processes can be performed through automation, and this represents an area where development and process skills are important. In tuning and recognizing other performance factors, SQL

Server Agent alerts can be set up based on performance criteria. The ability to monitor the server for this type of information can be a huge administrative benefit.

Performance Counter Alerts

The SQL Server Agent can monitor performance conditions in a similar fashion to how the System Monitor is used. A System Monitor counter can be used as the basis for specifying a performance condition to monitor. The condition causes an alert to fire if the performance threshold is reached. You can define the area of SQL Server performance to be monitored by defining the object, counter, instance, and threshold condition just as you do with the system/performance monitor. The difference is that the monitoring can be performed on an ongoing basis without any additional overhead.

The counter selected represents the specific property to be monitored. Because the performance data is collected on a periodic basis, there is often a delay between the threshold being hit and the performance alert firing.

Performance alerts can be used to activate maintenance jobs, such as backing up and clearing a log file when it is close to becoming full. You may also want individuals to be contacted in the event of potential problems such as an inordinate number of deadlocks per second. It is easier to allow for proactive management and solve potential problems before they can affect the end user.

Database Maintenance Plan Wizard

The Database Maintenance Plan Wizard is a good starting point for any server maintenance. The wizard can be used to help set up core maintenance tasks. At least a minimum amount of maintenance is necessary on any server. The wizard ensures that your database performs well, is backed up on a scheduled basis, and measures are taken to check for inconsistencies.

After you answer a few elementary questions, the wizard puts in place the necessary jobs to ensure that at least a minimum of upkeep operations are performed on the database system. Until you have mastered the remainder of the procedures developed in this chapter, this should remain the basis for your maintenance plan development.

The Profiler and Analyzer

By far the most substantial tools available to tune and maintain SQL Server are the combination of the SQL Server Profiler, SQL Query Analyzer, and automated maintenance through the use of jobs, alerts, and operators.

The SQL Profiler gives you a detailed report of activities captured from the server. With this amount of information available, troubleshooting server problems and diagnosing resource utilization becomes a lot easier.

The SQL Query Analyzer enables you to diagnose and fine-tune individual commands and processes. When you want to optimize a single application, procedure, and/or database, the analyzer gives you the most granularity available for viewing SQL Server statistical data.

The SQL Server Agent, operators, jobs, and alerts provide for a mechanism whereby maintenance operations can be scheduled to occur on a regular basis. This facility can be in itself an application architecture to build around.

SECURING OBJECTS

▶ Define object-level security, including column-level permissions, by using GRANT, REVOKE, and DENY.

SQL Server provides an auditing facility as a way to trace and record activity. SQL Server 2000 also provides the SQL Profiler for performing more in-depth monitoring. Auditing can be enabled or modified only by system administrators, and every modification of an audit can also be audited to prevent administrative abuse. The ability to create, use, alter, and remove objects can also be tightly controlled through the use of statement and object permissions.

SQL Server can accommodate two types of auditing: standard auditing and C2 auditing. Standard auditing provides some level of auditing but does not require the same number of policies as C2 auditing. C2 auditing requires that you follow very specific security policies. C2 security is more than just a machine standard, but has aspects to cover the whole computer facility. You can use SQL Profiler to perform both types of auditing.

C2 Security

Permission sets determine which network identifiers, groups, and roles can work with specific objects, and what degree of interaction is allowed. Chapter 6 covered security, and because permission sets are more an Administrator concern at this level, this chapter touches on a few more considerations but does not go into too much depth. If you are preparing for the companion exam, it is recommended that you learn more about this broad topic.

For more information about C2 certification, see the C2 Administrator's and User's Security Guide. This guide is in downloadable form from the Microsoft Technet site. URL information is provided at the end of this chapter under "Suggested Readings and Resources."

Statement and Object Permissions

Activities involved in creating a database or an item in a database, such as a table or stored procedure, require a class of permissions called statement permissions. Careful control over who can create and alter objects is very important. Essentially, statement permissions allow for the creation and alteration of objects. Statement permissions are:

- ◆ BACKUP DATABASE
- ◆ BACKUP LOG
- ◆ CREATE DATABASE
- ◆ CREATE DEFAULT
- ◆ CREATE FUNCTION
- ◆ CREATE PROCEDURE
- ◆ CREATE RULE
- ◆ CREATE TABLE
- ◆ CREATE VIEW

Because object ownership is established upon creation of objects, and too many owners can add unnecessary overhead, you should ensure that anyone creating objects is doing so under dbo ownership.

Object permissions determine to what level data can be accessed or whether a procedure can be executed. The list of object permissions is as follows:

◆ SELECT, INSERT, UPDATE, and DELETE permissions applied to data from a table and/or view

◆ SELECT and UPDATE statement permissions, which can be selectively applied to individual columns of a table or view

◆ SELECT permissions, which may be applied to user-defined functions

◆ INSERT and DELETE statement permissions, which affect the entire row, and therefore can be applied only to the table and view and not to individual columns

◆ EXECUTE statement permissions, which affect stored procedures and functions

Setting of permissions can allow audit processes to determine successful and failed attempts to use the permissions.

Security Audits

You use SQL Profiler for auditing events in several categories. A list of these categories and their descriptions is as follows:

◆ End user activity. Login, SQL, and enabling of application roles

◆ DBA activity. Includes configuration of database and server

◆ Security events. grant/revoke/deny, add/remove/configure

◆ Utility events. backup/restore/bulk insert/BCP/DBCC

◆ Server events. shutdown, pause, start

◆ Audit events. add audit, modify audit, stop audit

With the SQL Profiler you can determine the date and time of an event, who caused the event to occur, the type of event, the success or failure of the event, the origin of the request, the name of the object accessed, and the text of the SQL statement.

Auditing can have a significant performance impact. Before you select any object for auditing, balance the trade-off between the likelihood of a security breach and the overhead of the audit. Carefully consider an audit strategy before merely turning on auditing for all objects. If SQL Server is started with the -f flag, auditing does not run.

CASE STUDY: MENAUBI FOODS

ESSENCE OF THE CASE

▶ Online and network updates potentially occur at the same time.

▶ Complex structure of tables.

▶ Both applications stop responding.

SCENARIO

Menaubi Foods is a wholesale distributor of non-perishable food items to locations around the globe. The company runs a SQL Server 2000 machine that is used through a web site for online queries and updates. The server is also used on the local LAN, where a Visual Basic application provides accounting information and updates the same.

The database consists of a complex structure of tables that have been fully normalized for efficient storage. During some accounting updates, the Internet application stops responding, and after a time the machine running the accounting application must be rebooted. How would you go about finding the problem?

ANALYSIS

There are potentially a few problems in this scenario. The most likely is some form of error in the accounting application. There also seems to be a deadlock or blocking situation preventing the Internet application from responding.

Run the Profiler, set up for a replay trace, and ensure that you are tracking locking information as well as the standard template data. The trace could then be replayed on a test machine to diagnose the problem. It also might be beneficial to reinstall the accounting application. If you suspect locking, the quickest, most direct way to confirm this is to use the Enterprise Manager or the stored procedures sp_who or sp_lock.

CHAPTER SUMMARY

Troubleshooting, performance tuning, and resource optimization require in-depth knowledge of how SQL Server operates, as well as knowledge of the applications to which the database server is being applied. We have seen numerous tools and options that can be used to assist in this process.

The first problem you will face on the exam will be which tool to use, given a set of circumstances. Second, you will need to present a course of action for monitoring and troubleshooting. Third, you will need to read and diagnose the output and then select an appropriate solution. A person who implements databases needs to be comfortable in all these areas, and you will find a few of each type of question on the exam.

Throughout this book, a great deal of information has been provided that could potentially apply to this vast topic. Everything from appropriate database design, to the correct use of technologies, to the proper definition and use of SQL Server objects all will play a role. Expect exam questions that cover a variety of these topics wound into a single scenario.

Now that you have completed the entire book and have an understanding of all the concepts covered, the exam should be a cake-walk for you. If you have completed the Case Studies, Exercises, and Step by Steps of the chapter, you will have obtained valuable practical experience with the product. In the appendixes of this book are a couple of other elements that you can use for final preparation. Quick facts about the exam, more sample exam questions, and terminology definitions can all be found in the pages that follow.

KEY TERMS

- Query Analyzer
- SQL Profiler
- System Monitor
- Current Activity window
- T-SQL
- error logs
- Performance Monitor
- blocked process
- Windows application log
- jobs
- alerts
- operators
- sp_who
- sp_lock
- sp_spaceused
- sp_monitor
- meta data
- statistics

CHAPTER SUMMARY

- scalar function
- `sp_configure`
- reconfigure
- `SET`
- built-in function
- DBCC
- fragmentation
- trace
- filter
- trace flags
- SNMP
- TCP/IP

- row lock
- page lock
- extent lock
- database lock
- table lock
- `xp_sqlmaint`
- `sp_dboption`
- `sp_help`
- execution plan
- query optimizer
- statement permissions
- object permissions

Exercises

The following exercises take you through the variety of troubleshooting, performance tuning, and resource optimization tools available to the SQL Server administrator.

12.1 Exploring DBCC

Exercise 12.1 compares the output of CHECKALLOC to that of CHECKDB.

Estimated Time: 5 minutes.

1. If not already open, load the SQL Query Analyzer. Supply the logon connection information if requested.

2. Enter a query to check the consistency of disk space allocation structures:

   ```
   DBCC CHECKALLOC ('Northwind')
   ```

3. Compare the results against a check of the allocation and structural integrity of all the objects. (CHECKDB includes CHECKALLOC.)

   ```
   DBCC CHECKDB ('Northwind')
   ```

   Note that the output of the CHECKALLOC command covers a lot more detail than CHECKDB, although CHECKDB is more thorough.

12.2 Defining a Playback Trace

Exercise 12.2 traces SQL Server activity with a trace description that enables the activity to be played back.

Estimated Time: 20 minutes.

1. If not already open, load the SQL Profiler. Supply the logon connection information if requested.

2. Start a new trace definition. Supply the logon connection information if requested.

3. Enter **Playback** for the name of the trace and select the QLProfilerTSQL_Replay template. Store the replay to a table named Playback and select a database for storage, other than Master or Northwind.

   It is a good idea and standard practice to have a database prepared that will store traces from a variety of other databases. Make sure that you name the stored traces well and document circumstances surrounding the capture.

4. Select Run to begin the data capture.

5. Open an instance of the SQL Query Analyzer and select Northwind from the database drop-down list box.

6. Execute a series of simple queries similar to the following list:

   ```
   SELECT * FROM Employees
   GO

   SELECT * FROM Employees
     WHERE Title LIKE 'Sales%'
   GO

   SELECT * FROM Customers
     WHERE ContactTitle LIKE 'Own%'
   GO
   ```

7. Return to the Profiler window and stop the trace. Save the trace results and close the Trace window.

   Note that after a trace has been captured and saved to a table, you can reopen it and replay the trace later.

APPLY YOUR KNOWLEDGE

12.3 Replaying the Playback Trace

Exercise 12.3 replays the trace captured in Exercise 12.2.

Estimated Time: 15 minutes.

1. If not already open, load the SQL Profiler. Supply the logon connection information if requested.

2. From the File menu, select Open and then Trace Table. Supply the logon connection information if requested.

3. Locate the database and table from the capture in Exercise 12.2 and select OK to open the trace.

4. Click in the window and select the query:

```
SELECT * FROM Employees
 WHERE Title LIKE 'Sales%'
```

5. From the Replay menu, select Run to Cursor. Supply the logon connection information to your machine when requested. In the Query Selection dialog box, select the defaults and click Start to begin playback.

   Notice that the events replay up to the point of the query.

6. From the Replay menu select Start to enable the remainder of the query to be replayed.

Review Questions

1. Which DBCC operations should be performed on a regular basis? How frequently should they be executed?

2. In what situations would the SQL Query Analyzer be used instead of the Profiler?

3. Which stored procedures can be used to get information similar to what is found in the Enterprise Manager Current Activity window?

4. What aspects of alerts and operators make them useful in maintaining a SQL Server environment?

5. How would you go about auditing a SQL Server?

Exam Questions

1. You are evaluating the database design given to you by another developer. This database was to be designed with an emphasis on query performance, and an attempt has been made to meet the design goal. Replying to this directive, the developer has sketched out a design for several indexes for the tables. These indexes have been put together with the highest expected query usage kept in mind. As you review his design, you notice that the new indexes provide varying degrees of benefit to a variety of queries. Which of his indexes is likely to be the most effective?

   A. An index on gender for 134,000 registered voters.

   B. An index on the sales agent's last initial for 25,000 orders.

   C. An index for the StateCode Primary Key column in a US_States table.

   D. An index for the State column in a PacificTime_ZIP_Codes table.

APPLY YOUR KNOWLEDGE

2. As a database implementer you are developing several new stored procedures on an existing SQL Server 2000 database that resides at your company headquarters. You are experimenting with a Query Analyzer session that contains each of the individual queries to be used in these procedures. After running a given SELECT query and using the graphical showplan feature to understand the execution plan, you want to prove that internal statistics are available for a particular column used in the query. How would you best find this information?

A. Disable the graphical showplan display.

B. Hold the mouse over each individual node relating to the desired column.

C. Use a SET SHOWPLAN statement.

D. Examine each individual node relating to the desired column without mousing over it.

3. You are consulting for a manufacturing company that is running a single SQL Server 2000 computer. The server contains a database named Sales. The database has a group of tables that are used to examine sales trends. The database options are set to their default values.

Analysts who use the database report that query performance has become slower. You analyze the clustered Primary Key on the Invoices table and receive the following results:

```
DBCC SHOWCONTIG scanning 'Invoices' table...
Table: 'Invoices' (21575115); index ID: 1,
➥database ID: 6
TABLE level scan performed.
 - Pages
➥Scanned..............................: 200
 - Extents
➥Scanned..............................: 50
 - Extent
➥Switches.............................: 40
 - Avg. Pages per
➥Extent...............................: 4.0
```

```
 - Scan Density [Best Count:Actual
➥Count].......: 60.00%
➥[3:5]
 - Logical Scan
➥Fragmentation...................: 0.00%
 - Extent Scan
➥Fragmentation...................: 40.00%
 - Avg. Bytes Free per
➥Page.....................: 146.5
 - Avg. Page Density
➥(full)....................: 98.19%
DBCC execution completed. If DBCC printed
➥error messages,
contact your system administrator.
```

You want to improve performance of queries that join tables to the Invoices table. What are three possible T-SQL statements you can execute to achieve this goal? (Each correct answer represents a complete solution. Choose three.)

A. DBCC UPDATEUSEAGE
   ('Sales','Invoices','PK_Invoices')

B. CREATE UNIQUE CLUSTERED INDEX PK_
   Invoices On

   Invoices(InvoiceID) WITH DROP_EXISTING

C. DBCC INDEXDEFRAG
   ('Sales','Invoices','PK_Invoices')

D. DBCC DBREINDEX (Sales.dbo.Invoices,
   'PK_Invoices')

E. UPDATE STATISTICS 'Invoices'

F. DBCC CHECKALLOC (Sales, REPAIR_FAST)

4. You are a database implementer of a SQL Server 2000 environment that has a single database server. The server contains all your company's databases, including an investment-tracking database. Each day more than 100 operators make approximately 5,000 changes to customer investments. In addition, daily and monthly reports are created from the investment data.

APPLY YOUR KNOWLEDGE

Another development team at your company needs to optimize a database application. They need a sample of database query activity to discover whether they can speed up the transactions. The developers also want to replay the sample on another SQL Server computer.

You need to capture the sample, but you want to minimize any increase to the workload of the server. What should you do?

A. Run SQL Profiler on a client computer. Configure SQL Profiler to monitor database activity, and log data to a .trc file.

B. Run SQL Profiler on the server. Configure SQL Profiler to monitor database activity, and log data to a database table.

C. Run System Monitor on a client computer. Configure System Monitor to monitor database activity, and log data to a .blg file.

D. Start SQL Server from a command prompt. Specify trace flag 1204 to enable verbose logging.

5. You are the administrator of a SQL Server computer. Users report that the database times out when they attempt to modify data. You use the Current Activity window to examine locks held in the database as shown in the Figure 12.12.

spid 51   spid 52   spid 53
          (Blocking)   (Blocked By
                            52)

FIGURE 12.12
Current Activity window.

You need to discover why users cannot modify data in the database, but you do not want to disrupt normal database activities. What should you do?

A. Use the spid 52 icon in the Current Activity window to discover which SQL statement is being executed.

B. Use the sp_who stored procedure to discover who is logged in as spid 52.

C. Use SQL Profiler to capture the activity of the user who is logged in as spid 52.

D. Use System Monitor to log the locks that are granted in the database.

6. You are working on a SQL Server 2000 computer that contains a database that stores product data for your company. You need to execute an existing stored procedure that examines prices for your company's products and can modify them if necessary. You execute the stored procedure after business hours, but it does not complete. You execute the sp_lock stored procedure and receive the following output.

spid	dbid	ObjId	IndId	Type	Mode
61	7	0	0	DB	S
64	7	0	0	DB	S
72	7	0	0	DB	S
72	7	2145623952	1	PAG	IS
72	7	2145623952	0	TAB	IS
72	7	2145623952	1	KEY	S
78	7	0	0	DB	S
78	7	2145623952	1	PAG	IX
78	7	2145623952	0	TAB	IX
78	7	2145623952	1	KEY	X

You want the stored procedure to complete successfully. What should you do?

APPLY YOUR KNOWLEDGE

A. Execute the stored procedure, and specify the WITH RECOMPILE option.

B. Execute the DBCC FREEPROCCACHE statement.

C. Release the locks that are held by connections 61 and 64.

D. Release the locks that are held by connections 72 and 78.

7. You are working on a SQL Server 2000 computer that contains a database named Orders, which is used to record customer orders for the products your company sells. Your company's order volume exceeds 1 million orders per day. Each order uses approximately 100KB of space in the database. Users report that the database responds slowly when they enter new orders. You use SQL Profiler to monitor the activity on the database and receive the data shown in the Figure 12.13.

   You need to modify the database to improve performance. What should you do?

StartTime	EventClass
2000-08-30 01:53:13.033	Data File Auto Grow
2000-08-30 01:53:15.147	Data File Auto Grow
2000-08-30 01:53:17.320	Data File Auto Grow
2000-08-30 01:53:19.323	Data File Auto Grow
2000-08-30 01:53:21.567	Data File Auto Grow
2000-08-30 01:53:23.470	Data File Auto Grow
2000-08-30 01:53:26.063	Data File Auto Grow
2000-08-30 01:53:28.157	Data File Auto Grow
2000-08-30 01:53:30.060	Data File Auto Grow
2000-08-30 01:53:32.150	Data File Auto Grow
2000-08-30 01:53:33.993	Data File Auto Grow

FIGURE 12.13
Data received by using SQL Profiler.

A. Double the size of the data file.

B. Configure the database to automatically grow by 10%.

C. Separate the database into two physical files.

D. Increase the size of the transaction log file.

8. You are working on a SQL Server 2000 computer that contains a database named Sales. The company's web-based application uses the Sales database to store sales transactions. The company web site has grown in popularity, and database utilization has increased. You need to collect data about the utilization of server resources so that you can provide capacity planning. You want to automate the collection process so that information is gathered as quickly as possible. What should you do?

A. Configure System Monitor to collect data and store it in a SQL Server table.

B. Create a SQL Server Agent job that executes the sp_statistics stored procedure daily and places the results in a text file.

C. Use SQL Profiler to trace server activity and store the results in SQL Server tables.

D. Configure SQL Server alerts to store information in the Windows application event log.

APPLY YOUR KNOWLEDGE

Answers to Review Questions

1. CHECKDB should be run on a periodic basis to check storage allocation; INDEXDEFRAG should be run if the index structure appears to be too fragmented; SHRINKDATABASE should be run if there is an excessive amount of free space in the database files.

2. The SQL Query Analyzer is used to troubleshoot applications and query problems, and would be used when fine-tuning is to be done at a level that requires focusing on individual commands. The SQL Profiler is used to track SQL Server events on a broader scale.

3. The sp_who stored procedure provides information about the current user session, and sp_lock provides information on current processes and SQL Server locking in effect.

4. Alerts can be set up to monitor situations that may need to be addressed by an administrator. The administrators can be set up as operators so that if the alert occurs, the administrator can be contacted via email, pager, or net send.

5. The SQL Profiler is used to audit a server. You should carefully select the objects that you need to audit because this operation can add a significant amount of overhead to the server.

Answers to Exam Questions

1. **C.** Gender is never a good column to supply an index against because it has only two possible values. In general, a column with a high percentage of unique values is the best choice for indexing. An agent's last initial has 26 possibilities in a table of 25,000, which is still a rather poor choice. An index created on State value would be a good choice in either C or D, but C provides the best ratio. For more information, consult Chapter 10.

2. **B.** A feature of the graphical showplan display enables you to see information about each node in the display by holding the mouse over the node. A display shows the node analysis based on the contents of the entire query. Of the choices available, this would be the best mechanism to use to gain the desired information. For more information, see the section entitled "Query Analyzer."

3. **B, C, D.** Because of index fragmentation, the reduction in performance in this database could be improved by rebuilding, re-creating, or defragmenting the current index. For more information, see the "Validation DBCC Operations" section.

4. **A.** Although it would be most desirable to run the query on another SQL Server, it is always best to select a machine other than the production machine to absorb the overhead of the Profiler itself. For more information, see the section "SQL Server Profiler."

APPLY YOUR KNOWLEDGE

5. **A.** Although knowing who has the login may be useful later, the first thing to look for is what is executing that is causing the block. For more details, see "Current Activity" in SQL Server Books OnLine.

6. **D.** Procedures 72 and 78 are holding locks against the database and preventing the stored procedure from executing. For more information, see the section "sp_lock."

7. **B.** The data file is growing at too small an increment, which causes growth to occur in small, too-frequent increments. You may even want to set the growth rate higher than 10 percent, but of the available choices this is the best solution. For more information, consult the section "Alternative Mechanisms."

8. **C.** To monitor detailed activity of SQL Server, you should use the SQL Server Profiler and configure a trace to take in the necessary data and filter for the desired objects. For more details, see the "SQL Server Profiler" section.

Suggested Readings and Resources

1. SQL Server Books Online

   - Transact-SQL Reference DBCC

   - Administering SQL Server—Automating Administrative Tasks

   - Optimizing Database Performance

2. Internet Web Links:

   - C2 Administrator's Guide

   ```
   http://www.microsoft.com/technet/
   prodtechnol/sql/maintain/security/
   sqlc2.asp
   ```

   - SQL Server Performance Tuning and Optimization

   ```
   http://www.sql-server-performance.com/
   ```

   This is an excellent site for looking further into any of the topics covered in this chapter and then some.

PART II

FINAL REVIEW

Fast Facts

Study and Exam Prep Tips

Practice Exam

Now that you have finished the book and are well-versed in SQL Server 2000 database design issues, you're ready for the exam. This element of the book has been put together as a final set of study notes for use in the parking lot prior to sitting the actual exam. "Fast Facts" is exactly what its name implies: It's designed to aid you in the quick study of specific information contained in this book.

The following information has been squeezed out of the book and divided into the same topics covered by each chapter; it summarizes the facts you need to know and often the information that is more difficult to memorize. "Fast Facts," however, are not a substitute for "knowledge," which is a process, not an end in-and-of-itself. It is important that you understand the concepts behind these facts, as solely memorizing facts will not help you pass the exam.

A lot of care has been taken to select only the most essential facts for quick review. Here you will find information addressing some of the finer points that will help you answer questions on the actual exam.

Fast Facts

SQL SERVER 2000 REQUIREMENTS

As mentioned in Chapter 1, there are a couple of things required before you can set up your SQL Server. Internet Explorer 5.0 or later is needed solely for the Microsoft Management Console (MMC) and to view help topics in Books Online. There are still some hardware requirements that must be met before SQL Server can be installed, some of which are listed here. After making sure all the prerequisites are taken care of, you can then start the Setup Wizard by simply inserting the CD and clicking on Install SQL Server Components.

EXAM 70-229: DESIGNING AND IMPLEMENTING DATABASES WITH MICROSOFT SQL SERVER 2000 ENTERPRISE EDITION

The following hardware is needed to install the Enterprise version of SQL Server 2000:

◆ Computer:

Intel or compatible

Pentium 166 MHz or higher

◆ Memory:

64MB minimum, 128MB or more recommended

◆ Hard disk space:

SQL Server database components: 95-270MB, 250MB typical

Analysis Services: 50MB minimum, 130MB typical

English Query: 80MB

Desktop Engine only: 44MB

Books Online: 15MB

◆ Monitor:

VGA or higher resolution

800×600 or higher resolution required for the SQL Server graphical tools

◆ Other Peripherals:

CD-ROM drive

SQL Server 2000 Enterprise Edition

This edition is comprehensive, as outlined in Chapter 1: It includes the complete set of SQL Server database and analysis features and is uniquely characterized by several features that make it the most scalable and available edi-

tion of SQL Server 2000. It scales to the performance levels required to support the largest Web sites and enterprise online transaction processing (OLTP) and data warehousing systems. Its support for failover clustering also makes it ideal for any mission-critical, line-of-business application. Additionally, this edition includes several advanced analysis features that are not included in SQL Server 2000 Standard Edition. This edition requires the use of Indexed views.

DATABASE DESIGN FOR SQL SERVER 2000

ER Modeling

Data modeling concepts are the basis for everything we do in the industry as DBAs. As seen in Chapter 2, an ER data model consists of three main components that are present in any model format:

◆ **Entities.** In data modeling, entities can be closely compared to the physical element of a table in SQL Server. An entity is a collection of related data elements such as customers or products.

◆ **Attributes.** Attributes are the characteristics given to an entity such as Salary and FirstName. Attributes of an entity represent a set of properties of a data element within an entity. They will become the columns or fields in the physical database.

◆ **Relationships.** Relationships show a logical link between two or more entities. A customer entity may be related to orders, a product entity may be related to sales, and so on.

Primary Keys

Primary keys consist of sets of attributes whose values uniquely identify the rows in a entity. Primary keys give an ID to a row and make the row unique throughout the entity. This means that rows can be located easily by this identifier. Additionally, primary keys can be made up of multiple columns known as a composite key.

Foreign Keys

Foreign keys help in the relational process between two entities. When a primary key is created on a parent entity, it can be connected to the foreign key of another entity. You can also link two entities by relating a foreign key to a unique column not defined as the primary key.

One-To-One Relationship

This type of relationship occurs when one row or data element of an entity is associated with only one row or element in the second entity. It is not surprising that one-to-one relationships are uncommon in the real world. They are used mostly when an entity has an extraordinarily large number of attributes—then the entity is split in two to make it easier to manage. An extra entity also might be desired when developing the physical storage locations of the data. By separating seldom-used data from more frequently used information, faster data retrieval and updates can be accommodated.

One-To-Many Relationship

One-to-many relationships exist when a single instance of an entity (the parent entity) relates to many instances of another entity (the child entity). One-to-many relationships are the most common type of relationship. It is a natural occurrence in the real world—for example, a customer will have many orders, and a manufactured product will have many components.

Many-to-Many Relationship

This type of relationship occurs when many rows or data elements in an entity are associated with many rows or data elements in another entity. For example, a many-to-many relationship occurs between the Trainee and Course entities. Many Trainees can enroll to a single course, and one trainee can be enrolled into numerous courses. This type of relationship is not uncommon in the real world. However, SQL Server doesn't actually directly implement many-to-many relationships. A many-to-many relationship is implemented using three entities. The two main entities are connected together using a third entity. The third entity contains keys and interrelationship information. Each entity is connected to the new entity as a one-to-many relationship. To discover the cardinality of a relationship, you look at the correlation between the entities.

Entity Integrity

Entity integrity defines a unique row attribute as an identifier for individual entities. Generally, the regulations of this type of data integrity are easy to follow. Simple ways of enforcing this type of integrity are using primary keys, UNIQUE constraints, and unique indexes when the entity design moves into the physical stage of design. Entity integrity specifies that primary keys on every instance of an entity must be present, unique, and have values other than null content.

Domain Integrity

Domain integrity is restricting the data entered to a domain or range of values, and thus preventing incorrect data from entering the system.

Referential Integrity

Referential integrity specifies that every foreign key value map to a primary key or other unique value in related tables. Referential integrity guarantees the smooth navigation of moving from entity to entity, so it is extremely important to ensure proper referential integrity definition. Referential integrity ensures that no orphaned records exist. Orphaned data is a term used when data in a child entity exists that points to a non-existent parent.

Advanced Referential Integrity Options

When defining relationships to be used in a SQL Server database system, two new options exist that allow more control over the actions that can occur affecting key values. Cascade Update Related Fields and Cascade Delete Related Records allows updates or deletions of key values to cascade through the tables defined to have foreign key relationships that can be traced back to the table on which the modification is made.

A cascading deletion will occur when you delete a row with a key referenced by foreign keys in existing rows in other tables; all rows containing those foreign keys are also deleted.

A cascading update occurs when you update a key value in a row where the key value is referenced by foreign keys in existing rows in other tables. All foreign key values are also updated to the new value specified for the key.

SQL Server Data Types

The following list (excerpted from Chapter 2) details SQL Server data types:

- ◆ `bigint`. Integer data from -2^{63} (-9223372036854775808) through $2^{63}-1$ (9223372036854775807).

- ◆ `int`. Integer data from -2^{31} ($-2,147,483,648$) through $2^{31} - 1$ ($2,147,483,647$).

- ◆ `smallint`. Integer data from 2^{15} ($-32,768$) through $2^{15} - 1$ ($32,767$).

- ◆ `tinyint`. Integer data from 0 through 255.

- ◆ `bit`. Integer data with either a 1 or 0 value.

- ◆ `decimal`. Fixed precision and scale numeric data from $-10^{38} +1$ through $10^{38} -1$.

- ◆ `numeric`. Functionally equivalent to decimal.

- ◆ `money`. Monetary data from -2^{63} ($-922,337,203,685,477.5808$) through $2^{63} - 1$ ($+922,337,203,685,477.5807$), accuracy to a ten-thousandth.

- ◆ `smallmoney`. Monetary data values from $-214,748.3648$ through $+214,748.3647$, accuracy to a ten-thousandth.

- ◆ `float`. Floating precision data from $-1.79E + 308$ through $1.79E + 308$.

- ◆ `real`. Floating precision data from $-3.40E + 38$ through $3.40E + 38$.

- ◆ `datetime`. Date and time data from January 1, 1753, through December 31, 9999, with an accuracy of three-hundredths of a second, or 3.33 milliseconds.

- ◆ `smalldatetime`. Date and time data from January 1, 1900, through June 6, 2079, with an accuracy of one minute.

◆ char. Fixed-length single-byte data with a maximum length of 8,000 characters.

◆ varchar. Variable-length single-byte data with a maximum of 8,000 characters.

◆ text. Variable-length single-byte data with a maximum length of $2^{31} - 1$ (2,147,483,647) characters.

◆ nchar. Fixed-length Unicode, dual-byte data with a maximum length of 4,000 characters.

◆ nvarchar. Variable-length Unicode, dual-byte data with a maximum length of 4,000 characters.

◆ sysname. A system-supplied user-defined data type that is functionally equivalent to nvarchar(128) and is used to reference database object names.

◆ ntext. Variable-length Unicode, dual-byte data with a maximum length of $2^{30} - 1$ (1,073,741,823) characters.

◆ binary. Fixed-length binary data with a maximum length of 8,000 bytes.

◆ varbinary. Variable-length binary data with a maximum length of 8,000 bytes.

◆ image. Variable-length binary data with a maximum length of $2^{31} - 1$ (2,147,483,647) bytes.

◆ cursor. A reference to a cursor.

◆ sql_variant. A data type that stores values of various SQL Server-supported data types, except text, ntext, timestamp, and sql_variant.

◆ table. A special data type used to store a resultset for later processing.

◆ timestamp. A database-wide unique number that gets updated every time a row gets updated.

◆ uniqueidentifier. A globally unique identifier (GUID).

PHYSICAL DATABASE DESIGN AND IMPLEMENTATION

Database Creation

During the physical implementation discussed in Chapter 3, important issues with regard to appropriate use of the CREATE DATABASE statement are as follows:

◆ The default growth increment measure is MB but can also be specified with a KB or % suffix. When % is specified, the growth increment size is the specified percentage of the size of the file at the time the increment occurs.

◆ A maximum of 32,767 databases can be defined on a server.

◆ The minimum size for a log file is 512K.

◆ Each database has an owner. The owner is the user who creates the database. The database owner can be changed through sp_changedbowner.

◆ The Master database should be backed up after a user database is created.

◆ The default unit of measure for the size and maxsize settings is MB if you supply a number but no measure is provided. If options are not supplied, maxsize will default to unlimited and file growth will be 10 percent.

Shrinking Files

You can shrink each file within a database to remove unused pages; this applies to both data and log files. It is possible to shrink a database file manually, as a group, or individually. You use the DBCC statement with the SHRINKDATABASE or SHRINKFILE parameters (DBCC parameters will be shown in the Fast Facts section at the end of this text). Use DBCC SHRINKDATA-BASE to shrink the size of the data files in the specified database, or you can selectively choose a specific file and shrink its size using DBCC SHRINKFILE.

You can set the database to automatically shrink at periodic intervals by right-clicking on the database and selecting the database properties page from within the Enterprise Manager.

Column Properties

A complete list of potential column properties (see Chapter 3) is as follows:

◆ **Column Name.** This should be meaningful so as to describe the column content.

◆ **Data Type.** Any one of 25 possible definitions provides the basis for the data a column will contain. Choices include several possibilities for each data type.

◆ **Length.** For many data types, the length is predetermined. You must, however, specify a length for character, Unicode (nCHAR), and binary data. A length must also be specified for variable length data columns. If a char or nCHAR data type is only a single character, then no length has to be defined.

◆ **Allow Nulls.** You can provide an indicator for allowing NULL content for any variable except those assigned as primary keys.

◆ **Primary Key.** This enforces unique content for a column and can be used to relate other tables. Must contain a unique non-NULL value.

◆ **Description.** Provides an explanation of the column for documentation purposes. (This is an extended table property).

◆ **Default Value.** Provides a value for a column when not explicitly given during data entry. A default object must be created and then bound to a column, but the preferred technique is to pro-

vide the default definition, directly attached to the column in the create/alter table definition. It is defined at the database level and can be utilized by any number of columns in a database.

◆ **Precision.** The number of digits in a numeric column.

◆ **Scale.** The number of digits to the right of a decimal point in a numeric column.

◆ **Identity.** Inserts a value automatically into a column based on seed and increment definitions.

◆ **Identity Seed.** Provides the starting value for an Identity column.

◆ **Identity Increment.** Defines how an Identity will increase/decrease with each new row added to a table.

◆ **Is RowGuid.** Identifies a column that has been defined with the "Unique Identifier" data type as being the column to be used in conjunction with the ROWGUIDCOL function in a SELECT list.

◆ **Formula.** Provides a means of obtaining the column content through the use of a function or calculation.

◆ **Collation.** Can provide for a different character set/sort order than other data. (Use with extreme caution, if at all, as it will impair development ability.)

Check Constraints

A Check constraint may be desired to ensure that a value entered meets given criteria based on another value entered. In working with a physical structure, real data constraints are one of the main points of focus in Chapter 3. A table level Check constraint is defined at the bottom of the Alter/Create Table statement, unlike a column Check constraint, which is defined as part of the column definition.

Clustered Indexing

The selection of the appropriate column(s) to base a clustered index on is important for a number of reasons. As previously mentioned, a clustered index represents the order in which the data is physically stored on disk. For this reason, you can define only a single clustered index for any table. If you choose not to use a clustered index in a table, then the data on disk will be stored in a heap. If present, a clustered index will be used by all nonclustered indexes to determine the physical location of the data. Additionally, clustered indexes are particularly useful when a range of data will be queried, such as with the BETWEEN statement.

Nonclustered Indexing

Nonclustered indexes provide a means of retrieving the data from the database in an order other than that in which the data is physically stored. Nonclustered indexes are often used as covering indexes where all the columns specified in the query are contained within the same index.

Indexing is dealt with in a number of chapters in the book and will have equal importance on the exam. The basics of an indexing strategy were introduced in Chapters 2 and 3. Considerable attention was also given to their interaction with views and their affect on performance in Chapters 10 and 12, respectively.

Encryption Can Secure Definitions

Data encryption is a mechanism that can be used to secure data, communications, procedures, and other sensitive information. When encryption techniques are applied, sensitive information is transformed into a non-readable form that must be decrypted to be viewed.

Encryption will slow performance regardless of the method implemented because extra processing cycles are required whenever encryption or decryption occurs.

Schema Binding

Schema binding involves attaching an underlying table definition to a view or user-defined function. With binding, a view or function is connected to the underlying objects. Any attempt to change or remove the objects will fail unless the binding has first been removed. Normally you can create a view, and the underlying table might be changed so that the view no longer works. To prevent the underlying table from being changed, the view can be "schema bound" to the table. Any table changes, which would break the view, are not allowed. Schema binding is a technique that can be used with user-defined functions (see Chapter 9) and views, including indexed views (see Chapter 7).

Indexed Views

To allow for the use of indexed views, a number of session-level options must be set "on" when you create the index. You will need to set NUMERIC_ROUNDABORT "off." Options that need to be set are as follows:

- ◆ ANSI_NULLS
- ◆ ANSI_PADDING
- ◆ ANSI_WARNINGS
- ◆ ARITHABORT
- ◆ CONCAT_NULL_YIELDS_NULL
- ◆ QUOTED_IDENTIFIERS

Other than the specific set of options, nothing more needs to be done for the optimizer to utilize an Index with a query on a view. Essentially, the optimizer handles the View query in the same manner that it would a standard query against a table. The view cannot reference another view, only underlying tables are permitted, and you must create the view with the SCEMABINDING option. The creation of an indexed view is supported only by the Enterprise and Developer Editions.

There are a series of limitations to the content of the SELECT statement for the view definition. They are as follows:

◆ No use of *

◆ A column name used as a simple expression cannot be specified in more than one view column.

◆ No derived tables.

◆ Rowset functions are not permitted.

◆ UNION, outer joins, subqueries, or self-joins cannot be used only simple joins.

◆ No TOP, ORDER BY, COMPUTE, or COMPUTE BY clause.

◆ DISTINCT is not permitted.

◆ COUNT(*) cannot be used but COUNT_BIG(*) is allowed.

◆ Aggregate functions: AVG, MAX, MIN, STDEV, STDEVP, VAR, or VARP.

◆ A SUM function cannot reference a nullable expression.

◆ No use of full-text predicates CONTAINS or FREETEXT.

Data Integrity Options

Table 1 lists the data integrity options.

TABLE 1
MAINTAINING DATA INTEGRITY

Technique	Integrity Achieved	Usage	Timing(Log)
Primary Key	Entity	Identify each row	Before
Foreign Key	Referential/Domain	Ensure no orphan child elements	Before
Unique Index	Entity	Ensure KEY entries are exclusive	Before
Unique Constraint	Entity	No duplicate column values	Before
Identity	Entity	Auto incremented values	Before
Check Constraint	Domain	Ensure correct column entry	Before
Not NULL	Domain	A value must be present	Before
Default	Domain	Provides initial value	Before
Rule	Domain	Ensure correct column entry	Before
Trigger	Referential/Domain	Respond to add, change, delete	After
Stored Procedures	Referential/Domain/Entity	Process controlled operations	Before

QUERYING AND MODIFYING DATA

SQL SELECT

Basic query concepts and more advanced techniques were covered in Chapters 4 and 5, respectively. Using the T-SQL SELECT statement is the most common way to access data. The majority of all data retrieval statements begin with these four main fundamental parts of a SELECT operation:

◆ SELECT. Specifies the columns from the tables that need to be retrieved

◆ FROM. Specifies where the table(s) and the columns are located

◆ WHERE. Specifies a condition in order to filter data down

◆ ORDER BY. Specifies how you want to order the data after it's been retrieved

◆ Example:

```
SELECT * FROM Northwind.dbo.CUSTOMERS
    ORDER BY CompanyName
    (* retrieves all columns)

SELECT [all|distinct] columnlist
FROM tablelist
WHERE º
ORDERBY columnname type
```

The descriptions for the arguments are shown in Table 2.

TABLE 2
T-SQL SELECT STATEMENT ARGUMENTS

Argument	Description
all	*Optional.* Returns all rows, whether unique or not. This is the default.
distinct	*Optional.* Selects only unique rows.
columnlist	*Required.* The name of the column(s) you went to retrieve from the tables or * for all columns.
tablelist	*Required.* Specifies in which table(s) the columns are stored. In cases of joins, you may have more than one table specified.
Where *condition*	*Optional.* These are conditions that limit the number of rows returned.
OrderBy	*Optional.* This is a statement that tells how the resultset will be shown. This can either be ordered ascending (ASC) or descending (Desc).
GroupBy	*Optional.* Allows for the grouping of results. Also will sort the groups in ascending sequence if no aggregate function is supplied.
Having	*Optional.* Is used to filter a listing by removing groups that don't meet the defined criteria.
Compute (By)	*Optional.* Provides for data summarization.

◆ **Table.** The arguments of the basic SELECT statement

SELECT options must always be used in the correct sequence, which can be summarized by using a phrase to match the first letter of each clause in the SELECT. S F W G H O C (Select From Where Group Having Order Compute) is a mechanism used by this author for years, which goes somewhat like this:

Some Funny Walrus Goes Hysterical Over CocaCola

DATEADD, DATEDIFF, DATENAME, DATEPART

The date functions use part of the date you specify, such as month or day.

◆ Date_part determines which unit of measure of time. A listing of the possible values accepted are shown in Table 3.

◆ Date is a datetime or smalldatetime value.

TABLE 3
POSSIBLE VALUES FOR date_part.

Date_part name	Abbreviation
Year	yy, yyyy
Quarter	qq, q
Month	mm, m
dayofyear	dy, y
Day	dd, d
week	wk, ww
hour	hh
minute	mi, n
second	ss, s
millisecond	ms

Inserting Data

Despite the many ways to insert data into an existing table, such as using the Enterprise Manager, the exam deals with the primary coding method using the INSERT statement.

We can summarize the syntax of the INSERT INTO statement as follows:

```
INSERT [INTO] table_or_view [(column_list)]
➡VALUES data_values
```

Inserting Data Using *SELECT*

The SELECT INTO statement can perform a data insertion and create the table for the data in a single operation. The new table is populated from the data provided by a FROM clause. A simple example of its use follows:

```
SELECT * INTO ObsoleteProducts
FROM Products Where Discontinued = 1
```

A SELECT statement can be used within the INSERT statement to add values into a table from one or more other tables or views.

```
INSERT INTO Northwind.dbo.Customers
        SELECT EmployeeID, 'Northwind',
            FirstName + ' ' + LastName,
            'Employee', Address, City,
        ➡Region,
            PostalCode, Country, HomePhone,
        ➡NULL
    FROM Northwind.dbo.Employees
```

Deleting Data

Data that is not needed can be deleted using the DELETE statement. The DELETE statement removes one or more records from a table based on a condition in the WHERE clause. A simplified version of the DELETE statement is

```
DELETE table or view FROM table_sources WHERE
➡search_condition
```

Updating Data

Data that already exists might need to be modified with newer values as time passes; this type of data modification is known as updating. Data can be updated similar to how data is deleted and inserted. Data can be updated using the UPDATE statement. An UPDATE execution is actually an INSERT and DELETE operation. The DELETE operation occurs when the old value is removed and the INSERT occurs when the new value is added, thus creating an UPDATE effect. Sometimes an update is performed as an in-place update.

ADVANCED DATA RETRIEVAL AND MODIFICATION

Joins

There are three basic join types. An inner join shows results only where there are matches between the elements. In other words, if you were querying the database and only wanted to see the people who have addresses, you'd use an inner join. An inner join will leave out all records that don't have a match.

An outer join can show all records from one side of the relationship, and records that match if available from the other side and NULL values for records that do not have a match. An outer join between the Person and Sales table could show you each person and the amount of purchases they've made, and also show NULL values for people who haven't made purchases yet, but are in the table.

The final type of join is a cross-join. A cross-join returns all possible combinations of rows between the two sides of the join. The number of records in the resultset is equal to the number of records on one side of the join multiplied by the number of records on the other side of a join. No correlation between the two records is attempted—all the records from both sides are returned. Performing a cross-join on two large tables is probably not a good idea. The number of rows in the returnset, or in intermediate sets used by SQL Server, can get out of hand quickly, causing server-wide performance degradation.

Using GROUP BY

The GROUP BY operator creates subgroups within a query that can be used by aggregate functions. For example, look at the Sales table. Right now, the Sales

table has one record for each sale, but you really want to know how many total items each person bought. Here's how GROUP BY will solve that problem:

```
SELECT PersonID, sum(QtyPurchased) as
TotalQtyPurchased
FROM Sales
GROUP BY PersonID
```

There are, of course, some rules associated with the use of GROUP BY within a query:

◆ The items in the SELECT statement that are not part of an aggregate function have to appear in the GROUP BY clause.

◆ You can have multiple aggregates in one SELECT statement. For example, you can find MIN and MAX values for a particular column in one SELECT statement.

◆ The items in aggregate functions in the SELECT statement cannot appear outside aggregate functions in the SELECT statement. So, although you can do SELECT MIN(value), MAX(value), you can't do SELECT value, MIN(value), MAX(value), even if you use the appropriate GROUP BY.

Using GROUP BY and HAVING

The HAVING keyword appears after GROUP BY in a SELECT statement, and it is used to filter data after the GROUP BY. You can actually use HAVING without using GROUP BY, in which case HAVING will act like a part of the WHERE clause. The HAVING operator is typically used with aggregate functions to filter out rows that don't meet certain criteria.

Using COMPUTE and COMPUTE BY

So far, the operators you've looked at do not ever create data rows. That changes now. The COMPUTE and COMPUTE BY operators create summary data across your aggregates and add it into your rowset. There are the inevitable rules, however:

◆ If you use COMPUTE without using BY, you can use the COUNT aggregate; otherwise, you can't.

◆ If you use COMPUTE with BY, you need to have an ORDER BY, with the same columns in the same order. You can have additional items in the ORDER BY, but you at least need to have what is specified in the COMPUTE BY.

◆ You can't use COMPUTE or COMPUTE BY with SELECT INTO.

◆ You can't use COMPUTE or COMPUTE BY as the SELECT statement that feeds a cursor (cursors are covered in Chapter 6).

Using *OPENROWSET* and *OPENQUERY*

The OPENROWSET function returns a rowset to SQL Server. It's used in a SELECT statement in the same place as a table. Here are the parameters for the OPENROWSET function:

◆ provider_name. This is the name of the provider, as specified in the registry. It is not optional.

◆ datasource. This is the name of the file, server, or whatever the OLE-DB provider needs to figure out what it should be talking to.

◆ user_id. This is the username that the provider understands. Some providers may not need a username, so this could be blank.

◆ password. This is the password that the provider understands. Some providers may not need a password, so this could be blank.

◆ provider_string. This is a free text field that has everything else the provider needs to initiate the connection. Only the provider knows for sure what this is; you'll have to dig through piles of documentation.

◆ catalog. This is the name of the database, catalog, or whatever the provider understands. It's the top level of the hierarchy of object names. It's also likely to be blank if the provider doesn't use it.

◆ schema. This is the name of the owner of the object. It may be blank if the provider doesn't use it.

◆ object. This is the name of the object being manipulated. Believe it or not, this could be blank if there's only one object in the datasource, such as a text file.

◆ query. This is a string that's provider-specific, and it's passed directly to the provider as a query. It may be an SQL query, or it may be something else. It's also not processed by SQL Server, so you should make sure that the syntax is valid before you send it; otherwise, you'll get a very incomprehensible error message.

OPENQUERY allows for the execution of a pass-through query to be performed on a linked server. The linked server can be any OLE DB data source. The OPENQUERY function can be referenced in the FROM clause of a query in the same manner as the use of a table name. The OPENQUERY function can also be used as a target for an INSERT, UPDATE, or DELETE statement. The syntax for its use is

```
OPENQUERY (linked_server,'query')
```

where linked_server is the name of the linked server and 'query' is the string executed.

Linked Server

You can think of a linked server as a prebuilt set of arguments for OPENROWSET stored in a database object. You can just create an object called a linked server, and create it with all the attributes that you'd normally use in a call to OPENROWSET. Then, instead of having to type in all those parameters over and over again, you can just use the linked server. When a linked server is used, it is important to remember the four-part naming of objects in queries: *server.database.owner.object.*

XML

XML is breaking into the Internet, setting a new data standard and providing another mechanism of getting data from point A to point B. SQL Server's use of XML is discussed in Chapter 5. To put data into XML format, the SELECT statement includes an operator called FOR XML. This specifies to SQL Server that instead of returning a rowset, it should return an XML document. There are three different options for generating the XML: RAW, AUTO, and EXPLICIT.

In AUTO mode, SQL Server returns the rowset in an automatically generated nested XML format. If the query has no joins, it doesn't have a nesting at all. If the query has joins, then it returns the first row from the first table, and then all the correlated rows from each joined table as a nested level.

What if you don't want XML that is elaborately formatted? You then can use the RAW mode. RAW mode returns each row as an element with the identifier "row".

Another way to extract data with the FOR XML clause is by using the option EXPLICIT. The EXPLICIT option enables you to specify the format of the XML that will be created. To define the format, you have to alias the first column of output to the name Tag, name the sec-

ond column Parent, and then each consecutive column has to be aliased to relate it to a specific Tag. The column names after Parent are named like this: [ElementName!TagNumber!AttributeName!Directive], complete with the square brackets around the alias. (See Table 4 for a list of directives.)

TABLE 4
DIRECTIVES FOR USE IN XML COLUMN ALIASES

Directive	Description
ID	This is used to define an element as an anchor for a referral; other objects can then refer back to this one with IDREF and IDREFS. If you're not using the XMLDATA option, this option doesn't do anything.
IDREF	This links the element with another element that is specified with the ID directive. Once again, if you're not using the XMLDATA option, this doesn't do anything.
IDREFS	Same thing as IDREF.
hide	This specifies that the attribute should not be displayed. This is handy for creating an element that you want to sort on, but you don't necessarily want to have in the resultset.
element	This will force the creation of a new element with the name specified in the alias and the data coming from the column data.
xml	This directive specifies that the data in the column is already XML and shouldn't be parsed. It can be used only with the hide directive.
xmltext	The column will be wrapped up into a tag that will be stuck into the rest of your document. It also can be used only with the hide directive.
cdata	This will wrap the column data in a CDATA section with no encoding at all. Can be used only with string and text types, and it can be used only with the hide directive.

The OPENXML function works similarly to how OPEN-ROWSET and OPENQUERY work in that it returns a rowset that can be used in a SELECT statement. The full XML process is defined in the following list:

◆ Use the sp_xml_preparedocument system stored procedure to create a document handle.

◆ Use the OPENXML statement to define the format of the XML document and return the rowset.

◆ Use the sp_xml_removedocument system stored procedure to destroy the document handle.

Data Transformation Services

SQL Server 2000 provides a great tool that will import and export data for you, called the Data Transformation Services Import/Export Wizard. This tool uses SQL Server DTS to copy data into and out of SQL Server using nice, easy-to-understand graphical tools.

PROGRAMMING SQL SERVER 2000

Scripts, Batches, and Transactions

T-SQL programs are technically called *scripts*. A script is usually contained within a text file on disk, which is then loaded into some tool (the Query Analyzer, or the command-line equivalent called OSQL) and can be executed. A script is made of one or more *batches*. Each batch is made up of zero, one, or more transactions. Programming is discussed in Chapter 6.

Variable Types

You can create variables of nearly any type that you can store in a table, with the restriction that you can't create variables of type TEXT, NTEXT, or IMAGE. So, you can create int, tinyint, smallint, datetime, smalldatetime, uniqueidentifier, varchar, nvarchar, char, nchar, and so on. You can (and should) specify lengths where appropriate, such as varchar(30) or nchar(15). You can create a string variable that holds up to 8,000 bytes, so you can build a varchar(8000) or an nvarchar(4000) in a variable (remember that the nchar and nvarchar types are double-wide characters, so they take up twice as much room as a varchar).

Global Variables

Global variables are not variables. They are actually system functions that return various pieces of information about the current user environment for SQL Server. At one point, they were called "Global Variables," but that nomenclature is dying out. A global variable is a variable with two at-signs in front of it, like @@CONNECTIONS, which returns the current number of user connections. You cannot declare global variables, and you cannot directly change them with a SET statement or a SELECT statement. So, if you use one of these special functions somewhere, realize that although it looks like a variable and can act like one, you can't assign any data to it—you can only read data from it. Table 5 shows a list of the global variables in SQL Server 2000.

TABLE 5
GLOBAL VARIABLES IN SQL SERVER 2000

Global Variable	Description
@@CONNECTIONS	Returns the current number of connections that applications currently have open to SQL Server.
@@CPU_BUSY	The time, in milliseconds, that SQL Server has been busy since the last time it was restarted.
@@CURSOR_ROWS	The number of rows that are in the previously opened cursor. If no cursor has been opened, returns 0; if the cursor is asynchronous, returns a negative number representing the number of rows that have been used so far; if the number is positive, it's the number of rows in the cursor; and if the value is -1, the cursor is dynamic, so there's no telling how many rows are in it. We'll talk more about cursors later in this chapter.
@@DATEFIRST	Returns the number of the first day of the week. For example, if the first day of the week is set to Sunday, it will return 1; if it's set to Monday, it will return 2, and so on.
@@DBTS	Returns the current value of the time-stamp for the database. This has absolutely no relation to system time and is used only to manage certain inserts.
@@ERROR	Returns the error number for the last SQL statement executed.
@@FETCH_STATUS	Returns the status of the last cursor fetch operation: 0 for success, −1 for failure, or −2 for missing record.
@@IDENTITY	Returns the value used for the last INSERT INTO an identity column for the current connection.
@@IDLE	Returns the time in milliseconds that SQL Server has been idle since the last restart.
@@IO_BUSY	Returns the time in milliseconds that SQL Server has spent waiting for IO to return from a read or write request.
@@LANGID	Returns the language identifier of the current language in use.
@@LANGUAGE	Returns the name of the language currently in use. This is probably more useful than the ID number.
@@LOCK_TIMEOUT	Returns the number of milliseconds that the current connection will wait for a lock to clear to complete its work.
@@MAX_CONNECTIONS	Returns the maximum number of simultaneous user connections allowed on the current SQL Server.
@@MAX_PRECISION	This is the precision used by the DECIMAL and NUMERIC data types on the server. By default, this is 38.
@@NESTLEVEL	This is the current nesting level during stored procedure execution. We'll cover this more in Chapter 9.
@@OPTIONS	Returns an integer representing the settings of the user options for the current connection. See discussion in text under the heading "User Options".
@@PACK_RECEIVED	Returns the number of network packets received by the SQL Server since it was last restarted.
@@PACK_SENT	Returns the number of packets sent by the SQL Server since it was last restarted.
@@PACKET_ERRORS	Returns the number of packet errors that SQL Server has seen since it was last restarted.
@@PROCID	Returns the stored procedure identifier of the currently executing stored procedure.
@@REMSERVER	Returns the name of the SQL Server running the remote stored procedure.
@@ROWCOUNT	Returns the number of rows returned by the last statement. See the discussion in the text following the heading "Using @@ROWCOUNT".

continues

TABLE 5   *continued*
GLOBAL VARIABLES IN SQL SERVER 2000

Global Variable	Description
@@SERVERNAME	Returns the name of the current server.
@@SERVICENAME	Returns the name of the service that SQL Server is running under.
@@SPID	Returns the current process identifier used by SQL Server.
@@TEXTSIZE	This is the maximum number of bytes that will be returned in a resultset to the current connection from selecting a TEXT or IMAGE column.
@@TIMETICKS	Returns the number of microseconds that occur in one tick of the computer's clock.
@@TOTAL_ERRORS	Returns the total number of disk read/write errors that SQL Server has had since last restart.
@@TOTAL_READ	Returns the total number of physical disk reads that SQL Server has done since it was last started.
@@TOTAL_WRITE	Returns the total number of physical disk writes that SQL Server has done since it was last started.
@@TRANCOUNT	Returns the number of transactions "deep" the current statement is in a nested transaction.
@@VERSION	Returns the version string (date, version, and processor type) for the SQL Server.

Using Cursors

Cursors are a way to take the results of a SELECT statement and assign the output from the recordset to a set of variables one at a time. This allows you to walk through the recordset one record at a time and use the information in the recordset to do interesting things.

Creating a cursor has 5 steps. First, you have to DECLARE the cursor with the DECLARE CURSOR statement. Next, open the cursor with the OPEN statement. After that, you have to FETCH rows from the cursor, and when you're done you have to CLOSE the cursor and DEALLOCATE it. Table 6 shows a list of T-SQL cursor extensions.

TABLE 6
T-SQL CURSOR EXTENSIONS

Extension	Description
LOCAL	This is the optional state for a cursor. It means the cursor is available only for the current batch and the current connection. To change the default behavior, set the Default to Local Cursor database option.
GLOBAL	Global in this case means "Global to the current connection." Declaring a cursor as global will make it available to subsequent batches or stored procedures that are run by the connection. The cursor is not available to other connections, even if the connection is from the same user.
FORWARD_ONLY	This tells SQL Server that the cursor is going to run only from the beginning of the recordset to the end of the recordset. The cursor is not allowed to go backward or skip around. The only fetch that works is FETCH NEXT. This is an optimization; it allows SQL Server to consume less overhead for the cursor.
STATIC	This does the same thing as the INSENSITIVE keyword in the SQL-92 syntax.
KEYSET	If you use this extension, your cursor will not be able to access data inserted by other users after the cursor is opened. If a row is deleted by another user, an @@FETCH_STATUS of -2 (row is missing) message will be returned if you attempt to fetch a deleted row. This type of cursor has less overhead than a DYNAMIC cursor, but (unless FORWARD_ONLY is also specified) all the different FETCH options are available.
DYNAMIC	A DYNAMIC cursor is the opposite of a KEYSET cursor. All inserts and deletes done by users are immediately available to the cursor. However, FETCH ABSOLUTE will not work with a DYNAMIC cursor because the underlying data may change what position the records are in.
FAST_FORWARD	This is a cursor that has all the properties of a FORWARD_ONLY and READ_ONLY cursor, and is designed to go forward quickly with little overhead.
READ_ONLY	Does not allow updates to the cursor.
SCROLL_LOCKS	This causes SQL Server to exclusively lock each row that is touched by the cursor as they are read in, to prevent other users from updating the record.
OPTIMISTIC	This causes SQL Server to not lock any rows during the scrolling of the cursor. The script will just hope that none of the rows being changed by the cursor are being changed simultaneously by somebody else. Attempting to change a row through the cursor will result in an error.
TYPE_WARNING	If your cursor somehow changes type implicitly, a warning will be issued.

Lock Isolation Levels

SQL Server knows that sometimes it's critical that the data you are reading from the database is one hundred percent committed data, while sometimes you just want the data to be read quickly, and incomplete or uncommitted transactions just don't matter.

To allow for this, SQL Server supports four different transaction isolation levels:

◆ READ UNCOMMITTED. This isolation level will show you all the data without getting a shared lock before reading the data. Another connection may change the data while it is being read. This can be great for applications that are doing system monitoring or reporting, where minimal impact to the rest of the system is desired. This is also called "dirty reads."

◆ READ COMMITTED. This will acquire a shared lock during the read of the data but won't keep the shared lock for the entire transaction. The resulting data will be complete, but may change after successive reads, showing new data or missing data with each successive read. This is the default transaction isolation level and is generally an acceptable tradeoff between reading dirty data and minimizing contention.

◆ REPEATABLE READ. This acquires a shared lock on the rows for the duration of the transaction, but still allows other users to add rows into the result-set. This means that later reads may contain more data, but they won't contain any less.

◆ Serializable. This will acquire a shared lock on the entire range of data that is being queried, preventing inserts or updates from happening for the duration of the transaction. This is a very dangerous thing to do from a concurrency perspective, because it generates a lot of locks and can more easily result in deadlock problems.

Setting the isolation levels is performed through the use of the SET TRANSACTION ISOLATION LEVEL command. When set, the level will affect all SELECT operations issued through the connection.

Designing and Managing Transactions

If you don't explicitly tell SQL Server to treat a group of statements as a transaction, it implicitly puts each statement in its own transaction. For the purposes of an implicit transaction, the only statements that really count are the statements that interact with a database: SELECT, INSERT, UPDATE, and DELETE.

To explicitly put a group of statements into a transaction, you can use the BEGIN TRANSACTION command. This command tells SQL Server that all commands that follow are part of the transaction up until the end of the transaction, which is noted with a COMMIT TRANSACTION. In the event of a problem with the data being manipulated, you can also call ROLLBACK TRANSACTION. If there is an error during the execution of the transaction, such as a server shutdown, a disk error of some type, or lock contention, then the transaction will automatically roll back.

Statement Permissions

Statement permissions are assigned to allow users to do things like create databases, define user-defined functions and stored procedures, and back up the database or transaction log. Statement permissions are assigned by using the GRANT statement.

Object Permissions

Object permissions are permissions granted to access objects in certain ways. For tables and views, you can grant SELECT, DELETE, UPDATE, and INSERT permissions, and for stored procedure and function objects you can grant EXECUTE permissions. Permissions are granted to users, so the user must exist in the database prior to granting permission. To give a user permission to access certain database objects, use the GRANT command.

User Roles

In order to provide the capability to grant multiple users access to the same objects the same way, SQL Server provides a mechanism for creating collections of users, called *roles*.

Fixed Roles

SQL Server provides you with a set of roles you can use to assign different levels of permission to users. There are two types of fixed roles. Fixed server roles are server-wide permissions that can be used regardless of the database you are in. Then there are fixed database roles, which apply to only one database.

Application Roles

One of the handy features of this security model is the ability to have an application role. An application role is similar to other roles, but the role has no members associated with it. The GRANT and REVOKE statements work the same way with an application role as with any other role. To create an application role, use the sp_addapprole system stored procedure. Application roles have no members because they operate on a password. The use of the role is restricted to those who know the password as opposed to membership.

WORKING WITH VIEWS

Views

Views can be used to define numerous combinations of rows and columns from one or more tables (see Chapter 7). When views use only a portion of the columns in a table, then the table data is referred to as being *vertically filtered*. When Views use only a portion of the rows in a table, then the table data is referred to as being *horizontally filtered*. Filtering data is a great advantage of using views. For example, if you need only a subset of data from a table, then a view will prevent users from accidentally (or purposely) seeing too much data, because the most that can be seen is what is con-

tained in the view. The following list provides more information about views:

- A view is nothing more than a SELECT statement that has been given a name and saved in the database. The view does not contain the data, but defines where the data comes from. The view can often be treated like a table.

- Because a view is only a SELECT statement, you are able to filter the data that is returned to include some or all of a table's rows or columns. You are able to stick to the important data.

- The view's definition can consist of rows and columns from one or more tables in the current or other databases.

- A view can contain a maximum of 1,024 columns.

- Defaults, triggers, and rules are not allowed to be associated with a view. The only exception to this rule is the new INSTEAD OF trigger.

- A view can use data that may be anywhere (such as another database) as long as the view is created in current database.

- View names must follow the rules for identifiers.

- Views cannot be created using the ORDER BY clause unless they use the TOP clause (for example, TOP 100 PERCENT).

- Views cannot be created using the COMPUTE BY or SELECT INTO clauses.

- View names must adhere to uniqueness rules. Two users may create a view name "MyView" because the object owner will make the fully qualified names unique.

- Views cannot be created on temporary tables.

- Temporary views cannot be created.

- Views can be nested up to 32 levels.

Partitioned Views

A partitioned view combines horizontally partitioned data from *member* tables across one or more servers (distributed partitioned views). A member table can be thought of as a segment from a larger table. There are two types of partitioned views in SQL Server: A local partitioned view and a distributed partitioned view. A local partitioned view is a partitioned view where all member tables reside on the local instance of SQL Server.

When creating partitioned views, there are some considerations that should be noted:

◆ Local Partitioned Views do not need to use CHECK constraints. Not using CHECK constraints will also provide the same results as with using a CHECK constraint, except that the Query Optimizer will have to perform a lengthy search against all member tables meeting the query search condition. Using Check constraints will reduce the cost of queries.

◆ When creating partitioned views, be sure that all columns of each member table are included in the partitioned view definition. Also, make sure that the same column is not referenced twice in the SELECT list. Make sure that all identical columns in all tables are of the same data type.

◆ When referencing member tables in a view, be sure to use the FROM clause to specifically declare a reference each table will be used.

◆ Be sure that Primary Keys are defined on the same column for each member table.

◆ It is possible to create updateable partitioned views. This requires that each table's SELECT statement refers to only one base table, the UNION ALL operator is used to join the resultsets together, and non-local tables use the full four-part identifier in their name.

Broken Ownership Chains

One problem that can arise when you are using views and other database objects occurs when you have different owners for objects in your database. Whenever there is a change in ownership, the owner of each object has to grant permissions to the object. When the ownership of objects in a chain are changed, there is a break in ownership or you have a broken ownership chain. To prevent ownership chains, have all objects created and owned by dbo.

USE OF TRIGGERS

The use of triggers in SQL Server 2000 represents an important part of process development (see Chapter 8). INSERT triggers are used to modify and disallow data during an attempt to change a record. UPDATE triggers are used to restrict or allow update modifications made to a certain table. DELETE triggers work in reverse to how INSERT triggers work. They restrict the removal of data from a table, whereas an INSERT trigger restricts the data that goes inside a table.

Recursive Triggers

Triggers are used to keep the flow of data within the boundaries of proper business logic, and this is why they are so widely used. Their capability is equal to stored procedures, and they are able to change records in *other* tables. There are two types of recursion, and each type of recursion has a solution within the SQL Server. The two types of recursion are direct and indirect. Before any recursion takes place, the database option of Recursive Triggers must be set to On. This option can be set with sp_dboption and defaults to Off.

INSTEAD OF Triggers

Prior to SQL Server 2000, the only type of trigger available was an AFTER trigger—a trigger that contains a set of statements that fire *after* a modification to a table, after constraints have been applied. INSTEAD OF triggers are newly introduced into SQL Server 2000 and execute *instead of* the triggering action.

Because there can be only one INSTEAD OF trigger of each type on a table, there is no need or reason to attempt to set the fire order of INSTEAD OF triggers. There can be many AFTER triggers of each type set on a single table, however, which means that there is a reason to set the order of triggers. To change the fire order of triggers, you can use the sp_settriggerorder stored procedure. With the exception of first and last, you have no control over how triggers will fire.

STORED PROCEDURES AND USER-DEFINED FUNCTIONS

Stored Procedures

In any database system, you will be required to develop custom procedures and functions. Use of stored procedures and the new functionality of user–defined functions are covered in Chapter 9. A stored procedure can have input parameters, which make it possible to tell the stored procedure things like the parameters for the queries it should run. A stored procedure can return results in several ways: with an integer return code, with one or more resultsets, and with output parameters.

To pass back a number to the calling process, use the RETURN statement. The RETURN statement immediately exits the stored procedure, so don't use it until the stored procedure is done. Stored procedures can also

pass data to the calling application by using output parameters. Output parameters are declared like other parameters in the CREATE PROCEDURE statement with the word OUTPUT after them.

Cursor Status

If you're in doubt about the validity of the cursor variable, you can use the CURSOR_STATUS() function. This function returns different values depending on the condition of the cursor—provided you know the type of cursor (local, global, or variable). The syntax is CURSOR_STATUS('<type>', '<variable>'). The single ticks are mandatory. For example, to diagnose the preceding cursor, you could use CURSOR_STATUS ('variable', '@OutputCursor'). Table 7 shows what the CURSOR_STATUS function returns.

TABLE 7
CURSOR_STATUS RETURN VALUES

Return Value	Explanation
1	The cursor is allocated, open, valid, and has at least one row if it is a static cursor, or may have zero rows if it is dynamic.
0	The cursor is allocated and open, but it is empty. This can happen only on static cursors.
−1	The cursor is closed.
−2	An error occurred because the variable wasn't assigned or the cursor was closed and deallocated.
−3	The cursor doesn't exist.

Error Handling

If @@ERROR is set to something besides zero, then an error occurred while attempting to run the statement. The @@ERROR variable can be used to handle errors that won't stop a batch (or a stored procedure) from running, such as constraint violations or problems with aggregate functions that don't have enough data.

User-Defined Functions

User-defined functions have been on the most-requested-feature lists of most SQL Server programmers for a very long time. We use the system-defined functions, such as USER_NAME(), @@SERVERNAME, CONVERT(), and GETDATE() constantly—they provide the functionality that makes T-SQL useful in many respects. By passing back basic values, user-defined functions can be used in many places where stored procedures just wouldn't work.

The following list shows system-defined functions not allowed inside a user-defined function:

@@CONNECTIONS	@@PACK_SENT	GETDATE()
@@CPU_BUSY	@@PACKET_ERRORS	GETUTCDATE()
@@IDLE	@@TIMETICKS	NEWID()
@@IO_BUSY	@@TOTAL_ERRORS	RAND()
@@MAX_CONNECTIONS	@@TOTAL_READ	TEXTPTR
@@PACK_RECEIVED	@@TOTAL_WRITE	

BOOSTING PERFORMANCE WITH INDEXES

Clustered Indexes

Effects on performance can be notably improved or detrimentally negative based on appropriate use of indexes. This plays an important part in SQL Server development and on the exam, so we placed this related information into a topic of its own, which is covered in Chapters 10 and 12. As seen in the previous sections, a clustered index is a type of index in which the logical order of the key values determines the physical order of the data stored on disk. Because a clustered index shows how the physical data of a table is stored, there can be only one clustered index per table.

Nonclustered Indexes

Nonclustered indexes are indexes in which the logical order of the key values in the index is different from the physical order of the rows in the indexed table.

Index Selectivity

To find the selectivity of a query, use the following formula:

```
Selectivity ratio = [100 * (Total number of
➥distinct index rows)] / (Total number of rows
➥in the table)]
```

Here are some guidelines you should look at when choosing not to index a column:

◆ If the index is never used by the query optimizer.

◆ If the column values exhibit low selectivity, often greater than 95% for non-clustered indexes.

◆ If the column(s) to be indexed are very wide.

◆ If the table is rarely queried.

◆ Do not index columns that are not used in WHERE clauses, aggregated, or used in sorting.

Indexed Views

Here are some of the benefits of indexed views:

◆ They increase performance of queries that use joins and aggregates to process numerous rows.

◆ Data residing in an indexed view is automatically updated when a base table gets modified.

◆ Views that aggregate and join data are improved because when an index is created on a view, the view is executed and the resultset is stored in the database.

◆ The first time you create an index on a view, it has to be of type unique clustered; after this has been created, additional nonclustered indexes can be created.

Indexed Views Requirements and Restrictions

There are some prerequisites that need to be taken before creating an indexed view:

◆ The first index on a view must be a clustered index.

◆ Non-deterministic functions are not allowed in the view's definition.

◆ The view must be created using WITH SCHEMABINDING (which prevents the dropping and altering of tables participating in the indexed view).

◆ Modification of session-level settings are required. These are outlined in Table 8.

> **NOTE**
>
> **Non-Deterministic Functions Are Not Allowed on Indexed Views** Deterministic functions are functions that return the same result each time they are called. ABS is a deterministic function because it always returns the same outcome each time a new argument is supplied. GETDATE, on the other hand, is non-deterministic because it always results in a new value each time it is evaluated.

TABLE 8
MANDATORY SETTINGS

Session Level Setting	Value
ANSI_NULLS	On
ANSI_WARNINGS	On
ARITHABORT	On
CONCAT_NULL_YEILDS_NULL	On
QUOTED_IDENTIFIERS	On
ANSI_PADDING	On
NUMERIC_ROUNDABORT	Off

IMPLEMENTING AND UNDERSTANDING REPLICATION METHODOLOGIES

In putting together a complete enterprise-wide solution to data handling, the topic of replication and its pros and cons will no doubt come up. A thorough understanding of replication concepts is necessary to understand where this technology can be best implemented. Chapter 11 deals with all the concepts at length.

Replication is the process of carrying, modifying, and distributing data and database objects (stored procedures, extended properties, views, tables, user-defined functions, triggers, and indexes) from one source server to another, in a consistent fashion, independent of location. Replication can be implemented over the Internet to distribute data among diverse locations, allowing anonymous and disconnected users to access data. Replication is a huge topic. There are multiple types and an infinite number of forms any implementation can use. The following section describes just why replication is implemented.

MONITORING AND TUNING SQL SERVER DATABASES

Tools

Troubleshooting and getting the best performance out of an existing environment can be quite a challenge. Fortunately SQL Server has many tools that make this task a lot easier. Monitoring and troubleshooting are covered at length in Chapter 12.

To best troubleshoot any object, you first must have some knowledge of the circumstances surrounding the system and observations that will form the basis of the study. The following list represents the tools that are used to diagnose SQL Server implementations:

◆ **Query Analyzer.** Used to diagnose T-SQL statements and activity and aid in application performance tuning and optimization tasks.

◆ **SQL Profiler.** Provides access to all SQL Server activity and objects. Used for detailed monitoring of selected server-wide events.

◆ **System Monitor.** Provides a broad spectrum of server analysis. Used primarily for hardware and operating system activity as well as interactions between the operating system and SQL Server.

◆ **Current activity window.** This is what's happening now. View user, process, and lock information based on the present utilization.

◆ **Transact-SQL.** Many commands are available that can be used from the Query Analyzer or other T-SQL connection.

◆ **Error logs.** This won't necessarily tell you all of the whys, but it is an excellent start to find out the whats.

Simple Network Management Protocol (SNMP)

Simple Network Management Protocol (SNMP) is an application protocol that is part of the larger TCP/IP protocol suite. SNMP provides for network management services that report and diagnose operating system and protocol information. Using SNMP, you can monitor an instance of any server that has been configured to report its information. SQL Server can be monitored running on Windows NT 4.0, Windows 98, and UNIX, as well as other platforms.

SNMP requires that a service report information to an agent who can then send data to monitoring computers. Using different tools, an administrator can view and report on a variety of information from the operating system, SQL Server software, and database objects. SNMP uses management information databases (MIB) for each service that it diagnoses. This database provides the necessary hierarchy to allow an agent to query the server for the desired data.

System Monitor

The following list represent the SQL Server objects that are installed for the use of the Windows 2000 System Monitor and NT Server Performance Monitor tools and what the counter provides:

◆ **Access Methods.** Allocation of SQL Server database objects.

◆ **Backup Device.** Information about backup devices.

◆ **Buffer Manager.** Information about the memory buffers used by SQL Server.

◆ **Cache Manager.** Information about the SQL Server cache.

◆ **Databases.** Information about a SQL Server database.

◆ **General Statistics.** Information about general server-wide activity.

◆ **Latches.** Information about the latches on internal resources.

◆ **Locks.** Information about the individual lock requests made by SQL Server.

◆ **Memory Manager.** Information about SQL Server memory usage.

◆ **Replication Agents.** Information about the SQL Server replication agents.

◆ **Replication Dist.** The number of commands and transactions read from the distribution database and delivered to the `Subscriber` databases by the Distribution Agent.

◆ **Replication Logreader.** The number of commands and transactions read from the `Publisher` databases and delivered to the distribution database by the Log Reader Agent.

◆ **Replication Merge.** Information about SQL Server merge replication.

◆ **Replication Snapshot.** Information about SQL Server snapshot replication.

◆ **SQL Statistics.** Provides information about aspects of SQL queries.

◆ **User Settable Object.** Allows for custom monitoring. Each counter can be a custom stored procedure or any T-SQL statement that returns a value to be monitored.

This element of the book provides you with some general guidelines for preparing for a certification exam. It is organized into four sections. The first section addresses your learning style and how it affects your preparation for the exam. The second section covers your exam preparation activities and general study tips. This is followed by an extended look at the Microsoft certification exams, including a number of specific tips that apply to the various Microsoft exam formats and question types. Finally, changes in Microsoft's testing policies, and how these might affect you, are discussed.

LEARNING STYLES

To better understand the nature of preparation for the test, it is important to understand learning as a process. You probably are aware of how you best learn new material. You may find that outlining works best for you, or, as a visual learner, you may need to "see" things. Whatever your learning style, test preparation takes place over time. Obviously, you shouldn't start studying for these exams the night before you take them; it is very important to understand that learning is a developmental process. Understanding it as a process helps you focus on what you know and what you have yet to learn.

Thinking about how you learn should help you recognize that learning takes place when you are able to match new information to old. You have some previous experience with computers and networking. Now you are preparing for this certification exam. Using this book, software, and supplementary materials will not just add incrementally to what you know; as you study, the organization of your knowledge actually restructures as you integrate new information into your existing knowledge base. This leads you to a more comprehensive

Study and Exam Prep Tips

understanding of the tasks and concepts outlined in the objectives and of computing in general. Again, this happens as a result of a repetitive process rather than a single event. Keep this model of learning in mind as you prepare for the exam, and you will make better decisions concerning what to study and how much more studying you need to do.

Study Tips

There are many ways to approach studying just as there are many different types of material to study. However, the tips that follow should work well for the type of material covered on the certification exams.

Study Strategies

Although individuals vary in the ways they learn information, some basic principles of learning apply to everyone. You should adopt some study strategies that take advantage of these principles. One of these principles is that learning can be broken into various depths. Recognition (of terms, for example) exemplifies more of a surface level of learning, in which you rely on a prompt of some sort to elicit recall. Comprehension or understanding (of the concepts behind the terms, for example) represents a deeper level of learning. The ability to analyze a concept and apply your understanding of it in a new way represents a further depth of learning.

Your learning strategy should enable you to know the material at a level or two deeper than mere recognition. This will help you perform well on the exams. You should know the material so thoroughly that you can easily handle the recognition-level types of questions used in multiple-choice testing. You should also be able to apply your knowledge to solve new problems.

Macro and Micro Study Strategies

One strategy that can lead to this deeper learning is to prepare an outline that covers all the objectives and subobjectives for the particular exam you are preparing for. You should delve a bit further into the material and include a level or two of detail beyond the stated objectives and subobjectives for the exam. Then expand the outline by coming up with a statement of definition or a summary for each point in the outline.

An outline provides two approaches to studying. First, you can study the outline by focusing on the organization of the material. Work your way through the points and sub-points of your outline with the goal of learning how they relate to one another. For example, be sure you understand how each of the main objective areas is similar to and different from the others. Then, do the same thing with the subobjectives; be sure you know what subobjectives pertain to each objective area and how they relate to one another.

Next, you can work through the outline, focusing on learning the details. Memorize and understand terms and their definitions, facts, rules and strategies, advantages and disadvantages, and so on. In this pass through the outline, attempt to learn detail rather than the big picture (the organizational information that you worked on in the first pass through the outline).

Research has shown that attempting to assimilate both types of information at the same time seems to interfere with the overall learning process. Separate your studying into these two approaches, and you will perform better on the exam.

Active Study Strategies

The process of writing down and defining objectives, subobjectives, terms, facts, and definitions promotes a more active learning strategy than merely reading the material does. In human information-processing terms, writing forces you to engage in more active encoding of the information. Simply reading over it exemplifies more passive processing.

Next, determine whether you can apply the information you have learned by attempting to create examples and scenarios on your own. Think about how or where you could apply the concepts you are learning. Again, write down this information to process the facts and concepts in a more active fashion.

The hands-on nature of the step-by-step tutorials and exercises at the ends of the chapters provides further active learning opportunities that reinforce concepts as well.

Common-Sense Strategies

Finally, you should also follow common-sense practices when studying. Study when you are alert, reduce or eliminate distractions, and take breaks when you become fatigued.

Pre-Testing Yourself

Pre-testing enables you to assess how well you are learning. One of the most important aspects of learning is what has been called "meta-learning." Meta-learning has to do with realizing when you know something well or when you need to study some more. In other words, you recognize how well or how poorly you have learned the material you are studying.

For most people, this can be difficult to assess objectively on their own. Practice tests are useful in that they reveal more objectively what you have learned and what you have not learned. You should use this information to guide review and further studying. Developmental learning takes place as you cycle through studying, assessing how well you have learned, then reviewing, and then assessing again until you feel you are ready to take the exam.

You may have noticed the practice exam included in this book. Use it as part of the learning process. The *ExamGear, Training Guide Edition* test simulation software included on the CD also provides you with an excellent opportunity to assess your knowledge.

You should set a goal for your pre-testing. A reasonable goal would be to score consistently in the 90% range.

See Appendix D, "Using the *ExamGear, Training Guide Edition Software*," for more explanation of the test simulation software.

EXAM PREP TIPS

Having mastered the subject matter, the final preparatory step is to understand how the exam will be presented. Make no mistake: A Microsoft Certified Professional (MCP) exam will challenge both your knowledge and your test-taking skills. This section starts with the basics of exam design, reviews a new type of exam format, and concludes with hints targeted to each of the exam formats.

The MCP Exam

Every MCP exam is released in one of three basic formats. What's being called "exam format" here is really little more than a combination of the overall exam structure and the presentation method for exam questions.

Understanding the exam formats is key to good preparation because the format determines the number of questions presented, the difficulty of those questions, and the amount of time you have to complete the exam.

Each exam format uses many of the same types of questions. These types or styles of questions include several types of traditional multiple-choice questions, multiple-rating (or scenario-based) questions, and simulation-based questions. Some exams include other types of questions that ask you to drag and drop objects on the screen, reorder a list, or categorize things. Still other exams ask you to answer these types of questions in response to a case study you have read. It's important that you understand the types of questions you will be asked and the actions required to properly answer them.

The rest of this section addresses the exam formats and then tackles the question types. Understanding the formats and question types will help you feel much more comfortable when you take the exam.

Exam Format

The three basic formats for the MCP exams are the traditional fixed-form exam, the adaptive form, and the case study form. As its name implies, the fixed-form exam presents a fixed set of questions during the exam session. The adaptive form, however, uses only a subset of questions drawn from a larger pool during any given exam session. The case study form includes case studies that serve as the basis for the various types of questions.

Fixed-Form

A fixed-form computerized exam is based on a fixed set of exam questions. The individual questions are presented in random order during a test session. If you take the same exam more than once, you will not necessarily see the exact same questions. This happens because two or three final forms are typically assembled for every fixed-form exam Microsoft releases. These are usually labeled forms A, B, and C.

The final forms of the fixed-form exams are identical in terms of content coverage, number of questions, and allotted time, but the questions are different. You may notice, however, that some of the same questions appear on, or rather are shared among, different final forms. When questions are shared among multiple final forms of an exam, the percentage of sharing is generally small. Many final forms share no questions, but some older exams may have a 10–15% duplication of exam questions on the final exam forms.

Fixed-form exams also have a fixed time limit in which you must complete the exam. The *ExamGear, Training Guide Edition* software on the CD-ROM that accompanies this book provides fixed-form exams.

Finally, the score you achieve on a fixed-form exam, which is always reported for MCP exams on a scale of 0 to 1,000, is based on the number of questions you answer correctly. The passing score is the same for all final forms of a given fixed-form exam.

The typical format for a fixed-form exam is as follows:

◆ 50–60 questions.

◆ 75–90 minutes for testing time.

◆ Question review is allowed, including the opportunity to change your answers.

Adaptive Form

An adaptive-form exam has the same appearance as a fixed-form exam, but its questions differ in quantity and process of selection. Although the statistics of adaptive testing are fairly complex, the process is concerned with determining your level of skill or ability with the exam subject matter. This ability assessment begins with the presentation of questions of varying levels of difficulty and ascertaining at what difficulty level you can reliably answer them. Finally, the ability assessment determines whether that ability level is above or below the level required to pass that exam.

Examinees at different levels of ability see quite different sets of questions. Examinees who demonstrate little expertise with the subject matter continue to be presented with relatively easy questions. Examinees who demonstrate a high level of expertise are presented with progressively more difficult questions. Individuals of both levels of expertise may answer the same number of questions correctly, but because the higher-expertise examinee can correctly answer more difficult questions, he or she receives a higher score and is more likely to pass the exam.

The typical design for the adaptive form exam is as follows:

- ◆ 20–25 questions.

- ◆ 90-minute testing time (although this is likely to be reduced to 45–60 minutes in the near future).

- ◆ Question review is not allowed; you have no opportunity to change your answers.

The Adaptive-Exam Process

Your first adaptive exam will be unlike any other testing experience you have had. In fact, many examinees have difficulty accepting the adaptive testing process because they feel that they were not provided the opportunity to adequately demonstrate their full expertise.

You can take consolation in the fact that adaptive exams are painstakingly put together after months of data gathering and analysis and that adaptive exams are just as valid as fixed-form exams. The rigor introduced through the adaptive testing methodology means that there is nothing arbitrary about the exam items you'll see. It is also a more efficient means of testing, requiring less time to conduct and complete than traditional fixed-form exams.

As you can see in Figure 1, a number of statistical measures drive the adaptive examination process. The measure most immediately relevant to you is the ability estimate. Accompanying this test statistic are the standard error of measurement, the item characteristic curve, and the test information curve.

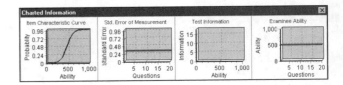

FIGURE 1
Microsoft's adaptive testing demonstration program.

The standard error, which is the key factor in determining when an adaptive exam will terminate, reflects the degree of error in the exam ability estimate. The item characteristic curve reflects the probability of a correct response relative to examinee ability. Finally, the test information statistic provides a measure of the information contained in the set of questions the examinee has answered, again relative to the ability level of the individual examinee.

When you begin an adaptive exam, the standard error has already been assigned a target value below which it must drop for the exam to conclude. This target value reflects a particular level of statistical confidence in the process. The examinee ability is initially set to the mean possible exam score (500 for MCP exams).

As the adaptive exam progresses, questions of varying difficulty are presented. Based on your pattern of responses to these questions, the ability estimate is recalculated. At the same time, the standard error estimate is refined from its first estimated value of one toward the target value. When the standard error reaches its target value, the exam is terminated. Thus, the more consistently you answer questions of the same degree of difficulty, the more quickly the standard error estimate drops, and the fewer questions you will end up seeing during the exam session. This situation is depicted in Figure 2.

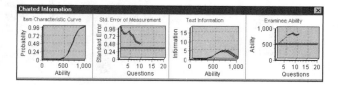

FIGURE 2
The changing statistics in an adaptive exam.

As you might suspect, one good piece of advice for taking an adaptive exam is to treat every exam question as if it were the most important. The adaptive scoring algorithm attempts to discover a pattern of responses that reflects some level of proficiency with the subject matter. Incorrect responses almost guarantee that additional questions must be answered (unless, of course, you get every question wrong). The scoring algorithm must adjust to information that is not consistent with the emerging pattern.

Case Study Form

The case study-based format first appeared with the advent of the 70-100 exam (Solution Architectures). The questions in the case study format are not the independent entities that they are in the fixed and adaptive formats. Instead, questions are tied to a case study, a long scenario-like description of an information technology situation. As the test taker, your job is to extract from the case study the information that needs to be integrated with your understanding of Microsoft technology. The idea is that a case study provides you with a situation that is even more like a "real life" problem situation than the other formats provide.

The case studies are presented as "testlets." These are sections within the exam in which you read the case study, then answer 10 to 15 questions that apply to the case study. When you finish that section, you move onto another testlet with another case study and its

associated questions. There may be as many as five of these testlets that compose the overall exam. You are given more time to complete such an exam because it takes time to read through the cases and analyze them. You may have as much as three hours to complete the exam—and you may need all of it. The case studies are always available through a linking button while you are in that testlet. However, after you leave a testlet, you cannot come back to it.

Figure 3 provides an illustration of part of such a case study.

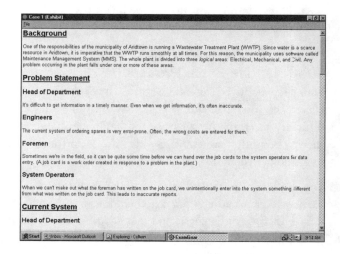

FIGURE 3
An example of a case study.

Question Types

A variety of question types can appear on MCP exams. Examples of many of the various types appear in this book and the *ExamGear, Training Guide Edition* software. We have attempted to cover all the types that were available at the time of this writing. Most of the question types discussed in the following sections can appear in each of the three exam formats.

The typical MCP exam question is based on the idea of measuring skills or the ability to complete tasks. Therefore, most of the questions are written so as to present you with a situation that includes a role (such as a system administrator or technician), a technology environment (100 computers running Windows 98 on a Windows 2000 Server network), and a problem to be solved (the user can connect to services on the LAN, but not the intranet). The answers indicate actions that you might take to solve the problem or create setups or environments that would function correctly from the start. Keep this in mind as you read the questions on the exam. You may encounter some questions that call for you to just regurgitate facts, but these will be relatively few and far between.

The following sections look at the different question types.

Multiple-Choice Questions

Despite the variety of question types that now appear in various MCP exams, the multiple-choice question is still the basic building block of the exams. The multiple-choice question comes in three varieties:

◆ **Regular multiple-choice.** Also referred to as an "alphabetic question," it asks you to choose one answer as correct.

◆ **Multiple-answer multiple-choice.** Also referred to as a "multi-alphabetic question," this version of a multiple-choice question requires you to choose two or more answers as correct. Typically, you are told precisely the number of correct answers to choose.

◆ **Enhanced multiple-choice.** This is a regular or multiple-answer question that includes a graphic or table to which you must refer to answer the question correctly.

Examples of such questions appear at the end of each chapter.

Multiple-Rating Questions

These questions are often referred to as "scenario questions." Similar to multiple-choice questions, they offer more extended descriptions of the computing environment and a problem that needs to be solved. Required and optional results of the problem-solving are specified, as well as a solution. You are then asked to judge whether the actions taken in the solution are likely to bring about all or part of the required and desired optional results. There is, typically, only one correct answer.

You may be asking yourself, "What is multiple about multiple-rating questions?" The answer is that rather than having multiple answers, the question itself may be repeated in the exam with only minor variations in the required results, optional results, or solution introduced to create "new" questions. Read these different versions very carefully; the differences can be subtle.

Examples of these types of questions appear at the end of the chapters.

Simulation Questions

Simulation-based questions reproduce the look and feel of key Microsoft product features for the purpose of testing. The simulation software used in MCP exams has been designed to look and act, as much as possible, just like the actual product. Consequently, answering simulation questions in an MCP exam entails completing one or more tasks just as if you were using the product itself.

The format of a typical Microsoft simulation question consists of a brief scenario or problem statement, along with one or more tasks that you must complete to solve the problem. An example of a simulation question for MCP exams is shown in the following section.

A Typical Simulation Question

It sounds obvious, but your first step when you encounter a simulation question is to carefully read the question (see Figure 4). Do not go straight to the simulation application! You must assess the problem that's presented and identify the conditions that make up the problem scenario. Note the tasks that must be performed or outcomes that must be achieved to answer the question, and then review any instructions you're given on how to proceed.

FIGURE 4
Typical MCP exam simulation question with directions.

The next step is to launch the simulator by using the button provided. After clicking the Show Simulation button, you will see a feature of the product, as shown in the dialog box in Figure 5. The simulation application partially obscures the question text on many test center machines. Feel free to reposition the simulator and to move between the question text screen and the simulator by using hotkeys or point-and-click navigation, or even by clicking the simulator's launch button again.

It is important for you to understand that your answer to the simulation question is not recorded until you move on to the next exam question. This gives you the added capability of closing and reopening the simulation application (using the launch button) on the same question without losing any partial answer you may have made.

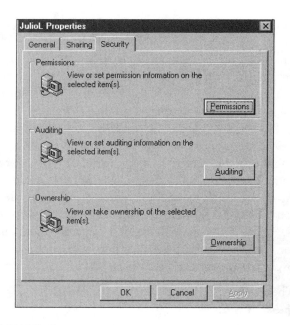

FIGURE 5
Launching the simulation application.

The third step is to use the simulator as you would the actual product to solve the problem or perform the defined tasks. Again, the simulation software is designed to function—within reason—just as the product does. But don't expect the simulator to reproduce product behavior perfectly. Most importantly, do not allow yourself to become flustered if the simulator does not look or act exactly like the product.

Figure 6 shows the solution to the example simulation problem.

Two final points will help you tackle simulation questions. First, respond only to what is being asked in the question; do not solve problems that you are not asked to solve. Second, accept what is being asked of you. You may not entirely agree with conditions in the problem statement, the quality of the desired solution, or the sufficiency of defined tasks to adequately solve the problem. Always remember that you are being tested on your ability to solve the problem as it is presented.

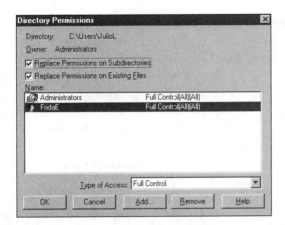

FIGURE 6
The solution to the simulation example.

The solution to the simulation problem shown in Figure 6 perfectly illustrates both of those points. As you'll recall from the question scenario (refer to Figure 4), you were asked to assign appropriate permissions to a new user, Frida E. You were not instructed to make any other changes in permissions. Thus, if you were to modify or remove the administrator's permissions, this item would be scored wrong on an MCP exam.

Hot Area Question

Hot area questions call for you to click a graphic or diagram to complete some task. You are asked a question that is similar to any other, but rather than clicking an option button or check box next to an answer, you click the relevant item in a screen shot or on a part of a diagram. An example of such an item is shown in Figure 7.

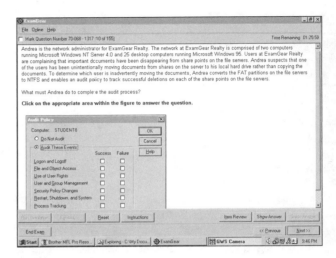

FIGURE 7
A typical hot area question.

Drag-and-Drop-Style Questions

Microsoft has utilized two different types of drag-and-drop questions in exams. The first is a select-and-place question. The other is a drop-and-connect question. Both are covered in the following sections.

Select-and-Place

Select-and-place questions typically require you to drag and drop labels on images in a diagram so as to correctly label or identify some portion of a network. Figure 8 shows you the actual question portion of a select-and-place item.

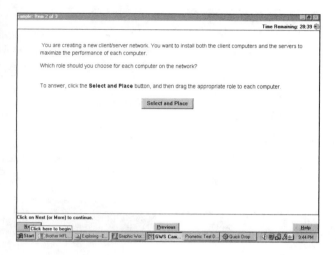

FIGURE 8
A select-and-place question.

Figure 9 shows the window you would see after you chose Select and Place. It contains the actual diagram in which you would select and drag the various server roles and match them up with the appropriate computers.

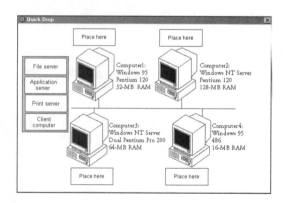

FIGURE 9
The window containing the diagram.

Drop and Connect

Drop-and-connect questions provide a different spin on the drag-and-drop question. The question provides you with the opportunity to create boxes that you can label, as well as connectors of various types with which to link them. In essence, you are creating a model or diagram to answer the question. You might have to create a network diagram or a data model for a database system. Figure 10 illustrates the idea of a drop-and-connect question.

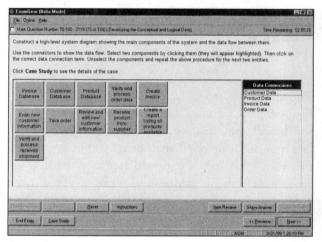

FIGURE 10
A drop-and-connect question.

Ordered List Questions

Ordered list questions require you to consider a list of items and place them in the proper order. You select items and then use a button to add them to a new list in the correct order. You have another button that you can use to remove the items in the new list in case you change your mind and want to reorder things. Figure 11 shows an ordered list item.

Tree Questions

Tree questions require you to think hierarchically and categorically. You are asked to place items from a list into categories that are displayed as nodes in a tree structure. Such questions might ask you to identify parent-child relationships in processes or the structure of keys in a database. You might also be required to show order within the categories much as you would in an ordered list question. Figure 12 shows a typical tree question.

As you can see, Microsoft is making an effort to utilize question types that go beyond asking you to simply memorize facts. These question types force you to know how to accomplish tasks and understand concepts and relationships. Study so that you can answer these types of questions rather than those that simply ask you to recall facts.

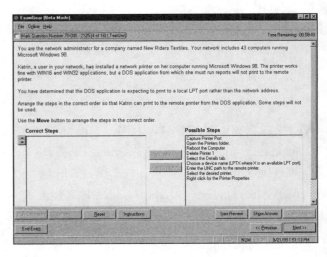

FIGURE 11
An ordered list question.

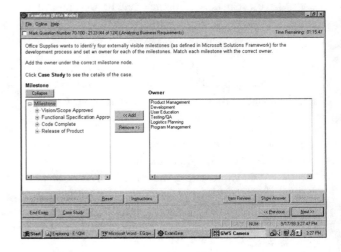

FIGURE 12
A tree question.

Putting It All Together

Given all these different pieces of information, the task now is to assemble a set of tips that will help you successfully tackle the different types of MCP exams.

More Exam Preparation Tips

Generic exam-preparation advice is always useful. Tips include the following:

◆ Become familiar with the product. Hands-on experience is one of the keys to success on any MCP exam. Review the exercises and the Step by Steps in the book.

◆ Review the current exam-preparation guide on the Microsoft MCP web site. The documentation Microsoft makes available over the web identifies the skills every exam is intended to test.

◆ Memorize foundational technical detail, but remember that MCP exams are generally heavier on problem solving and application of knowledge than on questions that require only rote memorization.

◆ Take any of the available practice tests. We recommend the one included in this book and the ones you can create using the *ExamGear* software on the CD-ROM. As a supplement to the material bound with this book, try the free practice tests available on the Microsoft MCP web site.

◆ Look on the Microsoft MCP web site for samples and demonstration items. These tend to be particularly valuable for one significant reason: They help you become familiar with new testing technologies before you encounter them on MCP exams.

During the Exam Session

The following generic exam-taking advice that you've heard for years also applies when you're taking an MCP exam:

◆ Take a deep breath and try to relax when you first sit down for your exam session. It is very important that you control the pressure you may (naturally) feel when taking exams.

◆ You will be provided scratch paper. Take a moment to write down any factual information and technical detail that you committed to short-term memory.

◆ Carefully read all information and instruction screens. These displays have been put together to give you information relevant to the exam you are taking.

◆ Accept the non-disclosure agreement and preliminary survey as part of the examination process. Complete them accurately and quickly move on.

◆ Read the exam questions carefully. Reread each question to identify all relevant detail.

◆ Tackle the questions in the order in which they are presented. Skipping around will not build your confidence; the clock is always counting down (at least in the fixed form exams).

◆ Don't rush, but also don't linger on difficult questions. The questions vary in degree of difficulty. Don't let yourself be flustered by a particularly difficult or wordy question.

Fixed-Form Exams

Building from this basic preparation and test-taking advice, you also need to consider the challenges presented by the different exam designs. Because a fixed-form exam is composed of a fixed, finite set of questions, add these tips to your strategy for taking a fixed-form exam:

◆ Note the time allotted and the number of questions on the exam you are taking. Make a rough calculation of how many minutes you can spend on each question, and use this figure to pace yourself through the exam.

◆ Take advantage of the fact that you can return to and review skipped or previously answered questions. Record the questions you can't answer confidently on the scratch paper provided, noting the relative difficulty of each question. When you reach the end of the exam, return to the more difficult questions.

◆ If you have session time remaining after you complete all the questions (and if you aren't too fatigued!), review your answers. Pay particular attention to questions that seem to have a lot of detail or that require graphics.

◆ As for changing your answers, the general rule of thumb here is *don't*! If you read the question carefully and completely and you felt like you knew the right answer, you probably did. Don't second-guess yourself. If, as you check your answers, one clearly stands out as incorrect, however, of course you should change it. But if you are at all unsure, go with your first impression.

Adaptive Exams

If you are planning to take an adaptive exam, keep these additional tips in mind:

◆ Read and answer every question with great care. When you're reading a question, identify every relevant detail, requirement, or task you must perform and double-check your answer to be sure you have addressed every one of them.

◆ If you cannot answer a question, use the process of elimination to reduce the set of potential answers, and then take your best guess. Stupid mistakes invariably mean that additional questions will be presented.

◆ You cannot review questions and change answers. When you leave a question, whether you've answered it or not, you cannot return to it. Do not skip any question, either; if you do, it's counted as incorrect.

Case Study Exams

This new exam format calls for unique study and exam-taking strategies. When you take this type of exam, remember that you have more time than in a typical exam. Take your time and read the case study thoroughly. Use the scrap paper or whatever medium is provided to you to take notes, diagram processes, and actively seek out the important information. Work through each testlet as if each were an independent exam. Remember, you cannot go back after you have left a testlet. Refer to the case study as often as you need to, but do not use that as a substitute for reading it carefully initially and for taking notes.

FINAL CONSIDERATIONS

Finally, a number of changes in the MCP program impact how frequently you can repeat an exam and what you will see when you do.

◆ Microsoft has instituted a new exam retake policy. The new rule is "two and two, then one and two." That is, you can attempt any exam twice with no restrictions on the time between attempts. But after the second attempt, you must wait two weeks before you can attempt that exam again. After that, you will be required to wait two weeks between subsequent attempts. Plan to pass the exam in two attempts or plan to increase your time horizon for receiving the MCP credential.

◆ New questions are being seeded into the MCP exams. After performance data is gathered on new questions, the examiners will replace older questions on all exam forms. This means that the questions appearing on exams will regularly change.

◆ Many of the current MCP exams will be republished in adaptive form. Prepare yourself for this significant change in testing; it is entirely likely that this will become the preferred MCP exam format for most exams. The exception to this may be the case study exams, because the adaptive approach may not work with that format.

These changes mean that the brute-force strategies for passing MCP exams may soon completely lose their viability. So if you don't pass an exam on the first or second attempt, it is likely that the exam's form will change significantly by the next time you take it. It could be updated from fixed-form to adaptive, or it could have a different set of questions or question types.

Microsoft's intention is not to make the exams more difficult by introducing unwanted change, but to create and maintain valid measures of the technical skills and knowledge associated with the different MCP credentials. Preparing for an MCP exam has always involved not only studying the subject matter but also planning for the testing experience itself. With the recent changes, this is now more true than ever.

Exam Title: 70-229 Designing and Implementing Databases with Microsoft SQL Server 2000, Enterprise Edition

Length: 1 hour, 45 minutes   45 questions total

Needed To Pass: 703/1000 (at time of authoring)

We have put together this practice exam to help you determine whether you are ready for the exam. The 70-229 exam that this book has been preparing you for is comparable to its predecessor (the 70-029: SQL 7 Design) in difficulty, but there is considerably more focus on the new functions and programming features added in SQL Server 2000. This practice exam should also give you a good idea of the feel of the actual exam. For example, both the live exam and this practice will be somewhat weighted with new features of SQL Server 2000. You will note a strong emphasis on XML, partitioned and indexed views, and user-defined functions, as well as the other new features of the product.

Before taking this practice exam, try to set yourself into a mode that simulates taking the real exam. Time the exam; give yourself exactly one hour and forty-five minutes. Watch the time closely and try to complete the entire practice within the time limit. After you have completed the exam, you can refer to the answers that follow. Along with the answers, we have provided the relevant chapter references within the book and other topics you can cross-reference for more information. Such a thorough review will help you fill any gaps that may be indicated by questions you answered incorrectly. On the whole, the 70-229 questions are somewhat similar to the traditional MCSE-style multiple-choice questions; and several drag-and-drop questions are added for variety.

Practice Exam

EXAM QUESTIONS

1. You are building a practice database that will be used to perform experiments before moving processing over to the production system on a new SQL Server 2000 computer. The database that you will be implementing is for a pharmaceutical company that operates a wholesale operation over the web and through a catalog ordering system. You have built several new tables with scripts similar to the following:

```
CREATE TABLE ProductTable
( ProductID          uniqueidentifier Primary
                     ➡Key Clustered,
  ProductName        varchar(30),
  CatalogShortID     int,
  CatalogFullID      uniqueidentifier,
  price              float
)
```

The only differences in the scripts are the table and column names. Your development team has told you that they are building several generic queries that can be run on this or any number of similar tables throughout the database. Because the column names differ slightly from one table to the next, they would like to build the queries so that the Primary Key values can be extracted without necessarily calling the key column by name. They also require the key to have a unique value supplied by SQL Server upon insertion of new data. They've decided to use the ROWGUIDCOL keyword in their queries.

What must be done when the table is created to allow the solution to work? (Select two.)

A. Change the data type of CatalogFullID.

B. Provide a default for the CatalogFullID.

C. Define the CatalogFullID as a ROWGUIDCOL.

D. Change the data type of the ProductID.

E. Provide a default for the ProductID.

F. Define the ProductID as a ROWGUIDCOL.

2. You have prepared the logical design for a very large database system that will act as the back end for an Internet application, as well as being accessed from the corporate WAN. The data in the system will be spread over a number of databases. You need to support a large number of concurrent users who will be accessing the database across various bandwidth speeds. Which SQL Server technologies could assist in allowing the users access while providing good performance? (Choose all that apply.)

A. Analysis services

B. Replication

C. Partitioned views

D. English query

E. Meta data services

3. You are working as a database administrator for a manufacturing firm that supplies articles constructed of glass to several international firms. In building several new objects in a SQL Server 2000 database, you develop a script to create a set of tables as follows:

```
CREATE TABLE BaseTable
( BaseID    bigint identity (45, 17),
  SupplyID  varchar(300) unique,
  General   char(300),
  Admin     char(600),
  Corpor    char(600),
  LeftBase  char(600),
  RtBase    char(300),
  KitFace   char(300)
)

CREATE TABLE ReferalTable
( RefID     int,
  SupplyID  varchar(300)
Foreign Key References BaseTable(SupplyID),
  Tally int
)
```

What elements in this script are suspect and would not permit the two tables to be created? (Select all that apply.)

A. Varchar fields cannot be used as Foreign Keys.

B. BaseTable rows exceed the maximum allowable row length.

C. There is no evidence the script should encounter problems.

D. The increment of an identity key should be the divisor of the identity's seed.

E. There is no Primary Key for Foreign relationship.

F. The BaseID should be used as the FK relationship.

4. An automobile dealership tracks inventory in a SQL Server database. The database contains information on the autos in stock. A VehicleInventory table is used to hold information for the automobiles in stock. A partial listing of attributes is as follows: VehicleIDNo(20 char), InvoiceNo(bigint), Make(20 char), Model(15 char), Year(smalldatetime), Colorcode(int), PurchasePrice(smallmoney), StickerPrices(smallmoney). Which of the columns would you choose as a Primary Key?

A. Use a compound key with Make, Model, and Year.

B. Create a surrogate identity key.

C. Use the VehicleIDNumber as the key.

D. Use the InvoiceNumber as the key.

E. Use a compound key with InvoiceNo and VehicleIDNo.

5. You are evaluating the database design given to you by another developer. This database was to be designed with an emphasis on query performance, and an attempt has been made to meet the design goal. Replying to this directive, the developer has sketched out several indexes for the tables. These indexes have been put together keeping in mind the highest expected query usage. As you review his design, you notice that the new indexes will provide varying degrees of benefit to a variety of queries. Which of his indexes is likely to be the most effective?

A. An index on gender for 134,000 registered voters.

B. An index on the sales agent's last initial for 25,000 orders.

C. An index for the StateCode Primary Key column in a US_States table.

D. An index for the State column in a PacificTime_ZIP_Codes table.

6. You are working in a database that has an nchar(5) attribute used to store solely numeric data. You believe that an alternate data type may reduce disk space used. You want to use the smallest amount of disk space for storage of this attribute. Which of the following data types would you select?

A. char(5)

B. real

C. smallint

D. int

E. bigint

7. You're conducting a class to help some junior-level developers hone their database-development skills. You enter a discussion with them about local and global variables, and are trying to clarify the differences between the two. Which of the following statements can you always make about these two kinds of variables? (Select two.)

   A. Global variables are really functions.

   B. All values returned are object-context-specific.

   C. They use different characters to denote themselves.

   D. All values returned are connection-context-specific.

   E. Both of them are available to all connections.

8. As a database implementer, you are creating an historical database for a local library that stores data and photographs about important dates in local history. In the database you will need to be able to store dates from the beginning of 14th century to the current date. You want to minimize the storage space used by the data. Which type of data type would you use?

   A. `datetime`

   B. `smalldatetime`

   C. `bigint`

   D. `int`

   E. `char(8)`

9. You are exploring some of SQL Server 2000's new features. The feature you are particularly interested in is for supporting XML documents. To experiment with the capability to output XML documents, you have developed the following query:

```
USE Northwind
GO
SELECT t.TerritoryID, e.EmployeeID as
➥EMPLOYEE,
    e.LastName, e.FirstName, t.EmployeeID
FROM Employees e INNER JOIN
➥EmployeeTerritories t
    ON e.EmployeeID = t.EmployeeID
WHERE t.EmployeeID = (SELECT min(EmployeeID)
➥FROM Employees)
ORDER BY TerritoryID
```

You are able to submit this script in a Query Analyzer session and return tabular results from the server. What must you do before this query can return its results as an XML document?

   A. Remove the `ORDER BY` clause.

   B. Remove the `JOIN` clause.

   C. Remove one or both of the duplicate column headers.

   D. Add a clause to the `SELECT` statement

   E. Remove the subquery from the query.

10. You are preparing a database structure for a large local construction company. At any one time the firm has 5 or more active sites, each site having anywhere between 25 and 200 homes. In charge of each site is a site supervisor who organizes the subcontractors at each phase of the building process, including landscaping, framing, drywalling, electrical, plumbing, and so on. Any subcontractor who is planning on working on a given site must be found in a database of approved vendors. The company would like a structure that would allow for storage of the subcontractors' personal information and information about the sites that includes the subcontractors assigned to each site. How would you set up this structure?

   A. Site entity and Contractor entity

   B. Site entity, Contractor entity, and Site/Contractor entity

C. Site entity, Process entity, Contractor entity

D. Site entity, Contractor entity, and Site/ Process entity

11. As a database implementer, you are developing several new stored procedures on an existing SQL Server 2000 database that resides at your company headquarters. You are experimenting with a Query Analyzer session that contains each of the individual queries to be used in these procedures. After running a given SELECT query and using the Graphical Showplan feature to understand the execution plan, you want to prove that internal statistics are available for a particular column used in the query. How would you best find this information?

A. Disable the graphical Showplan display.

B. Hold the mouse over each individual node relating to the desired column.

C. Use a SET SHOWPLAN statement.

D. Examine each individual node relating to the desired column without mousing over it.

12. A small manufacturing company has a considerable number of data sources because no standardization has occurred across any platform. One of the database servers has SQL Server installed; the others come from a variety of vendors. For a project you are working on you need to gather data from the SQL Server and merge it together with data from two other sources. You then need to bring the data from all sources into Excel where it will later be used for charting purposes. How would you accomplish this?

A. Export the data from the other sources into a comma-delimited file for import to SQL Server. Then export from SQL Server the data that is to be imported into Excel.

B. Export the data from all three sources so that it can be imported into Excel.

C. Use SQL Server to transfer all the data from all sources directly into Excel.

D. Use Excel to transfer data from all three sources into a spreadsheet.

13. You have developed a new database for your company to use when testing new applications. When the database was first created, data recovery was not a major concern. As a result of this oversight, the database initially carried a log file of only 5MB (with autogrow, but no autoshrink) and had its Truncate Log on Checkpoint option set. Midway through tests, however, one of the developers turned the option off, and consequently the log automatically grew to its current size of 150MB. Concerned about the low amount of free space remaining on the disk drive holding the log, you turn the option on once again. What configuration can you expect after the next checkpoint is passed?

A. SQL Server will never truncate this particular log.

B. The log would have been truncated, but the log allocation remains at 150MB.

C. The log would have been truncated, and the log allocation returns to 5MB.

D. The log would have been truncated, and the log allocation would shrink somewhat, but not back to 5MB.

14. You are the database administrator for a small private educational institution. You would like to use SQL Server as a gateway to a variety of data sources that have been used for a number of different applications. As a primary goal you would like to get a copy of all data stored on the SQL Server. What technologies would be used to solve this problem? (Select all that apply.)

A. OLE-DB

B. ANSI

C. ISO

D. ODBC

E. Analysis Services

F. SQL Profiler

15. You are the developer for a local manufacturing company and are currently working on the sales database. This database is used by three custom applications. Users of these three applications are members of a Windows 2000 domain group. The custom applications will connect to the database using application roles. Each of the roles was assigned a unique password. You need to ensure that the desired users have access to the database through the custom application. What do you do?

A. Assign correct permissions to each Windows 2000 group.

B. Assign correct permissions to each application role.

C. Assign the Windows 2000 group to the appropriate application roles.

D. Provide each user with a password to the appropriate application role.

16. A large shipping company uses a dual processor SQL Server to track load information for a fleet of transport vehicles that handle shipments throughout North America. Each shipment carries a variety of goods from fresh produce, to hardware, to automobiles, and so on. The data being collected will be shared with other vendors through a variety of applications. A technology is required that will provide a data structure and formatting rules and be easily transferable between business-to-business applications. Which technology is best suited for this structure?

A. HTML

B. IIS

C. XML

D. Replication

E. Triggers

17. Your company supplies building materials to contractors throughout the Midwest. You are the database developer of a SQL Server 2000 computer with dual processors and 1GB RAM. You are working with a database named `Policies` that holds a variety of corporate documents and data. You have designed a stored procedure, containing a cursor, that will run against the database. An analyst from the IT department in your firm reports that there is an initial delay when the query is executed. After that, the query performance runs well. How can you improve performance?

A. `sp_configure` "cursor threshold", 0.

B. `sp_dboption` "Policies" set cursor close on commit on.

C. Set Transaction isolation level to serializable.

D. `ALTER` db "Policies" set `Cursor_default` local.

18. You are the administrator of a SQL Server 2000 computer at your company's warehouse. All product orders are shipped out from this warehouse. Orders are received at 30 sales offices throughout the country. Each sales office offers a range of products specific to its own region.

Each sales office contains one SQL Server 2000 computer. These servers connect to the warehouse through dial-up connections once a day. Each sales office needs data pertaining to only its own region.

You need to replicate inventory data from the server at the warehouse to the servers at the sales offices. You have decided to use transactional replication. You want to minimize the amount of time needed to replicate the data.

Which actions should you take? (Choose three.)

A. Create one publication for each subscriber.

B. Create a standard publication for all subscribers.

C. Enable horizontal partitioning.

D. Enable vertical partitioning.

E. Use pull subscriptions.

F. Use push subscriptions.

19. You are the database developer for a large scientific research company. You are designing a SQL Server 2000 database that will host a distributed application used by several companies. You create a stored procedure that contains confidential information. You want to prevent the companies from viewing the confidential information, but not hamper their use of the procedure.

A. Remove the text of the procedure from the `syscomments` table.

B. Encrypt the definition of the stored procedure.

C. Deny `SELECT` on syscomments for the Public role.

D. Deny `SELECT` on sysobjects for the Public role.

E. Encrypt the output from the stored procedure.

20. Your company has just purchased an accounting application from a vendor. The application stores its data in a database named `Accounting`. The tables in this database contain columns that function as Primary Keys, but `PRIMARY KEY` and `FOREIGN KEY` constraints are not used.

You need to replicate data from this database to another SQL Server computer. This server will use the replicated data to generate reports. Most reports will run each month, but the accounting department needs to be able to run reports at any time. Reports should be accurate through the last full working day.

You cannot make any changes to the database, but you need to implement replication. Which two actions should you take? (Each correct answer represents part of the solution. Choose two.)

A. Implement merge replication.

B. Implement snapshot replication.

C. Implement transactional replication.

D. Schedule replication to run continuously.

E. Schedule replication to run during off-peak hours.

21. You are a database developer for an international corporation that ships products worldwide. Andrea, a Visual Basic developer, is also a member of your IT team. Andrea needs to alter views. But you need to prevent her from viewing and changing tables and their data. Currently she belongs to the Public database role. What needs to be done?

A. Add her to the `db_owner` database role.

B. Add her to the `db_ddl` admin database role.

C. Grant her Create View permission.

D. Grant her Alter View permission.

22. You are working for a large scientific research corporation that performs a variety of tests for numerous government agencies. In preparation for a major system upgrade, a large set of data changes are going to be made on the system you administer. You would like to implement a number of changes without affecting any of the existing data. Which of the following operations can be made without affecting any existing data values? (Select all that apply.)

    A. INSERT.

    B. UPDATE.

    C. Change column name.

    D. Increase column length.

    E. Decrease column length.

23. You are the database design technician for a large shipping firm that transports goods throughout North America. You are designing an Inventory and Shipping database that will be used as the heart of the corporate order-taking system. You must ensure that referential integrity of the database is maintained. What are the three constraint definitions you would choose? A partial database description is as follows:

    ```
    ORDER Table
    OrderID PK
    CustomerID
    ShipDate

    PRODUCT Table
    ProductID PK
    SupplierID

    ORDER DETAILS Table
    OrderID PK
    ProductID PK

    SUPPLIER Table
    SupplierID PK
    ```

    A. Create a Foreign Key constraint on the Products table that references the Order Details table.

    B. Create a Foreign Key constraint on the Products table that references the Supplier table.

    C. Create a Foreign Key constraint on the Order table that references the Order Details table.

    D. Create a Foreign Key constraint on the Order Details table that references the Order table.

    E. Create a Foreign Key constraint on the Order Details table that references the Products table.

    F. Create a Foreign Key constraint on the Supplier table that references the Products table.

24. As a database implementer, you are creating a one-time report to supply the office staff with a revenue breakdown from the last year of sales. The data source for the report contains cryptic column headings that cover several different categories. You must provide the report in a manner users can easily understand. Which of the following would be the best solution? (Select 2; each answer represents half of the correct solution.)

    A. Provide friendly aliases for the table names.

    B. Provide friendly aliases for the column names.

    C. Create a VIEW with corresponding definition.

    D. Create a corresponding DEFAULT definition.

    E. Execute a corresponding query from the Analyzer.

    F. Create a front-end program to execute the required query.

25. You are working as a database designer for an independent consulting firm. A variety of your clients need to support an XML document export from SQL Server. After developing a query capable of producing a working XML document, you would now like to build an XML schema document describing the validation rules for the generated document. What steps would you take to produce only a schema document from it?

    A. Add XML notation to the query's column headers.

    B. Ensure you have a live Internet connection.

    C. Add or extend the WHERE clause.

    D. Replace the FOR XML clause with a different clause.

    E. Add a keyword to the FOR XML clause.

26. You are working for a service organization that provides temporary personnel. You are trying to update the information in a table named Customers. You also need to remove and change records in the Orders and Order Details tables. You execute several attempts at a variety of UPDATE and DELETE queries, each without success. Where would you begin to look for a solution to the problem? (Select all that apply.)

    A. You are using a login that does not have the required permissions.

    B. A DEFAULT is defined that disagrees with your attempted changes.

    C. Referential integrity has been defined on the table structure.

    D. You don't have permission to create temporary tables.

    E. Backup operations have not yet been performed.

27. You are working for a large manufacturing firm that produces a variety of goods for sale throughout the continental USA. You are working with a Sales database that has an Inventory table. An application provides new sales information that updates the Inventory table. When the process executes, it gives an error message: Transaction was deadlocked on resources with another process, etc. The stored procedure looks like the following:

```
CREATE PROCEDURE UpdateInventory @IntID int
As
BEGIN
DECLARE @Count int
BEGIN TRANSACTION
SELECT @Count = Available From Inventory
➥with (HoldLock)
WHERE InventoryID = @IntID
IF (@Count >0)
   UPDATE Inventory SET Available = @Count
➥- 1
      Where InventoryID = @IntID
COMMIT TRANSACTION
END
```

Which of the following operations would be most likely to solve the problem and allow the process to complete?

    A. Change the table hint to UPDATE.

    B. Remove the table hint.

    C. Change the table hint to Repeatable Read.

    D. Set transaction isolation level Serializable.

    E. Set transaction isolation level Repeatable Read.

28. As one of several administrators, you support users who have been using a front-end application to INSERT new records into an existing table called Products. Several users report that they are unable to add product information to the table. Which of the following is not likely to be a possible cause of the problem?

A. The database files have had their properties changed.

B. The database properties have been changed.

C. The transaction log is full.

D. Backups are taking place.

E. User permissions have changed.

29. You are designing a database for a retail company that owns 300 stores. Every month, each store submits approximately 1,500 sales records. The sales records are loaded into a SQL Server 2000 database at the corporate headquarters. A DTS package transforms the sales records as they are loaded. The package writes the transformed sales records to the Sales table, which has a column for integer Primary Key values. The IDENTITY property automatically assigns a key value to each transformed record.

    After loading this month's sales data, you discover that a portion of the data contains errors. You stop the loading of the data to identify and delete the problem records. You want to reuse the key values that were assigned to the records that you deleted. You want to assign the deleted key values to the next sales records you load. You also want to disrupt users' work as little as possible. What should you do?

    A. Export all records from the Sales table to a temporary table. Truncate the Sales table, and then reload the records from the temporary table.

    B. Export all records from the Sales table to a text file. Drop the Sales table, and then reload the records from the text file.

    C. Use the DBCC CHECKIDENT statement to reseed the Sales table's IDENTITY property.

D. Set the Sales table's IDENTITY_INSERT property to ON. Add new sales records that have the desired key values.

30. You have entered a query using a TOP function to limit the number of records being viewed to five. When you see the results of the query, the dates being viewed were not the first five in the data. What could be the source of the problem?

    A. The resultset has not been grouped.

    B. The data contains NULL values.

    C. There is an incorrect ORDER.

    D. Table aliases were used.

    E. Schema binding has been applied.

31. You are implementing a database on a SQL Server 2000 computer. The server contains a database named Inventory. The database contains a table that is used to store information about equipment scheduling. Users report that some equipment schedules have an end date that is earlier than the start date. You need to ensure that the start date is always earlier than or equal to the end date. You also want to minimize physical I/O. You do not want users to change the Transact-SQL statements they use to modify data within the database. What should you do?

    A. Create a constraint that compares the start date to the end date.

    B. Create a trigger that compares the start date to the end date.

    C. Create a rule that compares the start date to the end date.

    D. Create a stored procedure that tests the start and end dates before inserting the row into the database.

32. As a database design technician, you work for a large manufacturing organization that maintains a large production database system on a single SQL Server 2000 machine. In attempting to enter a query to add a record to a table, you find that it is not possible. Which of the following is not a likely cause for the error?

    A. Data doesn't meet constraint.

    B. Referential integrity.

    C. Database is read-only.

    D. Permissions.

    E. Other applications are locking data.

    F. SQL Server Agent is not started.

33. You are implementing a database on a SQL Server 2000 computer. The server contains a database named `Inventory`. Users report that several rows in the `UnitsStored` field contain negative numbers. You examine the database's table structure. You correct all the negative numbers in the table. You must prevent the database from storing negative numbers. Which Transact-SQL statement should you execute?

    A.
```
ALTER TABLE dbo.StorageLocations ADD
CONSTRAINT

CK_StorageLocations_UnitsStored

CHECK (UnitsStored >= 0)
```

    B.
```
CREATE TRIGGER CK_UnitsStored On
StorageLocations

FOR INSERT, UPDATE AS

IF (SELECT Inserted.UnitsStored FROM
➥Inserted) < 0

ROLLBACK TRAN
```

    C.
```
CREATE RULE CK_UnitsStored As @Units >= 0

GO

sp_bindrule "CK_UnitsStored",

"StorageLocations.UnitsStored"

GO
```

    D.
```
CREATE PROC UpdateUnitsStored

(@StorageLocationID int, @UnitsStored
➥bigint) AS

IF @UnitsStored < 0

RAISERROR (50099, 17, 1)

ELSE

UPDATE StorageLocations

SET UnitsStored = @UnitsStored

WHERE StorageLocationID =
➥@StorageLocationID
```

34. A local branch of a large hotel chain maintains guest information on a single SQL Server 2000 computer. You are creating an application that will change the contents of a database programmatically through a Visual Basic interface on a local area network. Which technology would you utilize?

    A. ADO

    B. RDO

    C. DAO

    D. SQL DMO

    E. XML

35. You are implementing a database on a SQL Server 2000 computer. The server contains a database named `Inventory`. The database has a `Parts` table that has a field named `InStock`. When the parts have shipped, a table named `PartsShipped` is updated. When the parts are received, a table named `PartsReceived` is updated. You want the database to update the `InStock` field of the `Inventory` table automatically. What should you do?

   A. Add triggers to the `PartsShipped` and the `PartsReceived` tables that update the `InStock` field in the `Parts` table.

   B. Create a user-defined function that calculates current inventory by running aggregate queries on the `PartsShipped` and `PartsReceived` tables.

   C. Use a view that creates an `InStock` field as part of an aggregate query.

   D. Create stored procedures for modifying the `PartsShipped` and `PartsReceived` tables that also modify the `InStock` field in the `Parts` table. Use these procedures exclusively when modifying data in the `PartsShipped` and `PartsReceived` tables.

36. One of the local small merchants has a thriving business with a central manufacturing operation and three retail stores in the surrounding counties. You are preparing a report that will list sales figures for each store, and you would like to calculate subtotals and totals accordingly. Which of the following SELECT clauses will be required?

   A. ORDER BY, COMPUTE

   B. ORDER BY, COMPUTE BY

   C. GROUP BY, COMPUTE

   D. GROUP BY, COMPUTE BY

   E. ORDER BY, GROUP BY, COMPUTE, COMPUTE BY

37. You are working for a large international distributor of toiletry items. You are implementing a database on a new installation of SQL Server 2000. The server contains a database named `Inventory` that has a `Parts` table with a Primary Key that is used to identify each part stored in the company's warehouse. Each part has an unique UPC code that the accounting department uses to identify it. You want to maintain the referential integrity between the `Parts` table and the `OrderDetails` table. You want to minimize the amount of physical I/O that is used for access to the database. Which two T-SQL statements should you execute? (Select 2. Each correct answer represents part of the correct solution.)

   A. CREATE UNIQUE INDEX IX_PUPC On Parts(UPC)

   B. CREATE UNIQUE INDEX IX_ODUPC On OrderDetails(UPC)

   C. CREATE TRIGGER INUPOD1 On OrderDetails

      FOR INSERT, UPDATE As

      IF NOT EXISTS (SELECT Parts.UPC FROM Parts

       INNER JOIN Inserted.UPC

       ON Parts.UPC = Inserted.UPC)

      BEGIN

      ROLLBACK TRANSACTION

      END

   D. CREATE TRIGGER INUPP1 On Parts

```
FOR INSERT, UPDATE As

IF NOT EXISTS (SELECT OrderDetails.UPC

FROM OrderDetails INNER JOIN

Inserted ON OrderDetails.UPD =

➡Inserted.UPC)

BEGIN

ROLLBACK TRANSACTION

END
```

E. ```
ALTER TABLE dbo.OrderDetails ADD
➡CONSTRAINT

FK_OrderDetails_Parts FOREIGN KEY(UPC)

REFERENCES dbo.Parts(UPC)
```

F. ```
ALTER TABLE dbo.Parts ADD CONSTRAINT

FK_Parts_OrderDetails FOREIGN KEY (UPC)

REFERENCES dbo.Parts(UPC)
```

38. A greenhouse operation has the unique problem of dealing with live merchandise that is vulnerable to a unique set of circumstances. The database is stored on a single SQL Server 2000 computer that is accessed 24 hours a day from a web site. Periodically, an inventory update procedure alters the categories for various plants and other inventory. The update will encompass 90% of the records in a database that has over 12,000 rows. Which of the following answers represents the best solution?

   A. Perform one singular update.

   B. Divide the process into smaller batches using GROUPINGS.

   C. Vertically partition the data.

   D. Use WHERE clauses to perform small batch updates.

   E. Create a new database based on data from the old system combined with data from the update.

39. You are working as a database designer for a large U.S.-based scientific research firm. You are working on a DTS package that has been installed on a SQL Server 2000 computer. The DTS package queries multiple databases and writes the results to a text file. This package is run from a Windows 2000 batch file. The batch file uses the dtsrun utility to execute the package. You want to ensure that connection properties, such as login names and passwords, cannot be read or modified by users. Which two actions would you take to ensure this is done? (Select two. Each correct answer represents part of the correct solution.)

   A. Save the DTS package so that it has an owner password.

   B. Save the DTS package so that it has a user password.

   C. Encrypt the package details in the command line of the dtsrun utility.

   D. Store the DTS package in the Meta Data Services repository.

   E. Store the DTS package as a Microsoft Visual Basic file.

40. You work as an application developer for a large warehouse operation. The stock is organized by aisle and bin numbers that are stored in character columns and maintained in a SQL Server 2000 database. You want to prepare a query to list the products by their location (aisle, bin). Which of the following queries would suit the requirements?

   A. ```
SELECT (Aisle + Bin) Location, ProductID,
ProductName

FROM Products

ORDER BY Location
```
```

B. `SELECT (Aisle + Bin) Location, ProductID,`
`ProductName`

`FROM Products`

`GROUP BY Location`

C. `SELECT (Aisle + Bin) Location, ProductID,`
`ProductName`

`FROM Products`

`GROUP BY Aisle + Bin`

D. `SELECT (Aisle + Bin) Location, ProductID,`
`ProductName`

`FROM Products`

`GROUP BY Aisle + Bin, ProductID,`
`➥ProductName`

E. `SELECT (Aisle + Bin) Location, ProductID,`
`ProductName`

`FROM Products`

`ORDER BY Aisle, Bin`

41. You are working for a large international firm with headquarters in Miami and regional offices in Detroit, San Francisco, Houston, Boston, and Denver. You are the database designer responsible for a variety of databases stored on a SQL Server 2000 computer. The server contains a database named `EmployeeData` that your company's human resources department uses for a variety of applications. This database contains several tables that gather and distribute information from all regional offices.

The `Employees` table holds information for employee names, addresses, departments, and base salaries. The `Bonuses` table records information on bonuses that have been paid to individual employees. The `Awards` table holds information about awards that have been presented to individual employees.

The human resources department wants to make employee names, addresses, and award information available to anyone who has permission to access the server. However, you should allow users in only the human resources department to access salary and bonus information. You need to enable company users to access only the appropriate employee information. How would you accommodate the request?

A. Create a trigger on the `Salary` column that prevents unauthorized users from making changes to the data in the column.

B. Create a stored procedure that retrieves all the data from the `Employees` and `Awards` tables, inserts the data into a temporary table, and then grants the current user `SELECT` permissions on the temporary table. Grant the `Guest` database user `EXECUTE` permissions on the stored procedure.

C. Move the sensitive information out of the `Employees` table into a new table. Grant the `Guest` database user `SELECT` permission on the `Employees` and `Awards` tables.

D. Create a view that contains the name, address, and award information. Grant the `Guest` database user `SELECT` permissions on the view.

42. You administer the database server for a large lumber and building materials supplier. Your company ships to sites throughout a 500-mile radius from your center of operations. You want to query the materials used at a single site. Which of the following queries would suit your needs?

A. `SELECT Materials, Weight, Quantity FROM`
`Inventory`

`ORDER BY Site`

B. `SELECT Materials, Weight, Quantity FROM Inventory`

`WHERE Site = 4`

C. `SELECT Materials, Weight, Quantity FROM Inventory`

`GROUP BY Site`

D. `SELECT Materials, Weight, Quantity FROM Inventory`

`ORDER BY Site`

`GROUP BY Materials, Weight, Quantity`

E. `SELECT Materials, Weight, Quantity FROM Inventory`

`GROUP BY Materials, Weight, Quantity`

43. You are working as an independent database consultant for a variety of companies that use a number of different products in all areas of different n-tier systems. You have been asked by one of your clients to develop a process that will import a file from a predetermined server location. The file is a comma-delimited text-based flat file created by a third-party data source.

The fields in this flat file have been designed to match exactly with a table stored on the client's SQL Server 2000 system. The client needs the application as soon as possible and wants it to be fast, efficient, and easy to maintain. It must be possible to execute the process through a simple call from within the SQL Server Query Analyzer environment and allow the file to be imported at will.

The file is created in such a manner that it is always being appended to. Each night, several thousand rows are added to the end of the file without removing previous data. The SQL Server table holding the imported data is built from this file as well as two other data sources that are processed in a separate procedure. Your solution is to import only new records to the table; that is, it cannot import the same flat-file record twice, nor can it import records that have been added from either of the two other processes. At the end of each import, you need to know how many new records were added from the flat file during the single process.

What is the best SQL Server technology to use for this process?

A. Use a SQL script and a `BULK INSERT` operation.

B. Use the `bcp` command utility.

C. Build a DTS with T-SQL tasks and standard tasks.

D. Use DTS with standard tasks and transformations.

E. Use a stored procedure and a `SELECT INTO` operation.

F. Use a stored procedure and an `INSERT INTO` operation.

44. You have several new database designers that have been hired by your company to join several existing development teams. The current teams are working on a variety of projects that use Visual Basic, ASP, DHTML, and Visual C++ for development of internal projects. After each project is completed, it is then turned over to a specialized team that adjusts the project so that it can be resold to other companies as a finished product.

    You are working with the new employees on aspects of SQL Server 2000 database design and the constructs of all new features. The new employees have a variety of backgrounds in SQL Server and other third-party data sources. You are illustrating some of the standard mechanisms used to design the corporate databases as well as building appropriate error handling into stored procedures.

    You execute the following script from the SQL Server 2000 Query Analyzer against the Northwind database on your local machine:

    ```
    CREATE PROCEDURE CaseTest
    AS
    BEGIN TRANSACTION
     UPDATE Employees SET LastName = "Jones"
        WHERE EmployeeID > 0
    IF @@ERROR <> 0
     BEGIN
     ROLLBACK TRAN
     RETURN
     END

    UPDATE Employees SET LastName = "Smith"
    IF @@ERROR <> 0
     BEGIN
     ROLLBACK TRAN
     RETURN
     END
    COMMIT TRANSACTION
    ```

    After you run the procedure, you direct the students to run linked-server queries to your server in a Query Analyzer session and display all rows in Northwind's Employees table. All students report that the LastName value of each employee row is the same value, "smith", noted to be all in lowercase. All your updates specifically denote a mixed case value. You run your procedure again, with the same result. What is causing the anomaly?

    A. Check your SQL Server collation settings.

    B. Restart Query Analyzer on the linked servers.

    C. ALTER your procedure to correct the conversion error.

    D. Check the current settings for the database options.

    E. Correct the CONSTRAINT on the Employees table.

    F. Correct the INSTEAD OF trigger on the Employees table.

45. You are designing a database that will serve as a back end for several large web sites. The web sites themselves will use XML to communicate with each other and pass data back and forth. You would like to control the data displayed on the user browser, based on interactions with the user, without placing any unnecessary load on the server. In many cases, columns and rows need to be eliminated from the display based on the criteria supplied. You would like to minimize round trips to the server for data exchange purposes. What technology is the best to apply?

A. Use a user-defined function with SCHEMABIND-
ING set to the XML recordsets.

B. Create an indexed view of the XML recordset,
specifying only the columns needed, and supply a WHERE condition based on the rows
selected.

C. Create standard views of SQL Server data and
use XML to export the requested data.

D. Use FOR XML and OPENXML options to send data
requests and updates directly from the client
machine to the SQL Server.

E. Use HTML and an XML schema to provide
the necessary view of the data.

ANSWERS TO EXAM QUESTIONS

1. **E, F.** Although any number of columns in a table
can be defined with the uniquidentifier data
type, only one column can be the ROWGUIDCOL.
This single column must be defined in this manner for any procedures to use the ROWGUIDCOL
function in place of a column name. To provide a
value by the server for a uniqueidentifier data
type, you should provide a default definition that
uses the NEWID() functions to generate a GUID
upon insertion of data.

You can find information on data types in
Chapter 1, and information on DEFAULT, NEWID(),
and ROWGUIDCOL usage in Chapter 3. Also, in SQL
Server Books Online you can read more information under the topic heading "Using uniqueidentifier Data."

2. **B, C.** Partitioned views and replication enable
you to spread the load of a very large database
system across several machines. The benefit of
additional processing power and getting the data
closer to the user could be recognized by both
features, assuming they were properly partitioned
and configured.

Replication is discussed in full in Chapter 11 and
partitioned views in Chapter 7. In SQL Server
Books Online, the complete background information can be found under the topic "Publishing
Data and Database Objects."

3. **C.** There is no reason a varchar data type can't be
used as a Primary or Foreign Key. It is more pertinent that the Primary Key values be unique and
that the Foreign Key relationship be properly
defined. The maximum size for a data row in
SQL Server is 8,060. We are obviously nowhere
near this maximum. The increment of an
Identity column can be any desired value. As
long as the Foreign Key relationship points to a
unique value, it does not have to be declared as a
Primary Key.

Chapter 3 defines the Foreign Key relationship
and the guidelines for its use. SQL Server Books
Online has a complete section on defining this
activity under "FOREIGN KEY Constraints."

4. **B.** An automobile's VIN number, though unique,
is character data and is much too large to use as
an effective Primary Key. This is a perfect situation for an automatically incremented numeric
surrogate key that would take up a lot less storage
space. A surrogate key may be preferred, because
it is small and has no reason to ever change.

For information on setting appropriate Primary Keys and supplying the definitions, see Chapters 2 and 3. SQL Server Books Online covers Primary Keys extensively under the topic "PRIMARY KEY Constraints."

5. **C.** Gender is never a good column to supply an index against because it has only two possible values. In general, a column that has the highest percentage of unique values, based on the total number of rows in a table, is the best choice for indexing. An agent's last initial has 26 possibilities in a table of 25,000, which is still a rather poor choice. An index created on the State value would be a good choice in either C or D, but C would provide the best ratio.

   Index definitions are covered in Chapter 3, and the optimization of indexing strategies is covered in Chapter 10. SQL Server Books Online provides two similar topics under "Indexes" and "Index Tuning Recommendations."

6. **D.** According to byte sizes, int (4 bytes) would take less than half the space of the current nchar(5) setting (10 bytes). Smallint would even be better, but has an upper limit of 32,767. Using the char(5) data type would cut the space used in half, but using actual numeric storage would be better. Whenever a variable is going to contain only numbers, numeric storage is always more efficient.

   Chapter 2 covers the complete set of SQL Server data types, and SQL Server Books Online goes into further depth under the topic "Data Types."

7. **A, C.** In SQL Server 7 and beyond, global variables defined by a prefix @@ are now referred to as global functions and can be accessed through all connections and have an object context. Local variables are defined by a single @ prefix, are connection-context-specific, and are available to the connection of only the current session.

Variables are covered in Chapter 6, and SQL Server Books Online has many sections covering this topic. Possibly the most helpful for this situation are "Global Variables" and "Variables: Declare."

8. **D.** This is a tricky question to solve, and if it were not for the space restriction there would be a temptation to use characters for the storage. At 8 bytes a piece (double that of int) the easier technique would be to track days from the beginning of recorded time in an integer. (2001–1300)×365 1/4 would require 6 digits, and therefore int is the closest to the size required. Datetime allows dates to go no further back than the 1700s, and smalldatetime to the 1900s.

   Chapter 2 covers the complete set of SQL Server data types, and SQL Server Books Online goes into further depth under the topic "Data Types."

9. **D.** The results of almost any SQL Server SELECT operation can be given in the form of an XML document regardless of the columns, clauses, and other options in the SELECT statement proper. To produce the XML document you must add the FOR XML clause to the SELECT operation and specify the appropriate XML option for the desired output—either RAW or AUTO. EXPLICIT could alternatively be used if the format of the query was also altered.

   Chapter 5 deals completely with XML and related operations. SQL Server Books Online covers XML through a variety of topics, beginning with "XML Integration of Relational Data."

10. **B.** The many-to-many relationship in this scenario occurs because many contractors can work on a single site, and a single contractor can work at many sites. The connection needs to involve both sites and contractors for an appropriate relationship to be drawn.

For information on logical entity design and physical table design, see Chapters 2 and 3. SQL Server Books Online covers relationships in a variety of topics. The most helpful in this situation would likely be "Table Relationships."

11. **B.** A feature of the Graphical Showplan display enables you to see information about each node in the display by holding the mouse over the top of the node. This causes a display to show the node analysis based on the contents of the entire query. Of the choices available, this would be the best mechanism to use to gain the desired information.

Chapter 12 provides information on using the graphical execution plan display option. SQL Server Books Online covers this topic well under the heading "Graphical Showplan."

12. **C.** SQL Server is ideal for this situation. Depending on the actual details of the process, this can be performed directly using either replication or data transformation services (DTS). Given the complexity of the scenario, it is likelier that DTS would be used because of its limitless flexibility.

DTS is covered in Chapter 5, and replication is in Chapter 11. SQL Server Books Online covers DTS under the topic "Programming DTS Applications," and replication beginning under "Introducing Replication."

13. **B.** Having the size growing to the 150MB mark will be the size allocated unless the file is shrunk. Truncating and/or backing up the log removes the dead wood from the log, but does not affect the log size.

Transaction logs are dealt with fully in Chapter 3, and SQL Server Books Online has a variety of related topics, the best of which in this situation is "Shrinking the Transaction Log."

14. **A, D.** OLE-DB and ODBC are industry-standard technologies for drivers supplied to allow data to be read from an underlying data source. ODBC (open database connectivity) is a mature interface supported by almost all database engines. OLE-DB is a set of driver APIs that has growing usage and also allows for access to data in a generic form. ANSI and ISO are both organizations and not technologies.

This topic is fully covered in Chapters 1, 2, and 3. SQL Server Books Online can also be referenced under the topic "Heterogeneous Data Sources."

15. **B.** The custom applications will invoke role-based security for the duration of their execution. When this operation is performed, only the permissions applied to the application role are in effect. Assigning the correct levels of permissions to each of the application roles, therefore, is the only approach that would be successful in this case.

Application roles and role-based security are covered in Chapter 6. SQL Server Books Online covers security throughout, but the most relevant topic to this situation is "Application Roles."

16. **C.** XML, now supported through a number of new features, provides a mechanism whereby the data can be transmitted from one application to the other, while maintaining the data structure and other formatting provided by XML schemas and style sheets.

Chapter 5 deals completely with XML and related operations. SQL Server Books Online covers XML through a variety of topics, beginning with "XML Integration of Relational Data."

17. **A.** Use of the cursor threshold can enable operations to continue in a procedure while rowsets are being generated asynchronously. If you set the cursor threshold to –1, all keysets are generated synchronously, which benefits small cursor sets. If you set the cursor threshold to 0, all cursor keysets are generated asynchronously. The option should not be set too low in applications that generate small resultsets, because small resultsets are better built synchronously.

    Configuration options and their use are discussed fully in Chapter 3. You can find additional information on these options in SQL Server Books Online under the topic "Configuration Options Specifications."

18. **A, C, E.** It is necessary to design the structure of the database so that the publications can include an article specific to each location. This means you need a compound Primary Key containing regional information and an article for each subscriber that is horizontally partitioned based on the region. Also, because the connection is initiated by the subscriber dial-up, you must set up pull subscriptions.

    Replication is covered in Chapter 11. SQL Server Books Online covers replication beginning under "Introducing Replication."

19. **B.** If you encrypt a stored procedure, the details of the procedure become unreadable to a human being but can still be used and deciphered by SQL Server.

    Stored procedures are covered fully in Chapter 9, and definition encryption is covered fully in Chapter 3. SQL Server Books Online covers both topics thoroughly. Reference the topic "Stored Procedures" for more information on their use and "With Encryption" for definition encrypting.

20. **B, E.** Because there is no Primary Key, and no other changes to the database can be performed, the only alternative that does not require one of these two things to occur is snapshot replication. Because the data does not need to be up-to-the-minute, then a scheduled data refresh occurring overnight or during other non-peak times is most appropriate.

    Replication is covered in Chapter 11. SQL Server Books Online covers replication beginning under "Introducing Replication."

21. **C.** The db_owner and ddladmin fixed database roles allow for the creation and alteration of many different kinds of objects within the database. To limit Andrea solely to views, you would have to provide her with that specific permission. There is no such permission as Alter View.

    Role-based security is covered in Chapter 6. SQL Server Books Online covers security throughout, but the most relevant topic to this situation is "Fixed Database Roles."

22. **A, C, D.** If you were to select UPDATE, the purpose of the command is exactly what you want to avoid. You should be able to increase the data storage size and alter a column name without affecting the internal data. However, decreasing the size for data storage results in data truncation or loss. INSERT, used appropriately, will add data but not alter any existing values.

    INSERT and UPDATE operations are covered fully in Chapter 4, whereas table definitions are covered in Chapter 3. SQL Server Books Online covers all three topics in full in "UPDATE," "INSERT," and "Creating and Maintaining Databases."

23. **B, D, E.** According to the partial table definitions, there is a `SupplierID` in the `Products` table and a `ProductID` and `OrderID` in the `Order Details` table. The relationships to define, therefore, would be from these tables to the table that contains the remaining information.

    For information on logical entity design and physical table design, see Chapters 2 and 3. SQL Server Books Online covers relationships in a variety of topics. The most helpful in this situation would likely be "Table Relationships."

24. **B, E.** The key to this question is that this operation is going to be performed as a "one-time" thing, so the creation of data objects would likely be avoided, and therefore views would not be warranted. A script that performs the activity could easily be saved, if needed, in the future. Table aliases may help in your development, but in this scenario column aliases provide the end-user with the necessary data definition.

    Views are covered in their entirety in Chapter 7. SQL Server Books Online covers this topic in detail under "Views."

25. **E.** To have the Schema information output with the XML data document, you must use the `XML-DATA` option on the `FOR XML` clause. Without this option, the `XML` data is output without schema.

    Chapter 5 deals completely with XML and related operations. SQL Server Books Online covers XML through a variety of topics, beginning with "XML Integration of Relational Data."

26. **A, C.** Backup should not affect the alterations as SQL Server as backup is performed with the data online, and a `DEFAULT` should not restrict input. The most likely causes are referential integrity considerations and the permission to perform such updates.

    Permissions are covered fully in Chapter 6, whereas referential integrity is covered in Chapters 2 and 3. SQL Server Books Online covers both these functions. Security and permissions are related to numerous topics, but start with "Managing Permissions." For information on referential integrity usage, begin with the "Enforcing Referential Integrity Between Tables" topic.

27. **A.** If locking is altered to an `UPDATE` level lock when the initial `SELECT`, you can read data without blocking other processes that need to read data as well. Later in the process you may update it with the assurance that the data has not changed since the `SELECT`.

    Locking and hints are covered thoroughly in Chapter 6. SQL Server Books Online covers this same information in the topic "Locking Hints."

28. **D.** Database properties, file properties, and user permission changes could all have been implemented by another administrator, which could affect the end users and cause the problem defined. Also, if the transaction log becomes full, the database no longer accepts updates and deletions.

    Permissions are covered fully in Chapter 6. SQL Server Books Online covers security and permissions are related to numerous topics. Start with "Managing Permissions."

29. **C.** The `DBCC CHECKIDENT` operations check the current identity value for the specified table and, if needed, correct the value. `Reseed` will set the next ID to the largest current ID + 1 and work in this case *only* if the records deleted are ones at the end of the ID range.

    For more information on this and other DBCC operations, refer to Chapter 12. DBCC is covered fully in SQL Server Books Online under "DBCC Overview."

30. **C.** You are likely not ordering the data to achieve the desired results. Grouping of the resultset doesn't seem to be warranted because the question is asking for five rows. NULL values should not affect this query, though in some instances Null data can interfere with the results.

    ORDER and TOP are covered fully in Chapter 4, or refer to SQL Server Books Online, "Order" and "Top N."

31. **A.** When given a choice between a constraint, trigger, rule, and stored procedure, the constraint is often the best option. In this case, a constraint catches the error with the least amount of work and overhead on the server. A trigger or stored procedure is more useful when greater functionality is needed. A trigger is also helpful for processes that are reactionary based on data input, deletion, or alterations. A rule is rarely a good option because of its limited functionality and larger overhead. A stored procedure in this case is not valid because of the requirement that the users not change their statements. Otherwise, it is often recommended that programmatic data access (anything that isn't an ad-hoc one-time query) be done through a stored procedure for the purpose of maintainability (stored procedures provide centralized code base), reliability (no chance of mistyping an Insert statement with unfortunate or potentially even tragic results), and speed (precompiled, more reliable reuse of query plans than ad-hoc queries).

    For more information on the appropriate use of constraints, see Chapters 2 and 3. Triggers are covered in detail in Chapter 8. Stored procedures are dealt with at length in Chapter 9. SQL Server Books Online also covers these options under their respective headings: "Constraints," "Rules," "Triggers," and "Stored Procedures."

32. **F.** Each of the reasons, excluding the Agent, are very possibly a cause of the symptoms being given. The SQL Server Agent handles non-data activity on the server related to Operators, Jobs, and Events configured on the system. If the Agent is not running, only these particular processes are interrupted, not the entire database.

    See Chapters 2 and 3 to look at the variety of options that might prevent updates. SQL Server Books Online has an excellent "Troubleshooting" section that also covers these options.

33. **A.** When given a choice between a constraint, trigger, rule, and stored procedure, the constraint is often the best option. In this case, a constraint catches the error with the least amount of work and overhead on the server. A trigger or stored procedure is more useful when greater functionality is needed. A trigger is also helpful for processes that are reactionary, based on data input, deletion, or alterations. A rule is rarely a good option because of its limited functionality and larger overhead.

    For more information on the appropriate use of constraints, see Chapter 2 and 3. Triggers are covered in detail in Chapter 8. Stored procedures are dealt with at length in Chapter 9. SQL Server Books Online also covers these options under their respective headings: "Constraints," "Rules," "Triggers," and "Stored Procedures."

34. **A.** An XML implementation may be more suited to an active server page, Internet application than a LAN application. RDO and DAO represent older technologies that aren't as efficient and versatile as ADO. SQL-DMO is for development of system applications that interact with SQL Server on a non-data level.

    See these options in Chapters 1, 2, and 3. Also SQL Server Books Online covers this in the "ADO."

35. **A.** Triggers are perfect for any automated processing that needs to be done to update, insert, or delete other data based on data activity on the server. Be aware, though, that triggers can also make it hard to diagnose why data is "mysteriously" changing in a table. A stored procedure may have been the best solution in other cases. When all data access is done through stored procedures, the need for triggers is reduced. Admittedly, triggers protect you from an ill-conceived ad-hoc INSERT statement, which stored procedures cannot do; of course, this is mitigated by proper permissions to keep the riff-raff out of the database.

   Triggers are discussed in depth in Chapter 8. SQL Server Books Online also covers them at length under the "Triggers" topic.

36. **E.** ORDER BY and GROUP BY with COMPUTE will result in final totals and that is all. COMPUTE BY requires the use of ORDER BY. To produce an ordered, grouped listing with both intermediate and final totals, all four clauses need to be used.

   The basic SELECT operation and clauses are covered in Chapter 4. The GROUP and COMPUTE options are covered in Chapter 5. If you begin with the SELECT clause in SQL Server Books Online, you'll find a variety of good examples and ideas on where they can be used.

37. **A, E.** According to the problem description, a Foreign Key relationship is needed from the OrderDetails table to a uniquely defined element in the Parts table.

   For information on logical entity design and physical table design, see Chapters 2 and 3. SQL Server Books Online covers relationships in a variety of topics. The most helpful in this situation would likely be "Table Relationships."

38. **D.** A single update of this nature would lock the database out for an extended period of time. Because the majority of the data is going to be acted against through the update, and the data is needed around the clock to service the web site, you are probably better off breaking the update into smaller batches. Each batch would process a segment of the data based on WHERE conditions.

   Batch updates of this nature are covered in Chapter 9. SQL Server Books Online has additional information available under the topic "Effects of Transactions and Batches on SQL Server Performance."

39. **A, B.** By setting an owner and user password, you can control who is allowed to make updates to a DTS package as well as who can execute the process.

   Chapter 5 deals with DTS operations. SQL Server Books Online has additional material under "DTS."

40. **A.** When using an alias for a column, ORDER BY will allow for the actual alias name to be used, whereas GROUP BY requires that the columns be used individually.

   The basic SELECT operation and clauses are covered in Chapter 4. GROUP and COMPUTE options are covered in Chapter 5. If you begin with the SELECT clause in SQL Server Books Online, you'll find a variety of good examples and ideas on where they can be used.

41. **D.** In this situation the benefit of Views really comes out. They are particularly useful in situations where there is sensitive information or a complex data structure.

   Views are covered in their entirety in Chapter 7. SQL Server Books Online covers this topic in detail under "Views."

42. **B.** There is no need for ORDER or GROUP. In this solution, the best query is a simple SELECT query with a WHERE condition for the site.

    The basic SELECT operation and clauses are covered in Chapter 4. GROUP and COMPUTE options are covered in Chapter 5. If you begin with the SELECT clause in SQL Server Books Online, you'll find a variety of good examples and ideas on where they can be used.

43. **C.** Although each of the answers will potentially solve the problem, those easiest to develop, use, and maintain would be those that use DTS processes. Of the two DTS procedures, there are no transformations needed; it is more than just a simple DTS operation, and some standard tasks will be needed.

    Chapter 5 deals with DTS operations. SQL Server Books Online has additional material under "DTS."

44. **F.** Potentially an INSTEAD OF operation is altering the data before it gets into the table. Conversion of upper, lower, and mixed case would not usually be performed by the other types of potential problems listed.

    Triggers are discussed in depth in Chapter 8. SQL Server Books Online also covers this at length under the "Triggers" topic.

45. **E.** SCHEMABINDING refers only to SQL Server objects, specifically tables, views, and user-defined functions. An XML schema cannot be bound in this manner. XML resides in memory and is processed against its own internal set of rules, referred to as a schema. An XML schema interacts directly with the data to supply logic and display attributes to the user on the user's browser.

    Chapter 5 deals with XML and related operations. SQL Server Books Online covers XML through a variety of topics, beginning with "XML Integration of Relational Data."

APPENDIXES

Glossary

A

ADO (ActiveX Data Objects) An easy-to-use application programming interface (API) that wraps OLE DB for use in languages, such as Visual Basic, Visual Basic for Applications, Active Server Pages, and Microsoft Internet Explorer Visual Basic Scripting.

aggregate functions Functions that provide summary data over sets returning a singular value.

alert A user-defined response to a SQL Server event. Alerts can either execute a defined task or send an email and/or pager message to a specified operator.

ALTER A command used to change a database object, such as a function or procedure. Using ALTER allows the object to be changed without losing permissions and other database settings.

ALTER TRIGGER The ALTER TRIGGER statement is used to change the definition of a trigger. Its syntax and arguments are similar to CREATE TRIGGER.

ALTER VIEW The ALTER VIEW statement is used to easily reshape the definition of a view without affecting permissions granted. Its syntax is similar to the CREATE VIEW statement's syntax.

analysis server The server component of Analysis Services that is specifically designed to create and maintain multidimensional data structures and provide multidimensional data in response to client queries.

articles Data structures made from selected columns from a table, or an entire table, that need to be bundled into a publication to be used for replication. A publication is composed of one or more articles. An article represents some or all columns, and some or all rows in a single table.

attributes The characteristics given to an entity, such as PhoneNumber and State; they are usually represented as rows inside an entity. An attribute in data modeling can be thought of as the columns of a table implemented in SQL Server.

B

batch Multiple batches can be combined in a single script or procedure using the GO Keyword to separate the batches. A collection of zero, one, or more T-SQL statements sent to SQL Server to be run together.

BCP A command prompt bulk copy utility that copies SQL Server data to or from an operating system file in a user-specified format.

binding In SQL application programming interfaces (APIs), binding is associating a resultset column or a parameter with a program variable, so that data is moved automatically into or out of a program variable when a row is fetched or updated.

blocked process A process that cannot continue until a lock that another process holds is released.

Books Online A comprehensive help facility and electronic reference manual.

built-in function   A group of predefined functions provided as part of the T-SQL and Multidimensional Expressions (MDX) languages.

C

cascading actions   Cascading delete or cascading update operations that either delete a row containing a Primary Key or updates a Primary Key value referenced by Foreign Key columns in existing rows in other tables. On a cascading delete, all the rows whose Foreign Key values reference the deleted Primary Key value are also deleted. On a cascading update, all the Foreign Key values are updated to match the new Primary Key value.

CASE expression   A complex expression that handles multiple-branch conditional logic.

CAST   The CAST function converts data from one type to another and is based on the ANSI SQL-92 standard as opposed to the CONVERT function.

CHECK constraint   Defines what values are acceptable in a column. You can apply CHECK constraints to multiple columns, and you can apply multiple CHECK constraints to a single column. When a table is dropped, CHECK constraints are also dropped.

Client Network utility   The Client Network utility is used to manage the client net-libraries and define server alias names. It can also be used to set the default options used by DB-Library applications.

client/server   A physically or logically implemented system where a device or application called the server requests services or data from another device or application and the server fulfills the request.

clustered index   A clustered index in SQL Server is a type of index in which the logical order of key values determines the actual data rows; thereby the data rows are kept sorted. Using a clustered index causes the actual data rows to move into the leaf level of the index.

collation (sequence)   A set of rules that determines how data is compared, ordered, and presented. Character data is sorted using collation information, including locale, sort order, and case sensitivity.

column list   The column list, or select list, is the part of the SELECT statement that specifies the columns being accessed.

comment   Inline documentation used to explain what a set of T-SQL statements is doing. This is also a technique used to temporarily prevent statements from running for diagnostic and troubleshooting reasons; usually used in the sense "comment out."

constraint   A property assigned to a table column that prevents certain types of invalid data values from being placed in the column. For example, a UNIQUE or PRIMARY KEY constraint prevents you from inserting a value that is a duplicate of an existing value; a CHECK constraint prevents you from inserting a value that does not match a search condition; and NOT NULL prevents you from inserting a NULL value.

CREATE   A command used to create a database object, such as a view or stored procedure.

CREATE TRIGGER   Using the CREATE TRIGGER statement is the T-SQL way to create a trigger, but they can also be created using the Enterprise Manager. As with CREATE VIEW, you can specify useful arguments, such as WITH ENCRYPTION.

Current Activity window   The window view in the Enterprise Manager that enables you to see current processes, objects, and locks held by SQL Server.

cursor   A construct that holds a rowset from a SELECT statement, which can then be stepped through row by row for various operations.

D

data warehouse   A database specifically structured for query and analysis. A data warehouse typically contains data representing the business history of an organization.

database lock   The largest of locking increments affecting the entire database.

DBRE DBREINDEX   A Database Console Command used to rebuild indexes. Out of the different ways of rebuilding an index, the preferred is DBREINDEX because it does not require that you rebuild indexes individually, but it enables you to rebuild multiple indexes in a single shot.

deadlock   A state in which two users or processes cannot continue processing because they each have a resource that the other needs.

DELETE   The DELETE T-SQL statement can be used to delete data from a table. A fast way to delete all rows is TRUNCATE TABLE.

DELETE trigger   DELETE triggers are FOR or AFTER triggers that can restrict data from being deleted from a table, or to perform any other action with the deleted data—such as logging the deletion or generating an alert. They fire automatically when a DELETE statement is executed against the table.

denormalization   The process of adding planned redundancy to an already fully normalized data model.

derived table   In a FROM clause, you can use a SELECT statement in parentheses as one of the tables you are selecting from. This is called a derived table.

deterministic   A function is deterministic if it always returns the same output when presented with the same input. Mathematical functions, such as SQRT, are deterministic because they always return the same output given the same input.

distributed partitioned view   A distributed partitioned view collects data from two or more instances of SQL Server; a new feature to SQL Server 2000.

distributor   In SQL Server terminology, the Distributor is the server that contains the distribution database, data history, and transactions; as its name implies, its job is to distribute data to Subscribers.

DROP   A command used to drop a database object, such as a view or stored procedure. Using DROP removes all the permissions for the object, as well as the object itself. For example, the DROP VIEW statement is used to remove a view or indexed view from the database. Dropping a view removes the definition of a view from the database and an entry in the sysobjects while not affecting the underlying tables and views.

E

encryption   A method for keeping sensitive information confidential by changing data into an unreadable form.

English Query   Refers to a Microsoft application development product that enables users to ask questions in English, rather than in a computer language, such as SQL. For example, you might ask, "How many customers bought products last year?" rather than prepare an equivalent SQL statement.

entity   The main object in an entity-relationship model, which can be deduced by case study examination. Entities represent the things, places, people, concepts, and things involved in a real-world situation, and contain within them properties or attributes that relate to them.

entity decomposition   The breaking down of attributes so that they are made into a more basic form. Entity decomposition needs to be undertaken before applying attributes into the final data model.

execution plan   The method in which the query optimizer has chosen to execute a SQL operation.

extent lock   A lock covering eight contiguous data or index pages.

F

filegroups   In SQL Server, a named collection of one or more files that forms a single unit of allocation. Also for administration of a database.

FILLFACTOR   An attribute of an index that defines the amount of free space allotted to each page of the index. FILLFACTOR can be used to allocate space for future expansion. FILLFACTOR is a value from 1 through 100 that specifies the percentage of the index page to be left empty.

filter   A set of criteria that controls the set of records returned as a resultset. Filters can also define the sequence in which rows are returned.

Foreign Key   A column or multiple columns whose values match the Primary Key of another table. Foreign Keys help in the relational process between two entities by connecting the foreign attribute in the child entity to a Primary Key in a parent entity.

fragmentation   Occurs when data modifications are made. You can reduce fragmentation and improve read-ahead performance by dropping and re-creating a clustered index.

FROM   The FROM part of the SELECT statement specifies the tables being accessed. Specifying what tables are being accessed is compulsory for any SELECT data retrieval statement.

full-text catalog   A full-text catalog is a special storage space used to house full-text indexes. By default, all full-text indexes are housed in a single catalog.

full-text index   A special index that efficiently tracks the words you're looking for in a table. They help in enabling special searching functions that differ from those used in regular indexes.

G

GROUP BY operator   The operator that creates aggregated sets from a single select statement.

H

HTML (Hypertext Markup Language)   A system of marking up, or tagging, a document so that it can be published on the World Wide Web. Documents prepared in HTML include reference graphics and formatting tags. You use a web browser (such as Microsoft Internet Explorer) to view these documents.

I

identity   A column in a table that has been assigned the identity property. The identity property generates unique numbers.

IIS   Microsoft Internet Information Server.

IN operator   The operator that compares a single value to a set, and returns true if the single value occurs within the set.

index   In a relational database, a database object that provides fast access to data in the rows of a table, based on key values. Indexes can also enforce uniqueness on the rows in a table. SQL Server supports clustered and non-clustered indexes. The primary key/unique constraint automatically causes an index to be built. In full-text searches, a full-text index stores information about significant words and their location within a given column.

Index Tuning wizard   A graphical tool that enables you to select and create powerful indexes and statistics for a Microsoft SQL Server 2000 database without prior knowledge of index and database internal structural designs.

indexed view   A view that has an index defined onto it. Indexes on views enable view resultsets to be stored in the database's physical storage after an index is created. In contrast to this, in a non-indexed view, the view is activated at runtime and the resultset is dynamically built.

INSERT   T-SQL command used to add one or more records to a table.

INSERT INTO   The INSERT INTO T-SQL statement can be used to insert rows of data into a table when needed.

INSERT trigger   FOR or AFTER triggers that can be used to verify the data being inserted or to perform any other action with the data. They fire automatically when an INSERT statement is made against the underlying table.

INSTEAD OF trigger   A trigger new to SQL Server 2000, which replaces the action that an INSERT, DELETE, or UPDATE trigger might take.

Internet host name (DNS name)   Fully qualified name that is associated with the computer on the Internet (for example, `mycomputer.mydomain.com`)

J

job   A specified series of operations, called steps, performed sequentially by a SQL Server agent.

join   The act of combining the data in two tables based on values found in each of the tables.

K-L

LIKE   The LIKE predicate is used to search through character strings by specifying a search string. A LIKE search is primarily used for searches based on wildcard characters, such as the percent sign (%).

linked server   A database object that represents a particular data source and the attributes, including security and collation attributes, necessary to access the data source.

local partitioned view   A partitioned view where all member tables reside on the local instance of SQL Server.

lock   A method of ensuring concurrency. Locking enables users to temporarily "check out" an object, preventing other users from changing the object, for the purpose of ensuring consistency.

log file   A file or set of files containing a record of the modifications made in a database.

M

many-to-many relationship   This type of relationship occurs when many rows or things in an entity (many instances of an entity) are associated with many rows or things in another entity. This type of relationship is not uncommon in the real world. SQL Server doesn't actually allow direct implementation of many-to-many relationships; nevertheless, you can do so by creating two one-to-many relationships to a new entity.

Master database   The database that controls the operation of each instance of SQL Server. It is installed automatically with each instance of SQL Server and keeps track of user accounts, remote user accounts, and remote servers that each instance can interact with. It also tracks ongoing processes, configurable environment variables, system error messages, tapes and disks available on the system, and active locks.

merge replication   The process of transferring data from the Publisher to the Subscriber, allowing the Publisher and Subscriber to update data while connected or disconnected and then merging the updates after they both are connected. Merge replication begins with a snapshot. Thereafter, no data is replicated until the Publisher and Subscriber do a "merge." The merge can be scheduled or done via an ad-hoc request. Merge replication's main benefit is that it supports subscribers who are not on the network much of the time. Transactions, which are committed, however, may be rolled back as the result of conflict resolution.

meta data   Information about the properties of data, such as the type of data in a column (numeric, text, and so on) or the length of a column. It can also be information about the structure of data or information that specifies the design of objects, such as cubes or dimensions.

MIB (Management Information Base)   The SNMP protocol used to define a hierarchical list of objects

MMC (Microsoft Management Console)   A common console framework for server and network management applications known as snap-ins.

Model database   A database installed with SQL Server that provides the template for new user databases. SQL Server 2000 creates a new database by copying the contents of the Model database and then expanding it to the size requested.

msdb database   The msdb database is used by the SQL Server agent for scheduling alerts and jobs and for recording server operator information.

N

NetBIOS computer name   The Windows network name associated with the computer.

non-clustered index   An index in which the logical order of the index is different than the physical, stored order of the rows on disk. In contrast to clustered indexes, non-clustered indexes are totally separated from the actual data rows, causing an unsorted order of data based on non-clustered keys. Non-clustered indexes differ from the clustered indexes at the leaf level. The leaf level of a non-clustered index contains the key value and the row locator. The row locator is either the physical row address (if there is no clustered index) or the clustered index key value (if a clustered index exists).

non-deterministic   A function is non-deterministic if it can return different results when provided with the same input. The RAND function is non-deterministic because it returns a different randomly generated number each time it is called.

normalization   Developed by Dr. E. F. Codd in 1970, database normalization is the process of simplifying data and database design to achieve maximum performance and simplicity. This process involves the removing of useless and redundant data.

O

ODBC (Open Database Connectivity)   A data access application programming interface (API) that supports access to any data source for which an ODBC driver is available. ODBC is aligned with the American National Standards Institute (ANSI) and International Standards Organization for (ISO) standards for a database Call Level Interface (CLI).

OLE-DB   A COM-based application programming interface (API) for accessing data. OLE-DB supports accessing data stored in any format (databases, spreadsheets, text files, and so on) for which an OLE-DB provider is available.

one-to-many relationships These relationships exist when a single instance of an entity (the parent entity) relates to many instances of another entity (the child entity). One-to-many relationships are the most common relationships in the real world.

one-to-one relationship Occurs when one row or thing of an entity is associated with only one row or thing of another. One-to-one relationships are uncommon in the real world.

Online Analytical Processing (OLAP) A technology that uses multidimensional structures to provide rapid access to data for analysis. The source data for OLAP is commonly stored in data warehouses in a relational database.

Online Transaction Processing (OLTP) A data processing system designed to record all the business transactions of an organization as they occur. An OLTP system is characterized by many concurrent users actively adding and modifying data.

operator An individual that can potentially receive messages from SQL Server via email, pager, or Net send.

ORDER BY A sub-statement found in the SELECT statement used to order the rows in the resultset in either descending or ascending order: DESC and ASC, respectively.

OSQL (ODBC Structured Query Language) An interactive command prompt utility provided with SQL Server that enables users to execute T-SQL statements or batches from a server or workstation and view the results returned.

P

page lock A lock that covers 8KB of data.

partitioned view A table that has been replaced with multiple, smaller tables. Each smaller table has the same format as the original table, but with a subset of the data. Each partitioned table has rows allocated to it based on some characteristic of the data, such as specific key ranges. The rules that define into which table the rows go must be unambiguous. For example, a table is partitioned into two tables. All rows with Primary Key values lower than a specified value are allocated to one table, and all rows equal to or greater than the value are allocated to the other. Partitioning can improve application processing speeds and reduce the potential for conflicts in multi-site update replication. You can improve the usability of partitioned tables by creating a view. The view, created by a union of select operations on all the partitioned tables, presents the data as if it all resided in a single table.

performance monitor The NT implementation of system monitor.

Primary Key A column or set of columns that uniquely identify all the rows in a table. Primary Keys do not allow null values. No two rows can have the same Primary Key value; therefore, a Primary Key value always uniquely identifies a single row. More than one key can uniquely identify rows in a table; each of these keys is called a candidate key. Only one candidate can be chosen as the Primary Key of a table; all other candidate keys are known as alternate keys. Although tables are not required to have Primary Keys, it is good practice to define them. In a normalized table, all the data values in each row are fully dependent on the Primary Key. For example, in a normalized employee table that has EmployeeID as the Primary Key, all the columns should contain data related to a specific employee. This table does not have the column DepartmentName because the name of the department is dependent on a department ID, not on an employee ID.

Profiler SQL Profiler is a tool that captures SQL Server 2000 events from a server. The events are saved in a trace file that can later be analyzed or used to replay a specific series of steps when you want to diagnose a problem.

publication A container for articles that is capable of being replicated. A publication, which may include one or more articles, is the basic unit of replication. A publication has a single, specific replication type: either snapshot, transactional, or merge. When a subscriber chooses a publication, all the articles contained within the publication are part of the subscription.

Publisher In respect with replication, the Publisher is the server that produces data so that it can be replicated to Subscribers.

Q

Query Analyzer SQL Query Analyzer is an interactive, graphical tool that enables a database administrator or developer to write queries, execute multiple queries simultaneously, view results, analyze the query plan, and receive assistance to improve the query performance.

query optimizer The SQL Server database engine component responsible for generating efficient execution plans for SQL statements.

R

RAID (redundant array of independent disks)
A disk system that comprises multiple disk drives (an array) to provide higher performance, reliability, storage capacity, and lower cost. Fault-tolerant arrays are categorized in six RAID levels: 0 through 5. Each level uses a different algorithm to implement fault tolerance.

rebuilding indexes Helps in collecting the defragmented pages of information and bringing index data back to its original form. This increases the overall performance by making it easier for SQL Server to read pages to get data.

recompile The queries used by stored procedures and triggers are optimized only when they are compiled. As indexes or other changes that affect statistics are made to the database, compiled stored procedures and triggers may lose efficiency. By recompiling stored procedures and triggers that act on a table, you can reoptimize the queries.

reconfigure Command used to update the currently configured value of a configuration option changed with the sp_configure system stored procedure.

recursive trigger A recursive trigger is a trigger that updates, deletes, or inserts data into its own table or another table, which houses a trigger, and then fires another trigger.

relational database A collection of information organized in tables. Each table models a class of objects of interest to the organization (for example, Customers, Parts, Suppliers). Each column in a table models an attribute of the object (for example, LastName, Price, Color). Each row in a table represents one entity in the class of objects modeled by the table (for example, the customer name John Smith or the part number 1346). Queries can use data from one table to find related data in other tables.

Relational Database Management System The controlling software for databases in which data is organized into related objects within a database rather than tied to a file. Each of these objects is related to another in some way.

relationship A connection between entities ties a parent entity to a child entity through the Primary Key in one entity to a Foreign Key in another.

replication A process that copies and distributes data and database objects from one database to another and then synchronizes information between databases for consistency.

Replication agent Tool that enables SQL Server to perform the different types of replication processes when distributing data.

replication configurations Different physical scenarios in which replication is set up; these provide specific benefits and uses that are relevant to the configuration you use. Replication models, which include Single Publisher/Multiple Subscriber, Single Subscriber/Multiple Publishers, and Multiple Publishers/Multiple Subscribers, are the physical implementation. Each of the replication types may be implemented using any of the these models.

roles A SQL Server security account is a collection of other security accounts that can be treated as a single unit when managing permissions. A role can contain SQL Server logins, other roles, and Windows logins or groups.

row lock The finest granularity of locking available on SQL Server allowing for a single data record to be locked.

rules A database object that is bound to columns or user-defined data types, and specifies what data values are acceptable in a column. CHECK constraints provide the same functionality and are preferred because they are in the SQL-92 standard.

S

schema In the SQL-92 standard, a collection of database objects that are owned by a single user and form a single namespace. A namespace is a set of objects that cannot have duplicate names. For example, two tables can have the same name only if they are in separate schemas; no two tables in the same schema can have the same name. In T-SQL, much of the functionality associated with schemas is implemented by database user IDs. In database tools, schema also refers to the catalog information that describes the objects in a schema or database. In analysis services, a schema is a description of multidimensional objects, such as cubes and dimensions.

SCHEMABINDING An option for a user-defined function or a view that prevents changes to the objects referenced by the function or view unless you first drop the view. This makes the views and functions more reliable, because they can rely on their database objects always being present.

scope The lifetime of an object. Specifically, a variable has a scope within a single batch, which means it ceases to exist outside the batch.

script A collection of batches, usually stored in a text file.

SELECT The T-SQL statement used to return data to an application or another T-SQL statement, or to populate a cursor. The SELECT statement returns a tabular result set consisting of data that is typically extracted from one or more tables. The result set contains data from only those rows that match the search conditions specified in the WHERE or HAVING clauses.

Server Network utility The Server Network utility is used to manage the server net-libraries.

Service Manager SQL Server Service Manager is used to start, stop, and pause the SQL Server 2000 components on the server. These components run as services on Microsoft Windows NT or Microsoft Windows 2000 and as separate executable programs on Microsoft Windows 95 and Microsoft Windows 98.

SET The statement used to alter environment settings for a session.

snapshot replication A type of replication wherein data and database objects are distributed by copying published items via the Distributor and on to the Subscriber exactly as they appear at a specific moment in time. Snapshot replication provides the distribution of both data and structure (tables, indexes, and so on) on a scheduled basis. It may be thought of as a "whole table refresh." No updates to the source table are replicated until the next scheduled snapshot.

SNMP (Simple Network Management Protocol)
Used for troubleshooting and querying TCP/IP servers.

SQL Profiler   A tool used to trace SQL Server activity.

statement permissions   An attribute that controls whether a user can execute CREATE or BACKUP statements.

statistics   SQL Server keeps statistics about the distribution of the key values in each index and uses these statistics to determine what index(es) to use in query processing.

stored procedure   A collection of T-SQL statements with a well-defined set of inputs, called input parameters, and a well-defined set of outputs, which may be output parameters, return values, or cursors. Stored procedures allow the encapsulation of various database operations.

string concatenation   Combining of two strings, such as the results of the first name and last name columns. String concatenation can be performed using the plus (+) operator.

Structured Query Language (SQL)   A language used to insert, retrieve, modify, and delete data in a relational database. SQL also contains statements for defining and administering the objects in a database. SQL is the language supported by most relational databases, and is the subject of standards published by the International Standards Organization (ISO) and the American National Standards Institute (ANSI). SQL Server 2000 uses a version of the SQL language called T-SQL.

Subscriber   The server that receives replicated data (in the form of publications) from the Publisher.

System Monitor   The performance monitoring tool available in Windows 2000 operating systems.

T

table   A two-dimensional object, consisting of rows and columns, used to store data in a relational database. Each table stores information about one of the types of objects modeled by the database.

table lock   A lock on a table, including all data and indexes.

TCP/IP (Transmission Control Protocol/Internet Protocol)   An industry standard network protocol used by most companies for internetworking computer equipment.

tempdb   The database that provides a storage area for temporary tables, temporary stored procedures, and other temporary working storage needs.

TOP   The TOP keyword can be used in conjunction with the SELECT statement to select the top *n* rows or a percentage of the resultset rows.

trace   The SQL Profiler method for recording server events.

trace flags   Flags that can be enabled to aid in troubleshooting.

transactional replication   A type of replication where data and database objects are distributed by first applying an initial snapshot at the Subscriber and then later capturing transactions made at the Publisher and propagating them to individual Subscribers. Transactional replication, as with all replication types, begins with a synchronizing snapshot. After the initial synchronization, transactions, which are committed at the Publisher, are automatically replicated to the Subscribers.

Transact-SQL (T-SQL)   The language containing the commands used to administer instances of SQL Server, create and manage all objects in an instance of SQL Server, and to insert, retrieve, modify, and delete all data in SQL Server tables. T-SQL is an extension of the language defined in the SQL standards published by the International Standards Organization (ISO) and the American National Standards Institute (ANSI).

trigger A trigger is a stored procedure that is fired when data is modified from a table using any of the three modification statements: DELETE, INSERT, or UPDATE. FOR and AFTER are synonymous, and are usually implied when referring to triggers, rather than INSTEAD OF triggers. Triggers are often created to enforce referential integrity or consistency among logically related data in different tables.

T-SQL See *Transact-SQL*.

U

UNION operator An operator that can combine two SELECT statements into one large rowset.

UNIQUE constraint Constraints that enforce entity integrity on a non-Primary Key. UNIQUE constraints ensure that no duplicate values are entered and that an index is created to enhance performance.

UNIQUE index An index in which no two rows are permitted to have the same index value, thus prohibiting duplicate index or key values. The system checks for duplicate key values when the index is created and checks each time data is added with an INSERT or UPDATE statement.

UPDATE The act of modifying one or more data values in an existing row or rows, typically by using the UPDATE statement. Sometimes, the term *update* refers to any data modification, including INSERT, UPDATE, and DELETE operations.

UPDATE STATISTICS A command that updates statistical information for an index. Index statistics need to be up to date for the optimizer to decide upon the fastest route of access.

UPDATE trigger UPDATE triggers are FOR or AFTER triggers that can be used to evaluate UPDATE statements issued against a table to modify existing data. They can be used to allow or reject data modification attempts, to log the attempt, or to generate an alert. They fire automatically when an UPDATE statement is executed against the table.

updateable Subscribers Subscribers that are capable of updating and modifying data when it is replicated. This option can be used with snapshot replication and transactional replication. A transactional or snapshot publication may allow updateable Subscribers. Changes made on the Subscriber's replica are propagated to the Publisher either in real time via DTC, or near real time via a queue.

user A user is a database-wide security context.

user-defined function A collection of T-SQL statements with a well-defined set of input parameters, but only one output—which can be a scalar value or a table. User-defined functions allow the encapsulation of various logical and database operations, but cannot be used to affect changes to a database.

V

variable A construct that can temporarily hold values for use in a Transact-SQL batch.

view A view is a relational database object that can be referenced and built by using SELECT statements to join data from one or more base tables. Views are similar to tables in that data can be retrieved and modified and indexes can be built.

W

WHERE   A sub-statement found in the SELECT statement that uses any of various filter conditions, such as BETWEEN, IN, and LIKE, to limit the number of rows retrieved.

Windows application log   The operating system event log used to record application events sent by SQL Server services.

WITH ENCRYPTION   The WITH ENCRYPTION clause protects the definition of your view. If you specify this, you encrypt the definition of your view because you may not want users to display it. Encrypting using WITH ENCRYPTION disallows anyone from using sp_heptext to display your view or viewing it via the Enterprise Manager.

WITH SCHEMABINDING   The WITH SCHEMABINDING option specifies that the view be bound to the schema. This has to be specified when you want to create views with indexes. Also, when WITH SCHEMABINDING is specified, you have to adhere to the owner.object syntax when referencing tables or views in the creation of your view.

X-Z

XML (Extensible Markup Language)   A hypertext programming language used to describe the contents of a set of data and how the data should be output to a device or displayed in a web page. Used to move data between systems.

Overview of the Certification Process

You must pass rigorous certification exams to become a Microsoft Certified Professional. These closed-book exams provide a valid and reliable measure of your technical proficiency and expertise. Developed in consultation with computer industry professionals who have experience with Microsoft products in the workplace, the exams are conducted by two independent organizations. Virtual University Enterprises (VUE) testing centers offer exams at more than 2,700 locations in 128 countries. Sylvan Prometric offers the exams at more than 2,000 Authorized Prometric Testing Centers around the world as well.

To schedule an exam, call VUE at 888-837-8734 (or register online at http://www.vue.com/ms/msexam.html) or Sylvan Prometric Testing Centers at 800-755-EXAM (3926) (or register online at http://www.2test.com/register). At the time of this writing, Microsoft offered eight types of certification, each based on specific areas of expertise. Please check the Microsoft Certified Professional web site for the most up-to-date information (www.microsoft.com/mcp/).

TYPES OF CERTIFICATION

◆ **Microsoft Certified Professional (MCP).** Persons with this credential are qualified to support at least one Microsoft product. Candidates can take elective exams to develop areas of specialization. MCP is the base level of expertise.

◆ **Microsoft Certified Database Administrator (MCDBA).** Qualified individuals can derive physical database designs, develop logical data models, create physical databases, create data services by using Transact-SQL, manage and maintain databases, configure and manage security, monitor and optimize databases, and install and configure Microsoft SQL Server.

◆ **Microsoft Certified Systems Engineer (MCSE).** These individuals are qualified to analyze the business requirements for a system architecture, design solutions, deploy, install, and configure architecture components, and troubleshoot system problems.

◆ **Microsoft Certified Solution Developer (MCSD).** These individuals are qualified to design and develop custom business solutions by using Microsoft development tools, technologies, and platforms. The new track includes certification exams that test users' abilities to build web-based, distributed, and commerce applications by using Microsoft products, such as Microsoft SQL Server, Microsoft Visual Studio, and Microsoft Component Services.

◆ **Microsoft Certified Trainer (MCT).** Persons with this credential are instructionally and technically qualified by Microsoft to deliver Microsoft Education Courses at Microsoft-authorized sites. An MCT must be employed by a Microsoft Solution Provider Authorized Technical Education Center or a Microsoft Authorized Academic Training site.

IN THE FIELD

RETIRING CERTIFICATIONS

With the advent of Windows 2000, several certifications are being retired. These include the following:

- **Microsoft Certified Professional+Internet (MCP+Internet).** Although still listed on the Microsoft Training and Certification site at the time of this writing, this certification is retiring. Although the certification for current holders stays in effect until December 31, 2001, all the exams were retired by February 28, 2001.

- **Microsoft Certified Professional+Site Building (MCP+Site Building).** Although still listed on the Microsoft Training and Certification site at the time of this writing, this certification is retiring. The Microsoft Certified Professional+Site Building certification retires on June 30, 2002. An upgrade certification path is not planned.

- **Microsoft Certified Systems Engineer+Internet (MCSE+Internet).** Microsoft retired most of the exams leading to the Microsoft Certified Systems Engineer+Internet certification on February 28, 2001. All those who earned the MCSE+Internet certification by February 28, 2001, will retain the certification until December 31, 2001. An upgrade certification path is not planned.

NOTE
For up-to-date information about each type of certification, visit the Microsoft Training and Certification World Wide Web site at http://www.microsoft.com/trainingandservices. You also may contact Microsoft through the following sources:

- Microsoft Certified Professional Program: 800-636-7544

- http://register.microsoft.com/contactus/contactus.asp

CERTIFICATION REQUIREMENTS

An asterisk following an exam in any of the lists in the rest of this chapter means that it is slated for retirement.

How to Become a Microsoft Certified Professional

To become certified as a MCP, you need only to pass any Microsoft exam (with the exception of Microsoft Windows 2000 Accelerated Exam for MCPs Certified on Microsoft Windows NT 4.0, #70-240).

How to Become a Microsoft Certified Database Administrator

Two MCDBA tracks are still listed on the Microsoft Training and Certification site—one tied to Windows 2000, the other based on Windows NT 4.0. However, most of the exams for the Windows NT 4.0 track were retired by February 28, 2001. Thus, only the Windows 2000 track is covered here.

Windows 2000 Track

To become an MCDBA in the Windows 2000 track, you must pass three core exams:

Core Exams

- ◆ Installing, Configuring, and Administering Microsoft Windows 2000 Server, #70-215

  OR Microsoft Windows 2000 Accelerated Exam for MCPs Certified on Microsoft Windows NT 4.0, #70-240 (only for those who have passed exams #70-067*, #70-068*, and #70-073*)

◆ Administering Microsoft SQL Server 7.0, #70-028

OR Installing, Configuring, and Administering Microsoft SQL Server 2000, Enterprise Edition, #70-228

◆ Designing and Implementing Databases with Microsoft SQL Server 7.0, #70-029

OR Designing and Implementing Databases with Microsoft SQL Server 2000, Enterprise Edition, #70-229

Elective Exams

You must also pass one elective exam from the following list (note that #70-240 can be counted twice—as both a core and elective exam in the MCDBA track):

◆ Implementing and Administering a Microsoft Windows 2000 Network Infrastructure, #70-216 (only for those who have *NOT* already passed #70-067*, #70-068*, and #70-073*)

OR Microsoft Windows 2000 Accelerated Exam for MCPs Certified on Microsoft Windows NT 4.0, #70-240 (only for those who have passed exams #70-067*, #70-068*, and #70-073*)

◆ Designing and Implementing Distributed Applications with Microsoft Visual C++ 6.0, #70-015

◆ Designing and Implementing Data Warehouses with Microsoft SQL Server 7.0 and Microsoft Decision Support Services 1.0, #70-019

◆ Implementing and Supporting Microsoft Internet Information Server 4.0, #70-087*

◆ Designing and Implementing Distributed Applications with Microsoft Visual FoxPro 6.0, #70-155

◆ Designing and Implementing Distributed Applications with Microsoft Visual Basic 6.0, #70-175

How to Become a Microsoft Certified Systems Engineer

You must pass operating system exams and two elective exams to become an MCSE. The MCSE certification path is divided into two tracks: Windows 2000 and Windows NT 4.0.

However, most of the core exams for the Windows NT 4.0 track were retired by February 28, 2001. Thus, only the Windows 2000 track is covered here. To retain the MCSE certification, those certified in the Windows NT 4.0 track must upgrade their certification to the Windows 2000 requirements by December 31, 2001.

Windows 2000 Track

The Windows 2000 track requires you to pass five core exams (or an accelerated exam and another core exam) You must also pass two elective exams.

Core Exams

The Windows 2000 track core requirements for MCSE certification include the following for those who have *NOT* passed #70-067, #70-068, and #70-073:

◆ Installing, Configuring, and Administering Microsoft Windows 2000 Professional, #70-210

◆ Installing, Configuring, and Administering Microsoft Windows 2000 Server, #70-215

◆ Implementing and Administering a Microsoft Windows 2000 Network Infrastructure, #70-216

◆ Implementing and Administering a Microsoft Windows 2000 Directory Services Infrastructure, #70-217

The Windows 2000 track core requirements for MCSE certification include the following for those who have passed #70-067*, #70-068*, and #70-073*:

◆ Microsoft Windows 2000 Accelerated Exam for MCPs Certified on Microsoft Windows NT 4.0, #70-240

All candidates must pass one of these additional core exams:

◆ Designing a Microsoft Windows 2000 Directory Services Infrastructure, #70-219

OR Designing Security for a Microsoft Windows 2000 Network, #70-220

OR Designing a Microsoft Windows 2000 Infrastructure, #70-221

OR Designing Highly Available Web Solutions with Microsoft Windows 2000 Server Technologies, #70-226

Elective Exams

Any MCSE elective exams that are current (not slated for retirement) when the Windows 2000 core exams are released can be used to fulfill the requirement of two elective exams. In addition, core exams 219-221 can be used as elective exams as well, as long as they are not already being used to fulfill the "additional core exams" requirement outlined earlier. Exam #70-222, Upgrading from Microsoft Windows NT 4.0 to Microsoft Windows 2000, can also fulfill this requirement. Finally, selected third-party certifications that focus on interoperability can count for this requirement although none has been identified at this time.

How to Become a Microsoft Certified Solution Developer

The MCSD certification is outlined in the following sections. Undoubtedly changes will come to this certification with the release of the .NET technologies.

The MCSD Track

You must pass three core exams and one elective exam. The three core exam areas are listed here, as are the elective exams from which you can choose.

Core Exams

The core exams include the following:

Desktop Applications Development (one required)

◆ Designing and Implementing Desktop Applications with Microsoft Visual C++ 6.0, #70-016

OR Designing and Implementing Desktop Applications with Microsoft Visual FoxPro 6 0, #70-156

OR Designing and Implementing Desktop Applications with Microsoft Visual Basic 6.0, #70-176

Distributed Applications Development (one required)

◆ Designing and Implementing Distributed Applications with Microsoft Visual C++ 6.0, #70-015

OR Designing and Implementing Distributed Applications with Microsoft Visual FoxPro 6.0, #70-155

OR Designing and Implementing Distributed Applications with Microsoft Visual Basic 6.0, #70-175

Solution Architecture (required)

◆ Analyzing Requirements and Defining Solution Architectures, #70-100

Elective Exam

You must pass one of the following elective exams:

◆ Designing and Implementing Distributed Applications with Microsoft Visual C++ 6.0, #70-015

◆ Designing and Implementing Desktop Applications with Microsoft Visual C++ 6.0, #70-016

◆ Designing and Implementing Data Warehouses with Microsoft SQL Server 7.0, #70-019

◆ Developing Applications with C++ Using the Microsoft Foundation Class Library, #70-024

◆ Implementing OLE in Microsoft Foundation Class Applications, #70-025

◆ Implementing a Database Design on Microsoft SQL Server 6.5, #70-027

◆ Designing and Implementing Databases with Microsoft SQL Server 7.0, #70-029

◆ Designing and Implementing Databases with Microsoft SQL Server 2000 Enterprise Edition, #70-229

◆ Designing and Implementing Web Sites with Microsoft FrontPage 98, #70-055*

◆ Designing and Implementing Commerce Solutions with Microsoft Site Server 3.0, Commerce Edition, #70-057

◆ Application Development with Microsoft Access for Windows 95 and the Microsoft Access Developer's Toolkit, #70-069*

◆ Designing and Implementing Solutions with Microsoft Office 2000 and Microsoft Visual Basic for Applications, #70-091

◆ Designing and Implementing Collaborative Solutions with Microsoft Outlook 2000 and Microsoft Exchange Server 5.5, #70-105

◆ Designing and Implementing Web Solutions with Microsoft Visual InterDev 6.0, #70-152

◆ Designing and Implementing Distributed Applications with Microsoft Visual FoxPro 6.0, #70-155

◆ Designing and Implementing Desktop Applications with Microsoft Visual FoxPro 6.0, #70-156

◆ Developing Applications with Microsoft Visual Basic 5.0, #70-165*

◆ Designing and Implementing Distributed Applications with Microsoft Visual Basic 6.0, #70-175

◆ Designing and Implementing Desktop Applications with Microsoft Visual Basic 6.0, #70-176

Becoming a Microsoft Certified Trainer

As of January 1, 2001, all MCTs must hold a premier Microsoft Certified Professional (MCP) certification (Microsoft Certified Systems Engineer, Microsoft Certified Solution Developer, or Microsoft Certified Database Administrator). To fully understand the requirements and process for becoming an

MCT, you need to obtain the Microsoft Certified Trainer Guide document from:

```
http://www.microsoft.com/trainingandservices/
content/downloads/MCT_guide.doc
```

At this site, you can read the document as a web page or display and download it as a Word file. You can also download the application form from the site. The MCT Guide explains the process for becoming an MCT. The general steps for the MCT certification are as follows:

1. Complete and mail a Microsoft Certified Trainer application to Microsoft. You must include proof of your skills for presenting instructional material. The options for doing so are described in the MCT Guide.

2. Obtain and study the Microsoft Trainer Kit for the Microsoft Official Curricula (MOC) courses for which you want to be certified. Microsoft Trainer Kits can be ordered by calling 800-688-0496 in North America. Those of you in other regions should review the MCT Guide for information on how to order a Trainer Kit.

3. Take and pass any required prerequisite MCP exam(s) to measure your current technical knowledge.

4. Prepare to teach a MOC course. Begin by attending the MOC course for the course for which you want to be certified. This is required so that you understand how the course is structured, how labs are completed, and how the course flows.

5. Pass any additional exam requirement(s) to measure any additional product knowledge that pertains to the course.

6. Submit your course preparation checklist to Microsoft so that your additional accreditation may be processed and reflect on your transcript.

> **WARNING**
> You should consider the preceding steps a general overview of the MCT certification process. The precise steps that you need to take are described in detail on the web site mentioned earlier. Do not misinterpret the preceding steps as the exact process you must undergo.

If you are interested in becoming an MCT, you can obtain more information by visiting the Microsoft Certified Training WWW site at `http://www.microsoft.com/trainingandservices` and choosing MCT under Technical Certifications or by calling 800-688-0496.

What's on the CD-ROM

This appendix is a brief rundown of what you'll find on the CD-ROM that comes with this book. For a more detailed description of the newly developed *ExamGear, Training Guide Edition* exam simulation software, see Appendix D, "*Using the ExamGear, Training Guide Edition Software.*" All items on the CD-ROM are easily accessible from the simple interface. In addition to *ExamGear, Training Guide Edition,* it includes the electronic version of the book in Portable Document Format (PDF) as well as several utility and application programs.

EXAMGEAR, TRAINING GUIDE EDITION

We believe that *ExamGear, Training Guide Edition,* is the best exam software available. In addition to providing a means of evaluating your knowledge of the Training Guide material, *ExamGear, Training Guide Edition* features several innovations that help you to improve your mastery of the subject matter.

For example, the practice tests allow you to check your score by chapter to determine what topics you need to study more. In another mode, *ExamGear, Training Guide Edition* allows you to obtain immediate feedback on your responses in the form of explanations for the correct and incorrect answers.

Although *ExamGear, Training Guide Edition* exhibits most of the full functionality of the retail version of *ExamGear,* including the exam format and all question types, this special version is written to the Training Guide content. It is designed to aid you in assessing how well you understand the Training Guide material and allow you to experience the most common question formats you will see on the actual exam. It does not include all the Microsoft question types like the full *ExamGear* retail product. However, it serves as an excellent method for assessing your knowledge of the Training Guide content and gives you the experience of taking an electronic exam.

Again, for a more complete description of *ExamGear, Training Guide Edition* features, see Appendix D, "*Using the ExamGear, Training Guide Edition Software.*"

EXCLUSIVE ELECTRONIC VERSION OF TEXT

The CD-ROM also contains the electronic version of this book in Portable Document Format (PDF). The electronic version comes complete with all figures as they appear in the book. You will find that the search capabilities of the reader come in handy for study and review purposes.

Using the ExamGear, Training Guide Edition Software

This training guide includes a special version of *ExamGear*—a revolutionary test engine that is designed to give you the best in certification exam preparation. *ExamGear* offers sample and practice exams for many of today's most in-demand technical certifications. This special Training Guide edition is included with this book as a tool to utilize in assessing your knowledge of the Training Guide material, while also providing you with the experience of taking an electronic exam.

This appendix describes in detail what *ExamGear, Training Guide Edition* is, how it works, and what it can do to help you prepare for the exam. Note that although the Training Guide edition includes nearly all the test simulation functions of the complete, retail version, the questions focus on the *Training Guide* content, rather than on simulating the actual Microsoft exam.

EXAM SIMULATION

One of the main functions of *ExamGear, Training Guide Edition* is exam simulation. To prepare you to take the actual vendor certification exam, the Training Guide edition of this test engine is designed to offer the most effective exam simulation available.

Question Quality

The questions provided in the *ExamGear, Training Guide Edition* simulations are written to high standards of technical accuracy. The questions tap the content of the Training Guide chapters and help you review and assess your knowledge before you take the actual exam.

Interface Design

The *ExamGear, Training Guide Edition* exam simulation interface provides you with the experience of taking an electronic exam. This enables you to effectively prepare for taking the actual exam by making the test experience a familiar one. Using this test simulation can help eliminate the sense of surprise or anxiety that you might experience in the testing center, because you will already be acquainted with computerized testing.

STUDY TOOLS

ExamGear provides you with several learning tools to help prepare you for the actual certification exam.

Effective Learning Environment

The *ExamGear, Training Guide Edition* interface provides a learning environment that not only tests you through the computer, but also teaches the material you need to know to pass the certification exam. Each question comes with a detailed explanation of the correct answer and provides reasons why the other options were incorrect. This information helps to reinforce the knowledge you have already and also provides practical information you can use on the job.

Automatic Progress Tracking

ExamGear, Training Guide Edition automatically tracks your progress as you work through the test questions. From the Item Review tab (discussed in detail later in this appendix), you can see at a glance how well you are scoring by objective, by unit, or on a question-by-question basis (see Figure D.1). You can also configure *ExamGear* to drill you on the skills you need to work on most.

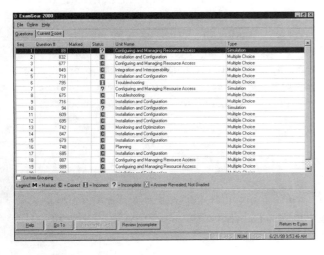

FIGURE D.1
Item review.

How *EXAMGEAR, TRAINING GUIDE EDITION* WORKS

ExamGear comprises two main elements: the interface and the database. The *interface* is the part of the program that you use to study and to run practice tests. The *database* stores all the question-and-answer data.

Interface

The *ExamGear, Training Guide Edition* interface is designed to be easy to use and provides the most effective study method available. The interface enables you to select among the following modes:

- ◆ **Study Mode.** In this mode, you can select the number of questions you want to see and the time you want to allow for the test. You can select questions from all the chapters or from specific chapters. This enables you to reinforce your knowledge in a specific area or strengthen your knowledge in areas pertaining to a specific objective. During the exam, you can display the correct answer to each question along with an explanation of why it is correct.

- ◆ **Practice Exam.** In this mode, you take an exam that is designed to simulate the actual certification exam. Questions are selected from all test-objective groups. The number of questions selected and the time allowed are set to match those parameters of the actual certification exam.

- ◆ **Adaptive Exam.** In this mode, you take an exam simulation using the adaptive testing technique. Questions are taken from all test-objective groups. The questions are presented in a way that ensures your mastery of all the test objectives. After you have a passing score, or if you reach a point where it is statistically impossible for you to pass, the exam is ended. This method provides a rapid assessment of your readiness for the actual exam.

> **NOTE** Microsoft has backed away from the adaptive format somewhat, but it is possible that they could return to it at any time.

Database

The *ExamGear, Training Guide Edition* database stores a group of 150 test questions along with answers and explanations. The questions are organized by the book chapters.

INSTALLING AND REGISTERING EXAMGEAR, TRAINING GUIDE EDITION

This section provides instructions for *ExamGear, Training Guide Edition* installation and describes the process and benefits of registering your Training Guide edition product.

Requirements

ExamGear requires a computer with the following:

◆ Microsoft Windows 95, Windows 98, Windows NT 4.0, Windows 2000, or Windows ME.

A Pentium or later processor is recommended.

◆ A minimum of 32MB of RAM.

As with any Windows application, the more memory, the better your performance.

◆ A connection to the Internet.

An Internet connection is not required for the software to work, but it is required for online registration and to download product updates.

◆ A web browser.

A web browser is not required for the software to work, but it is invoked from the Online, Web Sites menu option.

Installing *ExamGear, Training Guide Edition*

Install *ExamGear, Training Guide Edition* by running the setup program that you found on the *ExamGear, Training Guide Edition* CD. Follow these instructions to install the Training Guide edition on your computer:

1. Insert the CD in your CD-ROM drive. The Autorun feature of Windows should launch the software. If you have Autorun disabled, click Start, and choose Run. Go to the root directory of the CD and choose start.exe. Click Open and then click OK.

2. Click the button in the circle. A Welcome screen appears. From here you can install *ExamGear*. Click the ExamGear button to begin installation.

3. The Installation wizard appears onscreen and prompts you with instructions to complete the installation. Select a directory on which to install *ExamGear, Training Guide Edition*.

4. The Installation wizard copies the *ExamGear, Training Guide Edition* files to your hard drive, adds *ExamGear, Training Guide Edition* to your Program menu, adds values to your Registry, and installs the test engine's DLLs to the appropriate system folders. To ensure that the process was successful, the setup program finishes by running *ExamGear, Training Guide Edition*.

5. The Installation wizard logs the installation process and stores this information in a file named INSTALL.LOG. This log file is used by the uninstall process in the event that you choose to remove *ExamGear, Training Guide Edition* from your computer. Because the *ExamGear* installation adds Registry keys and DLL files to your computer, it is important to uninstall the program appropriately (see the section *"Removing ExamGear, Training Guide Edition from your Computer"*).

Registering *ExamGear, Training Guide Edition*

The Product Registration wizard appears when *ExamGear, Training Guide Edition* is started for the first time, and *ExamGear* checks at startup to see whether you are registered. If you are not registered, the main menu is hidden, and a Product Registration wizard appears. Remember that your computer must have an Internet connection to complete the Product Registration wizard.

The first page of the Product Registration wizard details the benefits of registration; however, you can always elect not to register. The Show This Message at Startup Until I Register option enables you to decide whether the registration screen should appear every time *ExamGear, Training Guide Edition* is started. If you click the Cancel button, you return to the main menu. You can register at any time by selecting Online, Registration from the main menu.

The registration process is composed of a simple form for entering your personal information, including your name and address. You are asked for your level of experience with the product you are testing on and whether you purchased *ExamGear, Training Guide Edition* from a retail store or over the Internet. The information will be used by our software designers and marketing department to provide us with feedback about the usability and usefulness of this product. It takes only a few seconds to fill out and transmit the registration data. A confirmation dialog box appears when registration is complete.

After you have registered and transmitted this information to Que, the registration option is removed from the pull-down menus.

Registration Benefits

Registering enables Que to notify you of product updates and new releases.

Removing *ExamGear, Training Guide Edition* from Your Computer

In the event that you elect to remove the *ExamGear, Training Guide Edition* product from your computer, an uninstall process has been included to ensure that it is removed from your system safely and completely. Follow these instructions to remove *ExamGear* from your computer:

1. Click Start, Settings, Control Panel.

2. Double-click the Add/Remove Programs icon.

3. You are presented with a list of software that is installed on your computer. Select *ExamGear, Training Guide Edition* from the list and click the Add/Remove button. The *ExamGear, Training Guide Edition* software is then removed from your computer.

It is important that the INSTALL.LOG file be present in the directory where you have installed *ExamGear, Training Guide Edition* should you ever choose to uninstall the product. Do not delete this file. The INSTALL.LOG file is used by the uninstall process to safely remove the files and Registry settings that were added to your computer by the installation process.

USING *EXAMGEAR, TRAINING GUIDE EDITION*

ExamGear is designed to be user friendly and very intuitive, eliminating the need for you to learn some confusing piece of software just to practice answering questions. Because the software has a smooth learning curve, your time is maximized because you start practicing almost immediately.

General Description of How the Software Works

ExamGear has three modes of operation: Study Mode, Practice Exam, and Adaptive Exam mode (see Figure D.2). All three sections have the same easy-to-use interface. Using Study Mode, you can hone your knowledge as well as your test-taking abilities through the use of the Show Answers option. While you are taking the test, you can expose the answers along with a brief description of why the given answers are right or wrong. This gives you the ability to better understand the material presented.

The Practice Exam section has many of the same options as Study Mode, but you cannot reveal the answers. This way, you have a more traditional testing environment with which to practice.

The Adaptive Exam questions continuously monitor your expertise in each tested topic area. If you reach a

point at which you either pass or fail, the software ends the examination. As in the Practice Exam, you cannot reveal the answers.

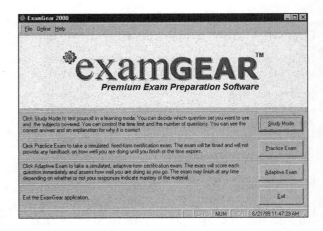

FIGURE D.2
The opening screen offers three testing modes.

Menu Options

The *ExamGear, Training Guide Edition* interface has an easy-to-use menu that provides the following options:

File	Print	Prints the current screen.
	Print Setup	Enables you to select the printer.
	Exit ExamGear	Exits the program.
Online	Registration	Starts the Registration wizard and enables you to register online. This menu option is removed after you have successfully registered the product.
	Check for Product Updates	Opens the ExamGear web site to available updates.
	Web Sites	Starts your browser and connects you to Que or ExamGear site.
Help	Contents	Opens *ExamGear, Training Guide Edition*'s help file.
	About	Displays information about *ExamGear, Training Guide Edition,* including serial number, registered owner, and so on.

File

The File menu allows you to exit the program and configure print options.

Online

In the Online menu, you can register *ExamGear, Training Guide Edition*, check for product updates (update the *ExamGear* executable as well as check for free, updated question sets), and surf web pages. The Online menu is always available, except when you are taking a test.

Registration

Registration is free and allows you access updates. Registration is the first task that *ExamGear, Training Guide Edition* asks you to perform. You will not have access to the free product updates if you do not register.

Check for Product Updates

This option takes you to *ExamGear, Training Guide Edition*'s web site, where you can update the software. Registration is required for this option to be available. You must also be connected to the Internet to use this option. The *ExamGear* web site lists the options that have been made available since your version of *ExamGear* was installed on your computer.

Web Sites

This option provides a convenient way to start your web browser and connect to either the Que or ExamGear home page.

Help

As it suggests, this menu option gives you access to *ExamGear*'s help system. It also provides important information, such as your serial number, software version, and so on.

Starting a Study Mode Session

Study Mode enables you to control the test in ways that actual certification exams do not allow:

◆ You can set your own time limits.

◆ You can concentrate on selected skill areas (chapters).

◆ You can reveal answers or have each response graded immediately with feedback.

◆ You can restrict the questions you see again to those missed or those answered correctly a given number of times.

◆ You can control the order in which questions are presented—(random order or in order by skill area (chapters).

To begin testing in Study Mode, click the Study Mode button from the main Interface screen. You are presented with the Study Mode configuration page (see Figure D.3).

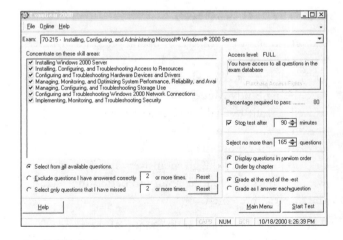

FIGURE D.3
The Study Mode configuration page.

At the top of the Study Mode configuration screen, you see the Exam drop-down list. This list shows the activated exam that you have purchased with your *ExamGear, Training Guide Edition* product, as well as any other exams you may have downloaded or any Preview exams that were shipped with your version of *ExamGear*. Select the exam with which you want to practice from the drop-down list.

Below the Exam drop-down list, you see the questions that are available for the selected exam. Each exam has at least one question set. You can select the individual question set or any combination of the question sets if there is more than one available for the selected exam.

Below the Question Set list is a list of skill areas or chapters on which you can concentrate. These skill areas or chapters reflect the units of exam objectives defined by Microsoft for the exam. Within each skill area you will find several exam objectives. You can select a single skill area or chapter to focus on, or you can select any combination of the available skill areas/chapters to customize the exam to your individual needs.

In addition to specifying what question sets and skill areas you want to test yourself on, you can also define what questions are included in the test based on your previous progress working with the test. *ExamGear, Training Guide Edition* automatically tracks your progress with the available questions. When configuring the Study Mode options, you can opt to view all the questions available within the question sets and skill areas you have selected, or you can limit the questions presented. Choose from the following options:

◆ **Select from All Available Questions.** This option causes *ExamGear, Training Guide Edition* to present all available questions from the selected question sets and skill areas.

◆ **Exclude Questions I Have Answered Correctly** *X* **or More Times.** *ExamGear* offers you the option to exclude questions that you have previously answered correctly. You can specify how many times you want to answer a question correctly before *ExamGear* considers you to have mastered it (the default is two times).

◆ **Select Only Questions That I Have Missed** *X* **or More Times.** This option configures *ExamGear, Training Guide Edition* to drill you only on questions that you have missed repeatedly. You may specify how many times you must miss a question before *ExamGear* determines that you have not mastered it (the default is two times).

At any time, you can reset *ExamGear, Training Guide Edition*'s tracking information by clicking the Reset button for the feature you want to clear.

At the top-right side of the Study Mode configuration sheet, you can see your access level to the question sets for the selected exam. Access levels are either Full or Preview. For a detailed explanation of each of these access levels, see the section "Obtaining Updates" in this appendix.

Under your access level, you see the score required to pass the selected exam. Below the required score, you can select whether the test will be timed and how much time will be allowed to complete the exam. Select the Stop Test After 90 Minutes check box to set a time limit for the exam. Enter the number of minutes you want to allow for the test (the default is 90 minutes). Deselecting this check box allows you to take an exam with no time limit.

You can also configure the number of questions included in the exam. The default number of questions changes with the specific exam you have selected. Enter the number of questions you want to include in the exam in the Select No More than *X* Questions option.

You can configure the order in which *ExamGear, Training Guide Edition* presents the exam questions. Select from the following options:

◆ **Display the Questions in Random Order.** This option is the default option. When selected, it causes *ExamGear, Training Guide Edition* to present the questions in random order throughout the exam.

◆ **Order by Skill Area.** This option causes *ExamGear* to group the questions presented in the exam by skill area. All questions for each selected skill area are presented in succession. The test progresses from one selected skill area to the next, until all the questions from each selected skill area have been presented.

ExamGear offers two options for scoring your exams. Select one of the following options:

◆ **Grade at the End of the Test.** This option configures *ExamGear, Training Guide Edition* to score your test after you have been presented with all the selected exam questions. You can reveal correct answers to a question, but if you do, that question is not scored.

◆ **Grade as I Answer Each Question.** This option configures *ExamGear* to grade each question as you answer it, providing you with instant feedback as you take the test. All questions are scored unless you click the Show Answer button before completing the question.

You can return to the *ExamGear, Training Guide Edition* main startup screen from the Study Mode configuration screen by clicking the Main Menu button. If you need assistance configuring the Study Mode exam options, click the Help button for configuration instructions.

After you have finished configuring all the exam options, click the Start Test button to begin the exam.

Starting Practice Exams and Adaptive Exams

This section describes practice and adaptive exams, defines the differences between these exam options and the Study Mode option, and provides instructions for starting them.

Differences Between the Practice and Adaptive Exams and Study Modes

Question screens in the practice and adaptive exams are identical to those found in Study Mode, except that the Show Answer, Grade Answer, and Item Review buttons are not available while you are in the process of taking a practice or adaptive exam. The Practice Exam provides you with a report screen at the end of the exam. The Adaptive Exam gives you a brief message indicating whether you've passed or failed the exam.

When taking a practice exam, the Item Review screen is not available until you have answered all the questions. This is consistent with the behavior of most vendor's current certification exams. In Study Mode, Item Review is available at any time.

When the exam timer expires, or if you click the End Exam button, the Examination Score Report screen comes up.

Starting an Exam

From the *ExamGear, Training Guide Edition* main menu screen, select the type of exam you want to run. Click the Practice Exam or Adaptive Exam button to begin the corresponding exam type.

What Is an Adaptive Exam?

To make the certification testing process more efficient and valid, and therefore make the certification itself more valuable, some vendors in the industry are using a testing technique called *adaptive testing*. In an adaptive exam, the exam "adapts" to your abilities by varying the difficulty level of the questions presented to you.

The first question in an adaptive exam is typically an easy one. If you answer it correctly, you are presented with a slightly more difficult question. If you answer that question correctly, the next question you see is even more difficult. If you answer the question incorrectly, however, the exam "adapts" to your skill level by presenting you with another question of equal or lesser difficulty on the same subject. If you answer that question correctly, the test begins to increase the difficulty level again. You must correctly answer several questions at a predetermined difficulty level to pass the exam. After you have done this successfully, the exam is ended and scored. If you do not reach the required level of difficulty within a predetermined time (typically 30 minutes) the exam is ended and scored.

Why Do Vendors Use Adaptive Exams?

Many vendors who offer technical certifications have adopted the adaptive testing technique. They have found that it is an effective way to measure a candidate's mastery of the test material in as little time as necessary. This reduces the scheduling demands on the test taker and allows the testing center to offer more tests per test station than they could with longer, more traditional exams. In addition, test security is greater and this increases the validity of the exam process.

Studying for Adaptive Exams

Studying for adaptive exams is no different from studying for traditional exams. You should make sure that you have thoroughly covered all the material for each of the test objectives specified by the certification exam vendor. As with any other exam, when you take an adaptive exam, you either know the material or you don't. If you are well prepared, you will be able to pass the exam. *ExamGear, Training Guide Edition* allows you to familiarize yourself with the adaptive exam testing technique. This will help eliminate any anxiety you might experience from this testing technique and allow you to focus on learning the actual exam material.

ExamGear's Adaptive Exam

The method used to score the adaptive exam requires a large pool of questions. For this reason, you cannot use this exam in Preview mode. The adaptive exam is presented in much the same way as the practice exam. When you click the Start Test button, you begin answering questions. The adaptive exam does not allow Item Review, and it does not allow you to mark questions to skip and answer later. You must answer each question when it is presented.

Assumptions

This section describes the assumptions made when designing the behavior of the *ExamGear, Training Guide Edition* adaptive exam.

◆ You fail the test if you fail any chapter or unit, earn a failing overall score, or reach a threshold at which it is statistically impossible for you to pass the exam.

◆ You can fail or pass a test without cycling through all the questions.

◆ The overall score for the adaptive exam is Pass or Fail. However, to evaluate user responses dynamically, percentage scores are recorded for units and the overall score.

Algorithm Assumptions

This section describes the assumptions used in designing the *ExamGear, Training Guide Edition* Adaptive Exam scoring algorithm.

Unit Scores

You fail a unit (and the exam) if any unit score falls below 66%.

Overall Scores

To pass the exam, you must pass all units and achieve an overall score of 86% or higher.

You fail if the overall score percentage is less than or equal to 85%, or if any unit score is less than 66%.

Inconclusive Scores

If your overall score is between 67 and 85%, it is considered to be *inconclusive*. Additional questions will be asked until you pass or fail or until it becomes statistically impossible to pass without asking more than the maximum number of questions allowed.

Question Types and How to Answer Them

Because certification exams from different vendors vary, you will face many types of questions on any given exam. *ExamGear, Training Guide Edition* presents you with different question types to allow you to become familiar with the various ways an actual exam may test your knowledge. This section describes each of the question types that can be presented by *ExamGear* and provides instructions for answering each type. You will not see all of these questions types in the Training Guide edition. All the questions types are available in the standalone ExamGear product.

Multiple Choice

Most of the questions you see on a certification exam are multiple choice (see Figure D.4). This question type asks you to select an answer from the list provided. Sometimes you must select only one answer, often indicated by answers preceded by option buttons (round selection buttons called radio buttons). At other times, multiple correct answers are possible, indicated by check boxes preceding the possible answer combinations (as shown in Figure D.4).

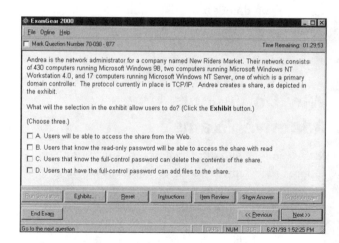

FIGURE D.4
A typical multiple-choice question.

You can use three methods to select an answer:

◆ Click the option button or check box next to the answer. If more than one correct answer to a question is possible, the answers will have check boxes next to them. If only one correct answer to a question is possible, each answer will have an option button next to it. *ExamGear, Training Guide Edition* prompts you with the number of answers you must select.

◆ Click the text of the answer.

◆ Press the alphabetic key that corresponds to the answer.

You can use any one of three methods to clear an option button:

◆ Click another option button.

◆ Click the text of another answer.

◆ Press the alphabetic key that corresponds to another answer.

You can use any one of three methods to clear a check box:

◆ Click the check box next to the selected answer.

◆ Click the text of the selected answer.

◆ Press the alphabetic key that corresponds to the selected answer.

To clear all answers, click the Reset button.

Remember that some of the questions have multiple answers that are correct. Do not let this throw you off. The *multiple correct* questions do not have one answer that is more correct than another. *ExamGear, Training Guide Edition* prompts you with the number of answers you must select. In the *single correct* format, only one answer is correct.

Drop and Connect

The *Drop and Connect* question presents you with a number of objects and connectors. The question prompts you to create relationships between the objects by using the connectors essentially to diagram the relationship. In Figure D.5, the gray squares on the left side of the question window are the objects you can select. The connectors are listed on the right side of the question window in the Connectors box.

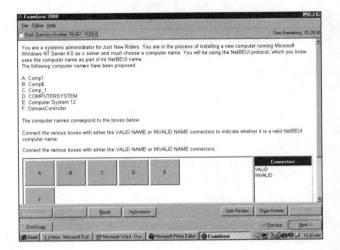

FIGURE D.5
Example of a Drop and Connect question.

To select an object, click it with the mouse. When an object is selected, it changes color. To drag an object, select it by clicking it with the left mouse button, and hold the left mouse button down. You can move (or drag) the object to another area on the screen by moving the mouse while holding the left mouse button down.

To create a relationship between two objects, take the following actions:

1. Select an object and drag it to an available area on the screen.

2. Select another object and drag it to a location near where you dragged the first object.

3. Select the connector that you want to place between the two objects. The relationship should now appear complete. Note that you must have two objects selected to create a relationship. If you try to select a connector without first selecting two objects, you will be presented with the error message shown in Figure D.6.

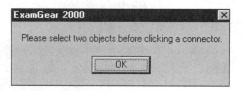

FIGURE D.6
You must select two objects to create a relationship, otherwise you receive this error.

Initially, the direction of the relationship established by the connector is from the first object selected to the second object selected. To change the direction of the connector, right-click the connector and choose Reverse Connection.

You can use either of two methods to remove the connector:

◆ Right-click the text of the connector you want to remove and choose Delete.

◆ Select the text of the connector you want to remove and press the Delete key.

To remove from the screen all of the relationships you have created, click the Reset button.

Keep in mind that connectors can be used multiple times. If you move connected objects, it will not change the relationship between the objects; to remove the relationship between objects, you must remove the connector that joins them. When ExamGear 2000 scores a drag-and-drop question, only objects with connectors to other objects are scored.

Select and Place

The *Select and Place* question requires you to label several items in a way that correctly assign various characteristics to them. For example, you might be given a list of IP addresses and asked to label them as Valid or Invalid. The list of items appears in the left-most pane on the screen, and the characteristics appear on the right. You begin by placing your cursor in the box to the right of the item. You then move your mouse pointer over to the far right column and double-click the correct characteristic. This type of question is shown in Figure D.7.

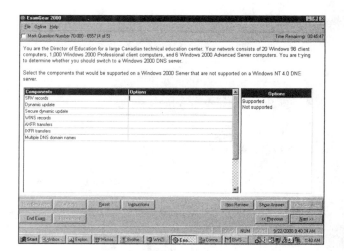

FIGURE D.7
A Select and Place question.

Ordered List

In the *ordered-list* question type (see Figure D.8), you are presented with a number of items and are asked to perform two tasks:

1. Build an answer list from items on the list of choices.

2. Put the items in a particular order.

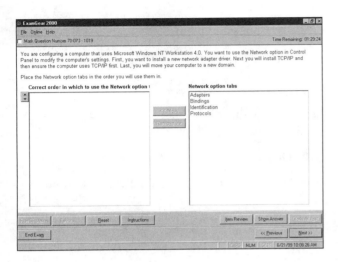

FIGURE D.8
A typical ordered-list question.

You can use any one of the following three methods to add an item to the answer list:

◆ Drag the item from the list of choices on the right side of the screen to the answer list on the left side of the screen.

◆ From the available items on the right side of the screen, double-click the item you want to add.

◆ From the available items on the right side of the screen, select the item you want to add; then click the Move button.

To remove an item from the answer list, you can use any one of the following four methods:

◆ Drag the item you want to remove from the answer list on the left side of the screen back to the list of choices on the right side of the screen.

◆ On the left side of the screen, double-click the item you want to remove from the answer list.

◆ On the left side of the screen, select the item you want to remove from the answer list, and then click the Remove button.

◆ On the left side of the screen, select the item you want to remove from the answer list, and then press the Delete key.

To remove all items from the answer list, click the Reset button.

If you need to change the order of the items in the answer list, you can do so using either of the following two methods:

◆ Drag each item to the appropriate location in the answer list.

◆ In the answer list, select the item that you want to move, and then click the up or down arrow button to move the item.

Keep in mind that items in the list can be selected twice. You may find that an ordered-list question will ask you to list in the correct order the steps required to perform a certain task. Certain steps may need to be performed more than once during the process. Don't think that after you have selected a list item, it is no longer available. If you need to select a list item more than once, you can simply select that item at each appropriate place as you construct your list.

Ordered Tree

The *ordered-tree* question type (see Figure D.9) presents you with a number of items and prompts you to create a tree structure from those items. The tree structure includes two or three levels of nodes.

An item in the list of choices can be added only to the appropriate node level. If you attempt to add one of the list choices to an inappropriate node level, you are presented with the error message shown in Figure D.10

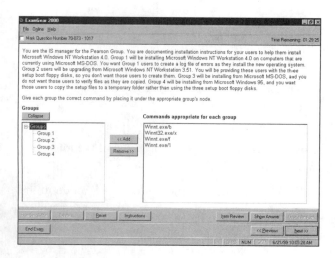

FIGURE D.9
A typical ordered-tree question.

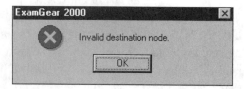

FIGURE D.10
The Invalid Destination Node error message.

Like the ordered-list question, realize that items in the list can be selected twice. If you need to select a list item more than once, you can simply select that item for the appropriate node as you construct your tree.

Also realize that not every tree question actually requires order to the lists under each node. Think of them as simply tree questions rather than ordered-tree questions. Such questions are just asking you to categorize hierarchically. Order is not an issue.

You can use either of the following two methods to add an item to the tree:

◆ Drag the item from the list of choices on the right side of the screen to the appropriate node of the tree on the left side of the screen.

◆ Select the appropriate node of the tree on the left side of the screen. Select the appropriate item from the list of choices on the right side of the screen. Click the Move button.

You can use either of the following two methods to remove an item from the tree:

◆ Drag an item from the tree to the list of choices.

◆ Select the item and click the Remove button.

To remove from the tree structure all the items you have added, click the Reset button.

Simulations

Simulation questions (see Figure D.11) require you to actually perform a task.

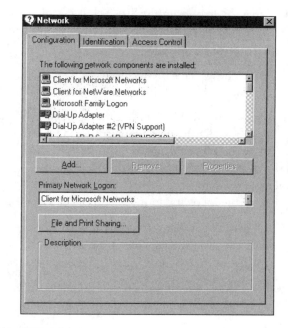

FIGURE D.11
A typical simulation question.

The main screen describes a situation and prompts you to provide a solution. When you are ready to proceed, you click the Run Simulation button in the lower-left corner. A screen or window appears on which you perform the solution. This window simulates the actual software that you would use to perform the required task in the real world. When a task requires several steps to complete, the simulator displays all the necessary screens to allow you to complete the task. When you have provided your answer by completing all the steps necessary to perform the required task, you can click the OK button to proceed to the next question.

You can return to any simulation to modify your answer. Your actions in the simulation are recorded, and the simulation appears exactly as you left it.

Simulation questions can be reset to their original state by clicking the Reset button.

Hot Spot Questions

Hot spot questions (see Figure D.12) ask you to correctly identify an item by clicking an area of the graphic or diagram displayed. To respond to the question, position the mouse cursor over a graphic. Then press the right mouse button to indicate your selection. To select another area on the graphic, you do not need to deselect the first one. Just click another region in the image.

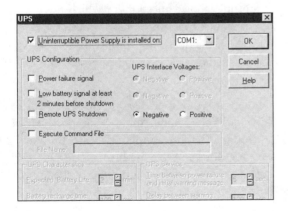

FIGURE D.12
A typical hot spot question.

Standard *ExamGear, Training Guide Edition* Options

Regardless of question type, a consistent set of clickable buttons enables you to navigate and interact with questions. The following list describes the function of each of the buttons you may see. Depending on the question type, some of the buttons will be grayed out and will be inaccessible. Buttons that are appropriate to the question type are active.

◆ **Run Simulation.** This button is enabled if the question supports a simulation. Clicking this button begins the simulation process.

◆ **Exhibits.** This button is enabled if exhibits are provided to support the question. An *exhibit* is an image, video, sound, or text file that provides supplemental information needed to answer the question. If a question has more than one exhibit, a dialog box appears, listing exhibits by name. If only one exhibit exists, the file is opened immediately when you click the Exhibits button.

◆ **Reset.** This button clears any selections you have made and returns the question window to the state in which it appeared when it was first displayed.

◆ **Instructions.** This button displays instructions for interacting with the current question type.

◆ **Item Review.** This button leaves the question window and opens the Item Review screen. For a detailed explanation of the Item Review screen, see the "Item Review" section later in this appendix.

◆ **Show Answer.** This option displays the correct answer with an explanation of why it is correct. If you choose this option, the current question will not be scored.

◆ **Grade Answer.** If Grade at the End of the Test is selected as a configuration option, this button is disabled. It is enabled when Grade As I Answer Each Question is selected as a configuration option. Clicking this button grades the current question immediately. An explanation of the correct answer is provided, just as if the Show Answer button were pressed. The question is graded, however.

◆ **End Exam.** This button ends the exam and displays the Examination Score Report screen.

◆ **<< Previous.** This button displays the previous question on the exam.

◆ **Next >>.** This button displays the next question on the exam.

◆ **<< Previous Marked.** This button is displayed if you have opted to review questions that you have marked using the Item Review screen. This button displays the previous marked question. Marking questions is discussed in more detail later in this appendix.

◆ **<< Previous Incomplete.** This button is displayed if you have opted to review questions that you have not answered using the Item Review screen. This button displays the previous unanswered question.

◆ **Next Marked >>.** This button is displayed if you have opted to review questions that you have marked using the Item Review screen. This button displays the next marked question. Marking questions is discussed in more detail later in this appendix.

◆ **Next Incomplete>>.** This button is displayed if you have opted to review questions, using the Item Review screen, that you have not answered. This button displays the next unanswered question.

Mark Question and Time Remaining

ExamGear provides you with two methods to aid in dealing with the time limit of the testing process. If you find that you need to skip a question, or if you want to check the time remaining to complete the test, use one of the options discussed in the following sections.

Mark Question

Check this box to mark a question so that you can return to it later using the Item Review feature. The adaptive exam does not allow questions to be marked because it does not support Item Review.

Time Remaining

If the test is timed, the Time Remaining indicator is enabled. It counts down minutes remaining to complete the test. The adaptive exam does not offer this feature because it is not timed.

Item Review

The Item Review screen allows you to jump to any question. *ExamGear, Training Guide Edition* considers an *incomplete* question to be any unanswered question or any multiple-choice question for which the total number of required responses has not been selected. For example, if the question prompts for three answers and you selected only A and C, *ExamGear* considers the question to be incomplete.

The Item Review screen enables you to review the exam questions in different ways. You can enter one of two *browse sequences* (series of similar records): Browse Marked Questions and Browse Incomplete Questions. You can also create a custom grouping of the exam questions for review based on a number of criteria.

When using Item Review, if Show Answer was selected for a question while you were taking the exam, the question is grayed out in Item Review. The question can be answered again if you use the Reset button to reset the question status.

The Item Review screen contains two tabs. The Questions tab lists questions and question information in columns. The Current Score tab provides your exam score information, presented as a percentage for each unit and as a bar graph for your overall score.

The Item Review Questions Tab

The Questions tab on the Item Review screen (see Figure D.13) presents the exam questions and question information in a table. You can select any row you want by clicking in the grid. The Go To button is enabled whenever a row is selected. Clicking the Go To button displays the question on the selected row. You can also display a question by double-clicking that row.

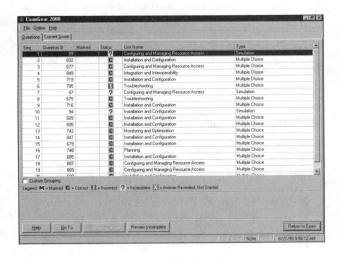

FIGURE D.13
The Questions tab on the Item Review screen.

Columns

The Questions tab contains the following six columns of information:

◆ **Seq.** Indicates the sequence number of the question as it was displayed in the exam.

◆ **Question Number.** Displays the question's identification number for easy reference.

◆ **Marked.** Indicates a question that you have marked using the Mark Question check box.

◆ **Status.** The status can be M for Marked, ? for Incomplete, C for Correct, I for Incorrect, or X for Answer Shown.

◆ **Chapter Name.** The chapter associated with each question.

◆ **Type.** The question type, which can be Multiple Choice, Drop and Connect, Select and Place, Simulation, Hot Spot, Ordered List, or Ordered Tree.

To resize a column, place the mouse pointer over the vertical line between column headings. When the mouse pointer changes to a set of right and left arrows, you can drag the column border to the left or right to make the column more or less wide. Simply click with the left mouse button and hold that button down while you move the column border in the desired direction.

The Item Review screen enables you to sort the questions on any of the column headings. Initially, the list of questions is sorted in descending order on the sequence number column. To sort on a different column heading, click that heading. You will see an arrow appear on the column heading indicating the direction of the sort (ascending or descending). To change the direction of the sort, click the column heading again.

The Item Review screen also allows you to create a *custom grouping*. This feature enables you to sort the questions based on any combination of criteria you prefer. For instance, you might want to review the question items sorted first by whether they were marked, then by the unit name, then by sequence number. The Custom Grouping feature allows you to do this. Start by checking the Custom Grouping check box (see Figure D.14). When you do so, the entire questions table shifts down a bit onscreen, and a message appears at the top of the table that reads `Drag a column heading here to group by that column`.

Simply click the column heading you want with the left mouse button, hold that button down, and move the mouse into the area directly above the questions table (the custom grouping area). Release the left mouse button to drop the column heading into the custom grouping area. To accomplish the custom grouping previously described, first check the Custom Grouping check box. Then drag the Marked column heading into the custom grouping area above the question table. Next, drag the Unit Name column heading into the custom grouping area. You will see the two column headings joined together by a line that indicates the order of the custom grouping. Finally, drag the Seq column heading into the custom grouping area. This heading will be joined to the Unit Name heading by another line indicating the direction of the custom grouping.

Notice that each column heading in the custom grouping area has an arrow indicating the direction in which items are sorted under that column heading. You can reverse the direction of the sort on an individual column-heading basis using these arrows. Click the column heading in the custom grouping area to change the direction of the sort for that column heading only. For example, using the custom grouping created previously, you can display the question list sorted first in descending order by whether the question was marked, in descending order by unit name, and then in ascending order by sequence number.

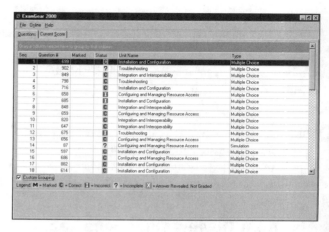

FIGURE D.14
The Custom Grouping check box allows you to create your own question sort order.

The custom grouping feature of the Item Review screen gives you enormous flexibility in how you choose to review the exam questions. To remove a custom grouping and return the Item Review display to its default setting (sorted in descending order by sequence number), simply uncheck the Custom Grouping check box.

The Current Score Tab

The Current Score tab of the Item Review screen (see Figure D.15) provides a real-time snapshot of your score. The top half of the screen is an expandable grid. When the grid is collapsed, scores are displayed for each unit. Units can be expanded to show percentage scores for objectives and subobjectives. Information about your exam progress is presented in the following columns:

◆ **Chapter Name.** This column shows the unit name for each objective group.

◆ **Percentage.** This column shows the percentage of questions for each objective group that you answered correctly.

◆ **Attempted.** This column lists the number of questions you answered either completely or partially for each objective group.

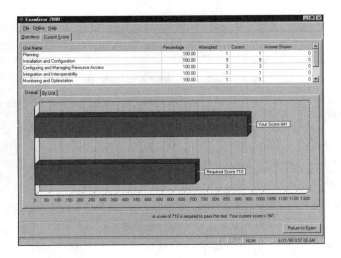

FIGURE D.15
The Current Score tab on the Item Review screen.

◆ **Correct.** This column lists the actual number of questions you answered correctly for each objective group.

◆ **Answer Shown.** This column lists the number of questions for each objective group that you chose to display the answer to using the Show Answer button.

The columns in the scoring table are resized and sorted in the same way as those in the questions table on the Item Review Questions tab. Refer to the earlier section, "The Item Review Questions Tab," for more details.

A graphical overview of the score is presented below the grid. The graph depicts two red bars: The top bar represents your current exam score and the bottom bar represents the required passing score. To the right of the bar graph is a legend that lists the required score and your score. Below the bar graph is a statement that describes the required passing score and your current score.

In addition, the information can be presented on an overall basis or by exam unit. The Overall tab shows the overall score. The By Unit tab shows the score by unit.

Clicking the End Exam button terminates the exam and passes control to the Examination Score Report screen.

The Return to Exam button returns to the exam at the question from which the Item Review button was clicked.

Review Marked Items

The Item Review screen allows you to enter a browse sequence for marked questions. When you click the Review Marked button, questions that you have previously marked using the Mark Question check box are presented for your review. While browsing the marked questions, you will see the following changes to the buttons available:

◆ The caption of the Next button becomes Next Marked.

◆ The caption of the Previous button becomes Previous Marked.

Review Incomplete

The Item Review screen allows you to enter a browse sequence for incomplete questions. When you click the Review Incomplete button, the questions you did not answer or did not completely answer are displayed for your review. While browsing the incomplete questions, you will see the following changes to the buttons:

◆ The caption of the Next button becomes Next Incomplete.

◆ The caption of the Previous button becomes Previous Incomplete.

Examination Score Report Screen

The Examination Score Report screen (see Figure D.16) appears when the Study Mode, Practice Exam, or Adaptive Exam ends—as the result of timer expiration, completion of all questions, or your decision to terminate early.

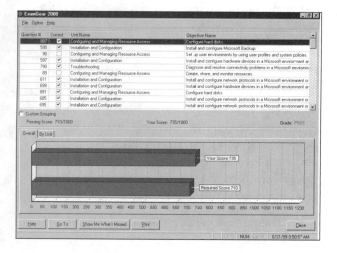

FIGURE D.16
The Examination Score Report screen.

This screen provides you with a graphical display of your test score, along with a tabular breakdown of scores by unit. The graphical display at the top of the screen compares your overall score with the score required to pass the exam. Buttons below the graphical display allow you to open the Show Me What I Missed browse sequence, print the screen, or return to the main menu.

Show Me What I Missed Browse Sequence

The Show Me What I Missed browse sequence is invoked by clicking the Show Me What I Missed button from the Examination Score Report or from the configuration screen of an Adaptive Exam.

Note that the window caption is modified to indicate that you are in the Show Me What I Missed browse sequence mode. Question IDs and position within the browse sequence appear at the top of the screen, in place of the Mark Question and Time Remaining indicators. Main window contents vary, depending on the question type. The following list describes the buttons available within the Show Me What I Missed browse sequence and the functions they perform:

◆ **Return to Score Report.** Returns control to the Examination Score Report screen. In the case of an adaptive exam, this button's caption is Exit, and control returns to the adaptive exam configuration screen.

◆ **Run Simulation.** Opens a simulation in Grade mode, causing the simulation to open displaying your response and the correct answer. If the current question does not offer a simulation, this button is disabled.

◆ **Exhibits.** Opens the Exhibits window. This button is enabled if one or more exhibits are available for the question.

◆ **Instructions.** Shows how to answer the current question type.

◆ **Print.** Prints the current screen.

◆ **Previous or Next.** Displays missed questions.

CHECKING THE WEB SITE

To check for ExamGear updates or other product information, go to the following web site:
`http://www.quepublishing.com/certification`

Contacting Que Publishing

At Que, we strive to meet and exceed the needs of our customers. We have developed *ExamGear, Training Guide Edition* to surpass the demands and expectations of network professionals seeking technical certifications, and we think it shows. What do you think?

If you need to contact Que regarding any aspect of the *ExamGear, Training Guide Edition* product line, feel free to do so. We look forward to hearing from you. Contact us at the following address:

Que Publishing
201 West 103 Street
Indianapolis, IN 46290

You can also reach us on the World Wide Web:

`http://www.quepublishing.com`

Technical Support

Technical support is available at the following phone number during the hours specified:

317-581-3833

Monday through Thursday, 10:00 a.m.–3:00 p.m. Central Standard Time.

Friday, 10:00 a.m.–12:00 p.m. Central Standard Time.

Customer Service

If you have a damaged product and need a replacement or refund, please call the following phone number:

800-858-7674

Product Updates

Product updates can be obtained by choosing *ExamGear, Training Guide Edition*'s Online pull-down menu and selecting Check for Products Updates. You'll be taken to a private web site with full details.

License Agreement

YOU SHOULD CAREFULLY READ THE FOLLOWING TERMS AND CONDITIONS BEFORE BREAKING THE SEAL ON THE PACKAGE. AMONG OTHER THINGS, THIS AGREEMENT LICENSES THE ENCLOSED SOFTWARE TO YOU AND CONTAINS WARRANTY AND LIABILITY DISCLAIMERS. BY BREAKING THE SEAL ON THE PACKAGE, YOU ARE ACCEPTING AND AGREEING TO THE TERMS AND CONDITIONS OF THIS AGREEMENT. IF YOU DO NOT AGREE TO THE TERMS OF THIS AGREEMENT, DO NOT BREAK THE SEAL. YOU SHOULD PROMPTLY RETURN THE PACKAGE UNOPENED.

License

Subject to the provisions contained herein, Que Publishing hereby grants to you a nonexclusive, nontransferable license to use the object-code version of the computer software product (Software) contained in the package on a single computer of the type identified on the package.

Software and Documentation

Que shall furnish the Software to you on media in machine-readable object-code form and may also provide the standard documentation (Documentation) containing instructions for operation and use of the Software.

License Term and Charges

The term of this license commences upon delivery of the Software to you and is perpetual unless earlier terminated upon default or as otherwise set forth herein.

Title

Title, ownership right, and intellectual property rights in and to the Software and Documentation shall remain in Que and/or in suppliers to Que of programs contained in the Software. The Software is provided for your own internal use under this license. This license does not include the right to sublicense and is personal to you and therefore may not be assigned (by operation of law or otherwise) or transferred without the prior written consent of Que. You acknowledge that the Software in source code form remains a confidential trade secret of Que and/or its suppliers and therefore you agree not to attempt to decipher or decompile, modify, disassemble, reverse engineer, or prepare derivative works of the Software or develop source code for the Software or knowingly allow others to do so. Further, you may not copy the Documentation or other written materials accompanying the Software.

Updates

This license does not grant you any right, license, or interest in and to any improvements, modifications, enhancements, or updates to the Software and Documentation. Updates, if available, may be obtained by you at Que's then-current standard pricing, terms, and conditions.

Limited Warranty and Disclaimer

Que warrants that the media containing the Software, if provided by Que, is free from defects in material and workmanship under normal use for a period of sixty (60) days from the date you purchased a license to it.

THIS IS A LIMITED WARRANTY AND IT IS THE ONLY WARRANTY MADE BY QUE. THE SOFTWARE IS PROVIDED "AS IS" AND QUE SPECIFICALLY DISCLAIMS ALL WARRANTIES OF ANY KIND, EITHER EXPRESS OR IMPLIED, INCLUDING, BUT NOT LIMITED TO, THE IMPLIED WARRANTY OF MERCHANTABILITY AND FITNESS FOR A PARTICULAR PURPOSE. FURTHER, COMPANY DOES NOT WARRANT, GUARANTEE, OR MAKE ANY REPRESENTATIONS REGARDING THE USE, OR THE RESULTS OF THE USE, OF THE SOFTWARE IN TERMS OR CORRECTNESS, ACCURACY, RELIABILITY, CURRENTNESS, OR OTHERWISE AND DOES NOT WARRANT THAT THE OPERATION OF ANY SOFTWARE WILL BE UNINTERRUPTED OR ERROR FREE. QUE EXPRESSLY DISCLAIMS ANY WARRANTIES NOT STATED HEREIN. NO ORAL OR WRITTEN INFORMA-

TION OR ADVICE GIVEN BY QUE, OR ANY QUE DEALER, AGENT, EMPLOYEE, OR OTHERS SHALL CREATE, MODIFY, OR EXTEND A WARRANTY OR IN ANY WAY INCREASE THE SCOPE OF THE FOREGOING WARRANTY, AND NEITHER SUBLICENSEE OR PURCHASER MAY RELY ON ANY SUCH INFORMATION OR ADVICE. If the media is subjected to accident, abuse, or improper use, or if you violate the terms of this Agreement, then this warranty shall immediately be terminated. This warranty shall not apply if the Software is used on or in conjunction with hardware or programs other than the unmodified version of hardware and programs with which the Software was designed to be used as described in the Documentation.

LIMITATION OF LIABILITY

Your sole and exclusive remedies for any damage or loss in any way connected with the Software are set forth below.

UNDER NO CIRCUMSTANCES AND UNDER NO LEGAL THEORY, TORT, CONTRACT, OR OTHERWISE, SHALL QUE BE LIABLE TO YOU OR ANY OTHER PERSON FOR ANY INDIRECT, SPECIAL, INCIDENTAL, OR CONSEQUENTIAL DAMAGES OF ANY CHARACTER INCLUDING, WITHOUT LIMITATION, DAMAGES FOR LOSS OF GOODWILL, LOSS OF PROFIT, WORK STOPPAGE, COMPUTER FAILURE OR MALFUNCTION, OR ANY AND ALL OTHER COMMERCIAL DAMAGES OR LOSSES, OR FOR ANY OTHER DAMAGES EVEN IF QUE SHALL HAVE BEEN INFORMED OF THE POSSIBILITY OF SUCH DAMAGES, OR FOR ANY CLAIM BY

ANOTHER PARTY. QUE 'S THIRD-PARTY PROGRAM SUPPLIERS MAKE NO WARRANTY, AND HAVE NO LIABILITY WHATSOEVER, TO YOU. Que's sole and exclusive obligation and liability and your exclusive remedy shall be: upon Que's election, (i) the replacement of our defective media; or (ii) the repair or correction of your defective media if Que is able, so that it will conform to the above warranty; or (iii) if Que is unable to replace or repair, you may terminate this license by returning the Software. Only if you inform Que of your problem during the applicable warranty period will Que be obligated to honor this warranty. SOME STATES OR JURISDICTIONS DO NOT ALLOW THE EXCLUSION OF IMPLIED WARRANTIES OR LIMITATION OR EXCLUSION OF CONSEQUENTIAL DAMAGES, SO THE ABOVE LIMITATIONS OR EXCLUSIONS MAY NOT APPLY TO YOU. THIS WARRANTY GIVES YOU SPECIFIC LEGAL RIGHTS AND YOU MAY ALSO HAVE OTHER RIGHTS WHICH VARY BY STATE OR JURISDICTION.

MISCELLANEOUS

If any provision of the Agreement is held to be ineffective, unenforceable, or illegal under certain circumstances for any reason, such decision shall not affect the validity or enforceability (i) of such provision under other circumstances or (ii) of the remaining provisions hereof under all circumstances, and such provision shall be reformed to and only to the extent necessary to make it effective, enforceable, and legal under such circumstances. All headings are solely for convenience and shall not be considered in interpreting this Agreement. This Agreement shall be governed by and construed under New York law as such law applies to agreements between New York residents entered into and to be performed entirely within New York, except as required by U.S. Government rules and regulations to be governed by Federal law.

YOU ACKNOWLEDGE THAT YOU HAVE READ THIS AGREEMENT, UNDERSTAND IT, AND AGREE TO BE BOUND BY ITS TERMS AND CONDITIONS. YOU FURTHER AGREE THAT IT IS THE COMPLETE AND EXCLUSIVE STATEMENT OF THE AGREEMENT BETWEEN US THAT SUPERSEDES ANY PROPOSAL OR PRIOR AGREEMENT, ORAL OR WRITTEN, AND ANY OTHER COMMUNICATIONS BETWEEN US RELATING TO THE SUBJECT MATTER OF THIS AGREEMENT.

U.S. GOVERNMENT RESTRICTED RIGHTS

Use, duplication, or disclosure by the Government is subject to restrictions set forth in subparagraphs (a) through (d) of the Commercial Computer-Restricted Rights clause at FAR 52.227-19 when applicable, or in subparagraph (c) (1) (ii) of the Rights in Technical Data and Computer Software clause at DFARS 252.227-7013, and in similar clauses in the NASA FAR Supplement.

Index

M

When **IT** really matters, test with VUE®

You've studied the *Training Guide*. Tested your skills with *ExamGear*™.
Now what? Are you ready to sit the exam?
If the answer is yes, be sure to test with VUE.

Why VUE? Because with VUE, you get the best technology and even better service. Some of the benefits are:

- **VUE allows you to register and reschedule your exam in real-time, online, by phone, or at you local testing center**
- **Your test is on time and ready for you, 99% of the time**
- **Your results are promptly and accurately provided to the certifying agency, then merged with your test history**

VUE has over 2,400 quality-focused testing centers worldwide, so no matter where you are, you're never far from a VUE testing center.

VUE is a testing vendor for all the major certification vendors, including Cisco®, Microsoft®, CompTIA® and Novell®.

**HURRY! SIGN UP FOR YOUR EXAM NOW!
TEST WITH VUE. WHEN *IT* REALLY MATTERS.**